DATE DUE

Feb 3, 05	

The Juvenile Justice System

Delinquency, Processing, and the Law

Fourth Edition

Dean John Champion
Texas A & M International University

PEARSON

Prentice
Hall

Upper Saddle River, New Jersey 07458

OCT 0 6 2004

Library of Congress Cataloging-in-Publication Data

Champion, Dean J.
   The juvenile justice system : delinquency, processing, and the law /
Dean John Champion.— 4th ed.
      p. cm.
Includes bibliographical references.
   ISBN 0-13-112287-8
   1. Juvenile justice, Administration of—United States. 2. Juvenile
courts—United States. I. Title.
   KF9779.C425 2003
   345.73'08—dc21

                                                          2003009824

Publisher: Stephen Helba
Executive Editor: Frank Mortimer, Jr.
Assistant Editor: Sarah Holle
Production Editor: Linda Duarte, Pine Tree Composition, Inc.
Production Liaison: Barbara Martine Cappuccio
Director of Manufacturing and Production: Bruce Johnson
Managing Editor: Mary Carnis
Manufacturing Buyer: Cathleen Peterson
Creative Director: Cheryl Asherman
Cover Design Coordinator: Miguel Ortiz
Cover Design: Carey Davies
Cover Image: Robert Essel NYC/CORBIS
Editorial Assistant: Barbara Rosenberg
Marketing Manager: Tim Peyton
Formatting and Interior Design: Pine Tree Composition, Inc.
Printing and Binding: Courier Westford

Chapter Opening Photo Credits: 1. Richard Hutching, PhotoEdit; 2. Michael Newman, PhotoEdit; 3. Lester Sloan, Woodfin Camp & Associates; 4. Kevin Cooper, AP/Wide World Photos; 5. Mel Curtis, Getty Images, Inc.; 7. Scott Cunningham, Merrill Education; 8. John Neubauer, PhotoEdit; 9. Michael Albans, AP/Wide World Photos; 10. Lou Jones, Getty Images Inc.; 11. A. Ramey, Stock Boston; 12. Michael Newman, PhotoEdit; 13. Donna DeCesare.

Additional Photo Credits: p. 69 – Mark Richards, PhotoEdit; p. 171 – AP/Wide World Photos; p. 192 – AP/Wide World Photos; p. 203 – John Hickey, AP/Wide World Photos; p. 245 – John McCutchen, AP/Wide World Photos; p. 315 – AP/Wide World Photos; p. 354 – The Oakland Press/Jose Juarez, A/P Wide World Photos; p. 434 – BI Inc.; p. 456 – John Discher, AP/Wide World Photos; p. 458 – BI Inc.; p. 475, 491, 496 – Corrections Corporation of America.

Pearson Prentice Hall™ is a trademark of Pearson Education, Inc.
Pearson® is a registered trademark of Pearson plc
Prentice Hall® is a registered trademark of Pearson Education, Inc.

Pearson Education LTD.
Pearson Education Singapore, Pte. Ltd
Pearson Education, Canada, Ltd
Pearson Education–Japan
Pearson Education Australia PTY, Limited
Pearson Education North Asia Ltd
Pearson Educaçion de Mexico, S.A. de C.V.
Pearson Education Malaysia, Pte. Ltd

10 9 8 7 6 5 4 3 2 1

ISBN 0-13-112287-8

Contents

Chapter 3

Theories of Delinquency

Chapter 4

An Overview of the Juvenile Justice System

Chapter 5

The Legal Rights of Juveniles

163

Chapter 6

Juveniles and the Police

211

Chapter 7

Intake and Preadjudicatory Processing   240

Chapter 8

Prosecutorial Decision Making in Juvenile Justice   268

Chapter 9

Classification and Preliminary Treatment: Waivers and Other Alternatives

297

Chapter 12

Juvenile Probation and Community-Based Corrections

Chapter 13

Juvenile Corrections: Custodial Sanctions and Parole

Preface

The Juvenile Justice System: Delinquency, Processing and the Law, fourth edition, is a complete examination of the juvenile justice system. It examines how juvenile offenders are defined and classified and draws on current literature to depict significant stages of juvenile processing.

Current juvenile cases are used to illustrate the legal bases for decisions about juveniles. Landmark Supreme Court cases are included, although persuasive decisions from various state courts are presented to show juvenile justice trends. A legalistic perspective is used, therefore, to highlight the different rights juveniles have acquired and how different components of the juvenile justice system relate to them. An integral feature of this book is the distinction between status offenses and delinquent offenses. This difference has significant consequences for all juveniles affected.

The history of juvenile courts is described, including crucial events that have influenced the course of juvenile justice. Increasingly, juveniles are extended rights commensurate with the rights of adults. An indication of this trend is the growing use of waivers (certifications or transfers) to criminal court. This option is intended to expose more serious juvenile offenders to more severe punishment forms compared with the possible punishments that juvenile judges may impose. However, the spreading use of waivers has not always achieved the intended result of more severe penalties for juveniles, since many juveniles who are waived to criminal courts receive minimal punishments if punished at all.

One explanation is that most juveniles who are transferred to criminal courts are not necessarily the most serious, dangerous, or violent juvenile offenders. A majority of those transferred continue to be property offenders, drug users, public order and status offenders. Once juveniles are waived to the jurisdiction of criminal courts, their age becomes a mitigating factor. Quite often, this factor trivializes the seriousness of their offending and lessens the punishments imposed. Many cases against juveniles are dropped or reduced to less serious charges. Thus, many juveniles who are tried as adults receive sentences that are comparatively less severe than those that would otherwise be contemplated and imposed by juvenile judges. However, one potential penalty that receives increasing attention is the death penalty applied to juveniles. Current case law about imposing the death penalty as a punishment for juveniles is examined, and several juvenile death penalty cases are described.

Juveniles are not only classified according to type of offense, but they are also tracked according to the nature of offenses committed across years. Delinquency is defined and measured according to several popular indices, such as the *Uniform Crime Reports* and the *National Crime Victimization Survey*. The fact is that no single resource discloses the true amount of delinquency in the United States.

The major components of the juvenile justice system are featured, including law enforcement, prosecution and the courts, and corrections. Corrections is presented in a broad context, with each correctional component described. Correctional strategies ranging from diversion to full-fledged incarceration are featured, together with a discussion of the favorable and unfavorable dimensions of such programs. One interesting feature is a section devoted to recidivism among juveniles, depending upon the nature of the treatment program described. Thus, community-based correctional programs are assessed, together with probation and parole alternatives for managing a growing juvenile offender aggregate. Electronic monitoring and home confinement are described as strategic and technological means of coping with growing numbers of juvenile offenders.

Every effort has been made to include the most up-to-date sources, references, and other materials. Thus, at the time this book went into production, the most currently available material was used as the bases for tables, figures, and juvenile justice statistics. The most current material is not always that current, however. For example, government documents about juvenile justice statistics are published from twelve to eighteen months from the time the information is actually collected and analyzed. Therefore, it is not unusual for a government document published in 2002 to report "recent" juvenile delinquency statistics for 2000. This situation is common, since governmental compilation and reporting of such information is a slow and tedious process. It is very unlikely, therefore, that the government will report 2002 information in 2002. However, the historical factual information about juveniles and the juvenile justice system does not change. Also, there are very few changes in juvenile laws from year to year. Of course, new information is constantly being generated by researchers and government agencies. As a textbook ages, therefore, those seeking more current information about juvenile delinquency trends and other statistical information can obtain additional data from several sites on the Internet. Several relevant Internet sites have been listed at chapter ends. I have sought to provide the reader with the best and most recent information available at the time this manuscript was prepared.

Features and Ancillaries

Several important features and ancillaries have been prepared for this book. First, there are *chapter objectives* that outline what each chapter is designed to accomplish. *Key terms* that are fundamental to understanding the juvenile justice system, the criminal justice system, and various programs and processes are highlighted in boldface. A complete *glossary* of these terms is provided in an *appendix*. Each chapter contains a *summary*, highlighting the chapter's main points. At chapter ends, a *list of suggested readings* is provided. These are intended to supplement materials presented in each chapter. Thus, if students wish to learn more about any specific topic, these references may be consulted easily. Also included at chapter ends are *questions for review*. Students are encouraged to study these questions and learn to answer them based on chapter information provided. These questions may also be used in preparation for semester or quarter examinations.

For instructors, an Instructor's Manual and Test Bank has been provided. This Instructor's Manual and Test Bank includes chapter objectives and summary information. It also includes true/false, multiple choice, and short-answer essay questions that can be used for examination purposes. Any instructor who adopts this book may request an Instructor's Manual and Test Bank on computer diskette in one of several popular software formats. A diskette containing this information is furnished upon request by contacting the author directly at the addresses provided below.

Acknowledgments

A textbook is the result of the hard work of many persons. From the outset when this book was originally envisoned, I would like to thank Chris Cardone, the former criminal justice editor at Macmillan Publishing Company, for signing this project. Subsequently, Macmillan was acquired by Prentice Hall, and the editorship changed. Continuing strong support for subsequent editions of this work was provided successively by editors Robin Baliszewski, Neil Marquardt, Kim Davies, and most recently, Frank Mortimer. All of you have been instrumental in seeing to the perpetuation of this work in its various editions.

My thanks are also extended to Sarah Holle, who has always been supportive. She has provided valuable assistance in this project's completion by soliciting reviews from juvenile justice scholars and coordinating the review process. Synthesizing these reviews and furnishing me with critical feedback have contributed significantly to improving the book's contents, completeness, and accuracy. I am indebted to Sarah for doing such a wonderful job. Before Sarah assumed these important responsibilities, she was preceded by Rosemary Florio, who performed similar tasks. Although Rosemary retired from Prentice Hall, she can rest assured that Sarah Holle is continuing this work with equivalent rigor and quality.

Thanks are also extended to Linda Duarte and Pine Tree Composition, Inc., in Lewiston, Maine, for their exceptional work. Linda is the Director of Full Service Production, and she did a great job identifying manuscript problems and inconsistencies when they occurred. This is a tedious task, and anyone performing such a task should get a medal. Thanks, Linda, for your professional finishing touch to the format and content of what I have written.

Finally, I wish to thank the reviewers of my fourth edition. Reviewers are essential for new and improved editions. Their constructive criticisms have substantially affected the final result. Reviewers provide valuable feedback and commentary, both to the organization of the book and its contents. While I accept full responsibility for any errors of fact, I would like to acknowledge the significant contributions of the following reviewers: Alan K. Marston, Southern Maine Technical College, Portland, ME; Dawn B. Young, Bossier Parish Community College, Bossier City, LA; Kim Tobin, Westfield State College, Westfield, MA; and Stephen C. Richards, Northern Kentucky University, Highland Heights, KY.

Dean John Champion
Texas A & M International University
Department of Social Sciences
5201 University Blvd.
Laredo, TX 78041
E-mail: dchampion@tamiu.edu

About the Author

Dean John Champion is Professor of Criminal Justice, Texas A & M International University, Laredo, Texas. Dr. Champion has taught at the University of Tennessee-Knoxville, California State University-Long Beach, and Minot State University. He earned his Ph.D. from Purdue University and B.S. and M.A. degrees from Brigham Young University. He also completed several years of law school at the Nashville School of Law.

Dr. Champion has written over 30 texts and/or edited works and maintains memberships in eleven professional organizations. He is a lifetime member of the American Society of Criminology, Academy of Criminal Justice Sciences, and the American Sociological Association. He is a former editor of the Academy of Criminal Justice Sciences/Anderson Publishing Company Series on *Issues in Crime and Justice* and the *Journal of Crime and Justice.* He is a contributing author for the *Encarta Encyclopedia 2000* for Microsoft. He has been a Visiting Scholar for the National Center for Juvenile Justice and is a former president of the Midwestern Criminal Justice Association. He has also designed and/or offered numerous online courses for the University of Phoenix and University of Alaska-Fairbanks.

Among his published books for Prentice-Hall are *Administration of Criminal Justice: Structure, Function, and Process* (2003); *Basic Statistics for Social Research* (1970, 1981); *Research Methods for Criminal Justice and Criminology* (1993, 2000); *The Juvenile Justice System: Delinquency, Processing, and the Law* (1992, 1998, 2001, 2004 forthcoming); *Corrections in the United States: A Contemporary Perspective* (1990, 1998, 2001, 2005 forthcoming); *Probation, Parole, and Community Corrections* (1990, 1996, 1999, 2005 forthcoming); *Policing in the Community* (w/George Rush) (1996); and *The Administration of Justice Systems* (2001). Works from other publishers include *The Sociology of Organizations* (McGraw-Hill, 1975); *Research Methods in Social Relations* (John Wiley & Sons, Inc., 1976); *Sociology* (Holt, Rinehart, and Winston, 1984);

The U.S. Sentencing Guidelines (Praeger Publishers, 1989); *Juvenile Transfer Hearings* (w/G. Larry Mays) (Praeger Publishers, 1991); and *Measuring Offender Risk* (Greenwood Press, 1994); *The Roxbury Dictionary of Criminal Justice: Key Terms and Leading Supreme Court Cases* (Roxbury Press, 1997, 2001); and *Criminal Justice in the United States 2/e* (Wadsworth, 1998). Dr. Champion's specialty interests include juvenile justice, criminal justice administration, corrections, and statistics/methods.

CHAPTER 1

An Introduction to Juvenile Justice in the United States

Chapter Outline

Key Terms

Act to Regulate the Control of Dependent, Neglected, and Delinquent Children
Actuarial justice
Addams, Jane
Adversarial proceedings
Banishment
Beccaria, Cesare
Beyond a reasonable doubt
Bridewell Workhouse
Chancellors
Chancery courts
Children's tribunals

Childsavers
Child-saving movement
Civil tribunals
Common law
Compulsory School Act
Convictions
Court of record
Court reporters
Courts of equity
Criminal justice
Criminal justice professional
Criminologists
Criminology

Defense attorneys
Gemeinschaft
Gesellschaft
Get-tough movement
Hospital of Saint Michael
Houses of refuge
Illinois Juvenile Court Act
Indentured servants
Indentured servant system
Infants
Jurisdiction
Juvenile courts
Juvenile delinquency

Juvenile delinquents
Juvenile justice system
Juvenile offenders
Juveniles
New York House of Refuge
Parens patriae
Philadelphia Society for Alleviating the Miseries of the Public Prisons

Poor Laws
Preponderance of the evidence
Prosecution and the courts
Prosecutors
Reeve
Reform schools
Shire
Society for the Prevention of Pauperism

Solitary confinement
Standard of proof
Status offenders
Sweat shops
Transportation
Truants
Walnut Street Jail
Workhouses

Chapter Objectives

As a result of reading this chapter, you will have accomplished the following objectives:

1. Understand the basic components of the juvenile justice system.

2. Know about the early origins of juvenile courts in the United States.

3. Understand significant historical events in the evolution of the juvenile justice system.

4. Become familiar with the doctrine of *parens patriae* and how juveniles continue to be affected by this doctrine.

5. Understand the difference between juvenile delinquents and status offenders.

6. Differentiate between and understand the primary characteristics of juvenile and criminal courts.

7. Understand alternative philosophies for managing juvenile offenders.

INTRODUCTION

- *Johnny B., 13 years of age, is from Michigan. One morning in June 2002 he was dropped off at school by his mother. But rather than going into the school building, Johnny B. waited until his mother had driven away and then went to the home of a teenage friend, Alex L., 14, nearby. There, they drank whiskey that was taken from Alex L.'s father's liquor cabinet. They smoked marijuana cigarettes that they had made from marijuana bought earlier in the week from another student at school. Alex L. decided to show Johnny B. his father's Colt .45 automatic pistol, which Alex L. had taken from his father's gun cabinet. He handed it to Johnny B. and said, "My dad used this in Desert Storm." Johnny B. stood up, pointed the gun at Alex L., pulled the hammer back, and pulled the trigger, pretending to shoot him. But the gun discharged, sending a .45 slug through Alex L.'s chest. Alex L. died instantly. Johnny B. was taken into custody by police following a report from a nearby neighbor who thought he heard a gunshot at Alex L.'s home. Johnny B. was in shock and said he didn't know the gun was loaded. He said that it was just "horseplay" and that he didn't intend to kill his friend, Alex L. Alex L.'s parents were stunned and angered. They sought to have Johnny B. charged with the murder of their son. Further, they threatened to sue school officials for permitting mari-juana to be sold on school property.* [Adapted from the Associated Press, "Available Gun Leads to Teen's Death." June 14, 2002].

• *Alfred G., 14, was arrested by police in Omaha, Nebraska, and charged with the death of Stephen James, a 15-year-old. Alfred G., a high school ninth-grader, reportedly is a gang member. At first, he refused to talk to police about the incident and denied any involvement in it. However, informants said that Alfred G. was the shooter, and they indicated where police could find the gun used by him to kill James. Confronted with overwhelming circumstantial evidence, Alfred G. confessed to the murder and said that it was part of a gang initiation. Apparently, the gang he wanted to join required him to shoot someone as a part of the initiation experience to show his loyalty and commitment. James was the member of a rival gang in the area. Alfred G. was subsequently transferred to criminal court to be tried as an adult. The prosecutor sought second-degree murder charges against Alfred G. He faced 15 years to life in prison if convicted.* [Adapted from the Associated Press, "Boy Dies as Result of Gang Initiation." July 12, 2002].

• *It happened in Philadelphia, Pennsylvania. On June 16, 2002, Thomas A., 13, and some friends were "hanging out" in an arcade, playing video games. Erik P., 14, and another companion, Arthur T., entered the arcade later. Arthur T. wanted to play his favorite video game, but Thomas A. was already playing it. Arthur T. waited for about 10 minutes, and he began to get restless. He got up and went over to the video game and suggested that Thomas A. should "give it a rest" and leave. To make his point, Arthur T. shoved the machine and tilted it, causing the game to stop. This angered Thomas A., who then hit Arthur T. in the face with his fist. Arthur T. pulled out a knife and thrust it into Thomas A.'s stomach. Thomas A. fell to the floor of the arcade, bleeding. Arthur T. and his friend fled the scene shortly thereafter. Although medical personnel arrived and performed CPR, they could not save Thomas A., who died about an hour later from the knife wound. Eyewitnesses led police to the home of Arthur T., who was well-known to arcade personnel. He was taken into custody by police. Subsequently, a hearing was conducted to determine whether Arthur T. should be transferred to criminal court to face second-degree murder charges. The judge granted the transfer motion, and Arthur T. was booked at the local jail and held without bond pending a later trial. He faced up to 25 years if convicted of the second-degree murder charge.* [Adapted from the Associated Press, "Arcade Argument Turns Deadly When Video Game Player Stabs 13-Year-Old." July 19, 2002].

Each of the above scenarios illustrates a teen death as the result of a violent act. In the first incident, the shooting death of a teenager is most likely accidental. In the second incident, a teen death is the result of a gang initiation. In the third incident, an argument over a video game in an arcade results in a teen's being stabbed to death.

There is a great deal of juvenile violence. Much of this violence is gang related (Miller 2001). In 2002 there were over 30,000 gangs in the United States with a total membership in excess of one million youths. Despite widespread gun control efforts, the availability and accessibility of firearms and other dangerous weapons is virtually unabated. During the period 1980–1996, juvenile violence escalated at an alarming rate, although it declined slightly from 1996–2002. Although we do not know how much juvenile violence there is today, we do know that the very nature of juvenile violence has escalated appreciably (Cunningham and Henggeler 2001). While there may be proportionately fewer violent youths in U.S. society in 2002 compared with previous years, the level of their violence has risen to intolerable levels. There has been a rash of mass murders at elementary and secondary schools, with great loss of life among teachers and students. The shooters have ranged in age from 10 to 18. Greater access to firearms, greater reliance on gang associations for friendships and ego-building, less control over one's emotional state, deteriorating family values, loss of parental control over incorrigible youths, and more frequent school disorder and disruption suggest that something is seriously wrong with the youth of U.S. society. Juvenile violence takes many forms. It may be drive-by or freeway shootings and road rage, a drug deal turned deadly, gang fighting, bullying or menacing at schools, and/or increasing assaults and teen rapes (Crews and Montgomery 2001).

Fortunately, there are relatively few violent juvenile offenders (Steinberg 2002). Of the 3 million juveniles taken into custody by police each year, less than 10 percent of these juveniles are involved in violent crimes. The large majority of juveniles commit property crimes, such as theft, burglary, malicious mischief, defacing public property, and other nuisance offenses. A portion of these juveniles commit offenses that would not be crimes if adults committed them. Truancy, runaway behavior, and curfew violation are some of the many offenses committed by juveniles that are not criminal conduct (Fried 2001).

Not everyone agrees about which solutions are best to reduce or eliminate juvenile offending of any kind. A clear and universally acceptable mandate about what should be done with youths who offend in different ways does not exist. Consistent standards of punishment and/or treatment are mixed and often contradictory. Surveys of public opinion about juvenile violence suggest that those juveniles who commit violent acts should be tried as adults and should be subject to adult punishments, even the death penalty. If they commit an adult crime, they should do adult time. Other observers say that youths ought to be treated rather than punished. According to this view, every child, regardless of the offense, is capable of becoming rehabilitated. Juveniles are not fully formed adults emotionally, and therefore they should not be held accountable according to the same punitive standards that are applied to adult offenders. The unresolved debate about what to do with juvenile offenders has continued for many decades.

Some persons argue that all juveniles are entitled to due process, justice, and just deserts. Stressed are proportional punishments to fit the nature of the offense and the incapacitation of those youths deemed to be dangerous to society. This legalistic emphasis is profound and pervasive, and it is deeply rooted in several significant U.S. Supreme Court decisions about the legal rights of juveniles. The other extreme is the traditional view that emphasizes individualized treatments, understanding adolescent behavior, and modifying unacceptable juvenile conduct with socially and psychologically therapeutic interventions (van Dalen 2001). Presently accepted as a vital component of U.S. jurisprudence is the juvenile justice system. This chapter introduces the juvenile justice system and highlights several mechanisms that are designed to deal with both violent and nonviolent juvenile offenders.

Juvenile courts are civil and low-profile entities. However, they have become increasingly adversarial during the 1990s and into the 21st century. **Defense attorneys** and **prosecutors** are standard features of contemporary juvenile court proceedings, and the differences between criminal courts and juvenile courts are diminishing. However, juvenile courts retain many of their historical antecedents. Much of what juvenile court prosecutors and judges do is influenced by these antecedents. The juvenile justice system is replete with reforms in recent years, and these reforms have included many new and conflicting philosophies. A portion of this chapter examines the roles of prosecutors and defense attorneys and how these roles have been modified.

Some of the highlights of the historical evolution of the juvenile court and its original conception will be reviewed. The influence of historical tradition on juvenile justice procedures remains strong. However, both prosecutors and defense attorneys alike are having to adjust their thinking about how juveniles are presently treated in the aftermath of numerous juvenile justice reforms. New juvenile laws are being enacted in most jurisdictions, and assorted legal bodies, such as the American Bar Association and the American Law Institute, are undertaking the complicated tasks of formulating revised juvenile model procedural and penal codes.

THE JUVENILE JUSTICE SYSTEM

The **juvenile justice system,** similar to **criminal justice,** consists of a more or less integrated network of agencies, institutions, organizations, and personnel that process juvenile offenders. This network is made up of law enforcement agencies, prosecution and the courts; corrections, probation, and parole services; and public and private community-based treatment programs that provide youths with diverse services. The preceding definition is qualified by the phrase "more or less integrated" because the concept of juvenile justice has different meanings for individual states and the federal government. Also, in some jurisdictions, the diverse components of the juvenile justice system are closely coordinated, while in other jurisdictions, these components are at best loosely coordinated, if they are coordinated at all. There is no single nationwide juvenile court system. Instead, there are fifty-one state systems, including the District of Columbia, and most of them are divided into local systems delivered through either juvenile or family courts at the county level, local probation offices, state correctional agencies, and private service providers. These systems, do, however, have a common set of core principles that distinguish them from criminal courts for adult offenders, including:

1. Limited jurisdiction (up to age 17 in most states)
2. Informal proceedings
3. Focus on offenders, not their crimes
4. Indeterminate sentences
5. Confidentiality (Wood 2001, 117).

A Process or System?

Many **criminologists** and **criminal justice professionals** express a preference for the word *process* rather than the word *system* when they refer to juvenile justice. This is because system connotes a condition of homeostasis, equilibrium, or internal balance among system components. In contrast, *process* focuses on the different actions and contributions of each of these components in dealing with juvenile offenders at various stages of the processing through the juvenile justice system. Furthermore, *system* implies coordination among elements in an efficient production process; in reality, however, communication and coordination among juvenile agencies, organizations, and personnel in the juvenile justice system are often inadequate or nonexistent (Wooden and Blazak 2001).

Further clouding the concept of juvenile justice is the fact that different criteria are used to define the broad classes of juveniles among local, state, and federal jurisdictions. Within each of these jurisdictions, certain mechanisms exist for redefining particular juveniles as adults so that they may be legally processed by the adult counterpart to juvenile justice, the criminal justice system. Despite these definitional ambiguities and systemic interfaces among jurisdictions, most scholars who investigate juveniles understand what is meant by juvenile justice. As with pornography, these scholars and investigators recognize the juvenile justice process whenever they see its components, even if they may not always be able to define it precisely.

About This Book

This book is about the juvenile justice system. Because of the multifaceted nature of this system or process, the wide variety of characteristics of its intended clients, and its interrelatedness with the criminal justice system, we may acquire a better understanding of its nature, purposes, and development if we can place it within a historical framework. Thus, the first part of this chapter describes the historical emergence of juvenile justice in the United States. Key events are noted, and their significance and influence on contemporary juvenile agencies and organizations is discussed. Early versions of juvenile justice were affected by and patterned substantially after early English common law and the role of kings and their agents in public affairs; we will trace the origins of our system in English law. Interestingly, certain functions and objectives of contemporary juvenile justice systems have their origins in fifteenth-century England, although particular ideas about how youths of all ages were to be defined, judged, punished, or treated also existed in biblical times.

This historical introduction is followed by a description of the juvenile court. This is a relatively recent concept. It is both pivotal and pervasive in most juvenile justice systems. Coexisting with juvenile courts are criminal courts designed to adjudicate adult offenders. Several important characteristics of both types of courts will be described, along with some of their differences. One feature that distinguishes these courts from one another is the age range of the clientele over which each exercises jurisdiction. The matters dealt with by these court systems vary as well. Some of these major differences will be highlighted.

Throughout the juvenile justice system in both colonial and modern times is the pervasive doctrine of **parens patriae.** This doctrine originated from early English common law in the twelfth century. Meaning literally "the parent of the country," *parens patriae* referred originally to the fact that the king of England was both a sovereign and a guardian of persons under legal disability, including children (Black 1990, 1114). This concept has been particularly influential regarding juvenile court practices as contrasted with criminal courts. In recent decades, there have been numerous reforms throughout the juvenile justice system, and the traditional juvenile court decision making has been transformed as it applies to youths (Fader et al. 2001).

Finally, alternative managerial philosophies exist that favor various modes of juvenile control. Some of these philosophies are in direct conflict and all have competing implications for affected juveniles. A description of these philosophies is in order at the outset, since all currently available juvenile services and programs have been variously influenced by them (Kempf-Leonard and Peterson 2000). Presently, little consensus exists among juvenile justice scholars and researchers about which philosophy is best or most useful. The result is a programmatic Tower of Babel, replete with conflicting values, interests, and aims with regard to the goals and purposes of the juvenile justice system (Wilson and Petersilia 2002).

This conflict is highlighted by competing juvenile justice reforms that have been attempted over the last 100 years. Moral entrepreneurs emphasized religion as an integrating and rehabilitative medium for wayward youths, while domestic reformers proclaimed that placing children in model homes would solve delinquency problems. Charitable reformers established cultural centers in impoverished neighborhoods, while progressive reformers suggested psychological adjustment as a cure for deviance. All of these reformers failed to anticipate that clients themselves would resist these different forms of assistance and intervention (Knupfer 2001). Many reformers did not question their assumption that by reforming individuals they could change society. In many respects, these reformers were wrong (Dodge 2001).

THE HISTORY OF JUVENILE COURTS

Juvenile courts are a relatively recent U.S. creation. However, modern U.S. juvenile courts have various less formal European antecedents. In biblical times, Roman law vested parents with the almost exclusive responsibility for disciplining their offspring. One's age was the crucial determinant of whether youths were subject to parental discipline or to the more severe penalties invoked for adult law violators. While the origin of this cutting point is unknown, the age of 7 was used in Roman times to separate infants from those older children who were accountable to the law for their actions. During the Middle Ages, English **common law** established under the monarchy adhered to the same standard. In the United States, several state jurisdictions currently apply this distinction and consider all children below the age of 7 to be not accountable for any criminal acts they may commit.

Under the laws of England during the 1500s, **shires** (counties) and other political subdivisions were organized to carry out the will of the king. Each shire had a **reeve,** or chief law enforcement officer. In later years, the term *shire* was combined with the term *reeve* (shire-reeve) to create the word *sheriff,* a term that is now applied to the chief law enforcement officer of most U.S. counties. While reeves enforced both criminal and civil laws and arrested law violators, other functionaries, called **chancellors,** acted on the king's behalf and dispensed justice according to his wishes. These chancellors held court and settled disputes that included simple property trespass, property boundary disagreements, and assorted personal and property offenses, including public drunkenness, thievery, and vagrancy. The courts conducted by chancellors were known as **chancery courts** or **courts of equity.** Today, some jurisdictions in the United States, such as Tennessee, have chancery courts where property boundary disputes and contested wills may be adjudicated by chancellors. These courts have other jurisdiction as well, although they deal primarily with equity cases (e.g., breaches of contract, specific performance actions, and child custody cases).

In eighteenth-century England, no distinctions were made regarding age or gender when punishments were administered. Youthful offenders age 7 or older experienced the same harsh punishments imposed on adults. Stocks and pillories, whipping posts, branding, ducking stools, and other forms of corporal punishment were administered to juveniles as well as to adult offenders for many different types of crimes. In some instances, **banishment** was used as a way of punishing more serious offenders. Some offenders were transported to Pacific islands that were owned by the British and converted into penal colonies. This was known as **transportation.** Many prisoners died in these colonies. The death penalty was invoked frequently, often for petty crimes. Incarceration of offenders was particularly sordid, as women, men, and youths were confined together in jails for lengthy periods. No attempts were made to classify these offenders by gender or age, and all prisoners slept on hay loosely thrown on wooden floors.

Workhouses and Poor Laws

Eighteenth-century jails were patterned largely after **workhouses** that were still common nearly two centuries earlier. In 1557, for example, **Bridewell Workhouse** was established in London. Although the manifest aim of such places was to punish offenders, Bridewell and other similar facilities were created primarily for the purpose of providing cheap labor to satisfy mercantile interests and demands. Interestingly, jailers and sheriffs profited greatly from leasing their inmates to various merchants in order to perform semiskilled and skilled labor (Spruit et al. 1998). These same jailers claimed that the worked performed by inmates for mercantile interests was largely therapeutic and rehabilitative, although in reality the primary incentive for operating such houses was profit and personal gain. Exploitation of inmates for profit in these and other workhouses was perpetuated by jailers and sheriffs for many decades, and the general practice was accepted by an influential constituency of merchants and entrepreneurs.

At the time of the Bridewell Workhouse, English legislators had already established several statutes known as the **Poor Laws.** These laws targeted debtors who owed creditors, and sanctions for those unable to pay their debts were imposed. Debtors' prisons were places where debtors were incarcerated until they could pay their debts. Since debtors needed to work to earn the money required to pay off their debts, and since opportunities for earning money for prison labor were almost nonexistent, imprisonment for debts was tantamount to a life sentence. Many offenders were incarcerated indefinitely or until someone, perhaps a relative or influential friend, could pay off their debts for them.

The Poor Laws were directed at the poor or socioeconomically disadvantaged. In 1601, additional statutes were established that provided constructive work for youths deemed by the courts to be vagrant, incorrigible, truant, or neglected. In general, education was not an option for these youths—it was an expensive commodity available almost exclusively to children from the upper social strata, and it provided a major means of achieving higher still status over time. For the masses of poor, education was usually beyond their reach; they spent most of their time earning money to pay for life's basic necessities. They had little or no time to consider education as a realistic option (Beier 1985).

Indentured Servants

Many youths during this time became apprentices, usually to master craftsmen, in a system of involuntary servitude. This servitude was patterned in part after the **indentured servant system. Indentured servants** entered voluntarily into contractual agreements with various merchants and businessmen to work for them for extended periods of up to seven years. This seven-year work agreement was considered by all parties to be a mutually beneficial way of paying for the indentured servant's passage from England to the colonies. In the case of youthful apprentices, however, their servitude, for the most part, was compulsory. Furthermore, it usually lasted until they reached adulthood or age 21 (Christianson 1998).

During the colonial period, English influence on penal practices was apparent in most New England jurisdictions. Colonists relied on familiar traditions for administering laws and sanctioning offenders. It is no coincidence, therefore, that much criminal procedure in U.S. courts today traces its origins to legal customs and precedents inherent in British jurisprudence during the 1600s and 1700s (Duffield and Bradley 1997). However, relatively little attention was devoted to the legal status of juveniles during this period and to how to manage them. In fact, more than a few juveniles were summarily executed for relatively petty offenses (Hale 1997).

Hospital of Saint Michael

In other parts of the world during the same era, certain religious interests were gradually devising institutions that catered primarily to youthful offenders. For example, in Italy, a corrective facility was established in 1704 to provide for unruly youths and other young people who violated criminal laws. This facility was the **Hospital of Saint Michael,** constructed in Rome at the request of the Pope. The institution was misleadingly named, however, since the youths it housed were not ill. Rather, they were assigned various tasks and trained to perform semiskilled and skilled labor—useful tools that would enable them to find employment more easily after their release from Saint Michael. During rest periods and evening hours, youths were housed in individual cells (Griffin and Griffin 1978).

The Quakers and Walnut Street Jail

Reforms relating to the treatment and/or punishment of juvenile offenders occurred slowly. Shortly after the Revolutionary War, religious interests in the United States moved forward with various proposals designed to improve the plight of the oppressed, particularly those who were incarcerated in prisons and jails. In 1787, the Quakers in Pennsylvania established the **Philadelphia Society for Alleviating the Miseries of the Public Prisons.** This largely philanthropic society was comprised of prominent citizens, religious leaders, and philanthropists who were appalled by existing prison and jail conditions. Adult male, female, and juvenile offenders continued to be housed in common quarters and treated like animals. The High Street Jail in Philadelphia was one eyesore that particularly attracted the Society's attention. Because members of the Quaker faith visited this and other jail facilities regularly to bring food, clothing, and religious instruction to inmates, they were in strategic positions to observe the totality of circumstances in which those confined found themselves.

In 1790, an older Philadelphia jail facility originally constructed in 1776 was overhauled and refurbished. It was renamed the **Walnut Street Jail.** This facility has considerable historical significance for corrections, since it was the first real attempt by jail authorities to classify and segregate offenders according to their age, gender, and crime seriousness. The Walnut Street Jail was innovative in at least three respects. First, it pioneered what is now known as **solitary confinement.** Sixteen large solitary cells were constructed to house prisoners on an individual basis during evening hours. Second, prisoners were segregated from other prisoners according to offense seriousness. More violent criminals were placed with others like them. First-offenders or petty offenders were similarly grouped together and segregated from more violent convicts. Third, women and children were maintained in separate rooms during evening hours, away from male prisoners (Roberts 1985).

The Walnut Street Jail promoted rehabilitation. It attempted to train its inmates for different types of labor, such as sewing, shoemaking, or carpentry. Unskilled laborers were assigned tasks such as beating hemp for ship caulking. Most prisoners received modest wages for their skilled or unskilled labor, although much of this pay was used to pay for their room and board. Finally, religious instruction was provided to inmates by Quaker teachers. This provision is indicative of the dramatic influence of religion in shaping prison policies and practices relating to inmate treatment and benefits (Stastny and Tyrnauer 1982).

The Child Savers and Houses of Refuge

As more families gravitated toward large cities such as New York, Philadelphia, Boston, and Chicago during the early 1800s to find work, increasing numbers of children roamed the streets, most often unsupervised by working parents who could not afford child care services. Lacking familial controls, many of these youths committed acts of vandalism and theft. Others were simply idle, without visible means of support, and were designated as vagrants. Again, religious organizations intervened in order to protect unsupervised youths from the perils of life in the streets. Believing that these youths would subsequently turn to lives of crime as adults, many reformers and philanthropists sought to save them from their plight.

Thus, in different cities throughout the United States, various groups were formed to find and control these youths by offering them constructive work programs, healthful living conditions, and above all, adult supervision. Collectively, these efforts became widely known as the **child-saving movement. Childsavers** came largely from the middle and upper classes, and their assistance to youths took many forms. Food and shelter were provided to children who were in trouble with the law or who were simply idle. Private homes were converted into settlements where social, educational, and other important activities could be provided for needy youths. The childsavers were not limited to the United States. In Scotland and England during the 1850s, child-saving institutions were abundant, with similar philosophies and interests compared with U.S. child-saving organizations. In England particularly, middle-class values were imposed on the children of the working class through institutional education, training, and discipline. Eventually, several juvenile reformatories were established for the purpose of institutional control (Sangster 2000).

In the United States, more than a few child-saver organizations sought to impose their class, ethnic, and racial biases on the poor, immigrants, and minority women. A middle-class gender ideology of maternal care was imposed upon working-class and lower-class mothers. Many of these mothers were declared as unfit and in need of state control, since they did not conform to the cultural ideal espoused by middle- and upper-class childsavers (Kasinsky 1994). Thus, there was the general charge that childsavers sought to control and resocialize the children of the dangerous classes for the benefit of the capitalist entrepreneurs (Salerno 1991). But not everyone agrees that childsavers exploited children. In certain cities, such as Wilmington, Delaware, the child-saving movement emphasized education rather than work. Furthermore, the ultimate aims of this movement in Delaware and several other states were largely altruistic and humanitarian.

The **New York House of Refuge** was established in New York City in 1825 by the **Society for the Prevention of Pauperism** (Cahalan 1986, 101). Subsequently imitated in other communities, **houses of refuge** were institutions largely devoted to managing status offenders, such as runaways or incorrigible children. Compulsory education and other forms of training and assistance were provided to these children. However, the strict, prison-like regimen of this organization was not entirely therapeutic for its clientele. Many of the youthful offenders who were sent to such institutions, including the House of Reformation in Boston, were offspring of immigrants. Often, they rebelled when exposed to the discipline of these organizations, and many of these youths eventually pursued criminal careers as a consequence (Hess and Clement 1993). It would appear that at least some of these humanitarian and philanthropic efforts by childsavers and others had adverse consequences for many affected juveniles.

Another facility with a notorious reputation for how it treated juveniles was the Western House of Refuge (WHR) in Rochester, New York, which operated during the 1880s. Juvenile inmates of this facility were considered deviant and criminal. In reality, the youths institutionalized at the WHR were primarily orphaned, abused, or neglected. Their treatment consisted of hard labor and rigid discipline (Smith 1989). Not all houses of refuge were like the Western House of Refuge, however. In California, for instance, several houses of refuge were operated in ways that stressed vocational training, educational instruction, and some amount of aftercare when youths were ultimately released (Schlossman and Pisciotta 1986).

Up until the late 1830s, there was little or no pattern to the division of labor between parental, religious, and state authority. As private interests continued to include larger numbers of juveniles within the scope of their supervision, various jurisdictions sought to regulate and institutionalize these assorted juvenile assistance, treatment, and/or intervention programs. In many communities, city councils sanctioned the establishment of facilities to accommodate youths who were either delinquent, dependent, or neglected.

Ex Parte Crouse

In 1839, a decision in a state case gave juvenile authorities considerable power over parents in the management and control of their own children. *Ex parte Crouse* (1839) was a case involving a father who attempted to secure the release of his daughter, Mary Ann Crouse, from the Philadelphia House of Refuge (Shelden 1998). The girl had been committed to the Philadelphia facility by the court because she was considered unmanageable. She was not given a trial by jury. Rather, her commitment was made arbitrarily by a presiding judge. A higher court rejected the father's claim that parental control of children is exclusive, natural, and proper, and it upheld the power of the state to exercise necessary reforms and restraints to protect children from themselves and their environments. While this decision was only applicable to Pennsylvania citizens and their children, other states took note of it and sought to invoke similar controls over errant children in their jurisdictions. Essentially, children in Pennsylvania were temporarily deprived of any legal standing to challenge decisions made by the state in their behalf.

Reform Schools and *People ex rel. O'Connell v. Turner* (1870)

Throughout the remainder of the nineteenth century, different types of institutions were established to supervise unruly juveniles. At roughly mid-century, **reform schools** in several jurisdictions were created. One of the first state-operated reform schools was opened in Westboro, Massachusetts, in 1848 (U.S. Department of Justice 1976). By the end of the century, all states had reform schools of one sort or another. All of these institutions were characterized by strict discipline, absolute control over juvenile behavior, and compulsory work at various trades. Another common feature was that they were controversial.

The primary question raised by reform school critics was Do reform schools reform? Since many juveniles continued to commit delinquent acts after being released from these schools and eventually became adult criminals, the rehabilitative value of reform schools was seriously challenged. The Civil War exacerbated the problem of unruly youths, since many families were broken up. Orphans of dead soldiers were commonplace in the post–Civil War period. Such children were often committed to reform schools, regardless of whether they had committed criminal offenses. Many status offenders were sent to reform schools, simply because they were vagrants. Many of these children did not need to be reformed. Rather, they needed homes and noninstitutional care.

One state, Illinois, was particularly aggressive when it came to confining juveniles in reform schools. Many of these incarcerated juveniles were children of immigrant workers in and around Chicago, and often they were rounded up and imprisoned for simple loitering or playing in the city streets. The Chicago Reform School was especially notorious as a site where such youths were sent and confined. In 1870, however, the Illinois Supreme Court heard and decided a case that ultimately prohibited such juvenile arrests by police and incarcerations. This was the case of *People ex rel. O'Connell v. Turner* (1870). Few legal challenges of state authority were made by complaining parents, because of the awesome power of the state and its control over juvenile matters. However, an Illinois case paved the way for special courts for juveniles and an early recognition of their rights. A youth, Daniel O'Connell, was declared vagrant and in need of supervision and committed to the Chicago Reform School for an unspecified period. O'Connell's parents challenged this court action, claiming that his confinement for vagrancy was unjust and untenable. Existing Illinois law vested state authorities with the power to commit any juvenile to a state reform school as long as a "reasonable justification" could be provided. In this instance, vagrancy was a reasonable justification. The Illinois Supreme Court distinguished between misfortune (vagrancy) and criminal acts in arriving at its decision to reverse Daniel O'Connell's commitment. In effect, the court nullified the law by declaring that reform school commitments of youths could not be made by the state if the "offense" was simple misfortune. They reasoned that state's interests would be better served if commitments of juveniles to reform schools were limited to those committing more serious criminal offenses rather than those who were victims of misfortune. The Illinois Supreme Court further held that it was unconstitutional to confine youths who had not been convicted of criminal conduct or afforded legal due process to be confined in the Chicago Reform School (Shepherd 2002, 2). One result of this decision was the eventual closure of the Chicago Reform School two years later. As one alternative to incarceration, Chicago and other Illinois youths without adult supervision were placed under the care of social service agencies and benevolent societies. Both individuals and groups established settlements for displaced or wayward youths.

Community-Based Private Agencies

In 1889, **Jane Addams** established and operated Hull House in Chicago, Illinois. Hull House was a settlement home used largely by children from immigrant families in the Chicago area. In those days, adults worked long hours, and many youths were otherwise unsupervised and wandered about their neighborhoods looking for something to do. Using money from various charities and philanthropists, Addams supplied many children with creative activities to alleviate their boredom and monotony. Addams integrated these activities with moral, ethical, and religious teachings. In her own way, she was hoping to deter these youths from lives of crime with her constructive activities and teaching (Ayers 1997). Thus, her approach was consistent with the philosophy of **Cesare Beccaria,** the father of classical **criminology.** Beccaria wrote in 1764 that the purpose of punishment was deterrence and that punishment should be measured according to the seriousness of the criminal acts committed.

Truancy Statutes

In 1852, **truants** were created as a class of juvenile offenders in Massachusetts, where the first compulsory school attendance statute was passed. Many other states adopted similar statutes, until all jurisdictions had compulsory school attendance provisions by 1918 (Virginia Commission on Youth 1998). Some historians have erroneously credited Colorado as having drafted the first juvenile court provisions. In fact, the Colorado legislature passed the Compulsory School Act of 1899, the same year that the first juvenile court was established in Illinois. The Colorado action was aimed at preventing truancy, specifically mentioning those youths who were habitually absent from school, wandered about the streets during school hours, and had no obvious business or occupation. Colorado legislators labeled such youths juvenile disorderly persons, but this action did not lead to the creation of a Colorado juvenile court (von Eye and Schuster 2001).

The Illinois Juvenile Court Act.   The Illinois legislature established the first juvenile court on July 1, 1899 by passing the **Act to Regulate the Treatment and**

Control of Dependent, Neglected, and Delinquent Children, or the **Illinois Juvenile Court Act.** This act provided for limited courts of record, where notes might be taken by judges or their assistants to reflect judicial actions against juveniles. The jurisdiction of these courts, subsequently designated as **juvenile courts,** would include all juveniles under the age of 16 who were found in violation of any state or local law or ordinance. Also, provision was made for the care of dependent and/or neglected children who had been abandoned or who otherwise lacked proper parental care, support, or guardianship. No minimum age was specified that would limit the jurisdiction of juvenile court judges. However, the act provided that judges could impose secure confinement on juveniles 10 years of age or over by placing them in state-regulated juvenile facilities such as the state reformatory or the State Home for Juvenile Female Offenders. Judges were expressly prohibited from confining any juvenile under 12 years of age in a jail or police station. Extremely young juveniles would be assigned probation officers who would look after their needs and placement on a temporary basis.

Illinois's Juvenile Court Act says much about the times and how the legal status of juveniles was interpreted and applied. The full title of the Act is revealing. According to the Act, it was applicable only to

> . . . children under the age of sixteen (16) years not now or hereafter inmates of a State institution, or any training school for boys or industrial school for girls or some institution incorporated under the laws of this State, except as provided [in other sections] . . . . For purposes of this act the words dependent child and neglected child shall mean any child who for any reason is destitute or homeless or abandoned; or dependent upon the public for support; or has not proper parental care or guardianship; or who habitually begs or receives alms, or who is found living in any house of ill fame or with any vicious or disreputable person; or whose home, by reason of neglect, cruelty or depravity on the part of its parents, guardian or other person in whose care it may be, is an unfit place for such a child; and any child under the age of eight (8) years who is found peddling or selling any article or singing or playing any musical instrument upon the streets or giving any public entertainment. The words delinquent child shall include any child under the age of 16 years who violates any law of this State or any city or village ordinance. The word child or children may mean one or more children, and the word parent or parents may be held to mean one or both parents, when consistent with the intent of this act. The word association shall include any corporation which includes in its purposes the care or disposition of children coming within the meaning of this act.

Even more insightful is what happens when such children are found. What are the limits of court sanctions? Illinois law authorized juvenile court judges to take the following actions in their dealings with dependent and neglected children:

> When any child under the age of sixteen (16) years shall be found to be dependent or neglected within the meaning of this act, the court may make an order committing the child to the care of some suitable State institution, or to the care of some reputable citizen of good moral character, or to the care of some training school or an industrial school, as provided by law, or to the care of some association willing to receive it embracing in its objects the purpose of caring or obtaining homes for dependent or neglected children, which association shall have been accredited as hereinafter provided. . .

For juvenile delinquents, similar provisions were made. Judges were authorized to continue the hearing for any specific delinquent child "from time to time" and "may commit the child to the care and guardianship of a probation officer." The child might be permitted to remain in *its* own home, subject to the visitation of the probation officer. [Emphasis mine] Judges were also authorized to commit children to state training or industrial schools until such time as they reach the age of their majority or adulthood.

Juveniles as Chattel

The choice of the word *it,* used here in reference to children, shows how youths were viewed in those days. In early English times, children were considered chattel, lumped together with the cows, pigs, horses, and other farm property one might lawfully possess. The Act itself was sufficiently ambiguous so as to allow judges and others considerable latitude or discretion about how to interpret juvenile behaviors. For example, what is meant by proper parental care or guardianship? What is habitual begging? Is occasional begging acceptable? Would children be subject to arrest and juvenile court sanctions for walking city streets playing a flute or other musical device? Who decides what homes and establishments are unfit? Where are the criteria that describe a home's fitness? It has almost always been presumed that juvenile court judges know the answers to these questions, and their judgments, regardless of their foundation, rationality, or consistency with due process, are seldom questioned.

These statements reflect the traditionalism that juvenile court judges have manifested over the years (Moore and Wakeling 1997). Taking dependent and neglected or abandoned children and placing them in training or industrial schools is the functional equivalent of adult incarceration in a prison or jail. By a stroke of the pen, the Illinois legislature gave juvenile court judges absolute control over the lives of all children under age 16 in the State of Illinois. During the next ten years, twenty states passed similar acts to establish juvenile courts. By the end of World War II, all states had created juvenile court systems. However, considerable variation existed among these court systems, depending on the jurisdiction. Not all of these courts were vested with a consistent set of responsibilities and powers.

Children's Tribunals

Earlier versions of juvenile courts were created in Massachusetts in 1874. For instance, there were **children's tribunals,** sometimes referred to as **civil tribunals.** These informal mechanisms were used to adjudicate and punish children charged with crimes. They were entirely independent from the system of criminal courts for adults. Usually, judges would confer with the equivalent of a social worker and then decide how best to deal with a wayward youth. Under the tribunal system, youths were not entitled to representation by counsel, and the proceedings occurred in secret, away from public view. Furthermore, there were no formal presentations of evidence against the accused youth, no transcripts, no cross-examination of witnesses, and no right to appeal a judicial decision.

Some years later, Colorado implemented an education law in 1899 known as the **Compulsory School Act.** Although this act was primarily targeted at youths who were habitually absent from school, it also encompassed juveniles

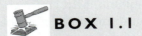 **BOX 1.1**

 **PERSONALITY HIGHLIGHT**

Abundio Rene Cantú
Student Aid Clerk, Office of the U.S. Attorney for the Southern District

Statistics:

A.A. (criminal justice), Laredo Community College; B.A. (legal studies), University of Texas at San Antonio; M.A. (criminal justice), Texas A & M International University

Background and Interests:

I am currently employed with the Office of the United States Attorney for the Southern District of Texas in Laredo. I was hired as a graduate student aid clerk and have always been interested in working in the many areas of the legal system. The areas of juveniles, corrections, and domestic violence have always been of great interest to me. I never thought that I would have the opportunity to go to college, because I had never really given it much thought until my parents were killed by a drunk driver in April 1995. This is when I started to take a great interest in criminal justice and the legal system, because I got a lot of exposure to lawyers and the courts because of this situation.

I graduated from John B. Alexander High School in December 1997. After finishing high school, I enrolled at Laredo Community College and started taking all of my basic courses. It was during my sophomore year that I got an opportunity to go to Washington, DC, and work for the U.S. Department of Labor as an intern under the National Hispanic Association of Colleges and Universities Internship Program. I lived in the District of Columbia from January 1999 to May 2000, when I returned to Laredo to graduate from Laredo Community College. In January 2000 I received a scholarship to attend the University of Texas at San Antonio where I majored in criminal justice with an emphasis on legal studies. I received my B.A. degree in criminal justice in December 2001. I have worked at the local, state, and federal levels of government agencies throughout my college career through various internship programs. I worked in the area of domestic violence at the Webb County District Attorney's Office, and at the San Antonio City Attorney's Office. I did many things for both of these agencies during the time spent there as an intern. I was in charge of conducting intakes for the attorneys at both agencies, and I usually took the intakes for the Mexican victims of domestic violence because I am bilingual in English and Spanish. It was a real challenge for me because these are real people with real problems in very tough situations. You have to always be very professional when dealing with these victims, especially if there are children involved.

One interesting experience I had when dealing with these victims at the City Attorney's Office was when we had a lady come into the office and report that her husband had been abusing her and her children for over eighteen years and she finally decided to do something about it. This is when you know that there is a problem, but because the victim feared her husband would cause further injury to her and her children, she kept quiet all of this time. These crimes are serious. Experience shows that the levels of violence in these relationships tend to escalate, and many police departments cite domestic violence as their number one problem. Tough laws and effective prosecutions of abusers, combined with education and a cooperative approach among law enforcement and social service agencies, will take time to be effective. Until then we all must take a greater role in reporting domestic abuse. Our efforts to break the silence can make a difference.

In the Laredo office, I was in charge of assisting the domestic violence counselor, Mr. Rick Flores, with intakes and filling out all necessary paperwork to obtain protection orders for both adult and juvenile victims. At the San Antonio Attorney's Office, I was also in charge of conducting victim intakes as well as trial preparation for cases that were going to be prosecuted. Since domestic violence is a problem affecting many communities throughout the United States, I plan on becoming a domestic violence advocate for women and children as well as any individuals who are in these terrible situations. I want people to know that there is help for them and I would like to help these victims in any way I can.

The impact of domestic violence upon children in these families is quite apparent. It is sad to see families with preteen children who are emotionally distraught. The dysfunctional family environment cannot help but disable children and cause them not to function normally in other aspects of their social life. More than a few of these children learn by example, and if the domestic violence examples they are exposed to in their homes are any indication, they will grow up and likely behave in ways similar to their parents. It is a repetitive process that can only be terminated with solid intervention programs such as the ones I have seen and worked with in these different counties.

Advice to Students:

My advice to any student who is interested in pursuing a career in the area of criminal justice is to establish goals for yourself and do not give up on those goals until you have accomplished them. Remember, nothing in life comes free and easy. If there is something that you one day plan on becoming, you must always stay focused and never lose confidence in your abilities to attain your goals. Frank Sinatra once sang, in reference to finding success in New York, "If you can make it there, you'll make it anywhere." By the same token, if you target certain professions as goals, with hard work and determination, you can make it anywhere too. Working with families and victims of domestic violence is a very rewarding activity for me personally. When I see a family gain stability, or whenever the violence is eliminated, the youths in these families have a much better chance of leading normal lives and not becoming delinquent or problem children.

who wandered the streets during school hours, without any obvious business or occupation. These youths were termed "juvenile disorderly persons," and they were legislatively placed within the purview of truant officers and law enforcement officers who could detain them and hold them for further action by other community agencies. While both Massachusetts and Colorado created these different mechanisms specifically for dealing with juvenile offenders, they were not juvenile courts in the same sense as those established by Illinois in 1899 (Hahn 1984). Furthermore, these truancy-oriented courts were not an exclusively U.S. creation. In England, for example, precourt tribunals have been established to decide whether families should be taken to court because of a child's nonattendance at school. The intent of such tribunals is to normalize families and destroy deviant identities juveniles might acquire because of their school absences. Both parents and children must reassure the judge that regular school attendance will be forthcoming (Pratt and Grimshaw 1985).

Informal Welfare Agencies and Emerging Juvenile Courts

The juvenile court has evolved from an informal welfare agency into a scaled-down, second-class criminal court as the result of a series of reforms that have diverted less serious offenders from juvenile court and moved more serious offenders to criminal courts for processing (Feld 1993b). Several policy responses have been recommended as options. These include (1) restructuring the juvenile courts to fit their original therapeutic purposes; (2) accepting punishment as the purpose of delinquency proceedings, but coupling it with criminal procedural safeguards; and/or (3) abolishing juvenile courts altogether and trying young offenders in criminal courts, with certain substantive and procedural modifications (Cohn 1994).

The Lack of Juvenile Court Uniformity

Currently, little uniformity exists among jurisdictions regarding juvenile court organization and operation (Butts 1996b). Even within state jurisdictions, great variations exist among counties and cities relating to how juvenile offenders are processed. Historically, family or domestic courts have retained jurisdiction over most, if not all, juvenile matters. Not all jurisdictions have juvenile courts, per se. Rather, some jurisdictions have courts that adjudicate juvenile offenders as well as decide child custody (Secret and Johnston 1996). Thus, while it is true that all jurisdictions presently have juvenile courts, these courts are not always called juvenile courts.

From *Gemeinschaft* to *Gesellschaft* and Reconceptualizing Juveniles

Before the establishment of juvenile courts, how were juvenile offenders processed and punished? How were dependent and neglected children treated? Social scientists would probably describe village and community life in the 1700s and 1800s by citing the dominant social and cultural values that existed then. The term **gemeinschaft** might be used here to describe the lifestyle one might find in such settings. It is a term used to characterize social relations as being highly dependent upon verbal agreements and understandings and informality. Ferdinand Tönnies, a social theorist, used *gemeinschaft* to convey the richness of tradition that would typify small communities where everyone was known to all others. In these settings, formal punishment, such as incarceration in prisons or jails, was seldom used. More effective than incarceration were punishments that heightened public humiliation through stocks and pillars and other corporal measures. There was sufficient social pressure exerted so that most complied with the law. Thus, in *gemeinschaft* communities, people would probably fear social stigma, ostracism, and scorn more than their loss of freedom through incarceration.

In these communities, children would remain children through adolescence, eventually becoming adults as they commenced to perform trades or crafts and earned independent livings apart from their families. Children performed apprenticeships over lengthy periods under the tutorship of master craftsmen and others. Many of the terms we currently use to describe delinquent acts and status offenses were nonexistent then. As the nation grew, urbanization and the increasing population density of large cities changed social relationships gradually but extensively. Tonnies described the nature of this gradual shift in social relationships from a *gemeinschaft*-type of social network to a **gesellschaft**-type of society. In *gesellschaft* societies, social relationships

are more formal, contractual, and impersonal. There is greater reliance on codified compilations of appropriate and lawful conduct as a means of regulating
social relations.

As urbanization gradually occurred, children were reconceptualized. During the period of Reconstruction following the Civil War, there were no child
labor laws, and children were exploited increasingly by industry and business.
Children were put to work in factories in their early years, where they were
paid low wages in **sweat shops,** usually manufacturing companies where long
hours were required and persons worked at repetitive jobs on assembly lines.
By the end of the nineteenth century, in part because of these widespread
nonunionized and unregulated sweat shop operations and compulsory school
attendance for youths in their early years, loitering youths became increasingly
visible and attracted the attention of the general public and law enforcement.

Specialized Juvenile Courts

Special courts were subsequently established to adjudicate juvenile matters.
The technical language describing inappropriate youthful conduct or misbehav-
iors was greatly expanded and refined. These new courts were also vested with
the authority to appoint probation officers and other persons considered suitable to manage juvenile offenders and enforce new juvenile codes that most
cities created. Today, most larger police departments have specialized juvenile
sections or divisions, where only juvenile law violations or suspicious activities are investigated. In retrospect, Platt (1969) suggests that the original aggregate of childsavers had much to do with inventing delinquency and its
numerous, specialized subcategories as we now know them. At least they contributed to the formality of the present juvenile justice system by defining a
range of impermissible juvenile behaviors that would require an operational
legal apparatus to address. Once a juvenile justice system was established and
properly armed with the right conceptual tools, it was a relatively easy step to
enforce a fairly rigid set of juvenile behavioral standards and regulate most aspects of their conduct. This seems to be a part of a continuing pattern designed
to criminalize the juvenile courts and hold juveniles accountable to the same
standards as adult offenders (Feld 1995).

As juvenile court systems became more widespread, it was apparent that
these proceedings were quite different from criminal courts in several respects.
Largely one-sided affairs, these proceedings typically involved the juvenile
charged with some offense, a petitioner claiming the juvenile should be declared delinquent, a status offender, dependent, or neglected, and a judge who
would weigh the evidence and decide the matter. Juveniles themselves were
not provided with opportunities to solicit witnesses or even give testimony in
their own behalf. Defense attorneys were largely unknown in juvenile courtrooms, since there were no significant issues to defend.

Juvenile court proceedings were closed to the general public, primarily to
protect the identities of the youthful accused. While these proceedings were
conducted behind closed doors for this manifest purpose, a latent function of
such secrecy was to obscure from public view the high-handed and discriminatory decision making that characterized many juvenile court judges. In short,
they didn't want the general public to know about the subjectivity and arbitrary
nature of their decisions. On the basis of allegations alone, together with uncor-
roborated statements and pronouncements from probation officers and others,

juvenile court judges were free to declare any particular juvenile either delinquent or nondelinquent. The penalties that could be imposed were wide-ranging, from verbal reprimands and warnings to full-fledged incarceration in a secure juvenile facility. Virtually everything depended upon the opinions and views of presiding juvenile court judges. And their decisions were not appealable to higher courts (Johnston and Secret 1995).

Throughout much of the twentieth century, juveniles had no legal standing in U.S. courts. Their constitutional rights were not at issue, because they did not have any constitutional protections in the courtroom. No rules of evidence existed to govern the quality of evidence admitted or to challenge the reliability or integrity of testifying witnesses. In most jurisdictions, juveniles were not entitled to jury trials, unless the juvenile court judge approved. And most juvenile court judges opted for bench trials rather than granting jury trials to juvenile defendants. Because these proceedings were exclusively civil in nature, the rules of criminal procedure governing criminal courts did not apply. Juveniles did not acquire criminal records. Rather, they acquired civil adjudications of delinquency. Yet, the incarceration dimension of the juvenile justice system has almost always paralleled that of the criminal justice system. Industrial or training schools, reform schools, and other types of secure confinement for juveniles have generally been nothing more than juvenile prisons. Thus, for many adjudicated juvenile offenders sentenced to one of these industrial schools, these sentences were the equivalent of imprisonment.

Kangaroo Courts in Action

Such unchecked discretion among juvenile court judges continued well into the 1960s. One explanation is mass complacency or apathy among the general public about juvenile affairs. Juvenile matters were relatively unimportant and trivial. Another explanation is the prevalent belief that juvenile court judges knew what is best for adjudicated offenders and usually prescribed appropriate punishments. Juvenile court judges and others often viewed juveniles as victims of their environment and peer associations. It might be easier to justify why new environments are required, including incarceration for the purpose of training, education, and rehabilitation, if the adverse effects of former environments can be illustrated. However, in 1967, the U.S. Supreme Court decided the case of *In re Gault.* This was perhaps the first major Supreme Court case that applied more stringent standards to juvenile court judge decision making, thus making them more accountable to the general public.

Briefly, Gerald Gault was a 15-year-old Arizona youth who allegedly made an obscene telephone call to an adult female neighbor. The woman called police, suggested that the youth, Gault, was the guilty party, and Gault was summarily taken into custody and detained for nearly two days. The woman was never brought to court as a witness, and the only evidence she provided was her initial verbal accusation made to police on the day of Gault's arrest. Gault himself allegedly admitted that he dialed the woman's number, but he claimed that a boyfriend of his actually spoke to the woman and made the remarks she found offensive. Partly because Gault had been involved in an earlier petty offense and had a "record," the judge, together with the probation officer, decided that Gault was dangerous enough to commit to the Arizona State Industrial School, Arizona's main juvenile penitentiary, until he reached 21 years of age or until juvenile corrections authorities decided he was rehabilitated and could be safely released. According to Arizona law, the sentence was unappealable. Any adult convicted of the same offense may have been fined $50 and/or sentenced to a 30-day jail term. But in Gault's case, he received six years in a juvenile prison, complete with correctional officers with firearms, high walls, locked gates, and barbed wire.

Appropriately, the U.S. Supreme Court referred to the court of the judge who originally sentenced Gault as a kangaroo court. Gault's sentence was reversed and several important constitutional rights were conferred upon all juveniles as a result. Specifically, all of Gault's due process rights had been denied. He had been denied counsel, had not been protected against self-incrimination, had not been permitted to cross-examine his accuser, and had not been provided with specific notice of the charges against him. Now all juveniles enjoy these rights in every U.S. juvenile court. It is important to note that Arizona was not alone in its harsh and one-sided treatment of juvenile offenders. What occurred in the Gault case was occurring in juvenile courts in most other jurisdictions at the time. The Gault case served to underscore the lack of legal standing of juveniles everywhere, and substantial juvenile justice reforms were occurring.

The Increasing Bureaucratization and Criminalization of Juvenile Justice

After the *Gault* case and several other important Supreme Court decisions affecting juveniles, the nature of juvenile courts began to change. But this transformation was anything but smooth. Even the U.S. Supreme Court continued to view juvenile courts as basically rehabilitative and treatment-centered apparatuses, thus reinforcing the traditional doctrine within the context of various constitutional restraints. Nevertheless, episodic changes in juvenile court procedures and the juvenile justice system generally suggested that it was becoming increasingly criminalized. Furthermore, many juvenile courts have moved away from traditional methods of conducting adjudicatory hearings for juveniles. Instead of individualized decision making and a rehabilitative orientation, many judges are increasingly interested in mechanisms that streamline the processing of juvenile cases and offenders. In fact, some juvenile courts have used mathematical models to establish profiles of juvenile offenders to expedite the adjudicatory process. This has been termed **actuarial justice** by some authorities, and it means that the traditional orientation of juvenile justice and punishment has been supplanted by the goal of efficient offender processing (Kempf-Leonard and Peterson 2000). In Minnesota and other jurisdictions, the development of new Rules of Procedure for Juvenile Court and the current administrative assumptions and operations of these courts, with limited exceptions, often render them indistinguishable from criminal courts and the procedures these courts follow (Feld 1993b).

WHO ARE JUVENILE OFFENDERS?

Juvenile Offenders Defined

Depending upon the jurisdiction, **juvenile offenders** are classified and defined according to several different criteria. According to the 1899 Illinois Act that created juvenile courts, the **jurisdiction** of such courts would extend to all juve-

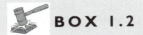 **BOX 1.2**

Rick Richardson
Juvenile Probation Officer, Yellowstone County, Billings, Montana

Statistics:

B.A. (criminal justice), Montana State University–Bozeman; Eastern Montana College–Billings; Montana State University–Billings; Chadwick University, Birmingham, Alabama

Work Experience:

I started out working for the Billings Police Department (BPD) in Montana. I worked as a uniformed street patrol officer for eight years. I was transferred to the Juvenile Detective Division and worked for twelve years specializing in investigations of sex crimes against juveniles and satanic/ritual abuse of juveniles. Also, I was a volunteer board member of the Tumbleweed Runaway Program and a board member of the Sexual Abuse Task Force. I conducted workshops related to local area cult activity. I was promoted to sergeant and returned to uniformed street patrol as a shift supervisor. Subsequently, I was transferred back into the Detective Division as a supervisor.

My early years with the BPD during the 1970s were interesting. At that time, BPD officers were allowed broad discretionary powers. For instance, we were given the latitude to decide minor violations informally, without making arrests or filling out lengthy reports. Drunk drivers were usually given rides home by officers rather than cited or arrested. They were given verbal reprimands, however, to not get caught drunk again without consequences. In domestic violence cases, which are the most dangerous types of police calls, it didn't matter whether one or the other spouse had a black eye or was bleeding from wounds inflicted during fights. We knew that the other spouse wouldn't press charges anyway. Usually, we separated the spouses for an evening and then got them back together.

One incident stands out, however, as an exception. We responded to a spouse abuse call and approached a house in a usually quiet neighborhood. As we walked toward the house where some spouses were allegedly arguing, a man suddenly appeared on the front porch with a shotgun pressed against a woman's head. He yelled out that he would "blow her head off" if we got in his way. I huddled behind my cruiser and took careful aim. At one point, I had a clean shot to take him out, but I hesitated. I was fearful that a muscle contraction might cause the shotgun to go off, killing the woman anyway. We followed him as he walked away from the home, with the woman in his arm and the shotgun pressed against her head. They were several houses down the street when I heard the woman tell the man, "Quit pointing that gun at my head. You know it's not loaded anyway." The man said, "I just want to get out of here so they don't take me to jail." Subsequently, he threw the shotgun on the ground and we moved in and arrested him. The adrenaline rush I felt began to subside, and I pondered what might have happened if I had pulled the trigger and killed him.

Many changes in law enforcement practices occurred over the next few decades, removing much discretion from police officers. Mandatory arrest policies went into effect for arguing spouses. Drunks were no longer given rides home. They were cited and taken to jail. We began using nonlethal weapons in our tactics training. Community-oriented policing became the rule rather than the exception. During the 1990s, after I had put in over twenty years in law enforcement, I decided to retire from the BPD.

In 1995, I decided to commence a new career in law enforcement as a Juvenile Probation Officer with Yellowstone County, Billings, Montana. The department, Court Services, as of 2002 was subsumed under the direction of the Montana Supreme Court. Duties included supervising youth who committed offenses that, if committed by adults, would be crimes, as well as supervising youths who had been placed on probation as delinquents and those deemed in need of intervention or had violated any probation condition. Supervision of youth assigned under the guidelines of the Montana Youth Court Act range from informal dispositions (consent adjustments) to consent decrees and formal probation with petitions. The vast majority of youth are first-time misdemeanants committing crimes such as theft, illegal possession of controlled substances, and status offenses such as minors in possession of alcohol/tobacco, and curfew violations. While we would like to spend the majority of our working hours with more serious juvenile offenders, that just doesn't happen around here because of the large case assignments and limited resources.

The Youth Intake and Assessment Center was supposed to speed up processing of first-time minor offenders and make them immediately accountable for their actions. That system provides risk assessments designed for case management and identifies services the youth and families might need. Limited funding for staff has resulted in a backlog of youth referred to the center rather than the intended purpose of streamlining the intake/dispositional process. An example is cited below.

I was called by a police detective to come over to the police department and view an audio/videotape taken from one of the local convenience stores from the night before. On this tape was the murder of a middle-aged store clerk. The detective was inquiring if the juvenile probation office staff knew who the young male was who was shown on the video shooting the clerk, while holding the semi-automatic pistol gang style. The youth appeared familiar, but no one, including myself, knew his identity. The film was released, in part, to the local news media and within a few hours, the youth had been identified and arrested for this murder. I check the youth's juvenile record with our department files and found that he had a minor offense that was handled as a counseled and warned disposition. Nothing else in this youth's file indicated that he had a violent nature that would lead him to kill just a few months later. Why didn't the risk assessment identify this youth as a potential violent juvenile offender, and if it did, why wasn't it acted upon? Those were questions the department had to answer when this case came to trial. This youth's case was subsequently transferred out of Youth Court and into District Court where the youth was on trial for murder as an adult offender. He was 16 at the time of the offense.

Advice to Students:

A career in law enforcement, whether as a police officer or a juvenile probation officer, has its rewards in terms of personal and professional growth. The bonds made with peers last a lifetime. Police and probation work offer a variety of interesting work experiences, and the opportunity to specialize in areas of your interest are readily available. Working in a helping profession also has a down side. Long hours, shift work, and average pay can become frustrating. Individuals seeking to become law enforcement officers should weigh the pros and cons before deciding to dedicate themselves to these professions. Police and probation departments recognize the need for higher education, with most departments rewarding officers for achieving bachelor's and master's level degrees through incentives of higher pay, promotions, and time off. Trends in law enforcement constantly change, and continuing education in the criminal justice field is necessary and vital in order to keep abreast of these changes.

niles under the age of 16 who were found in violation of any state or local law or ordinance (Gittens 1994). About a fifth of all states place the upper age limit for juveniles at either 15 or 16. In most other states, the upper age limit for juveniles is 17, except for Wyoming, where the upper age limit is 18. Ordinarily, the jurisdiction of juvenile courts includes all **juveniles** between the ages of 7 and 18 (Black 1990, 867). Federal law considers juveniles to be any persons who have not attained their eighteenth birthday (18 U.S.C., Sec. 5031, 2002). Viewed another way, criminal court jurisdiction over a majority of offenders in the United States usually begins with their eighteenth birthday.

The Age Jurisdiction of Juvenile Courts

While fairly uniform upper age limits for juveniles have been established in all U.S. jurisdictions (either under 16, under 17, or under 18 years of age), there is no uniformity concerning lower age limits. English common law considered juveniles under the age of 7 incapable of formulating criminal intent; therefore, they were not within the jurisdiction of criminal courts. Today most U.S. jurisdictions recognize this common law age of 7, and youths under the age of 7 are generally not held accountable for whatever they do. Instead of punishments imposed for those under the age of 7, various kinds of treatment, including social therapy and psychological counseling, are required. Some states have further age-accountability provisions. In Tennessee, for instance, juveniles between the ages of 7 and 12 are presumed accountable for their delinquent acts, although this presumption may be overcome by their attorneys through effective oral arguments and clear and convincing evidence.

Many juvenile courts throughout the United States have no lower age limits for juveniles. While it is very unlikely that any juvenile court will adjudicate a 3-year-old, many of these courts have the power to decide matters involving children of any age. This control often involves placement of children or infants in foster homes or under the supervision of community service or human welfare agencies. Neglected, unmanageable, abused, or other children in need of supervision are placed in the custody of these various agencies, at the discretion of juvenile judges. Thus, juvenile courts generally have broad discretionary powers over most persons under the age of 18.

The Treatment and Punishment Functions of Juvenile Courts

The idea that in order for juvenile courts to exercise jurisdiction over juveniles, these youths must be offenders and must have committed offending acts (i.e., illegal acts or crimes) is misleading. Many youths appearing before juvenile judges have not violated any criminal laws. Rather, their status as juveniles renders them subject to juvenile court control, provided certain circumstances exist. These circumstances may be the quality of their adult supervision, if any. Other circumstances may be that they run away from home, are truant from school, or loiter on certain city streets during evening hours. Runaways, truants, or loiterers are considered **status offenders,** since their acts would not be criminal if committed by adults (Feld 1993b).

Additionally, children who are physically, psychologically, or sexually abused by parents or other adults in their homes are brought within the scope of juvenile court authority. However, the majority of youthful offenders who

 **BOX 1.3**

TEEN PLEADS GUILTY TO MOTHER'S MURDER

Arnell VanDuyne, 16

It happened in Clovis, New Mexico. On July 5, 2001, Norma Young, 41, was found in her home murdered. At first, police were baffled over the discovery. Norma Young was a mother, and she operated a day care center in her home. On the day of her murder, she had been playing with other children in the home. After interviewing the young children, police focused their investigation on a foster child who had been adopted by Young three years earlier. He was Arnell VanDuyne, 16. When police looked for VanDuyne, they couldn't find him. An all-points bulletin was issued for his arrest, and he was subsequently located in Cannin, Texas. He led police on a high-speed chase before being caught. He had fled the scene in Young's automobile, and he had stolen her credit cards and money.

Later during an interrogation, VanDuyne confessed to police and told them what had happened. He said that he became angry with Young when she told him to clean out his dresser. She later checked and told him that he wasn't doing it right. VanDuyne then subdued Young, tied her hands behind her back, and attempted to rape her. Subsequently, he beat her to death with a baseball bat in front of six small children. VanDuyne told authorities, "I can't give you all Norma back and I know that. I'm sorry for what I done. I can't take it back."

According to VanDuyne's defense counsel, James Wilson, VanDuyne should be shown mercy in sentencing. This is because of his difficult early life, according to Wilson. Wilson said that VanDuyne's natural mother used to lock him up in a closet in a crack house for several days when he was a toddler. But Norma Young's husband, Paul Young, said, "To kill someone who takes you in as she had done herself is inhumane and unjustified." The 16-year-old VanDuyne was sentenced to life in prison.

Should a juvenile's prior treatment as a toddler be regarded as a significant factor in his sentencing for murder? Should the judge be lenient with VanDuyne in this case? What do you think?

Source: Adapted from Heather Clark and the Associated Press. "Teen Pleads Guilty to Mother's Murder." November 21, 2001.

appear before juvenile courts are those who have violated state or local laws or ordinances. These youths are **juvenile delinquents.** Federal law says that **juvenile delinquency** is the violation of any law of the United States by a person prior to his (or her) eighteenth birthday, which would have been a crime if committed by an adult (18 U.S.C., Sec. 5031, 2002). In law, juveniles are referred to as **infants.** A legal definition of a juvenile delinquent is any infant of not more than a specified age who has violated criminal laws or engages in disobedient, indecent, or immoral conduct, and is in need of treatment, rehabilitation, or supervision (Black 1990, 777).

It is evident from these definitions that juvenile courts may define juveniles and juvenile delinquency according to their own standards and that for many jurisdictions, a delinquent act is whatever these courts say it is. Despite U.S. Supreme Court proclamations to the contrary, juvenile court judges continue to determine which juvenile rights will be observed or ignored. This ambiguity is unsettling to many critics of the juvenile justice system, who feel that the authority of juvenile judges is too broad and ought to be restricted. Incorrigibility, for instance, most often arises in everyday disputes between parents and children. The courts, thus far, have mediated these disputes largely in favor of adults. At least some persons contend that juvenile courts should not intervene in less-than-life-threatening events that arise from normal parent–child relations (Moore and Wakeling 1997). However, the vast bulk of incorrigibility charges that result in court-imposed sanctions on juveniles involve ordinary parent–child disputes. For some persons, these disputes are not appropriately a part of the business of U.S. courts (Schneider 1992). Other persons contend, however, that society has thrust upon children a degree of pseudomaturity, such as is manifested by juvenile court plea bargaining and other criminal court-like procedures (Sanborn 1993a). It is important at the outset to understand that much of this state authority originated under the early English doctrine of *parens patriae*.

PARENS PATRIAE

Parens patriae is a concept that originated with the king of England during the twelfth century. It means literally the father of the country. Applied to juvenile matters, *parens patriae* means that the king is in charge of, makes decisions about, and has the responsibility for all matters involving juveniles. Within the scope of early English common law, parental authority was primary in the early upbringing of children. However, as children advanced beyond the age of 7, they acquired some measure of responsibility for their own actions. Accountability to parents was shifted gradually to accountability to the state, whenever youths 7 years of age or older violated the law. In the name of the king, chancellors in various districts adjudicated matters involving juveniles and the offenses they committed. Juveniles had no legal rights or standing in any court. They were the sole responsibility of the king or his agents. Their future often depended largely upon chancellor decisions. In effect, children were wards of the court, and the court was vested with the responsibility to safeguard their welfare.

Chancery courts of twelfth and thirteenth century England and later years performed many tasks, including the management of children and their affairs, as well as the management of the affairs of the mentally ill and incompetent. Therefore, an early division of labor was created, involving a three-way relationship between the child, the parent, and the state. The underlying thesis of *parens patriae* was that the parents are merely the agents of society in the area of childrearing and that the state has the primary and legitimate interest in the upbringing of its children. Thus, *parens patriae* established a type of fiduciary or trust-like parent-child relation, with the state able to exercise the right of intervention to delimit parental rights (Fader et al. 2001).

Since children could become wards of the court and subject to their control, a key concern for many chancellors was for the future welfare of these children. The welfare interests of chancellors and their actions led to numerous rehabilitative and/or treatment measures. Some of these measures included placement of children in foster homes or their assignment to various work tasks for local merchants. Parental influence in these child placement decisions was minimal. In the context of *parens patriae,* it is fairly easy to trace this early philosophy of child management and its influence to subsequent events in the United States, such as the child-saver movement, houses of refuge, and reform schools. These latter developments were both private and public attempts to rescue children from their hostile environments and meet some or all of their needs through various forms of institutionalization.

MODERN INTERPRETATIONS OF *PARENS PATRIAE*

Parens patriae in the 1990s is very much alive throughout all juvenile court jurisdictions in the United States, although some erosion of this doctrine has occurred during the past three or four decades. The persistence of this doctrine is evidenced by the wide range of dispositional options available to juvenile court judges and others involved in earlier stages of offender processing in the juvenile justice system. Most of these dispositional options are either nominal or conditional, meaning that the confinement of any juvenile for most offenses is regarded as a last resort. Nominal or conditional options involve relatively mild sanctions (e.g., verbal warnings or reprimands, diversion, probation, making financial restitution to victims, performance of community service, participation in individual or group therapy, or involvement in educational programs), and these sanctions are intended to reflect the rehabilitative ideal that has been a major philosophical underpinning of *parens patriae* (Kempf-Leonard and Peterson 2000).

However, the strong treatment or rehabilitative orientation reflected by the *parens patriae* concept is in conflict with the contemporary juvenile justice themes of accountability, justice, and due process. Contemporary juvenile court jurisprudence stresses individual accountability for one's actions. Increasingly, there is a trend toward just-deserts and justice in the juvenile justice system. This **get-tough movement** is geared toward providing law violators with swifter, harsher, and more certain justice and punishment than the previously dominant rehabilitative philosophy of U.S. courts (Fader et al. 2001).

For juveniles, this means greater use of nonsecure and secure custody and incarcerative sanctions in state group homes, industrial schools, or reform schools. For those juveniles charged with violent offenses, this means transferring larger numbers of them to the jurisdiction of criminal courts for adults, where more severe sanctions such as life imprisonment or the death penalty may be imposed. Not all authorities agree that this is a sound trend, however (McLaren 2000). It has been suggested that while many people favor a separate juvenile justice system different from the criminal justice system, they exhibit a strong preference for a system that disposes most juveniles to specialized treatment or counseling programs in lieu of incarceration, even for repeat offenders (Fader et al. 2001; Lutze 2001).

Influencing the *parens patriae* doctrine are the changing rights of juveniles. Since the mid-1960s, juveniles have acquired greater constitutional rights commensurate with those enjoyed by adults in criminal courts. Some researchers believe that as juveniles are vested with greater numbers of constitutional rights, a gradual transformation of the juvenile court is occurring toward one of greater criminalization (Feld 2000). Interestingly, as juveniles obtain a greater range of constitutional rights, they become less susceptible to the influence of *parens patriae*.

Another factor is the gradual transformation of the role of prosecutors in juvenile courts. As prosecutors become more involved in pursuing cases against juvenile defendants, the entire juvenile justice process is perceived by some researchers as weakening the delinquency prevention role of juvenile

BOX 1.4

The York Haven, Pennsylvania, Kiddie Sex Ring

A group of seventeen students at Northeastern Middle School and York Haven Elementary School in York Haven, Pennsylvania, was discovered to have originated and perpetuated an intense sex ring. They ranged in age from 7 to 16, and their activities included virtually every sexual perversion and deviant sex act known. Newberry Township Police Chief Bill Myers said, "These kids knew that what they were doing wasn't right, but they didn't know it was as bad as it was. There was a naivete about the legal and moral consequences." Subsequently, six children were charged in juvenile court on various counts of rape, involuntary deviate sexual intercourse, and indecent assault. Several incidents of incest were found but not pursued criminally. The sexual activity had gone on for two and one-half years with just a few children involved at first. Then the group grew gradually to seventeen students of various ages. The assaults and sex acts occurred in the homes of the children when parents were away or in wooded areas in abandoned shacks. More children would have been charged but they were younger than the 10-year-old minimum for criminal charges, according to investigating detectives. Police learned about the sex ring after a sleepover sixteenth birthday party for one girl that was attended by another 16-year-old girl, two 11-year-old boys, and a 13-year-old boy. Supposedly, what happened was that they were playing "spin the bottle," and things got well beyond that. The story was that one bottle pointed toward one of the males and he had to have intercourse with one of the girls. This turned out to be the tip of the iceberg. Following the birthday party, it was discovered that one of the 11-year-old boys had been molesting a 7-year-old neighbor and told it to the victim's mother. When the woman went to police, the daughter admitted that she had been having sex with an 11-year-old boy.

What should be the punishment for these children who ran the sex ring? Is there sufficient evidence to justify crimes among the participants? What do you think?

Source: Adapted from the Associated Press, "17 Children Involved in Neighborhood Sex Ring." July 5, 1999.

courts. Thus, more aggressive prosecution of juvenile cases is perceived as moving away from delinquency prevention for the purpose of deterring youths from future adult criminality. The intentions of prosecutors in most cases are to ensure that youths are entitled to due process, but the social costs may be to label these youths in ways that will propel them toward adult criminality rather than away from it (Cooper et al. 1994).

JUVENILE AND CRIMINAL COURTS: SOME PRELIMINARY DISTINCTIONS

Some of the major differences between juvenile and criminal courts and indicated below. These generalizations are more or less valid in most jurisdictions in the United States.

1. Juvenile courts are civil proceedings exclusively designed for juveniles, whereas criminal courts are proceedings designed to try adults charged

with crimes. In criminal courts, adults are targeted for criminal court actions, although some juveniles may be tried as adults in these same courts. The civil–criminal distinction is important because a civil adjudication of a juvenile court case does not result in a criminal record for the juvenile offender. In criminal courts, either a judge or jury finds a defendant guilty or not guilty. In the case of guilty verdicts, offenders are convicted and acquire criminal records. These **convictions** follow adult offenders for the rest of their lives. However, when juveniles are tried in juvenile courts, their juvenile court adjudications are sealed or expunged and generally forgotten, with exceptions, once they reach adulthood or the age of their majority.

2. Juvenile proceedings are more informal, whereas criminal proceedings are more formal. Attempts are made in many juvenile courts to avoid the formal trappings that characterize criminal proceedings. Juvenile court judges frequently address juveniles directly and casually. Formal rules of criminal procedure are not followed relating to the admissibility of evidence and testimony, and hearsay from various witnesses is considered together with hard factual information and evidence. Despite attempts by juvenile courts to minimize the formality of their proceedings, however, juvenile court procedures in recent years have become increasingly formalized. In some jurisdictions at least, it is difficult to distinguish criminal courts from juvenile courts in terms of their formality.

3. In thirty-nine states, juveniles are not entitled to a trial by jury, unless the juvenile court judge approves. In all criminal proceedings, defendants are entitled to a trial by jury if they want one, and if the crime or crimes they are accused of committing carry incarcerative penalties of more than six months. Judicial approval is required for a jury trial for juveniles in most jurisdictions. This is one of the remaining legacies of the *parens patriae* doctrine in contemporary juvenile courts. Eleven states have legislative mandated jury trials for juveniles in juvenile courts if they are charged with certain types of offenses, if they are certain ages, and if they make a timely request for a jury trial.

4. Juvenile court and criminal court are **adversarial proceedings.** Juveniles may or may not wish to retain or be represented by counsel (*In re Gault,* 1967). In almost every juvenile court case, prosecutors allege various infractions or law violations against juveniles, and these charges may be rebutted by juveniles or others. If juveniles are represented by counsel, these defense attorneys are permitted to offer a defense to the allegations. Criminal courts are obligated to provide counsel for anyone charged with a crime, if defendants cannot afford to retain their own counsel (*Argersinger v. Hamlin,* 1972). Every state has provisions for providing defense attorneys to indigent juveniles who are adjudicated in juvenile court.

5. Criminal courts are **courts of record,** whereas transcripts of most juvenile proceedings are made only if the judge decides. **Court reporters** record all testimony presented in most criminal courts. All state criminal trial courts are courts of record, where either a tape-recorded transcript of proceedings is maintained, or a written record is kept. Thus, if trial court verdicts are appealed later by either the prosecution or defense, transcripts of these proceedings can be presented by either side as evidence of errors committed by the judge or other violations of one's due process rights. Original convic-

tions may be reversed or they may be allowed to stand, depending upon whatever the records disclose about the propriety of the proceedings. Juvenile courts are not courts of record. Thus, it is unlikely that in any given juvenile proceeding, a court reporter will keep a verbatim record of the proceedings. One factor that inhibits juvenile courts from being courts of record is the sheer expense of hiring court reporters for this work. Courts of record are expensive to maintain. Certainly in some of the more affluent jurisdictions, some juvenile court judges may enjoy the luxury of a court reporter to transcribe or record all court matters. But this is the exception rather than the rule. Furthermore, the U.S. Supreme Court has declared that juvenile courts are not obligated to be courts of record (*In re Gault,* 1967).

6. The **standard of proof** used for determining one's guilt in criminal proceedings is **beyond a reasonable doubt.** In juvenile courts, the less rigorous civil standard of **preponderance of the evidence** is used in most juvenile court matters. However, the U.S. Supreme Court has held that if any juvenile is in jeopardy of losing his or her liberty as the result of an adjudication by a juvenile court judge, then the evidentiary standard must be the criminal court standard of beyond a reasonable doubt (*In re Winship,* 1970). Losing liberty means to be locked up for any period of time, whether it is for one day, one month, or one or more years. Thus, juveniles who face charges in juvenile court where the possible punishment is confinement in a secure juvenile facility for any period of time are entitled to the beyond-a-reasonable-doubt criminal standard in determining their guilt. Therefore, it is expected of juvenile court judges that they will always apply this standard when adjudicating a juvenile's case and where one's loss of liberty is a possibility.

7. The range of penalties juvenile court judges may impose is limited, whereas in most criminal courts, the range of penalties may include life-without-parole sentences or the death penalty. The jurisdiction of juvenile court judges over youthful offenders typically ends when these juveniles reach adulthood. Some exceptions are that juvenile courts may retain jurisdiction over mentally ill youthful offenders indefinitely after they reach adulthood. In California, for instance, the Department of the Youth Authority supervises youthful offenders ranging in age from 11 to 25.

The purpose of this comparison is to show that criminal court actions are more serious and have harsher long-term consequences for offenders compared with juvenile court proceedings. Juvenile courts continue to be guided by a strong rehabilitative orientation in most jurisdictions, where the most frequently used punishments are either verbal reprimands or probationary dispositions. Secure confinement is viewed by most juvenile court judges as a last resort, and such a punishment is reserved for only the most serious youthful offenders, with exceptions. Probably less than 10 percent of all adjudicated delinquent offenders are incarcerated in secure juvenile facilities. However, in criminal courts, convicted offenders are more frequently jailed or imprisoned. Criminal courts also use probation as a punishment in about 60 percent of all criminal cases, especially for first offenders or those who have committed less serious crimes. Although increasing numbers of juvenile courts are adopting more punitive sanctions similar to those of criminal courts, many youths continue to receive treatment-oriented punishments rather than incarceration in secure juvenile facilities.

 **BOX 1.5**

BOY GETS MAN'S SENTENCE OF 50 YEARS FOR BEING SEDUCED INTO COMMITTING MURDER

Robert Hudson, 15

It happened in Ebensburg, Pennsylvania. A teenage boy was pressured by his lover into killing the father of her two children. The murder occurred on March 11, 1999 when Robert Hudson, 15, was baby-sitting for Robert Hawks, 35, and Michelle Clark, 32. Clark became attracted to Hudson and seduced him sexually. After a short affair, Clark suggested to Hudson that he should kill Robert Hawks, the father of her two children. That evening while Hudson was baby-sitting, he took a gun and ambushed Hawks in the attic of Hawks' home. Hawks was shot to death and pronounced dead later by the coroner. Hudson claimed that Clark threatened to abandon him if he did not help her kill Hawks. At first, Clark wanted a hit man to kill her live-in boyfriend and father of her children. The reason she wanted Hawks dead was so that she could obtain custody of her children. Hudson was appre-

hended by police shortly after the shooting and confessed. He said, "I'm sorry . . . I wish I could do something about it. Sometimes I wish I could take his place." Hudson was sentenced as an adult to a 25- to 50-year term in prison. His accomplice, Michelle Clark, pleaded guilty to criminal solicitation of homicide, conspiracy to commit homicide, and statutory sexual assault. She was sentenced to 12 to 30 years in prison. Following the sentencing, the father of Hawks, Anson Hawks, said, "My son is dead, and he'll [Hudson] possibly be walking the streets in twenty-five years."

Was a 50-year sentence adequate in Hudson's case? Were there any mitigating circumstances? Should Michelle Clark have received a similar sentence for pressuring Hudson into committing murder? What do you think?

Source: Adapted from the Associated Press. "Boy Seduced into Murder Gets up to 50 Years." April 20, 2001.

SUMMARY

The juvenile justice system is a more or less integrated network of agencies, institutions, and personnel that process juvenile offenders. Because of the existing lack of close coordination between agencies and organizations, some critics have labeled it a process. During the past several decades, the juvenile justice process has undergone substantial reforms. There is no indication that this reformation will abate in the near future.

Juveniles are currently managed and processed through civil authority. English influence on the juvenile justice process is strong. In the twelfth century, the King of England established the doctrine of *parens patriae,* where he functioned as the father of the country and made decisions relating to juveniles and their welfare. Because of the geographical limitations on his jurisdiction, he appointed chancellors to act and make decisions about juveniles in his own behalf. Today, several jurisdictions have chancery courts, where chancellors preside and continue to affect juveniles' lives.

Early English common law presumed that all infants under the age of 7 were not accountable for their actions. Parents were largely responsible for maintaining discipline among their children. From age 7 to adulthood, youths would be accountable to various authorities besides their parents for any wrongful actions, and the punishments they received were most often different from those imposed on adults who committed crimes. In colonial times, youthful offenders were assigned various skilled and semiskilled tasks to perform for merchants. Little, if any, attention was given to their legal rights. Shortly after the United States was established, houses of refuge were constructed in New York and other states. These houses sought to provide idle youths with productive work and educational experiences.

The child-saver movement, often having religious foundations, was strong during the 1800s. Basically, this movement believed that children could be rescued from societal circumstances that might otherwise cause their delinquency and lead to lives as adult criminals. Over the years, state authority encroached on private interests and eventually exerted extensive control over large numbers of errant juveniles. Parental authority over children decreased accordingly as state interests became primary. Eventually, specialized courts, juvenile courts, were created to further formalize how youths would be managed and processed.

Juvenile courts are largely a U.S. creation, with the first juvenile court established in Illinois in 1899. Currently, all jurisdictions throughout the United States have juvenile courts. These courts perform various functions, including adjudications of juveniles as either delinquent or nondelinquent. Juvenile judges impose assorted punishments in accordance with state and local statutes as well as their own discretion about what is best for youths in their courts. Although jurisdictions vary according to how juveniles are defined, most jurisdictions define juveniles as being under age 18. In about a fifth of all jurisdictions, no minimum age is prescribed to limit the jurisdiction of juvenile courts.

Some major differences between juvenile courts and criminal courts for adults are that juvenile courts are civil, and an adjudication as delinquent does not mean that a youth will acquire a criminal record. Compared with criminal courts, juvenile courts are less formal, less likely to be courts of record and keep running transcriptions of court proceedings, and have less severe penalties as punishments. Both types of courts are adversarial. While the standard of proof in both types of courts is "beyond a reasonable doubt" whenever one's freedom is in jeopardy, juvenile courts in many jurisdictions also utilize the civil standard, "preponderance of the evidence."

QUESTIONS FOR REVIEW

1. What is meant by the juvenile justice system? Is it a system or a process? Why do some people consider it a process?

2. What was the Bridewell Workhouse? What were the functions of workhouses in early England? How did the poor laws influence those confined to workhouses?

3. Who were the childsavers? What was the child-saving movement and what was its significance in the subsequent emergence of the juvenile court?

4. What were the cases of *Ex parte Crouse* and *People ex rel. O'Connell v. Turner*? What was their significance for juvenile justice?

5. What was the Illinois Juvenile Court Act and what was its significance for juvenile courts?

6. What is the age jurisdiction of most juvenile courts in the United States? Who are juvenile offenders?

7. What is meant by *parens patriae?* How has this concept influenced juvenile courts in the United States?

8. What are four major differences between criminal courts and juvenile courts?

9. Are juveniles in all states entitled to a jury trial in juvenile court proceedings? What is the standard of proof in juvenile court proceedings where a juvenile can lose his or her liberty?

10. What are the general functions of juvenile courts? Are juvenile courts primarily treatment centered or punishment centered? What are some reasons for your answer?

SUGGESTED READINGS

American Correctional Association. 2002. *Juvenile justice today: Essays on programs and policies.* Laurel, MD: American Correctional Association.

Crews, Gordon A. and Reid H. Montgomery 2001. *Chasing shadows: Confronting juvenile violence in America.* Upper Saddle River, NJ: Prentice Hall.

Wilson, James Q. and Joan Petersilia 2002. *Crime: Public policies for crime control.* Oakland, CA: Institute for Contemporary Studies Press.

Wooden, Wayne S. and Randy Blazek 2001. *Renegade kids, suburban outlaws: From youth culture to delinquency. 2d ed.* Belmont, CA: Wadsworth.

INTERNET CONNECTIONS

American Bar Association's Juvenile Justice Center
http://www.abanet.org/crimjust/juvjus/home.html

American Civil Liberties Union
http://www.aclu.org

Building Blocks for Youth
http://www.buildingblocksforyouth.org/issues/jjdpa/factsheet.html

Center on Crime, Communities, and Culture
http://www.soros.org/crime/

National Center for Missing Children
http://www.scubed.com/public_service/index.html

National Clearinghouse on Child Abuse
http://www.calib.com/nccanch

Youth Change (problem-youth problem solving)
http://www.youthchg.com

Chapter Outline

Key Terms

National Juvenile Court Data
  Archive
National Youth Survey
Net-widening
Office of Juvenile Justice and
  Delinquency Prevention
  (OJJDP)

Pathways
Pittsburgh Youth Study (PYS)
Relabeling
Runaways
Self-reports, self-report
  information

*Sourcebook of Criminal Justice
  Statistics*
Status offenses
Stigmas, stigmatize, stigmatization
Uniform Crime Reports (UCR)
Victimization

Chapter Objectives

As a result of reading this chapter, you will have accomplished the following objectives:

1. Determine what is meant by juvenile delinquency.
2. Distinguish between juvenile delinquents and the broad class of status offenders, including runaways, truants, and curfew violators.
3. Understand the deinstitutionalization of status offenders.
4. Learn important differences between the *Uniform Crime Reports* and *National Crime Victimization Survey* as key indicators of delinquent behavior.
5. Learn about other important sources of information about juvenile offending, including the *National Juvenile Court Data Archive*, self-report information, and the *Sourcebook of Criminal Justice Statistics*.
6. Learn about violent and nonviolent delinquent conduct and whether there is any career escalation among juvenile offenders.
7. Determine some of the major differences between male and female juveniles and their offending patterns.

INTRODUCTION

- *It happened in Chicago, Illinois. On January 23, 2002, four teenage girls were standing in a restaurant parking lot on Wells Street at 12:30 A.M. They appeared to be highly animated, conversing with one another, laughing, and smoking. A Chicago Police Department cruiser pulled into the parking lot and two officers exited their vehicle. The four girls didn't appear to be upset or startled. As the officers approached the girls, they detected the odor of marijuana. They asked the girls for identification. Only one of the girls had a driver's license, which she gave to the officers. It indicated that she was Marcia C., 16 years old, and that she lived in a Chicago suburb about twenty miles from the downtown parking lot. The other girls gave their names and ages, respectively 15, 15, and 14. The oldest girl, Marcia C., said that they had been to a party earlier that evening and that she had driven the younger girls to the downtown parking lot where someone was going to meet them "between 12:00 midnight and 1:00 A.M." to transport the girls back to their homes. Marcia C. had agreed to bring them to the parking lot of the well-known Chicago restaurant and wait with them until their ride arrived. She pointed out a red Camaro as "her car," which was situated nearby in the parking lot. The officers investigated and determined that the girls were smoking plain cigarettes. They inquired about the marijuana odor, and Marcia C. said that a few persons at the party they attended had been smoking pot. The girls said that they had nothing to drink other than Coca Cola, although they admitted to underage smoking. While the officers continued to investigate, a late-model Cadillac pulled into the parking lot aside the girls and a couple in their forties emerged. They identified themselves as the mother and father of two of the girls and said they had arranged to meet with Marcia C. in the restaurant parking lot to drive their daughters and their friend back home in a direction opposite to that where Marcia C. resided. The officers pointed out to the parents that their daughters had been smoking when the officers had arrived and that this was illegal. They also noted that Chicago had a curfew ordinance prohibiting juveniles being on city streets late at night unaccompanied by an adult. After issuing a verbal warning, the officers got back in their cruiser and drove away.* [Adapted from the Associated Press, "Curfew Law Draws Complaints from Chicago Citizens." January 28, 2002].

• *A Nevada state trooper was driving north on Interstate 15 outside of Las Vegas late one evening when he spotted two youthful-looking hitchhikers, one female, the other male. He stopped his cruiser and approached them, asking for identification. The female produced an ID that showed her age as 18 and her name as "Rachel Smith" from Indianapolis, Indiana. The male showed an ID that indicated he was "John Houston," 21, from St. George, Utah. Somehow, their appearances did not match the ages on their IDs. The officer asked them to empty their pockets on the trunk lid of his cruiser. Among other things, the male was carrying a pocket knife. The female emptied the contents of her purse to yield some small, glassine envelopes that the officer suspected contained cocaine. The drugs and knife were confiscated. The trooper placed both persons in his cruiser and drove them to the nearest jail in Las Vegas, where they were detained pending further investigation. Subsequently, they were identified as Mark H., 15, from Grand Rapids, Michigan, and his girlfriend, Martha M., 14, also from Grand Rapids. They had been missing for two weeks and were considered runaways. The parents of both youths were contacted. They flew to Las Vegas and escorted their children back to Grand Rapids after filling out some police forms.* [Adapted from the Associated Press, "Juvenile Runaways from Michigan Nabbed in Las Vegas." April 13, 2002].

• *A New York City police officer was making her rounds late one evening in the Bronx. She heard some noises emanating from an alleyway. When she investigated, she saw two youths climbing out of a rear window of a drug store. They had what appeared to be pillowcases stuffed with unknown items. She called for backup, and, at gunpoint, she ordered the youths to place their hands over their heads and stand facing the drugstore back wall. Shortly thereafter, she was joined by two other officers who assisted her in frisking the youths. One youth was carrying a loaded .22 caliber automatic pistol, while the other youth was carrying a loaded Colt .45 automatic firearm. The contents of their pillowcases yielded numerous bottles of prescription drugs, mostly narcotic pain relievers. Later, at the police station, the two youths were booked, fingerprinted, and photographed. Both youths were 16 years old and had extensive juvenile records. One of the youths was on probation for burglary. The other youth had several prior arrests for aggravated assault and robbery. Warrants were issued by a local magistrate to search the homes of the youths. Detectives discovered large quantities of prescription drugs, cocaine, heroin, methamphetamines, and several other firearms. Some of the drugs were identified as having been stolen from other drugstores in the Bronx, and the guns had been reported stolen in adjacent states. As it turned out, one of the firearms seized had been used in the murder of an adult male victim four months earlier, although neither youth admitted to being involved in the murder. A juvenile court prosecutor said that she was going to request that these boys be charged as adults and stand trial in criminal court on the drug and weapons charges, as well as for the various burglaries.* [Adapted from the Associated Press, "Boys Apprehended in Bronx Drug Theft Linked to Murder for Hire." June 1, 2002].

These three scenarios are only a few of the hundreds of thousands of incidents involving youths each year. They depict police encounters with a wide range of juvenile suspects. As can be seen from the above depictions, some of these encounters involve relatively minor offending, such as curfew violation or runaway behavior. However, some encounters involve situations that are potentially lethal for investigating police officers. While curfew violation and running away from home are not crimes if adults engage in them, they are considered "offenses" if juveniles commit them. This is precisely because of their status as juveniles. In more than a few U.S. jurisdictions, juvenile courts would hear and decide these cases. In some of these instances, serious consequences might result in some form of probation supervision or control. In the case of the armed juvenile burglars, these juveniles have extensive records of offending. They are clearly in a more serious class of juvenile offender compared with curfew violators and runaways. They, too, will be processed by the juvenile court. But there is a far greater likelihood that they will be subject to more serious punishments if it is found that they are guilty of the crimes alleged against them. Conceivably, they might be incarcerated in a juvenile facility for a period of months or years.

Youths ages 13 to 18 make up about 10 percent of the U.S. population. However, members of this same age group account for 20 percent of all arrests annually (*World Almanac Books* 2002). Such an overrepresentation of juveniles among those arrested for crimes in the United States has attracted the attention and interest of many organizations and agencies. Is there currently a crime wave of youthful offenders? Is juvenile violence increasing? Is there anything we can do about it?

This chapter examines delinquency and how it is officially and unofficially defined. Each jurisdiction has different policies that pertain to the treatment and punishment of juvenile offenders. Numerous programs have been designed to manage the juvenile offender population and are in various stages of implementation throughout the United States today. No single program seems to have universal appeal. Widely different juvenile audiences are targeted by each of these programs, and the success of each is measured according to several types of standards. Because some of these programs are preventive in nature and involve interventions with children designated at risk in their early years, it is often impossible to calculate their long-term value and effectiveness.

For many years, the juvenile justice system has included within its jurisdiction youths who represent a wide variety of offense categories. Not all of these categories involve crimes. Thus, an important distinction is made between youthful offenders who engage in serious offenses as well as those who are involved in less serious activities known as status offenses. Recently, different jurisdictions have separated more serious offenders from less serious ones in the early stages of youth entry into the juvenile justice system. This process will be described.

The chapter also examines primary sources of information about juvenile offenders, including the *Uniform Crime Reports* and the *National Crime Victimization Survey*. These official sources of information are flawed in various respects. However, they do portray offense trends in different jurisdictions. While the accuracy of this information is suspect, it nevertheless is used by agencies and organizations as a measure or gauge of program effectiveness. The strengths and weaknesses of these sources will be described, together with certain criticisms each has received. In addition to these official sources, unofficial information about juvenile offenses is provided by juveniles themselves in the form of self-reports. Juveniles are questioned about their offending activities, and on the basis of anonymous responses, comparisons of this self-report data are made against that provided by official sources. However, self-reports may not be perfectly accurate indicators of delinquent activity, either. The value of such self-report information will be examined.

The final portion of this chapter will discuss the general questions of whether juveniles who are adjudicated for minor offenses progress eventually to more serious offense activity. Does career escalation occur among juvenile offenders? Are youths committing more violent acts over successive years? Also, are there major differences in the nature of juvenile offending behavior that might be attributable to gender? These and other similar questions will be highlighted.

DELINQUENCY: DEFINITIONS AND DISTINCTIONS

Juveniles

The jurisdiction of juvenile courts depends upon the established legislative definitions of juveniles among the different states. The federal government has no juvenile court. Rather, federal cases involving juveniles infrequently are heard in federal district courts, but adjudicated juveniles are housed in state or local facilities if the sentences involve incarceration. Ordinarily, upper and lower age limits are prescribed. However, these age limits are far from uniform among jurisdictions. Common law has been applied in some jurisdictions where the minimum age of accountability for juveniles is 7. In some states, no lower age limits exist to restrict juvenile court jurisdiction. Table 2.1 shows upper age limits for most U.S. jurisdictions (from Butts et al. 1996, 64–87).

Those states with the lowest maximum age for juvenile court jurisdiction include Connecticut, New York, and North Carolina. In these states, the lowest maximum age for juvenile court jurisdiction is 15. Those states having the lowest maximum age of 16 for juvenile court jurisdiction are Georgia, Illinois, Louisiana, Massachusetts, Michigan, Missouri, South Carolina, and Texas. All other states and the federal government use age 18 as the minimum age for criminal court jurisdiction (Butts et al. 1996). Under the Juvenile Justice and Delinquency Prevention Act of 1974, juveniles are persons who have not attained their eighteenth birthday (18 U.S.C., Sec. 5031, 2002).

Juvenile offenders who are especially young (under age 7 in most jurisdictions) are often placed within the control of community agencies such as departments of human services or social welfare. These children frequently have little or no responsible parental supervision or control. In many cases, the parents themselves may have psychological problems or suffer from alcohol or drug dependencies. Youths from such families may be abused and/or neglected and in need of supervision and other forms of care or treatment. Under common law in those states where common law applies, it is presumed that persons under the age of 7 are incapable of formulating criminal intent. While this presumption may be rebutted, in most cases, it isn't. Thus, if a 6-year-old child kills someone, deliberately or accidentally, he or she will likely be treated rather than punished.

TABLE 2.1

Age at Which Criminal Courts Gain Jurisdiction of Young Offenders

Age of Offender When Under Criminal Court Jurisdiction (years)	States
16	Connecticut, New York, North Carolina
17	Georgia, Illinois, Louisiana, Massachusetts, Missouri, South Carolina, Texas
18	Alabama, Alaska, Arizona, Arkansas, California, Colorado, Delaware, District of Columbia, Florida, Hawaii, Idaho, Indiana, Iowa, Kansas, Kentucky, Maine, Maryland, Michigan, Minnesota, Mississippi, Montana, Nebraska, Nevada, New Hampshire, New Jersey, New Mexico, North Dakota, Ohio, Oklahoma, Oregon, Pennsylvania, Rhode Island, South Dakota, Tennessee, Utah, Vermont, Virginia, Washington, West Virginia, Wisconsin, Federal districts
19	Wyoming

Source: Jeffrey A. Butts et al. (1996). *Juvenile Court Statistics 1993: Statistics Report.* Washington, DC: Office of Juvenile Justice and Delinquency Prevention.

Juvenile Delinquency

Juvenile delinquency or **delinquency** is defined by federal law as the violation of a law of the United States by a person prior to his or her eighteenth birthday that would have been a crime if committed by an adult (18 U.S.C., Sec. 5031, 2002). A broader, legally applicable, definition of juvenile delinquency is a violation of any state or local law or ordinance by anyone who has not yet achieved the age of majority (adapted from Black 1990, 428). Black (1990, 428) refers to a juvenile delinquent as a **delinquent child.** The **age of majority** depends upon the defining jurisdiction as shown in Table 2.1.

The most liberal definition of juvenile delinquency is whatever the juvenile court believes should be brought within its jurisdiction. This definition vests juvenile court judges and other juvenile authorities with broad discretionary powers to define almost any juvenile conduct as delinquent conduct. To illustrate the implications of such a definition for any juvenile, consider the following scenarios.

Scenario 1:   Three black teenage males are walking down a deserted downtown Detroit street in a high-crime neighborhood. It is 12:30 A.M. A police cruiser with two black female officers pulls alongside the boys and the officers ask the boys for identification. The boys are not carrying any identification, although they politely give their names, ages, and addresses to the officer. They are all 13 years old, and they claim to have been at a movie about five blocks from where they are now. On the basis of where they say they live, the officers determine that the boys are walking in the general direction of their neighborhood. The officers want to know if the boys are carrying any weapons. The boys reply "No, we don't have any weapons." One officer asks if they would mind if she searches them. One boy backs up, pushes up his hands, and says, "I don't want no cop's hands on me." After that remark, the officers exit their cruiser and force the boys against a nearby brick wall, where they are patted down and frisked. One boy is carrying a small pocket knife, while another boy is carrying a bottle opener. The officers decide to take the boys into custody. They handcuff each boy and place them in the rear seat of the cruiser. The boys are taken to the police station, and the parents of the boys are called. The parents of the three boys show up at the police station 15 minutes later. They are advised that two of the boys are being charged with carrying "concealed weapons" and will probably have to appear in juvenile court later. The other boy is released into the custody of his parents with a verbal reprimand from the officers that boys that age shouldn't be walking in dangerous neighborhoods late at night. Subsequently, a juvenile court prosecutor drops the concealed weapons charges and nothing more is done in the incident.

Scenario 2:   Two 12-year-old girls are driving in a stolen car in Miami, Florida, at 10:00 P.M. on a Saturday night. A sheriff's deputy on patrol notices the youthfulness of the car's driver as they pass his car, which is parked on a side street. The deputy follows the girls and radios the license plate of the vehicle they are driving. The dispatcher reports that the car belongs to a woman in an exclusive Miami neighborhood on the other side of town. The deputy turns on his cruiser lights and shines a spotlight on the back of the girls' vehicle, intending for the girls to stop. Instead, the girls attempt to elude the deputy and drive off at a high rate of speed. Eventually, the girls crash the car into another automobile as they attempt to pass through a busy intersection. The deputy determines that the girls are injured and calls for backup and emergency medical personnel, who show up a short time later. The girls are taken to a nearby medical center where they are placed under watch and treated for their injuries. In the meantime, the deputy and other officers attempt to contact the automobile's owner. The woman doesn't answer her telephone. Two officers drive out to her home and knock on the door. Lights are on inside the house, and a radio is playing loudly. The officers walk around to the back of the house and see what appears to be a bloody handprint on the back screen door. The pull out their pistols and enter the rear of the home, finding an elderly woman lying on the floor in a pool of blood. A knife is sticking out of her back, and the house appears to have been ransacked. It seems that the woman was a bible studies teacher thought to have a lot of money secreted away in her home. The two girls admit under subsequent questioning that they went to her home earlier that day on the pretense of enrolling in her bible studies class. When she admitted them to her home, they attacked her with a knife and a lead pipe. She fled to the kitchen where they killed her. They stole her car keys and found $55 in her purse. They drove her car to the apartment of a friend where they obtained some beer and drugs with some of their money. Then they got high and drove around town until they were spotted by the sheriff's deputy. They are charged with murder. Subsequently, a juvenile court judge adjudicates both girls delinquent on the murder charges, and they are disposed to the Florida Industrial School until they reach adulthood.

Scenario 3:   One afternoon in a busy department store, a security officer spotted two youths stealing several pairs of tennis shoes by placing them in a store shopping bag. As they exited the store with the stolen merchandise, the security officer moved in to detain them. With the assistance of two other officers, the boys were subdued and turned over to police officers. Upon questioning at the police station, the boys admitted to stealing the shoes. They said that the theft was a part of a gang initiation. A check of juvenile records revealed that the boys, 14-year-olds, had no prior arrests or incidents involving delinquent conduct. A juvenile court prosecutor plea bargained the case, where the boys admitted their guilt to the juvenile court judge in exchange for a disposition of probation for one year. The boys were further ordered to perform 100 hours of community service.

These and a thousand other scenarios could be presented. Are all of these scenarios the same? No. Are all of these scenarios of equivalent seriousness? No. Can each of these scenarios result in an adjudication of delinquency by a juvenile court judge? Yes. Whether juveniles are walking late at night in a high-crime neighborhood with knives and bottle openers, whether they have committed a murder, or whether they have stolen merchandise from a department store as a gang initiation act, it is possible that they may all be combined into one large category as delinquent. Some juvenile offending is more serious than other types of juvenile offending. Breaking windows or letting the air out of someone's automobile tires are less serious than armed robbery, rape, or murder. The wide range of offense seriousness has caused many jurisdictions to channel less serious cases away from juvenile courts and toward various community agencies where the juveniles involved can receive assistance rather than punishment. Should one's age, socioeconomic status, ethnicity or race, attitude, and other situational circumstances influence police response one way or another? The fact is that regardless of the offenses alleged, all juveniles are confronted by subjective appraisals and judgments from the police, prosecutors, and juvenile court judges on the basis of both legal and extralegal factors (Fader et al. 2001).

Most U.S. jurisdictions restrict their definitions of juvenile delinquency to any act committed by a juvenile that, if committed by an adult, would be considered a crime (Lauritsen 2001). Because of their status as juveniles, youths may also be charged with various noncriminal acts. Such acts are broadly described as **status offenses.** Status offenses are any acts committed by juveniles that would (1) bring the juveniles to the attention of juvenile courts and (2) not be crimes if committed by adults. Typical status offenses are running away from home, truancy, and curfew violations. Adults would not be arrested for running away from home, being truant from school, or walking the streets after some curfew time for juveniles. However, if juveniles do these sorts of things in particular cities, they may be grouped within the broad delinquency category, together with more serious juvenile offenders who are charged with armed robbery, forcible rape, murder, aggravated assault, burglary, larceny, vehicular theft, or illicit drug sales (Collins and Kearns 2001; Katz, Webb, and Schaefer 2000).

Underage drinking is a status offense.

STATUS OFFENDERS AND DELINQUENT OFFENDERS

Status offenders are of interest to both the juvenile justice system and the criminal justice system. While status offenses such as runaway behavior, truancy, or curfew violations are not crimes, many persons believe that there are several adverse concomitants of status offenses. One result is the belief by some persons that status offenders progress to more serious types of offending over time. However, there is little empirical support for this view (Fried 2001; Males 2000).

Runaways

In 2000, 141,976 **runaways** in the United States were reported to police (Maguire and Pastore 2002). This represents less than 1 percent of all offenses charged that year. Over half of these runaways are 15 to 17 years of age. Runaways consist of those youths who leave their homes, without permission or their parents' knowledge, and who remain away from home for prolonged periods ranging from several days to several years. Many runaways are eventually picked up by police in different jurisdictions and returned to their homes. Others return of their own free will and choice. Some runaways remain permanently missing, although they are likely a part of growing numbers of homeless youths roaming faraway city streets throughout the United States. Information about runaways and other types of status offenders is compiled annually through various statewide clearinghouses and the federally funded National Incidence Studies of Missing, Abducted, Runaway, and Thrownaway Children (NISMART).

Runaway behavior is complex and difficult to explain, although researchers tend to agree that many runaways generally have serious mental health needs (Cocozza and Skowyra 2000). Many of these youths seek out others like them for dependency and emotional support. Some runaways regard others like them as role models and peers, and often, delinquency among them occurs and increases through such peer modeling (Lindstrom 1996). Studies of runaways indicate that many boys and girls have psychological and/or familial adjustment problems and have been physically and sexually abused by their parents or close relatives. Evidence suggests that many runaways engage in theft or prostitution to finance their independence away from home and are exploited (Kassebaum, Marker, and Glancey 1997).

Although all runaways are not alike, there have been attempts to profile them. Depending upon how authorities and parents react to children who have been apprehended after running away, there may be either positive or negative consequences. Empathy for runaways and their problems is important for instilling positive feelings within them. Various runaway shelters have been established to offer runaways a nonthreatening residence and social support system in various jurisdictions. These shelters often locate particular services for runaways that will help meet their needs. Many children accommodated by these shelters report that they have been physically and sexually abused by family members. Thus, there is some coordination of these homes with various law enforcement agencies to investigate these allegations and assist parents in making their homes safer for their children (Harris 2000; Reynolds et al. 1999).

Truants and Curfew Violators

Other types of status offenders are truants and curfew and liquor law violators. Truants are those who absent themselves from school without either school or parental permission. Very little is known about the numbers or characteristics of truants in the United States (Baker, Sigmon, and Nugent 2001). Several reasons are that each school district defines truancy differently from other districts; sociodemographic characteristics of truants are not normally maintained, even by individual schools; and no consistent, central reporting mechanisms exist for data compilations about truants. For instance, in Wisconsin, a truant may be a youth who absents himself or herself from school without excuse for five or more consecutive school days. In other states, a truant may be defined as someone who misses one day of school without a valid excuse.

There are probably 200,000 or more truants in the United States on any given day. This figure is most likely an underestimate of the actual number of truants. On a city-by-city basis, where records of truants are maintained, we can glean much about the true magnitude of truancy. For instance, in Pittsburgh, Pennsylvania, on any given day, 3,500 students are absent from school, with about 70 percent of these absences unexcused. In Philadelphia, 2,500 students are truant each day. And in Milwaukee, Wisconsin, 4,000 students are absent from school each day without an excuse. One disturbing dimension of truancy is that about two-thirds of all juvenile males arrested while truant have tested positive for drug use (Witmer 2002, 1–2).

Truancy is not a crime. It is a status offense. Youths can be charged with truancy and brought into juvenile court for a status offense adjudication. Truancy is taken quite seriously in many jurisdictions, since evidence suggests that daytime crime and truancy are highly correlated. In Minneapolis, for example, when police officers began to cite truant students and take them into custody, daytime crime dropped by 68 percent. And in San Diego, California, about half of all violent juvenile offending occurs between 8:30 A.M. and 1:30 P.M. (Witmer 2002, 2).

In contrast, **curfew violators** are those youths who remain on city streets after specified evening hours when they are prohibited from loitering or not being in the company of a parent or guardian. In 2000, there were 156,711 youths charged with violating curfew and loitering laws in the United States (Maguire and Pastore 2002). This is less than 1 percent of all offenses reported to police that year.

Curfew violators tend to differ from runaways in that they are more serious offenders (Terrell 1997). However, truants and liquor law violators are more inclined to become **chronic offenders** and to engage in more serious, possibly criminal, behaviors. This is because truancy and curfew violations are viewed as undisciplined offenses (Hemmens and Bennett 1999). Some state jurisdictions, such as Maryland, have established programs to deal with chronic truancy. In Maryland, for example, Project Attend creates partnerships between local school systems and law enforcement agencies in school clusters where chronic truancy is a problem. Through arbitration, the attendance and academic achievement of identified chronic truants is improved significantly by including families and matching them with appropriate service providers (Simms 1998, 98).

In an effort to decrease the incidence of juvenile crime, many cities throughout the United States have enacted curfew laws specifically applicable to youths (Reynolds, Seydlitz, and Jenkins 2000). The theory is that if juveniles are obliged to observe curfews in their communities, then they will have fewer opportunities to commit delinquent acts or status offenses. For example, in New Orleans, Louisiana, in June 1994, the most restrictive curfew law went into effect. Under this law, juveniles under age 17 were prohibited from being in public places, including the premises of business establishments, unless accompanied by a legal guardian or authorized adults. The curfew on weeknights began at 8:00 P.M. and at 11:00 P.M. on weekends. Several exceptions were made for youths who might be traveling to and from work or who were attending school, religious, or civil events. A study of the impact of this strict curfew law was conducted, and it revealed that juvenile offending shifted to noncurfew hours. Furthermore, the enforcement of this curfew law by New Orleans police was difficult, since curfew violations often occurred outside of a police presence (Reynolds, Seydlitz, and Jenkins 2000). If anything, the curfew law tended to induce rebelliousness among those youths affected by the law (Reynolds et al. 1999). Curfew laws have not been an especially effective deterrent to status offending or delinquency generally.

Juvenile and Criminal Court Interest in Status Offenders

Among status offenders, juvenile courts are most interested in chronic or persistent offenders, such as those who habitually appear before juvenile court judges. Repeated juvenile court exposure by status offenders may eventually be followed by adult criminality, although there is little support for this view in the research literature. The chronicity of juvenile offending seems to be influenced by the amount of contact youths have with juvenile courts. Greater contact with juvenile courts is believed by some persons to **stigmatize** youths and cause them to acquire labels or **stigmas** as delinquents or deviants (Hagan and

 **BOX 2.1**

GOING TO JAIL FOR WRITING AN ESSAY?

Boy Writes Essay, Gets "A," Goes to Jail

It happened in Ponder, Texas. A 13-year-old boy wrote a Halloween horror story for his English class at school. The school assignment described a high school shooting where a teacher and two classmates are killed. The English teacher, Amanda Henry, thought the boy did such a good job that she gave him an "A" for the paper, plus extra credit for reading the paper aloud in class. The paper, written in the first person and with some misspellings, described a boy who becomes angry in school and shoots his classmates and a teacher. The boy actually used the English teacher, Mrs. Henry, as the teacher-victim in the shooting. Police officers were called by one of the students in class, who reported the paper and its contents. An investigation led to the 13-year-old's arrest and detention in jail for five days. Police said that the fact that "we're dealing with real people, named specifically in the classroom, that's a real problem." School superintendent Byron Welch said that the outcome might have been different had the boy used fictitious names instead of real names. The boy said, "I was supposed to write a horror story. I don't think I did anything wrong."

Should police be able to arrest and detain youths for papers they write for their English classes? What responsibility should rest with the teacher in this case to ensure that good taste should be exercised when preparing papers on any subject? Who is at fault here? Was any law violated? Was an arrest and five-day detention warranted here? What do you think?

Source: Adapted from the Associated Press, "Halloween Essay Lands Boy in Jail." November 4, 1999.

McCarthy 1997). Therefore, diversion of certain types of juvenile offenders from the juvenile justice system has been advocated and recommended to minimize **stigmatization.**

One increasingly popular strategy is to remove certain types of offenses from the jurisdiction of juvenile court judges (MacDonald and Chesney-Lind 2001). Because status offenders are comparatively less serious than juvenile delinquents who commit crimes, status offenders have been targeted by many state legislatures for removal from juvenile court jurisdiction. The removal of status offenders from the discretionary power of juvenile courts is a part of what is generally known as the **deinstitutionalization of status offenses** or **DSO.**

THE DEINSTITUTIONALIZATION OF STATUS OFFENSES

The Juvenile Justice and Delinquency Prevention Act of 1974

The U.S. Congress passed the **Juvenile Justice and Delinquency Prevention Act of 1974 (JJDPA)** in response to a national concern about growing juvenile delinquency and youth crime. This Act authorized the establishment of the **Office of Juvenile Justice and Delinquency Prevention (OJJDP),** which has been extremely helpful and influential in matters of disseminating information about juvenile offending and prevention and as a general data source. Box 2.2 is a history and summary of the JJDPA and its subsequent amendments.

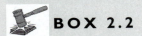 **BOX 2.2**

HISTORY AND SUMMARY OF THE JUVENILE JUSTICE AND DELINQUENCY PREVENTION ACT OF 1974 AND ITS SUBSEQUENT AMENDMENTS

Fact Sheet

The Juvenile Justice and Delinquency Prevention Act of 1974 (JJDPA) provides the major source of federal funding to improve states' juvenile justice systems. The JJDPA was developed with a broad consensus that children should not have contact with adults in jails and other institutional settings and that status offenders should not be placed in secure detention. Under the JJDPA and its subsequent reauthorizations, in order to receive federal funds, states are required to maintain these core protections for children:

Deinstitutionalization of Status Offenders (DSO)

Status offenders may not be held in secure detention or confinement. There are, however, several exceptions to this rule, including allowing some status offenders to be detained for up to 24 hours. The DSO provision seeks to ensure that status offenders who have not committed criminal offenses are not held in secure juvenile facilities for extended periods of time or in secure adult facilities for any length of time. Status offenses are offenses that only apply to children, such as skipping school, running away, breaking curfew, and possession or use of alcohol. These children, instead, should receive community-based services, such as day treatment or residential home treatment, counseling, mentoring, alternative education, and job development support.

Adult Jail and Lockup Removal

Juveniles may not be detained in adult jails and lockups except for limited times before or after a court hearing (6 hours), in rural areas (24 hours plus weekends and holidays), or in unsafe travel conditions. This provision does not apply to children who are tried or convicted in adult criminal court of a felony level offense. This provision is designed to protect children from psychological abuse, physical assault, and isolation. Children housed in adult jails and lockups have been found to be eight times more likely to commit suicide, five times more likely to be sexually assaulted, two times more likely to be assaulted by staff, and 50 percent more likely to be attacked with a weapon than children in juvenile facilities.

Sight and Sound Separation

When children are placed in an adult jail or lockup, as in exceptions listed above, "sight and sound" contact with adults is prohibited. This provision seeks to prevent children from psychological abuse and physical assault. Under "sight and sound," children cannot be housed next to adult cells; share dining halls, recreation areas, or any other common spaces with adults; or be placed in any circumstances that could expose them to threats or abuse from adult offenders.

Disproportionate Minority Confinement (DMC)

States are required to assess and address the disproportionate confinement of minority juveniles in all secure facilities. Studies indicate that minority youth receive tougher sentences and are more likely to be incarcerated than nonminority youth for the same offenses. With minority children making up one-third of the youth population but two-thirds of children in confinement, this provision requires states to gather information and assess the reason for disproportionate minority confinement.

Of particular interest here is the fourth Division, the State Relations and Assistance

Division. This Division addresses directly the matter of removing juveniles, especially status offenders, from secure institutions (facilities similar to adult prisons), jails, and lockups. The second Division, Research and Program Development, is concerned with examining how juvenile courts process juvenile offenders. Individual states and local jurisdictions are encouraged to devise ways of separating juvenile delinquents from status offenders and removing status offenders from the jurisdiction of juvenile courts. The Act suggests that status offenders should be processed by agencies and organizations other than juvenile courts, such as social or human services agencies and bureaus.

September 7, 1974: The JJDPA signed into law. It created a formula grant program, the Office of Juvenile Justice and Delinquency Prevention, the National Institute for Juvenile Justice and Delinquency Prevention, the Federal Coordinating Council, the National Advisory Committee; required each state to submit an annual plan for compliance; required each state to create an advisory group; established the separation requirement; and required that the state planning agency submit to the Law Enforcement Assistance Administration administrator an analysis of the plan's effectiveness.

October 5, 1974: The Departments of State, Justice, and Commerce, and Several Independent Agencies Act of 1975, which appropriated $25 million for fiscal year 1975 for the JJDPA was signed into law by the president.

July 10, 1975: Law Enforcement Assistance Administration issued guidelines for state receipt of formula grants; the DSO requirement provided that status offenders and nonstatus offenders shall not be placed in juvenile detention or correctional facilities, but must be placed in shelter facilities on a temporary or emergency basis; defined shelter facilities for status offenders; listed examples when a juvenile should be considered a status offender, a criminal-type offender, or a nonoffender; stated that for purpose of the separation requirement is to keep

delinquents totally separate from adults, except for incidental contact.

October 7, 1975: Law Enforcement Assistance Administration of Legal Counsel Legal Option.

October 3, 1977: The Juvenile Justice Amendments of 1977 were signed into law; increased the amount of time within which a state must comply with the DSO requirement to three years; stated that failure to reach full compliance with the DSO requirement within three years made the state ineligible for funding, unless the state was found to be in substantial compliance; required a state to provide an annual report reviewing progress made on the DSO requirement that the number of accused status offenders and nonoffenders held in juvenile detention or correctional facilities did not include those held less than 24 hours following initial police contact or those held less than 24 hours following initial court contact; expanded the separation requirement to include delinquents, status offenders, and nonoffenders.

August 16, 1978: The Law Enforcement Assistance Administration issued guidelines for the implementation of the 1977 amendments; each state was required to submit a report on its compliance with the DSO and the separation requirement; to demonstrate compliance the state must include information for both the baseline and the current reporting periods.

September 24, 1979: The Departments of State, Justice, and Commerce Act of 1980, which appropriated $100 million for fiscal year 1980 for the JJDPA, was signed into law by the president.

December 8, 1980: Juvenile Justice Amendments of 1980 were signed into law; amended the Act to require that states submit a three-year plan; established jail removal requirement and compliance provisions for the requirement; established the Office of Juvenile Justice and Delinquency Prevention as a separate entity; deleted the correctional institution or facility and added the definitions for

(continued)

BOX 2.2 (*Continued*)

secure detention facility and secure correctional facility; clarified that juveniles who are charged with or who have committed status offenses shall not be placed in secure detention facilities or secure correctional facilities; modified the DSO provision to exempt juveniles who commit offenses that constitute violations of valid court orders; modified the substantial compliance standard for the DSO requirement; provided for an emphasis on dealing with learning disabled and handicapped juveniles and juveniles who commit serious crimes; renumbered and amended monitoring provision.

December 31, 1981: The OJJDP published final regulations, except for regulations concerning the valid court orders; set forth the DSO requirement's main provisions; set forth the separation requirement's main provisions; set forth the jail removal requirement's main provisions and exceptions to the requirement; defined substantial compliance for each of the major provisions.

January 17, 1984: The OJJDP issued a position statement on the minimum requirements for the jail removal requirement; clarified the jail removal requirement's goals; set forth mandatory and recommended regulations if juveniles and adults are housed in one structure.

October 12, 1984: Juvenile Justice, Runaway Youth, and Missing Children's Act Amendments of 1984 of the Comprehensive Crime Control Act of 1984 was signed into law; established administrator of OJJDP as a presidential appointment; sought to provide for enhanced parental involvement and efforts to strengthen the family unit in addressing delinquency-related problems; amended the jail removal requirement to allow the OJJDP administrator to, through 1989, to make exceptions to the requirement; added "valid court order" to the definition section of the JJDPA; allowed three additional years to achieve full compliance

with the jail removal requirement if the state achieves substantial compliance.

June 20, 1985: The OJJDP published the final regulations on the jail removal requirement; adopted the requirements initially set forth on January 17, 1984; gave states until December 8, 1988 to achieve full compliance with the jail removal requirement; clarified the exceptions to the jail removal requirement; defined adult jail and adult lockup.

November 2, 1988: The OJJDP revised the criteria for de minimus exceptions to full compliance with the jail removal requirement; issued a policy to aid in the determination of when a juvenile held in nonsecure custody within a building that houses adults; defined secure detention and nonsecure detention.

November 18, 1988: The Juvenile Justice and Delinquency Prevention of the Anti-Drug Abuse Act of 1988 was signed into law; reauthorized Juvenile Justice Act through fiscal year 1992; placed emphasis on the problem of overrepresentation of minority youth in juvenile justice system; amended the substantial compliance provision.

August 8, 1989: The OJJDP final regulations on jail removal requirement; amended jail removal requirement to provide an alternative way of substantial compliance; clarified states' monitoring responsibilities.

November 4, 1992: The JJDPA Amendments of 1992 were signed into law; reauthorized juvenile justice and delinquency prevention formula grant program through fiscal year 1996; established a number of new grant programs, including initiatives targeted at eliminating gender bias in treatment of juvenile delinquents; amended the separation requirement to require that detained or confined juveniles do not have contact with incarcerated adults; placed an emphasis on cooperation between federal, state, and local agencies in service delivery and program administration; emphasized delinquency prevention and diversion to services, including recreation programs, prevention and treatment in rural areas, prevention and treatment of hate crimes, family strengthening and involvement in treatment of delinquents; specified services for juveniles in custody, graduated sanctions and risk-need assessments; amended the DSO requirement to require that alien juveniles in custody also be deinstitutionalized; amended the separation requirement to prevent juveniles from having contact with part-time or full-time security staff or direct-care staff of a jail or lockup for adults; amended the jail removal requirement to allow the administrator to promulgate regulations through 1997 making exceptions regarding the detention of juveniles; amended the substantial compliance provision with respect to the jail removal requirement.

Source: Adapted from Shay Bilchik (1995). *Unlocking the Doors for Status Offenders: The State of the States.* Washington, DC: Office of Juvenile Justice and Delinquency Prevention, pps. 50–60.

Changes and Modifications in the JJDPA

In 1977 Congress modified the Act by declaring the juveniles should be separated by both sight and sound from adult offenders in detention and correctional facilities. Also in 1977, states were given five years to comply with the DSO mandate. Nonoffenders, such as dependent and neglected children, were also included. Congress relaxed certain JJDPA rules and gave states additional latitude regarding their placement options for status offenders and nonoffenders, including no placement.

In 1980 Congress recommended that states should refrain from detaining juveniles in jails and lockups. Explicit compliance with this recommendation by any state is complicated by several factors. First, many juveniles appear to be adults when arrested for various offenses. Second, the relatively easy access to false identification cards and driver's licenses makes a precise determination of age difficult. Sometimes it may take days or weeks for police to determine the identity and age of any particular youth being held in a jail or lockup. Congress also directed that states should examine their secure confinement policies relating to minority juveniles and to determine reasons and justification for the disproportionately high rate of minority confinement. Congress also established an exception to DSO by declaring that juveniles who violate a valid court order can be placed in secure confinement for a period of time.

By 1992, Congress directed that any participating state would have up to 25 percent of its formula grant money withheld to the extent that the state was not in compliance with each of the JJDPA mandates. Thus, it is clear that state compliance with these provisions of the JJDPA was encouraged and obtained by providing grants-in-aid to various jurisdictions wanting to improve their juvenile justice systems and facilities. There has been almost universal compliance with the JJDPA mandate throughout the various state juvenile justice systems, and it has served as a significant catalyst for major reform initiatives (Schiraldi and Ziedenberg 1997).

Deinstitutionalization of Status Offenses Defined

The most popular meaning of DSO is the removal of status offenders from juvenile secure institutions. However, the JJDPA has extended the meaning of DSO to include alternative ways of ensuring that status offenders are separated from delinquent offenders. Presently, DSO occurs in three major ways: (1) decarceration, (2) diverting dependent and neglected children to social services, and (3) divestiture of jurisdiction.

Decarceration.   **Decarceration** means to remove status offenders from secure juvenile institutions, such as state industrial schools. Prior to the Juvenile Justice and Delinquency Prevention Act of 1974, it was common practice in most states to incarcerate both status and delinquent offenders together in reform schools or industrial schools. But more than a few people, scholars and the general public alike, questioned this practice. Why should truants, curfew violators, runaways, and difficult-to-control children be placed in prison-like facilities together with adjudicated juvenile murderers, rapists, burglars, thieves, robbers, arsonists, and other violent and property felony offenders? Qualitatively, there are substantial differences between status offenders and delinquent offenders. Do status offenders deserve to be treated the same as delinquent offenders for such drastically different offending behaviors? No.

Prevalent opinion suggests that causing status offenders to live and interact with delinquents in secure confinement, especially for prolonged periods of time, is definitely detrimental to status offenders (Gray 1999). The mere exposure of status offenders to the criminogenic influence of and close association with hard-core delinquents adversely affects the social and psychological well-being of status offenders. The damage to a status offender's self-concept and esteem is incalculable (Evans et al. 1996). This particular problem has been acknowledged outside of the United States as well. Countries, such as China, have implemented similar reforms in their juvenile justice systems in recent years in order to separate less serious juvenile offenders from more serious ones (Chen 2000). Sensing the many problems associated with combining status offenders with delinquent offenders in secure institutions no doubt was a compelling factor leading to the passage of the JJDPA.

Subsequently, most states have implemented decarceration policies for status offenders. For instance, Pennsylvania does not place status offenders in secure facilities. However, in some predominantly rural states, such as Montana and North Dakota, some status offenders continue to be disposed to secure institutions by juvenile court judges. One reason is that juvenile court judges view incarcerating these youths as an appropriate punishment and a potential cure for their status offending. Another reason is that these state legislatures have not devised alternative strategies for treating status offenders through other state agencies or services. A third reason is that often facilities simply do not exist in rural areas to meet status offender needs and provide the social services they require. Thus, the only alternative for their treatment and punishment is to be locked up in secure juvenile facilities together with delinquent offenders.

In order to expedite the decarceration of status offenders from secure juvenile facilities, the federal government has made available substantial sums of money to the states for the purpose of establishing alternative social services. Usually, states who agree to accept federal money in exchange for implementing DSO are given several years over which to implement these reforms in how status offenders are processed. Thus, a period of time is allocated in which to phase out the incarceration of status offenders and phase in the creation of alternative social service agencies designed to accommodate them and meet their needs (Curtin 1997). For instance, in Maryland, the Montrose Residential Training School was used to house a broad array of adjudicated juvenile offenders, including status offenders and delinquents, during the 1980s. In 1988 it was closed. However, the closure was gradual and occurred over a period of time (Gottfredson and Barton 1997).

Diverting Dependent and Neglected Children to Social Services.   A second type of DSO deals with **dependent and neglected children.** While the juvenile court continues to exercise jurisdiction over dependent and neglected youths, diversion programs have been established to receive these children directly from law enforcement officers, schools, parents, or even self-referrals. These diversion programs provide crisis intervention services for youths, and their aim is to return juveniles eventually to their homes. However, more serious offenders may need more elaborate services provided by shelter homes, group homes, or even foster homes (Fader et al. 2001).

Divestiture of Jurisdiction.   The third type of deinstitutionalization is called **divestiture** of jurisdiction. Under divestiture, juvenile courts cannot detain, petition, adjudicate, or place youths on probation or in institutions for any status offense. However, several studies of DSO implementation policies reveal that there are gaps in coordinating interjurisdictional practices involving juveniles. Often, particular agencies continue to operate in their own philosophical contexts in contrast with, and sometimes in opposition to, legislative mandates for juvenile processing changes (Feld 2000).

Potential Outcomes of DSO

Five potential outcomes of DSO are:

1. DSO has reduced the number of status offenders in secure confinement, especially in local facilities. Greater numbers of jurisdictions are adopting deinstitutionalization policies and the actual number of institutionalized status offenders is decreasing (Florida Department of Juvenile Justice 1999).

2. **Net-widening,** or pulling youths into the juvenile justice system who would not have been involved previously in the system, has increased as one result of DSO. Many state jurisdictions have drawn large numbers of status offenders into the net of the juvenile justice system following DSO. In past years, many status offenders would have been ignored by police or handled informally. But when specific community programs were established for status offenders, the net widened and many status offenders were placed in these programs regardless of whether they needed specific social services.

3. **Relabeling,** or defining youths as delinquent or as emotionally disturbed who in the past would have been defined and processed as status offenders, has occurred in certain jurisdictions following DSO. For instance, po-

BOX 2.3

ON FEEDING A 13-MONTH-OLD BABY WINDSHIELD WASHER FLUID

Braxton Bowers, 14, Charged with Murder and Sexual Assault

In Rockford, Illinois, a 14-year-old boy is facing murder and sexual assault charges in adult court resulting from feeding windshield washer fluid to his 13-month-old niece after the toddler scratched him. The boy, Braxton Bowers, was ordered to stand trial in adult court after he appeared before Juvenile Court Judge Steven Nash. Nash remarked at the time of the transfer, "There may be no hope of rehabilitation if in fact he is the perpetrator of such fundamentally brutal, vicious acts." If Braxton were subsequently convicted, he could face confinement in a juvenile facility until age 17, at which time he would be placed in an adult prison for the rest of his life without the possibility of parole. Had the case remained in juvenile court, the most serious punishment the judge could impose on Braxton would be confinement in a juvenile facility until Braxton turned 21 years of age. According to police investigators, Braxton was baby-sitting Amber, his 13-month-old niece and his 4-year-old sister. He said that the baby scratched him while he was changing her diaper, and so he mixed the washer fluid with juice in a bottle and gave it to her. Prosecutor Lorinda Lamken said that a coroner's investigation revealed that there was definite evidence of sexual assault. A defense counsel appointed for Braxton said that Braxton did not know the fluid would kill his niece, Amber.

What punishment would you impose if Braxton Bowers were convicted of murder and sexual assault? Is age 14 too young to be tried as an adult in criminal court? What do you think?

Source: Adapted from the Associated Press, "Boy Charged in Baby's Death." January 23, 2000

lice officers can easily relabel juvenile curfew violators or loiterers as larceny or burglary suspects and detain these youths (Reynolds et al. 1999). In many instances, juvenile court judges have resisted DSO reforms for similar reasons (e.g., loss of discretionary control and power over status offenders).

4. DSO has had little, if any, impact on recidivism rates among status offenders. More than a few jurisdictions report that removing status offenders from juvenile court jurisdiction or not institutionalizing them will decrease their recidivism (Gottfredson and Barton 1997).

5. DSO has created several service delivery problems, including inadequate services, nonexistent services or facilities, or the general inability to provide services within a voluntary system. This is because there is so much variation among status offenders that it is difficult to establish standardized programming and services that will be effective for all of them (Harris 2000; Katz, Webb, and Schaefer 2000).

Regardless of the relative merits of DSO and the ambiguity of research results concerning its short- and long-term effects, there is no doubt that DSO is widespread nationally and has become the prevailing juvenile justice policy.

DSO has set in motion numerous programs in all jurisdictions to better serve the needs of a growing constituency of status offenders (Stanley 2001). This necessarily obligates growing numbers of agencies and organizations to contemplate new and innovative strategies—rehabilitative, therapeutic, and/or educational—to cope with these youths with diverse needs. Greater cooperation between the public, youth services, and community-based treatment programs is required to facilitate developing the best program policies and practices (Cameron and MacDougal 2000).

THE *UNIFORM CRIME REPORTS* AND *NATIONAL CRIME VICTIMIZATION SURVEY*

Two official sources of information about both adult and juvenile offenders are the *Uniform Crime Reports (UCR)* and the *National Crime Victimization Survey (NCVS)*.

Uniform Crime Reports

The **Uniform Crime Reports (UCR)** is published annually by the Federal Bureau of Investigation (FBI) in Washington, DC. The *UCR* is a compilation of arrests for different offenses according to several time intervals. Periodic reports of arrests are issued quarterly to interested law enforcement agencies. All rural and urban law enforcement agencies are requested on a voluntary basis to submit statistical information about twenty-nine different offenses. Most of these agencies submit arrest information, and thus the *UCR* represents over 15,000 law enforcement agencies throughout the United States (Ruback and Menard 2001).

Crime in the *UCR* is classified into two major categories, Part I and Part II offenses. Part I offenses are considered the most serious, and eight serious felonies are listed. These include murder and nonnegligent manslaughter, forcible rape, robbery, aggravated assault, burglary, larceny-theft, motor vehicle theft, and arson. Table 2.2 shows a listing of the eight major **index offenses** (Part I offenses) and their definitions.

Table 2.2 shows **index crimes** for 1999. The first eight offenses are major offenses classified as **felonies.** Felonies are violations of criminal laws that are punishable by terms of imprisonment of one year or longer in state or federal prisons or penitentiaries. These offenses are known as index offenses because they provide readers with a sample of key or index crimes that can be charted quarterly or annually according to different jurisdictions and demographic and socioeconomic dimensions (e.g., city size, age, race, gender, urban-rural). Thus, the crime categories listed are not intended to be an exhaustive compilation. However, it is possible to scan these representative crime categories to obtain a general picture of crime trends across years or other desired time segments.

Table 2.3 shows various index offenses, including both felonies and misdemeanors, according to the age of arrestees. The second grouping of offenses

TABLE 2.2

Uniform Crime Report, Part I: Crimes and Their Definition

Crime	Definition
Murder and nonnegligent manslaughter	Willful (nonnegligent) killing of one human being by another
Forcible rape	Carnal knowledge of a female, forcibly and against her will; assaults or attempts to commit rape by force or threat of force are included
Robbery	Taking or attempting to take anything of value from the care, custody, or control of a person or persons by force or threat of force or violence and/or by putting the victim in fear
Aggravated assault	Unlawful attack by one person upon another for the purpose of inflicting severe or aggravated bodily injury
Burglary	Unlawful entry into a structure to commit a felony or theft
Larceny-theft	Unlawful taking, carrying, leading, or riding away of property from the possession or constructive possession of another, including shoplifting, pocket picking, purse snatching, and thefts of motor vehicle parts or accessories
Motor vehicle theft	Theft or attempted theft of a motor vehicle, including automobiles, trucks, buses, motorscooters, and snowmobiles
Arson	Any willful or malicious burning or attempt to burn, with or without intent to defraud, a dwelling house, public building, motor vehicle or aircraft, and the personal property of another

Source: U.S. Department of Justice, Federal Bureau of Investigation, *Crime in the United States* (Washington, DC: U.S. Government Printing Office, 1999).

in Table 2.3, commencing with "Other Assaults" and ending with "Runaways," portrays both misdemeanors and status offenses. A **misdemeanor** is a violation of criminal laws that is punishable by an incarcerative term of less than one year in city or county jails. Status offenses listed, including runaway behavior, truancy, and violation of curfew, are not considered crimes, although they are reported together with criminal offenses to give a more complete picture of arrest activity throughout the United States (Baker, Sigmon, and Nugent 2001). These offenses listed are not an exhaustive compilation. Rather, a sample listing of crimes based on arrests is provided.

Because of the age breakdown presented in Table 2.3, it is possible to examine juvenile arrest statistics for different offenses and age categories. For example, by inspecting Table 2.3, we can determine that juveniles under age 18 accounted for 17.4 percent of all arrests in 1999. For violent crimes, those under age 18 accounted for 16.2 percent of them. For property crimes, juveniles under age 18 accounted for 32.3 percent of all arrests. Specific crime categories may be consulted as well. For instance, 919 juveniles were arrested in 1999 for murder and nonnegligent manslaughter. About 249,100 juveniles were arrested that same year for larceny-theft (Maguire and Pastore 2002, 362–363).

Besides this factual information about juvenile offenders, the *UCR* may also be used to gauge the incidence of arrests across different age categories. An inspection of Table 2.3 shows that for runaways, arrests increase for juveniles and peak at about ages 13 to 14. For subsequent years, the numbers of arrests for runaway behavior decrease. For curfew violations and loitering, the peak year for juveniles appears to be 16. Thereafter, declines in arrests are observed. Interestingly, liquor law violations involving juveniles show an upward trend across years. The numbers of arrests for liquor law violations increase dramatically from age 10 to 18.

Other information disclosed by the *UCR* concerning juveniles is that those 14 years of age or younger made up about 21.4 percent of the U.S. population in 1999, yet they accounted for only 5.5 percent of all arrests. However, those ages 15 to 19 made up 7.2 percent of the U.S. population that same year, but they accounted for 21.9 percent of all arrests, the largest percentage of arrests for all age categories (Maguire and Pastore 2002, 355). Furthermore, between 1990 and 1999, there was a 2.9 percent *decrease* in the number of arrests of persons age 18 and older. However, there was an 11 percent *increase* in the number of arrests of persons under age 18 (Maguire and Pastore 2002, 361). This figure is one of the reasons why the public is concerned generally about the rising incidence of delinquency.

National Crime Victimization Survey

Compared with the *UCR,* the **National Crime Victimization Survey (NCVS)** is conducted annually by the United States Bureau of the Census. It is a random survey of approximately 60,000 dwellings, about 127,000 persons age 12 or over, and approximately 50,000 businesses. Subsamples of persons are questioned by interviewers who compile information about crime victims. Those interviewed are asked whether they have had different types of crime committed against them during the past six months or year. Through statistical analysis, the amount of crime throughout the general population can be estimated (Levitt 1998).

The *NCVS* provides information about criminal victimizations and incidents. A **victimization** is the basic measure of the occurrence of a crime and is a specific criminal act that affects a single victim. An **incident** is a specific criminal act that may involve one or more victims (Fisher, Cullen, and Turner 2000). Because the *NCVS* reflects an amount of crime allegedly perpetrated against a large sample of victims, it is believed more accurate as a national crime estimate than the *UCR.* Thus, whenever comparisons of crime from the *UCR* are made against the *NCVS,* the *NCVS* reports from two to four times the amount of crime as indicated by law enforcement agency arrest figures in the *UCR.* But because of certain flaws inherent in both estimates of national crime, some observers believe both reports are underestimates of the true amount of crime in the United States.

TABLE 2.3

Arrests by offense charged and age, United States, 1999 (8,546 agencies; 1999 estimated population 171,831,000)

Offense charged	Total all ages	Under 15 years	Under 18 years	18 years and older	Under 10 years	10 to 12 years	13 to 14 years	15 years	16 years	17 years	18 years	19 years
Total	9,141,201	506,817	1,588,839	7,552,362	24,530	117,679	364,608	298,239	372,066	411,717	460,578	460,633
Percent[a]	100.0%	5.5	17.4	82.6	0.3	1.3	4.0	3.3	4.1	4.5	5.0	5.0
Murder and nonnegligent manslaughter	9,727	114	919	8,808	1	10	103	119	270	416	729	696
Forcible rape	18,759	1,221	3,182	15,577	40	373	808	592	649	720	895	878
Robbery	73,619	4,888	18,735	54,884	133	1,073	3,682	3,643	4,696	5,508	6,291	5,530
Aggravated assault	318,051	16,139	45,080	272,971	830	4,292	11,017	7,980	9,863	11,098	12,389	12,672
Burglary	192,570	24,561	64,481	128,089	1,486	6,388	16,687	12,057	13,525	14,338	15,113	12,096
Larceny-theft	794,201	100,635	249,100	545,101	4,871	28,180	67,584	45,551	51,349	51,565	48,353	39,066
Motor vehicle theft	94,335	8,508	33,255	61,080	108	1,080	7,320	7,597	8,637	8,513	7,416	6,169
Arson	10,811	3,874	5,791	5,020	743	1,287	1,844	847	558	512	413	333
Violent crime[b]	420,156	22,362	67,916	352,240	1,004	5,748	15,610	12,334	15,478	17,742	20,304	19,776
Percent[a]	100.0%	5.3	16.2	83.8	0.2	1.4	3.7	2.9	3.7	4.2	4.8	4.7
Property crime[c]	1,091,917	137,578	352,627	739,290	7,208	36,935	93,435	66,052	74,069	74,928	71,295	57,664
Percent[a]	100.0%	12.6	32.3	67.7	0.7	3.4	8.6	6.0	6.8	6.9	6.5	5.3
Total Crime Index[d]	1,512,073	159,940	420,543	1,091,530	8,212	42,683	109,045	78,386	89,547	92,670	91,599	77,440
Percent[a]	100.0%	10.6	27.8	72.2	0.5	2.8	7.2	5.2	5.9	6.1	6.1	5.1
Other assaults	844,728	64,980	151,645	693,083	3,419	18,121	43,440	27,240	29,989	29,436	28,683	28,960
Forgery and counterfeiting	69,853	585	4,481	65,372	23	90	452	649	1,257	2,010	3,298	3,802
Fraud	225,934	1,730	7,940	217,994	94	379	1,257	1,181	2,018	3,011	6,109	8,867
Embezzlement	11,208	68	1,101	10,107	4	6	58	64	348	621	776	747
Stolen property; buying, receiving, possessing	80,426	5,044	18,865	61,561	126	901	4,017	3,535	4,588	5,698	6,418	5,524
Vandalism	182,043	33,736	76,319	105,724	3,218	9,859	20,659	12,984	15,033	14,566	12,383	9,467
Weapons; carrying, possessing, etc.	113,880	8,945	27,596	86,284	482	2,074	6,389	4,899	6,361	7,391	8,185	7,570
Prostitution and commercialized vice	63,927	126	877	63,050	18	15	93	111	223	417	1,201	1,590
Sex offenses (except forcible rape and prostitution)	60,120	5,384	10,641	49,479	397	1,609	3,378	1,879	1,634	1,744	2,049	2,004
Drug abuse violations	1,007,002	20,428	128,286	878,716	330	2,352	17,746	22,304	35,592	49,962	67,123	64,509
Gambling	7,023	95	835	6,188	3	13	79	143	213	384	431	418
Offenses against family and children	92,849	2,137	6,093	86,756	360	485	1,292	1,152	1,370	1,434	2,363	2,381
Driving under the influence	931,235	391	13,803	917,432	91	72	228	661	3,540	9,211	21,631	28,340
Liquor laws	427,873	10,748	103,734	324,139	190	907	9,651	15,605	30,448	46,933	69,773	69,024
Drunkenness	437,153	1,861	14,082	423,071	89	151	1,621	2,207	3,396	6,618	12,051	13,164
Disorderly conduct	421,662	42,467	113,303	308,359	1,359	10,384	30,724	22,049	23,883	24,904	23,563	21,190
Vagrancy	20,213	326	1,597	18,616	21	57	248	307	414	550	965	852
All other offenses (except traffic)	2,416,544	78,007	275,397	2,141,147	4,003	16,019	57,985	52,744	66,900	77,746	101,674	114,528
Suspicion	4,907	330	1,153	3,754	13	77	240	198	254	371	303	256
Curfew and loitering law violations	114,220	31,513	114,220	×	828	5,107	25,578	25,251	31,847	25,609	×	×
Runaways	96,328	37,996	96,328	×	1,250	6,318	30,428	24,690	23,211	10,431	×	×

Note: See Note, Table 4.1. This table presents data from all law enforcement agencies submitting complete reports for 12 months in 1999 (Source, p. 403). Population figures are estimates calculated from U.S. Census Bureau data. For definitions of offenses, see Appendix 3.
[a]Because of rounding, percents may not add to total.
[b]Violent crimes are offenses of murder and nonnegligent manslaughter, forcible rape, robbery, and aggravated assault.
[c]Property crimes are offenses of burglary, larceny-theft, motor vehicle theft, and arson.
[d]Includes arson.
Source: U.S. Department of Justice, Federal Bureau of Investigation, *Crime in the United States, 1999* (Washington, DC: USGPO, 2000), pp. 222, 223.

20 years	21 years	22 years	23 years	24 years	25 to 29 years	30 to 24 years	35 to 39 years	40 to 44 years	45 to 49 years	50 to 54 years	55 to 59 years	60 to 64 years	65 years and older
410,001	359,019	321,146	283,264	267,445	1,186,201	1,079,480	1,058,525	770,305	446,646	224,755	109,867	54,514	59,983
4.5	3.9	3.5	3.1	2.9	13.0	11.8	11.6	8.4	4.9	2.5	1.2	0.6	0.7
672	564	552	456	391	1,525	1,015	824	556	329	211	129	53	106
778	787	689	576	538	2,508	2,411	2,195	1,461	813	470	270	153	155
4,207	3,635	2,843	2,298	2,137	8,899	7,274	5,853	3,399	1,487	609	203	102	117
12,218	12,212	11,458	10,641	10,078	46,364	42,617	40,687	28,620	15,960	8,377	4,130	2,105	2,443
9,063	6,748	5,592	4,851	4,300	19,133	17,498	15,759	10,134	4,628	1,902	681	294	297
29,905	24,422	20,840	17,778	16,468	77,106	76,339	74,317	55,317	32,052	15,884	7,619	3,910	5,725
4,550	3,624	3,128	2,499	2,165	9,854	8,257	6,658	3,857	1,765	656	259	105	118
286	209	213	171	162	616	692	656	537	344	188	87	51	62
17,875	17,198	15,542	13,971	13,144	59,296	53,317	49,559	34,036	18,589	9,667	4,732	2,413	2,821
4.3	4.1	3.7	3.3	3.1	14.1	12.7	11.8	8.1	4.4	2.3	1.1	0.6	0.7
43,804	35,003	29,773	25,299	23,095	106,709	102,786	97,390	69,845	38,789	18,630	8,646	4,360	6,202
4.0	3.2	2.7	2.3	2.1	9.8	9.4	8.9	6.4	3.6	1.7	0.8	0.4	0.6
61,679	52,201	45,315	39,270	26,239	166,005	156,103	146,949	103,881	57,378	28,297	13,378	6,773	9,023
4.1	3.5	3.0	2.6	2.4	11.0	10.3	9.7	6.9	3.8	1.9	0.9	0.4	0.6
28,435	29,385	28,019	26,120	25,618	120,237	113,443	109,540	75,260	39,962	19,590	9,342	4,775	5,714
3,831	3,234	2,910	2656	2,583	12,086	10,812	9,065	5,874	3,028	1,287	541	176	189
9,716	9,503	9,333	8,753	8,431	40,570	36,681	32,755	21,964	12,592	6,493	3,119	1,489	1,619
616	553	494	397	466	1,816	1,377	1,221	755	464	242	101	42	40
4,459	3,607	3,069	2,489	2,282	9,527	8,204	7,191	4,658	2,267	1,000	441	222	203
7,258	6,535	5,252	4,421	3,955	15,948	13,180	12,023	7,631	3,885	1,860	818	438	670
6,142	5,653	4,769	3,947	3,494	13,392	9,515	8,731	6,288	3,829	2,191	1,214	604	760
1,713	1,714	1,734	1,710	1,924	11,528	13,094	12,159	7,670	3,704	1,580	774	448	507
1,926	1,800	1,566	1,402	1,364	6,591	7,127	7,593	5,657	3,844	2,692	1,584	939	1,341
55,456	47,932	41,514	35,331	32,470	137,816	122,434	118,953	84,035	43,196	17,581	6,144	2,346	1,876
345	312	277	235	218	667	508	488	468	690	367	325	179	260
2,414	2,759	2,714	2,755	2,982	15,303	15,974	15,931	10,754	5,406	2,493	1,157	570	800
30,131	38,287	36,840	34,107	32,990	150,712	134,731	139,746	109,931	71,887	41,882	22,579	11,851	11,787
53,486	11,944	8,295	6,130	5,409	19,888	17,609	19,946	17,389	11,807	6,481	3,517	1,723	1,718
12,900	16,795	14,783	13,285	12,441	56,527	58,456	68,877	59,601	40,270	21,627	11,583	5,891	4,820
18,322	19,535	16,461	13,632	12,242	46,776	39,086	38,278	27,497	15,764	7,903	3,836	1,945	2,329
707	641	592	469	394	2,097	2,572	3,096	2,685	1,759	843	479	259	206
110,216	106,370	97,033	86,002	81,802	358,136	318,078	305,475	217,999	124,755	60,257	28,904	13,817	16,101
249	259	176	153	141	579	496	508	308	159	89	31	27	20
×	×	×	×	×	×	×	×	×	×	×	×	×	×
×	×	×	×	×	×	×	×	×	×	×	×	×	×

Strengths of These Measures

One strength of these indicators of crime in the United States is the sheer numbers of offenses reported. Few alternative sources of information about crime in the United States exhibit such voluminous reporting. Also, regional and seasonal reports of criminal activity are provided. The *UCR* also reports the proportion of different types of crime that are **cleared by arrest.** Cleared by arrest means that someone has been arrested and charged with a particular crime. Another favorable feature of both the *UCR* and *NCVS* is that numbers of arrests and reported crimes can be compared across years. Therefore, the *UCR* reports percentage increases or decreases in the amount of different types of crime for many different jurisdictions and over various time periods. And although the *NCVS* does not purport to survey all crime victims, the randomness inherent in the selection of the target respondents is such that generalizations about the U.S. population are considered reasonably valid (Finkelhor and Ormrod 2001b).

A primary advantage of the *NCVS* over the *UCR* is that victims offer interviewers information about crimes committed against them. In many instances, these respondents disclose that they do not report these crimes to police. The reasons for not reporting crimes to police vary, although these victims often believe that the police cannot do much about their victimization anyway. Sometimes, rape victims are too embarrassed to report these incidents, or they may feel that they were partially to blame. Furthermore, in some of these cases, family members or close friends may be the perpetrators, and victims may be reluctant to press criminal charges (Lauritsen 2001).

Weaknesses of These Measures

Certain limitations of the *UCR* and *NCVS* are well documented. Focusing upon the *UCR* first, we may cite some of the more important weaknesses of these statistics. For instance, *UCR* figures do not provide an annual per capita measure of crime frequency. Not all law enforcement agencies report crime to the FBI, and those that do may fail to report crime uniformly. Because law enforcement agencies are not compelled to submit annual information to the FBI, some agencies fail to report their arrest activity. Also, crimes of the same name vary in definition among jurisdictions. For instance, there are rapes in North Dakota, but there is no "rape" crime category. Rape is a form of "gross sexual imposition." And so is child sexual abuse. This conceptual Tower of Babel contributes to inaccurate and/or incomplete crime reporting.

The *UCR* only reports arrests, not the actual amount of crime. When arrests are reported in the *UCR,* only the most serious offenses are often reported. Thus, if a robbery suspect is apprehended, she may possess burglary tools, a concealed weapon, and stolen property. She may have caused physical injuries to victims. All of these events are crimes, but only the robbery, the most serious offense, will be reported to the FBI. Therefore, there is much basis for the belief that these official reports of crime are at best underestimates. Arrest activity in the *UCR* may be attributable to fluctuations in police activity rather than actual fluctuations in criminal activity. Finally, although they only make up a fraction of national criminal activity, federal crimes are not reported in the *UCR.*

Anonymous self-reports disclose more offending information than is reported by official sources of delinquency.

Both the *NCVS* and *UCR* overemphasize street crimes and underemphasize corporate crimes. Self-reported information contained in the *NCVS* is often unreliable. Sometimes victims interviewed may not be able to identify certain actions against them as crimes. For instance, date-rapes may be reported as assaults. Also, persons may not be able to remember clearly certain criminal events. Fear of reprisals from criminals may compel some victims not to disclose their victimizations to interviewers (Felson, Baumer, and Messner 2000). Some victimization data reported in the *NCVS* may be either exaggerated or more liberally reported. For various reasons, interviewees may lie to interviewers in disclosing details of crimes committed against them.

Despite these criticisms, the *UCR* and *NCVS* provide valuable data for interested professionals. The fact that virtually all law enforcement agencies rely to some extent on these annual figures as valid indicators of criminal activity in the United States suggests that their utility in this regard is invaluable. Supplementing this information are other, more detailed, reports of selected offense activity. The U.S. Department of Justice Bureau of Justice Statistics publishes an incredible amount of information annually about different dimensions of crime and offender characteristics and behavior. This supplemental information, together with the data provided by the *UCR* and *NCVS,* may be combined to furnish us with a more complete picture of crime in the United States. Several alternative data sources are discussed in the following section.

OTHER SOURCES

One of the best compendiums of data specifically about juveniles and juvenile court adjudications is the **National Juvenile Court Data Archive.** While the federal government has collected data pertaining to juveniles since 1926, the data were dependent upon the voluntary completion of statistical forms by juvenile courts in a limited number of U.S. jurisdictions. In 1975, however, the Office of Juvenile Justice and Delinquency Prevention (OJJDP) assumed responsibility for acquiring court dispositional records and publishing periodic reports of juvenile offenses and adjudicatory outcomes.

The National Juvenile Court Data Archive contains over 800,000 annual automated case records of juveniles in various states. Numerous data sets are currently available to researchers and may be accessed for investigative purposes. These data sets are nonuniform, although they ordinarily contain information such as age at referral, gender, race, county of residence, offense(s) charged, date of referral, processing characteristics of the case (e.g., incarceration and manner of handling), and the case disposition (National Council of Juvenile and Family Court Judges 1998).

Another compendium of offender characteristics of all ages is the ***Sourcebook of Criminal Justice Statistics*** published annually by the Hindelang Criminal Justice Research Center and supported by grants from the U.S. Department of Justice (Maguire and Pastore 2002). This is perhaps the most comprehensive source that we have discussed, since it accesses numerous governmental documents and reports annually to keep readers abreast of the latest crime figures. Among other things, it describes justice system employment and spending, jail and prison management and prisoner issues, judicial misconduct and complaints, correctional officer characteristics, crime victim characteristics and victimization patterns, delinquent behavior patterns and trends, and considerable survey information. Literally hundreds of tables are presented that summarize much of the information reported by various private and governmental agencies. Useful annotated information is provided to supplement the tabular material.

Statistics pertaining to juvenile offenders include juvenile admissions and discharges from public and private incarcerative facilities, average length of stay of juveniles in these facilities, a profile of juvenile custody facilities, demographic information about juveniles detained for lengthy terms, criminal history or prior records of juveniles, illegal drug and alcohol use among juveniles, waiver information, and offense patterns according to socioeconomic and demographic factors. Each annual sourcebook is somewhat different from those published in previous years, although much of the material in subsequent editions has been updated from previous years.

Self-Report Information

While these official sources of crime and delinquency are quite useful, a common criticism is that they tend to underestimate the amount of offense behaviors that actually occur in the United States (Levy 2001). For many years, those interested in studying juvenile offense behaviors have frequently relied upon data derived from **self-reports.** The self-report is a data collection method involving an unofficial survey of youths or adults where the intent is to obtain information about specific types of behavior not ordinarily disclosed through traditional data collection methods, including questionnaires, interviews, polls, official agency reports, or sociodemographic summaries. This information is called **self-report information.** The exact origin of the use of self-reports is unknown. However, in 1943, Austin L. Porterfield investigated hidden delinquency, or delinquency neither detected by nor reported to police. He surveyed several hundred college students, asking them to disclose whether they had ever engaged in delinquent acts. While all of the students reported that they had previously engaged in delinquent acts, most also reported that they had not been caught by police or brought to the attention of the juvenile courts (Porterfield 1943).

In 1958, James Short and Ivan Nye became the first investigators to conduct the first self-report study of a delinquent population. They obtained self-report information from hundreds of delinquents in several Washington state training schools. They compared this information with self-report data from hundreds of students in three Washington state communities and three Midwestern towns. Their findings revealed that delinquency was widespread and not specific to any social class. Further, both the seriousness and frequency of juvenile offending were key determinants of juvenile court treatment of youthful offenders and public policy relating to delinquents (Short and Nye 1958).

Self-report surveys are believed to be more accurate and informative compared with official sources of crime and delinquency information. Before self-report surveys of such information are presented, it is helpful to become familiar with some of the more popular crime and delinquency information sources and their strengths and weaknesses.

The research applications of self-reports are both extensive and diverse. An inspection of research articles compiled by the *Criminal Justice Abstracts* between the years 1968–1998 by this author revealed that 202 articles utilized self-reports for different purposes. Two-thirds of the articles involved studies of juveniles, while article subject-matter was dominated by the themes of drug/alcohol use, sex offenses, spousal abuse, status offending and delinquency, and early childhood sexual, psychological, or physical abuse.

Generally, self-report studies accomplish two important research objectives: (1) describing and understanding behavior and (2) predicting behavior. Self-report information provides considerable enriching details about persons under a variety of circumstances. Self-reports furnish important descriptive information about what people think and do. Such descriptions include how persons were treated as children and the events that were most significant to them as they grew to adulthood. The more that is learned about the significant occurrences in one's life, the better the predictive schemes to explain present and to forecast future behaviors. Self-reports, therefore, are an important source of information for descriptive and theoretical purposes. From a theoretical standpoint, self-reports represent one important means of theory verification.

Some of the popular self-report surveys conducted annually are the **National Youth Survey** and the **Monitoring the Future Survey.** These large-scale surveys of high school students focus upon particular behaviors (Chaffin, Bonner, and Hill 2001). In addition, the Institute for Social Research at the University of Michigan annually solicits information from a national sample of 3,000 high school students. These informative reports are frequently cited in the research literature, which attests to the integrity, reliability, and validity of this information among noted juvenile justice professionals (Matsueda and Anderson 1998; Mazerolle 1998).

These national surveys involve administering confidential questionnaires and checklists to high school students (Everle and Maiuro 2001). Students are asked to indicate which behaviors they have engaged in during the past six months or the previous year. Assuming that their responses are truthful, researchers believe that the results are a more accurate reflection of delinquent behaviors than are official sources, such as the *UCR*. Ordinarily, simple check-lists are given to students and they are asked to identify those behaviors they have done, not necessarily those for which they have been apprehended. Considered unofficial sources of information about delinquency and delinquency patterns, these self-disclosures are considered by many professionals to be more accurate than official sources. An example of such a checklist is shown in Table 2.4.

Self-reports enable researchers to determine whether there are changing offending patterns among juveniles over time. Substantial information exists that characterizes violent juvenile offenders and catalogs the many potential causal factors that are associated with violence, such as gang involvement (Curry, Decker, and Egley 2002). Self-reported data about juvenile offenses suggests that a sizable gap exists between official reports of delinquent conduct and information disclosed through self-reports (Rosenblatt and Furlong 1997). Self-reports reveal much more delinquency than is reported by either the *UCR* or *NCVS*. However, since *NCVS* information is also a form of self-disclosure, some investigators have found greater compatibility between delinquency self-reporting and the *NCVS* than between delinquency self-reporting and the *UCR*, which reports only arrest information. In any case, self-reports of delinquency or status offense conduct have caused researchers to refer to these undetected offending behaviors as **hidden delinquency.**

Some investigators question whether self-report information is reliable. Do youths tell the truth about their conduct, whatever the reported behavior? Some reported information is more easily refuted or confirmed by independent means. In the cases of illicit alcohol, tobacco, or drug use, independent tests may be conducted to determine the veracity of self-report information. In one school district, for instance, over 50 percent of all high school students interviewed disclosed through self-reports that they smoked. Subsequently, analyses of saliva specimens from these same students revealed that less than 10 percent of them tested positive for tobacco use. For several reasons unknown to the researchers, about half of these high schoolers reported that they used tobacco when most of them didn't use tobacco. Were they bragging? Was this peer pressure in action? In view of the evidence, this is the strong implication.

In another test of the reliability of self-reports, Dembo and his associates studied 114 arrested youths who were processed at the Hillsborough County, Florida, Juvenile Assessment Center (Dembo et al. 1995). Youths furnished investigators with self-reports of their drug use. They also provided hair specimens that were later used in drug testing. In Dembo's research, about half of all processed youths tested positive for either marijuana or cocaine and had used these substances within the most recent 90-day period. Actual self-reports from these youths were fairly consistent with the drug test results.

The relation between one's early childhood and the onset of status offending or delinquency has been heavily investigated. Typically, parent–child association and attachment are linked with delinquent conduct. Samples of delinquents and nondelinquents are asked to provide self-reports of their early upbringing, including their perceived closeness with parents and the disciplinary methods used to sanction misconduct. Different themes are researched. For instance, the etiology of delinquency as related to different family processes according to race/ethnicity has been studied (Smith and Krohn 1991). Does a sample of inner-city high-risk youths reflect important differences in family processes according to race/ethnicity?

TABLE 2.4

An Hypothetical Checklist for Self-Report Disclosures of Delinquent or Criminal Conduct among High School Students

"How often during the past six months have you committed the following offenses?" Check whichever best applies to you.

Offense	Frequency				
	0 times	1 time	2 times	3 times	4 or more times
Smoked marijuana	_____	_____	_____	_____	_____
Stole something worth $50 or less	_____	_____	_____	_____	_____
Got drunk on beer or wine	_____	_____	_____	_____	_____
Got drunk on hard liquor	_____	_____	_____	_____	_____
Used crack or cocaine	_____	_____	_____	_____	_____

Information about runaways is almost exclusively gleaned from self-report studies (Whitbeck, Hoyt, and Ackley 1997). For example, it has been found that runaways compared with other types of status offenders have greater levels of family violence, rejection, and sexual abuse. Not unexpectedly, based upon self-report experiences, runaways were from families where there was less parental monitoring of juvenile behavior, warmth, and supportiveness.

In a more general analysis of early childhood experiences involving adolescent maltreatment and its link with delinquency, self-reports were used by Ireland, Smith, and Thornberry (2002) to identify the frequency of delinquency and drug use among youths involved in the Rochester Youth Development Study. This was a multiwave panel study of adolescent development, involving youths starting at age 14 and interviewed every six months for nine consecutive waves. A general delinquency index included thirty-two offenses ranging from minor offenses like public disorder to robbery and assault with a deadly weapon. Over time, youths involved in the multiwave panel were separated according to the persistence and prevalence of their offending behavior. Childhood maltreatment was defined as a broad spectrum of aberrant behaviors that are harmful to children, including physical, sexual, neglect, and emotional, and that place children at risk for problem behaviors, including delinquency, during adolescence. A set of self-reported delinquency and drug use questions asked whether the respondents had committed particular offenses in the six-month interval between the last and current interview, and if so, the frequency of the behavior. The basic hypothesis postulated by these researchers was that exposure to any type of abusive condition disrupts the normal course of development and leads to maladaptive behaviors, including delinquency and drug use at later ages. It was expected that although different types of maltreatment may have effects of varying magnitude, the general expectation was that all types will generate negative behaviors. Mild support was found for the hypothesis tested, in that self-disclosed maltreatment during adolescence does increase the risk for delinquent behaviors in early adolescence.

Not all of this research is dependent upon recollections of one's childhood and familial past. For instance, thirty-nine community-based organizations in Miami, Florida, have provided risk-focused delinquency prevention services for over 900 families (Kakar, 1998). These organizations provided families with parenting skills and counseled both adults and juveniles about how to cope with day-to-day family problems and stresses. Self-reports from family members indicated that the program was effective and accomplishing its goal of delinquency prevention.

School violence is an increasingly important topic of discussion among parents, school officials, and juvenile justice professionals (Danner and Carmody 2001). Although the media suggests that school violence is pervasive, the sensationalism attached to school shootings does not necessarily mean that school violence is increasing. For instance, a study of 3,364 high school seniors drawn from 113 public and 19 private schools across the United State revealed that between 1982 and 1988, school victimizations occurred at relatively low rates (Hanke 1996). Boys were victimized more frequently than girls, and nonwhites were victimized more frequently than whites. Most victimizations were single occurrences, with dangerous weapons used in only limited instances. Verbal threats not involving injury or weapons were most commonly observed. These victimizations were noted through the use of self-reports, where juveniles were asked whether they had been victimized at school. Other researchers have reported more serious and frequent violence, especially in schools with larger proportions of at-risk youth (Levine 1996).

A frequently cited relation is between drug/alcohol abuse and delinquency. In Hillsborough County, Florida, the Juvenile Assessment Center was established as an intervention project to help at-risk youths and their families (Dembo, Pacheco, and Schmeidler 1997). Self-reports of 114 project participants led researchers to conclude that a significant association exists between self-reported drug use and involvement in delinquent behavior. Self-reports of crime and delinquency are a valuable source of information to researchers. Research projects with exploratory, descriptive, and/or experimental study objectives benefit from the use of self-report data. Descriptions of different types of delinquents and the development of useful intervention strategies for delinquency prevention have been assisted greatly by the use of self-reports. The broad application of self-reports in virtually every facet of criminology and criminal justice suggests the long-term application of this data collection method.

VIOLENCE AND NONVIOLENCE: CAREER ESCALATION?

How much violent crime is committed by juveniles? Are juveniles likely to escalate to more serious offenses during their youthful years as they become more deeply involved in delinquent conduct? Are there certain kinds of juvenile offenders who are more or less susceptible to intervention programs and treatments as means of reducing or eliminating their propensity to engage in delinquent conduct? Are schools new battlezones for gang warfare and other forms of violence? Certainly the media have helped to heighten our awareness of the presence and violence of youth gangs in various cities. Startling information about extensive drug and alcohol use among juveniles is frequently broadcasted or reported (Pleydon and Schner 2001). Is there currently an unstoppable juvenile crime wave prevalent throughout the United States?

School Violence

Violence among school children has received increased attention in recent years (Mills 2001). The media suggest that school violence is pervasive. In Miami, Florida, for example, high school students have reported both serious and frequent victimization. In many of these victimizations, dangerous weapons such as firearms were used to effect the victimization (Small and Tetrick 2001, 3–5). But school violence is not restricted to schools in lower socioeconomic areas or where large numbers of at-risk youths are found. More affluent settings are increasingly sites of violence. On April 20, 1999, two youths entered Columbine High School in Littleton, Colorado and proceeded to murder thirteen of their fellow students and a teacher. They used semiautomatic weapons and shotguns, together with an array of pipe bombs and other explosive devices. Surrounded by police, the two youths took their own lives rather than risk capture. This carnage came on the heels of similar mass murders committed by youths at elementary and secondary schools in Mississippi, Arkansas, and Oregon during 1998–1999.

Surprisingly, there are over 100 violent student deaths at elementary and secondary schools each year. A majority of these deaths do not receive national media coverage (Kaufman et al. 1998, 6). For instance, in the first half of the 1998–1999 school year, about 135 children were killed at school, killed on school property, at a school-sponsored event, or on the way to or from school. Furthermore, teachers are also victims of crime at school. Between 1994 and 1998, for example, an average of 133,700 violent crimes and 217,400 thefts were committed by students against teachers each year. Teachers in urban school settings were more likely to be victims of violent crimes than were teachers in suburban or rural schools (Small and Tetrick 2001, 8).

Fortunately, most school violence is seldom fatal. In 1996 students ranging in age from 12 to 18 were victims of about 255,000 incidents of nonfatal serious violent crimes in their schools. There were 671,000 similar incidents involving this age group outside of school (Kaufman et al. 1998, 5). During the period 1996–1997, 57 percent of all public schools reported either a serious violent crime, such as murder or rape, or less serious violent crimes (e.g., assault) to the police.

A general response to school violence throughout the United States has led to the development of several aggressive policy changes. School systems are training their teachers and students how to react in ways that will rapidly contain potentially serious school violence. Special response police forces are being trained to be more effective in providing ancillary support for school administrators and staff. Intensive prevention training for all involved parties, after-school academic enrichment programs, enforcement of and punishment for firearms possession and drug use/sales on campus, and developing a standardized system of early detection and assessment of at-risk students are being implemented on a national basis (Bell 2002; California School Violence Prevention and Response Task Force 2000; Jones 2001). Evidence of the success of these initiatives is the dramatic reduction in school violence subsequent to

 **BOX 2.4**

Minerva H. Evans
Classroom Teacher, C.M. Macdonnell Elementary, Laredo Independent School District, Laredo, Texas

Statistics:

B.A. (psychology), Texas A & M International University; B.S. (elementary education), Texas A & M International University; M.A. (forthcoming, sociology and psychology), Texas A & M International University

Work History and Experience:

I was born and reared in Laredo, Texas, a small border town that is now booming due to the passage of NAFTA. As the city became more metropolitan, new issues and concerns have arisen that are reflected in the elementary classroom. I teach primary elementary school, and I mostly work with first- and second-graders. I am currently pursuing a master's degree in sociology. My experience in the classroom has enabled me to make a direct correlation between theory and real-life situations. Since our city has grown, new people have come to Laredo from other parts of the country, and of course, we do have a very high immigrant population coming into the schools from all parts of Mexico. The social trends in Laredo have affected many of our students in many ways. More people are now employed, and hence we now see more latchkey kids, a term I was only familiar with in the past from the sociological literature.

One experience of such a child has moved and influenced me to seek alternative ways to help other children in the same situation. My third year as a first-grade teacher found me starting school with a child that was already at the age of 6 labeled as a "discipline child." It seems that this child ruled kindergarten. He did not follow any of the school rules, and therefore he spent most of his kindergarten year in the principal's office. Of course, I knew that on top of the discipline problem, I was getting a child who had missed a lot of instruction because of his own misbehavior. Instead of

complaining, I accepted the challenge and decided that this child was going to learn academics, although most of all, he was going to learn to behave so that he could find out for himself that by doing so, it would be to his ultimate benefit.

The child tested my patience for the first few weeks. I set rules for him to follow, and I also showed him that I would not bend. I treated him fairly and equally like everyone else. I also started to give him some responsibilities within the classroom. I would call on him often to read or to share an answer. At first, I noticed a look of dismay, with him thinking that I would not call on him. But the more I put him on the spot, the more he wanted to participate. After a while, he was always raising his hand. Many times I had to redirect him because he was very aggressive and would not allow other children to answer. I established a very clear and definite routing with him. He knew exactly where to sit every day. He knew what was going to happen every single minute of the day. I tried never to deviate from the set schedule so that he would feel secure and confident about what he was doing.

After having this child working with me in the classroom, I tried to get his mother to come in to see why he was still having problems with behavior outside of the classroom. After several conferences, I realized that his mother was a single parent who was a habitual drug user. She spent most of her time out of the house, looking for her next "fix." This child was left alone in his home to fend for himself. His mother had no idea if he ate, had or did homework, bathed, or played. This child did not know what to expect at home every day he got home from school. The uncertainty of his life was creating chaos and confusion in his school life. School was the only place where he interacted with other children or adults.

I immediately sought counseling and intervention for this young child, who now became my major concern. Through weekly counseling and referrals to other agencies within the community, this child was practically a transformed person by the end of the first grade. At school, rules were structured and explicit. He knew the consequences of his behavior, and I am quite sure that he felt secure in this structured environment. At home there were no rules. His mother was eventually jailed, which of course had a dramatic effect on the child. But his uncle took him in and provided nurturing and a sense of belonging that he desperately needed at home.

During his second-grade year, this child—who had previously tormented his kindergarten teacher, alienated his peers, and cussed out the P.E. coach—was now a peaceful child who sought to please his teachers and his foster parents. His grades dramatically improved and he strove to be better at everything he undertook.

I have since made it a personal goal to reach out to those at-risk children and try every conceivable way to give them breaks, allow them to flourish, and just be kids having fun in school. As I read more and more in my graduate courses, I am convinced that our society is ever-changing, and that these changes have an effect on people and the community at large. We must deal with these changes in positive ways. Society's problems are brought into the classroom, not only by students, but also by parents who do not know what to do in certain situations. I believe that it is not only my responsibility to educate the child, but also the parents.

Advice to Students:

Take the challenge, especially with the problem child. Take the time to search all of the resources that are available at the school and throughout the community that can ultimately benefit the child. Do not accept the label that a child has when he or she first arrives in your classroom. Children live up to our expectations. Society changes constantly, and these changes affect the children in our classrooms. If we are to deal with and eliminate the problems in our society, first we have to work with and help our children to become positive, productive members of that society. Under no circumstances give up on any child.

1996 and through 2000 (Pollack and Sundermann 2001). One of the contributing factors to this decline in school violence has been the establishment of a zero tolerance policy in many school systems, which imposes more stringent penalties on youthful offenders who bring dangerous weapons to their schools (Casella 2001).

At-Risk Youths and the Pittsburgh Youth Study

Who are **at-risk youths?** It is difficult to forecast which youths will become delinquent and which ones won't. For many decades, researchers have attempted to profile so-called at-risk youths by assigning to them various characteristics that seem to be associated with hardcore delinquents. In 1986 and for the next decade, investigators conducted a longitudinal study of 1,517 inner-city boys from Pittsburgh, Pennsylvania. The **Pittsburgh Youth Study (PYS)** followed three samples of boys for over a decade to determine how and why boys became involved in delinquent and other problem behaviors (Browning and Loeber 1999:1). Initially, boys were randomly selected from the first, fourth, and seventh grades and tracked over time.

Eventually, three developmental pathways were defined, each displaying progressively more serious problem behaviors. The first pathway, authority-conflict, involves youths who exhibit stubbornness prior to age 12, and then they move on to defiance and avoidance of authority. The second pathway, covert, includes minor covert acts, such as lying, followed by property damage and moderately serious delinquency, and then serious delinquency. The third pathway, overt, starts with minor aggression, followed by fighting and violence. Risk factors identified and associated with delinquency among the Pittsburgh youth include impulsivity, lower IQ, certain negative personality characteristics (e.g. antisocial behavior), forces in an individual's environment, including parents, siblings, and peers, and factors related to family, school, and neighborhood.

At-risk youth in the PYS tended to have greater impulsivity, lower IQ, a lower threshold for experiencing negative emotions, such as fear, anxiety, and anger, and were more inclined to be involved in thrill-seeking and acting without caution. Family risk factors included poor supervision by parents, family receipt of public assistance (welfare), and lower socioeconomic status. The greatest demographic variable associated with delinquency was having a broken family. Living in a bad neighborhood doubled the risk for delinquency.

These aggregate data are interesting, but they fail to enable researchers to forecast with accuracy which youths will become delinquent and which ones won't. Maybe this is too much to ask without more definitive criteria for identifying potential juvenile offenders. Nevertheless, a profile of at-risk youths has slowly been generated to the extent that various intervention programs can be attempted in certain jurisdictions. The theory is that if at-risk youth can be identified according to proven prior characteristics from delinquency research, then perhaps one or more interventions can be attempted to work with some or all of those youths who are at risk.

In a series of independent investigations, Greenwood (1999, 1) has studied early childhood interventions applied to particular at-risk youths. Using experimental groups compared with control groups of youths, Greenwood reports that those at-risk youths who received various interventions and social assistance in their early years exhibited higher emotional and cognitive development, improved educational outcomes, enhanced economic self-sufficiency, and decreased criminal activity compared with a matched control group of youths (Greenwood 1999, 1). Greenwood's analysis included evaluations of nine different childhood intervention programs, including the Early Training Project, the Perry Preschool Project, and the Infant Health and Development Project. Greenwood concluded that in some situations at least, carefully targeted childhood interventions can yield measurable benefits and that some of those benefits endure for some time after the program has ended.

Juvenile courts have attempted their own form of intervention involving at-risk youths. Since the mid-1970s, the National Council of Juvenile and Family Court Judges has sought to focus national attention on abused and neglected children (Mentaberry 1999, 1). Youths placed in foster care and/or suffering from various forms of sexual or physical abuse in their families are considered at-risk and in need of special treatment from various social services. It has been found, for instance, that a strategy for assisting at-risk youths is to educate family and juvenile court judges in ways to improve their court practices. By 1999, the Permanency Planning for Children Department has established seventeen Model Courts in sixteen states. These Model Courts have implemented a number of programs to deal with at-risk youths and their families. Such programs can easily be replicated in other jurisdictions. For instance, court calendars are generated to ensure that judicial decision makers are assigned to specific dependency cases and will remain on those cases until the children involved achieve permanence, either by being safely reunited with their rehabilitative families or by being placed in permanent adoptive homes. Family group conferencing and mediation programs are also incorporated into several of these Model Court jurisdictions. Proper handling of cases involving these types of at-risk youths tends to decrease the likelihood that placed youths will become delinquent in their future years.

Gang Violence

Juvenile justice professionals are interested in the increased incidence of gang formation and membership behavior (Howell and Lynch 2000). The gang phenomenon seems widespread throughout the United States rather than localized in major city centers. **Gangs** are found in most jurisdictions and seem to organize along racial or ethnic lines, often for mutual protection against other gangs. Various independent investigations of gang presence and activities have been undertaken in recent years, including Project GANGMILL, by the National Gang Crime Research Center in Chicago. This investigation studied 3,489 gang members in seven states and twenty-two correctional facilities (National Gang Crime Research Center 2000, 38). General findings from these investigations parallel other broader investigations of gangs in the United States conducted by various federal agencies.

The gang problem in the United States is increasing (Howell and Decker 1999). There has been a rapid proliferation of youth gangs in the United States since 1980, despite our best intervention and gang prevention efforts. In 1980, for instance, there were 2,000 gangs in 286 jurisdictions, with over 100,000 gang members. In 1999 there were more than 26,000 gangs in 4,800 jurisdictions, with over 840,500 gang members (Egley 2000, 1). About 11 percent of all gang members are female (National Gang Crime Research Center 2000, 38–40). While definitive national trend data are unavailable concerning female gang

Gangs are pervasive in most cities and towns, and they often form along racial or ethnic lines.

members and the types of offenses they commit, independent investigations of selected jurisdictions suggest that the number of female gangs in the United States is increasing.

In 1992 the Chicago City Council held hearings to identify strategies to combat youth violence attributable to gangs and gang membership. Subsequently, the Gang Congregation Ordinance was passed. This ordinance authorized Chicago police officers to investigate youths on city streets, where the youths appeared to be loitering or congregating in groups. Further, police were authorized to order such groups of youths to disperse (Regini 1998, 25–26). Similar ordinances were passed in other cities, such as Los Angeles. This ordinance gave police officers considerable discretion to determine which youths were gang members and to intervene whenever they believed gangs were present. The intent of the ordinance was to discourage neighborhood gang activity and reduce gang-related violence. However, the American Civil Liberties Union and other interested rights organizations protested and sought injunctions against police from taking gang-busting actions in those cities where such ordinances were passed. In 1999 the U.S. Supreme Court held these ordinances to be unconstitutional. Among the reasons were the fact that the ordinances were unconstitutionally vague and failed to specify what behaviors were prohibited. Further, no definitive criteria were established whereby gang members could be distinguished from nongang members. More than a few police officers and police departments regarded this Supreme Court decision as a major setback in their efforts to combat gang violence.

Kids Who Kill

Juveniles who commit homicide are relative rare (Fox and Zawitz 1999, 1). Of the 14,697 homicide offenders reported by the *UCR* in 2000, 832 (5.6 percent) of these involved juveniles under age 18 (Maguire and Pastore 2002, 23). Some juveniles have begun their careers of gang violence, including murder and attempted murder, as early as age 6. An increasing amount of youth violence, including homicide, is linked to gang membership (Flannery and Huff 1999). There were 650 gang-related juvenile murders in 2000. Actually, gang-related murders declined from 1996 (858 murders) to 1999 (580 murders), but the number of murders increased again in 2000.

Apart from gang-related murders, many youths kill one or more of their family members, such as their mothers or fathers. Studies of youths who kill their parents show that they are often severely physically or sexually abused and that they are particularly sensitive to stressors in the home environment (Heide 1999). Many juvenile murderers have chemical dependencies for which they require treatment (Hillbrand et al. 1999). Juvenile murderers also exhibit greater psychotic and conduct disorder symptoms compared with other types of juvenile offenders (Myers and Scott 1998).

Some juvenile murders are sexually motivated and occur when victims threaten to tell others (Glick and Sturgeon 1999). But even something as specific as sexually motivated juvenile murder is poorly misunderstood by the public. A wide variety of explanations is provided for explaining or rationalizing adolescent murders, although any excuse is rarely accepted as mitigating (Flannery and Huff 1999). One frequently cited reason for gang violence was that it was an expected part of gang initiation rites (National Gang Crime Re-

search Center 2000, 52–53). Most often cited as mitigating factors in juvenile homicides are troubled family histories and social backgrounds, psychological disturbances, mental retardation, indigence, and substance abuse. Treatments often include psychotherapy, psychiatric hospitalization, institutional placement, and psychopharmacological agents (Heide 1999).

Juvenile Violence Trends

Violence committed by juveniles has increased during the last few decades. Between 1986 and 1996, the juvenile violent crime index soared. Chesney-Lind et al. (1998) indicate that juvenile arrests for violent crimes increased by 200 percent during this ten-year period. However, since 1996, there has been a mild decline in juvenile violence. This decline in juvenile violence has not been substantial, less than 15 percent. However, this slight decline may be one indication that various youth crime intervention programs are working (U.S. Department of Justice 2002).

One concomitant of youth violence is access to firearms. Gun-related violence is both a criminal justice and a public health problem. In 1997 there were 7 murders per 100,000 U.S. residents. But in 2000, the murder rate had dropped to 3.5 per 100,000 (U.S. Department of Justice 2002). This is the lowest murder rate in the United States since 1965. However, preliminary projections by the Federal Bureau of Investigation at the time of this writing showed that for 2001, the murder rate had increased by 3.1 percent (Federal Bureau of Investigation 2002). This increase excludes the September 11, 2001 World Trade Center loss of lives through terrorist acts.

The impact of gun violence is especially strong for juveniles and young adults. There were 1,300 murder victims under the age of 18 in 2000. This is over 50 percent lower than the peak year of 1993, when there were 2,900 juvenile deaths. About half of these deaths were from firearms. Various policies and laws have been implemented to intervene in gun-related violence. Sources of illegal guns are increasingly interrupted; penalties have been increased for illegal possession and carrying of guns; and persons who supply at-risk youths for violence (e.g., probationers, gang members, and drug traffickers) are being prosecuted more aggressively. Simultaneously, programs are in place to treat and deal with those youthful offenders who have mental disorders and/or substance abuse problems (U.S. Department of Justice 2001).

Career Escalation

Do status offenders progress to more serious offending, such as juvenile delinquency? Do juvenile delinquents become adult offenders? This phenomenon is known as **career escalation.** Presently, there is little agreement among professionals that either status offenders or delinquents progress toward more serious offending as they get older (Zimring 1998). This generalization applies to both male and female offenders. One problem is that different **pathways,** or developmental sequences over the term of one's adolescence, are associated with serious, chronic, and violent offenders (Kempf-Leonard, Tracy, and Howell 2001). Thus, a single trajectory or pathway cannot be used as a general forecast of career escalation, whenever it occurs. Furthermore, comparative research on career escalation among delinquent youths suggests that situational factors, such

 **BOX 2.5**

PERSONALITY HIGHLIGHT

Fructuoso San Miguel, III
Assistant Chief, Laredo, Texas, Police Department

Statistics:

M.S. (criminal justice and public administration), Texas A & M International University; master's certificate, Texas Commission on Law Enforcement Officer Standards and Education (TCLEOSE); FBI National Academy; International Association of Chiefs of Police (IACP)

Background and Interests:

I began my career with the Laredo Police Department in 1982. I was promoted to Investigator in 1986, and I was assigned to the Detectives Section where I worked cases involving juveniles and sex crimes. In 1992, I was promoted to the rank of sergeant and reassigned to the Patrol Section where I supervised a patrol squad. In 1996, I was promoted to the rank of lieutenant and was assigned the position of Watch Commander for the Patrol Section. In 1997, I was promoted to Deputy Chief of Police. In 2001, I was promoted to Assistant Chief of Police, where I currently oversee the auxiliary and patrol operation services at the Laredo Police Department.

I earned my master's degree in criminal justice with a minor in public administration from Texas A & M International University in Laredo, Texas. I received my master's certificate from the Texas Commission on Law Enforcement Officer Standards and Education (TCLEOSE), and I am a 2000 FBI National Academy graduate. I am also an active member of the International Association of Chiefs of Police (IACP).

Experiences:

Being a police officer has allowed me to interact with many individuals, both adult and juvenile offenders. Unfortunately, many of these interactions have not been pleasant, since they involved arresting those whose behavior violated the law. However, because of these interactions, I was exposed to the re-

alities of the criminal justice system. This was especially true when as an investigator I was assigned to investigate sexual assaults.

One case in particular caused me to question the efficacy of the system, specifically the role of correctional institutions designed to rehabilitate inmates. The case that is such a clear example involved the sexual assault of a 22-year-old male. The perfunctory investigation of this case led to an unusual suspect—a recently released male inmate, approximately 30 years of age. Upon conducting an interrogation, the suspect readily admitted to sex with the victim but was adamant that it was consensual, since the male victim was a prostitute. Subsequent interviews with the suspect indicated that the cause of such a degrading crime pointed directly to his prison experience. According to the suspect, he was sexually abused in prison and was eager to inflict such violence upon someone, as an act of revenge. Although the sexual assault of inmates by others in a correctional institution is something that is common knowledge as an officer, I never before questioned why such an institution geared to reform or rehabilitate inmates produced such violent tendencies in released inmates. Of course, these violent tendencies may be present before individuals interact with inmates, but this clearly was not the case with this suspect.

The interrogations revealed that he did not have a history of violent criminal activity and had never sexually assaulted anyone. Although it should not be an excuse, institutional life was the primary contributing factor or cause of this crime, in my opinion. The case further caused me to question the criminal justice system when I learned that the victim was later accused of sodomy with an 8-year-old boy. Despite my work investigating this crime and other sexual asaults, I do believe that the criminal justice system has improved in the last few decades, and I regard my profession as very rewarding.

as whether youths come from abusive families and where drug and/or alcohol dependencies are evident, are more significant predictors of future, more serious offending rather than the sheer onset of status of delinquent offending (Cooke 2001; Estrada 2001).

With little more information than whether youths commit particular status or delinquent acts at particular ages, long-term predictions of future career escalation among these juveniles are simply unwarranted (Zimring 1998). Arrest rates for juvenile offenders change drastically within short-term cycles of three years, rather than long-term cycles of more than three years. Also, there are different varieties of juvenile violence. About half of all juvenile violence is gang related. This type of violence is quite different from the violence exhibited by youths who kill their parents or other youths out of anger or frustration (Hillbrand et al. 1999; Van Hofer 2000). In fact, researchers have been aware of these different types of violence and their origins for several decades (Pennell and Curtis 1982).

Interest in career escalation among juveniles heightened during the 1970s and 1980s, when delinquency and crime increased appreciably (Piper 1983; Rankin and Wells 1985). Statistical correlations between rising crime and delinquency rates and the amount of status and delinquent offending led to the tentative conclusion that career escalation was occurring. In retrospect, and after a closer examination of adult recidivists, a clear pattern of career escalation among juvenile offenders has not been revealed. More than any other factor, domestic violence and an abusive family environment seem to be critical determinants of whether certain youths from such families will become chronic and persistent offenders (Darby et al. 1998; Kelleher 1998).

FEMALE VERSUS MALE DELINQUENCY: CATALOGING THE DIFFERENCES

In 2000, 24 percent of all juvenile arrests involved females. However, of the total number of juveniles held in either public or private juvenile secure facilities in 2000, approximately 10 percent of these detainees were female (American Correctional Association 2002). Also, about 15 percent of all youths in juvenile community correctional programs were female (American Correctional Association 2002). An independent investigation of a large cross-section of gang members in seven states and twenty-two juvenile correctional institutions discloses similar proportionate results (National Gang Crime Research Center, 2000). These figures indicate that female juvenile arrestees are committed to secure facilities at a lower rate than male juveniles and that females are also returned to their communities more frequently after serving shorter secure confinement terms (Maguire and Pastore 2002).

Profiling Female Juveniles

Are there significant differences between male and female juveniles concerning the nature of their offending? Yes. Female juveniles get into trouble more quietly. They tend to be involved to a greater degree in less serious types of offending, including runaway behavior, curfew violations, unruly behavior, larceny-theft, and drug abuse. In fact, the juvenile female offender of the 1990s and 2000s appears to be similar in demographic characteristics to female juvenile offenders of the 1980s. Survey data show that many youthful female offenders have prior histories of being sexually or physically abused, come from a single-parent home, and lack appropriate social and work-related skills (Office of Juvenile Justice and Delinquency Prevention 2002).

Evidence indicates that growing numbers of female juveniles are entering the juvenile justice system annually, at younger ages, and for more violent offending (Zaslaw 1999, 33). Over 60 percent of all female juveniles charged with juvenile delinquency in 1997 were under age 16 (Scahill 2000, 1). Additionally, increasing numbers of female juveniles are being transferred to criminal courts for prosecution as adult offenders. Compared with 1988 figures, there were 400 female juveniles transferred to criminal court jurisdiction in 1997, up 37 percent (Scahill 2000, 1). Approximately 42 percent of these cases involved a violent offense as the most serious charge. Several important risk factors have been identified and associated with greater amounts of female offending. Although every girl who gets into trouble with the juvenile justice system is unique, she is likely to share elements of the following profile with other female juvenile delinquents:

1. She's now 14 to 16 years old, although she may have started acting out a few years earlier.
2. She's poor and has grown up in a neighborhood with a high crime rate.
3. She's likely to belong to an ethnic minority group (50 percent of female juveniles in detention are black, 13 percent are Hispanic, and 34 percent are Caucasian).
4. She's had a history of poor academic performance and may be a high school dropout.
5. She's been a victim of physical, sexual, and/or emotional abuse or exploitation.
6. She has used and abused drugs and/or alcohol.
7. She has gone without attention for medical and mental health needs.
8. She feels that life is oppressive and lacks hope for the future (Office of Juvenile Justice and Delinquency Prevention 2002, 2).

Trends in Female Juvenile Offending

However, in recent years, the pattern of female delinquent offending compared with male delinquent offending has been changing. Between 1990 and 2000, there has been a substantial increase in the number of female juvenile arrestees compared with their male counterparts. In 1990, for instance, only 11 percent of all juvenile arrestees were female. But in 2000, this figure had risen to 24 percent. Furthermore, arrests of female juveniles for violent offenses increased during the 1990–2000 period. About 15 percent of all female arrestees in 2000 involved allegations of violent crimes. This figure compares with only 7 percent of all juvenile violent crime arrestees for 1990. One reason for this increase is the increased involvement of female juveniles in gangs (National Gang Investigator's Association 2002).

The most common reason for female juveniles to join gangs is for protection, often from abusive sexual or physical encounters with their fathers at home. Another important reason is simple rebellion against parents (Bloom et al. 2002). For many female juvenile gang members, their membership gives them status among their peers and enables them to profit in illicit drug activities. It is difficult to estimate the numbers of females who are gang members. Conservatively, about 10 percent of all juvenile gang members in the United States today are female, although estimates have ranged between 9 and 22 percent, depending upon the survey conducted (National Youth Gang Center 2000). Although female gangs commit fewer violent crimes compared with male gangs, 38 percent of female youth gang offending involves violent crimes, while 37 percent of their offending involves drug offenses (Moore and Hagedorn 2001, 5). Therefore, female youth gangs should be taken seriously.

Is there a new breed of violent juvenile female offender emerging? No. Is female delinquency skyrocketing out of control? No. We don't know whether female juveniles are becoming more violent, although some evidence suggests that they are (Kakar, Friedemann, and Peck 2002). We *do* know that juvenile courts are processing larger numbers of female juveniles and that greater numbers of delinquency adjudications involve females. We suspect that in past years many juvenile court judges acted in a paternalistic manner toward female juveniles, and that often their offenses were downgraded or downplayed in seriousness (Moore and Hagedorn 2001 4–5). However, in more recent years, there has been more equitable treatment of female juveniles by the juvenile courts (Scahill 2000).

Myths and Misconceptions: Changing Views of Juvenile Females

A historical observation by Gelsthorpe (1987) indicates that there are four main themes guiding responses toward males and females in the juvenile justice system. First, males are more likely than females to offend at some point during their adolescence, although self-reports from female juveniles in a nationwide survey revealed that in 2000, 91 percent of them disclosed that they had committed at least one delinquent act (Office of Juvenile Justice and Delinquency Prevention 2002). Females who offend during adolescence are often considered abnormal in some way. Second, much male offending is property-related, while it is assumed that female delinquency is predominantly sexual. Third, female delinquents seem to come from broken homes at a higher rate than their male counterparts. Therefore, their delinquency is often attributed to deficient family relationships (Rebellon 2002). Fourth, female delinquents are characterized as having greater mental instability and nonrational behavior, whereas male juvenile offenders are characterized as rational and adventurous, simply testing the bounds of their adolescence (Glick and Goldstein 1995). Most of this historical analysis of male and female juvenile differences is pure myth and misconceived (Zaslaw 1999). A similar analysis along political-legal lines has been made by Curran (1984). Curran examined the long-range impact of the women's movement in the United States during the period 1960–1980. A prevailing belief is that the women's movement brought about many changes in both the

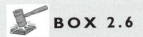 **BOX 2.6**

15-YEAR-OLD FEMALE GETS TEN YEARS FOR MURDER

The Case of Randee Sailer, Beulah, North Dakota

A judge ordered the maximum 10-year sentence for a 15-year-old Beulah, North Dakota, girl for the strangulation death of her 4-year-old half brother. Randee Sailer, 15, was tried as an adult following an indictment for murder in the death of her younger brother. Randee pleaded guilty to manslaughter in June 1999 in a plea bargain with prosecutors. She strangled to death her half brother, Jarret Sasse, in a Stanton, North Dakota, park in the summer of 1998. The maximum sentence of 10 years was recommended by prosecutor Jonathan Byers, who said that Randee "hasn't demonstrated self-control or expressed remorse for killing the boy. Although we can hope for change that she will some day have remorse, I don't think that this court or society is willing to trust that that's going to happen at this point." Countering the prosecutor's claim of Randee's lack of remorse, defense attorney Tom Tuntland said that Randee was sorry for her actions. "Randee does not express remorse very well," said Tuntland, who was interviewed following her sentence. Tuntland also expressed pessimism that Randee would receive the sort of help she would need to improve in prison. He didn't think that prison would make Randee a better person when she returns to society at age 25. Randee's family members were pleased with the sentence, however. In fact, some members didn't feel that the 10-year sentence was sufficient. It seems that Randee was also suspected in the death of Jarret Sasse's 2-year-old sister, Morgan. Jarret's aunt, Cheryl Gramm, said that Randee had tortured Jarret, pinching, scratching, biting, and abusing him. "We were seeking the help of our pastor, police, and friends on how to handle these feelings—the feelings that you, Randee, not only murdered Jarret, but Morgan also," said Gramm. Tuntland, the defense counsel, objected half way through Gramm's remarks, saying they were nothing more than an attempt to try to pin something on Randee for which she is not on trial, for which she is not being punished." In the case of Morgan Sasse, the coroner described her death as "very unusual." She died several months before Jarret, in February 1998. The state medical examiner later determined that the child died of an inflammation of the throat and trachea. Randee Sailer was asked if she wanted to make a statement at the time of sentencing. She declined because she was "too nervous to address the court."

Was Sailer's sentence proper? Should 15-year-old admitted murderers receive only 10 years for their crimes? At what age should we expect youths to be accountable for their actions? What do you think?

Source: Adapted from the Associated Press, "Judge Sentences 15-Year-Old Beulah Girl to 10 Years." September 11, 1999.

quality and quantity of female offenses during this period, as well as the way in which women were generally treated in both the criminal and juvenile justice systems. However, Curran disagrees with this view. Rather, he suggests that certain political and legal changes in the United States during the 1960–1980 period furnish a better explanation for how female juvenile offenders have been treated. Further, changes in the rate of female delinquency are likely attributable to these same factors.

Two major events triggered the change from a liberal to a conservative approach to juvenile justice throughout the United States. First, states passed legislation in response to public perceptions of increased violent crime among juveniles. Second, status offenses were removed from the jurisdiction of juvenile courts in many jurisdictions. Greater priority was given to getting tough with juvenile offenders. Regarding female juveniles, Curran has identified three major political-legal periods: (1) the paternalistic period (1960–1967), during which female delinquents were dealt with more severely than boys by the juvenile courts "for their own good"; (2) a due process period (1968–1976) that reflected the impact of various legal decisions such as *In re Gault* (1967); and (3) a law-and-order phase (1977–1980), during which the court adjusted to the new conservatism of the late 1970s (Curran 1984). Therefore, presumed changing rates in female juvenile offending were more attributable to changing policies in the treatment of female juveniles rather than actual increases in the rate of female criminality. However, as we have seen, the nature of female juvenile offending is definitely changing and increasing (Kakar, Friedemann, and Peck 2002 57). While policy changes and juvenile court views toward female offenders have probably occurred during the 1980s and 1990s, increased female juvenile offending has been observed. At the very least, female delinquency is becoming increasingly similar to male delinquency in a number of respects, and court treatment of male and female juveniles in becoming more equalized (Kempf-Leonard and Sample 2000).

SUMMARY

Juveniles are persons who have not yet attained their eighteenth birthday, although in a limited number of jurisdictions, the maximum age of a juvenile is 16. Common law in many states places juvenile offender accountability at age 7. Delinquency refers to offenses committed by youths who have not reached the age of their majority and that would otherwise be considered crimes if committed by adults. However, many juveniles commit status offenses, or acts that would not be considered crimes if adults committed them. Status offenses include runaway from home, violating curfew, liquor law violations, and truancy. Deinstitutionalization of status offenses, DSO, is a popular juvenile justice reform. One reason for its popularity is that status offenders are protected from the trappings of juvenile courts and the possible adverse effects of labeling that may result from exposure to these courts. Also, delinquents who commit crimes are logically more serious types of offenders than status offenders. But some experts believe that status offenders will escalate to more serious offenses over time and should be treated the same as delinquents.

Traditionally, juvenile courts have operated within the context and spirit of *parens patriae,* a belief that these courts know what is best for juveniles and can decide matters in their best interests. Therefore, some judicial opposition to DSO and other less punitive alternatives (ADR and peer juries) are evident. Net-widening has occurred, as larger numbers of juveniles, particularly status offenders, are brought into community-based treatment programs that have been created especially for nonviolent offenders. Juvenile detention rates in many jurisdictions have increased rather than decreased. Recidivism rates among these youths have remained unaffected, and some evidence of relabeling by police and others has occurred, where law enforcement officers relabel behaviors as delinquent that would have been considered trivial and/or nondelinquent in pre-DSO periods.

Major sources of information about delinquency and status offenses are the *Uniform Crime Reports* (*UCR*) and *National Crime Victimization Survey* (*NCVS*). These sources respectively reflect arrest information and reports from crime victims. Selected crimes are reported in the *UCR* known as index offenses. Felonies and misdemeanors are reported, as well as certain status offenses such as liquor law violations, running away from home, and curfew violations. These are known as official sources of information about delinquent conduct, although they have been extensively criticized. Other sources of information about juvenile delinquency include the National Juvenile Court Data Archive, the *Sourcebook of Criminal Justice Statistics,* and self-report information from various surveys such as the National Youth Survey and the Monitoring the Future survey (Jang 2002).

Most delinquency is nonviolent, although there is a hard core of chronic, persistent, violent juvenile offenders. Most juvenile violent offenders are male. There is no juvenile crime wave, although there was an apparent increase in delinquency during the period 1960–1975. Many of the policies devised to deal with juvenile offenders have been based on a trend that no longer exists. Although the public is often influenced by the conspicuous nature of gang violence in forming their impressions about the extent of delinquency in the United States, there is little evidence that delinquency is increasing dramatically compared with previous years or that delinquents are becoming increasingly violent in the acts they commit (Miller and Decker 2001).

Certain male-female differences exist in delinquent conduct, where much female delinquency is related to nonviolent offenses such as fraud and running away from home. Female delinquents seem to come from less stable, single-parent homes and are more deprived socioeconomically than many of their male counterparts. Provisions for female juveniles are lacking in many community-based public and private treatment programs. This is because the juvenile justice system has been geared primarily to service large numbers of male delinquents. The paternalistic nature of juvenile courts has resulted in the differential treatment of female offenders, where they are often detained for minor offenses for their own protection. Prevailing beliefs about female juvenile offenders are that they are less emotionally stable than males and exhibit nonrational behavior. Little consistent support for these views has been found by researchers, however.

QUESTIONS FOR REVIEW

1. What is meant by juvenile delinquency? What is the significance of common law and the circumstances under which youths are not held accountable for their actions?

2. Is juvenile delinquency defined the same way in all jurisdictions? If not, what are some variations?

3. What are status offenders? What are three types of status offenders and their characteristics?

4. What is meant by the deinstitutionalization of status offenses? What are three meanings of DSO and their definition?

5. What are four potential outcomes of DSO?

6. What is the *Uniform Crime Reports?* What type of information does it provide? How does it differ from the *National Crime Victimization Survey?*

7. What are some strengths and weaknesses of the *UCR* and *NCVS?*

8. What is self-report information? Is it more or less accurate compared with data reported by the *UCR* or *NCVS?* What are some reasons for your answer? What are several problems accompanying self-report information?

9. Who are at-risk youths and why are they of interest to criminal justice professionals?

10. What is career escalation? Does career escalation occur for any particular type of juvenile offender, such as a violent delinquent or a status offender? What are some juvenile violence trends?

SUGGESTED READINGS

Jones, Tony L. 2001. *Effective response to school violence: A guide for educators and law enforcement personnel.* Springfield, IL: Charles C. Thomas.

Knupfer, Anne Meis. 2001. *Reform and resistance: Gender, delinquency, and America's first juvenile court.* New York: Routledge.

Myers, David L. 2001. *Excluding violent youths from juvenile court: The effectiveness of legislative waiver.* New York: LFB Scholarly Publishing LLC.

INTERNET CONNECTIONS

Children Now
http://www.childrennow.org/

Children's Legal Protection Center
http://www.childprotect.org/

Children's Defense Fund
http://www.childrensdefense.org/

Drug Reform Coordination Network
http://www.drcnet.org/

General Victim's Assistance Information
http://www.ncjrs.org/victhome.htm

National Council on Crime and Delinquency
http://www.nccd.com

National Organization for the Reform of Marijuana Laws
http://www.norml.org/

North Carolina Center for the Prevention of School Violence
http://www2.ncsu.edu/ncsu/cep/PreViolence/CtrPreSchVio.htm

CHAPTER 3 | *Theories of Delinquency*

Chapter Outline

Key Terms
Chapter Objectives
Introduction
Classical and Biological Theories
Psychological Theories
Sociological Theories
Extraneous Factors

An Evaluation of Explanations
   of Delinquent Conduct
Models for Dealing with Juvenile
   Offenders
Delinquency Prevention
   Programs and Community
   Interventions

Summary
Questions for Review
Suggested Readings
Internet Connections

Key Terms

Anomie, anomie theory
Assumptions
Atavism
Big Brothers/Big Sisters Program
Biological determinism
Bonding theory
Bullying Prevention Program
CASASTART Program
Children at risk
Classical school

Classical theory
Community reintegration model
Concentric zone hypothesis
Conformity
Consent decrees
Containment theory
C.O.P.Y. Kids
Crime control model
Cultural transmission theory
D.A.R.E.

Determinism
Differential association theory
Differential reinforcement theory
Drift theory
Due process model
Ectomorphs
Ego
Endomorphs
Faith in Families Multi-Systematic
   Therapy Program (MST)

Chapter Objectives

As a result of reading this chapter, you will have accomplished the following objectives:

1. Understand alternative theories of juvenile conduct.
2. Differentiate between classical, biological, and psychological theories of delinquency.
3. Understand several important sociological theories of juvenile delinquency.
4. Learn about several key psychological theories of juvenile delinquency.
5. Understand how to appreciate the importance of different theoretical explanations in terms of their successful use in forecasting delinquent behavior and creating intervention programs.

INTRODUCTION

- *It happened in St. Paul, Minnesota, on January 9, 1997. Thai Lor, 19, and his 17-year-old brother, Kao Lor, were playing a Nintendo game. Their father had told each of them that they could play Nintendo for 30 minutes. When 30 minutes had expired, Thai Lor, the older brother responsible for carrying out the rules of the Lor family, began to shut down the Nintendo game. Kao Lor grabbed a knife and cut the Nintendo game controller cord in defiance of the 30-minute playing deadline. Thai Lor grabbed a nearby handgun and shot his younger brother, Kao, in the head. Kao died instantly. Subsequently convicted of second-degree murder, Thai Lor was sentenced to 22 1/2 years in prison. He will be eligible for parole after serving at least 15 years of this sentence. [Adapted from the Associated Press, "Video Game Killing Nets 22 1/2 Years." August 14, 1997.]*

- *It could have been another massacre on a middle school campus. Two 12-year-old boys amassed an arsenal of deadly weapons and ammunition, including a .25-caliber semiautomatic pistol, a .22-caliber rifle, a crossbow with arrows, a knife, ammunition, and cash. The boys gathered their weapons from one of their residences. The plan was that they would go to school with the weapons and shoot anyone who got in their way. One of the boys wanted to "get even" with some of the boys who "mess with him." The other boy said that while he didn't particularly want to shoot anyone, some of the boys had humiliated him at school and that the other boy had given him a gun to even the score. A neighbor happened to see the boys trying to hide the guns and other weapons in an alley near their home. Police were contacted and investigated. When police approached the boys' home, one boy threatened one of the officers by pointing a gun at him, while the other boy was found in the bathroom, holding a handgun to his right temple. Officers defused the situation and retrieved the weapons. One boy was charged with aggravated assault on a public servant and conspiracy to commit capital murder, while the other boy was charged with conspiracy to commit capital murder.* [Adapted from the Associated Press, "Boys Allegedly Plan Shooting." May 20, 2000.]

• *It wasn't particularly pleasant. The incident began in June 1998, in Tampa, Florida. Vicki Robinson, mother of 15-year-old Valessa Robinson, was attempting to separate her daughter from a 19-year-old drifter, Adam Davis. The plan was that Vicki would send her daughter away to a school for troubled teens. It didn't work out that way. One afternoon, Valessa choked her mother, injected her with bleach, and then stabbed her to death on the kitchen floor as she writhed in pain from the bleach. Subsequently, police arrested Valessa and she was charged with first-degree murder. A jury in Tampa found Valessa guilty of third-degree murder in April 2000, rejecting the first-degree murder charge that could have resulted in life imprisonment for the teenager. The prosecutor was disappointed with the third-degree murder conviction. State's attorney Shirley Williams said, "Valessa initiated the killing, then held her struggling mother down. She made statements afterward that she had wanted to kill her mother over the affair with Davis." The jurors deliberated for 17 hours before reaching their verdict.* [Adapted from the Associated Press, "Teen Found Guilty in Mom's Death." April 22, 2000.]

• *You are 15. You have access to a computer. You scan the Internet looking for interesting websites. One site intrigues you. It is the Pentagon. You make various attempts to enter the Pentagon security system, but your attempts are frustrated by high-tech security measures. But one bright day, you successfully break through and are admitted into a highly classified system that monitors threats from nuclear, biological, chemical, conventional, and special weapons. In June 1999, this very thing happened at the Marshall Space Flight Center in Huntsville, Alabama. Approximately $1.7 million in NASA proprietary software was downloaded to an individual's personal computer system over a three-week period. The computer at the Marshall Center was run by the Defense Threat Reduction Agency, a NASA and Pentagon security affiliate. The computer hacker who accessed these sensitive documents was only 15. Known as "comrade" to his Internet friends, the unnamed youth (because of his age) illegally entered the Pentagon computer system and intercepted at least 3,300 e-mail transmissions and stolen passwords. A Justice Department official said that this was the first juvenile hacker to successfully enter the Pentagon files. A spokesman for Internet Security Systems, Inc. of Atlanta, Georgia, Chris Rouland, said that the case was unusual, not because the youngster was caught, but because he managed to break into the computers in the first place. The Attorney General of the United States, Janet Reno, commented on the offense. "Breaking into someone else's property, whether it's a robbery or a computer intrusion, is a serious crime." Through a plea bargain agreement reached between the U.S. Attorney's Office and the boy's defense counsel, the youth admitted to breaking into thirteen different computers at the Marshall Center for a two-day period in June 1999. NASA officials said it cost $41,000 to check and repair the system during the three-week shutdown after the illegal entry was discovered. The boy, now 16, was sentenced to serve six months in a Florida detention center. This was the first time a juvenile hacker had been incarcerated for his crimes.* [Adapted from Catherine Wilson and the Associated Press, "Teen Gets Six Months for Hacking." September 22, 2000.]

These scenarios describe incidents of second-degree murder, conspiracy to commit murder, premeditated murder, and computer hacking. A common thread running throughout these scenarios is that they involve juveniles. None of these juveniles had a prior record of delinquency or misconduct. The events in these scenarios were seemingly unpredictable. Were there any clues that one juvenile or another in any of these scenarios would behave as they did? Parents, school officials, ministers, police, social service organizations, and many other interested persons and agencies struggle to devise ways of identifying troubled teens or those most likely to commit crimes.

For many interested professionals who study juvenile behavior generally and delinquency specifically, certain factors are believed to be important determinants of one's lawful as well as unlawful behaviors. If these factors can be identified, isolated, and/or measured, we may eventually learn how to control them. This means that it may be possible to modify certain situational factors that influence juveniles to commit delinquent acts and other offenses. These behavioral modifications, manipulations, or controls exerted over factors believed to precipitate delinquent conduct may also indicate the means whereby such offending conduct or behaviors can be regulated or reduced, perhaps even eliminated.

This chapter examines several popular **theories** of delinquent conduct. Theories are integrated explanatory schemes that predict relationships between two or more phenomena. They provide rational foundations to account for or explain things and help us to understand why juveniles are processed different ways by the juvenile justice system. Integral components of theories include **propositions** and **assumptions,** or different kinds of statements about the real world that vary in their tentativeness or uncertainty (Merton 1957). Theories are also more or less plausible, meaning that some explanations for events are more plausible or believable than others.

At the outset it is important to understand that no single theory of delinquent conduct has been universally accepted by all criminologists or students of juvenile delinquency (Piquero 2002). This is true, in part, because there are many different types of juvenile delinquency in need of explanation, and each theory is either more or less effective at explaining certain types of delinquency compared with other theories (Haas, 1988). Also, each theory has its own coterie of supporters as well as accompanying weaknesses and strengths when contrasted with other theories designed to explain or account for the same delinquent conduct. In fact, some of these theories are outright contradictory and compete for recognition and adoption. Additionally, gender differences in delinquent offending patterns pose challenging questions for certain theories to answer, especially where such theories emphasize explanations of male offending almost exclusively. Female delinquency is as important as male delinquency, and it deserves an explanation as well (Shoemaker 2000). For many researchers, among high-risk youths, gender is a dynamic and complex socially defined activity whose dimensions intertwine with delinquent activity. Thus, our theories of delinquency must be altered to encompass an interactive and contextually sensitive concept of gender differentiation (Bottcher 2001; Mazerolle et al. 2000).

Furthermore, if we become acquainted with the many different explanatory schemes that theorists have used over the years to account for delinquent behaviors, we may acquire a better understanding of the different programs and treatment methods that have been devised by practitioners to modify delinquent conduct, reduce its incidence, or perhaps eliminate it. This is because different theories suggest specific strategies for coping with delinquents or promote certain solutions over others, and each delinquency prevention or intervention program is, in turn, influenced by these different proposed solutions (Romero et al. 2001).

Changes within the juvenile justice system itself, particularly during the 1960s, 1970s, and 1980s, may also be explained or better understood by paying attention to theories that attempt to account for delinquent conduct or forecast its incidence. Although the precise association between delinquency theories and juvenile justice system reforms is unknown, available evidence suggests that juvenile justice is reactionary and modifies, tailors, and adjusts itself according to recent research developments and findings (Muncie 1999).

Seemingly, many delinquency intervention and prevention programs at local, state, and federal levels have been established largely as the result of isolated research investigations that suggest causal, yet tenuous, relations between delinquency and assorted factors (e.g., alcohol and drug use, peer influence, achievement motivation and school success, family structure, personality and self-concept, work values, and institutional—primarily school and church—responsibilities) (Muncie 1999; Sorenson and Brownfield, 1995). Thus, emerging delinquency treatment and interventionist programs tend to reflect these factors and reinforce their importance by influencing and modifying juvenile justice policies at all levels, including offender handling and disposition at the time of detection, arrest, and initial processing, adjudicatory procedures by prosecutors and juvenile judges, and correctional alternatives.

This chapter consists of six parts. Sections on classical theories, psychological theories, sociological theories, and extraneous factors examine delinquent conduct from several different perspectives or dimensions. After reading this material, it will be apparent that each theory does a better job accounting for particular kinds of delinquent conduct compared with all other theories. Also, some of these explanatory and predictive schemes are more popular, meaning that they are more widely adopted by professionals and significantly influence and enhance their research work. However, it must be remembered that no theory of delinquent conduct has been accepted by all those who study delinquency.

Further, a general limitation applicable to all theories is that no theory yet devised has been found to account for all types of delinquency. For instance, explanations for violence among juveniles may not apply equally effectively to property offenders or to the etiology of juvenile gangs, their emergence and persistence. A fifth section provides several criteria that may be used for evaluating the predictive and explanatory utility of each theory. While the forthcoming presentation of delinquency theories is not inclusive, it is nevertheless representative and will provide the reader with an ample array of explanations for juvenile delinquency.

Finally, we will describe several intervention programs that have been established in recent years to either reduce or prevent various types of juvenile delinquency. Not all of these programs are equally effective. Neither are they used in all jurisdictions throughout the United States. However, we may gain some insight into how the theories that have been described earlier have influenced this array of programs. Almost every intervention program has as its basis a theoretical scheme designed to explain certain delinquency forms. The intervention itself is intended to manipulate environment in an effort to divert juveniles from circumstances that give rise to delinquent behavior. The few programs that are mentioned in this section do not comprise an exhaustive compilation. Rather, they are designed to show the types of programming that have been attempted and are currently in progress in different jurisdictions. There will always be different interventions attempted, as researchers seek to find the right combination of preventive factors that enable youths to become law-abiding and avoid the influence of gangs and/or delinquent peers.

CLASSICAL AND BIOLOGICAL THEORIES

In this section, several classical and biological theories of criminality and delinquency will be examined. These include (1) classical theory, (2) positivist theory or biological determinism, (3) sociobiology, and (4) the XYY theory.

Classical Theory

Classical theory is a criminological perspective indicating that people have free will to choose either criminal or conventional behavior. People choose to commit crime for reasons of greed or personal need. Crime can be controlled by criminal sanctions, which should be proportionate to the guilt of the perpetrator.

Philosophers have speculated about the causes of crime for centuries, and they have elaborated diverse explanations for criminal conduct. In the 1700s, criminologists devised several explanations for criminal behavior that have persisted to the present day. Deeply rooted in the general principles of Christianity, the classical school of criminology originated with the work of Cesare Beccaria (1738–1794), *On Crimes and Punishments* (1764). Subsequent scholars who adopted perspectives about crime different from those of Beccaria labeled his views as classical, since they included an inherent conflict between good and evil and provided a standard against which other views of crime could be contrasted.

The **classical school** assumes that people are rational beings who exercise free will in choosing between good actions and evil ones. At the other end of the continuum is **determinism,** the view that a specific factor, variable, or event is a determinant of one's actions or behaviors. Determinism rejects the notion of free will and choice, relying instead on properties that cause human beings to behave one way or another. Within the classical context, however, societal progress and perpetuation are paramount, and individuals must each sacrifice a degree of their freedoms in order that all persons can pursue happiness and attain their respective goals. Evil actions operate adversely for societal progress and merit punishment. Because evil acts vary in their seriousness, the severity of punishments for those actions should be adjusted accordingly. Beccaria believed that punishments should be swift, certain, and just, where the penalties are appropriately adjusted to fit particular offenses. The primary purposes of punishment are deterrence and just deserts. In an ideal world, people will refrain from wrongdoing in order to avoid the pain of punishment. Furthermore, whatever punishment is imposed is equivalent or proportional in severity with the amount of social and physical damage caused by those found guilty of crimes. Fines and/or imprisonment were common penalties for those found guilty of property crimes and violent offenses.

The origins of different sentencing schemes in the United States today can be traced to Beccaria's classical theory. Most states have mandatory sentences for specific offenses, including using a firearm during the commission of a felony. Also, most state statutes carry sentences of determinate lengths and/or fines that are roughly commensurate with crime severity.

Less than two decades after Beccaria outlined his philosophy of crime and punishment, Jeremy Bentham (1748–1832), an English philosopher, advanced a similar scheme in his book, *An Introduction to the Principles of Morals and Legislation* (1790). Bentham was known for his belief that **hedonism,** the pursuit of pleasure, was a primary motivator underlying much social and personal action. Simply, humans seek to acquire pleasure and avoid pain. Thus, in this pleasure–pain framework, Bentham formulated his views about the worth and intent of punishment. Like Beccaria, Bentham believed that punishments' objectives were to deter crime and to impose sanctions sufficient to outweigh any pleasures criminals might derive from the crimes they commit. Therefore, many would-be offenders might desist from crime because the threat of punishment would more than offset the projected pleasure derived from criminal actions. Those more persistent offenders would be subject to painful punishments adjusted according to the severity of their offenses.

Under the prevailing common law of that period, those under the age of 7 were not held accountable for their actions or subject to the same kinds of punishments prescribed for adults. However, older youths eventually were vested with responsibilities for their own actions and were subject to similar adult punishments. One contemporary view of juvenile delinquents is that juveniles must accept responsibility for their actions. If they choose to ignore societal values and persist in violating the law, they must be held accountable for these offenses and punished accordingly.

In reality, the classical school of criminology is not so much an explanation of why crime or delinquency exists, but rather, it is a statement about how various offenses should be punished in order to frustrate criminal conduct.

 **BOX 3.1**

GETAWAY DRIVER 11 YEARS OLD

It was a stolen car

It happened in Alpharetta, Georgia. A reckless driver was spotted by police speeding south on Georgia Highway 400, a major freeway connecting Atlanta to the northern suburbs. During the hot pursuit, speeds reached in excess of 110 miles per hour. Police believed they were following a dangerous man. The car was reported stolen. Eventually, the police successfully stopped the speeding vehicle and caused the driver to surrender. He turned out to be 11 years old. Police eventually charged the 11-year-old with reckless driving, vehicular theft, and forgery because he possessed a counterfeit $100 bill. Chris Lagerbloom, a spokesperson for the police, said, "We've never seen anything like this before with someone this young. When they attempted to stop him, he sped off. He topped out at about 100 miles per hour."

What is an appropriate punishment for an 11-year-old for committing vehicular theft and forgery? At what age should youths be held accountable for their actions? What do you think?

Source: Adapted from the Associated Press, "11-Year-Old Was Driver in Chase." November 29, 1999.

However, some elements of explanation are contained in classical thought. Bentham, for instance, would probably speculate that persistent criminal offenders are gamblers, in a sense, since they regard the calculated risk of being caught and punished for crimes as secondary to the pleasurable benefits derived from committing crimes. The pleasure of crime outweighs the pain of punishment. Beccaria might argue that criminals are comprised of those who have failed to inculcate societal values or respect for the common good.

This perspective has received attention from contemporary theorists such as Kohlberg (1981) who constructed a theory of moral development to account for both deviant and conforming behaviors. This theory is properly classified in a social learning context, and it will be discussed briefly in the section on psychological theories presented below. Although Kohlberg's theory of moral development has been both supported and rejected by adherents and critics, some experts believe that his views may have intuitive value for furnishing insight into more aberrant modes of criminality. Further, the theory may improve our understanding of a wide range of delinquent acts if integrated into a perspective that is sensitive to how varying social contexts shape individual inclinations (Delorto and Cullen 1985).

Biological Theories

Determinism is strongly evident in biological theories of criminal and delinquent behavior. Generally, theories of determinism seek to associate criminal, delinquent, and deviant conduct with biological, biochemical, or genetic bases in a direct, causal relation. According to this view, juvenile delinquency is a selective phenomenon in that it does not occur spontaneously. Delinquents are destined to become delinquent because of factors beyond their own control and/or because of the presence of certain internal factors, while nondelinquents are destined to be nondelinquent because of the presence of different internal factors. The idea that there are known, predisposing factors that cause delinquent behaviors conveniently shifts the responsibility for delinquent conduct from youths themselves to some internal or external source.

Although the attribution of criminality and delinquency to biological causes dates to pre-biblical times, such determinism, **biological determinism,** was given a degree of academic dignity in the work of an Italian physician and criminologist, Cesare Lombroso (1835–1909), during the 1860s. Considered by many professionals to be the father of criminology, Lombroso was influenced by the work of Charles Darwin (1809–1882). Darwin's major writing, *The Origin of the Species,* was both revolutionary and evolutionary, arguing in part that human beings evolved from lower animal forms over thousands of years. Natural selection and survival of the fittest were key principles of Darwin's evolutionary theory. Lombroso was intrigued by these principles and applied them in his explanation of criminal conduct.

For Lombroso, criminals were products of heredity. Successive generations of human beings inherited not only physical features genetically from their ancestors, but they also inherited behavioral predispositions such as propensities toward criminal conduct or antisocial proclivities. Since heredity is more or less binding on future generations, it made sense to Lombroso and many of his disciples that certain physical characteristics would also be inexorably related to criminal behavior. Therefore, physical appearance would be a telling factor whether certain persons would be predisposed to criminality or other types of deviant behavior. This led Lombroso to conjecture extensively about criminal types and born criminals. Height, weight, hair and eye color, physiognomic features such as jaw sizes and angles and ear lobe shapes, finger lengths and hand sizes, and assorted other anatomical characteristics were painstakingly measured and charted by Lombroso. Samples of both willing and unwilling volunteers were obtained for his analyses, including populations of Italian prisoners and soldiers. Eventually, Lombroso concluded that many of the physiological characteristics shared by criminals were indicative of stunted evolutionary growth. Indeed, Lombroso considered criminals to be throwbacks typical of earlier evolutionary stages. This view of criminals is **atavism,** strongly suggestive of subhuman qualities.

Lombroso's views became known popularly as **positivism,** and the **positive school of criminology** originated. This view rejected the free will and choice doctrines espoused by Beccaria and other classical theorists. Rather, criminal conduct more likely emanated from biochemical and genetic factors peculiar to criminal types. Physical features of criminal types were describable, and inferences could be made about their inherited propensities toward various forms of criminal conduct. Lombroso made further refinements by concluding that certain physical features (e.g., sloping foreheads, compressed jaws, large earlobes, long, slender fingers, excessive facial and body hair) would tend to indicate the type of criminal behavior expected from those observed.

Although Lombroso limited his theoretical and empirical work primarily to adult criminals, his strong focus upon the heredity factor was easily generalizable to juveniles. Thus, he simultaneously provided explanations for both criminal and delinquent conduct that relied almost exclusively on genetic factors. In later years, however, Lombroso changed his opinion about the key role played by genetics in promoting criminal behavior. His beliefs were changed, in part, as the result of extensive scientific studies of both juveniles and adults that disclosed little relation between physiological features and criminal behaviors (Ferri 1901; Goring 1913). Also, the growth of other social sciences such as sociology and psychology led him to assign a more prominent role to one's social milieu as a prerequisite to criminal or delinquent conduct.

Despite the fact that specific biological features or characteristics could not be positively connected with specific types of criminal conduct, certain professionals in the early 1900s continued to regard biological determinism as a plausible explanation for criminality and delinquency. During the 1930s, Hooton (1939) and Kretschmer (1936) established physical typologies of criminals that were given some credence by the academic community. In the 1940s, William H. Sheldon (1949) provided what later became both a popular and an elaborate description of genetic types that seemingly manifested certain kinds of criminal characteristics. Sheldon defined three major categories of body types, including **mesomorphs,** strong, athletic individuals, **ectomorphs,** or thin, submissive beings, and **endomorphs,** or fat persons. He assigned point valuations to each person observed and attempted to describe behaviors most typical of them. Mesomorphs were believed to typify those who manifested criminal or delinquent behaviors. Unfortunately, little consistency existed in his descriptions of those sharing these bodily characteristics. Particularly disturbing was the fact that many nondelinquents and noncriminals were classified as mesomorphs. His work was soundly criticized by other professionals who concluded that no relation between body type and criminality could be established positively (Sutherland 1951).

Although Sheldon's work was widely criticized and subsequently discounted, some researchers continue to investigate the relation between biology and criminal propensities and regard such a connection as plausible. For instance, research conducted by Sheldon and Eleanor Glueck in 1950 targeted 1,000 white male youths, 500 of whom were delinquent and 500 of whom were nondelinquent (Glueck and Glueck 1950). Mesomorphic characteristics similar to those described by Sheldon were found among 60 percent of the delinquents studied, while only 30 percent of the nondelinquents shared these characteristics. While the Gluecks interpreted their findings conservatively and never said that delinquency is caused by mesomorphic characteristics, they nevertheless described delinquents generally as more agitated and aggressive compared with nondelinquents. Over five decades later, we can look back at the Gluecks' study and argue, particularly in view of the rise in the incidence of juvenile gangs in many of the nation's larger cities, that more muscular youths are probably more likely to be gang members than less muscular youths. Further, the fact that the Gluecks confined their analysis to white male juveniles means that they excluded from consideration several races and ethnic groups that have become increasingly conspicuous in U.S. society and associated with certain forms of delinquency. Additionally, the Gluecks have been criticized on both methodological and statistical grounds (Laub 1987).

Sociobiology.   In recent decades, several criminologists have reaffirmed the significance of the biological contribution to criminality and delinquency (Kendrick and Sheets 1993; Rowe and Osgood 1984; Wilson and Herrnstein 1985). Genetic researchers and biologists have evolved **sociobiology,** or the study of the biological basis for social action (Wilson 1975, 16). While this new field is not necessarily biological determinism or positivism revisited, it nevertheless stimulates interest in and directs our attention toward the role of genetics in human behavior. Presently, it is believed that a connection exists, but we are unable to elaborate this connection (Braithwaite et al. 1993).

The XYY Theory.   Closely associated in principle with the sociobiological explanation of criminality and delinquency is the **XYY theory.** This theory asserts that certain chromosomatic abnormalities may precipitate violence and/or criminal conduct. *X* chromosomes designate female characteristics and are regarded as passive, while *Y* chromosomes designate male characteristics and are regarded as aggressive. Normally, an *XX* chromosomatic combination produces a female, while the *XY* chromosomatic combination yields a male. Sometimes, an extra *Y* chromosome insinuates itself into the *XY* formula to produce an *XYY* type. The input from this additional aggressive chromosome is believed responsible, at least in some instances, for criminal behaviors among those observed to possess it. Unfortunately, this chromosomatic combination exists in less than 5 percent of the population, and thus it lacks sufficient predictive utility when considered on its own merits (Marsh and Katz 1985).

Besides designating specific body types, physical features, and heredity as crucial manifestations or causes of delinquency and criminal behavior, other biological or physical causes have been advanced in previous years. Feeblemindedness, mental illnesses, low intelligence, physical deformity including assorted stigmata, and glandular malfunction or imbalance have been variously described as concomitants of delinquency and criminality (Barnum 1987; Gordon 1986). Walsh (1987), for instance, studied 256 delinquents in Toledo, Ohio, and Boise, Idaho. He examined their IQ levels and types of offenses committed. While he found that those delinquents with higher IQ levels tended not to engage in violent acts, he also found that those juveniles with lower IQ levels evidenced an inordinate amount of property crime, crime most likely to offer instant gratification to offenders. He argued accordingly that low IQ apparently predisposed delinquents to impulsive and spontaneous property crimes, while higher IQ disposed youths to commit crimes that required planning and offered deferred gratification. Presently, however, most professionals are not prepared to acknowledge IQ as a valid indicator of delinquent propensities.

Other Biologically Related Explanations.   Much research exists regarding the relation of criminal and delinquent behavior to physical deformities and glandular malfunctions. While these ideas that glandular malfunctions and physical defects are somehow causally related to various forms of deviant behavior are interesting, no consistent groundwork has been provided that empirically supports any of these notions. Regarding stigmata, for instance, Irving Goffman (1961) has observed that often, unusual behaviors are elicited from those possessing stigmata by defining audiences of others who regard such stigmata with repulsion. Thus, those with stigmas of one type or another, such as facial disfigurement, react to the reactions of others toward them, sometimes behaving as they believe others expect them to behave. It is not the stigma that causes deviant behavior, but rather, the reactions of stigmatized persons who respond to the reactions of others. No scientific continuity has been conclusively established between stigmata and criminality. Some relatively recent investigations have attempted to correlate antisocial and delinquent behavior with early exposure to lead and other toxicants. These investigations have also included examinations of delinquent youth exposed to marijuana use by one or both parents and determined by prenatal and postnatal exposures to the drug. Interestingly, a positive correlation has been drawn between prenatal exposure to certain drugs and toxicants from mothers and subsequent behavioral problems of children from their infant years through adolescence (Dietrich et al. 2001).

A key feature of many community-based juvenile correctional programs is counseling designed to assist juveniles acquire more positive self-concepts and self-assurance. Sometimes, disfigurements or physical inadequacies might cause some of these youths to feel rejected by others or left out of group activities. Wilderness experiences and outdoors survival courses are designed, in part, to bolster youth's confidence in the ability to set goals and accomplish them. If youths can cope with living in the wilderness, by learning camping, cooking, and other pioneer crafts, then they might assume that other problems can be overcome as well. While it is impossible to tell for sure whether biological explanations of delinquent conduct have contributed to the establishment of such programs, it is clear that many individual and group activities involving youthful offenders are geared toward developing coping skills. And often, coping with one's own physical and/or psychological inadequacies is an essential part of growing out of the delinquent mode of conduct.

PSYCHOLOGICAL THEORIES

Theories that attribute criminal and delinquent behaviors to personality maladjustment or to some unusual cognitive condition are categorically known as **psychological theories.** These theories focus upon the learning process, the process whereby humans acquire language, self-definitions, definitions of others, and assorted behavioral proprieties. Because the precise mechanisms involved in the learning process are elusive and cannot be inspected or investigated directly, each psychological theory is inherently subjective and may be debated endlessly regarding its relative merits and explanatory effectiveness. In this section, two psychological explanations for delinquent conduct will be examined: (1) psychoanalytic theory and (2) social learning theory.

Psychoanalytic Theory

Some of the early pioneers of psychological theories of human behavior were Sigmund Freud, Karen Horney, and Carl Jung. These theorists conjectured about personality systems, how they are formed, and how personality and behavior are inexorably intertwined. The most popular psychologist historically was probably Sigmund Freud (1856–1939). At least Freud was one of the few early theorists who presented a very systematic explanatory scheme for personality emergence and development. Freud's investigations and writings eventually became widely known as **psychoanalytic theory.**

At the core of psychoanalytic theory, according to Freud, are three major personality components known respectively as the **id, ego,** and **superego.** The id is the uncontrolled "I-want" component prevalent among all newborn infants. The desire of the id is for immediate gratification. Thus, infants typically exhibit little or no concern for others as they seek to acquire things they like or admire. As infants mature to young children, the id is suppressed to a degree by the ego, another personality component. The ego is a recognition of others and a respect of their rights and interests. Eventually, higher-level moral development occurs through the superego or conscience. When children begin to feel guilty when they have deprived others of something wrongfully, this is a manifestation of the superego in action, according to Freud. Eventually, a **libido** emerges, which is a basic drive for sexual stimulation and gratification. The onset of puberty is a common event signally the importance of the libido. Again, the ego and superego function to keep the libido in check.

Deviant behavior generally and criminal behavior and delinquency specifically may be explained as the result of insufficient ego and superego development. The id dominates and seeks activities that will fulfill the urges or needs it stimulates. Parent–child relations are often cited as primary in the normal development of the ego and superego. Therefore, if some children lack control over their impulses and desires, the blame is often placed at the parents' feet for their failure to inculcate these important inhibitors into the youth's personality system.

Psychoanalytic theory stresses one's early childhood experiences as crucial for normal adult functioning to occur. Traumatic experiences may prevent proper ego or superego development. Adults may develop neuroses or psychoses that may be traceable to bizarre childhood events. In a 1950s movie based upon an actual case, *The Three Faces of Eve,* actress Joanne Woodward portrayed a country housewife with multiple personalities or schizophrenia. A psychiatrist, portrayed by actor Lee J. Cobb, sought to psychoanalyze the woman to discover which early childhood events may have been responsible for her current mental condition. Under hypnosis, the woman disclosed that when she was a young child attending a wake or funeral in a relative's home, she was forced by her parents to kiss the face of her aunt who had recently died

 **BOX 3.2**

JUVENILES INCRIMINATE THEMSELVES WITH HOME VIDEOS

Human Head Baseball

A 16-year-old in Sparta, Michigan, bludgeoned a man to death. Then he cut off the man's head and took it home with him. In his kitchen, he placed the head in the kitchen sink and slashed the head repeatedly with a butcher knife. He removed the brain from the head and discarded it in the trash. Then he wrapped the head in plastic and played "kickball" with it outside with several friends. In Fort Lauderdale, Florida, five teenagers vandalized and burglarized eight homes and a school. At one home they took a live sea trout and put it in a microwave oven. They watched as the sea trout wiggled uncomfortably and eventually blew up inside the microwave oven. In Los Angeles, several teens shot various victims with "paint balls" or paint projectiles shot from guns. They "whooped it up" as the victims fell down after being hit, writhing in pain. In Washington, DC, five teens robbed, beat, and urinated on a victim. After the incident, the teens conducted an interview with each other, pretending that they were on a news documentary. The teens involved in these scenarios dubbed their acts a "game," "bashing," and "human head baseball." In each of the above incidents, the youths involved videotaped their various acts. Police recovered the videos from each of these crime scenes and were able to make arrests that led to ironclad convictions

against these youths in court. The videotapes were overwhelmingly persuasive to juries who heard their cases.

Sex crime investigators say that videotaping different kinds of criminal activities is not new. Individuals have engaged in various sex acts and photographed or videotaped these acts for decades. Most of these sex-related videos come from the perpetrators' desire to relive their experiences at a later time. Interestingly, police reports suggest that videotaping of youth crimes is on the increase, and that more frequently, police investigators are uncovering incriminating videotapes of crimes perpetrated by brazen criminals. One of the most blatant examples of videotaping criminal activity occurred when James Jordan, father of basketball star Michael Jordan, was murdered. The two teens involved in his murder spent several days partying and showing off the property they had stolen from Mr. Jordan. All of this activity was videotaped by them and used by prosecutors later to obtain convictions. Increasing numbers of search warrants are being issued with specific directives to obtain copies of any videotape that may be left at the crime scene.

What do you think caused these youths to commit these acts? Are any of these acts evidence of hedonism? What do you think?

Source: Adapted from Edward F. Davis and Anthony J. Pinizzotto, "Caught On Tape: Using Criminals' Videos Against Them." *FBI Law Enforcement Bulletin* 67:13–15, 1998.

and was reposing in a coffin. Her repulsion and shock were sufficient to suppress this event deep into her subconscious mind. Certain coping mechanisms were triggered that apparently led to the formation of different personality systems.

While the case of Eve in the movie was to some extent related to adult deviant behavior and relied heavily on a psychoanalytic explanation, it did not deal directly with delinquency. However, psychoanalytic theory has been used either implicitly or explicitly in subsequent studies of juvenile sex offenders and others who commit crimes such as arson. A study of juvenile rapists, for instance, disclosed that compared with a matched sample of juvenile nonrapists, rapists tended to exhibit higher rates of social isolation, physical problems, and problems with sexual identification. In fact, it was concluded that it may be useful to view juvenile rape as a violent, impulsive act committed by youths with a low level of ego integration (Corder et al. 1986). Also, in a study of arson committed by juveniles, it was indicated that childhood firestarting behavior is a relatively common but serious psychiatric problem. Firestarting emerges from a confluence of factors, including learning contingencies that shape and mold normal childhood interest in fire, family and historical events that can lead to a conduct-disorder problem, and triggering factors that lead to specific instances of firestarting (Heath et al. 1988).

Many treatment programs have been established that operate to improve a youth's cognitive development. In Albany, New York, for example, the Juvenile Sex Offender Project (JSOP) was established by the St. Anne Institute to meet the needs of juvenile sex offenders ages 10 to 19 (Lombardo and DiGiorgio-Miller 1988). Interestingly, each candidate for treatment was selected only after a detailed assessment procedure that examined psychosocial development, family processes, and past involvement with legal systems. Empathy for victims, an ego-related function, was stressed in the JSOP. The psychoanalytic approach continues to be widely used in treatment programs for errant adolescents. However, indications are that psychoanalytic theory is increasingly used together with other approaches that encourage systemic family therapy (Jarjoura and May 2000).

Social Learning Theory

Social learning theory is somewhat different from psychoanalytic theory. Traumatic early childhood experiences may be important determinants of subsequent adult personality characteristics, but the primary factors influencing whether one conforms to or deviates from societal rules are those experiences

Talking out one's problems with others may assist in promoting better coping skills.

youths have while learning from others such as their parents. Adults in any institutional context (e.g., schools, churches, homes) provide role models for children to follow. Homes that are beset with violence and conflict between spouses are poor training grounds for children. Children often learn to cope with their problems in ways that are labeled antisocial or hostile. Even the punishments parents impose on children for disobeying them are translated into acceptable behaviors that children can direct toward their own peers.

In its most simplified form, social learning theory implies that children learn to do what they see significant others do. Poor parental role models have been emphasized as a probable cause of poor adolescent adjustment and delinquent behavior (Bandura and Walters 1959). Also perceiving the importance of the family in the early social development of children is Carlson (1986). Carlson believes that children who use violence to resolve disputes with other children likely have learned such behaviors in homes where violence is exhibited regularly by parents.

If delinquency is fostered through social learning, then, it seems, certain social learning intervention models might be useful for assisting youths to learn different, more acceptable behaviors. In fact, provided that certain youths who exhibit learning or developmental disabilities in school can be identified accurately, teachers may modify their classroom curricula in ways that increase opportunities, skills, and rewards for these children (Moore, Sprengelmeyer, and Chamberlain 2001). This view has received support from researchers in other parts of the world, including Canada (Stutt, 1986).

Several researchers have examined the relation between delinquency and whether children have learning disabilities (Fishbein and Thatcher 1986). Children with learning disabilities suffer a double disadvantage, in a sense, since their learning disabilities have likely contributed to poor school performance and social adjustments. Such learning disabilities may impair their judgment regarding peer associations, and it is possible that they might have encounters with the law more frequently than other children. When they are evaluated at intake or later in juvenile court, their school records are "evidence" against them. Some persons may erroneously conclude that learning disabilities produce delinquent conduct, when, in fact, other factors are at work. Teachers themselves may become impatient with children with learning disabilities, particularly if their conditions are unknown in advance. A lack of rewards from teachers may have deep emotional impacts for some of these children, thus creating a vicious cycle of failure for them.

Alternative explanations of delinquent conduct have incorporated elements from several different theoretical schemes. For example, a twenty-year longitudinal study of delinquency spanning the years 1954 through 1974 examined the predictive utility of both biological and psychosocial factors in early and middle childhood (Werner 1987). A sample of 698 children were examined. Pediatricians and psychologists conducted extensive observations and applied batteries of aptitude tests. It was eventually determined that a child's low standard of living tended to increase the likelihood that the child would be exposed to both biological and psychological risk factors. But it was only the joint effect of these factors together with early familial instability that precipitated serious delinquent patterns. Mother–child relations were generally more important in adolescent development in one's childhood, while father–child relations became more important in one's teen years. The social dimension was prominent in this research.

These psychological theories stress one's early moral and cognitive development as influential in relation to one's later behaviors. Many delinquency prevention programs have been designed as interventions in one's early years. Therefore, it is not unusual to see attempts by public agencies and professionals to intervene through early training or educational programs in schools. The California Office of Criminal Justice Planning, for example, designed a curriculum for children in grades K-4 for reducing their vulnerability to certain crimes. They were taught about personal safety, how to recognize child abuse situations, how to protect personal property from others, and certain types of responsible behaviors, including respecting the rights of others (California Office of Criminal Justice Planning 1984).

Davidson et al. (1987) has described the aims of different delinquency prevention programs that target young school children. One such program is Elan One, a Maine program that emphasizes certain key elements, including acquiring feelings of interpersonal competence, understanding the impact of peer pressure, learning respect for authority, and receiving cognitive therapy to reinforce one's values and suggest future behavioral options. This particular program stresses individual learning. Other programs, such as Illinois's Ounce of Prevention program, attempt to involve the entire family in school-based interventions that assist youths and their families learn more effective social skills (Zigler and Hall 1987). Such familial support in one's early years serves to reinforce values believed important by program planners.

Finally, the Perry Preschool project in Ypsilanti, Michigan, was an attempt to identify certain children who exhibited a strong likelihood of dropping out of school (Berrueta-Clement, et al. 1984). These youths at risk were targeted in their preschool years and placed in special education classes. Their special training was supplemented by weekly home visits. Compared with a birth cohort of youths not receiving such training, but who were also identified as high risks for failure, the experimental group of Perry Preschoolers experienced less than half the rate of arrests. Further, more of these youths stayed in school longer and tended to graduate, with some even obtaining graduate degrees. For some interventionists, then, exposure to special kinds of training in one's formative years does much to promote more socially and psychologically healthy school and home environments. The psychological school's impact here is quite apparent.

SOCIOLOGICAL THEORIES

It is worth noting that the theories advanced thus far have related deviant, criminal, and/or delinquent behaviors to factors almost exclusively within individuals (i.e., either their minds or bodies or both). These theories have been described elsewhere as inside notions (e.g., the positivist view, glandular malfunction, XYY theory, sociobiology, low IQ), primarily because they identify internal factors as causally important for explaining deviation of any kind (Walsh 2000). While these inside notions have persisted over the years to provide plausible explanations for why criminals and delinquents commit their various offenses, other rival explanations have been advanced that shift certain causes of deviant conduct to factors outside of or external to individuals. Sociologists have encouraged strong consideration of social factors as major variables that can account for the emergence and persistence of delinquent conduct (Warr 1993).

It is perhaps most realistic to regard these different perspectives as mutually overlapping rather than as mutually exclusive. Thus, we might view social learning theory as predominantly a psychological theory with certain sociological elements. The biological factor may figure significantly into the delinquency equation, particularly when considering the matter of developmental disabilities of a physical nature in the social learning process (Benda and Corwyn 2000). A pragmatic view will be adopted here, and we will regard any explanation as useful, provided that it is accompanied by some predictive utility.

 BOX 3.3

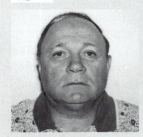

Michael J. Palmiotto
Professor of Criminal Justice
Wichita State University

Statistics:

Ph.D. University of Pittsburgh, M.P.A. John Jay College of Criminal Justice (CUNY), and B.S. Mercy College (Dobbs Ferry, New York)

Interests:

Presently, I am a Professor of Criminal Justice at Wichita State University whose specialization is policing. I teach undergraduate and graduate courses in criminal justice and policing. These courses include but are not limited to Introduction to Criminal Justice, Law Enforcement, Police Administration, Community Policing, and Crime Prevention. My publications include ten books, numerous book chapters, and articles in refereed and professional journals. Two of my recent books were published by Prentice-Hall: *Police Misconduct: A Reader for the 21st Century,* published in 2001, and *Policing and Training Issues,* which was published in 2003.

Background:

I grew up in the suburbs north of New York City. Upon graduating from Ossining High School, I entered the Marines. While in the Marines I was assigned temporary duty as an M.P. in Vasaquez, Puerto Rico. This assignment whet my appetite for police work. Upon being released from the Marines, I became a police officer in White Plains, New York. While attending mandatory police training, a fellow recruit informed me that the local community college had a criminal justice program. Upon completing police recruit training, I signed up the next semester for classes on a part-time basis. Classes were taken on a part-time basis until I was able to complete my doctorate at the University of Pittsburgh.

Upon completing my bachelor's degree, I began applying for academic positions. I obtained one at the Community College of Beaver County in Monaca, Pennsylvania. After a few years I was made the head of the criminal justice program. A short time after being program head, the local police chiefs requested that I establish a mandatory police recruit training program. In a short period of time I was able to obtain the approval from the Pennsylvania State Police Training Commission to offer training at the college. While head of the Criminal Justice program and Police Training, I continued my education and eventually obtained my doctorate from the University of Pittsburgh. Shortly after receiving my doctorate, I was offered an academic position at Western Illinois University; since that time I have been an academic professor involved in research and scholarship.

Explanations for Delinquency:

There are a variety of theories about why juveniles may be involved in crime and become classified as delinquent. Disciplines contributing to delinquency theory include sociology, psychology, and biology, all of which may have some validity. However, the theories as to why juveniles commit criminal acts often cannot be compared, since they may not focus on the same subject. It appears that most theories that make an effort to a certain extent have at least a limited value in explaining delinquents' actions. Sociologists who claim that delinquency is learned have some validity. Don't all of us learn from our parents, siblings, and playmates? Psychologists claim that a child who has been verbally abused for an extended period of time by his parents can lose self-confidence and develop a low self-concept of himself. Don't we all know someone like this? When older people develop dementia, isn't that biological? It seems to me that various disciplines make valid contributions to explaining delinquency, but no one theory can be used to explain all delinquent behavior.

In my opinion, in the early twenty-first century we have many young people who have not been given a moral foundation. Too many of us are selfish, greedy, and self-centered. This description not only applies to our young people but to many of our older citizens. Many of us are not gentlemen or ladies, as was prevalent in an earlier period of time. By being a gentlemen or lady, I simply mean respecting other people. We should be civil to all people, regardless of their position, finances, national origin, race, or gender. We could all use the words "thank you" and "please" more frequently. There are people in our society who look upon their fellow human beings as objects and not as equal fellow humans. The term "recreational murder" has been termed to identify the crime perpetrated by those offenders who get a buzz and thrill out of killing another human being for kicks.

If delinquency is to be licked, we need to put other people ahead of ourselves. Our parents, wives, husbands, and children need to be placed first. Our needs must to take a back seat to the needs of our loved ones. If this means doing without unnecessary material goods, then this should be done. This also includes living up to our adult responsibilities. If we have a child, the child's needs are placed ahead of our own. At one time, not only the parents but also the extended family of grandparents, aunts, uncles, and older cousins all played a major role in raising children. Inappropriate behavior was corrected. Today who raises the child? When both parents put their careers and desires for material goods ahead of their children, who is there to raise the child? Children need attention; children need to be cared for; and, most of all, they need to be loved not only by their parents but also by everyone who comes to know them and comes in contact with them.

The point of my comment is not to criticize anyone who, because of financial need, must work or hold several jobs to take care of their loved ones but to emphasize that our children need our love more than we need a new car or coat. I want to emphasize that I have observed many great mothers and fathers, but all parents need to be great mothers and fathers. Those children who don't have mothers and fathers are being cheated. Perhaps great mothers and mothers will not completely eliminate delinquency, but I bet they could put a major dent in juvenile delinquency. We need more great mothers and fathers if we want to lower juvenile delinquency even more.

Advice to Students:

For those students studying the juvenile justice system, I recommend that they take additional courses in juvenile delinquency, child development, child psychology, and abnormal behavior. I would also recommend that students who think they have an interest with working with juveniles do an internship—this requires working with juveniles. An internship is an excellent way for students to find out if they want to work with juveniles.

The Concentric Zone Hypothesis and Delinquency

During the early 1900s, large cities such as Chicago, Illinois, were undergoing rapid expansion as one result of the great influx of laborers from farms and rural regions to city centers to find work. Urbanization emanated from the center of cities outward, and such expansion caused some of the older neighborhoods within the inner city to undergo dramatic transition. Sociologists at the University of Chicago and elsewhere studied the urban development of Chicago. Social scientists Ernest W. Burgess and Robert E. Park defined a series of concentric zones around Chicago, commencing with the core or "Loop" in downtown Chicago and progressing outward away from the city center in a series of concentric rings. The outward ring or zone immediately adjacent to the central core was labeled by Burgess and Park as an **interstitial area** or **zone of transition.** This was the immediate periphery of downtown Chicago and was characterized by slums and urban renewal projects. This area was also typified by high delinquency and crime. These researchers believed that other cities might exhibit similar growth patterns and concentric zones similar to those identified in the Chicago area. Thus, the **concentric zone hypothesis** of urban growth originated, accompanied by descriptions of different social and demographic characteristics of those inhabiting each zone.

Concurrent with Burgess's and Park's efforts was an investigation of delinquency patterns in Chicago conducted by Clifford Shaw and Henry McKay (1972). These researchers studied the characteristics of delinquent youths in the zone of transition and compared the backgrounds of these youths with other youths inhabiting more stabilized neighborhoods in the zones further removed from the inner core of downtown Chicago. They based their subsequent findings and probable causes of delinquency on the records of nearly 25,000 delinquent youths in Cook County, Illinois, between 1900 and the early 1930s. Essentially, Shaw and McKay found that over the thirty-year period, delinquency within the interstitial zone was widespread and tended to grow in a concomitant fashion with the growth of slums and deteriorating neighborhoods. For many of these youths, both of their parents worked in factories for long hours. Large numbers of juveniles roamed these Chicago streets with little or no adult supervision. Family stability was lacking, and many youths turned toward gang activities with other youths as a means of surviving, gaining recognition and status, and achieving certain material goals.

Compared with other zones, zones in transition were typically overcrowded, replete with families of lower socioeconomic statuses. No zones were completely free of delinquency, however. But in other zones, families were more affluent and stable, and accordingly, less delinquency was observed compared with delinquency within interstitial areas. Shaw and McKay explained delinquency in these transitional areas as likely attributable to a breakdown in family unity and pervasive social disorganization. Interstitial areas lacked recreational facilities and schools and churches were run down. As a result, youths literally played in the streets, with little or nothing to do to occupy their time other than to form gangs and commit delinquent acts. Because many of the same gangs formed at the turn of the century were still in existence in the early 1930s, Shaw and McKay believed that gang members perpetuated gang traditions and gang culture over time through cultural transmission.

One immediate effect of Shaw's and McKay's work was to divert explanations of delinquency away from biological explanations such as genetics and physical abnormalities (Gold 1987). The long-range influence of the pioneering work of Shaw and McKay is evident in contemporary studies seeking to link neighborhood characteristics with delinquent conduct (Heitgerd and Bursik 1987; Walker 1992). Generally, these studies have been supportive of Shaw's and McKay's work, although other factors closely associated with those residing in slum areas have also been causally linked with delinquency (Sampson 2002). One of these factors is socioeconomic status (SES) (Wickstrom and Loeber 2000).

Studies investigating the relation between SES and delinquency have generally found more frequent and more violent types of juvenile conduct among youths of lower SESs (Wolfgang and Ferracuti 1967), while less frequent and less violent conduct has been exhibited by youths from families in the upper SESs (LeFlore 1988; Tygart 1988). Some of this research also suggests that juveniles who are identified with lower SESs seem more likely to do less well in school than other juveniles from higher SESs.

We might conjecture that students from families of lower SESs may reflect different values and achievement orientations compared with youths from higher SESs. This factor may figure significantly in the rate of juveniles' school successes or failures. School dropouts or underachievers may, in fact, turn toward other underachievers or dropouts for companionship, recognition, and prestige. Thus, a complex and vicious cycle is put into motion, with certain conditions and characteristics of lower SES leading to poor academic performance, growing antisocial behavior, and subsequent delinquent conduct. However, describing the concomitants of delinquents or their prominent characteristics does not necessarily pinpoint the true causal factors associated with their conduct in any predictive sense. After all, many lower SES youths adjust well to their academic work and refrain from delinquent activities. Also, many seemingly well-adjusted and academically successful youths from higher SESs may engage in certain forms of delinquent conduct.

Some research has associated having money or possessing monetary resources as being positively related to delinquent conduct. Thus, especially among higher SES youth, having money becomes a risk factor to criminal conduct in that it reduces family attachments, leads to increased dating, and increases illicit drug use. It may be that efforts to facilitate adolescents' entrance into the adult world of earning, spending, credit, and financial obligation may produce unintended consequences, namely increased use of drugs and greater misbehavior. The attraction of purchasing wanted luxury items, such as clothes, CDs, cellular phones, and expensive cars, may be overwhelming when compared with the mere promise that delayed gratification somehow will improve one's life at some distant, uncertain point in the future. The proceeds from adolescents' employment and parental allowance may facilitate values and behaviors that divorce youths from the responsibility accompanying entrance into the adult world of economic relationships. In a sense, then, parents and employers may be the economic agents responsible for subsidizing adolescents' delinquent involvement and drug use (Wright et al. 2001, 262).

The Subculture Theory of Delinquency

During the 1950s, sociologist Albert Cohen (1955) focused upon and described a delinquent subculture, or a **subculture of delinquency.** Delinquent subcultures exist, according to Cohen, within the greater societal culture. But these subcultures contain value systems and modes of achievement and gaining status and recognition apart from the mainstream culture (Davies and Pearson 1999). Thus, if we are to understand why many juveniles behave as they do, we must pay attention to the patterns of their particular subculture.

The notion of a delinquent subculture is fairly easy to understand, especially in view of the earlier work of Shaw and McKay. While middle- and upper-class children learn and aspire to achieve lofty ambitions and educational goals and receive support for these aspirations from their parents as well as from predominantly middle-class teachers, lower-class youths are at a distinct disadvantage at the outset. They are born into families where these aspirations and attainments may be alien and rejected. Their primary familial role models have not attained these high aims themselves. At school, these youths are often isolated socially from upper- and middle-class juveniles, and therefore, social attachments are formed with others similar to themselves. Perhaps these youths dress differently from other students, wear their hair in a certain style, or use coded language when talking to peers in front of other students. They acquire a culture unto themselves and one that is largely unknown to other students. In a sense, much of this cultural isolation is self-imposed. But it functions to give them a sense of fulfillment, reward, self-esteem, and recognition apart from other reward systems. If these students cannot achieve one or more of the various standards set by middle-class society, then they create their own standards and prescribe the means to achieve those standards.

Cohen is quick to point out that delinquency is not a product of lower SES per se. Rather, children from lower SESs are at greater risk than others of being susceptible to the rewards and opportunities a subculture of delinquency might offer in contrast with the system's middle-class reward structure. Several experiments have subsequently been implemented with delinquents, where these subcultures have been targeted and described, and where the norms of these subcultures have been used as intervening mechanisms to modify delinquent behaviors toward nondelinquent modes of action. The Provo Experiment was influenced, to a degree, by the work of Cohen (Empey and Rabow 1961). Samples of delinquent youths in Provo, Utah, were identified in the late 1950s and given an opportunity to participate in group therapy sessions at Pine Hills, a large home in Provo that had been converted to an experimental laboratory.

In cooperation with juvenile court judges and other authorities, Pine Hills investigators commenced their intervention strategies assuming that juvenile participants (1) had limited access to success goals, (2) performed many of their delinquent activities in groups rather than alone, and (3) committed their delinquent acts for nonutilitarian objectives rather than for money (Empey and Rabow 1961). These investigators believed that since the delinquents had acquired their delinquent values and conduct through their subculture of delinquency, they could unlearn these values and learn new values by the same means. Thus, groups of delinquents participated extensively in therapy directed at changing their behaviors through group processes. The investigators believed that their intervention efforts were largely successful and that the subcultural approach to delinquency prevention and behavioral change was fruitful.

A variation on the subcultural theme is the work of Wolfgang and Ferracuti (1967). It will be recalled that Wolfgang and other associates investigated large numbers of Philadelphia, Pennsylvania, boys in a study of birth cohorts. In that study, he found that approximately 6 percent of all boys accounted for

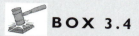

BOX 3.4

TEEN SHOOTER CLAIMS INSANITY

Conyers, Georgia. In May 1999, T.J. Solomon, 15, opened fire at Heritage High School in Conyers, Georgia, wounding six classmates with a .22 rifle. Subsequently, he was subdued by school teachers and other students when he ran out of ammunition. Since May, Solomon has been maintained in juvenile detention awaiting a subsequent disposition. Authorities decided to charge Solomon as an adult and try him in criminal court. If convicted, Solomon could receive life imprisonment. From the start, Solomon's attorneys have never denied that Solomon was the shooter. He has acknowledged that he opened fire on other students with the rifle and that he wounded several of them during the shooting spree. One of his attorneys,

Jana Jarris, said "We have never disputed that the shots were fired by Mr. Solomon. The depths of his illness, the circumstances surrounding the case—these are the things that will be examined at the trial." In late March 2000, Solomon entered a plea of not guilty by reason of insanity to all of the shooting charges. If he is found not guilty by reason of insanity, he could be institutionalized in a mental hospital or freed.

Should the insanity plea be accepted in cases such as this? How frequently is the insanity defense used in criminal cases? Does it excuse criminal conduct? Should Solomon be allowed to go free merely by alleging that he was insane at the time he shot other students? What do you think?

Source: Adapted from the Associated Press, "Georgia School Shooting Suspect Enters Insanity Plea." April 1, 2000.

over 50 percent of all delinquent conduct from the entire cohort of over 9,000 boys (Wolfgang, Figlio, and Sellin 1972). These were chronic recidivists who were also violent offenders. Wolfgang has theorized that in many communities, there are subcultural norms of violence that attract youthful males. They regard violence as a normal part of their environment, use violence, and respect the use of violence by others. On the basis of evidence amassed by Wolfgang and Ferracuti, it appeared that predominantly lower-class and less-educated males formed a disproportionately large part of this subculture of delinquency. Where violence is accepted and respected, its use is considered normal and normative for the users. Remorse is an alien emotion to those using violence and who live with it constantly. Thus, it is socially ingrained as a subcultural value.

This theme would suggest that violence and aggression are learned through socialization with others, even one's siblings (Berset 2001). However, Ellis (1985) has questioned this generalization. He has conducted extensive investigations of lower animals, including apes and other animals, and his reports show that aggressive and violent behaviors are exhibited by these animals despite the fact that they are not socialized or experience the same type of socialization as human beings. However, animal studies, though important because of their intuitive value, are often criticized because of the completely different sets of assumptions that are applied to studies of lower animals and human beings.

The subcultural perspective toward delinquent conduct is indicative of a strain between the values of society and the values of a subgroup of delinquent youths (Schneider 1999). Therefore, some researchers have labeled the subcultural perspective a **strain theory.** The strain component is apparent since, although many lower SES youths have adopted middle-class goals and aspirations, they may be unable to attain these goals because of their individual economic and cultural circumstances (Vigil 1999). This is a frustrating experience for many of these youths, and such frustration is manifested by the strain to achieve difficult goals or objectives (Broidy 2001; Mazerolle and Maahs 2000). While middle-class youths also experience strain in their attempts to achieve middle-class goals, it is particularly aggravating for many lower-class youths, since they sometimes do not receive the necessary support from their families (Miller 2001). Another strain theory is Robert Merton's theory of anomie.

The Anomie Theory of Delinquency

Anomie theory was used by the early French social scientist, Emile Durkheim. Durkheim investigated many social and psychological phenomena, including suicide and its causes. One precipitating factor leading to certain suicides, according to Durkheim, was anomie or normlessness. Durkheim intended that the term was to portray a condition where people's lives, their values, and various social rules were disrupted and they found it difficult to cope with their changed life conditions. Thus, they would experience **anomie,** a type of helplessness, perhaps hopelessness. Most persons usually adapt to drastic changes in their life styles or patterns, but a few may opt for suicide, since they lack the social and psychological means to cope with the strain of change.

Merton (1957) was intrigued by Durkheim's notion of anomie and how persons adapt to the strain of changing conditions. He devised a goals/means scheme as a way of describing different social actions that persons might use for making behavioral choices. Merton contended that society generally prescribes approved cultural goals for its members to seek (e.g., new homes, jobs, automobiles). Furthermore, appropriate, legitimate, or institutionalized means are prescribed for the purpose of attaining these goals. But not everyone is equally endowed with the desire to achieve societal goals nor are they necessarily committed to using the prescribed means to achieve these goals.

Merton described five different **modes of adaptation** that people might exhibit. These modes included **conformity** (persons accept the goals of society and work toward their attainment using societally approved means), **innovation** (persons accept the goals of society but use means to achieve goals other than those approved by society), **ritualism** (persons reject goals but work toward less lofty goals by institutionally approved means), **retreatism** (persons reject goals and reject the means to achieve goals—e.g., hermits, street people, or "bag ladies" typify those who retreat or escape from mainstream society and establish their own goals and means to achieve them), and **rebellion** (persons seek to replace culturally approved goals and institutionalized means with new goals and means for others to follow).

Of these, the innovation mode characterizes juvenile delinquents, according to Merton. Juvenile delinquency is innovative in that youths accept culturally desirable goals, but they reject the legitimate means to achieve these goals. Instead, they adopt illegitimate means such as theft, burglary, or violence. Many youths may crave new clothes, automobiles, and other expensive material items. Since they may lack the money to pay for these items, one alternative is to steal them. This is regarded by Merton as one innovative response arising from a condition of anomie and the strain it emits.

Many intermediate punishment programs today are designed to assist youths in devising new strategies to cope with everyday life rather than to use crime or delinquent conduct to achieve their goals. VisionQuest, Homeward Bound, and various types of wilderness experiences incorporate adaptive experiences as integral features of these programs. Those youths with substantial energy are sometimes placed in camps or on ranches where they can act out some of their feelings and frustrations. These programs deliberately cater to youths who are innovative, but who lack a clear sense of direction. Subsequent empirical tests of Merton's theory of anomie have found the theory to have considerable predictive power in explaining drug use/abuse and other forms of deviance (Menard 1995).

Labeling Theory

One of the more social sociological approaches to delinquent conduct is **labeling theory.** Labeling theory's primary proponent is Edwin Lemert (1951, 1967a, 1967b). Other social scientists have also been credited with originating this concept (Becker 1963; Kitsuse 1962). **Labeling** stresses the definitions people have of delinquent acts rather than delinquency itself. Applied to delinquent conduct, Lemert was concerned with two primary questions: (1) What is the process whereby youths become labeled as delinquent? and (2) What is the influence of such labeling upon these youths' future behavior? Lemert assumed that no act is inherently delinquent, that all persons at different points in time conform to or deviate from the law, that persons become delinquent through social labeling or definition, that being apprehended by police begins the labeling process, that youths defined as delinquent will acquire self-definitions as delinquents, and finally, that those defining themselves as delinquent will seek to establish associations with others also defined as delinquent.

Not every youth who violates the law, regardless of the seriousness of the offense, will become a hardcore delinquent. Some infractions are relatively minor offenses. For example, experimenting with alcohol and getting drunk or trying certain drugs, joyriding, and petty theft may be one-time events never to be repeated (Harrell et al. 2002). However, getting caught enhances the likelihood that any particular youth will be brought into the juvenile justice system for processing and labeling. Youths who have adopted delinquent subcultures are often those who have attracted the attention of others, including the police, by engaging in wrongful acts or causing trouble. Wearing the symbols of gang membership such as jackets emblazoned with gang names helps to solidify one's self-definition of being delinquent.

Lemert suggested that juvenile deviation may be **primary deviation** or **secondary deviation.** Primary deviation occurs when youths spontaneously violate the law by engaging in occasional pranks. Law enforcement authorities may conclude that these pranks are not particularly serious. However, if juveniles persist in repeating their deviant and delinquent conduct, they may exhibit secondary deviation. Secondary deviation occurs whenever the deviant conduct becomes a part of one's behavior pattern or lifestyle. Thus, delinquency is viewed as a social label applied by others to those youths who have relative frequent contact with the juvenile justice system (Adams 1996; Adams, Johnson, and Evans 1998). The strength of such social labeling is such that juveniles themselves adopt such social labels and regard themselves as delinquent. This, too, is a vicious cycle of sorts, in that one phenomenon (social labeling by others of some youths as delinquent) reinforces the other (labeled youths acquiring self-definitions as delinquent and engaging in further delinquent conduct consistent with the delinquent label).

Lemert's labeling perspective has probably been the most influential theory relative to policy decisions by juvenile courts to divert youths away from the formal trappings of court proceedings (Zhang 1997). The sentiment is that if we can keep youths away from the juvenile justice system, they are less inclined to identify with it. Accordingly, they are less likely to define themselves as delinquent and engage in delinquent conduct. This theory is also more broadly applicable to adult first offenders. Criminal courts often use diversion as a means of keeping first offenders out of the system. This is done, in part, to give them another chance to conform to the law and not acquire a criminal record. Diversion doesn't always work for either adults or juveniles, but at least we can better appreciate why the different justice systems employ it to deal with at least some adult and juvenile offenders in the early stages of their processing by the system.

Bonding Theory

Bonding theory or **social control theory** derives primarily from the work of Travis Hirschi (1969). This theory stresses processual aspects of youths becoming bonded or socially integrated into the norms of society. The greater the integration or bonding, particularly with parents and school teachers, the less likelihood that youths will engage in delinquent activity. Different dimensions of bonding include attachment (emotional linkages with those we respect and admire), commitment (enthusiasm or energy expended in a specific relationship), belief (moral definition of the rightness or wrongness of certain conduct), and involvement (intensity of attachment with those who engage in conventional conduct or espouse conventional values).

Hirschi investigated large numbers of high school students in order to test his bonding theory. More academically successful students seemed to be bonded to conventional values and significant others such as teachers and school authorities compared with less successful students. Those students who apparently lack strong commitment to school and to education generally are more prone to become delinquent than those students with opposite dispositions. However, since Hirschi limited his research to students in high school settings, he has been criticized subsequently for not applying his bonding theory to juvenile samples in other, nonschool settings. Furthermore, Hirschi has failed to explain clearly the processual aspects of bonding. Also, since rejecting or accepting conventional values and significant others is a matter of degree, and because youths may have many attachments with both delinquent and nondelinquent juveniles, bonding theory has failed to predict accurately which youths will eventually become delinquent. This is regarded as a serious limitation (Costello 2000; Wadsworth 2000).

EXTRANEOUS FACTORS

Obviously, many other explanations for delinquent conduct have been advanced by various theorists. Those selected for more in-depth coverage here are not necessarily the best theories to account for delinquency. Their inclusion is

BOX 3.5

Richard Lawrence
Professor of Criminal Justice
St. Cloud State University

Statistics:

B.A. (psychology), Bethel College; M.A. (psychology), St. Mary's University; Ph.D. (criminal justice), Sam Houston State University.

Background and Interests:

I am currently Professor of Criminal Justice at St. Cloud State University in Minnesota. I have also been a faculty member in the criminal justice programs at the University of Texas–San Antonio and at Central Missouri State University.

I grew up in a small town in Northwestern North Dakota. My parents were school teachers and they instilled in me the value of education and hard work. My career in criminal justice began as a Juvenile Probation Officer in San Antonio, Texas. After completing my master's degree in psychology at St. Mary's University, I was promoted to Research and Training Director at the Probation Department. I experienced firsthand the numerous juvenile justice developments in the early 1970s that included federally funded research and legislation, funding for delinquency prevention programs, and U.S. Supreme Court cases that changed existing juvenile court procedures. These changes focused attention on our profession, presented new challenges, and encouraged me to pursue graduate studies in criminal justice. I completed my Ph.D. at the Criminal Justice Center of Sam Houston State University in 1978.

Views on Delinquency:

My educational background in psychology, combined with personal observations from working with hundreds of juvenile delinquents and their families, provided me with some valuable personal views and insights on delinquency. I came to believe that most young juvenile offenders are doing the best they can do most of the time, given their background, social learning, personal skills for coping and decision making, and the environmental influences around them. Most delinquent youth lack positive role models, have not learned prosocial values, and lack the skills for sound decision making, goal setting, school achievement, and striving for success. We all need to feel loved, accepted, and like we are good at something. Deviant and delinquent youth have the same needs, but they often seek to fulfill those needs through unacceptable means.

This view does not fit all delinquent youth. Many youth get into trouble "just for kicks," "for the thrill of it," or because the benefits of crime outweigh the costs. Those of us who have worked with juvenile delinquents see firsthand the numerous reasons for their lawbreaking. Reasons for misbehavior are not justifications, however. Poverty, racial and ethnic discrimination, and the lack of educational and employment opportunities certainly explain a great deal of crime in our society, but those social problems do not justify criminal involvement. Similarly, youth who lack role models, prosocial values, and skills for success are more at risk for delinquency, drug use, and gang affiliation—but probation officers and youth advocates would do well to remind these youth that personal and social problems are not excuses for delinquency and that delinquent involvement is a *choice* that they have made. One of my favorite approaches for dealing with delinquents in fact

(continued)

BOX 3.5 (*Continued*)

was based on a **reality therapy model** first developed by Dr. William Glaser. It is a way of helping juveniles to take responsibility for their decisions and actions.

My preferred theory for explaining juvenile delinquency is Travis Hirschi's social control theory, because it combines the individual or psychology and the sociological perspectives, and it explains delinquent behavior among different socioeconomic, racial/ethnic, and subcultural groups better than most other theories. Self-report studies are vivid reminders that most of us have engaged in some forms of delinquent behavior. Social control theory focuses upon social bonds that help to reduce the likelihood of youths' delinquent involvement: attachment, commitment, involvement, and belief. The theory supports my own work on school crime and violence and how a lack of commitment to education, poor school performance, and noninvolvement in school activities are strongly associated with delinquent behavior and violence in the schools.

Advice to Students:

Enforcing the law with consistency and fairness and administering justice in an effort to protect victims and change offenders are among the most challenging and demanding roles of any profession. A career in criminal justice demands personal commitment, high ethical standards, and the ability to work with a variety of persons under many circumstances. Criminal justice professionals must have good communication skills, both oral and written. Your written reports and documents will be read and carefully reviewed by law enforcement officers, attorneys, judges, and correctional administrators. The accuracy and completeness of the reports may make the difference between a conviction or acquittal; good reports will help protect victims and get the proper sentence and correctional treatment for offenders. Data and information in criminal justice reports and documents are used in decision making that affects the lives of many persons. That reality can be intimidating, but for the well-prepared and committed professional, it is a challenge that brings personal satisfaction and something new and interesting each day on the job.

To prepare for a career in criminal justice, I recommend that students learn all they can about crime, criminals, law, and the justice process. But they should also take other social science courses in disciplines such as political science, psychology, and sociology. They should read widely, from academic and research sources and from newspapers and magazines, and note how crime prevention, law enforcement, and justice administration are applied in our world on a daily basis. They should write on a regular basis and summarize what they learn from their reading. They should keep a personal journal, recording thoughts, observations, and reflections. They should gain personal experience through field trips, visits to courtrooms, jails, prisons, and community corrections agencies. An internship is very important for students to apply theory and practice in a criminal justice agency, gain work experience, a job recommendation, and an advantage in a competitive job market. For students unable to do an internship, some volunteer work is invaluable. They should take advantage of any opportunities on campus and in the workplace to improve their understanding, skills, knowledge, and the ability to apply that knowledge in the workplace. They should ask to read the written work of criminal justice professionals: police reports, investigation reports, court reports, probation officers' presentence investigations (be sure to maintain confidentiality and ethical standards whenever visiting agencies and reading their documents). Students should ask questions and learn from experienced professionals in the field. They should observe carefully and critically and note the similarities and differences between what's learned in the classroom and what's observed in the real world of criminal justice. Learning about justice is almost as exciting as doing justice. These students are in for a real adventure!

intended to describe some of the thinking about why juveniles might be engage in delinquent conduct. Some of the other approaches that have been advocated include containment theory, neutralization or drift theory, differential association theory, and differential reinforcement theory.

Containment theory is associated with the work of sociologist Walter Reckless (1967). Reckless outlined a theoretical model consisting of pushes and pulls in relation to delinquency. By pushes he referred to internal personal factors, including hostility, anxiety, and discontent. By pulls he meant external social forces, including delinquent subcultures and significant others. The containment dimension of his theoretical scheme consisted of both outer and inner containments. Outer containments, according to Reckless, are social norms, folkways, mores, laws, and institutional arrangements that induce societal conformity. By inner containments, Reckless referred to individual or personal coping strategies to deal with stressful situations and conflict. These strategies might be a high tolerance for conflict or frustration and considerable ego strength. Thus, Reckless combined both psychological and social elements in referring to weak attachments of some youths to cultural norms, high anxiety levels, and low tolerance for personal stress. These persons are most inclined to delinquent conduct. A key factor in whether juveniles adopt delinquent behaviors is their level of self-esteem. Those with high levels of self-esteem seem most resistant to delinquent behaviors if they are exposed to such conduct while around their friends (Lawrence 1985).

Neutralization theory or **drift theory** was originally outlined by David Matza (1964). Matza said that most juveniles spend their early years on a behavioral continuum ranging between unlimited freedom and total control or restraint. These persons drift toward one end of the continuum or the other, depending upon their social and psychological circumstances. If youths have strong attachments with those who are delinquent, then they drift toward the unlimited freedom end of the continuum and perhaps engage in delinquent activities. However, Matza indicates that the behavioral issue is not clear-cut. Juveniles most likely have associations with normative culture, such as their parents or religious leaders, as well as the delinquent subculture, such as various delinquent youths. They may engage in delinquent conduct and regard their behavior as acceptable at the time they engage in it. Elaborate rationales for delinquent behavior may be invented by youths (e.g., society is unfair, victims deserve to be victims, nobody is hurt by our particular acts), and thus, they effectively neutralize the normative constraints of society that impinge upon them. Therefore, at least some delinquency results from rationalizations created by youths that render delinquent acts acceptable under the circumstances. Appropriate preventive therapy for such delinquents might be to undermine their rationales for delinquent behaviors through empathic means. Also, activities that are geared toward strengthening family bonds are important, since greater attachments with one's parents tend to overwhelm the influence of one's associations with delinquent peers (Costello 2000).

Differential association theory was first advanced by Edwin Sutherland (1939). In some respects, it is an outgrowth of the **cultural transmission theory** described by Shaw and McKay in their investigations of juvenile offenders in Chicago. Sutherland described a socialization process (learning through contact with others) whereby juveniles would acquire delinquent behaviors manifested by others among their close associates. It would certainly be an oversimplification of Sutherland's views to claim that associating with other delinquents would cause certain juveniles to adopt similar delinquent behaviors. Sutherland's scheme was more complex and multifaceted than that. He suggested that several interpersonal dimensions characterize relations between law violators and others who behave similarly. Sutherland said that differential association consists of the following elements: frequency, priority, duration, and intensity. Thus, engaging in frequent associations and long-lasting interactions with others who are delinquent, giving them priority as significant others, and cultivating strong emotional attachments with them will contribute in a significant way to a youth's propensity to commit delinquent acts.

Explicit in Sutherland's scheme is the phenomenon of attachments with others who are delinquent. Thus, this is at least one similarity differential association theory shares with containment theory and bonding. Sutherland sought to characterize relationships some juveniles have with delinquents as multidimensional relationships, and the association aspect was only one of several of these dimensions. Although Sutherland's work has been influential and has been widely quoted and utilized by criminologists, some experts have been critical of his theory on various grounds. He never fully articulated the true meaning of intensity, for instance. How intense should a relation be between a delinquent and a nondelinquent before making a difference and causing the nondelinquent to adopt delinquent patterns of behavior? How frequently should nondelinquents be in the company of delinquents before such contact becomes crucial and changes nondelinquent behavior? These and other similar questions were never fully addressed by Sutherland. Nevertheless, differential association has influenced certain correctional policies and treatment programs for both juveniles and adults.

Much like labeling theory, differential association theory has encouraged minimizing contact between hardcore criminal offenders and first offenders. The use of prison is often the last resort in certain cases, since it is believed that more prolonged contact with other criminals will only serve to intensify any criminal propensities first offenders might exhibit. If they were diverted to some nonincarcerative option, they might not become recidivists and commit new crimes. The same principle applies to delinquent first offenders and accounts for widespread use of noncustodial sanctions that seek to minimize a juvenile's contact with the juvenile justice system.

In 1966, Robert Burgess and Ronald Akers attempted to revise Sutherland's differential association theory and derived what they termed **differential reinforcement theory.** Differential reinforcement theory actually combines elements from labeling theory and a psychological phenomenon known as conditioning. Conditioning functions in the social learning process as persons are rewarded for engaging in certain desirable behaviors and refraining from certain undesirable behaviors. Juveniles perceive how others respond to their behaviors (negative reactions) and may be disposed to behave in ways that will maximize their rewards from others (Burgess and Akers 1966).

Also, in some respects, Burgess and Akers have incorporated certain aspects of the **looking-glass self** concept originally devised by the theorist, Charles Horton Cooley. Cooley theorized that people learned ways of conforming by paying attention to the reactions of others in response to their own behavior. Therefore, Cooley would argue that we imagine how others see us. We look for other's reactions to our behavior and make interpretations of these reactions as either good or bad reactions. If we define others' reactions as good, we will feel a degree of pride and likely persist in the behaviors. But, as Cooley indicated, if we interpret their reactions to our behaviors as bad, we might experience mortification. Given this latter reaction or at least our interpretation of it, we might change our behaviors to conform to what others might want and thereby elicit approval from them. While these ideas continue to interest us, they are difficult to conceptualize and investigate empirically. Akers and others have acknowledged such difficulties, although their work is insightful and underscores the reality of a multidimensional view of delinquent conduct.

AN EVALUATION OF EXPLANATIONS OF DELINQUENT CONDUCT

Assessing the importance or significance of theories of delinquency is difficult. First, almost all causes of delinquent conduct promulgated by experts during the past century continue to interest contemporary investigators. The most frequently discounted and consistently criticized views are biological ones, although as we have seen, sociobiology and genetic concomitants of delinquent conduct continue to raise questions about the role of heredity as a significant factor in explaining delinquency (Shoemaker 2000).

Psychological explanations seem more plausible than biological ones, although the precise relation between the psyche and biological factors remains unknown. If we focus upon psychological explanations of delinquency as important in fostering delinquent conduct, almost invariably we involve certain elements of one's social world in such explanations. Thus, one's mental processes are influenced in various ways by one's social experiences. Self-definitions, important to psychologists and learning theorists, are conceived largely in social contexts, in the presence of and through contact with others. It is not surprising, therefore, that the most fruitful explanations for delinquency are those that seek to blend the best parts of different theories that assess different dimensions of youths, their physique and intellectual abilities, personalities, and social experiences (Ellis and McDonald 2001). Intellectual isolationism or complete reliance on biological factors exclusively or psychological factors exclusively or sociological factors exclusively may simplify theory construction, but in the final analysis, such isolationism is unproductive (Binder and Geis 1984). Certainly, each field has importance and makes a contribution toward explaining why some youths exhibit delinquent conduct and why others do not.

From a purely pragmatic approach in assessing the predictive and/or explanatory utility of each of these theories, we may examine contemporary interventionist efforts that seek to curb delinquency or prevent its recurrence. One way of determining which theories are most popular and/or influence policy and administrative decision making relative to juveniles is to identify the ways youthful offenders are treated by the juvenile justice system when they have been apprehended and adjudicated (Houston 2001).

A preliminary screening of juvenile offenders may result in some being diverted from the juvenile justice system. One manifest purpose of such diversionary action is to reduce the potentially adverse influence of labeling on these youths (Anderson and Schoen 1985). A long-term objective of diversion is to minimize recidivism among divertees. While some experts contend that the intended effects of diversion, such as a reduction in the degree of social stigmatization toward status offenders, are presently unclear, inconsistent, and insufficiently documented, other professionals endorse diversion programs and regard them as effective in preventing further delinquent conduct among first offenders (DeAngelo 1988). In fact, the preponderance of evidence from a survey of available literature is that diversion, while not fully effective at preventing recidivism, nevertheless tends to reduce it substantially (Davidson et al. 1987; Shoemaker 2000). This evidence is largely supportive of less aggressive intervention strategies for dealing with minor delinquent offenders until after they have committed at least two or three other offenses (Lab 1984).

During the period 1983–1984, for example, the probation departments of Los Angeles and Contra Costa Counties, together with several community service agencies in Southern California, conducted a Youth at Risk Program, consisting of ten-day rural training courses for large samples of youths, ages 13 through 19 (MetaMetrics, Inc. 1984). These Youth at Risk programs included classes, outdoor recreational activities, and an emphasis upon self-reliance and individual responsibility. Youths participating in the program were the subject of a fifteen-month follow-up that sought to identify their recidivism rates. Compared with samples of delinquent youths not involved in this diversion program, the amount of recidivism among program participants was quite low. Program officials concluded that their program was a significant improvement over traditional processing methods by the juvenile justice systems in these same jurisdictions. Diversionary programs in Denver, Colorado, and in various Midwestern cities have yielded similar results (Davidson et al. 1987; Regoli, Wilderman, and Pogrebin 1985).

These and other similar diversionary studies have reported lower rates of recidivism among participating youths. Implicit in most of these studies has been the idea that minimizing formal involvement with the juvenile justice system has been favorable for reducing participants' self-definitions as delinquent and avoiding the delinquent label. Thus, labeling theory seems to have been prominent in the promotion of diversionary programs. Furthermore, many divertees have been exposed to experiences that enhance or improve their self-reliance and independence. Many youths have learned to think out their problems rather than act them out unproductively or antisocially. When we examine the contents of these programs closely, it is fairly easy to detect aspects of bonding theory, containment theory, and differential reinforcement theory at work in the delinquency prevention process.

Besides using diversion per se with or without various programs, there are elements or overtones of other theoretical schemes that may be present in the particular treatments or experiences juveniles receive as they continue to be processed throughout the juvenile justice system. At the time of adjudication, for example, juvenile court judges may or may not impose special conditions to accompany a sentence of probation. Special conditions may refer to obligating juveniles to make restitution to victims, perform public services, participate in group or individual therapy, or undergo medical treatment in cases of drug addiction or alcohol abuse. Some investigators have suggested that those youths who receive probation accompanied by special conditions are less likely to recidivate compared with those youths who receive probation unconditionally (Nagoshi 1986).

Learning to accept responsibility for one's actions, acquiring new coping skills to face crises and personal tragedy, improving one's educational attainment, and improving one's ego strength to resist the influence of one's delinquent peers are individually or collectively integral parts of various delinquency treatment programs, particularly where the psychological approach is strong.

For example, a juvenile education program was implemented at the East Lansing (Kansas) Penitentiary in the late 1970s. Delinquent youths currently on probation and residing in three Kansas counties near the penitentiary were obligated to participate in the program, which stressed introducing the juveniles to the realities of prison life (Locke et al. 1986). These juveniles participated from June to October 1980. In a follow-up investigation of their recidivism rates compared with a sample of other delinquents not exposed to the program, self-reported delinquency was considerably lower among previous program participants than among those who did not participate in the program. Researchers concluded that the experience of life in prison was to a degree therapeutic, and it appeared to change the perceived status of most participants.

Greenwood (1986b) has described programs in various jurisdictions that function as alternatives to state training schools. These programs include outdoor educational activities and wilderness challenges that encourage youths to learn useful skills and confront their fears. For those designated as **children at risk,** preschool programs such as Headstart, parent training programs such as the Oregon Learning Center, selected school programs intended to increase the achievement of lower income children, and voluntary youth service programs such as California's Conservation Corps provide many participating youths with opportunities to avoid delinquent behavioral patterns (Greenwood 1986b).

Together with psychodrama, behavioral-cognitive techniques were used by the Clinic of the Wayne County, Michigan Juvenile Court and were intended to reduce participants' acting-out, aggressive tendencies and build their ego strength. Jesness, a High School Personality Questionnaire, was administered to all adolescents participating in the program to chart before and after program changes. Researchers reported positive results, where juveniles tended to exhibit higher ego strength, less introversive tendencies, and less antisocial behavior after program participation. Intervention techniques included behavioral contracting, monetary reinforcement, and alternative behavior rehearsals, together with psychodrama, as methods for reducing these delinquents' acting-out tendencies (Carpenter and Sandberg 1985).

Minor offenders who shoplift can learn to be law-abiding with counseling rather than punishment.

Several psychologists have conducted an extensive review of group therapy literature as applied to the treatment of juvenile delinquents (Lavin, Trabka, and Kahn 1984). They conclude that group therapy is particularly effective for more aggressive adolescents. They also report that much of the research surveyed is conducted in residential settings, such as group homes. In these less traditional, nonthreatening circumstances, juveniles seem to be more amenable to behavioral change and improved conduct.

During the late 1970s, a program known as Getting It Together was established in a large city juvenile court jurisdiction (Carpenter and Sugrue 1984). The program emphasized a combination of affective (emotional) and social skills training designed to assist those with immature personalities and who exhibited neurotic behaviors. Over the next several years, many delinquent youths participated in this program. A majority reported improved self-esteem and socially mature behavior, better communication skills with authorities and parents, greater self-control, more positive values, and more adequate job skills. Ego strength levels for most participating youths improved, as did the quality of peer relationships and a reduction of various sexual problems. This program, in addition to other similar enterprises, has been guided to a great degree by social learning theory.

Program successes are often used as gauges of the successfulness of their underlying theoretical schemes. Since no program is 100 percent effective at preventing delinquency, it follows that no theoretical scheme devised thus far is fully effective. Yet, the wide variety of programs that are applied today to deal with different kinds of juvenile offenders indicates that most psychological and sociological approaches have some merit and contribute differentially to delinquency reduction (Jennings and Gunther 2000). Policy decisions are made throughout the juvenile justice system and are often contingent upon the theoretical views adopted by politicians, law enforcement personnel, prosecutors and judges, and correctional officials at every stage of the justice process. We may appreciate most theoretical views because of their varying intuitive value and selectively apply particular approaches to accommodate different types of juvenile offenders.

Regarding theories of delinquency generally, their impact has been felt most strongly in the area of policy making rather than in behavioral change or modification. Virtually every theory is connected in some respect to various types of experimental programs in different jurisdictions. The intent of most programs has been to change behaviors of participants. However, high rates of recidivism characterize all delinquency-prevention innovations, regardless of their intensity or ingenuity. Policy decisions implemented at earlier points have long-range implications for present policies in correctional work. Probationers and parolees as well as inmates and divertees, adults and juveniles alike, are recipients or inheritors of previous policies laid in place by theorists who have attempted to convert their theories into practical experiences and action.

Current policy in juvenile justice favors the get-tough orientation, and programs are increasingly sponsored that heavily incorporate accountability and individual responsibility elements. At an earlier point in time, projects emphasizing rehabilitation and reintegration were rewarded more heavily through private grants and various types of government funding. No particular prevention or intervention or supervision program works best. Numerous contrasting perspectives about how policy should be shaped continue to vie for recognition among professionals and politicians. The theories that have been described here are indicative of the many factors that have shaped our present policies and practices. The influence of these diverse theories is reflected in a variety of models that have been and continue to be used by juvenile justice practitioners. Several of these models are presented in the following section.

MODELS FOR DEALING WITH JUVENILE OFFENDERS

Six models for dealing with juvenile offenders are described here. Each of these models is driven by a particular view of juvenile delinquency and what might cause it. The causes of delinquency are many and diverse, and thus not everyone agrees with any particular explanation. Therefore, not every expert dealing with juvenile offenders agrees that one particular model is most fruitful as a basis for delinquency intervention. Rather, these models serve as a guide to the different types of decisions that are made on behalf of or against specific juvenile offenders. Because each model includes aims or objectives that are related to a degree with the aims or objectives of other models, there is sometimes confusion about model identities. For example, professionals may use a particular model label to refer to orientations that are more properly included in the context of other models. Some professionals say that they do not use any particular model, but rather, they rely on their own intuition for exercising a particular juvenile intervention.

Additionally, some recently developed interventionist activities have combined the favorable features of one model with those of others. These hybrid models are difficult to categorize, although they are believed to be helpful in diverting youths to more productive and nondelinquent activities. One way of overcoming this confusion is to highlight those features of models that most directly reflect the models' aims. The models discussed include (1) the rehabilitation model, (2) the treatment or medical model, (3) the noninterventionist model, (4) the due process model, (5) the "just deserts"/justice model, and (6) the crime control model.

The Rehabilitation Model

Perhaps the most influential model that has benefited first-offender juveniles is the **rehabilitation model.** This model assumes that delinquency or delinquent conduct is the result of poor friendship or peer choices, poor social adjustments, the wrong educational priorities, and/or a general failure to envision realistic life goals and inculcate appropriate moral values. In corrections, the rehabilitation model is associated with programs that change offender attitudes, personalities, or character (Weedon 2002). These programs may be therapeutic, educational, or vocational. At the intake stage, however, there is little, if any, reliance on existing community-based programs or services that cater to certain juvenile needs. Intake officers who use the rehabilitation model in their decision-making activities will often attempt to impart different values and personal goals to juveniles through a type of informal teaching.

If a youth is being processed at the intake stage for theft, for example, the intake officer may emphasize the harmful effects of the theft for the owner from whom the merchandise was taken. Intake officers who meet with nonviolent first-offenders usually do not want to see these juveniles move further into the juvenile justice system. Therefore, these officers may attempt to get juvenile offenders to empathize with their victims and to understand the harm they have caused by their actions. While theft is a serious offense, it is less serious than aggravated assault, rape, armed robbery, or murder. Intake officers rely heavily upon their personal experience and judgment in determining the best course of action to follow. When a juvenile is very young and has committed this single theft offense, this is an ideal situation where intake officers can exercise strategic discretion and temper their decisions with some leniency. But in the context of *parens patriae* and the rehabilitative framework guiding some of these officers, leniency does not mean outright tokenism or ineffective wrist-slapping. Doing nothing may send the wrong message to youths who have violated the law. The same may be said of police officers who encounter youths on streets and engage in police cautioning or stationhouse adjustments as alternative means of warning juveniles to refrain from future misconduct. Thus, it is believed that the informal intake hearing itself is sufficiently traumatic for most youths so that they will not be eager to reoffend subsequently. Advice, cautioning, and warnings given under such circumstances are likely to be remembered. It is also important to involve one's family members in these intake conferences. If a youth who has committed a delinquent act can see that his or her behavior has affected his or her family members, then the chances of recidivism may decline (Dembo 2001).

The Treatment or Medical Model

The **treatment model** or **medical model** assumes that delinquent conduct is like a disease, the causes of which can be isolated and attacked. Cures may be effected by administering appropriate remedies. The treatment model is very similar to the rehabilitation model. Indeed, some persons consider the treatment or medical model to be a subcategory of the rehabilitation model (Steen 2001). The aim of the treatment model is to provide conditional punishments for juveniles that are closely related to treatment. Intake officers have the authority to refer certain youths to select community-based agencies and services where they may receive the proper treatment. This treatment approach assumes that these intake officers have correctly diagnosed the illness and know best how to cure it. Compliance with program requirements that are nonobligatory for juveniles is enhanced merely by the possibility that the intake officer may later file a delinquency petition with the juvenile court against uncooperative youths.

In San Diego County, California, for instance, an Interagency Agreement plan was instituted in December 1982 for the purpose of reducing delinquency through consistent, early intervention and graduated sanctions and holding youths accountable for their acts (Pennell, Curtis, and Scheck 1990). Specific guidelines were used by police and intake officers for determining the best disposition of any particular case following a juvenile's arrest. First-time, nonserious offenders were to be handled informally, with an emphasis upon diversion to and participation in various community-based services and restitution for the purpose of establishing a youth's accountability. Recidivist youths would receive more in-depth counseling and referrals to formal probation, and eventually, formal petitions would be filed against them. The plan followed by San Diego intake officers appeared to have a favorable effect on reducing juvenile recidivism rates, where a pre- and post-test design was used over one- and two-year experimental periods.

In growing numbers of jurisdictions, social services are being utilized increasingly by juvenile courts and juvenile justice staff in order to treat various disorders exhibited by youthful offenders. Alcohol and drug dependencies characterize large numbers of arrested youths (Bilchik 1998). Therefore, treatment programs are provided for these youths in order that they can learn about and deal with their alcohol or drug dependencies. Some youths need psychological counseling. Others require anger management training and courses to improve their interpersonal skills. In Idaho, for instance, the juvenile justice system was overhauled by the legislature in 1995. Added services included two detention centers staffed by juvenile probation officers, an alternative school, psychological assessments of juveniles, treatment provisions by private agencies for juvenile sex offenders and drug/alcohol abusers, and mentoring provided by volunteers who also serve on diversion boards and youth court programs (Wright 1997). Juvenile mentoring in both secure and nonsecure settings is receiving greater recognition. The 1992 Reauthorization of the Juvenile Justice and Delinquency Prevention Act of 1974 has recognized mentoring as significant for addressing problems of school attendance and delinquent activity, and a **Juvenile Mentoring Program (JUMP)** has been established in various jurisdictions such as Florida (Swanson 1998, 38–39).

One drawback to the treatment model generally is that great variations exist among community agencies regarding the availability of certain services as remedies for particular kinds of juvenile problems (Kamerman and Kahn 1990). Also, the intake officer may incorrectly diagnose an offender's illness and prescribe inappropriate therapy. Certain types of deep-seated personality maladjustments cannot be detected through superficial informal intake proceedings. Simply participating in some community-based service or treatment program may be insufficient to relieve particular juveniles of the original or core causes of their delinquent behaviors. Nevertheless, intake screenings may lead to community-based agency referrals that eventually may or may not be productive. In most jurisdictions, these are conditional sanctions that may be administered by intake officers without judicial approval or intervention.

The Noninterventionist Model

As the name implies, the **noninterventionist model** means the absence of any direct intervention with certain juveniles who have been taken into custody. The noninterventionist model is best understood when considered in the context of labeling theory (Lemert 1967a). Labeling theory stresses that direct and frequent contact with the juvenile justice system will cause those having contact with it to eventually define themselves as delinquent. This definition will prompt self-definers to commit additional delinquent acts, since such behaviors are expected of those defined or stigmatized as such by others. Labeling theory advocates the removal of nonserious juveniles and status offenders from the juvenile justice system, or at least from the criminalizing influence and trappings of the juvenile courtroom. However, some persons question the validity of labeling theory as it is presently used to explain reductions in juvenile recidivism (Coumarelos and Weatherburn 1995).

The noninterventionist model is strategically applied only to those juveniles who the intake officer believes are unlikely to reoffend if given a second chance, or who are clearly status offenders without qualification (e.g., drug- or alcohol-dependent, chronic or persistent offenders). Intake officers who elect to act in a noninterventionist fashion with certain types of offenders may simply function as a possible resource person for juveniles and their parents. In cases involving runaways, truants, or curfew violators, it becomes a judgment call whether to refer youths and/or their parents to certain community services or counseling. The noninterventionist model would encourage no action by intake officers in nonserious or status offender cases, except under the most compelling circumstances. Since not all runaways are alike, certain runaways may be more in need of intervention than others, for instance. Again, the aim of nonintervention is to assist youths in avoiding stigma and unfavorable labeling that might arise if they were to be involved more deeply within the juvenile justice system. Even minor referrals by intake officers might prompt adverse reactions from offenders so that future offending behavior would be regarded as a way of getting even with the system.

The noninterventionist model is popular today, particularly because it fits well with the deinstitutionalization of status offenses (DSO) movement that has occurred in most jurisdictions. DSO was designed to divest juvenile courts of their jurisdiction over status offenders and remove status offenders from secure custodial institutions. Therefore, the primary intent of DSO was to minimize the potentially adverse influence of labeling that might occur through incarceration or if juveniles appear before juvenile court judges in a courtroom atmosphere (Coumarelos and Weatherburn 1995). Also, an intended function of DSO was to reduce the docket load for many juvenile court judges by transferring their jurisdiction over status offenders to community agencies and services. The noninterventionist strategy is significant here because it advocates doing nothing about certain juvenile dispositions. The works of Lemert (1967a) and Schur (1973) are relevant for the noninterventionist perspective. These have described **judicious nonintervention** and **radical nonintervention** as terms that might be applied to noninterventionist do-nothing policy.

Radical nonintervention counters traditional thinking about delinquency, which is to assume that the juvenile justice system merely needs to be improved. Radical nonintervention argues that many of the current approaches to delinquency are not only fundamentally unsound, but they are also harmful to youth whenever they are applied. Radical nonintervention assumes the following:

1. The delinquent is not basically different from the nondelinquent.
2. Most types of youthful misconduct are found within all socioeconomic strata.
3. The primary target for delinquency policy should be neither the individual nor the local community setting, but rather the delinquency-defining processes themselves.

Radical nonintervention implies that policies that accommodate society to the widest possible diversity of behaviors and attitudes rather than forcing as many individuals as possible to adjust to supposedly common societal standards are the best policies. Subsidiary policies would favor collective action programs instead of those that single out specific individuals and voluntary programs instead of compulsory ones (Schur 1973). However, some critics of nonintervention suggest that such nonintervention is defeatist. Thus, rather than adopt a "do no harm" stance, juvenile justice system officials should be more concerned with "doing good" with their various approaches and programs (Travis and Cullen 1984).

At the same time that some persons foster judicious nonintervention, others favor early intervention, especially for first offenders and those who are 13 years old or younger at the time of their first police contact (Greenwood 1999). An Early Offender Program (EOP) was established in 1985 in Oakland County, Michigan, through the Probate Court (Howitt and Moore 1991). The purpose of this program was to provide specialized, intensive, in-home interventions. Parents and youths would be visited in their homes by personnel working with the Probate Court. These personnel would assist the family through diverse and sometimes difficult interpersonal problems. Youths who were involved with drugs or had general chemical dependencies were assisted through community services as well as through home visits from counselors. Those youths with poor school adjustment received assistance from these counselors as well. This early in-home intervention proved quite valuable as a part of a general strategy to minimize recidivism among first offenders. Although there was some recidivism, it was slight. Those tending to recidivate most often were previously involved with drugs and had numerous adjustment problems in their schools. Whether there is no intervention or early intervention, some persons believe that all youths should be expected to do something, such as restitution, so as to grasp and appreciate the harm or inconvenience they have caused others (Roy 1995).

The Due Process Model

The notion of due process is an integral feature of the criminal justice system. Due process is the basic constitutional right to a fair trial, to have an opportunity to be heard, to be aware of matters that are pending, to a presumption of innocence until guilt is established beyond a reasonable doubt, to make an informed choice whether to acquiesce or contest, and to provide the reasons for such a choice before a judicial official. An important aspect of due process is that police officers must have probable cause to justify their arrests of suspected criminals. Therefore, one's constitutional rights are given considerable weight in comparison with any incriminating evidence obtained by police or others (Erickson and Crosnoe 2000).

Intake officers who rely heavily upon the **due process model** in their dealings with juveniles are concerned that the juveniles' rights are fully protected at every stage of juvenile justice processing (Wu 1997). Therefore, these officers pay particular attention to how evidence was gathered by police against certain juveniles and whether the juvenile's constitutional rights were protected and police officers advised the juvenile of the right to counsel at the time of the arrest and/or subsequent interrogation. The higher priority given to due process in recent years is considered by some researchers to be a significant juvenile justice reform (Bridges and Steen 1998). An intake officer's emphasis of due process requirements in juvenile offender processing stems, in part, from several important U.S. Supreme Court decisions during the 1960s and 1970s, although professional associations and other interests have strongly advocated a concern for greater protection of juvenile rights in recent years (U.S. General Accounting Office 1995a).

Because of the interest certain intake officers might take in one's right to due process, some intake hearings may be more formally conducted than others. Legal variables, such as present offense, numbers of charges, and prior petitions, would be given greater weight in the context of due process. Shelden and Horvath (1987) have noted that legal variables such as these have accounted for or explained as much as 40 percent of the variance in intake processing in the jurisdictions they have investigated. Thus, intake guidelines in these jurisdictions promote legal variables and downplay the significance of nonlegal factors. However, many offender dispositions seem to be affected by nonlegal variables as well, including the youth's attitude, grades in school, and school status. While mildly related to dispositions, gender, race, and social class are only moderately related to offender dispositions.

Extralegal variables include race, ethnicity, gender, family solidarity, and socioeconomic status. Studies of juvenile court dispositions in different jurisdictions such as Utah and Pennsylvania reveal that minority offenders are dealt with more severely than white offenders. In Utah, it has been found that minority youths are more likely than white youths to be placed in custodial institutions or disposed to longer periods of probation (Jenson et al. 1995). In Pennsylvania, 4,683 official juvenile case records were examined (DeJong and Jackson 1998). Black, white, and Hispanic youths were compared according to the severity of their dispositions following delinquency adjudications. Black youths tended to receive harsher dispositions compared with white or Hispanic youths. Furthermore, youths from single-parent families tended to be more harshly treated compared with other juvenile offenders, controlling for prior record and the nature of the present offense. Besides being treated differently compared with white offenders, black juveniles have been subjected to greater detrimental labeling by the juvenile justice system over time (Adams, Johnson, and Evans 1998). Differential treatment according to one's gender has also occurred in more than a few jurisdictions (Sealock and Simpson 1998). Ideally, juvenile justice decision making should be free of the influence of these and other extralegal variables, according to the due process model.

The Just-Deserts/Justice Model

There is a strong rehabilitative orientation prevalent throughout the juvenile justice system, where the emphasis is upon serving the best interests of offending youths and the delivery of individualized services to them on the basis of their needs (Schwartz 1999). *Parens patriae* explains much of the origin of this emphasis in the United States. However, the changing nature of juvenile offending during the last several decades and a gradual transformation of public sentiment toward more punitive measures have prompted certain juvenile justice reforms that are aimed at holding youths increasingly accountable for their actions and punishing them accordingly (Feld 1995).

The **just-deserts/justice model** is punishment-centered and seemingly revenge-oriented, where the state's interest is to ensure that juveniles are punished in relation to the seriousness of the offenses they have committed (Bazemore 1997). Further, those who commit identical offenses should be punished identically. This introduces the element of fairness into the punishment prescribed. The usefulness of this get-tough approach in disposing of various juvenile cases is controversial and has both proponents and opponents (Fader et al. 2001). It is significant that such an approach represents a major shift of emphasis away from juvenile offenders and their individualized needs and more toward the nature and seriousness of their actions. Just deserts as an orientation has frequently been combined with the justice model or orientation. The justice orientation is the idea that punishments should be gauged to fit the seriousness of offenses committed. Therefore, juveniles who commit more serious acts should receive harsher punishments, treatments, or sentences than those juveniles who commit less serious acts. Besides promoting punishment in proportion to offending behavior, the justice model includes certain victim considerations, such as provisions for restitution or victim compensation by offending juveniles.

The Crime Control Model

The **crime control model** theorizes that one of the best ways of controlling juvenile delinquency is to incapacitate juvenile offenders, either through some secure incarceration or through an intensive supervision program operated by a community-based agency or organization. Perhaps **consent decrees** may include provisions for the electronic monitoring of certain juvenile offenders in selected jurisdictions. These juveniles might be required to wear plastic bracelets or anklets that are devised to emit electronic signals and notify juvenile probation officers of an offender's whereabouts. Or juvenile offenders may be incarcerated in secure facilities for short- or long-term periods, depending upon the seriousness of their offenses (Pitts 2001).

The crime control perspective causes intake officers to move certain chronic, persistent, and/or dangerous juvenile offenders further into the juvenile justice system. If they believe certain juveniles pose serious risks to others or are considered dangerous, these intake officers might decide that juveniles should be held in secure confinement pending a subsequent detention hearing. If juveniles who are chronic or persistent offenders are incapacitated, they cannot reoffend. Treatment and rehabilitation are subordinate to simple control and incapacitation. Intake officers who favor the crime control view have few illusions that the system can change certain juvenile offenders. Rather, the best course of action for them is secure incarceration for lengthy periods, considering the availability of space in existing juvenile secure confinement facilities. In this way, they are directly prevented from reoffending, since they are totally incapacitated. The cost effectiveness of such incarceration of the most chronic and persistent juvenile offenders in relation to the monies lost resulting from thefts, burglaries, robberies, and other property crimes is difficult to calculate. Incarceration is costly, and immense overcrowding in existing juvenile secure confinement facilities already plagues most jurisdictions.

An alternative to incarceration for juveniles is to focus on those most susceptible to being influenced by the potential for incarceration if they continue to reoffend. More than a few intervention programs have emphasized the adverse implications for juveniles, such as incarceration, if they continue their delinquent behavior. The unpleasantness of prison settings is stressed. Programs, such as Scared Straight, are intended to scare some juveniles into becoming more law-abiding. For instance, selected juvenile delinquents are brought to a prison where they are confronted by several inmates. The inmates talk about what it is like to be locked up and subjected to abuse from other inmates. The intent of programs such as this is to frighten juveniles so much with what it might be like to be incarcerated that they will not be inclined to reoffend in the future. Scared Straight and similar programs have had limited success with certain juvenile offenders, although widespread success of these types of programs has not been achieved (Feder and Boruch 2000).

Crime control is also achieved to a degree through the establishment of after-school programs for youths considered at risk of becoming delinquent. It has been found that juveniles, particularly those who are unsupervised during after-school hours, are more inclined to commit delinquent acts compared with supervised youths (Gottfredson, Gottfredson, and Weisman 2001). Thus, one method of crime control is to focus upon those times when youths have the greatest opportunities to offend. Although unsupervised youths are more likely to commit delinquent acts at any time, their frequency of offending escalates especially during after-school hours (Gottfredson, Gottfredson, and Weisman 2001, 61–62). Sports events and other types of after-school activities that cause such youths to become more involved with other school peers are considered helpful at reducing the frequency of delinquency. However, other factors, such as urban ecological features (nearby malls, high schools, high unemployment areas), must be considered when devising particular types of after-school interventions (LaGrange 1999).

DELINQUENCY PREVENTION PROGRAMS AND COMMUNITY INTERVENTIONS

Since the 1980s much has been done to establish delinquency prevention programs in various communities and to involve both citizens and the police in joint efforts to combat juvenile crime (Houston 2001). Because of the great diversity of offending among juveniles, it has been necessary to devise specific types of programs to target certain juvenile offender populations. For instance, a significant amount of youth violence occurs in school settings. As a result, considerable resources have been allocated to address the problem of school violence and reduce its incidence (Dahlberg and Potter 2001). At the same time that school violence is targeted for reduction, certain programs seek to heighten

Delinquency prevention programs often teach participants useful skills.

the accountability of offenders who are most prominently involved in school violence (Holmes 2000, 29). Programs that implement accountability principles include school-based probation, the Handgun Intervention Program, and the Positive Adolescent Choices Training program, which provides skills training for high-risk youths between the ages of 12 and 16 (Decker 2000).

Some programs are aimed at youthful sex offenders. Sex offender services and counseling are provided in various communities to assist those youths with these specific problems (Berenson and Underwood 2001; Righthand and Welch 2001). Other programs target youths who are either gang-affiliated or at risk of becoming affiliated with a gang. Such programs attempt to educate youths about the risks of gang membership as well as some of the personal and social reasons youths seek out gangs initially (Miller 2001). Even youths who are presently incarcerated in secure facilities are considered potential subjects for intervention programs. Therefore, various forms of assistance and services are made available to youthful inmates in juvenile industrial schools for their rehabilitation and reintegration (Crowe 2000).

The State of Washington has adopted a "best practices" approach in an effort to identify the most successful interventions that might be useful in reducing juvenile delinquency. The Washington State Legislature passed the Community Juvenile Accountability Act in 1997, which is designed to distribute resources and ensure that local governments are supported in their efforts to implement empirically validated programs. The goals of the Act are to demonstrate reductions in recidivism and crime rates of juvenile offenders in juvenile courts. The juvenile courts are required to (1) determine the level of risk for re-offending posed by juvenile offenders so that the courts may target more intensive efforts at higher-risk youth and not use scarce resources for lower-risk youth; (2) identify the targets of intervention to guide the rehabilitative effort; (3) develop a case management plan focused on intervention strategies that are linked to reductions in future criminal behavior by reducing risk factors and strengthening protective and competency factors; (4) identify and implement intervention strategies and programs with demonstrated outcomes in reducing juvenile crime; (5) monitor the youth's progress in reducing risk factors and increasing protective factors to know whether the case management strategy is effective; (6) reduce paperwork through the use of computerized assessment and monitoring software; and (7) provide juvenile court management with information on the progress made to reduce risk factors and increase protective factors by court programs and contracted service providers (Van Dieten 2002, 41). Washington officials believe that there are complex challenges and obstacles that frustrate their efforts to fulfill these objectives. Nevertheless, they believe that attempting to use those interventions with some demonstrated degrees of success will result in the wisest allocation of scarce juvenile justice resources for the state.

Many persons believe that effective intervention programs designed to prevent delinquent conduct should be started early in a youth's life, probably through school programs (Bilchik 1998, 1). School systems are logical conduits through which intervention programs can be channeled. A wide range of ages is targeted by various intervention programs. Some of these programs are described below.

The Perry Preschool Program.   The **Perry Preschool Program** provides high-level early childhood education to disadvantaged children in order to improve their later school life and performance. This intervention combats childhood poverty and school failure by promoting young children's intellectual, social, and physical development. By increasing academic success, the Perry Preschool Program is also able to improve employment opportunities and wages, as well as decrease crime, teenage pregnancy, and welfare use. School staff view children, ages 3 and 4, as active, self-initiated learners. Small groups of twenty children are taught in classrooms over a two-year period, 2.5 hours per day, five days per week, for seven months a year. The program consists of ongoing mentoring and sensitivity to the noneducational needs of disadvantaged children and their families, including providing meals and recommending other social service agencies. Program outcomes have been less delinquency, including less contact with the juvenile justice system, fewer arrests at age 19, and less involvement in serious fights, gang fights, causing injuries, and police contact. Less antisocial behavior and misconduct during elementary school, higher academic achievement, fewer school dropouts, and greater economic independence have also been observed (Center for the Study and Prevention of Violence 2002).

The FAST Track Program. The **FAST Track Program** is both a rural and an urban intervention for both boys and girls of varying ethnicities. It is a long-term and comprehensive program that is designed to prevent chronic and severe conduct problems for high-risk children. It originates from the view that antisocial behavior stems from multiple factors, including the school, home, and individual (McGee and Baker 2002). FAST Track's goals are to increase communication and bonds between these three domains, improve children's social, cognitive, and problem-solving skills, improve peer relations, and ultimately decrease disruptive behavior at home and school. FAST Track targets grades 1 through 6, but it is most intense during the first grade. It includes parent training, bi-weekly home visits to reinforce parenting skills, social skills training for involved youths, academic tutoring three times a week, and a curriculum that improves youths' awareness skills, self-control, problem-solving skills, provides a positive peer climate, and improves teachers' classroom management skills. Program results have included better teacher–parent relations, improved interactions between parents and their children, better overall ratings by observers of youths' classroom behavior, more appropriate discipline techniques, more maternal involvement in school activities, and greater liking of student peers by FAST Track students (Center for the Study and Prevention of Violence 2002).

C.O.P.Y. Kids. **C.O.P.Y. Kids** (Community Opportunities Program for Youth) is a demonstration project that was undertaken in the summer of 1993 by the Spokane Police Department in Washington. Officers engaged in weekly interactions with 335 economically disadvantaged youths ranging in age from 11 to 15. Their program involved an attempt to assist these youths in improving their self-concepts, self-images, and to promote general law-abiding behavior. Parents were involved as well as a large supporting staff contingent. Youths were given an opportunity to participate in various crafts and jobs where they could acquire several useful skills for subsequent employment. At the conclusion of the program, youths were taken to a local bank, where $40 had been deposited into an account for each participating youth. Interviews with parents and workers suggested that these productive activities allowed children to develop a greater sense of responsibility. Particularly encouraging was the fact that these youths developed a more favorable image of police officers and the police department. Limited information existed to show any effects on curbing delinquency among those involved youths, although investigators believed that this plan was a useful deterrent to delinquent conduct.

The Bullying Prevention Program.   The **Bullying Prevention Program** is directed at reducing and preventing bullying in elementary, middle, and junior high schools. School staff are trained and vested with the responsibility of introducing and implementing the program. An anonymous questionnaire is administered to all students, soliciting feedback about the presence of school bullying. Class rules are established by a Bullying Prevention Coordinating Committee, with the assistance of school-based mental health professionals. Significant reductions in bullying behavior have been reported, including a significant reduction in antisocial behavior, such as vandalism, fighting, theft, and truancy. Students report a more favorable social climate throughout their school (Olweus, Limber, and Mihalic 1999).

The PATHS Program.   The **PATHS** (Promoting Alternative THinking Strategies) **Program** is a comprehensive curriculum designed to promote emotional and social competencies and reduce aggression and other related behavioral problems in elementary school-aged children. The PATHS curriculum is taught three times per week, for a minimum of 20 to 30 minutes per day. Teachers are provided with systematic, developmentally based lessons, materials, and instructions for teaching their students emotional literacy, self-control, social competence, positive peer relations, and interpersonal problem-solving skills to prevent or reduce behavioral and emotional problems. Reported program results include improved understanding and recognition of emotions, increased ability to tolerate frustration, use of more effective conflict-resolution strategies, improved thinking and planning skills, decreased anxiety/depressive symptoms, decreased conduct problems, and decreased aggression. Program costs over a three-year period range from $15 per student per year to $45 per student per year, depending upon whether an on-site coordinator is hired to assist in teacher training (Greenberg, Kusche, and Mihalic 1998).

D.A.R.E.   The Los Angeles Police Department has implemented a program for intervening with elementary school drug use called Drug Abuse Resistance Education or **D.A.R.E.** D.A.R.E. uses police officers familiar with drugs and drug laws who visit schools in their precincts and speak to youths about how to say "no" to drugs. Children are taught how to recognize illegal drugs, different types of drugs, as well as their adverse effects.

Big Brothers/Big Sisters Program.   The **Big Brothers/Big Sisters Program** is not new. It has been around for nearly a century. This program is designed to provide youths aged 6 to 18 from single-parent homes with adult support and friendship. Over 100,000 youth had been involved in Big Brothers/Big Sisters by 1998. Those adults seeking to be mentors for disadvantaged youth are screened rigorously. Matches between particular adults and youths are made on the basis of comparisons of written applications, interviews with the child and parent, and a home assessment. The needs of youth and the abilities of the adult volunteer are carefully weighed. Supervision and adult–child contact are accomplished through frequent activities scheduled one or more times per week. Adult volunteers are the equivalent of surrogate parents, and they offer youths the chance to interact with "fathers" or "mothers" they don't have in their actual home environments. This program offers youths a high degree of stability. Over the years, evaluation research has demonstrated that nearly half of all involved youths are less likely to initiate drug or alcohol use. A third are less likely to hit someone or engage in antisocial behavior. Furthermore, there is evidence that the program fosters higher quality relationships among a youth's peers. The program costs approximately $1,000 per year for making and supporting a match relationship (McGill, Mihalic, and Grotpeter 1998).

G.R.E.A.T. (Gang Resistance Education and Training).   The **G.R.E.A.T. Program** has been implemented in Phoenix, Arizona, between community leaders and educators and funded by the Bureau of Alcohol, Tobacco, and Firearms to intervene with gangs on a nationwide basis. This program uses police officers who visit schools and interact with students on a regular basis over a specified time period. Classroom sessions consist of eight, 1-hour periods where youths can learn to overcome peer pressure relative to drug use and joining delinquent gangs. The weekly topics are diverse, including cultural sensitivity and prejudice, crimes, victims and rights, drugs and neighborhoods, diverse responsibilities, goal setting, and conflict resolution and need fulfillment. This program was designed and targeted for children in after-school hours. Parental involvement is encouraged, and police organizations sponsor summer activities to give local youths alternative interesting projects. Evidence suggests that this program is having significant results, in that participating students are acquiring more prosocial attitudes compared with non-G.R.E.A.T. students (Esbensen et al. 2001:87).

The Juvenile Mentoring Program (JUMP).   The Juvenile Mentoring Program is a federal program administered by the Office of Juvenile Justice and Delinquency Prevention. The three principal goals of this program are to (1) reduce juvenile delinquency and gang participation by at-risk youth, (2) improve academic performance of at-risk youth, and (3) reduce the school dropout rate for at-risk youth. Mentoring is a one-on-one relation between a pair of unrelated individuals, one adult and one juvenile, that takes place on a regular basis over an extended period of time. It is almost always characterized by a special bond of mutual commitment and an emotional character of respect, loyalty, and identification. JUMP is designed to reduce juvenile delinquency and gang participation, improve academic performance, and reduce school dropout rates. To achieve these purposes, JUMP brings together caring, responsible adults and at-risk young people in need of positive role models. Mentors are college students, senior citizens, federal employees, businessmen, law enforcement and fire department personnel, and other interested private citizens. Those treated range in age from 5 to 20. By 2002 JUMP was involved in attempting to keep more than 9,200 at-risk youths in twenty-five states in school and off the streets through one-to-one mentoring (Cain 2002).

The Friends for the Love of Reading Project.   In Philadelphia, Pennsylvania, Division of Juvenile Justice Services, Deputy Commissioner Joyce Burrell implemented the **Friends for the Love of Reading Project,** which is based on the District of Columbia's Book Buddies Program (Howell 1999, 26). The objective of this program is to involve community residents with various high school youths who cannot read well. Volunteers work with particular youths and read to them as a part of a self-help program to improve reading skills. It was discovered that Philadelphia school districts had rather high dropout rates often traceable to poor reading ability. Many juveniles who eventually became involved with the law in delinquent activity were among those who did not graduate from school and had reading problems. A primary goal of the program is to involve parents, volunteers, and youths in an aggressive reading program in an effort to motivate them to stay in school and out of trouble. During 1997–1998, over 20,000 volunteers were recruited to work with youths on a one-to-one basis in the greater Philadelphia area. The program is believed to be effective at reducing school dropout rates, and ultimately, a sound method of delinquency prevention (Howell 1999).

The Faith in Families Multi-Systematic Therapy Program.   The **Faith in Families Multi-Systematic Therapy Program (MST)** is operated by the Henry and Rilla White Foundation of Bronson, Florida (Schossler and Powers 1999, 112). This program attempts to modify youth behaviors by working with their interpersonal environment, including the family, school, and peer groups. Family therapists are on call 24 hours a day to provide social and psychological support for youths and their families. The program includes weekly meetings with youths, their families, the family therapist, and juvenile court judge in a milieu termed therapeutic jurisprudence. The program incorporates cognitive behavior therapy and teaches children greater self-control, self-reflectiveness, and problem-solving skills in academic and interpersonal situations. Emphasis is upon thinking and planning before acting. Preliminary results of the program's effectiveness show a 85.7 percent successful completion rate and that antisocial behavior in at-risk youths can be identified and corrected.

The Casastart Program.   The **CASASTART Program** targets high-risk youths, ages 11 to 13, who are exposed to drugs and criminal activity. The program seeks to decrease individual, peer group, and family and neighborhood risk factors through case management services, after-school and summer activities, and increased police involvement. Eight core components of CASASTART include (1) community-enhanced policing/enhanced enforcement; (2) case management (13 to 18 families); (3) criminal/juvenile justice intervention; (4) family services, including parent programs, counseling, and organized parent–child activities; (5) after-school and summer activities for personal and social development, improving self-esteem, and studying one's cultural heritage; (6) education services, offering tutoring as well as work preparation opportunities; (7) mentoring through one-on-one relationships; and (8) incentives, both monetary and nonmonetary. CASASTART has reported lower rates of drug use among participants as well as more prosocial behavior (Center for the Study of Prevention and Violence 2002).

The Midwestern Prevention Project.   The **Midwestern Prevention Project** is a multifaceted program for adolescent drug abuse prevention. It is initiated in school settings and targets early adolescents to middle and late adolescence. The program attempts to help youth recognize the social pressures to use drugs, and it provides training skills about how to avoid drug use and drug use situations. The skills are initially learned in the school program and reinforced through the parent, media, and community organization components. Active learning techniques are used, such as role playing, modeling, and discussion, with student peers assisting teachers. Outcomes of this project have included reductions in smoking behavior and marijuana use maintained through grade 12 and increased parent-child communication. Program costs are approximately $175,000 over a three-year period, which includes teacher and parent training and curriculum for school-based programs. For each program, twenty teachers are trained, as well as principals and student peers, and twelve parents (Pentz, Mihalic, and Grotpeter 1998).

These are only a few of the many programs operating throughout the United States involving police and interested citizens in proactive and positive roles, where they are taking an active interest in preventing delinquent conduct through interacting closely with youths. These programs will not make juvenile offenders desist from delinquent conduct, but it will make many of them aware of a positive side of police officers. Further, it will have the positive effect of helping police officers understand juveniles and their motives.

SUMMARY

There are many theories of delinquency. Theories are integrated explanatory schemes that predict relationships between two or more phenomena. Theories of delinquency may be grouped into biological, psychological, and sociological explanations. Biological theories strongly imply a causal relation between physique and other genetic phenomena and delinquent behaviors. Psychological theories include psychoanalytic theory devised by Sigmund Freud and promoted by others. Social learning theory is similar to psychoanalytic theory, although it stresses imitation of significant others. Concentric zone theory postulates that ecological factors such as the nature of urban growth create living situations conducive to delinquent conduct.

A popular sociological view of delinquency is labeling theory. Those who engage in wrongdoing may come to adopt self-definitions as delinquents, particularly if significant others and the police define them as delinquents. Having frequent contact with the juvenile justice system enhances such labeling for many youths. Labeling theorists often argue that delinquents are "acting out" the behaviors others expect from them. Closely related to labeling theory is bonding theory, where juveniles develop either close or distant attachments to schools, teachers, and peers. Delinquency is regarded as a function of inadequate bonding or a weakening of social attachments. Other theories include containment theory, neutralization or drift theory, and differential association. Each of these views suggests the power or attraction of group processes in the onset of delinquent conduct.

Theories of delinquency are often evaluated according to how they influence public policy relating to juvenile conduct and its prevention or treatment. Diversionary programs that prevent further juvenile contact with the juvenile justice system are influenced largely by labeling theory, since it is believed that youths will become more deeply entrenched in juvenile conduct to the extent that they are exposed to the formal system and juvenile courts. Individual and group therapy, often a part of treatment programs for errant juveniles, seek to use ego development strategies coupled with various learning methods to improve self-definitions, reduce antisocial behaviors, and promote more healthy attitudes toward others. Programs that emphasize personal responsibility for one's actions or encourage youths to become more active in decision making seem to make a difference in reducing recidivism among program participants. No theory is universally accepted, however.

Alternative models for managing or treating juvenile offenders include the medical or treatment model, where delinquency is considered a disease or illness. Prescriptions are provided to cure the illness. These are often individual or group therapy, medical treatment in the case of alcohol and drug abusers, and educational experiences (O'Sullivan, Rose, and Murphy 2001). Closely related to the treatment or medical model is the rehabilitation model. Similar to the treatment model, the rehabilitation model emphasizes learning and coping experiences, victim restitution, and community service to contribute toward one's rehabilitation. The **community reintegration model** employs similar treatment strategies, although this model locates treatment facilities within the community to preserve a youth's identity with it.

The prevention/control model strives to reduce or eliminate delinquent behavior by targeting high risk or at-risk youths in their early years and instituting various interventions, such as learning strategies to overcome learning disabilities and improving one's self-concept. The "just-deserts" and justice models stress punishments that are equivalent to wrongful acts committed by youths, although the justice model promotes fairness in treatment. Finally, the reality therapy model uses shock experiences, such as temporary incarceration in a prison or jail, to awaken youths to the realities of prison life. Face-to-face encounters with incarcerated adult offenders are also a part of reality therapy. Various programs exist where police officers become involved with youth in delinquency prevention programs and show youths more favorable dimensions of police work.

QUESTIONS FOR REVIEW

1. What is a theory of delinquency? What are two important functions of theory? How do assumptions and propositions relate to theory?

2. What is meant by *determinism*? Explain the difference between determinism and free will. What types of theories are associated with determinism? Explain.

3. What are the major components of psychoanalytic theory? Describe the importance of one's formative years to psychoanalytic theory. In what respect is one's childhood regarded as one's "formative years"?

4. How does social learning theory differ from psychoanalytic theory?

5. How is cultural transmission theory related to the concentric zone hypothesis?

6. What seems to be the role of socioeconomic status in the complex picture of juvenile delinquency?

7. What is a delinquent subculture? How can we possibly use such information about a delinquent subculture to change delinquent behaviors in various communities?

8. How can strain theory and Merton's theory of anomie be distinguished? What mode of adaptation is most likely to be invoked by juvenile delinquents? What other modes of adaptation are there?

9. How are various theories of delinquent conduct evaluated?

10. What are four types of intervention programs? What is their relative successfulness in reducing delinquency?

SUGGESTED READINGS

Berenson, David and Lee Underwood. 2001. *Juvenile sex offender programming: A resource guide.* Washington, DC: U.S. Office of Juvenile Justice and Delinquency Prevention.

Miller, Walter B. 2001. *The growth of youth gang problems in the United States: 1970–1998.* Washington, DC: U.S. Office of Juvenile Justice and Delinquency Prevention.

Shoemaker, Donald J. 2000. *Theories of delinquency: An examination of explanations of delinquent behavior.* 4th ed. New York: Oxford University Press.

INTERNET CONNECTIONS

HandsNet
http://www.handsnet.org/

Human Rights and the Drug War
http://www.hr95.org/

Juvenile Justice Center
http://www.aba.net/crimjust/juvjus/home.html

Maryland Justice Policy Institute
http://www.mid-justice-policy-inst.org/

Marijuana Policy Project
http://www.mpp.org/

National Center for Institutional Alternatives
http://www.ncia.net/ncia/home.html

National Center for Youth Law
http://www.youthlaw.org/

CHAPTER 4 | *An Overview of the Juvenile Justice System*

Chapter Outline

Key Terms

Adjudication
Adjudication hearing, adjudicatory hearing
Aftercare
Aggravating circumstances
Arraignment
Arrest
Bail
Bail bond
Bench trials
Booking
Conditional dispositions

Corrections
Criminal informations
Criminal justice system, process
Custodial dispositions
Defendants
Dispose
Dispositions
Exculpatory evidence
Grand juries
Hard time
Inculpatory evidence
Indictments

Informations
Initial appearance
Intake
Intake hearings, intake screenings
Intake officer
Intermediate punishments
Jail removal initiative
Jails
Jury
Jury trials
Law enforcement officers
Lockups

Mistrial
Mitigating circumstances
No bills, no true bills
Nominal dispositions
Nonsecure custody, nonsecure confinement
Parole
Parole board
Petitions
Petit juries

Plea bargains, plea bargaining
Police discretion
Preliminary examination
Preliminary hearing
Presentments
Pretrial detention
Preventive detention
Prisons
Probable cause
Probation

Referrals
Release on own recognizance (ROR)
Restorative justice
Screening
Secure custody, secure confinement
Sentencing hearing
Taken into custody
True bills

Chapter Objectives

As a result of reading this chapter, you will accomplish the following objectives:

1. Understand the criminal justice system and how juvenile offenders are initially processed when taken into custody.
2. Understand the intake process for screening juveniles.
3. Learn about different prosecutorial options for pursuing cases against juveniles.
4. Acquire an understanding of the different types of juvenile court dispositions, including nominal, conditional, and custodial sanctions that may be applied.

INTRODUCTION

• An 11-year-old boy, Kenny A., was taken into custody by police officers in Knoxville, Tennessee, following the theft of a bicycle from a neighbor's child. It was Christmas afternoon. Kenny A.'s parents were poor. Both worked at low-paying jobs in a textile mill and an auto body repair shop. They couldn't afford to buy Kenny A. many presents. But the neighbor's child received a brand new red bicycle for Christmas. Kenny A. saw him riding the bicycle and decided he wanted it. He waited until the boy went into the house, then Kenny A. went to the neighbor's yard, took the red bicycle to his own house, and, using his father's spray paint cans, spray-painted the entire bicycle white. After the paint dried, Kenny A. rode the bicycle around the neighborhood. When the neighboring boy discovered his bicycle missing, he observed Kenny A. riding one just like it, only the bicycle was white. However, some of the red was showing through where Kenny A. had failed to cover all spots. The neighbor child told his dad about it, and the father called police. They investigated shortly thereafter and determined that Kenny A. was not the true owner of the bicycle. Kenny A.'s parents were shocked with what their son had done. A week later in juvenile court, a juvenile probation officer conducted an intake hearing where Kenny A. and the mother attended. The officer determined that this was Kenny A.'s first offense. He had no prior juvenile record and had otherwise been law-abiding. The officer asked Kenny A. why he stole the other boy's bicycle. "Because I didn't have one," he replied tearfully. The officer worked out an agreement with Kenny A. and his mother whereby Kenny A. would do work around the house and yard for the next year and pay back the neighbor for his bicycle loss. Kenny A. was warned by the officer that he shouldn't do that again and that was the end of the incident. [Adapted from the Associated Press, "Youth Repaints Stolen Bicycle." January 15, 2002].

• *It happened in an alleyway in downtown Detroit. Luther R. and Michael G. confronted a 12-year-old girl and demanded money. The girl tried to flee, but Luther and Michael tackled her and dragged her to a deserted building where they raped her repeatedly. They hit her with bricks and boards when finished, leaving her for dead. The girl was discovered by a homeless man who alerted police. Emergency medical personnel saved the girl's life and she survived to identify her attackers. Subsequently, police officers took Luther G. into custody. He identified Michael G. as his accomplice. Both were charged with aggravated rape and attempted murder. They were 11 and 12 respectively.* [Adapted from the Associated Press, "Pre-Teens Involved in Rape and Attempted Murder." July 1, 2002].

What should be done with kids who kill or rape other kids? How should violent offenders be processed? What punishments should be imposed for juvenile rapists and youths who commit murder or other violent crimes? How should young, first-time property offenders be handled by juvenile authorities? In 2000 over 2 million juveniles were arrested for various crimes in the United States (Maguire and Pastore 2002). Most of these juveniles are taken to jails or lockups where they are detained for brief periods. While approximately 90 percent of these juveniles are either referred to juvenile court jurisdiction or released to parents or guardians within hours following their arrest, the remainder are formally admitted to these jails or other places of confinement to await further action.

The juvenile justice system interfaces in several significant ways with the criminal justice system. Because a small portion of the juveniles who are arrested by police will eventually fall within the jurisdiction of the criminal justice system, it is important to understand the basic elements and stages of both systems. This chapter is an overview of the juvenile justice system and the criminal justice system. A description of the criminal justice system is provided, including the preliminary procedures often followed by law enforcement officers whenever youthful offenders are apprehended. Subsequent to arrest, juveniles must be identified and classified. Depending upon the seriousness of the offense(s) alleged, decisions are made by arresting officers, jail personnel, and/or judges whether to release certain juveniles to the custody of their parents or legal guardians, release them to juvenile authorities, or detain them for further action.

Preliminary classifications and dispositions of many juvenile offenders are routine and pose few problems for arresting officers and others. However, a proportion of those taken into custody may require special handling and treatment. They may be mentally or physically ill, under the influence of drugs or alcohol, or dangerous and pose threats to the safety and security of others or even to themselves. Discretionary actions in some of these cases are far from perfunctory. The process of classifying juveniles and establishing where jurisdiction lies is described.

Once jurisdiction is established and it is determined that the juvenile justice system is where certain youthful offenders should be sent, these juveniles are brought to juvenile halls or other juvenile facilities where they will await further disposition. While specific procedures followed in the processing of juveniles vary among jurisdictions, the intake process will be described. This process involves several alternative actions and may lead to further involvement in the juvenile justice system. Prosecutors in many jurisdictions decide whether to bring juveniles before juvenile courts for formal adjudicatory action by judges. The juvenile court is becoming increasingly adversarial as juveniles acquire greater numbers of constitutional rights commensurate with those enjoyed by adults in the criminal justice system. This chapter will provide an overview of adjudicatory alternatives available to juvenile court judges and describe the array of punishments that may be imposed on those found delinquent or in need of special care. Finally, a brief overview and description of juvenile corrections will be presented.

THE CRIMINAL JUSTICE SYSTEM

The **criminal justice system** or **criminal justice process** is an interrelated set of agencies and organizations designed to control criminal behavior, to detect crime, and to apprehend, process, prosecute, punish, or rehabilitate criminal offenders. Figure 4.1 is a diagram of the criminal justice system.

Figure 4.1 includes descriptions of both the criminal and juvenile justice systems, since cases that fall within the jurisdiction of the juvenile justice system are diverted to it following arrests. Sending a case to juvenile court occurs either because of arrests by police officers or through referrals from various community agencies or organizations (Arrigona, Birch, and Dailey 1996). Some cases that originate in juvenile courts may eventually be transferred to the jurisdiction of criminal courts. Because some juveniles may be included within the jurisdiction of adult criminal courts, it is important that we should have a working familiarity with these courts and the criminal justice system. The following discussion is only a review of criminal justice system fundamentals otherwise covered extensively in introductory criminal justice courses.

The traditional elements of the criminal justice system include law enforcement agencies or law enforcement, prosecution and the courts, and **corrections,** although law-making bodies such as state legislatures and Congress are sometimes included. The word *system* is misleading, in a sense, since the different criminal justice components are not as closely integrated and coordinated as a system would indicate. Some persons prefer to use *process* as a better way of depicting how arrested persons are treated during various phases of their processing. There is a criminal justice system and it exists as a system, although it is usually a loosely integrated one. For instance, law enforcement officers seldom ask prosecutors and the courts if they have arrested too many offenders for the system to handle. Also, prosecutors and the courts seldom ask jail and prison officials whether there is sufficient space to accommodate persons who are to be incarcerated for short or long periods. Below are descriptions of the various criminal justice system components.

Legislatures

Criminal laws originate largely as the result of legislative actions in most jurisdictions. *Jurisdiction* refers to the power of courts to hear cases, although we generally define a jurisdiction according to various political subdivisions, including townships, cities, counties, states, or federal districts. Thus, when criminals cross state or county lines, they leave the state or local jurisdictions where violations of the law occurred. Under certain circumstances, these jurisdictional boundaries may be crossed by pursuing authorities. At the federal

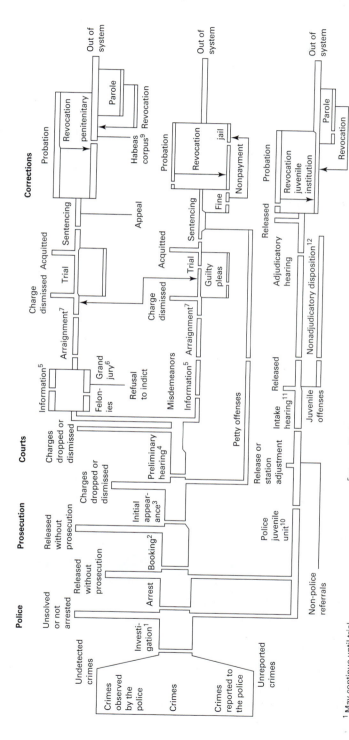

Police

Crimes observed by the police

Undetected crimes

Investigation[1]

Unsolved or not arrested

Released without prosecution

Arrest

Released without prosecution

Booking[2]

Prosecution

Released without prosecution

Initial appearance[3]

Charges dropped or dismissed

Non-police referrals

Police juvenile unit[10]

Courts

Charges dropped or dismissed

Preliminary hearing[4]

Charges dropped or dismissed

Felonies

Information[5]

Grand jury[6]

Refusal to indict

Misdemeanors

Information[5]

Petty offenses

Release or station adjustment

Intake hearing[11]

Released

Juvenile offenses

Nonadjudicatory disposition[12]

Crimes

Crimes reported to the police

Unreported crimes

Arraignment[7]

Charge dismissed

Trial

Acquitted

Sentencing

Charge dismissed

Arraignment[7]

Guilty pleas

Acquitted

Trial

Sentencing

Appeal

Released

Adjudicatory hearing

Corrections

Probation

Revocation

penitentiary

Parole

Habeas corpus[9]

Revocation

Out of system

Probation

Revocation

jail

Fine

Nonpayment

Out of system

Probation

Revocation

juvenile institution

Parole

Revocation

Out of system

Parole

[1] May continue until trial.
[2] Administrative record of arrest. First step at which temporary release on bail may be available.
[3] Before magistrate, commissioner, or justice of the peace. Formal notice of charge, advice of rights. Bail set. Summary trials for petty offenses usually conducted here without further processing.
[4] Preliminary testing of evidence against defendant. Charge may be reduced. No seperate preliminary hearing for misdemeanors in some systems.

[5] Charge filed by prosecutor on basis of information submitted by police or citizens. Alternative to grand jury indictment; often used in felonies, almost always in misdemeanors.
[6] Reviews whether government evidence sufficient to justify trial. Some states have no grand jury system; others seldom use it.
[7] Appearance for plea; defendant elects trial by judge or jury (if available); counsel for indigent usually appointed here in felonies. Often not at all on other cases.

[8] Charge may be reduced at any time prior to trial in return for plea of guilty or for other reasons.
[9] Challenge on constitutional grounds to legality of detention. May be sought at any point in process.
[10] Police often hold informal hearings, dismiss or adjust many cases without further processing.
[11] Probation officer decides desirability of further court action.
[12] Welfare agency, social services, counseling, medical care, etc., cases where adjudicatory handling not needed.

FIGURE 4.1 The Criminal and Juvenile Justice Systems

133

level, any federal agency may enforce certain federal laws in any state, territory, or U.S. possession.

The Congress of the United States passes criminal laws that are enforceable by various federal agencies, including the Federal Bureau of Investigation (FBI), Drug Enforcement Administration (DEA), and the Criminal Investigation Division (CID) of the Internal Revenue Service. State legislatures enact criminal laws that are enforced by state and local law enforcement officers. At the community level, city and county governments determine specific criminal laws, statutes, and ordinances that should be enforced, depending upon the circumstances of the locality. Some local ordinances are especially geared to regulate juvenile conduct. Such ordinances include curfews, truancy laws, and incorrigibility provisions, where parents or guardians cannot control the behaviors of their children. Virtually all ordinances aimed at juveniles are status ordinances, since these ordinances are not applicable to adults. Whenever juveniles violate these ordinances or commit prohibited criminal offenses, they fall within the purview of law enforcement.

Law Enforcement

There were over 20,000 police and sheriff's departments in the United States in 2000. These law enforcement agencies employed over 922,200 full-time sworn officers with general **arrest** powers (Maguire and Pastore 2002). The most visible **law enforcement officers** are uniformed police officers in local and state governments. Federal officers, especially FBI agents, DEA personnel, and others, may encounter juveniles who are involved in federal crimes, although most of the time their work is focused upon apprehending adult offenders. Usually, federal agents who apprehend juveniles will deliver them to local authorities for processing. It is unusual for federal courts to prosecute juvenile offenders, despite the fact that juveniles may commit one or more federal crimes.

Law enforcement officers who are most likely to have direct contact with juveniles are city police and sheriff's deputies. These officers patrol city and county

Loitering youths often attract police attention.

streets and general areas, and they may encounter juveniles acting suspiciously or in the act of committing offenses. They may respond to citizen reports of disturbances involving juveniles. In certain jurisdictions, special police forces are designated to deal with particular types of juvenile offenders. In Honolulu, Hawaii, for example, the Honolulu Police Department has created a Youth Gang Response System, a collaboration between state and county agencies that emphasizes programs and community services (Chesney-Lind and Matsuo 1995). Officers assigned to this program encounter all types of juvenile offenders, including truants, curfew violators, and runaways, and either return them to school or take them into custody. Also, in Hawaii and other jurisdictions, law enforcement officers may apprehend any juvenile suspected of violating criminal laws.

Whenever juveniles are taken into custody by police officers, they may be taken to a local police station and questioned. **Police discretion** is very important, since officers may make on-the-spot decisions either to warn and release juveniles in their initial encounters with them on city streets or take them to a jail or police department for further questioning. Circumstances often dictate which course of action is followed. Juveniles loitering late at night near a store

 **BOX 4.1**

TEEN-ASSISTED SUICIDE

On the Suicide of Jennifer Garvey, 15

It happened in Annapolis, Maryland. A 16-year-old boy watched as his troubled 15-year-old girlfriend shot herself to death as a part of an apparent suicide pact. The 16-year-old was subsequently charged with assisting in her suicide. The boy was charged as a juvenile under Maryland law. Under Maryland law, physician-assisted suicides are unlawful. This law took effect October 1, 1999. Under the law, anyone who provides the means another person uses to commit suicide could be sentenced up to one year in prison and fined $10,000. In the present case, the boy provided a .38 caliber handgun to Jennifer Garvey, 15, and she used the gun to kill herself on October 18, 1999 in a culvert in Crofton, near Annapolis. The gun had been stolen from the boy's stepfather. The couple had been dating for less than five months. Jennifer left a note to her family and friends, according to police. The note was intended to speak for both her and the 16-year-old, who had also agreed to commit suicide. It read in part, "You've kept us apart and hurt us with your insensitivity. Now we can be together." Jennifer was being treated for depression and went through with her part of the pact. But the boy changed his mind and ran to a friend's home. The charges against the 16-year-old are a highly unusual application of the assisted-suicide law, according to the Denver-based Hemlock Society, which advocates the right to die. "It's so remote from the thing we concern ourselves with that we don't know what to think about it," according to Faye Girsch, president of the Hemlock Society. "We're opposed to suicide for people who have a whole life to live. But charging the boy with the girl's death would offer little help to him or to Jennifer's family," Girsch said.

Should the 16-year-old boy be charged with murder? What amount of blame should he accept for Jennifer Garvey's death? What sort of punishment should be imposed if he is eventually found guilty of a crime? What do you think?

Source: Adapted from Seth Hettena, "Teen Accused in Assisted Suicide." *USA Today,* March 1, 2000:4A.

where a burglar alarm has been activated are likely targets for apprehension by police. The police have a right to be suspicious of these juveniles and to investigate the circumstances of their presence in the area until they are satisfied that the youths were not involved in a possible burglary.

Police discretion also influences where juveniles are taken if it is decided they should be detained. Extremely young juveniles may be taken directly to social service agencies where they can be reunited with their parents or guardians. Many juveniles may not be involved in delinquent activity, but their youthful appearance may suggest to police the need for adult supervision and/or parental involvement. Many runaways may be taken to shelters where they can be fed and clothed. Many male and female juveniles appear older than they really are. They may lie to police and give them false names, addresses, and ages. Police officers have a right to detain these juveniles until their identity can be established and/or it can be learned whether they have violated any criminal laws.

Prosecution and the Courts

When criminal suspects and others are arrested by law enforcement officers, they are usually booked. **Booking** involves obtaining descriptive information from those arrested, including their names, addresses, occupations, next of kin, photographs, and fingerprints. Booking varies in formality among jurisdictions. Essentially, the booking process is a formality as well as an account or written report of the arrest or detention. Police may consult other law enforcement agencies through a computer network to determine whether those arrested have prior records. Interested agencies such as the Bureau of Justice Statistics within the U.S. Department of Justice collect this statistical information to profile those admitted to jails and prisons.

Figure 4.1 also shows other stages of processing in the criminal justice system subsequent to the arrest and booking of suspects. Note that one early discretionary action is to divert certain offenders directly to the juvenile justice system. For adult offenders, however, they will likely move forward to the **initial appearance** stage. The initial appearance of **defendants** or those charged with crimes is before a magistrate or other court official, usually to advise defendants of the charges against them and to determine the amount of bail necessary to obtain their release. **Bail** or a **bail bond** is a surety in the form of money or property that may be posted by either a bonding company or others, including defendants themselves, to obtain their temporary release from custody and to ensure their subsequent appearance at trial.

Under the Eighth Amendment, only those entitled to bail may receive it. Bail is not an absolute right. Ordinarily, those not entitled to bail are either considered very dangerous to others or very likely to flee the jurisdiction to avoid prosecution for their crimes. Because of serious jail overcrowding problems and other considerations, bail is often waived in minor offense cases, and defendants are **released on** (their) **own recognizance (ROR)**. These persons usually have ties within the community, are employed, and are not considered dangerous or likely to flee.

During the period following a defendant's initial appearance, prosecutors, representing the states' interests, must decide whether to bring formal charges against these persons. Evidence of criminal activity collected by police officers (e.g., eye-witness reports, confessions, weapons, fingerprints) is carefully examined, and consideration is given to the seriousness of the alleged criminal activity and prior record of the defendant, if any. If defendants are represented by counsel, interactions may occur between prosecutors and defense counsels where agreements are reached known as **plea bargains.** Plea bargains are pre-conviction agreements between defendants and the state whereby defendants enter guilty pleas to certain criminal charges in exchange for some state benefit such as sentencing leniency (Conley 1994). Probably over 90 percent of all criminal convictions are secured through **plea bargaining** in most U.S. jurisdictions at both the state and federal levels. In many instances, if the cases against certain defendants are weak, prosecutors may elect to drop the charges and excuse these defendants from further processing.

Depending upon the circumstances, prosecutors may follow through with charges against defendants and take their cases to trial. Using this worst-case scenario (for the defendant), defendants who either do not plea bargain and plead not guilty will eventually be arraigned. An **arraignment** is a proceeding where (1) a list of specific charges is made available to defendants and their attorneys, (2) a formal plea to the charges is entered by the defendant, and (3) a trial date is established. Prior to being arraigned, however, those charged with especially serious crimes will be entitled to a **preliminary examination** or **preliminary hearing,** a proceeding where both the prosecutor and defense counsel may present some evidence against and on behalf of the defendant. Preliminary hearings establish whether **probable cause** exists. Probable cause is the determination or reasonable suspicion that a crime has been committed and the defendant likely committed it. These hearings are not trials and do not establish one's guilt or innocence. They are intended to determine probable cause, or whether sufficient evidence exists to proceed further.

The preliminary hearing is important also because it is an opportunity for judges and others to hear some of the evidence both in the defendant's favor and derogatory to the defendant. In some respects as Figure 4.1 specifies, this is a preliminary testing of the evidence. Two types of evidence are exculpatory and inculpatory. **Exculpatory evidence** is anything that may help show the defendant's innocence. **Inculpatory evidence** is anything that may show defendant guilt. At this stage, prosecutors sometimes decide to withdraw charges against defendants. Also at this stage, the presiding magistrate may conclude that insufficient evidence exists against the defendant to proceed any further. Thus, the criminal charges either may be dropped or dismissed outright. Figure 4.1 shows this particular phase sandwiched between the initial appearance and arraignment.

Also note in Figure 4.1 that upward and downward branches of the process following the preliminary hearing include **informations.** A brief explanation of these branches is in order. First, informations, sometimes known as **criminal informations,** are formal charges against defendants brought by prosecutors acting on their own authority. Typically, informations may be brought against any defendant for minor crimes or misdemeanors. This is reflected by the lower branch stemming from preliminary hearings. However, if the crime is a felony, this follows the upper branch.

While preliminary hearings or preliminary examinations are used in most jurisdictions for an early test of the evidence against defendants for the purpose of establishing whether probable cause exists to proceed further, about half of all states and the federal government use grand juries to bring charges against defendants charged with serious offenses. **Grand juries** are investigative bodies of citizens selected from residents of the jurisdiction. There is great variation among jurisdictions relating to the size and functions of grand juries. For example, federal grand juries consist of from 16 to 23 members and serve for 90-day or 120-day terms. Grand juries issue criminal charges against defendants known as **indictments** or **presentments.**

Indictments, also known as **true bills,** are the functional equivalent of criminal informations brought by prosecutors. Ordinarily, prosecutors present evidence to grand juries for their consideration. Defendants and their attorneys are barred from grand jury proceedings. When grand juries issue indictments, they are in effect saying, "We believe that probable cause has been established that a crime or crimes have been committed and John Doe (or the person or persons named in the indictment) probably committed the crimes." If the grand jury believes that insufficient evidence exists against defendants, they may issue **no bills** or **no true bills.** A no bill results in charges being dismissed against defendants, since probable cause that a crime was committed was not established.

The term *jury* is confusing to those unfamiliar with the criminal justice system. Because grand juries issue indictments or presentments against defendants, some persons believe immediately that those indicted must obviously be guilty of the crimes alleged, since a jury issued an indictment against them. This isn't so. Those juries charged with determining one's guilt beyond a reasonable doubt are known as **petit juries.** These petit juries, more commonly known as juries, are the citizens selected to hear evidence in trials. Thus, an important distinction exists between grand juries, who decide probable cause questions and whether further action should be taken against defendants, and petit juries, who decide the issue of guilt using the beyond a reasonable doubt standard in all criminal cases.

After a trial date is established from the point of arraignment, defendants may elect to have either **bench trials** or a **jury trials,** depending upon the seriousness of the crimes alleged. Bench trials are conducted exclusively by the judge who presides and determine's the defendant's guilt or innocence. Jury trials or trials by jury involve determinations of one's guilt or innocence by a jury of one's peers. These peers are selected by various methods from the community or jurisdiction where the trial occurs. All citizens charged with a crime are entitled to a jury trial as a matter of right under the U.S. Constitution, if the possible statutory incarcerative term accompanying the alleged offense is six months or longer (*Duncan v. Louisiana* 1968). There are some exceptions to this provision, however.

Trials are adversarial proceedings where a defendant's guilt or innocence is established. Jury trials vary in size among jurisdictions. In some states, for instance, juries may consist of six jurors. Traditionally, jury size in the majority of states and in federal district courts in criminal trials is twelve jurors. In these jury trials, if jurors cannot agree on a verdict, the jury is considered deadlocked or hung, and a **mistrial** is declared. Most jurisdictions require that juries must be unanimous, regardless of their finding. However, in a few states such as Louisiana and Oregon where jury size is twelve, majority verdicts of 9–3 or 10–2 are permitted (*Johnson v. Louisiana* 1972; *Apodaca v. Oregon* 1972).

When defendants are convicted of one or more crimes, their punishment is imposed in a **sentencing hearing.** Criminal court judges consider all circumstances and information available, and on the basis of their experience and judgment, together with statutory provisions mandated by legislatures, they impose sentences. Sentences do not necessarily involve incarceration (Brumbaugh and Birkbeck 1999). In many states, judges are permitted wide latitude in the sentences they impose on convicted offenders. Judges consider factors such as one's leadership role in the crime and whether physical injuries were inflicted on victims during the crime's commission. These circumstances are **aggravating circumstances** because they intensify the punishment convicted offenders receive. Other factors are considered, including whether offenders furnished helpful information to police that enabled them to apprehend others connected with the crime. An offender's youthfulness would be considered as well. Whether offenders were mentally ill when they committed their crimes would also be important. These factors are considered **mitigating circumstances** because they often result in less severe sentences imposed by judges.

Because of serious prison and jail overcrowding problems in most jurisdictions, however, judges often impose **probation** as a punishment. Probation is a conditional nonincarcerative sentence, where the offender is under the management of probation department personnel or probation officers. Probation is most often used for first offenders who have been convicted of minor crimes. However, evidence of its growing use in the United States annually for more serious crimes (e.g., felony probation) is well documented (Champion 2002). Regardless of whether convicted offenders receive probation or a sentence involving incarceration for designated terms, offenders move to the final component of the criminal justice process—corrections.

Corrections

Corrections consists of all agencies and personnel who deal with convicted offenders after court proceedings. As noted earlier, some convicted offenders may receive probation, or conditional sentences in lieu of incarceration. Other offenders may be confined in jails or prisons, again depending upon the seriousness of their offenses, the jurisdiction where the conviction occurred, and the availability of jail or prison space. In 2001 there were 1,965,495 inmates in jails and prisons in the United States (Beck, Karberg, and Harrison 2002, 1).

Jails are short-term facilities and locally operated by city or county governments. A few jails are state-operated. Most jail functions include but are not limited to detaining those arrested for various offenses and who are awaiting trial, maintaining witnesses in protective custody pending their testimony in court, providing confinement for short-term, petty offenders serving sentences of less than 1 year, and accommodating overflow from state or federal prisons in instances where chronic prison overcrowding exists. Jails are not usually designed for long-term confinement of prisoners. They have few, if any, recreational facilities and few services.

Prisons are long-term facilities. Most prisons have recreational yards, hospitals, work programs, and a host of other facilities to accommodate inmates who are confined for lengthy periods. Prisons are usually reserved for more serious offenders who have received incarcerative sentences of 1 year or longer from judges. In many jurisdictions, inmates of prisons and jails may be released short of serving their full sentences. This is usually accomplished through **parole.** Parole is a conditional release from incarceration for a designated duration, usually the remainder of one's original sentence. A **parole board** determines an inmate's parole eligibility and whether early release from prison will be granted.

BOX 4.2

AN EXAMPLE OF TEENAGE VIOLENCE

David Daniel Dodge, Everett, Washington

It happened in Everett, Washington. David Daniel Dodge, 17, set out to burglarize a neighbor's house. When he entered, he didn't hear any noises at first. When he heard noises, he fled the house and into the woods, where he obtained a large stick of wood. Then he returned to the house. Subsequently he was discovered by the 12-year-old female babysitter. The girl, Ashley Jones, was babysitting five children for a family. When Dodge was discovered by Jones, he struck her repeatedly with the wood. He carried Jones to the basement and raped her, as one of the children slept on a nearby couch. Then he left her for dead. Her body was discovered about 2:00 A.M. the next morning by the returning family. They called police, who investigated. Jones was taken to the hospital in critical condition. She died shortly thereafter from her head wounds. Dodge was subsequently arrested when it was discovered that he had run away from a juvenile halfway house in the neighborhood. He had a history of minor crimes but no record of violence, according to investigating officials. He was charged with murder, rape, and three counts of burglary and was scheduled to be tried as an adult.

Is there necessarily anything to the idea that minor property offenders eventually escalate to violent crimes, such as the one committed by Dodge? Is this necessarily a statement about the ineffectiveness of halfway houses for juveniles, or do you believe that this is an exception? What do you think?

Source: Adapted from the Associated Press, "Boy Charged in Sitter's Death." September 25, 1997.

There are many correctional options available for judges to impose besides probation and incarceration. A vast array of **intermediate punishments** exists. Intermediate punishments are sanctions that exist somewhere between incarceration and probation on the continuum of criminal penalties. Intermediate punishments might include electronic monitoring, house arrest or home confinement, or community-based correctional alternatives such as halfway houses or intensive supervised probation or parole. Many of these options are available to juvenile as well as adult offenders.

The remainder of this chapter examines the juvenile justice system and provides an overview of how juveniles are processed by it. Later chapters provide more detailed coverage of each of these stages. We will begin this discussion at the point where youths have been arrested or taken into custody by law enforcement officers or others.

AN OVERVIEW OF THE JUVENILE JUSTICE SYSTEM

The Ambiguity of Adolescence and Adulthood

Police have broad discretionary powers in their encounters with the public and dealing with street crime. Although some evidence suggests that police have shifted their policing priorities away from juveniles toward more serious adult offenders for various reasons (e.g., cases against juveniles are often dismissed or judges issue nothing more than verbal warnings to them and return them to the custody of their parents), police arrests and detentions of juveniles in local jails remain the major conduit of a juvenile's entry into the juvenile justice system.

Many juveniles are clearly juveniles. It is difficult to find youths age 13 or under who physically appear 18 or older. Yet, nearly 10 percent of all juveniles held for brief periods in adult jails annually are 13 years old or younger (Gilliard and Beck 1998). For juveniles in the 14 to 17 age range, visual determination of one's juvenile or nonjuvenile status is increasingly difficult. Thus, at least some justification exists for why police officers take many youthful offenders to jails initially for identification and questioning. Furthermore, the U.S. Supreme Court has condoned jailing juveniles under **preventive detention** in the case of *Schall v. Martin* (1984). In this particular case, a juvenile was detained by police on serious charges. He refused to give his name or other identification and was deemed by those in charge to be dangerous, either to himself or to others. His preventive detention was upheld by the U.S. Supreme Court as not violating his constitutional right to due process. Prior to this Supreme Court ruling, however, many states had similar laws that permitted both pretrial and preventive detention of suspects. Although **pretrial detention** presupposes a forthcoming trial of those detained and preventive detention does not, both terms are often used interchangeably or even combined, as in preventive pretrial detention (Alexander 2000).

Other ways that juveniles can enter the juvenile justice system include referrals from or complaints by parents, neighbors, victims, and others (social work staff, probation officers) unrelated to law enforcement. Dependent or neglected children may be reported to police initially. Following up on these complaints, police officers may take youths into custody until arrangements for their care can be made. Or police officers may arrest youths for alleged crimes.

Being Taken into Custody and Being Arrested

Being **taken into custody** and being arrested are different procedures. For law enforcement officers, whenever youths are taken into custody, they are not necessarily arrested, and they may not necessarily be arrested later. Being taken into custody means precisely what it says. Officers take certain youths into custody as a protective measure so that they can determine what is best for the juvenile. Some youths who are taken into custody might be those suffering from child sexual abuse or physical abuse inflicted by parents or others, runaways, or missing children. Youths wandering the streets may also be taken into custody by police if they are suspected of being truant from school.

When youths are arrested, this is more serious police action. An arrest means that the juvenile is suspected of committing a crime. Charges may be filed against arrested youths once it is determined who should have jurisdiction over them. Police authorities may determine that the juvenile court has jurisdiction, depending on the age or youthfulness of the offender. Or authorities may decide that the criminal court has jurisdiction and the youthful-appearing offender should be charged as an adult (Alexander 2000).

Juveniles in Jails

In 2001, there were 7,613 juveniles under the age of 18 being held in jails (Beck, Karberg, and Harrison 2002, 14). About 89 percent of these juveniles were being held as adults. This represents about 1 percent of all jail inmates held in jails for 2001. This figure is misleading, however. It does not reflect the total number of juveniles who are brought to jails annually after they have been arrested or taken into custody by police. Many youths are jailed for short time periods, merely on suspicion, even though they haven't committed any obvious offenses. Short time periods are often two or three hours. Some states, such as Illinois, have passed laws preventing police officers from detaining juveniles in adult jails for more than six hours. Such laws reflect the **jail removal initiative,** whereby states are encouraged not to house juveniles in adult jails, even for short periods (Ziedenberg and Schiraldi 1998). Despite the passage of new laws to minimize or eliminate holding juveniles in adult **jails** or **lockups,** even for short periods, juveniles continue to be held in jails for short time periods. If 1 percent of the 11 million admissions and releases to jails annually are juveniles, then a good estimate would be that at least 100,000 or more juveniles spend at least some time in jails annually, if only to determine their identity and release them into the custody of their parents or guardians after a few hours (Beck, Karberg, and Harrison 2002).

Referrals

Figure 4.2 is a diagram of the juvenile justice system. Although each jurisdiction in the United States has its own methods for processing juvenile offenders, Figure 4.2 is sufficiently general to encompass most of these processing methods. Focusing on the diagram in Figure 4.2, a majority of juvenile encounters with the juvenile justice system are through **referrals** from police officers (Butts, 1996a). Referrals are notifications made to juvenile court authorities that a juvenile requires the court's attention. Referrals may be made by anyone, such as concerned parents, school principals, teachers, neighbors and others. However, over 90 percent of all referrals to juvenile court are made by law enforcement officers. These referrals may be made for runaways; truants; curfew violators; unmanageable, unsupervised, or incorrigible children; children with drug or alcohol problems; or any youth suspected of committing a crime.

Each jurisdiction throughout the United States has its own policies relating to how referrals are handled. In Figure 4.2, following a police officer investigation, juveniles are either counseled and released to parents, referred to community resources, cited and referred to juvenile intake, followed by a subsequent release to parents; or transported to juvenile hall or shelter for further detention. Each of these actions is the result of police discretion. The nature of the discretionary action of police officers who take youths into custody for any reason is governed by what these officers have observed. If a youth has been loitering, especially in cities with curfew laws for juveniles, then the discretion of police officers might be to counsel the youth and turn him or her over to his or her parents without further action. In more than a few cases, youths are taken into custody, and parents or guardians for these youths cannot be found. In these cases, police officers turn the youths over to community resources for further action.

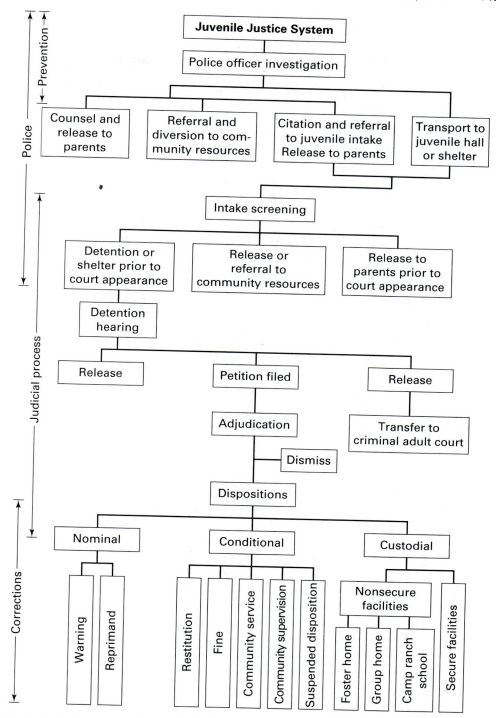

FIGURE 4.2   The Juvenile Justice System
Source: From the National Advisory Committee on Criminal Justice Standards and Goals, *Juvenile Justice and Delinquency Prevention* (Washington, D.C.: U.S. Government Priniting Office, 1967), p.9.

Subsequently, most of these youths are returned to the custody of their parents or guardians. However, some youths are apprehended while committing serious crimes. Police officers will likely transport these youths to a juvenile hall or shelter to await further action by juvenile justice system personnel.

 **BOX 4.3**

Luis A. Maldonado
Laredo Police Department (formerly School Resource Officer)

Statistics:

Texas A & M University–Kingsville; South Texas Regional Police Academy, Del Mar College; National Association of School Resource Officers (NASRO); Advanced Certification Training; S.W.A.T. Team Member

Background:

Presently, I hold the position of patrolman with the Laredo, Texas, Police Department. I have been privileged to be working in this department for the past six years. I am currently awaiting a promotion to investigator now that I have passed all test requirements for this position. I have been assigned to the School Resource Officer (SRO) program for the last four years. Prior to my employment with the Laredo Police Department, I was a sheriff's deputy with the Kleberg County Sheriff's Office in Kingsville, Texas, for about 1 1/2 years.

I've lived most of my life in Laredo. My mother, a long-time school teacher, has done a great job of rearing six kids. My oldest sister is also a teacher. Coincidentally, my older brother is also a police officer with the Laredo Police Department. And of the three remaining sisters, I am proud to say that one is a Time-Warner Communications representative, another is a college student in California, and the youngest is currently attending college at Texas A & M International University on a full scholarship.

I have always known that I wanted to do something in law enforcement since a young age. My mother used to tell me stories of how I was so fascinated by the police cars as they raced by with their bright lights and screaming sirens. Interestingly enough, I did not even look into actually taking my first steps toward the law enforcement world until I was ready for college. While in college, I had a friend who was a police officer with the Kingsville, Texas, Police Department. He invited me to come on my first

ride-along so that I could see if police work was for me. I knew instantly that I was looking into my future. I was captivated by the sounds of the police radio. My mind was never so alert as when we were out on the streets responding to emergency calls. I'm quite sure that I logged more hours in the ride-along program than I did at my part-time job in an arcade. After a few months of trying, I was able to get the Kleberg County Sheriff's Office to sponsor me into the Del Mar Regional Police Academy. In order to secure the only full-time position available at the time with the department, I had to graduate at the top of the class. After a year and a half, I left Kingsville and was fortunate enough to join the Laredo Police Department. I have been enjoying every minute of it ever since.

Interesting Experiences:

In the past few years as a school resource officer, I have encountered some very interesting situations and conditions. Police work out in the street as compared with police work on a school campus can be somewhat more challenging at times. On the street, cops can usually count on the fact that a majority of their calls will be handled on the spot with virtually no interference or influence. For example, an officer who encounters a person found to be in possession of an illegal substance, such as marijuana, would usually arrest and book the person without delay. As a School Resource Officer (SRO), you can encounter a few more obstacles for many reasons. In a school setting, an officer will deal with both juveniles and adults. In

Texas, an adult is any person over the age of 17. And so basically half of the student body is classified as adult and the other half as juvenile. An adult student arrested on campus can usually be taken into custody without having to involve the parents immediately. Even though the parents are called and advised of the situation, it is not a priority when the person is taken into custody. On the other hand, when a juvenile student is arrested on campus, it is advised that you first inform the school administration of the crime committed and its severity. Then, every effort should be made to contact the juvenile's parents or legal guardians. As a SRO, you must understand that the arrest of a person on a school campus affects and involves teachers, administrators, and parents all at once.

As a police officer, I have learned a lot about the human condition. After time, some police officers say that they develop an understanding as to why people commit crimes. Some say that they can even sense when a person is lying or trying to cover up a long-kept secret. I didn't really understand what they were really saying until my first year as an SRO. During my first year, I was assigned to a high school in West Laredo. West Laredo could be characterized as a middle- to low-income area. In this high school, I had several students whom I dealt with almost on a daily basis. One young man in particular, whom I will call "Bird," just could not seem to stay out of trouble. If he wasn't skipping class, he was stealing something. If he wasn't disrupting his class, he was sleeping in it. I could see that he was not an aggressive young man. But it did seem that he had a lot deeper issues than just laziness. One day I decided to pay Bird a visit at his home. He lived not far from the campus. As I arrived at Bird's house (no pun intended), I could see that it was not exactly the nicest house in the neighborhood. In fact, it was dilapidated and run down. I approached the door and knocked several times. Bird's dad greeted me. The father explained that he was the only parent in the home and that he had a hard time controlling Bird's behavior. Bird's mother had left some time ago. Then man invited me into the home. He then explained that he was not working but that he was receiving money from workman's compensation. I could not help but notice that he was intoxicated. It was not even noon yet, for crying out loud! The living conditions were substandard, in my opinion. It was then that I realized why Bird did some of the things that he did. What reasons would Bird (or someone like Bird) have not to join a gang? A gang could offer him friendship, protection, and even financial opportunities. Bird made claims that he sold drugs because he needed money to purchase his own clothing and food. He would assist his fellow gang members in the assaults of other persons in order stay in their good graces. In Bird's mind, he had nothing to lose and everything to gain. Even though we may know this to be false, it is nonetheless his reality. Once I began to understand this, I was better able to relate to these young people on a different level than before.

Advice to Students:

As students, you stand at the doors that lead down many roads. You must never forget that education is the key that opens many of these doors. If you are serious about pursuing a career in law enforcement, I would suggest visiting your police department and finding out if it has a ride-along program. This is usually the best way to become familiar with some aspects of police work without taking a risk you may later regret. Personally, not a day goes by that I don't thank God for looking after me and giving me the opportunity to be a police officer.

In New Mexico, for example, whenever a juvenile is referred to the juvenile justice system for any offense, the referral is first screened by the Juvenile Probation/Parole Office. Juvenile probation/parole officers (JPPOs) are assigned to initially screen a police report and file. This screening is performed, in part, to determine the accuracy of the report and if the information is correct. If the information is correct, then an intake process will commence, where the youth

Teens may be referred to counseling in lieu of formal juvenile court processing.

undergoes further screening by a JJPO assigned to the case by a supervisor (New Mexico Juvenile Justice Division 2002). Figure 4.3 is a decision tree for the New Mexico Juvenile Justice Division and provides us with an overview of how its processing of juvenile offenders works.

Figure 4.3 shows that once a referral has been made to the Juvenile Probation/Parole Office, a decision is made whether to file **petitions** or to handle the case informally. About 50 percent of all juvenile cases are handled informally. Petitions are official documents filed in juvenile courts on the juvenile's behalf, specifying reasons for the youth's court appearance. These documents assert that juveniles fall within the categories of dependent or neglected, status offender, or delinquent, and the reasons for such assertions are usually provided. Filing a petition formally places the juvenile before the juvenile court judge in many jurisdictions. But juveniles may come before juvenile court judges in less formal ways. About 45 percent of the cases brought before the juvenile court each year are nonpetitioned cases. Less than 1 percent of these cases result in out-of-home placements, 30 percent receive probation, 50 percent are dismissed, and the remainder are diverted, downgraded, or result in verbal warnings (Bilchik 1998; Butts and Snyder 1997).

When individual cases are handled informally, JPPOs in New Mexico jurisdictions have several options. Whenever youths are determined to require special care, are needy or dependent, or are otherwise unsupervised by adults or guardians, JPPOs may refer them to a Juvenile Early Intervention Program (JEIP). The JEIP is a highly structured program for at risk, nonadjudicated youths. Figure 4.4 shows a referral form used by New Mexico JPPOs to refer youths into this early intervention program.

Juveniles referred to the program will have been assessed to need services and/or supervision due to the nature of their current offense or situation, as well as their propensity for future misconduct as determined from a preliminary inquiry by the JPPO. The target group for the JEIP ranges in age from 10 to 12 at the time of the allegation against them. Status offenders, including truants, runaways, or curfew violators, may be referred to the JEIP. Both the juve-

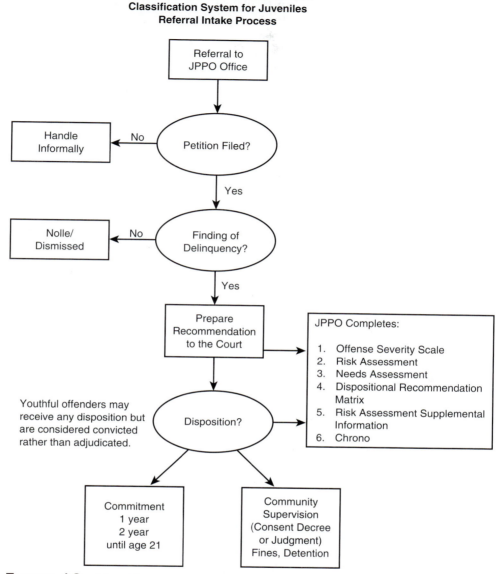

FIGURE 4.3   New Mexico Juvenile Justice Division Classification System for Juveniles Referral Intake Process

nile and his or her family must agree to participate in the JEIP and to follow through with recommendations for additional services. The JEIP consists of eight weekly sessions, including an overall presentation of the program and expectations, choices, self-esteem including a parent's group, peer pressure, gangs, drug and alcohol issues with parents included, feelings, and a final session that includes a review and graduation ceremony. Following completion of the program, a 30-day follow-up is conducted by JPPOs.

Depending upon the jurisdiction, however, the majority of alleged juvenile delinquents will be advanced further into the juvenile justice system. Some status offenders, especially recidivists, will also move further into the system. Some youths may be maintained in juvenile detention facilities temporarily to

REFERRAL FORM

Date: _____ File #: _____ Cause # (if appl.): _____

Client's Name: _____ DOB: _____ Age: _____

Address: _____ Zip: _____ Phone #: _____

Ethnicity: _____ Gender: _____ SS#: _____

Referral Source: _____ Primary Language Spoken: _____

Guardian's Name: _____ Relationship: _____

Guardian's Legal Status: _____

Current Offense: _____

School: _____ Grade: _____ Reg. Ed. _____ Special Ed. _____

Client's Mental Health Issues (meds, if any): _____

_____

_____

_____

Guardian's Mental Health Issues (meds, if any): _____

_____

_____

_____

Directions to client's residence:

FIGURE 4.4 Referral form used by New Mexico JPPOs to refer youths into an early intervention program

await further action. Other youths may be released to their parent's custody, but these youths may be required to reappear later to face further action. Most of these youths will subsequently be interviewed by an **intake officer** in a proceeding known as **intake.**

Intake

Intake varies in formality among jurisdictions (Glaser et al. 2001). Intake is a **screening** procedure usually conducted by a juvenile probation officer where one or several courses of action are recommended. Some jurisdictions conduct **intake hearings** or **intake screenings** where comments and opinions are solicited from significant others such as the police, parents, neighbors, or victims. In other jurisdictions, intake proceedings are quite informal, usually consisting of a dialogue between the juvenile and the intake officer. These are important proceedings, regardless of their degree of formality. Intake is a major screening stage in the juvenile justice process where further action against juveniles may be contemplated or required. Intake officers hear complaints against juveniles and informally resolve the least serious cases, or they are more often juvenile probation officers who perform intake as a special assignment. In many small jurisdictions, juvenile probation officers may perform diverse functions, including intake, enforcement of truancy statutes, and juvenile placements (Castellano and Ferguson 1998).

Intake officers also consider youths' attitudes, demeanor, age, offense seriousness, and a host of other factors. Has the juvenile had frequent prior contact with the juvenile justice system? If the offenses alleged are serious, what evidence exists against the offender? Should the offender be referred to certain community social service agencies, receive psychological counseling, receive vocational counseling and guidance, acquire educational or technical training and skills, be issued a verbal reprimand, be placed on some type of diversionary status, or be returned to parental custody? Interviews with parents and neighbors may be conducted as a part of an intake officer's information gathering (Florida Department of Juvenile Justice 2000).

In most jurisdictions, intake results in one of five actions, depending upon the discretion of intake officers: (1) dismissal of the case, with or without a verbal or written reprimand; (2) remand youths to the custody of their parents; (3) remand youths to the custody of their parents, with provisions for or referrals to counseling or special services; (4) divert youths to an alternative dispute resolution program, if one exists in the jurisdiction; (5) refer youths to the juvenile prosecutor for further action and possible filing of a delinquency petition. Many observers including juvenile court judges regard the intake process as a key opportunity to impose punishments, prescribe treatments, and issue threats or verbal warnings (Hodges and Kim 2000).

Returning to an examination of Figure 4.2, following an intake screening, some of the options available to intake officers noted above are indicated. Theoretically, at least, only the most serious juveniles will be referred to detention to await a subsequent juvenile court appearance. In order for a youth to be detained while awaiting a juvenile court appearance, a detention hearing is usually conducted. Most of the time, youths considered for such detention are either a danger to themselves or to others or they are likely to flee the jurisdiction to avoid prosecution in juvenile court. Others may be released to the custody of their parents or they may be referred to one or more community resources. Usually, these community resources are intended to meet the specific needs of particular juvenile offenders. Or the intake officer may release the juvenile to his or her parents prior to a subsequent juvenile court appearance. For serious cases, a petition is filed with the juvenile court. The juvenile court prosecutor further screens these petitions and decides which ones merit an appearance before the juvenile court judge. In Alaska, for example, a petition for adjudication of delinquency is used to bring delinquency cases before the juvenile court. An illustration of such a petition is shown in Figure 4.5.

Notice in Figure 4.5 that allegations are made concerning the delinquent acts committed by the juvenile. Furthermore, supporting information accompanies the petition that presumably establishes probable cause and supports the facts alleged. The petitioner signs the petition under oath and avers that the statements made are true. Their occupation and relationship with the juvenile are also included, as well as their telephone number and address. It is up to the prosecutor to determine whether action should be taken on petitions filed. Figure 4.5 alleges delinquency, or one or more crimes committed by the named juvenile. Other petitions may allege status offending, such as truancy, runaway behavior, curfew violation, or violation of drug or liquor laws. These petitions are similar in form to Figure 4.5. Delinquency petitions throughout most U.S.

In the matter of:)
)
)   CASE NO. _____CP
)
A minor under 18 years of age   )
Date of Birth: _____)

PETITION FOR ADJUDICATION OF DELINQUENCY

The petitioner requests that the above-named juvenile be adjudicated as a delinquent under A.S 47.12.020 and that an appropriate disposition be entered.

The petitioner alleges that:

Probable cause supporting the above allegation(s) is that:

The juvenile's address is _____.

The juvenile's father is: _____, whose address is

_____.

The juvenile's mother is: _____, whose address is

_____.

The juvenile's guardian/custodian/grandmother is _____, whose address is

_____.

06-9541 (Rev. 10/97) YC   PETITION FOR ADJUDICATION OF DELINQUENCY

2.b.1

FIGURE 4.5 Alaskan petition for adjudication of delinquency

<u>In the Matter of:</u> _____ Case No._____

Petitioner swears or affirms upon information and belief to the above statements.

_____
          Date

                                  _____
                                  PETITIONER (signature)

                                  _____
                                  PRINT NAME AND OCCUPATION/RELATIONSHIP

                                  _____
                                  ADDRESS AND PHONE NUMBER

SUBSCRIBED AND SWORN TO before me on _____.
                                                       Date

      (SEAL)   _____
                                        CLERK/NOTARY PUBLIC

                               My Commission Expires:_____

CERTIFICATE OF SERVICE
I certify that on <u>July 21,</u>_____
a copy of this document was sent
to: _____

By:_____Notary

06-9541   (Rev. 10/97) YC   PETITION FOR ADJUDICATION OF DELINQUENCY
                                                   2.b.2

FIGURE 4.5 (CONTINUED)

jurisdictions resemble the Alaska delinquency petition. Regarding petitions filed with the juvenile court, not all petitions result in formal action by a juvenile court prosecutor. Like prosecutors in criminal court, juvenile court prosecutors prioritize cases they will prosecute. Such case prioritizing depends upon the volume of petitions filed, the time estimated for the juvenile court judge to hear and act on these petitions, the sufficiency of evidence supporting these petitions, as well as an array of other factors (Young 1999).

Alternative Prosecutorial Actions

Cases referred to juvenile prosecutors for further action are usually, though not always, more serious cases. Exceptions might include those youths who are chronic recidivists or technical program violators and nonviolent property offenders (e.g., status offenders, vandalism, petty theft, public order offenders).

Juvenile court prosecutors have broad discretionary powers. They may cease prosecutions against alleged offenders or downgrade the offenses alleged from felonies to misdemeanors or from misdemeanors to status offenses. Much depends upon the docket load or case activity of their own juvenile courts. In some instances, prosecutors may divert some of the more serious juvenile cases for processing by criminal courts. The least serious cases are disposed informally. Prosecutors either file petitions or act on petitions filed by others, such as intake officers, the police, school officials, or interested family and citizens.

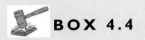 **BOX 4.4**

TEEN DRAWS EIGHT MONTHS FOR SHOOTING FIVE AT MIDDLE SCHOOL

Seth Trickey, 13-Year-Old Shooter

On December 6, 1999, a 13-year-old student, Seth Trickey, opened fire on a crowd of students at Fort Gibson Middle School in Muskogee, Oklahoma. Five students were wounded in the shooting, and Seth Trickey was captured by school officials. Prosecutors attempted to have Trickey certified as an adult under Oklahoma law in order for him to be tried in criminal court for his crimes. Prosecutors were unsuccessful in this regard, and Trickey's case was heard in juvenile court. In May 2000, Trickey was ordered by the juvenile court judge to be placed for a period of eight months in the Lloyd E. Rader Children's Center, a juvenile treatment center, in Sand Springs. According to Danita Engleman, the assistant district attorney, "In the juvenile justice system, this is not like a sentence. Some children go through the program in as little as eight months." If Trickey had been convicted as an adult, he could have been sentenced to life in prison.

Should 13-year-olds be tried as adults when they commit murder or attempted murder? Is an eight-month period in a treatment facility sufficient punishment for attempting to kill five people? Should the juvenile justice system be tougher on violent offenders such as Seth Trickey? What do you think?

Source: Adapted from the Associated Press. "Teen to Stay in Juvenile Center." May 29, 2000.

ADJUDICATORY PROCEEDINGS

Jurisdictions vary considerably concerning their juvenile court proceedings. Increasingly, juvenile courts are emulating criminal courts in many respects. Most of the physical trappings of criminal courts are present, including the judge's bench, tables for the prosecution and defense, and a witness stand. Further, there appears widespread interest in holding juveniles more accountable for their actions than was the case in past years (DiCataldo and Grisso 1995).

Besides the more formal atmosphere of juvenile courts, the procedure is becoming increasingly adversarial, where prosecutors and defense attorneys do battle against and on behalf of juveniles charged with various offenses. However, less than 50 percent of the juvenile offenders in jurisdictions such as Minnesota have the assistance of counsel, although they are entitled to counsel (Feld 1995). Both alleged status offenders and those charged with crimes are entitled to be represented by counsel in their court cases. In most jurisdictions, juvenile court judges have almost absolute discretion in how their courts are conducted. Juvenile defendants alleged to have committed various crimes may or may not be granted a trial by jury if they request one. In 1999 only 11 states provided jury trials for juveniles in juvenile courts, and these jury trials were restricted to a narrow list of serious offenses.

After hearing the evidence presented by both sides in any juvenile proceeding, the judge decides or adjudicates the matter in an **adjudication hearing,** sometimes called an **adjudicatory hearing.** An **adjudication** is a judgment or action on the petition filed with the court by others. If the petition alleges delinquency on the part of certain juveniles, the judge determines whether the juveniles are delinquent or not delinquent. If the petition alleges that the juveniles involved are dependent, neglected, or otherwise in need of care by agencies or others, the judge decides the matter. If the adjudicatory hearing fails to yield supporting facts for the petition filed, then the case is dismissed and the youth exits the juvenile justice system. If the adjudicatory hearing supports the allegations in the petition, then the judge must **dispose** the juvenile according to a range of punishments. An example of an adjudication form where action is taken by the juvenile court judge on facts alleged in a delinquency petition is illustrated in Figure 4.6.

In Figure 4.6, the adjudication form shows that a petition was filed with the court on a particular date, an adjudicatory hearing was conducted, and particular findings and conclusions are indicated. Notice in Figure 4.6 that juveniles may be adjudicated delinquent by the court, or they may be found in violation of one or more conditions of their probation, if they were originally disposed to probation by the juvenile court judge. This is because, like adult proceedings in criminal court, juvenile court judges retain jurisdiction over juveniles whenever they are placed on probation.

JUVENILE DISPOSITIONS

Disposing juveniles is the equivalent of sentencing adult offenders. When adult offenders are convicted of crimes, they are sentenced. When juveniles are adjudicated delinquent, they are disposed. At least twelve **dispositions** or

IN THE SUPERIOR COURT FOR THE STATE OF ALASKA
AT _____

In the Matter of:)
)
)
)
)   CASE NO. _____CP
A minor under 18 years of age.   )
)   ADJUDICATION UPON ADMISSION
Date of birth: _____   )

A petition was filed on _____ , 20 _____ , alleging that the
above-named juvenile is:

☐   a delinquent juvenile.

☐   a delinquent juvenile who has violated the conditions of his (probation) / (deferred
     institutional order) / (conduct agreement).

An adjudication hearing was held on the above petition on _____.
20 ____ Present were:

The court has considered the allegation in the petition and evidence presented and makes the
following FINDINGS AND CONCLUSIONS:

1.   The court has jurisdiction over the parties and the subject matter of the proceedings.

2.   The child has knowingly and voluntarily admitted pursuant to Delinquency
      Rule 14(b)(4) that :

      ☐   all allegations in the petition are true.

      ☐   the following allegations in the petition are true:

THEREFORE, IT IS ADJUDGED that the above-named juvenile is:

☐   a delinquent juvenile.

☐   a delinquent juvenile who has violated the conditions of his (probation) / (deferred
     institutional order) / (conduct agreement).

Recommended on _____   Effective Date: _____

_____   _____   _____
      Superior Court Master   Superior Court Judge   Date

                                          _____
                                               Type or Print Name

I certify that on _____
a copy of this adjudication was sent to:
      DHSS, Juvenile/Attorney, Parent/Guardian, Other: _____

Clerk: _____

CP-230 (5/88) (st.5)   Del.R. 14(b) (4)
ADJUDICATION UPON ADMISSION   AS 47.10.010

FIGURE 4.6   An example of an adjudication form where action is taken by the juvenile
court judge

punishments are available to juvenile court judges, if the facts alleged in petitions are upheld (Lansing 1999). These dispositions are: (1) nominal, (2) conditional, or (3) custodial options.

Nominal Dispositions

Nominal dispositions are either verbal warnings or stern reprimands and are the least punitive dispositional options. The nature of such verbal warnings or reprimands is a matter of judicial discretion. Release to the custody of parents or legal guardians completes the juvenile court action against the youth. Usually, nominal dispositions are most often applied to low-risk first offenders who are the least likely to recidivate and commit new offenses. The emphasis of nominal dispositions is upon rehabilitation and fostering a continuing positive, reintegrative relationship between the juvenile and his or her community (Altschuler and Armstrong 2001).

Conditional Dispositions

All **conditional dispositions** are probationary options. The most frequently imposed disposition is probation. Youths are placed on probation and required to comply with certain conditions during a probationary period lasting from several months to several years. Conditional dispositions usually require offenders to do something as a condition of probation. The nature of the conditions to be fulfilled depends on the needs of the offender and the nature of the offense committed. If youths have alcohol or drug dependencies, they may be required to undergo individual or group counseling and some type of therapy to cope with substance abuse. Sex offenders may be required to undergo psychological counseling and clinical evaluation (Hindman and Peters 2001).

Property offenders may be required to make restitution to victims or to compensate the court in some way for the damage they have caused. In a growing number of jurisdictions, **restorative justice** is practiced, where offenders and their victims are brought together for the purpose of mediation. Youths learn to accept responsibility for what they have done, and their accountability is heightened (Guarino-Ghezzi 1998). In Maryland, the Juvenile Causes Act has been revised with an emphasis upon balanced, restorative, and victim-centered justice. The aim of this legislation is to (1) promote public safety and the protection of the community, (2) heighten accountability of youths toward victims and the community for offenses committed, and (3) increase competency and improve character development to assist youths in becoming responsible and productive members of society (Simms 1998, 94).

Offenders with behavioral disorders may require more intensive supervision while on probation. Those considered high risks for recidivism may be required to undergo electronic monitoring and house arrest as a part of their supervision by juvenile probation officers. These and other similar control strategies are a part of the growing area of community corrections and intermediate punishments where greater emphasis is upon community reintegration and rehabilitation (Ardovini and Walker 2000). During the 1990s there has been a gradual intensification of punishments for juveniles, including probation dispositions. This emphasis on punishment is a reflection of state legislatures' tougher stance toward juveniles. Figure 4.7 is a conduct agreement form used

IN THE SUPERIOR COURT FOR THE STATE OF ALASKA
_____ JUDICIAL DISTRICT AT _____

In the Matter of:)
)
)   CASE NO. _____ CP
)
A minor under 18 years of age   )   ☐ **CONDUCT AGREEMENT**
Date of Birth: _____   )   ☐ **CONDITIONS OF PROBATION**
                                                          OR DEFERRED INSTITUTIONAL
                                                          PLACEMENT

1. I will obey all municipal, state and federal laws.

2. I will remain in the placement designated by my Probation/Intake Officer and obey the curfew hours set by my parents, guardian, custodian or Probation/Intake Officer.

3. I will notify my Probation/Intake Officer prior to changing my residence, employment or school.

4. I will obey the rules and instructions set forth by my parents, guardian, custodian, and Probation/Intake Officer.

5. I will attend school or vocational training when in session and conduct myself in accordance with school policy; otherwise, I will maintain steady employment.

6. I will report as directed to my Probation/Intake Officer.

7. I will appear at all scheduled court hearings.

8. I will not ingest illegal drugs or alcohol, and will submit to random urinalysis as requested.

9. I will not possess, have in my custody, handle, purchase or transport any firearm, knife, club or other type of weapon, ammunition or explosives. I will not carry any weapon on my person including pocket knives.

10. I will obey the following additional conditions: _____

_____

_____

_____

_____

_____

_____

Page 1 of 2   Del.R. 12(c), 23 & 24
06-9555 (10/97) YC   AS 47.12.120
CONDUCT AGREEMENT/CONDITIONS OF PROBATION
                                                       3.q.1

FIGURE 4.7   Conduct agreement form

In the Matter of: _____   Case No. _____ CP

I (have read)(have had read to me) and understand these conditions. I agree to obey them and understand that any violation may result in my being detained or having my probation revoked.

_____   _____   _____   _____
Probation/Intake Officer   Date   Juvenile   Date

We have read and understand these conditions. We agree to require the juvenile to obey them and to report any violations. We understand that if we fail to report a violation which is known to us, action may be taken against us in court. We further understand that any violation by the juvenile may result in his/her detention. We agree to bring the juvenile before the court when directed.

_____   _____
Parent/Guardian/Custodian   Date

ORDER

The above juvenile is hereby released under the terms and conditions agreed to in this document.

Recommended on_____   Effective Date: _____
                          Date

_____   _____   _____
Superior Court Master   Superior Court Judge   Date

                                          _____
                                          Type or Print Name

I certify that on_____
a copy of this document was sent to:

    DHSS
    Juvenile/Attorney
    Parent/Guardian
    Placement Facility
    Other:_____

Clerk: _____

Page 2 of 2
06-9555 (10/97) YC
CONDUCT AGREEMENT/CONDITIONS OF PROBATION

Del.R. 12(c), 23 & 24
AS 47.12.120
3.q.2

FIGURE 4.7 (CONTINUED)

 **BOX 4.5**

A CAREER OF VIOLENCE

Drifter Tommy Lynn Sells, 35: Career of Violence Starts at Age 13

It happened on New Year's eve, December 31, 1999 in Del Rio, Texas. A man slipped into a home through a window and went in search of someone to kill. He found two girls sleeping in one of the bedrooms. With a boning knife, he slit their throats, killing 13-year-old Kaylene Harris almost instantly. The other girl, Krystal Surles, 10 years old, lay bleeding and still, but nevertheless alive. The attacker left the home shortly thereafter. Krystal got up out of bed and ran a quarter of a mile to another home to report the murder. She was bleeding profusely through her throat wound. Since Krystal's vocal cords and muscles had been cut, she was only able to use hand gestures and other nonverbal communication. But she was able to provide police officers with an accurate description of her attacker. Later at police headquarters, Krystal picked out the picture of her attacker: 35-year-old ex-convict Tommy Lynn Sells. Sells was a drifter who was a former carnival worker. Subsequently, Sells was arrested by police and was being held in the Val Verde County Jail near the Mexican border. When confronted with the evidence against him, Sells confessed to murdering Kaylene Harris and assaulting Krystal Surles. Police were shocked to learn that Sells had committed other murders as well. Sells, a California native, told investigators that he committed his first serious assault when he was 13. He believes he killed someone when he was 17. Although Sells did not have an attorney at the time of his interrogation by police, he volunteered to provide police with some of his blood and tissue so that investigators can attempt to link him through DNA testing to particular crimes. However, Sells refused to give news interviews with anyone.

Sells told police that his killings are unpredictable. He says, "Sometimes its like a pressure cooker, you know. I'm about to blow up. I didn't have any plan, no purpose. No direction. I'd just go." Sells said that when he attacked the two girls in their home, he cut his way into the home through a window screen. Then he just went around to everybody's bedroom and looked in everybody's bedroom and came back to the girls' room. On the night of the attack, Krystal had been visiting the Harrises as her parents prepared to move from Kansas to Del Rio. Others in the house that night apparently did not hear the attack. Although charges have been filed only in the Del Rio murder and assault cases, Sells has admitted to the rape and murder of a 13-year-old girl in Lexington, Kentucky in May 1999. Furthermore, he admitted to murders in Alabama, California, Arizona, and Arkansas. He also admitted to armed robberies in Florida. Authorities said that Sells "seems remorseful at times and cries."

If Sells is convicted of murder, should he be executed? Although Sells admitted to multiple murders, he claims that in most instances, he was high on drugs and alcohol. According to police, many of the murders to which Sells confessed happened during "alcohol-induced blackouts," and thus Sells' memory about them is "fuzzy." Is alcohol an excuse for these murders? How would you sentence Sells if he is convicted? What do you think should be his appropriate punishment?

Source: Adapted from the Associated Press, "Man Confesses to Multiple Slayings." January 14, 2000.

by Alaska juvenile court judges whenever they place adjudicated juveniles on probation.

The terms and conditions of probation are outlined in Figure 4.9. Obeying the law, attending school, maintaining employment, reporting to the probation officer, attending vocational training or education courses, appearing at subsequent court hearings, refraining from using drugs and alcohol, and refraining from possessing dangerous weapons are standard probation conditions. Furthermore, the judge may add other conditions, such as mandatory counseling or therapy, depending upon the particular needs exhibited by the offender and which are brought to the attention of the court.

Custodial Dispositions

Custodial dispositions are classified according to **nonsecure custody** or **nonsecure confinement** and **secure custody** or **secure confinement**. Nonsecure custody consists of placing certain juveniles into foster homes, group homes, camps, ranches, or schools. These are temporary measures often designed to lead to more permanent placement arrangements for juveniles later. Juveniles have freedom of movement, and they can generally participate in school and other youthful activities. If they are living in group homes or are on camp ranches, there are curfews to be observed. It is assumed that if they are in the care of others in foster homes or shelters, such curfews will be implicitly (if not explicitly) enforced (Florida Department of Juvenile Justice 2000).

The secure custodial option is considered by most juvenile court judges as the last resort for serious juvenile offenders. Some of the reasons for this include overcrowding in secure juvenile facilities, a general reluctance among judges to incarcerate youths because of adverse labeling effects, and the potential effectiveness of certain intermediate punishments through community-service agencies. Fewer than 10 percent of all juveniles processed by juvenile courts annually are subsequently placed in either nonsecure or secure facilities (Butts and Snyder, 1997).

JUVENILE CORRECTIONS

In 2000 there were 38,459 juveniles in residential and nonresidential correctional programs other than probation (American Correctional Association 2002, 54). The range of juvenile corrections is almost as broad as programs for convicted adult offenders. In fact, since 1992 changes in juvenile court dispositions have been in the direction of increased incarceration of juveniles adjudicated delinquent for violent or other serious offenses without comparable attention to probation, community corrections, or other types of **aftercare** (Ashford, Sales, and Reid 2000).

Juveniles adjudicated delinquent may be placed on probation or in secure confinement, depending upon juvenile court judge opinions and evaluations. Depending upon juvenile probation officer caseloads in various jurisdictions, probation may be more or less intense, commensurate with intensive supervised probation for adults. One's placement in different types of probationary programs is dependent upon how the youth is originally classified. Interestingly, juvenile court judges have not consistently applied legal variables in their decision making about juvenile secure placements. In fact, some research suggests that nonlegal or extralegal variables are most influential (Taxman and Elis 1999). Hoge, Andrews, and Leschied (1995) studied 338 adolescent boys and girls who were adjudicated delinquent in a large urban U.S. region. They found that personal and situational variables often governed secure confinement decision making rather than legal criteria. More rational legal criteria for secure confinement decision making have been recommended (Altschuler and Armstrong 2001).

Whether it is intensive, probation may be conditional and involve restitution to victims and/or community services. In 2001, there were over 350,000 juveniles on probation in various state jurisdictions (American Correctional Association 2001). Juveniles may be placed in community-based residential programs or exposed to various therapies and treatments or training (Aloisi and LeBaroon 2001).

Confinement in state industrial schools is the juvenile equivalent of incarceration in a state prison for adults. This type of confinement is considered **hard time** for many juveniles. The California Youth Authority operates various facilities to house growing numbers of juvenile offenders in secure confinement. Lengths of commitment vary for offenders, depending upon the seriousness of their adjudication offenses (Maguire and Pastore 2002).

Juvenile Parole

When juveniles have served a portion of their incarcerative terms, they are paroled by a juvenile paroling authority to the supervision of an appropriate state or community agency. Such supervision may be in the form of intensive aftercare (Meisel 2001). In 2001, there were 80,000 juveniles on parole in various state jurisdictions (American Correctional Association 2001). In Utah, for instance, a nine-member board, the Utah Youth Parole Authority, makes early-release decisions over large numbers of incarcerated youths monthly. Operated by the Utah Division of Youth Corrections, this board conducted over 350 parole hearings in 2001 (American Correctional Association 2001). Although the board appears to be guided by certain eligibility criteria, one's institutional behavior while confined is considered quite important as an indicator of one's future community reintegration.

One example of aftercare provisions for juvenile parolees is the Intensive Aftercare Demonstration Project (IAP), which was implemented in Golden, Colorado in 1999 (Meisel 2001). The IAP adhered to a reintegrative confinement concept in order to reduce recidivism among juvenile parolees at greatest risk of reoffending. Successful intensive case supervision often assumes that providers develop positive relationships with their clients. A sample of 97 juveniles was recruited from the Lookout Mountain Youth Services Center in Golden and randomly assigned to treatment and received intensive aftercare services, while other youths were subject to control conditions of traditional aftercare. The IAP clients reported having stronger relationships with their case managers and viewed them as being more supportive and responsive compared with those in the control group. IAP clients with former gang affiliations also reported less influence of their former gangs compared with clients in the control group. Overall, the IAP participants viewed their relationships with community resource persons the most favorably and exhibited considerably less recidivism in follow-ups compared with their control group counterparts. Thus quality aftercare programs are encouraged for juvenile parolees (Meisel 2001).

SUMMARY

Approximately 2 million juveniles are arrested or taken into custody by police annually. The criminal justice system, an interrelated set of agencies and organizations designed to control criminal behavior, detect crime, and punish criminals, is a major receiver of juveniles initially after they are apprehended. The components of the criminal justice system include the legislature, law enforcement, prosecution and the courts, and corrections.

When juveniles are arrested, they are often brought to jails where they are detained while police officers investigate the circumstances leading to their apprehension. In some instances, certain jurisdictions automatically process juveniles as adults where serious felonies are involved. Adults are also booked after they have been apprehended, and are subject to an initial appearance before a magistrate. Other ways of entering the criminal justice system are through criminal informations or charges against defendants filed by prosecutors or indictments from grand juries.

Both juveniles and adults may enter into plea bargain agreements, whereby offenders plead guilty to certain charges in exchange for some type of leniency from the court. If cases are not plea bargained, defendants may take their cases to trial. Preceding trial, however, is an arraignment. This is a formal proceeding where the final list of charges is prepared, a plea is entered by the defendant, and a trial date established. If defendants are convicted, they are sentenced by the presiding judge who considers any aggravating or mitigating circumstances that might intensify the punishment or reduce it. Sentences include probation, intensive supervised probation, some type of community-based supervision, electronic monitoring, or incarceration in a jail or prison for a specified term. Inmates eventually are released after serving all or a portion of their sentences, either through parole or accumulation of good time credit.

The juvenile justice system parallels the criminal justice system in a number of respects. Police officers classify juveniles according to the offenses alleged, and preliminary dispositions of cases are made. At any point during processing, charges against juveniles may be dropped or dismissed. Youths may be returned to parental custody or placed in the care of community agencies or certain legal guardians. Those juveniles who move further into the juvenile justice system are screened through intake, a process of classification by a probation or court officer. Petitions are filed by various persons against certain juveniles, alleging either misconduct or specific needs in the case of dependent, neglected, and/or abused children. These petitions are presented in juvenile courts where the cases are adjudicated.

Nominal sanctions include verbal warnings or reprimands. Conditional sanctions include payment of fines or restitution to victims, community service, participation in drug- or alcohol-dependent programs, or in some educational training program or therapy treatment. Custodial sanctions include nonsecure and secure custody. Nonsecure custody may be placement in a foster or group home, or in a camp ranch. Secure custody is similar to prison incarceration and is manifested by the various industrial schools among the states. These facilities are typically designed for the more serious offenders, although many nonserious offenders are incarcerated because of a lack of appropriate community-based treatment programs in some jurisdictions.

QUESTIONS FOR REVIEW

1. What are the essential components of the criminal justice system? What are their primary characteristics?

2. What is the difference between a preliminary hearing and an arraignment?

3. What are the major differences between aggravating and mitigating circumstances?

4. What are some key differences between being arrested and being taken into custody? Which action is better for juvenile offenders and why?

5. What is a referral? Who can make referrals?

6. What is an adjudicatory proceeding? How does intake influence whether adjudicatory proceedings will occur?

7. What are three kinds of juvenile dispositions? What are some differences between them?

8. What are nominal dispositions? Which type of disposition does the juvenile court impose most frequently and why?

9. What are some differences between secure and nonsecure custody?

10. What is juvenile parole? In what respect is it a part of juvenile corrections?

SUGGESTED READINGS

Ellis, Rodney A. and Karen M. Sowers. 2001. *Juvenile justice practice: A cross-disciplinary approach to intervention.* Belmont, CA: Brooks/Cole.

Finkelhor, David and Richard Ormrod. 2000. *Juvenile victims of property crimes.* Washington, DC: U.S. Office of Juvenile Justice and Delinquency Prevention.

Houston, James G. 2001. *Crime, policy, and criminal behavior in America.* Lexington, NY: Edwin Mellen Press.

Roberson, Cliff. 2000. *Exploring juvenile justice.* 2d ed. Incline Village, NV: Copperhouse Publishing Company.

INTERNET CONNECTIONS

Activism 2000 Youth Project
http://www.youthactivism.com

Aspen Youth Services
http://www.aspenyouth.com

Center on Juvenile and Criminal Justice
http://www.cjcj.org/

Children and Family Justice Center
http://www.law.nwu.edu/edpts/clinic/cfjc/index.htm

CHAPTER 5 | *The Legal Rights of Juveniles*

Chapter Outline

Key Terms

Court unification
Double jeopardy
Family model

Habeas corpus
Hands-off doctrine
Litigation explosion

Miranda warning
Traditional model

Chapter Objectives

As a result of reading this chapter, you will realize the following objectives:

1. Understand the historical context within which juvenile rights were gradually acquired.
2. Learn about the hands-off doctrine as it once applied to juvenile cases.
3. Understand critical events in the emergence of juvenile rights.
4. Learn about key landmark cases advancing constitutional rights for juveniles charged with crimes.
5. Distinguish between criminal courts and juvenile courts in terms of the rights of offenders processed by each.
6. Understand the debate over whether the death penalty shall be applied to selected juvenile offenders who commit capital murder, including the pros and cons of this process.
7. Learn about several important death penalty cases involving juveniles.
8. Learn about court unification and some of the reasons for its implementation.

INTRODUCTION

• *A 21-year-old woman was jogging in a local Baltimore, Maryland, park one evening when she was suddenly ambushed by four teenagers. The youths dragged her into the bushes where they struck her with limbs from trees. They tied her up and gagged her. Then they raped her. Throughout the incident, she begged and pleaded to be released, but to no avail. When they were finished, one youth took out a .22 pistol and fired a shot at the woman's head. Luckily for the woman, the bullet only grazed her skull and she played dead until the youths left the scene. She managed to untie herself and called 911 from her cellular phone, which she had retrieved from her purse nearby. Apparently, the youths had overlooked the purse and its contents. Police response was rapid, and the four teenagers were apprehended as they were exiting the large park. Two of the youths admitted the crime during a brief police interrogation at the police department. Later at the police station, the woman, badly shaken by the incident, identified each of her attackers in a police line-up. Each was charged with aggravated rape and attempted murder. Because of their ages (three were 16 and one was 17), the juvenile court in Baltimore decided to transfer them to criminal court to stand trial for these crimes as adults. If convicted on all counts, they faced life imprisonment. However, a public defender representing the youths said that there were several police errors in making the arrest. He said that the youths were not properly Mirandized before being interrogated by police and that excessive force was used to extract confessions from them. [Adapted from the Associated Press, "Female Jogger IDs Teen Attackers in Park Assault." August 15, 2000].*

• *His name was Morteza Moqaddam, and he was 17 years old. He had been convicted of fatally stabbing a 22-year-old on December 13, 1999 after quarreling about smoking in public. He was to be hanged from a crane fixed atop a truck 30 feet from the electronics shop where he had committed the crime. He stood on the gallows with a rope around his neck and a dark hood over his head. He was handcuffed. Tears rolled down his cheeks as he awaited his inevitable execution: death by hanging. Shortly before sunrise, a judicial official had brought Moqaddam, dressed in a blue sweatshirt and sweatpants, out of a police car where he had been waiting. The official read out the death sentence and fixed a thick rope around Moqaddam's neck. But seconds before the execution was to be performed, the family of the murder victim decided that the boy should be spared.*

Officials say that the deceased boy's father spoke to the judicial officials at the last moment, saying that he had forgiven Moqaddam. The teen's family was overjoyed with the decision of the father, Ali Mohebbi. Moqaddam's mother said, "Ever since his son died I have been praying for him. I will never forget as long as I live how he gave me my son's life back." This incident happened in Tehran, Iran. Under Iran's Islamic legal system, whether the convicted boy would die was a decision left up to the relatives of the victim. About 4,000 spectators were on hand to witness the execution, and many of them pleaded with the victim's father to forgive the offender. The crowd rejoiced at the news, shouting "Allahu Akbar!" or "God is great!" Would such a policy of executing convicted juvenile murderers work in the United States? How much input should the relatives of victims have in deciding whether convicted juvenile murderers should receive the death penalty? What do you think? [Adapted from the Associated Press, "Iranian Teen-Ager Pardoned Seconds Before Hanging." January 3, 2000.]

- *It's a new twist on the otherwise unfortunate theme of school violence. In September 1999, a San Francisco boy was caught with an electric stun gun used by police officers to subdue unruly suspects. The eighth-grader, a 14-year-old, shoved an electric stun gun into a classmate's chest and pulled the trigger, and then he ran away. The incident happened at Hoover Middle School in a San Francisco suburb. A counselor at the middle school apprehended the suspect after witnesses and the 11-year-old victim identified him. The 11-year-old victim suffered extensive burns and welts on his chest following the incident. He was treated at a hospital and then released to his parents. The 14-year-old suspect was charged with one count of assault with a deadly weapon and one charge of possession of a deadly weapon. Are stun guns deadly weapons? How should the youth be judged who used the stun gun? What punishment should be imposed if the youth is found guilty of the offense? What do you think?* [Adapted from the Associated Press, "Boy Shocks Classmate with Stun Gun." September 8, 1999.]

Presently, we are uncertain about whether juvenile violence is escalating. The media have exposed us to seemingly more frequent and heinous incidents of juvenile violence in recent years, especially violence in schools. Highlighted are shooting incidents with high body counts. Gang warfare on city streets goes unabated. Greater juvenile violence, real or imagined, and increasingly bizarre incidents of violence involving juveniles have caused many persons to question whether our existing juvenile laws are adequate to deal with these offenders. In some instances, the get-tough approach seems the most feasible alternative in dealing with youths who commit more serious offenses. Some persons have adopted the view that if juveniles commit the crime, then they should do the time.

Driving this get-tough approach to juvenile offending are the following assumptions: (1) Youths are committing more serious offenses and (2) the onset of delinquency is occurring at much earlier ages. More youths involved in drive-by shootings are 10 years of age or younger. More capital offenses are being committed by younger children each year. Some juveniles are seasoned "hit men" by the time they are 11, and they have numerous "kills" attributed to them. The public is perplexed about this state of affairs and what to do about it. One increasingly popular solution is to hold juveniles more accountable for their actions and to exact harsher penalties whenever juveniles commit more serious crimes. As their accountability increases in juvenile courts, the courts have vested juveniles with more rights commensurate with their adult counterparts in criminal courts. This chapter describes the rights of juvenile offenders as well as some of the implications of these rights for their life chances.

Prior to the mid-1960s, almost every juvenile court in the nation made important, life-altering decisions affecting juveniles according to what the courts believed to be in the youths' best interests. These best interests were almost always subject to court definition and interpretation. This was and continues to be the fundamental doctrine of *parens patriae*. Since the mid-1960s, juveniles have achieved several significant legal milestones, including, but not limited to, the right to be represented by counsel, the right to cross-examine their accusers, and the right against self-incrimination. This chapter examines the contemporary range of legal rights extended to juveniles. Several landmark cases will be described where significant rights have been established through U.S. Supreme Court decisions. Some of the more important implications of these decisions for juvenile offenders will be discussed.

Juvenile rights are best understood in the context of the traditional *parens patriae* doctrine and how it has gradually been transformed by social and institutional changes. As one consequence of greater urbanization, Americans have enjoyed the advantages of greater professional and geographical mobility. Furthermore, the educational level of citizens has gradually increased. Today, citizens are more sophisticated than in previous times, and their legal understanding and interest has greatly improved. The dominant *parens patriae* doctrine remained unchallenged for decades. However, a growing wave of appeals of juvenile court decisions has resulted in an extensive erosion of the *parens patriae* doctrine by the U.S. Supreme Court.

The issue of capital punishment for juveniles will also be treated. This is especially important since the U.S. Supreme Court determined in 1988 that the death penalty may not be administered to any juvenile under the age of 16 at the time a capital crime was committed (*Thompson v. Oklahoma*, 1988) and upheld the executions of two other youths aged 16 and 17 respectively the following year. The application of the death penalty to juveniles is likely to generate large numbers of appeals in future years.

ORIGINAL JUVENILE COURT JURISDICTION: *PARENS PATRIAE*

Until the mid-1960s, juvenile courts had considerable latitude in regulating the affairs of minors. This freedom to act in a child's behalf was rooted in the largely unchallenged doctrine of *parens patriae*. Whenever juveniles were apprehended by police officers for alleged crimes, they were eventually turned over to juvenile authorities or taken to a juvenile hall for further processing. They were not advised of their right to an attorney, to have an attorney present during any interrogation, or to remain silent. They could be questioned by police at length, without parental notification or legal contact. In short, they had little, if any, protection against adult constitutional rights violations on the part of law enforcement officers and others. They had no access to due process because of their status or standing as juveniles (Feld 2000).

In the early years of juvenile courts, when juveniles appeared before juvenile court judges, they almost never had the opportunity to rebut evidence presented against them or to test the reliability of witnesses through cross-examination. This was rationalized at the time by asserting that juveniles did not understand the law and had to have it interpreted for them by others, principally juvenile court judges. Subsequent investigations of the knowledge youths have of their rights seems to confirm this assertion. These early adjudicatory proceedings were very informal. They were also conducted without defense counsel being present to advise their youthful clients. In one-sided affairs, facts were alleged by various accusers, often persons such as probation officers or police officers, and youthful defendants were not permitted to give testimony in their own behalf or cross-examine those giving testimony.

Prosecutors were seldom present in juvenile proceedings, since they were largely nonadversarial, and juvenile court judges handled most cases informally, independently, and subjectively, depending upon the youth's needs and the seriousness of the offense. If judges decided that secure confinement would best serve the interests of justice and the welfare of the juvenile, then the youth would be placed in a secure confinement facility (juvenile prison) for an indeterminate period. These decisions were seldom questioned or challenged. If they were challenged, higher courts would dismiss these challenges as frivolous or without merit.

The "Hands-Off" Doctrine

A major reason for the silent acceptance of juvenile court judges' decisions was that the U.S. Supreme Court had repeatedly demonstrated its reluctance to intervene in juvenile matters or question decisions made by juvenile court judges. In the case of *In re Gault* (1967), Justice Stewart typified the traditional orientation of former Supreme Courts by declaring:

> The Court today uses an obscure Arizona case as a vehicle to impose upon thousands of juvenile courts throughout the Nation restrictions that the Constitution made applicable to adversary criminal trials. I believe the Court's decision is *wholly unsound* [emphasis mine] as a matter of constitutional law, and sadly unwise as a matter of judicial policy . . . The inflexible restrictions that the Constitution so wisely made applicable to adversary criminal trials have no inevitable place in the proceedings of those public social agencies known as juvenile or family courts. (387 U.S. at 78–79)

The **hands-off doctrine** of the U.S. Supreme Court toward juvenile court matters was similar to their hands-off policy toward corrections. In the case of *Ruffin v. Commonwealth* (1871), a Virginia judge declared that "prisoners have no more rights than slaves." Thus, during the next seventy years, prisoners were used as guinea pigs in various biological and chemical experiments, particularly in the testing of gases used on the front lines in Europe during World War I. Such tests of chemical agents on prisoners were conducted at the Michigan State Prison at Jackson. Some prisons mandated inmate sterilization, because it was believed that criminal behavior was hereditary. No committees for the protection of human subjects existed to protest these inmate treatments. Inmates had absolutely no rights, including mail privacy, visitation, or other privileges, other than those rights dispensed or withheld by prison authorities (Myers 1973).

The U.S. Supreme Court commenced to change this state of affairs toward corrections in 1941 in the case of *Ex parte Hull* (1941). This case involved attempts by prisoners to petition the courts to hear various grievances or complaints. Prison superintendents and staff would routinely trash these petitions, contending that they were improperly prepared and hence, legally unacceptable. In the *Hull* decision, the Court held that no state or its officers could abridge inmates of their right to access the federal or state courts through their petitions. Once the *Hull* decision had been made, there was a proliferation of inmate rights cases in subsequent years known as a **litigation explosion** (Daniels 1984). Two decades later, a similar litigation explosion would occur. This time the subject matter would be juvenile rights (Roleff 1996).

In many respects, juveniles were treated like adult inmates in prisons (Myers 1973). Youths had no legal standing and virtually no rights other than those extended by the courts. The right to a trial by jury, a basic right provided any defendant who might be incarcerated for six months or more by a criminal court conviction, did not exist for juveniles unless juvenile court judges permitted such trials. Most juvenile court judges abhor jury trials for their juveniles and refuse to permit them. Even today, juveniles do not have an absolute right to a trial by jury, with few exceptions through state statutes. Thus, juveniles may be deprived of their freedom for many years on the basis of a personal judicial decision.

Because of the informality of juvenile proceedings in most jurisdictions, there were frequent and obvious abuses of judicial discretion. These abuses occurred because of the absence of consistent guidelines whereby cases could be adjudicated. Juvenile probation officers might casually recommend to judges that particular juveniles "ought to do a few months" in an industrial school or other secure confinement facility, and the judge might be persuaded to adjudicate these cases accordingly.

However, several forces were at work simultaneously during the 1950s and 1960s that would eventually have the conjoint consequence of making juvenile courts more accountable for specific adjudications of youthful offenders. One of these forces was increased parental and general public recognition of and concern for the liberal license taken by juvenile courts in administering the affairs of juveniles. The abuse of judicial discretion was becoming increasingly apparent. Additionally, there was a growing disenchantment with and apathy for the rehabilitation ideal, although this disenchantment was not directed solely at juvenile courts (Roleff 1996).

The juvenile court as originally envisioned by progressives was procedurally informal, characterized by individualized, offender-oriented dispositional practices. However, the contemporary juvenile court departs markedly from this progressive ideal. Today, juvenile courts are increasingly criminalized, featuring an adversarial system and greater procedural formality. This formality effectively inhibits any individualized treatment these courts might contemplate, and it has increased the perfunctory nature of sentencing juveniles adjudicated as delinquent (Feld 1995).

The transformation of juvenile courts into more formal proceedings as part of the national trend toward bureaucratization and as an institutional compromise between law and social welfare has been described (Sutton 1985). Bureaucracy stresses a fixed hierarchy of authority, task specialization, individualized spheres of competence, impersonal social relationships between organizational actors, and impartial enforcement of abstract rules. Thus, in the context of bureaucracy, decision making is routinized rather than arbitrary. Personalities and social characteristics are irrelevant.

Applied to juvenile court proceedings, juvenile court decision making would most likely be a function of the nature and seriousness of offenses committed and the factual delinquent history of juvenile defendants. Emotional considerations in bureaucratic structures are nonexistent. The bureaucratic approach would be that juveniles should be held to a high standard of accountability for their actions. Furthermore, an individualized, treatment-oriented sanctioning system would be inconsistent with bureaucracy and violative of its general principles of impartiality. This type of system for juvenile justice seems consistent with the sentiments of a large portion of U.S. citizens and their belief that juvenile courts should get tough with juvenile offenders. Despite this due-process and bureaucratic emphasis, juvenile courts have continued to retain many of their seemingly haphazard characteristics. Good policies have been established, but their implementation has remained inconsistent and problematic for many juvenile courts (Johnston and Secret 1995).

A major change from *parens patriae* state-based interests to a due-process juvenile justice model means that decision making about youthful offenders is increasingly rationalized, and the principle of just deserts is fundamental. This means that less discretionary authority will be manifested by juvenile court judges, as they decide each case more on the basis of offense seriousness and prescribed punishments rather than according to individual factors or circumstances (Fader et al. 2001). Table 5.1 provides a general chronology of events relating to juvenile rights during the last 200 years.

TABLE 5.1

Chronological Summary of Major Events in Juvenile Justice

Year	Event
1791	Bill of Rights passed by U.S. Congress
1825	New York House of Refuge established
1839	*Ex parte Crouse,* established right of juvenile court to intervene in parent–child matters
1841	John Augustus initiates probation in Boston
1853	New York Children's Aid Society established
1855	Death penalty imposed on 10-year-old, James Arcene, in Arkansas for robbery and murder; earliest juvenile execution was Thomas Graunger, 16-year-old, for sodomizing a horse and cow in 1642
1866	Massachusetts statute passed giving juvenile court power to intervene and take custody where parents are unfit
1868	Fourteenth Amendment passed by U.S. Congress, establishing right to due process and equal protection under the law
1874	Massachusetts established first Children's Tribunal to deal with youthful offenders
1889	Indiana established children's guardians to have jurisdiction over neglected and dependent children
1889	Hull House established in Chicago by Jane Addams to assist unsupervised children of immigrant parents
1899	Compulsory School Act, Colorado; statutory regulation of truants
1899	Illinois Act to Regulate the Treatment and Control of Dependent, Neglected, and Delinquent Children; first juvenile court established in United States
1901	Juvenile court established in Denver, Colorado
1907	Separate juvenile court with original jurisdiction in juvenile matters established in Denver, Colorado

(continued)

TABLE 5.1 (CONTINUED)

Chronological Summary of Major Events in Juvenile Justice

Year	Event
1912	Creation of U.S. Children's Bureau, charged with compiling statistical information about juvenile offenders; existed from 1912 to 1940
1918	Chicago slums studied by Shaw and McKay; delinquency related to urban environment and transitional neighborhoods
1938	Federal Juvenile Delinquency Act
1966	*Kent v. United States* case established juvenile's right to hearing before transfer to criminal court, right to assistance of counsel during police interrogations, right to reports and records relating to transfer decision, and right to reasons given by judge for transfer
1967	*In re Gault* case established juvenile's right to an attorney, right to notice of charges, right to confront and cross-examine witnesses, and right against self-incrimination
1970	*In re Winship* case established juvenile's right to criminal court standard of "beyond a reasonable doubt" where loss of freedom is a possible penalty
1971	*McKeiver v. Pennsylvania* case established that juvenile's right to a trial by jury is not absolute
1974	Juvenile Justice and Delinquency Prevention Act
1974	Office of Juvenile Justice and Delinquency Prevention, instrumental in promoting deinstitutionalization of status offenses
1975	*Breed v. Jones* case established that double jeopardy exists if juvenile is adjudicated as delinquent in juvenile court and tried for same offense later in criminal court; prohibits double jeopardy
1982	*Eddings v. Oklahoma* case established that death penalty applied to juveniles was not "cruel and unusual punishment" per se
1984	*Schall v. Martin* case established the constitutionality of the preventive detention of juveniles
1985	*New Jersey v. T.L.O.* case established lesser standard of search and seizure on school property; searches and seizures permissible without probable cause or warrant
1988	*Thompson v. Oklahoma* case established that death penalty applied to juveniles convicted of murder who were under age 16 at time of murder is cruel and unusual punishment
1989	*Stanford v. Kentucky* and *Wilkins v. Missouri* cases established that death penalty is not cruel and unusual punishment applied to juveniles convicted of murder and who were aged 16 or 17 at the time the murder was committed

Source: Compiled by author.

During the mid-1960s and through the 1980s, significant achievements were made in the area of juvenile rights. Although the *parens patriae* philosophy continues to influence juvenile proceedings, the U.S. Supreme Court has vested youths with certain constitutional rights. These rights do not encompass all of the rights extended to adults who are charged with crimes. But those rights conveyed to juveniles thus far have had far-reaching implications for how juveniles are processed. The general result of these U.S. Supreme Court decisions has been to bring the juvenile court system under constitutional control (Manfredi 1998). In the following section, several landmark cases involving juvenile rights will be described.

LANDMARK CASES IN JUVENILE JUSTICE

Several significant changes have been made in the juvenile justice system and how youths are processed in recent decades. In this section, we will examine several important rights bestowed upon juveniles by the U.S. Supreme Court during the period 1960–1990. Describing these rights will make clear those rights juveniles did not have until the landmark cases associated with them were decided. Then, a comparison will be made of juvenile rights and those rights enjoyed by adults charged with crimes in criminal courts. Despite sweeping juvenile reforms and major legal gains, there are still several important differences between the rights of juveniles and adults when both are charged with crimes (Feld 2000).

Currently, juvenile courts are largely punishment-centered, with the justice and just-deserts models influencing court decision making. Interests of youths are secondary, while community interests are seemingly served by juvenile court actions. Juveniles are being given greater responsibility for their actions, and they are increasingly expected to be held accountable for their wrongdoing (Feld 2001).

Each of the cases presented below represents attempts by juveniles to either secure rights ordinarily extended to adults. Given these cases, juveniles have fared well with the U.S. Supreme Court in past years. While juveniles still do not enjoy the full range of rights extended to adult offenders who are tried in criminal courts, juveniles have acquired due-process privileges that were not available to them prior to the 1960s. The first three cases presented, *Kent v. United States, In re Gault,* and *In re Winship,* comprise the "big three" of juvenile cases involving their legal rights. The remaining cases address specific rights issues, such as the right against double jeopardy, jury trials as a matter of right in juvenile courts, preventive detention, and the standards that should govern searches of students and seizures of contraband on school property.

Gerald Gault working in the auto shop of the Arizona State Industrial School.

Kent v. United States (1966)

Regarded as the first major juvenile rights case to preface further juvenile court reforms, *Kent v. United States* (1966) established the universal precedents of (1) requiring waiver hearings before juveniles can be transferred to the jurisdiction of a criminal court (excepting legislative automatic waivers as discussed in this and other chapters, although reverse waiver hearings must be conducted at the juvenile's request), and (2) juveniles are entitled to consult with counsel prior to and during such hearings (Grisso 1998).

The facts in the case are that in 1959, Morris A. Kent, Jr., a 14-year-old in the District of Columbia, was apprehended as the result of several housebreakings and attempted purse snatchings. He was placed on probation in the custody of his mother. In 1961, an intruder entered the apartment of a woman, took her wallet, and raped her. Fingerprints at the crime scene were later identified as those of Morris Kent, who was fingerprinted when apprehended for housebreaking in 1959. On September 5, 1961, Kent, 16, was taken into custody by police, interrogated for seven hours, and admitted the offense as well as volunteering information about other housebreakings, robberies, and rapes. Although the records are unclear about when Kent's mother became aware of Kent's arrest, she did obtain counsel for Kent shortly after 2:00 P.M. the following day. She and her attorney conferred with the Social Service Director of the Juvenile Court and learned there was a possibility Kent would be waived to criminal court. Kent's attorney advised the Director of his intention to oppose the waiver.

Kent was detained in a Receiving Home for one week. During that period, there was no arraignment and no determination by a judicial officer of probable cause for Kent's arrest. His attorney filed a motion with the juvenile court opposing the waiver as well as a request to inspect records relating to Kent's previous offenses. Also, a psychiatric examination of Kent was arranged by Kent's attorney. Kent's attorney argued that because his client was "a victim of severe psychopathology," it would be in Kent's best interests to remain within juvenile court jurisdiction where he could receive adequate treatment in a hospital and would be a suitable subject for rehabilitation.

Typical of juvenile court judges at the time, the juvenile court judge failed to rule on any of Kent's attorney's motions. He also failed to confer with Kent's attorney and/or parents. In a somewhat arrogant manner, the juvenile court judge declared that "after full investigation, I do hereby waive" jurisdiction of Kent and direct that he be "held for trial for [the alleged] offenses under the regular procedure of the U.S. District Court for the District of Columbia." He offered no findings, nor did he recite any reason for the waiver or make mention of Kent's attorney's motions. Kent was later found guilty of six counts of housebreaking by a federal jury, although the jury found him "not guilty by reason of insanity" on the rape charge. Because of District of Columbia law, it was mandatory that Kent be transferred to a mental institution until such time as his sanity is restored. On each of the housebreaking counts, Kent's sentence was 5 to 15 years, or a total of 30 to 90 years in prison. His mental institution commitment would be counted as time served against the 30- to 90-year sentence.

Kent's conviction was reversed by a vote of 5–4. This is significant, because it signified a subtle shift in Supreme Court sentiment relating to juvenile rights. The majority held that Kent's rights to due process and to the effective assistance of counsel were violated when he was denied a formal hearing on the waiver and his attorneys' motions were ignored. It is also significant that the Supreme Court stressed the phrase, "critically important," when referring to the absence of counsel and waiver hearing respectively. In adult cases, critical stages are those that relate to the defendant's potential loss of freedoms (i.e., incarceration). Because of the *Kent* decision, waiver hearings are now critical stages. Regarding the effective assistance of counsel, this was also regarded by the Court as a "critically important" decision. They observed that "the right to representation by counsel is not a formality. It is not a grudging gesture to a ritualistic requirement. It is of the essence of justice. . . . Appointment of counsel without affording an opportunity for a hearing on a 'critically important' decision is tantamount to a denial of counsel" (383 U.S. at 561).

In re Gault (1967)

The case of *In re Gault* (1967) is perhaps the most noteworthy of all landmark juvenile rights cases. Certainly it is considered the most ambitious. In a 7–2 vote, the U.S. Supreme Court articulated the following rights for all juveniles: (1) the right to a notice of charges, (2) the right to counsel, (3) the right to confront and cross-examine witnesses, and (4) the right to invoke the privilege against self-incrimination. The petitioner, Gault, requested the Court to rule favorably on two additional rights sought: (1) the right to a transcript of the proceedings and (2) the right to appellate review. The Court elected not to rule on either of these rights.

The facts in the case are that Gerald Francis Gault, a 15-year-old, and a friend, Ronald Lewis, were taken into custody by the Sheriff of Gila County, Arizona, in the morning of June 8, 1964. At the time, Gault was on probation as the result of "being in the company of another" who had stolen a wallet from a lady's purse," a judgment entered February 25, 1964. A verbal complaint had been filed by a neighbor of Gault, Mrs. Cook, alleging that Gault had called her and made lewd and indecent remarks. [With some levity, the Supreme Court said that "It will suffice for purposes of this opinion to say that the remarks or questions put to her were of the irritatingly offensive, adolescent, sex variety" (387 U.S. at 4)]. When Gault was picked up, his mother and father were at work. Indeed, they did not learn where their son was until much later that evening. Gault was being held at the Children's Detention Home.

Gault's parents proceeded to the Home. Officer Flagg, the deputy probation officer and superintendent of the Children's Detention Home where Gault was being detained, advised Gault's parents that a hearing would be held in Juvenile Court at 3:00 P.M. the following day. Flagg filed a petition with the court on the hearing day, June 9. This petition was entirely formal, stating only that "said minor is under the age of 18 years, and is in need of the protection of this Honorable Court; [and that] said minor is a delinquent minor." It prayed for a hearing and an order regarding the "care and custody of said minor." No factual basis was provided for the petition, and Gault's parents were not provided with a copy of it in advance of the hearing.

On June 9, the hearing was held, with only Gault, his mother and older brother, Probation Officers Flagg and Henderson, and the juvenile court judge present. The original complainant, Mrs. Cook, was not there. No one was sworn at the hearing, no transcript was made of it, and no memorandum of the substance of the proceedings was prepared. The testimony consisted largely of allegations by Officer Flagg about Gault's behavior and prior juvenile record. A subsequent hearing was scheduled for June 15. On June 15, another hearing was held, with all above present, including Ronald Lewis and his father, and Gerald's father. What actually transpired is unknown, although there are conflicting recollections from all parties who were there. Mrs. Gault asked why Mrs. Cook was not present. Judge McGhee said "she didn't have to be present at that hearing." Furthermore, the judge did not speak to Mrs. Cook or communicate with her at any time. Flagg spoke with her once by telephone on June 9. Officially, the charge against Gault was "Lewd Telephone Calls." When the hearing was concluded, the judge committed Gault as a juvenile delinquent to the Arizona State Industrial School "for a period of his minority" [until age 21]. [Parenthetically, if an adult had made an obscene telephone call, he would have received a $50 fine and no more than 60 days in jail. In Gerald Gault's case, he was facing nearly six years in a juvenile prison for the same offense].

A **habeas corpus** hearing was held on August 17, and Judge McGhee was cross-examined regarding his actions. After "hemming and hawing," the judge declared that Gault had "disturbed the peace" and was "habitually involved in immoral matters." Regarding the judge's reference to Gault's alleged "habitual immorality," the judge made vague references to an incident two years earlier when Gault had been accused of stealing someone's baseball glove and had lied to police by denying that he had taken it. The judge also recalled, again vaguely, that Gault had testified some months earlier about making "silly calls, or funny calls, or something like that."

After exhausting their appeals in Arizona state courts, the Gaults appealed to the U.S. Supreme Court. Needless to say, the Court was appalled that Gault's case had been handled in such a cavalier and unconstitutional manner. They reversed the Arizona Supreme Court, holding that Gault did, indeed, have the right to an attorney, the right to confront his accuser (Mrs. Cook) and to cross-examine her, the right against self-incrimination, and the right to have notice of the charges filed against him. Perhaps Justice Black summed up the current juvenile court situation in the United States when he said, "This holding strikes a well-nigh fatal blow to much that is *unique* [emphasis mine] about the juvenile courts in this Nation."

In re Winship (1970)

In re Winship was a less complex case compared with *Gault.* But it established an important precedent in juvenile courts relating to the standard of proof used in established defendant guilt. The U.S. Supreme Court held that "beyond a reasonable doubt," a standard ordinarily used in adult criminal courts, was henceforth to be used by juvenile court judges and others in establishing a youth's delinquency. Formerly, the standard used was the civil application of "preponderance of the evidence."

The facts in the *Winship* case are that Samuel Winship was a 12-year-old charged with larceny in New York City. He purportedly entered a locker and stole $112 from a woman's pocketbook. Under Section 712 of the New York Family Court Act, a juvenile delinquent was defined as "a person over seven and less than sixteen years of age who does any act, which, if done by an adult, would constitute a crime." Interestingly, the juvenile court judge in the case acknowledged that the proof to be presented by the prosecution might be insufficient to establish the guilt of Winship beyond a reasonable doubt, although he

did indicate that the New York Family Court Act provided that "any determination at the conclusion of [an adjudicatory hearing] that a [juvenile] did an act or acts must be based on a preponderance of the evidence" standard (397 U.S. at 360). Winship was adjudicated as a delinquent and ordered to a training school for 18 months, subject to annual extensions of his commitment until his eighteenth birthday. Appeals to New York courts were unsuccessful.

The U.S. Supreme Court heard Winship's case and, in a 6–3 vote, reversed the New York Family Court ruling. A statement by Justice Brennan succinctly states the case for the beyond a reasonable doubt standard: "In sum, the constitutional safeguard of proof beyond a reasonable doubt is as much required during the adjudicatory stage of a delinquency proceeding as are those constitutional safeguards applied in *Gault*—notice of charges, right to counsel, the rights of confrontation and examination, and the privilege of self-incrimination. We therefore hold, in agreement with Chief Justice Fuld in dissent in the Court of Appeals, that where a 12-year-old child is charged with an act of stealing which renders him liable to confinement for as long as six years, then, as a matter of due process, the case against him must be proved beyond a reasonable doubt" (397 U.S. at 368).

McKeiver v. Pennsylvania (1971)

The *McKeiver* case was important because the U.S. Supreme Court held that juveniles are not entitled to a jury trial as a matter of right. [It should be noted that as of 1990, twelve states legislatively mandated jury trials for juveniles in juvenile courts if they so requested such trials, depending upon the seriousness of the offense(s) alleged]. The facts are that in May, 1968, Joseph McKeiver, age 16, was charged with robbery, larceny, and receiving stolen goods. Although he was represented by counsel at his adjudicatory hearing and requested a trial by jury to ascertain his guilt or innocence, Judge Theodore S. Gutowicz of the Court of Common Pleas, Family Division, Juvenile Branch, of Philadelphia, Pennsylvania, denied the request. McKeiver was subsequently adjudicated delinquent. On subsequent appeal to the U.S. Supreme Court, McKeiver's adjudication was upheld. Again, of interest to criminal justice analysts, the remarks of a U.S. Supreme Court Justice are insightful. Justice Blackmun indicated: "If the formalities of the criminal adjudicative process are to be superimposed upon the juvenile court system, there is little need for its separate existence. Perhaps that ultimate disillusionment will come one day, but for the moment, we are disinclined to give impetus to it" (403 U.S. at 551).

Throughout the opinion delivered in the McKeiver case, it is apparent that the Supreme Court was sensitive to the problems associated with juvenile court procedure. Since criminal courts were already bogged down with formalities and lengthy protocol that frequently led to excessive court delays, it was not unreasonable for the Court to rule against perpetuating such formalities in juvenile courts. But we must recognize that in this instance, the Court merely ruled that it is not the constitutional right of juveniles to have the right to a jury trial upon their request. This proclamation had no effect on individual states that wished to enact or preserve such a method of adjudicating juveniles as delinquent or not delinquent. Therefore, about a fourth of the states today have legislative provisions for jury trials in juvenile courts. See the discussion below on the 1997 status of jury trials for juveniles.

Breed v. Jones (1975)

The *Breed v. Jones* case raised the significant constitutional issue of **double jeopardy**. Double jeopardy means being tried for the same crime twice. The Fifth Amendment provides us with the protection against double jeopardy. Thus, if someone is charged with a crime and acquitted, they cannot be tried again for that same offense. This would violate their Fifth Amendment right against double jeopardy. In *Breed v. Jones,* the U.S. Supreme Court concluded that after a juvenile has been adjudicated delinquent for a particular offense, the youth cannot be tried again as an adult in criminal court for that same offense.

The facts of the case are that on February 8, 1971 in Los Angeles, California, Gary Steven Jones, 17 years old, was armed with a deadly weapon and allegedly committed robbery. Jones was subsequently apprehended and an adjudicatory hearing was held on March 1. A petition was filed against Jones. After testimony was taken from Jones and witnesses, the Juvenile Court found that the allegations in the petition were true and sustained the petition. A dispositional hearing date was set for March 15. At that time, Jones was declared "not . . . amenable to the care, treatment and training program available through the facilities of the juvenile court" under a California statute. Jones was then transferred by judicial waiver to a California criminal court where he could be tried as an adult. In a later criminal trial, Jones was convicted of robbery and committed for an indeterminate period to the California Youth Authority. The California Supreme Court upheld the conviction.

When Jones appealed the decision in 1971, the U.S. Supreme Court reversed the robbery conviction. Chief Justice Warren Burger delivered the Court opinion: "We hold that the prosecution of [Jones] in Superior Court, after an adjudicatory proceeding in Juvenile Court, violated the Double Jeopardy Clause of the Fifth Amendment, as applied to the States through the Fourteenth Amendment." The Court ordered Jones' release outright or a remand to juvenile court for disposition. In a lengthy opinion, Justice Burger targeted double jeopardy as (1) being adjudicated as delinquent on specific charges in a juvenile court, and (2) subsequently being tried and convicted on those same charges in criminal court. Within the context of fundamental fairness, such action could not be tolerated.

Schall v. Martin (1984)

In the *Schall* case, the U.S. Supreme Court issued juveniles a minor setback regarding the state's right to hold them in preventive detention pending a subsequent adjudication. The Court said that the preventive detention of juveniles by states is constitutional, if judges perceive these youths to pose a danger to the community or an otherwise serious risk if released short of an adjudicatory hearing. This decision was significant, in part, because many persons advocated the separation of juveniles and adults in jails, those facilities most often used for preventive detention. Also, the preventive detention of adults was not ordinarily practiced at that time. [Since then, the preventive detention of adults who are deemed to pose societal risks has been upheld by the U.S. Supreme Court (*United States v. Salerno,* 1987)].

The facts are that 14-year-old Gregory Martin was arrested at 11:30 P.M. on December 13, 1977 in New York City. He was charged with first-degree robbery, second-degree assault, and criminal possession of a weapon. Martin lied to police at the time, giving a false name and address. Between the time of his arrest and December 29 when a fact-finding hearing was held, Martin was detained (a total of 15 days). His confinement was based largely on the false information he had supplied to police and the seriousness of the charges pending against him. Subsequently, he was adjudicated a delinquent and placed on two years' probation. Later, his attorney filed an appeal, contesting his preventive detention as violative of the Due Process Clause of the Fourteenth Amendment. The U.S.

TABLE 5.2

Comparison of Juvenile and Adult Rights Relating to Delinquency and Crime

Right	Adults	Juveniles
1. "Beyond a reasonable doubt" standard used in court	Yes	Yes
2. Right against double jeopardy	Yes	Yes
3. Right to assistance of counsel	Yes	Yes
4. Right to notice of charges	Yes	Yes
5. Right to a transcript of court proceedings	Yes	No
6. Right against self-incrimination	Yes	Yes
7. Right to trial by jury	Yes	No in most states
8. Right to defense counsel in court proceedings	Yes	No
9. Right to due process	Yes	No[a]
10. Right to bail	Yes	No, with exceptions
11. Right to cross-examine witnesses	Yes	Yes
12. Right of confrontation	Yes	Yes
13. Standards relating to searches and seizures:		
a. "Probable cause" and warrants required for searches and seizures	Yes, with exceptions	No
b. "Reasonable suspicion" required for searches and seizures without warrant	No	Yes
14. Right to hearing prior to transfer to criminal court or to a reverse waiver hearing in states with automatic transfer provisions	N/A	Yes
15. Right to a speedy trial	Yes	No
16. Right to *habeas corpus* relief in correctional settings	Yes	No
17. Right to rehabilitation	No	No
18. Criminal evidentiary standards	Yes	Yes
19. Right to hearing for parole or probation revocation	Yes	No
20. Bifurcated trial, death penalty cases	Yes	Yes
21. Right to discovery	Yes	Limited
22. Fingerprinting, photographing at booking	Yes	No, with exceptions
23. Right to appeal	Yes	Limited
24. Waivers of rights:		
a. Adults	Knowingly, intelligently	
b. Juveniles	Totality of circumstances	

(continued)

TABLE 5.2　(CONTINUED)

Comparison of Juvenile and Adult Rights Relating to Delinquency and Crime

Right	Adults	Juveniles
25. Right to hearing for parole or probation revocation	Yes	No, with exceptions
26. "Equal protection" clause of 14th Amendment applicable	Yes	No, with exceptions
27. Right to court-appointed attorney if indigent	Yes	No, with exceptions
28. Transcript required of criminal/delinquency trial proceedings	Yes	No, with exceptions
29. Pretrial detention permitted	Yes	Yes
30. Plea bargaining	Yes, with exceptions	No, with exceptions
31. Burden of proof borne by prosecution	Yes	No, with exceptions[b]
32. Public access to trials	Yes	Limited
33. Conviction/adjudication results in criminal record	Yes	No

[a]Minimal, not full, due-process safeguards assured.
[b]Burden of proof is borne by prosecutor in 23 state juvenile courts; the remainder make no provision or mention of who bears the burden of proof.
Source: Compiled by author.

Supreme Court eventually heard the case and upheld the detention as constitutional. Table 5.2 summarizes some of the major rights available to juveniles and compares these rights with selected rights enjoyed by adults in criminal proceedings.

IMPLICATIONS OF MORE CONSTITUTIONAL RIGHTS FOR JUVENILES

Some of the major implications of more constitutional rights for juveniles include: (1) more equitable treatment through less disparity in dispositions among juveniles judges; (2) greater certainty of punishment through the new justice orientation; (3) less informality in dispositions and less individualized rehabilitative treatments; (4) greater likelihood of acquiring a juvenile offender record, since procedures from intake through adjudication are increasingly codified; and (5) greater likelihood of being transferred to criminal courts through waivers, since the most serious cases will move forward more frequently to juvenile courts.

Almost all juvenile courts in the United States are civil courts. When juveniles are adjudicated delinquent by these courts, they do not acquire criminal records. Once youths reach the age of majority or adulthood, their juvenile records are expunged, forgotten, or sealed. They begin a fresh life as adults without a prior record of delinquency or criminal activity. This works to their advantage. However, the jurisdiction of juvenile courts in various states is changing. As we will see in subsequent chapters, the powers of juvenile court judges are being extended. Increasingly, it is possible for these judges to impose both juvenile and adult penalties on youths adjudicated delinquent. These dual sanctions are both innovative and controversial (Bilchik 1996). Furthermore, many states are lowering the age at which a juvenile may be tried as an adult in criminal court. In a deadly school shooting in Arkansas, for instance, the two shooters were 13 and 14 years of age, respectively. The 14-year-old was subsequently tried as an adult in criminal court. However, the 13-year-old was adjudicated in juvenile court where the harshness of penalties was severely limited. This was because the law as it was applied then meant that he could not be tried as an adult in criminal court, regardless of the heinousness of his actions. Only those age 14 or older could be tried as adults. As a result, the Arkansas legislature lowered the minimum age at which a juvenile could be tried as an adult in criminal court. Thus, if in the future, a 13-year-old juvenile committed murder in Arkansas, the juvenile could be prosecuted as an adult offender in criminal court (Associated Press 2001).

For the majority of jurisdictions as of 2002, while most juveniles remain within juvenile court jurisdiction, they are subject to harsher penalties as juveniles than might otherwise be the case if they were treated as adults. For instance, the case of *Gault* reported earlier in this chapter saw a boy disposed to nearly six years in a state industrial school for allegedly making an obscene telephone call, a low-level misdemeanor. For offenses such as this, adults would not be incarcerated. Rather, they would be fined a nominal amount. Currently, juvenile court judges have considerable power to influence a juvenile's liberty to the limits of one's infant status. Even now in most jurisdictions, if juvenile court judges wish, they may dispose youths to long-term secure confinement far beyond incarcerative terms for sentenced adults who have been convicted of similar offenses. This unfairness is a carryover from the *parens patriae* years of juvenile courts.

The Juvenile's Right to Waive Rights

With all of the legal rights extended to juveniles since 1966, there are more than a few occasions when juveniles may waive various rights, such as the right to counsel, at one or more critical stages of their juvenile justice system processing. For instance, a 1968 case decided following the *In re Gault* decision was *West v. United States* (1968). In the *West* case, a juvenile had waived his right to counsel, as well as several other important rights that had been extended to juveniles through the *Gault* case. A nine-point standard for analysis was established by the 5th Circuit Court of Appeals when the *West* disposition was imposed and an appeal followed. The nine-point standard was devised in order for judges to determine whether *any* juvenile is capable of understanding and waiving one or more of his or her constitutional rights. These nine points are:

1. Age
2. Education
3. Knowledge of the substance of the charge and the nature of the right to remain silent and the right to an attorney
4. Whether the accused is allowed contact with parents, guardian, attorney, or other interested adult

5. Whether the interrogation occurred before or after indictment

6. Methods used in interrogation

7. Length of interrogation

8. Whether the accused refused to voluntarily give statements on prior occasions

9. Whether the accused had repudiated an extrajudicial statement at a later date

While these nine points are interesting and relevant, the fact that they were articulated by the 5th Circuit Court of Appeals meant that they were not binding on federal district courts in other circuits. For that matter, since these were rights conveyed through a federal circuit, they were not binding on any particular state jurisdiction, even a state within the territory of the 5th Circuit Court of Appeals.

Subsequently, a totality of circumstances test in the case of *Fare v. Michael C.* (1979) was established by the U.S. Supreme Court and it has resulted in mixed decisions among appellate courts. For instance, in *Woods v. Clusen* (1986), the 7th Circuit Court of Appeals ruled that a 16 1/2-year-old's confession was inadmissible because the juvenile had been taken from his home at 7:30 A.M., handcuffed, stripped, forced to wear institutional clothing but no shoes or socks, shown pictures of the crime scene, and intimidated and interrogated for many hours. These police tactics were criticized by the court and the investigators were reprimanded for their failure to uphold and respect the offender's constitutional rights and provide fundamental fairness.

Research by Grisso (1980, 1998), for instance, shows that juveniles have little grasp of their constitutional rights. Grisso studied a large sample of juveniles and found that only 10 percent of them chose not to waive their rights where serious charges were alleged. Grisso found that they (1) demonstrated less comprehension than adults of their *Miranda* rights; (2) had less understanding of the wording of the **Miranda warning**; (3) misunderstood their right to counsel; and (4) did not understand their right to remain silent, believing that they could later be punished if they failed to tell about their criminal activities (*Miranda v. Arizona* 1966). Independent research has yielded findings consistent with the Grisso studies (Bailey 1983; Reineman 1969).

Another study was conducted to determine the degree of compliance of state juvenile codes with the actual rights juveniles have been extended by U.S. Supreme Court decisions (Caeti, Hemmens, and Burton 1996). Content analysis was used to examine all state statutes pertaining to legal counsel for juveniles. Among other things, the investigators wanted to determine whether there were statutory guarantees of a juvenile defendant's right to counsel; whether judicial discretion is permitted in the actual appointment of counsel for indigent juveniles; whether strict rights waivers were included; and whether defense counsel was mandated for all critical stages of juvenile justice processing.

First, these researchers found that all states, with the exception of Hawaii, Massachusetts, Michigan, Mississippi, Missouri, New Hampshire, North Carolina, North Dakota, Rhode Island, South Carolina, South Dakota, and West Virginia, had a specific juvenile statute identifying the juvenile's right to legal counsel. Table 5.3 shows a distribution of the states according to this and other

TABLE 5.3

Conditions under Which the Right to Counsel is Invoked[a]

State	Specific Juvenile Statute	Discretionary Appointment	Strict Waiver Requirements	Mandatory Appointment
Alabama	x	x		
Alaska	x			
Arizona	x	x		
Arkansas	x	x	x	
California	x	x		x
Colorado	x	x	x	
Connecticut	x	x	x	
Delaware				
Florida	x			
Georgia	x	x		
Hawaii				
Idaho	x	x		
Illinois	x	x		x
Indiana	x	x		
Iowa	x	x	x	
Kansas	x	x		x
Kentucky	x			
Louisiana	x		x	x
Maine	x			
Maryland	x	x	x	
Massachusetts		x	x	x
Michigan				
Minnesota	x			
Mississippi				
Missouri				
Montana	x	x	x	
Nebraska	x			
Nevada	x			
New Hampshire				
New Jersey	x		x	
New Mexico	x	x	x	x
New York	x			
North Carolina		x		x
North Dakota		x		
Ohio	x	x	x	
Oklahoma	x	x	x	
Oregon	x	x		
Pennsylvania	x	x	x	
Rhode Island		x		
South Carolina		x		
South Dakota		x	x	
Tennessee	x	x		
Texas	x	x	x	x
Utah	x	x		

(continued)

TABLE 5.3 (CONTINUED)

Conditions under Which the Right to Counsel is Invoked

State	Specific Juvenile Statute	Discretionary Appointment	Strict Waiver Requirements	Mandatory Appointment
Vermont	x	x		
Virginia	x	x	x	
Washington	x			
West Virginia		x		
Wisconsin	x	x		
Wyoming	x			

[a]Six states—Delaware, Hawaii, Michigan, Missouri, Mississippi, and New Hampshire—do not have statutory references to a juvenile's right to legal counsel in their state legal codes.
Source: Caeti, Hemmens, and Burton, 1996:622–623. Reprinted with permission of the *American Journal of Criminal Law* and the authors.

legal rights of juveniles regarding defense counsel appointments and waivers of the right to counsel. Only about half of all states have vested juvenile court judges with the discretion to appoint counsel for juveniles, while even fewer states provide strict rights waiver requirements and mandatory defense counsel appointments.

Subsequently, the researchers divided the states according to which ones were least and most protective of juveniles. They divided all states according to five categories. These are shown in Table 5.4. The first category in Table 5.4 shows six states where no specific statute exists guaranteeing juveniles the right to counsel.

The authors correctly indicate that despite the fact that these states are absent such statutes, the case of *In re Gault* is applicable to all states and ensures a juvenile's right to counsel at critical stages of their processing. Thus, there may not be a need to articulate this right as a legislated statute. The second category contains those states where minimal statements exist concerning a child's right to counsel at specific stages. They use Indiana as such a state where a statute says that "a child charged with a delinquent act is also entitled to be represented by counsel" (Caeti, Hemmens, and Burton 1996, 627). The third category contains states where statutory language extends the right to counsel to all juveniles at all stages or every stage of proceedings against them. The fourth category contains those states that provide counsel for juveniles beyond the stages articulated by *Gault.* These researchers cite Arkansas as a state where strict criteria are applicable in the event a juvenile wishes to waive certain constitutional rights. In the fifth and final category, states are shown where the right to counsel is extended, even to juveniles who do not face the prospect of secure confinement or any loss of freedom. Therefore, Table 5.4 is actually a continuum of the degree of statutory protection provided juveniles by various states, ranging from least protective to most protective (Caeti, Hemmens, and Burton 1996).

TABLE 5.4

Degree of Statutory Protection[a]

Category 1	Category 2	Category 3	Category 4	Category 5
Delaware	Alaska	Arizona	Alabama	California
Hawaii	District of Columbia	Colorado	Arkansas	Illinois
Michigan	Florida	District of Columbia	Connecticut	Kansas
Mississippi	Indiana	Georgia	Georgia	Louisiana
Missouri	Kentucky	Idaho	Iowa	New Mexico
New Hampshire	Maine	Maryland	Montana	North Carolina
	Minnesota	Massachusetts	Ohio	Texas
	Missouri	New Jersey	Oklahoma	
	Nebraska	North Dakota	Pennsylvania	
	Nevada	Ohio	Virginia	
	New York	Oregon	Wisconsin	
	North Dakota	Pennsylvania	Wyoming	
	Rhode Island	South Dakota		
	South Carolina	Tennessee		
	South Dakota	Utah		
	Tennessee	Vermont		
	Washington	Virginia		
	West Virginia	Washington		
		Wisconsin		

[a]Category 1 is least protective; category 5 is most protective.

Source: Caeti, Hemmens, and Burton, 1996:626. Reproduced with permission of the *American Journal of Criminal Law* and the authors.

The Continued Leniency of Juvenile Court Adjudications and Dispositions

Juvenile court actions continue to be fairly lenient. The sanction of choice among juvenile court judges is probation. Even those offenders who appear multiple times before the same judge are likely to continue to receive probation for their persistent offending. However, the many juvenile justice reforms that have occurred during the 1980s and 1990s have caused some persons to see little difference between how adults are processed by criminal courts and how juveniles are processed by juvenile courts (Feld 1993a). However, despite the increased criminalization of juvenile courts, there are significant differences that serve to differentiate criminal courts and criminal processing from how youths are treated or processed by the juvenile justice system.

Perhaps the most important implication for juveniles is that in most cases, juvenile court adjudications do not result in criminal records. These courts continue to exercise civil authority. Once juveniles reach adulthood, their juvenile records are routinely expunged and forgotten, with some exceptions. But having one's case adjudicated by a juvenile court operates to a youth's disadvantage in some respects. For instance, the rules governing the admissibility of evidence or testimony are relaxed considerably compared with the rules governing similar admissions in criminal courts. Thus, it is easier in juvenile courts to admit inculpatory evidence and testimony than in criminal courtrooms.

Further, cases against juveniles do not need to be as convincing as cases against criminal defendants. Lower standards of proof are operative relative to search and seizure and the degree of probable cause required. School children are particularly vulnerable in this regard, in view of *New Jersey v. T.L.O.* (1985). In this case, a 14-year-old girl was caught smoking a cigarette in the school bathroom, violating school rules. When confronted by the principal, she denied that she had been smoking. The principal examined her purse and discovered a pack of cigarettes, some rolling papers, money, marijuana, and other drug materials. This information was turned over to police, who charged the girl with delinquency. She was convicted. The girl's attorney sought to exclude the seized evidence because it was believed to be in violation of her Fourth Amendment right against unreasonable searches and seizures. The U.S. Supreme Court heard the case and ruled in favor of school officials, declaring that they only need reasonable suspicion, not probable cause, in order to search students and their possessions while on school property. When students enter their schools, they are subject to a lower standard than that applied to adult suspects when suspected of wrongdoing or carrying illegal contraband in violation of school rules.

Adversely, juveniles do not always receive jury trials if they request them (Sanborn 1993b). Less than a fourth of all states permit jury trials for juveniles by statute. In all other states, jury trials are available to juveniles only if judges permit them. In most cases, therefore, the judgment of the juvenile court is final, for all practical purposes. Appeals of decisions by juvenile court judges are relatively rare. Long-term dispositions of incarceration may be imposed by juvenile court judges at will, without serious challenge. Current profiles of long-term detainees in secure juvenile facilities suggests that judges impose dispositions of secure confinement frequently. Further, a majority of these long-term detainees are less serious property offenders with some chronicity in their rate of reoffending.

An Update on Jury Trials for Juvenile Delinquents

The National Center for Juvenile Justice (2001) has investigated various state jurisdictions to determine their present status concerning jury trials and other formal procedures for juveniles. The categories created by this investigation included the following: (1) states providing no right to a jury trial for juvenile delinquents under any circumstances; (2) states providing a right to a jury trial for juveniles delinquents under any circumstances; (3) states not providing a jury trial for juvenile delinquents except under specified circumstances; states providing the right to a jury trial for juvenile delinquents under specified circumstances; and (5) states with statutes allowing juvenile delinquents with a right to jury trial to waive that right.

1. States Not Providing Jury Trials for Juvenile Delinquents Under Any Circumstances: Alabama, Arizona, Arkansas, California, District of Columbia, Georgia, Hawaii, Indiana, Kentucky, Louisiana, Maryland, Mississippi, Nevada, New Jersey, North Dakota, Ohio, Oregon, Pennsylvania, South Carolina, Tennessee, Utah, Vermont, and Washington.

2. States Providing Jury Trials for Juvenile Delinquents Under Any Circumstance: Alaska, Massachusetts, Michigan, West Virginia.

3. States Not Providing Jury Trials for Juvenile Delinquents, Except Under Specified Circumstances: Colorado: All hearings, including adjudicatory hearings shall be heard without a jury; juvenile not entitled to a trial by jury when petition alleges a delinquent act which is a class 2 or class 3 misdemeanor, a petty offense, a violation of a municipal or county ordinance, or a violation of a court order if, prior to the trial and with the approval of the court, the district attorney has waived in writing the right to seek a commitment to the department of human services or a sentence to the county jail.

    District of Columbia: Probation revocation hearings heard without a jury.

    Florida: Adjudicatory hearings heard without a jury.

    Louisiana: Adjudication hearings heard without a jury.

    Maine: Adjudicatory hearing heard without a jury.

    Montana: Hearing on whether juvenile should be transferred to adult criminal court heard without a jury; probation revocation proceeding heard without a jury.

    Nebraska: Adjudicatory hearing heard without a jury.

    New Mexico: Probation revocation proceedings heard without a jury.

    North Carolina: Adjudicatory hearing heard without a jury.

    Texas: Detention hearing heard without a jury; hearing to consider transfer of child for criminal proceedings and hearing to consider waiver of jurisdiction held without a jury; disposition hearing heard without a jury, unless child in jeopardy of a determinate sentence; hearing to modify a disposition heard without a jury, unless child in jeopardy of a sentence for a determinate term.

    Wisconsin: No right to a jury trial in a waiver hearing.

    Wyoming: Probation revocation hearing heard without a jury; transfer hearing heard without a jury.

4. States Where Juvenile Delinquent Has a Right to a Jury Trial Under Specified Circumstances: Arkansas: If amount of restitution ordered by the court exceeds $10,000, juvenile has right to jury trial on all issues of liability and damages.

    Colorado: No right to a jury trial unless otherwise provided by this title; juvenile may demand a jury trial, unless the petition alleges a delinquent act that is a class 2 or class 3 misdemeanor, a petty offense, a violation of a municipal or county ordinance, or a violation of a court order if, prior to the trial and with the approval of the court, the district attorney has waived in writing the right to seek a commitment to the department of human services or a sentence to the county jail; any juvenile alleged to be an aggravated juvenile offender (defined in statute) has the right to a jury trial.

    Idaho: Any juvenile age 14 to 18 alleged to have committed a violent offense (defined in statute) or a controlled substance offense has the right to a jury trial.

    Illinois: Any Habitual Juvenile Offender (defined in statute) has the right to a jury trial.

    Kansas: Any juvenile alleged to have committed an act that would be a felony if committed by an adult has the right to a jury trial.

    Minnesota: Child who is prosecuted as an extended jurisdiction juvenile has the right to a jury trial on the issue of guilt.

> Montana: Any juvenile who contests the offenses alleged in the petition has the right to a jury trial.
>
> New Mexico: Jury trial on issues of alleged delinquent acts may be demanded when the offenses alleged would be triable by a jury if committed by an adult.
>
> Oklahoma: Child has right to a jury trial in adjudicatory hearing.
>
> Rhode Island: Child has right to jury when court finds child is subject to certification to adult court.
>
> Texas: Child has right to jury trial at adjudicatory hearing; child has right to a jury trial at disposition hearing only if child is in jeopardy of a determinate sentence; child has right to a jury trial at a hearing to modify the disposition only if the child is in jeopardy of a determinate sentence on the issues of the violation of the court's orders and the sentence.
>
> Virginia: If juvenile indicted, juvenile has the right to a jury trial; if found guilty of capital murder, court fixes sentence with intervention of a jury; where appeal is taken by child on a finding that he or she is delinquent and the alleged delinquent act would be a felony if done by adult, the child is entitled to a jury.
>
> Wyoming: Juvenile has right to jury trial at adjudicatory hearing.

5. States Providing Right to a Jury Trial for Juvenile Delinquents Where Juvenile Delinquents Can Waive Their Right to a Jury Trial:

> Colorado: Unless a jury is demanded, it shall be deemed waived.
>
> Illinois: Minor can demand in open court and with advice of counsel, a trial by the court without a jury.
>
> Massachusetts: Child can file written waiver and consent to be tried by the court without a jury; this waiver cannot be received unless the child is represented by counsel or has filed, through his [or her] parent or guardian, a written waiver of counsel.
>
> Montana: In the absence of a demand, a jury trial is waived.
>
> Oklahoma: Child has right to waive jury trial.
>
> Texas: Trial shall be by jury unless jury is waived.
>
> Wyoming: Failure of party to demand a jury no later than 10 days after the party is advised of his or her right, is a waiver of this right.

(*Source:* Compiled by author.)

Gelber (1990) has speculated what the juvenile court might be like during the first several decades of the twenty-first century. He envisions a court, conceivably renamed the Juvenile Services Consortium, with two tiers. The first tier will be devoted to adjudicating offenders under age 14. These offenders will always receive rehabilitative sanctions, such as probation or placement in conditional, community-based correctional programs. The second tier consists of those aged 14 to 18. For these juveniles, jury trials will be available, and these offenders will be subject to the same incarcerative sanctions that can be imposed by criminal courts.

Gelber's two-tiered juvenile court projection for the twenty-first century may not be far off the mark in relation to societal expectations for such courts in future years. The public mood seems to be in favor of deserts-based sentencing and toward due process for juvenile offenders. The two-tiered nature of Gelber's projected court organization would seemingly achieve this get tough result, although provisions would remain for treatment-centered rehabilitative sanctions for younger offenders. In a sense, this two-tiered court projection seems to be nothing more than lowering the age jurisdiction of criminal courts from 18 to 14. However, Gelber's intent is to preserve the jurisdictional integrity of the juvenile justice system in relation to the criminal justice system. In any case, this would be an effective compromise between those favoring the traditional rehabilitative posture of juvenile courts and those favoring a shift to more punitive court policies and practices.

THE DEATH PENALTY FOR JUVENILES

In 2001, there were 3,593 prisoners on death row awaiting the penalty of death. There were 431 death row inmates age 19 or younger, which accounted for approximately 12 percent of all death row inmates (Snell 2001, 9). Between 1642 and 2000 there were over 325 executions of youths in the United States when they were under age 18 when committing capital crimes.

The first documented execution of a juvenile occurred in 1642. Thomas Graunger, a 16-year-old, was convicted of bestiality. He was caught sodomizing a horse and a cow. Graunger was tried, convicted, and executed. The youngest age where the death penalty was imposed is 10. A poorly documented case of a 10-year-old convicted murderer in Louisiana occurred in 1855. A more celebrated case, that of 10-year-old James Arcene, occurred in Arkansas in 1885. Arcene was 10 years old when he robbed and murdered his victim. He was eventually arrested at age 23 before being executed (Streib 1987, 57).

Arguments for or against the death penalty for adults pertain to juveniles as well (Moon et al. 2000). The media have assisted in sensationalizing capital crimes by juveniles, and to some extent, this has caused a substantial number of persons to approve the death penalty for certain juveniles (Coleman 1998). Those favoring the death penalty say it is "just" punishment and a societal revenge for the life taken or harm inflicted by the offender. It is an economical way of dealing with those who will never be released from confinement. It may be administered humanely, through lethal injection. It functions as a deterrent to others to refrain from committing capital crimes. Opponents say it is cruel and unusual punishment. They claim the death penalty does not deter those who intend to take another's life. It is barbaric and uncivilized. Other countries do not impose it for any type of offense, regardless of its seriousness. It makes no sense to kill as a means of sending messages to others not to kill (Coalition for Juvenile Justice 1998).

For juveniles, the argument is supplemented by the fact that age functions as a mitigating factor. In any capital conviction, the convicted offender is entitled to a bifurcated trial where guilt is established first, and then the punishment is imposed in view of any prevailing mitigating or aggravating circumstances. Was the crime especially brutal? Did the victim suffer? Was the murderer senile or mentally ill? Or was the murderer a juvenile? Since age acts as a mitigating factor in cases where the death penalty is considered for adults, there are those who say the death penalty should not be applied to juveniles under any condition. Early English precedent and common law assumed that those under age 7 were incapable of formulating criminal intent, and thus, they were absolved from any wrongdoing. Between ages 7 and 12, a presumption exists that the child is capable of formulating criminal intent, and in every jurisdiction, the burden is borne by the prosecution for establishing beyond a reasonable doubt that the youth was capable of formulating criminal intent.

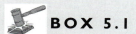 **BOX 5.1**

Kip Kinkel, Springfield High School (Oregon) Murderer

It happened at Springfield High School in Eugene, Oregon, on May 21, 1998. A 16-year-old, Kip Kinkel, had just shot his parents to death at their home. He headed for the high school with several firearms and ample ammunition. When he arrived at the school, he shot and killed two students and wounded twenty-six others before he was apprehended. At Kinkel's subsequent trial, doctors testified for the defense that Kinkel was a paranoid schizophrenic driven to kill by hallucinations. He was convicted of four murders and twenty-six counts of attempted murder. He entered a guilty plea to four counts of murder and the attempted murder counts, agreeing to serve 25 years in prison for the murders. The judge could impose an additional 220 years for the attempted murders. At Kinkel's sentencing hearing later, several of his victims spoke out against any type of judicial leniency. One woman, Jennifer Alldredge, said that she had been sitting in the cafeteria talking with friends about a surprise birthday party they were planning for her boyfriend, Jake Ryker. Ryker was subsequently wounded in the attack but ended up tackling Kinkel and ending the rampage. Ms. Alldredge was shot in the lung and hand. Ms. Alldredge said that she was still startled by loud noises and aware of people staring at her scars when she wears a bathing suit and ashamed for what happened to her. She faced Kinkel and yelled, "I hate you. I hate what you have done, I hate what I have become because of you. I'm so tired of having all this run my life."

Several parents recounted the horror they experienced when learning that their children had been shot. Fear still rules their lives, they said. Several students described how their grades have gone down and how they were plagued with nightmares. All of them asked the judge to sentence Kinkel to spend the rest of their life in prison so that they could feel safe. "If Mr. Kinkel is sitting in prison without the possibility of release for the rest of his life, it might—it just might—keep some other person from taking a gun to school," said Mark Walker, father of Ben Walker, a student who was killed in the shooting. He added, "That would be the only positive thing to come from this." Another victim was Ryan Crowley. His father, Michael Crowley, said that Ryan could not bear to be in the courtroom with Kinkel. He said Ryan was spared death only because Kinkel had run out of bullets before he put a .22 caliber rifle to Ryan's head and pulled the trigger. "Don't tell Kip there is no punishment for putting a gun to Ryan's forehead," said Michael Crowley. "Don't tell Ryan it doesn't matter." Kinkel sat slumped forward looking down, but glanced at the victims from time to time. He obeyed the request of one victim to look at him as she spoke. When Jake Ryker's turn came to speak, he walked to the defense table and faced Kinkel. "I'm not going to ask you to look at me, I demand it," said Ryker. Ryker recounted the pain of being shot and recalled how when Kinkel ran out of ammunition in his rifle and drew a 9mm pistol, Ryker shoved it away. Ryker said that he should have taken the pistol and killed Kinkel when he had the chance. "I don't care if you're sick, insane, or crazy. I can't stand here and look at you without wanting to kill you," said Ryker. Ms. Alldrege added, "I'm not falling for this poor, mentally sick, rich boy explanation." Other victims said that they believed that Kinkel was lying when he claimed that voices in his head made him open fire inside his high school cafeteria. Subsequently, Kip Kinkel was sentenced to 112 years in prison. On his own behalf, Kinkel read a prepared statement: "I absolutely loved my parents and had no reason to kill them. I had no reason to dislike or try to kill anyone at Thurston (the high school where the tragedy occurred). I am truly sorry for all of this. These events have pulled me to a state of deterioration and self-loathing that I didn't know existed." Kinkel stood with his hands clasped in front of him as the judge gave him what amounted to a life sentence. Kinkel was 15 when he went on the shooting spree. Thus, he was ineligible for the death penalty. Most of the victims seemed satisfied with his sentence, and they hoped that some day they could get on with their lives.

What do you think is the major effect of victim impact statements? To what extent should judges be influenced in their sentencing decisions by such statements? Victim impact statements have been ruled constitutional by the U.S. Supreme Court. Should they be permitted in all serious cases or are they unfairly prejudicial? Was Kinkel's sentence fair? What do you think?

Source: Adapted from the Associated Press, "Victims Tell Kinkel They Don't Believe Voices Made Him Kill." November 10, 1999:A5; Associated Press, "Kip Kinkel Sentenced to Life." November 11, 1999.

While each case is judged on its own merits, there are always at least two sides in an issue involving the murder of one by another. The survivors of the victim demand justice, and the justice they usually seek is the death of the one who brought about the death of their own. This is a manifestation of the eye-for-an-eye philosophy. In many respects, it is an accurate portrayal of why the death penalty is imposed for both juveniles and adults. It is supposed to be a penalty that fits the crime committed. But attorneys and family members of those convicted of capital crimes cannot help but feel compassion for their doomed relatives. Someone they love is about to lose his or her life. But hadn't

BOX 5.2

PERSONALITY HIGHLIGHT

Shani Gray
Ph.D. in progress (social psychology), Indiana University

Marla Sandys
Professor, Indiana University

Statistics:

Marla Sandys, Ph.D. (criminal justice), University of Kentucky

Background and Interests:

Shani Gray is a doctoral student in the Department of Criminal Justice at Indiana University. Her research interests include issues surrounding juvenile justice, juvenile waivers, community corrections programming, and the role of faith-based organizations in community crime control efforts. Marla Sandys is an Associate Professor of Criminal Justice at Indiana University. She earned her Ph.D. in social psychology from

the University of Kentucky. Her research interests include attitudes toward capital punishment, jury selection, and jury decision making in capital cases.

Opinions and Views:

Should juveniles be eligible for the death penalty? That question, in many respects, is akin to asking whether juveniles should ever be waived to adult court. The conditions that

(continued)

BOX 5.2 (*Continued*)

render a juvenile eligible to be waived to adult court ultimately serve as the conditions that subject him or her to the death penalty. As was established in *Kent v. United States* (1966), "an offense falling within the statutory limits . . . will be waived if it has prosecutive merit and if heinous or of an aggravated character, or—even though less serious—if it represents a pattern of repeated offenses which indicate that the juvenile may be beyond rehabilitation under Juvenile Court procedures, or if the public needs protection afforded by such action" (at 566). Moreover, the ruling held that juveniles must receive a waiver hearing before they are tried as adults. Thus, one could argue that juveniles who stand to face the death penalty are given the benefit of two additional levels of decision that are not accorded to their adult counterparts. If either the prosecutor charging the offenses or the judge overseeing the waiver hearing believes that the crime does not warrant eligibility for the death penalty, then the process can be stopped at that time.

Another similarity between juvenile waivers and eligibility for the death penalty is the selective nature of the decisions: Both situations pertain to a relatively small group of people who have committed what are supposed to be the most heinous crimes, those crimes that so shock the conscience of the community that the standard practice appears to be an inadequate response. For instance, should a 17-year-old who commits what would be considered a death-eligible offense for an adult, such as killing multiple people, be allowed to serve the four years until he or she reaches the age of maturity and then be released from the juvenile facility? If one believes that there are conditions under which juveniles should be treated as adults in the eyes of the law, then logic dictates that one possible outcome is a sentence of death.

The operative word in the previous sentence is *possible;* the death penalty, whether it be for juveniles or adults, is never mandatory. Even a person who is serving a life sentence who then murders a prison guard is not subject to a mandatory death sentence (*Sumner v. Schuman,* 1987). Rather, the law requires that decisions of life and death be made on the basis of aggravating and mitigating circumstances. Age of the offender is one of those compelling circumstances that is to inform decisions about the case at every stage of the judicial process. Should the juvenile be waived to adult court? Once waived, should the juvenile be charged with a capital offense? Should the state seek the death penalty? If convicted of the capital offense, should the juvenile be sentenced to death? The age of the offender is supposed to come into play at each one of these decision points; those who ultimately are sentenced to death are theoretically those whose youthfulness is overshadowed by the aggravating nature of their crime.

We know from attitudinal surveys that, in general, there is less support for capital punishment for juveniles than for adults. For instance, Sandys and McGarrell (1995) found that only 14 percent of their sample of 514 Indiana residents indicated any opposition in response to the general death penalty question. In contrast, a slim majority (51 percent) agreed that the death penalty should *not* be imposed on a person who was younger than 18 at the time of the crime. Most interesting for the purpose of this discussion, however, was their finding that a small number of respondents who indicated general opposition to capital punishment nonetheless indicated that they favored the death penalty for juveniles. Hence, the findings suggest that people are able to make those difficult distinctions between cases that might or might not warrant a sentence of death. In fact, there is some evidence to suggest that while age of the offender often is a persuasive mitigator, some jurors evaluate the age of the offender as an aggravator rather than a mitigator. If a juror is convinced that the offender is beyond rehabilitation, to use the term in *Kent,* then they might believe that there is nothing that could be done for this offender. In effect, the juror may look at a young offender and think that if this person is capable of committing this sort of offense at this young age, then there is no hope for him or her.

In some respects, the above argument was the one adopted by Indiana at the most recent hearing on a bill to raise the minimum age of eligibility for the death penalty from 16 to 18. Sandys attended the hearing and while all but one person spoke in favor of the bill, the Executive Director of the Prosecuting Attorneys Council said, in effect, that there are just some crimes, committed by some juveniles, that warrant death. The director conceded that those cases are rare, and that the use of the death penalty should be a last resort, especially as it applies to juveniles, but that there were cases that were so horrific that nothing less than death would seem appropriate. In effect, the Attorney General was arguing that the State wanted the option of the death penalty for juveniles as a means of possibly deterring some people, but more importantly, as a means of retributive justice. The committee hearing the bill and ultimate the legislature and the governor were not persuaded by the argument. As of July 1, 2002, Indiana presently requires that persons be at least 18 years old at the time of the offense in order to be eligible for a sentence of death.

From a broader perspective, one could argue that the U.S. Supreme Court determines what is constitutionally permissible by the states; it does not require that all states adopt a particular provision. As this applies to juveniles and the death penalty, we know that a slight majority of states with the death penalty (22 of 38 states plus the federal courts) allow for persons under 18 to be sentenced to death. Thus, one could advance the argument that this is an issue of states' rights: If particular states do not want juveniles to be eligible for the death penalty, then that is their right. In fact, sixteen states together with the federal courts have exercised this right, requiring that persons under their jurisdiction be at least 18 years old before being eligible for a sentence of death. Moreover, as public or legislative sentiment changes, so too can the laws. [While the following is not an argument for the death penalty for juveniles per se, it is an interesting take on proposed legislative changes. Some people who consider themselves ardent abolitionists, people who are completely opposed to capital punishment, nonetheless oppose raising the age of eligibility from 16 to 18 years old. The argument is *not* that they support the death penalty for juveniles, but rather, that any change to current law should be abolition and nothing less. To the extent that we make the death penalty more palatable—such as recent changes in the method of execution from the electric chair to lethal injection—we make it that much easier to accept the penalty, and that is seen by some as the wrong road to abolition. Many thanks to a death row inmate who wishes to remain anonymous for insisting that this point be included in any discussion of the recent legislative changes in Indiana.]

For instance, a mere thirteen years ago, Indiana allowed for children as young as 10 to be eligible for the death penalty. Then, when Paula Cooper's case was under review in 1989, the state raised the minimum age for the death penalty to 16 years of age. [Paula Cooper was a 15-year-old girl from Gary, Indiana, who was sentenced to death for killing her bible school teacher. Her death sentence was overturned and she received a term of years. As of May 2002, Paula Cooper graduated college through correspondence courses while still in prison.] Furthermore, within states, particular jurors on particular cases can determine whether particular juveniles should be sentenced to death. In fact, the U.S. Supreme Court acknowledges that its Eighth Amendment capital jurisprudence relies on assessment of "evolving standards of decency that mark the progress of a maturing society" (*Trop v. Dulles*, 1958 at 101). If juries stop voting to sentence juveniles to death, and if legislatures vote to increase the minimum age of the death penalty to 18, then the Court might conclude that capital punishment for juveniles is cruel and unusual punishment. That time has not come, although there are indications that the Court is poised to consider

(continued)

BOX 5.2 (*Continued*)

this issue in the near future. In the summer of 2002, the U.S. Supreme Court declared that the death penalty is unconstitutional for persons who are mentally retarded (*Atkins v. Virginia,* 2002). The same analysis that applies to persons who are mentally retarded applies to juveniles. Even more recently, Justices Stevens, Ginsburg, and Breyer, in dissents from an order declining to stay the execution of a person who had been sentenced to death as a juvenile, intimated that it was time for the Court to reconsider the issue of juveniles and the death penalty: "I think it would be appropriate for the Court to revisit the issue [the Eighth Amendment challenge to the execution of a person con-

victed of a crime committed when he was under 18 years of age] at the earliest opportunity" (*Patterson v. Texas* 2002, U.S. LEXIS 5341). Clearly, three of nine Justices is not a majority, but to voice such strong opinions in a dissent from an order to grant a stay is highly unusual. The coming years will no doubt bring the issue of juveniles and the death penalty to the Court's table, and while it is a foolish game to predict the Court's stance on the issue, it appears clear that the Court will agree to hear such a case and that the arguments touched upon here and throughout this text will be those proffered for consideration.

they taken someone's life in the process? But does taking another life bring back the dead victim? But does taking the life of the murderer fulfill some lofty societal purpose? The arguments about this issue are endless.

In 1977 in Fort Jackson, South Carolina, a 17-year-old mentally retarded youth and a 16-year-old companion were living with a 22-year-old soldier in a rented, rundown house. [The following account has been adapted from Streib 1987, 125–127]. Alcohol, THC, PCP, marijuana and other drugs were readily available. On a warm Saturday, October 29, after heavy drinking and consuming drugs, the three decided to look for a girl to rape. They drove to a baseball park in nearby Columbia. They parked next to a young couple, a 17-year-old boy and his 14-year-old girlfriend. On orders from the soldier, they shot the boy three times with a high-powered rifle, killing him instantly. Then they drove off with the girl to a secluded area where each raped her repeatedly. Finally, they finished her off by shooting her and mutilating her body.

James Terry Roach was electrocuted in South Carolina for a murder he committed as a teenager in 1977.

The three were soon arrested by police. The youngest youth agreed to testify against the soldier and the 17-year-old in exchange for a lighter punishment. Both the soldier and the 17-year-old eventually entered guilty pleas and were sentenced to death. After lengthy appeals, the soldier was executed by South Carolina authorities on January 11, 1985. Finally, on January 10, 1986, James Terry Roach, the 17-year-old who killed the boy and girl and mutilated the girl's body, was executed in the South Carolina electric chair. Justice was served. Or was it? A crowd cheered outside the prison walls as the execution of Roach occurred. Roach wrote his last letter, and as he was strapped into the electric chair, he read it with shaky hands: "To the families of the victims, my heart is still with you in your sorrow. May you forgive me just as I know that my Lord has done." Two one-minute surges of electricity hit him and he was pronounced dead at 5:16 A.M. (Streib 1987, 125–127). The minimum offender age for the death penalty in those states where the death penalty is imposed for capital crimes is as follows in Table 5.5.

Until recently, the U.S. Supreme Court has consistently refused to become embroiled in the capital-punishment-for-juveniles issue, although it has heard several juvenile death penalty cases in past years. One frequently cited case is *Eddings v. Oklahoma* (1982). The case raised the question of whether the death penalty as applied to juveniles was cruel and unusual punishment under the

TABLE 5.5

Minimum Age Authorized for Capital Punishment, 2000

Age 16 or Less	Age 17	Age 18	None Specified
Alabama (16)	Georgia	California	Arizona
Arkansas (14)[a]	New Hampshire	Colorado	Idaho
Delaware (16)	North Carolina[b]	Connecticut[c]	Louisiana
Florida (16)	Texas	Federal system	Montana[d]
Indiana (16)		Illinois	Pennsylvania
Kentucky (16)		Kansas	South Carolina
Mississippi (16)[e]		Maryland	South Dakota[f]
Missouri (16)		Nebraska	
Nevada (16)		New Jersey	
Oklahoma (16)		New Mexico	
Utah (14)		New York	
Virginia (14)[g]		Ohio	
Wyoming (16)		Oregon	
		Tennessee	
		Washington	

Note: Reporting by States reflects interpretations by State attorney generals' offices and may differ from previously reported ages.
[a]See Ark. Code Ann. 9-27-318(c)(2)(Supp. 1999).
[b]Age required is 17 unless the murderer was incarcerated for murder when a subsequent murder occurred; then the age may be 14.
[c]See Conn. Gen. Stat. 53a-46a(g)(1).
[d]Montana law specifies that offenders tried under the capital sexual assault statute be 18 or older. Age may be a mitigating factor for other capital crimes.
[e]The minimum age defined by statute is 13, but the effective age is 16 based on interpretation of U.S. Supreme Court decisions by the Mississippi Supreme Court.
[f]Juveniles may be transferred to adult court. Age can be a mitigating factor.
[g]The minimum age for transfer to adult court by statute is 14, but the effective age is 16 based on interpretation of U.S. Supreme Court decisions by the State attorney general's office.

Eighth Amendment of the U.S. Constitution. The U.S. Supreme Court avoided the issue. The Justices did not say it was cruel and unusual punishment, but they also did not say that it wasn't. What they said was that the youthfulness of the offender is a mitigating factor of great weight that must be considered. Thus, many jurisdictions were left to make their own interpretations of the high court opinion.

Reasons for Supporting the Death Penalty

The primary reasons for supporting the death penalty in certain capital cases are threefold: (1) retribution; (2) deterrence; and (3) just-deserts.

1. The death penalty is retribution. Retribution is defended largely on the basis of the philosophical just-desert rationale. Offenders should be executed because they did not respect the lives of others. Death is the just desert for someone who inflicted death on someone else. Retribution is regarded by some observers as the primary purpose of the death penalty (Whitehead 1998).

2. The death penalty deters others from committing murder. The deterrence function of the death penalty is frequently questioned as well. An exami-

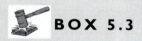   **BOX 5.3**

Brenda Sims Blackwell
Georgia State University

Statistics:

B.S. (criminal justice), Northern Arizona University; M.A. (sociology), University of Oklahoma; Ph.D. (sociology), University of Oklahoma

Current Interests and Specialties:

My primary research focuses on exploring the sources of gender differences in delinquency and crime, with a particular emphasis on examining power-control theory. However, I have also maintained an interest in corrections and the death penalty in particular. Early in my graduate career, I had the opportunity to work on a research project that examined the religious foundations of public support for the death penalty. More recently, since joining the faculty at Georgia State University, I have become involved in a research project that explores the impact of the death penalty on the families of both victims and offenders.

Support of the Death Penalty for Juveniles:

The death penalty is one of the hotly debated issues in not only criminology and criminal justice classes but also public discourse. When juveniles are the subject of the death penalty, emotions run particularly high. Indeed, public policy on execution has been more fluid for juveniles than adults. Historically, there were not separate court and correctional systems for juveniles, and thus, they were as subject to death sentences as adult offenders. However, largely as a result of the childsavers movement, a separate court system was established for juveniles, based on the notions that youth are more amenable to change and that children do not hold the same capacity of intent as do adults. From the late 1970s to the late 1990s, the United States experienced increasing rates of juvenile crime. In response to public outcry, we saw increases in the number of transfers of offenders from the juvenile and family courts into the adult criminal justice system; a number of these transfers occurred with the purpose of seeking the death penalty. In addition, we saw legislatures reconsidering the age levels at which transfers into the adult system were appropriate.

It is important to understand public opinions about correctional policies, particularly the death penalty, because the public clearly influences the direction of policy change. It is notable that while there is a high level of support for the death penalty for juveniles, it is not as strong as support for adult death sentences. Furthermore, those who oppose the death penalty for juveniles demonstrate stronger levels of opposition than those against the death penalty for adults. This likely indicates that the idea of sentencing youth to death is a more emotional issue than when adults are the subject. The philosophies behind the development of the juvenile court movement, of malleability and lower capacity for intent, are also reflected in such opposition.

Studies examining the correlates of support for the death penalty consistently indicate that the same factors are at work when juveniles and adults are considered. Specifically, those who support the death penalty for juveniles (and adults) are most typically male, white, younger, more affluent, less educated, and more politically conservative. In addition, religious background is consistently and significantly linked to support for the death penalty.

My research with Dr. Harold G. Grasmick and Dr. Robert J. Bursik, examining public support for the death penalty for both juveniles and adults, specifically focused on the effect of religion. We were particularly interested in the different ways that religion could impact public attitudes. In particular,

we posited that it is not solely religiosity, or the fact that one is religious, that leads to support for the death penalty. Instead, we noted that fundamentalists and evangelicals were more likely to support the death penalty than nonfundamentalists, in large part because of their religious views. Specifically, we noted that individuals who adhere to fundamentalist/evangelical beliefs are more punitive in nature, are more likely to take a literal interpretation of the Bible, are more likely to view God as punitive (rather than forgiving), and are more likely to attribute crime to an individual's character than their circumstance. Our findings provided support for our position. While levels of religiosity did not impact support, we did find that supporters of the death penalty for juveniles and adults were more likely to interpret the Bible in a literal manner. In addition, individuals who viewed God as punitive were more likely to support the death penalty for juveniles than those who viewed God as forgiving.

Advice to Students:

When doing a research project on the death penalty, it is easy to get lost in the literature that exists. Indeed, a vast amount of research has been conducted that explores various aspects of the death penalty. My advice is to narrow your focus to a very specific issue. For example, while a great deal of research has examined sources of support for the death penalty, narrowing the topic to focus on religious-based support significantly reduced the literature. In my own research, further narrowing the topic to support for the death penalty for juveniles allowed for a very thorough review of the literature, because there is less extant literature that has examined such a narrow topic. In addition, by restricting your topic in this way, it actually becomes easier to identify what is missing, yielding opportunities for developing your own project to fill these gaps. In sum, while it is natural to pick a broad topic, doing so is generally quite overwhelming. Narrowing your topic affords you the opportunity to thoroughly review the literature and to more readily identify gaps.

nation of homicide rates in Illinois during a forty-eight-year period (1933–1980) was conducted. It revealed that average homicide rates for three different periods did not fluctuate noticeably. These periods included (1) times when the death penalty was allowed; (2) years when the death penalty was allowed but no executions were performed; and (3) years when the death penalty was abolished (Decker and Kohfeld 1990). Persons favoring the abolition of the death penalty argue that no criminal act ever justifies capital punishment (Forst 1995).

3. The death penalty is a just-desert for commission of a capital offense. The just-deserts philosophy would argue that the death penalty is just punishment for someone who has committed murder (Sandys and McGarrell 1995). The U.S. Supreme Court has indirectly validated this reasoning by refusing to declare the death penalty cruel and unusual punishment.

Reasons for Opposing the Death Penalty

Some of the reasons persons use to oppose the death penalty are that (1) it is barbaric; (2) it may be applied in error to someone who is not actually guilty of a capital offense; (3) it is nothing more than sheer revenge; (4) it is more costly than life imprisonment; (5) it is applied arbitrarily; (6) it does not deter others from committing murder; and (7) most persons in the United States are opposed to the death penalty.

1. The death penalty is barbaric. Nancy Walker (2001) says that the death penalty is barbaric and violates international law. There are other avenues whereby convicted capital offenders can be punished. The United States is one of the few civilized countries of the modern world that still uses the death penalty. Portraits of persons condemned to death include accounts of their past lives by close friends and family members who oppose capital punishment in their cases. Even statements from various family members of victims express opposition to the death penalty because of its alleged barbarism.

2. The death penalty is unfair and may be applied erroneously. Some convicted offenders are wrongly convicted. Evidence subsequently discovered has led to freeing several persons who were formerly on death row awaiting execution. Bedau (1992) and the American Civil Liberties Union are strong death penalty opponents. This reason is one of their strongest arguments against its application. Thus, this view proposes an outright ban on the death penalty because of the mere possibility that some persons sentenced to death are actually innocent and should not be executed. A study by Michael Radelet, Hugo Bedau, and Constance Putnam (1992) showed, for instance, that over 400 persons have been wrongly convicted of capital crimes and sentenced to death as miscarriages of justice in the United States. Evidence eventually discovered and used to free these persons included the confessions of the real perpetrators, reversals on appeal, and unofficial judgments when crimes were found not to have occurred (e.g., missing bodies eventually discovered and found not to have been murdered).

3. The death penalty is nothing more than revenge. Some observers argue that by condoning the death penalty, the U.S. Supreme Court has sanc-

tioned vengeance, which is an unacceptable justification for imposing capital punishment. For persons who are retarded or intellectually disabled, it is likely that they cannot reach the level of culpability necessary to trigger the need for the death penalty. They cannot engage in cold calculus to weigh committing the crime against the potential death penalty used to punish it (Miller 1990).

4. The death penalty is more costly than life-without-parole sentences. Many opponents of capital punishment grasp the cost factor to show that executing prisoners under death sentences is more costly over time than imprisoning them for life (Bedau 1992). However, a key reason for the high cost of executing prisoners is that they have been entitled to file endless appeals and delay the imposition of their death sentences (Costanzo and White 1994). In 1996, Congress acted to limit the number of appeals inmates on death rows could file. Thus, it is expected in future years that the length of time between conviction and imposition of the death penalty will be greatly abbreviated. This shorter period of time will decrease the expense of death penalty appeals and undermine this particular argument.

5. The death penalty is still applied arbitrarily despite efforts by legislatures and Congress to make its application more equitable. Evidence suggests that although bifurcated trials have decreased the racial bias in death penalty applications, disproportionality of death sentences according to race and ethnicity have not been eliminated (Bohm and Vogel 1994). While some persons argue that some races and ethnic categories have higher rates of capital murder and thus are disproportionately represented on death row, other persons say that the death penalty continues to be applied in a discriminatory manner in many jurisdictions.

6. The death penalty does not deter others from committing murder. The literature strongly supports the idea that the death penalty apparently has no discernable deterrent effect. Persons will commit murder anyway, even knowing that there is a chance they may be caught eventually and executed for the crime. An examination of crime statistics and comparisons of those jurisdictions where the death penalty is applied and jurisdictions where it isn't applied show few, if any, differences in capital murder cases. Thus, the argument goes, if capital punishment fails to deter capital murder, then it should be abolished (Godfrey and Schiraldi 1995).

7. Most persons in the United States are against the death penalty. Bedau (1992) has suggested that there is growing lack of public support for the death penalty in the United States. However, several national surveys show that over 75 percent of those interviewed support the death penalty and its application (Simmons et al. 1995). Certainly, a knowledge of the death penalty and its deterrent and retributive effects makes a difference in whether persons support or oppose its use. Growing violent street crimes, especially violent street crimes resulting in the deaths of innocent victims, do nothing but trigger pro–capital punishment reactions from an increasingly frightened public (Moon et al. 2000).

All of the arguments that function as either pros or cons relative to the death penalty also apply directly to the issue of juvenile executions. However,

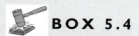 **BOX 5.4**

ANOTHER HIGH SCHOOL SHOOTING

It's Only Me, Andy Williams, 15

He is only 15, the target of teasing, and a meek and mild high schooler. His name is Andy Williams. He moved to California from Knoxville, Maryland, a rural hamlet. In Maryland, Williams was an honors student. He was a fun-loving kid and very popular with other boys and girls. His principal at Brunswick Middle School said that Williams was very happy in school. However, when he moved to California, all of that changed. He kept in touch with his former Maryland friends through e-mails. He told his friends that his new California schoolmates called him "gay." He said that they made fun of him for being from the country, the way he talked, dressed, and cut his hair. He also missed his mother, who moved to South Carolina following a divorce.

In California, Williams went to Santana High School in Santee, which is about 10 miles northeast of San Diego. He quickly adapted to the taunts from other schoolmates. He would joke with them when they called him a nerd or dork. People called him a pussy and teased him a lot. Ashlee Allsop was a student he dated when he moved to Santana High School. She said that other students made fun of him because he was skinny. She added that he never took it seriously and laughed about it. However, other students had different impressions of how Williams reacted. One student, Justin Kraft, 17, said that Williams was pissed off with everyone. There were some warning signs that something bad was going to happen. A man, Chris Reynolds, 29, lived with Williams' best friend, Josh Stevens, who is the son of Karen Reynolds who lived with Reynolds. Reynolds said that he would hear Williams make threats about getting even at school, about pulling a "Columbine," where numerous students were murdered in Colorado. When Reynolds asked Williams if he was joking, Williams would say, "Yeah." But Williams was not joking.

On March 5, 2001, Williams obtained a .22 caliber revolver from his father's dresser drawer and took it with him to school. When he arrived, some of his friends decided to frisk him to make sure he wasn't carrying a weapon. They patted him down and searched his book bag, but not thoroughly enough. They failed to find the gun inside the bag. It took him only six minutes to kill two students, Randy Gordon, 17, and Bryan Zuckor, 14, and wound fourteen others. He fired at least 30 shots and reloaded several times. When police arrived and subdued him, he surrendered meekly and said to them, "It's only me." Williams was subsequently charged with murder as an adult. Although he cannot be executed for his crimes since he was under 16 at the time of the murders, he can receive life without the possibility of parole. Ashlee Allsop, his girlfriend, said, "Andy is not a bad person at all . . . he was always there for his friends. I don't want him to be locked up forever. He's only 15."

What should Williams' punishment be? Should the judge sentence Williams to life without the possibility of parole? Do you think that someone like Williams can be rehabilitated? What do you think?

Source: Adapted from Jill Smolowe, Leslie Berestein, Maureen Harrington, and J. Todd Foster. "It's Only Me." *People,* March 7, 2001, 61–62.

the nature of juvenile justice reforms is such that a strong belief persists that substantial efforts must be made by juvenile courts and corrections to rehabilitate juveniles rather than incarcerate or execute them. In those states where executions are conducted, where should the line be drawn concerning the minimum age at which someone becomes liable, accountable, and subject to the death penalty?

U.S. SUPREME COURT DEATH PENALTY CASES

Several U.S. Supreme Court cases have been decided in recent years involving questions of executions of juveniles. These cases have been especially significant in providing a legal foundation for such executions. These include *Eddings v. Oklahoma* (1982), *Thompson v. Oklahoma* (1988), *Stanford v. Kentucky* (1989), and *Wilkins v. Missouri* (1989). As a prelude to discussing these cases, it should be noted that until 1988, sixteen states had minimum-age provisions for juvenile executions (under age 18), where the range in minimum age was from 10 (Indiana) to 17 (Georgia, New Hampshire, and Texas). When the *Thompson v. Oklahoma* case was decided in 1988, the minimum age for juvenile executions in all states was raised to 16. The following year, the U.S. Supreme Court upheld death sentences of a 16-year-old and a 17-year-old as well.

Eddings v. Oklahoma (1982)

On April 4, 1977, Monty Lee Eddings and several other companions ran away from their Missouri homes. In a car owned by Eddings' older brother, they drove, without direction or purpose, eventually reaching the Oklahoma Turnpike. Eddings had several firearms in the car, including several rifles that he had stolen from his father. At one point, Eddings lost control of the car and was stopped by an Oklahoma State Highway Patrol officer. When the officer approached the car, Eddings stuck a shotgun out of the window and killed the officer outright. When Eddings was subsequently apprehended, he was waived to criminal court on a prosecutorial motion. Efforts by Eddings and his attorney to oppose the waiver failed.

In a subsequent bifurcated trial, several aggravating circumstances were introduced and alleged, while several mitigating circumstances, including Eddings' youthfulness, mental state, and potential for treatment, were considered by the trial judge. However, the judge did not consider Eddings' "unhappy upbringing and emotional disturbance" as significant mitigating factors to offset the aggravating ones. Eddings' attorney filed an appeal that eventually reached the U.S. Supreme Court. Although the Oklahoma Court of Criminal Appeals reversed the trial judge's ruling, the U.S. Supreme Court reversed the Oklahoma Court of Criminal Appeals. The reversal pivoted on whether the trial judge erred by refusing to consider the "unhappy upbringing and emotionally disturbed state" of Eddings. The trial judge had previously acknowledged the youthfulness of Eddings as a mitigating factor. The *fact* of Eddings' age, 16, was significant, precisely because the majority of Justices did not consider it as significant. Rather, they focused upon the issue of introduction of mitigating circumstances specifically outlined in Eddings' appeal. Oklahoma was now in the position of lawfully imposing the death penalty on a juvenile who was 16 years old at the time he committed murder.

Thompson v. Oklahoma (1988)

In the case of William Wayne Thompson, he was convicted of murdering his former brother-in-law, Charles Keene. Keene had been suspected of abusing Thompson's sister. In the evening hours of January 22–23, 1983, Thompson and three older companions left his mother's house, saying "We're going to kill

Charles." Facts disclose that later that early morning, Charles Keene was beaten to death by Thompson and his associates with fists and handheld weapons, including a length of pipe. Thompson later told others, "We killed him. I shot him in the head and cut his throat in the river." Thompson's accomplices told police shortly after their arrest that Thompson had shot Keene twice in the head, and then cut his body in several places (e.g., throat, chest, and abdomen), so that, according to Thompson, "the fish could eat his body." When Keene's body was recovered on February 18, 1983, the medical examiner indicated that Keene had been shot twice in the head, had been beaten, and that his throat, chest, and abdomen had been cut.

Since Thompson was 15 years old at the time of the murder, juvenile officials transferred his case to criminal court. This transfer was supported, in part, by an Oklahoma statutory provision indicating that there was "prosecutive

 **BOX 5.5**

 **PERSONALITY HIGHLIGHT**

Dennis R. Longmire
Sam Houston State University

Statistics:

Ph.D. (criminal justice and criminology), University of Maryland, Institute for Criminal Justice and Criminology; M.A. (criminology), University of Maryland, Institute for Criminal Justice and Criminology; B.A. (sociology), Towson State College

Biographical Sketch:

I began my career as a criminologist after concluding my formal education in 1979. I worked for a year as an assistant professor of criminal justice at California State University–Long Beach and then moved to Ohio State University, where I worked as an assistant professor in the Department of Sociology. In 1984 I accepted the position of Assistant Dean of Graduate Studies at Sam Houston State University, where I also served as Associate Dean until 1993, when I left the administrative responsibilities behind to enjoy the life of a full professor. I am internationally recognized for my work in the death penalty abolition movement and serve as co-advisor to the Sam Houston State University's student group of Amnesty International. I am on the advisory boards of the Houston/Harris County Chapter of Murder Victim's Families for Reconciliation, the *Texas Death Row Journal,* and the Texas

Coalition to Abolish the Death Penalty. During Texas's last legislative session, I provided expert resource testimony for committees in both the House and Senate. As a resident of Huntsville, Texas, I regularly hold a prayer vigil at the corner of 12th Street and Avenue I on the evening of each execution, and I was recently featured in the *Contemporary Justice Review*'s "Justice Profile" for my work in this area.

What Attracted Me to the Field and the Study of the Death Penalty:

When I was taking a class in juvenile delinquency as an undergraduate student, I read about the Outward Bound Programs, which were designed to help delinquent youths develop patterns of inner strength that would give them necessary coping skills to avoid the temptations of crime and delinquency that seemed to be all too present in their (our) lives. At that time in my life, I knew that I wanted to do something aimed at prevention and reform rather than punishment and control. I naively thought that I would pursue a career in social work with a special focus on the needs of the youth and that I would be able to do this. I spent a brief time working with the juvenile probation system in Baltimore City and then as a correctional officer in a maximum security prison in Maryland (the infamous Paxtuent Institution). Both of these real-world experiences led me to the realization that there were serious problems with the systems of justice we had constructed to deal with juvenile and adult offenders, and that these systems needed to be reformed before we could even begin to reform the offenders. This realization led me to graduate studies at the University of Maryland where they had just instituted a new graduate program focusing on criminal justice and criminology.

Very early in my graduate studies, I came to a second realization about the systems of justice operating in the United States: They are driven more by who you are than by what you have done. Whether we talked about this in the context of arrest, prosecution, conviction, or delivery of sanction, conclusions were the same. At that time, the scholarship being written under the rubric of Marxist, critical, radical, humanist, or anarchist criminology seemed to offer the most accurate descriptions of the reality of how the systems of justice I had worked in actually operated and gave me a general frame of reference to draw from as I continued to struggle with questions about how these systems needed to be reformed. I was also introduced to the scholarship offered under the context of critical legal theory and quickly concluded that there was little hope that we could reform the entire system of justice at once, but that we could begin to make significant changes in different aspects of the system by focusing attention on specific areas of justice. The U.S. Supreme Court announced in its decision to reauthorize the death penalty in the collection of cases referred to as the *Gregg v. Georgia* in January 1976, and at that moment I realized that this was one area of reform that should be given priority over all others. While I could see that the biases in the systems of justice were endemic and that the entire system of law was, in my mind, in need of considerable reform. The most pressing issue seemed to be in the delivery of the ultimate sanction: the penalty of death. In my mind, there could be no real hope for justice as long as we continued to authorize states to exercise this ultimate form of punishment, knowing that everything leading up to it was influenced by the socioeconomic and political biases that were so much a part of the administration of law at that time in our history.

Unfortunately, as I understand the current statistics describing the way our justice systems work, little has changed since I began my career as a student of criminal/juvenile justice. Our juvenile and adult justice systems continue to target people of color and people with little economic or political status. Our laws continue to be enforced differentially depending on who you are rather than what you have done, and in many ways we have become even more calloused to these differences because of a false sense of equality that has been claimed following the civil rights movement. I continue to hope that we can reform the systems by calling attention to the inequities and biases that show themselves so obviously when we study the demographics of who is selected to receive the ultimate sanction.

Advice to Students:

The basic things I try to teach everyone who comes into contact with me is to think critically and to focus your critical thoughts toward the question of justice. Reflect on what this concept means to you and try to re-form your understanding of it on a daily basis. The field of criminal justice/criminology is driven by some fundamental belief in a principle called "justice," but relatively little time is spent reflecting on what this principle is and how it is reflected in the actions of lawmakers, law enforcers, and other administrators of justice working in the various agencies we refer to as criminal/juvenile justice agencies. Engage yourselves in the pursuit of justice rather than the enforcement of law and do not be afraid to ask questions about how or why the agencies operate the way they do.

merit" in pursuing the case against Thompson. Again, the subject of the defendant's youthfulness was introduced as a mitigating factor (among other factors), together with aggravating factors such as the "especially heinous, atrocious, and cruel" manner in which Keene had been murdered. Thompson was convicted of first-degree murder and sentenced to death.

Thompson filed an appeal that eventually reached the U.S. Supreme Court. The Court examined Thompson's case at length, and in a vigorously debated opinion, it overturned Thompson's death sentence, indicated in its conclusory dicta that "petitioner's counsel and various *amici curiae* have asked us to 'draw the line' that would prohibit the execution of any person who was under the age of 18 at the time of the offense. Our task, today, however, is to decide the case before us; we do so by concluding that the Eighth and Fourteenth Amendments prohibit the execution of a person who was under 16 years of age at the time of his or her offense" (108 S.Ct. at 2700). Accordingly, Thompson's death penalty was reversed. Officially, this Supreme Court action effectively drew a temporary line of 16 years of age as a minimum for exacting the death penalty in capital cases. This "line" awaited subsequent challenges, however.

Stanford v. Kentucky (1989)

Kevin Stanford was 17 when, on January 17, 1981, he and an accomplice repeatedly raped and sodomized and eventually shot to death 20-year-old Baerbel Poore in Jefferson County, Kentucky. This occurred during a robbery of a gas station where Poore worked as an attendant. Stanford later told police, "I had to shoot her [since] she lived next door to me and she would recognize me . . . I guess we could have tied her up or something or beat [her up] . . . and tell her if she tells, we would kill her . . . " A corrections officer who interviewed Stanford said that after Stanford made that disclosure, "he (Stanford) started laughing." The jury in Stanford's case found him guilty of first-degree murder and the judge sentenced him to death. The U.S. Supreme Court eventually heard his appeal, and in an opinion that addressed the "minimum age for the death penalty" issue, decided both this case and the case of Heath Wilkins in the paragraphs to follow.

Wilkins v. Missouri (1989)

Heath Wilkins, a 16-year-old at the time of the crime, stabbed to death Nancy Allen Moore, a 26-year-old mother of two who was working behind the counter of a convenience store in Avondale, Missouri. On July 27, 1985, Wilkins and his accomplice, Patrick Stevens, entered the convenience store to rob it, agreeing that with Wilkins' plan that they would kill "whoever was behind the counter" because "a dead person can't talk." When they entered the store, they stabbed Moore, who fell to the floor. When Stevens had difficulty opening the cash register, Moore, mortally wounded, offered to help him. Wilkins stabbed her three more times in the chest, two of the knife wounds penetrating Moore's heart. Moore began to beg for her life, whereupon Wilkins stabbed her four more times in the neck, opening up her carotid artery. She died shortly thereafter. Stevens and Wilkins netted $450 in cash and checks, some liquor, cigarettes, and rolling papers from the robbery/murder. Wilkins was convicted of first-degree murder and the judge sentenced him to death.

14-year-old Eric Smith was tried for murdering a 4-year-old in Savona, New York.

The U.S. Supreme Court heard both cases simultaneously, since the singular issue was whether the death penalty was considered cruel and inhumane as it pertained to 16-and 17-year-olds. At that time, not all states had achieved consensus about applying the death penalty to persons under the age of 18 as a punishment for capital crimes. Although several Justices dissented from the majority view, the U.S. Supreme Court upheld the death sentences of Stanford and Wilkins, concluding that "we discern neither a historical nor a modern societal consensus forbidding the imposition of capital punishment on any person who murders at 16 or 17 years of age. Accordingly, we conclude that such punishment does not offend the Eighth Amendment's prohibition against cruel and unusual punishment" (109 S.Ct. at 2980). Thus, this crucial opinion underscored age 16 as the minimum age at which the death penalty may be administered.

Apart from the question of whether the death penalty should be administered at all to anyone, there is no apparent consensus concerning the application of the death penalty to juveniles convicted of capital crimes. Arguments favoring the death penalty stress the accountability of these youthful offenders and the justice of capital punishment where capital crimes have been committed. Arguments opposing the death penalty for juveniles are often emotionally laden or address issues related only remotely to the death penalty issue (Bedau 1992). For instance, it is argued that juveniles are more amenable to treatment and rehabilitation, and thus, provisions should be made for this rehabilitation and treatment to occur (Whitehead 1998). Whatever the appeal of such an argument, the U.S. Supreme Court has, at least for the time being, resolved the age/death penalty issue with some degree of finality. Other factors will have to be cited as mitigating in a youth's defense, if a capital crime is alleged.

Currently, there are only a small number of juveniles on death rows in U.S. state prisons. Because of the declining frequency with which juveniles have been executed in recent years, the death penalty issue as it applies to juveniles does not seem as strong as it once was. There will always be many persons in society who will oppose the death penalty for any reason (Cook 1998). But it is doubtful that major changes will be made about the death penalty policy applied to capital juvenile offenders, unless the present composition of the U.S. Supreme Court changes significantly (Hodgkinson et al. 1996). While public sentiment is not always easy to measure, there seems to be strong sentiment for harsher penalties meted out to juveniles. This doesn't necessarily mean the death penalty or life imprisonment, but it does mean tighter laws and enforcement of those laws where juveniles are concerned.

PUBLIC SENTIMENT ABOUT THE DEATH PENALTY FOR JUVENILES

Views of criminologists are not that different from the views held by the general public about juvenile delinquency and what should be done to prevent or punish it (Coleman 1998). Victor Streib (1987, 189) has summarized succinctly a commonly expressed, though nebulous, solution that "our society must be willing to devote enormous resources to a search for the causes and cures of violent juvenile crime, just as we have done in the search for the causes and cures of such killer diseases as cancer. And we must not demand a complete cure in a short time, since no one knows how long it will take." Obviously, we have not cured cancer. We are even further away from discovering the etiology of delinquent behavior in all of its diverse forms and finding one or more satisfactory cures for it.

Early identification of at-risk youths who have suffered some type of child abuse from their parents has been linked with subsequent youth violence (Clayton 1999). Family dysfunction has been linked with assault behavior manifested by a sample of male juveniles in a Toronto, Canada, study (Awad and Saunders 1991). Explanations for youth violence are varied and complex. So far, we do not have a good grasp of the specific factors that produce violent behavior among adolescents. We can say, for instance, that in certain instances, childhood victimization has increased the overall risk of violent offending among affected juveniles. But we are not yet in a position to say which juveniles will commit specific violent types of offenses in their future years (Finkelhor and Ormrod 2001a).

However, our failure to identify background factors that can be manipulated experimentally to cause law-abiding behavior among samples of youths has not deterred us from investigating juvenile violence. Much of this research has been productive, in that some juveniles appear to have been assisted by suggested interventions. In 1985, for example, an Early Offender Program (EOP) was established in Oakland County, California. An experimental group of 145 youths was studied and compared with a control group of 61 juveniles. The Oakland County Probate Court provided specialized, intensive in-home interventions for those youths aged 13 or younger at the time of their first contact with the court. Data about these youths were gathered from case files, interviews, and court records. Over time, the EOP cases exhibited lower career recidivism rates compared with the control group who did not receive any type of intervention. Both parents and youths involved in the EOP reported positive changes in family situations, peer relations, school performance, and general conduct as a result of participating in EOP (Howitt and Moore 1991). Nevertheless, the general public has inconsistent views toward those juveniles who commit violent acts. Results from a survey of 681 householders were mixed when they were asked about different hypothetical scenarios involving juveniles who committed different kinds of violent offenses, including murder. About half of those surveyed recommended that the juveniles should be processed by juvenile court. Other respondents believed that criminal court was the best option for repeat offenders. Most respondents actually preferred criminal court for those offenders charged with murder and who had no history of child abuse (Stalans and Henry 1994).

UNIFICATION OF CRIMINAL AND JUVENILE COURTS

Presently, there are several different types of courts in every U.S. jurisdiction. Usually, these courts have general, original, and concurrent jurisdiction, meaning that some courts share adjudicatory responsibilities involving the same subject matter. In Arkansas, for example, chancery courts have jurisdiction over juvenile delinquency cases, although separate county courts may also hear cases involving juveniles. In Colorado, district courts have general jurisdiction over criminal and civil matters, probate matters, and juvenile cases. However, there are specific juvenile courts in Colorado that hear juvenile cases as well. Tennessee county courts, circuit courts, and juvenile courts have concurrent jurisdiction over delinquency and other types of juvenile cases (e.g., children in need of supervision, child custody cases).

Court unification is a general proposal that seeks to centralize and integrate the diverse functions of all courts of general, concurrent, and exclusive jurisdiction into a more simplified and uncomplicated scheme. One way of viewing court unification is that it is ultimately intended to abolish concurrent jurisdiction wherever it is currently shared among various courts in a common jurisdiction, although no presently advocated court unification model has been shown to be superior to others proposed. Thus, there are different ways of achieving unification, although not everyone agrees about which method is best (Lahey, Christenson, and Rossi 2000). One example of court unification is Pennsylvania.

Prior to 1969, Pennsylvania had two appellate courts and numerous local courts that functioned independently of one another (Yeager, Herb, and Lemmon 1989). Even the Pennsylvania Supreme Court lacked full and explicit administrative and supervisory authority over the entire judicial system. As the result of the Pennsylvania Constitutional Convention of 1967–1968, a new Judiciary Article, Article V of the Pennsylvania Constitution, was framed. Vast changes were made in court organization and operations. A Family Division was established to deal exclusively with all juvenile matters. A ten-year follow-up evaluation of Pennsylvania's court unification concluded that the present court organization is vastly superior to the pre-1969 court organization. Efficiency and economy were two objectives sought by these court changes. Both aims were achieved.

Earlier studies of jurisdictions representing various degrees of unification have been conducted to assess whether there is necessarily greater economy, coordination, and speed associated with maintaining records and processing cases (Henderson et al. 1984). Georgia, Iowa, Colorado, New Jersey, and Connecticut were examined. Data were collected from records maintained by state administrative officials and local trial courts, and interviews were conducted with key court personnel. A total of 103 courts were selected for analysis, including 20 courts of general jurisdiction, 69 courts of limited jurisdiction, and 15 juvenile courts. More centralized organizational schemes only partially fulfilled the expectations of these researchers. Henderson et al. (1984) report that under centralization, poorer areas were likely to do better financially, although courts in well-off areas faced tighter budget restrictions. Greater uniformity of operations was observed in most jurisdictions. Further, centralization of court organization tended to highlight problems in previously neglected areas, including family and juvenile services. Their findings relating to differences in the effectiveness and efficiency of case processing in trial courts in both decentralized and centralized systems were inconclusive, however.

Implications of Court Unification for Juveniles

For juveniles, court unification poses potentially threatening consequences. For example, in those jurisdictions where considerable fragmentation exists in the processing of juvenile cases or where concurrent jurisdiction distributes juvenile matters among several different courts, juveniles, especially habitual offenders, may be able to benefit because of a general lack of centralization in record-keeping. Thus, juveniles may be adjudicated delinquent in one juvenile court jurisdiction, but this record of adjudication may not be communicated to other courts in adjacent jurisdictions. In time, it is likely that a national record-keeping network will exist, where all juvenile courts may access information from other jurisdictions. Currently, however, the confidentiality of record-keeping is a structural constraint that inhibits the development of such extensive record-sharing. However, as has been reported in earlier chapters, one major change in juvenile justice record-keeping has been the creation of various state repositories of juvenile information that can be shared among interested agencies. This is considered a part of the get-tough movement and is intended to hold juveniles more accountable for their offending by giving authorities in different jurisdictions greater access to their prior offense records (Torbet et al. 1996).

Those who favor a separate and distinct juvenile justice system apart from the criminal justice system contend that the primary goal of juvenile courts should be individualized treatment, with therapy and rehabilitation as dominant factors (Dwyer and McNally 1987). However, other voices encourage perpetuating a separate juvenile justice system which not only is designed to treat and prevent delinquency, but is also designed to hold juveniles strictly accountable for their actions (Torbet et al. 1996). Thus, it is suggested that less use be made of secure confinement and greater use be made of probation and parole, with the primary objectives of offering restitution to victims, compensating communities and courts for the time taken to process cases, and performing community services to learn valuable lessons (Maloney, Romig, and Armstrong 1988).

Getting Tough and Court Unification

There is no question that the get-tough movement is still in force and is pervasive throughout the juvenile justice system. One indication of this is the increased use of waivers or transfers, as more juveniles are shifted to the jurisdiction of criminal courts (Glick 1998). We have seen certain implications of juveniles as they enter criminal courts for processing, although some of these implications are not entirely unfavorable. Increasing numbers of juvenile court judges are soliciting the involvement of members of the community in voluntary capacities to assist in monitoring adjudicated youths. Greater responsibilities are shifting toward parents in many jurisdictions, particularly when their children commit crimes against property and do extensive damage monetarily (Rottman and Hewitt 1996).

Public policy currently favors protecting juveniles as much as possible from the stigmatization of courts and criminal labeling, including the large-scale removal of youths from jails and prisons (Flango 1994). Accordingly, recommendations from the public include greater use of nonsecure facilities and programs as opposed to confinement in secure facilities. Especially manifest is the concern for very young offenders. More children age 12 or younger are entering the juvenile justice system annually (Butts and Snyder 1997). Clearly, effective programs and procedures for processing such youths need to be in place and operative. Encouragement for greater use of community-based services and treatment programs, special education services, and school-based, early intervention programs is apparent.

There is increasing bureaucratization of juvenile courts, indicated in part by greater formality of juvenile case processing. Juvenile proceedings are increasingly adversarial proceedings similar to criminal courts. Almost all of the criminal court trappings are found in juvenile courts, with some significant exceptions that have been noted above (Feld 1995). Most juvenile courts are not courts of record, and much informality exists regarding calling witnesses and offering testimony. Federal and state rules of evidence are relaxed considerably and do not attach directly to juvenile civil proceedings.

Juvenile courts are sometimes classified according to a **traditional model** or **family model** and due process distinction (Dahlen 1986). Traditional courts perpetuate the doctrine of *parens patriae,* and juvenile court judges retain a good deal of discretion in adjudicating offenders. They rely more heavily on confinement as a punishment. The due-process juvenile courtroom relies more heavily on preadjudicatory interactions between defense counsels and prosecutors, and nonjudicial handling of cases is more the rule rather than the exception. More frequently used in such courts are nonsecure facilities, community-based programs, probation, and diversion with conditions.

Politicizing Juvenile Punishments

The political approach to punishing juveniles is to rely heavily on the sentiments expressed by voting constituencies. State legislators are at the helm of juvenile justice reforms currently, and several organizations are in strategic positions to offer their guidance and assistance in formulating new juvenile policies. The American Bar Association, the American Legislative Exchange Council, and the Institute of Judicial Administration have provided legislators with model penal codes and proposed juvenile court revisions to introduce consistency throughout an inconsistent juvenile justice system (Treanor and Volenik 1987). The federally funded Juvenile Justice Reform Project, which has reviewed existing juvenile codes and statutes in all fifty states, has conducted an extensive national opinion survey of child-serving professionals (Rossum, Koller, and Manfredi 1987). Two model juvenile justice acts have been proposed—the Model Delinquency Act and the Model Disobedient Children's Act. Among other things, these acts respectively distinguish between delinquent and status offenders and make provisions for their alternative care, treatment, and punishment. Both acts are designed to hold juveniles responsible for their acts and to hold the system accountable for its treatment of these youths as well.

It is debatable whether these codes are functional and in the best interests of those youths served. Some persons say that these codes will weaken the current protection extended to dependent children or children in need of supervision. Furthermore, a serious erosion of judicial discretion may occur, accompanied by increased use of pretrial detention for juveniles where serious crimes are alleged. Also, status offenders may be jailed for violating court orders (Orlando, Breed, and Smith 1987). Indeed, it is difficult to devise a code of accountability founded on the principle of just-deserts that nevertheless performs certain traditional treatment functions in the old context of *parens patriae* (Treanor and Volenik 1987). Additionally, codes of any kind promote a degree of blind conformity or compliance with rules for the sake of compliance. With greater codification of juvenile procedures, less latitude exists for judges and others to make concessions and impose individualized dispositions where appropriate. The very idea of individualized dispositions, while appealing to just-deserts interests, invites abuse through discriminatory treatment on racial, ethnic, gender, and socioeconomic grounds.

SUMMARY

Historically, the United States has been influenced by the early English doctrine of *parens patriae,* where the King of England acted as the father of the country on behalf of minors and other dependent persons. This doctrine served to shape contemporary juvenile courts and the attitudes of court officers toward youths as well as the sentences they receive for their delinquent acts. The basic elements of *parens patriae* include state control over children's affairs, informal processing of juveniles to avoid adverse labeling effects, and benevolent and treatment-oriented sanctions that seek to rehabilitate and reform rather than to punish. The case of *Ex parte Crouse,* decided in 1839, was the first legal recognition of this doctrine in the United States, and it effectively separated parental interests in children from the interests of the court, giving the court the final power to make decisions for juveniles.

For many decades, the U.S. Supreme Court practiced a hands-off philosophy toward the juvenile court, since it was believed that juvenile courts act in the best interests of children. However, numerous blatant abuses of juvenile court authority led to substantial changes in how juveniles would be processed in future years. The U.S. Supreme Court vested juveniles with successive rights, commencing with the right to a hearing prior to being waived or transferred to criminal courts where potentially more severe punishments might be exacted. Subsequent rights given juveniles by the Supreme Court include the right to an attorney, the rights to confront and cross-examine witnesses, the right against self-incrimination, the right to notice of charges, and the right against double jeopardy. Eventually, juveniles were given minimum due process. In about a fourth of all states, juveniles may be entitled to a jury trial if one is requested. However, most other states leave this option to the discretion of juvenile court judges.

Generally, juvenile courts operate with less rigorous evidentiary standards compared with criminal courts. Juveniles may be held for preventive detention. The "beyond a reasonable doubt" standard is now used as the standard of guilt or innocence in juvenile courts, where the possibility of incarceration exists. Very much in favor of juvenile offenders is the fact that juvenile courts continue to exercise civil jurisdiction. Thus, adjudicated delinquents cannot acquire criminal records as the result of their misdeeds while juvenile offenders. Of course, we have seen that juveniles may be waived to criminal courts for processing, particularly where serious offenses have been alleged. Therefore, they may be treated as adults according to statutory authority, although they may still be minors. Perhaps the most serious implication of being treated as adults for juveniles is that they may have the death penalty imposed for capital crimes. In recent years the U.S. Supreme Court has upheld the death penalty as applied to 16- and 17-year-olds, although it has ruled that the death penalty is cruel and unusual punishment if administered to youths under age 16. The death penalty is controversial per se, although it fosters an unusually large amount of controversy whenever youths are concerned.

Criticisms of contemporary juvenile courts are that they are increasingly similar to criminal courts and have undergone a degree of criminalization. As juvenile courts become increasingly formalized and bureaucratic, some degree of judicial discretion is lost. This is both good and bad, since juvenile court judges might abuse this discretionary authority or they may make decisions that are quite lenient and in favor of youthful offenders. Informal adjudicatory proceedings are gradually being eliminated as the juvenile court system is increasingly adversarial. Proposals have been advanced that favor court unification, or combining juvenile courts with criminal courts for general types of offenses. Court unification is perceived by many experts as an economic necessity as our society becomes more complex and legalistic. However, opponents to court unification believe that much will be lost that currently benefits youths in juvenile courts, including more treatment-oriented and rehabilitative adjudications and sentences.

QUESTIONS FOR REVIEW

1. What is the get-tough movement and what does it have to do with juvenile rights?
2. What is the hands-off doctrine? What is the significance of the hands-off doctrine for U.S. Supreme Court decision making and juvenile rights?
3. What was the significance of (a) *Kent v. United States* and (b) *In re Gault*?
4. What is the standard of proof currently used in juvenile courts, where a juvenile's liberty is in jeopardy? What case was significant in evolving this standard of proof?
5. What is the case of *Breed v. Jones* and its significance for juvenile rights?
6. What is the minimum age for seeking the death penalty against a juvenile who has allegedly committed capital murder?
7. What are two significant cases that drew a minimum age line for seeking the death penalty against juveniles? What are the general facts of these two cases?
8. What are three arguments for and three arguments against the death penalty?
9. What was the significance of the case of *Thompson v. Oklahoma* and whether juveniles could be executed for committing capital crimes?
10. What is meant by court unification? What are some implications of court unification for juvenile offenders?

SUGGESTED READINGS

Bartollas, Clemens and Stuart J. Miller. 2001. *Juvenile justice in America. 3d ed.* Upper Saddle River, NJ: Prentice Hall.

Feld, Barry C. 2000. *Cases and materials on juvenile justice administration.* St. Paul, MN: West Group.

Lahey, Mary Anne, Bruce A. Christenson, and Robert J. Rossi. 2000. *Analysis of trial court unification in California: Final report.* Sacramento: Judicial Council of California.

INTERNET CONNECTIONS

Campaign Against Wrongful Executions
http://www.justice.policy.net/

Moratorium2000
http://www.moratorium2000.org/

Office of Juvenile Justice and Delinquency Prevention
http://www.ojjdp.ncjrs.org/

Youth Defense Counsels
http://www.juveniledefense.com

CHAPTER 6 | *Juveniles and the Police*

Chapter Outline

Key Terms
Chapter Objectives
Introduction
Police Discretion: Use and Abuse
Arrests of Juveniles

Status Offenders and Juvenile
   Delinquents
Divestiture and Its Implications:
   Net-Widening
Redefining Delinquency

Summary
Questions for Review
Suggested Readings
Internet Connections

Key Terms

Automatic transfer laws
Beats
Children in need of supervision
   (CHINS)
Community policing
Corporate gangs
Criminogenic environment

Discretionary powers
Expungement orders
National Youth Gang Survey
   (NYGS)
Proactive units
Reactive units
Restorative policing

Scavenger gangs
Sealing records of juveniles
Situationally based discretion
Stationhouse adjustments
Territorial gangs
Totality of circumstances
Youth squads

Chapter Objectives

As a result of reading this chapter, you will have accomplished the following objectives:

1. Learn about police discretion relative to juvenile offenders.
2. Assess the importance of youth squads in police departments that interdict delinquent conduct.
3. Understand differential response of youths to contacts with police.
4. Understand the ambiguity associated with juvenile arrests.
5. Understand how police officers distinguish between and process status and delinquent offenders.
6. Learn about several important delinquency intervention programs within communities and their effectiveness.

INTRODUCTION

• *It happened in New York City. A family from Iowa was touring the city for the week. They took in some Broadway plays and a tennis match. They were enjoying a day of shopping. Everything was going fine. As they entered a subway to go to their next event, two youths ran up behind the father, 51, and slashed his pants with a sharp knife. One youth grabbed the man's wallet, while the other pushed the family members away. The father's son, 23, attempted to intervene. The other youth stabbed him in the chest with a large knife and fled. Fortunately, a subway officer was entering the station and radioed for his fellow officers to intercept the youths. They were apprehended about five minutes later. In the meantime, the stabbing victim died of his wounds, while the father was treated at an emergency clinic for cuts to his buttocks. The youths turned out to be Gabriel H. and Rolando H., brothers, ages 16 and 17 respectively. They had lengthy juvenile records, including several violent offenses. Records indicated that neither youth had ever been incarcerated in a juvenile facility. They had received probation at each delinquency adjudication hearing. This time, because of the death of the Iowa man, the juvenile court prosecutor sought to transfer them to criminal court where they could be tried as adults. If convicted, they faced lengthy prison time. A police spokeswoman revealed that the two boys had been involved in a Big Brothers/Big Sisters program one year earlier, since they were from a fatherless home.* [Adapted from the Associated Press, "Subway Mugging Turns Deadly." April 3, 2002].

• *Police officers in Ames, Iowa spotted a late-model automobile driving slowly down a city street at 2:00 A.M. on a Saturday morning. What attracted their attention was that no one appeared to be driving the vehicle. They pulled alongside the vehicle, shone their spotlight in the driver's window, and spotted a blond head barely above the dashboard of the car. They announced on their loudspeaker for the car to pull over, which it did. When police investigated, they discovered the driver to be a 9-year-old boy. He told officers his name and address, and that because he couldn't sleep, he decided to "take a drive" in the family car. He said he took his father's car keys and quietly opened the garage door. He had watched his father drive the car many times and was familiar with what to do. He had driven about 15 miles before the police stopped him. His parents were notified and they arrived at the scene to retrieve their other car and their child. The incident was not pursued by the juvenile court.* [Adapted from the Associated Press, "Driverless Car Leads Police on Short Chase: Nine-Year-Old Driver Returned to Parents." January 4, 2002].

• *As over 100 high schoolers convened on the school auditorium for the junior prom at a high school in Boston, Massachusetts, a 1984 Oldsmobile drove by slowly and automatic gunfire erupted. The short burst of fire from the automatic weapon spit out 30 cartridges indiscriminately into the crowd of teenagers. Several students collapsed and a panic ensued. Eyewitnesses described the car of the suspected shooters to police, and an hour later, a car matching that description was stopped about four miles from the school. Three juvenile suspects, ages 15, 16, and 16, were taken into custody. Several weapons, including the automatic rifle, were seized. It turned out that the shooter was the ex-boyfriend of a girl who was attending the junior prom with a new boyfriend. Neither of them was injured in the shooting. However, nonlethal bullet wounds were inflicted on 11 students nearest the passing car. All but four injured students were treated and released. The remaining victims were hospitalized but were not considered in serious condition. The shooter and his companions were charged with attempted murder and conspiracy. A spokesman for the Boston Police Department was quoted as saying, "You should see the weapons we took from those kids. They have better firepower than we do!" The juvenile court prosecutor was considering action to have the juveniles transferred to criminal court for processing.* [Adapted from the Associated Press, "Drive-By Shooting at Boston High School Injures 11." June 1, 2002].

This chapter examines police discretion as it pertains to wide varieties of juvenile conduct. How should police officers react toward youths under different circumstances? When is formal action necessary or strongly suggested? What statutory provisions exist for handling certain types of encounters with juveniles? Under what circumstances should juveniles be arrested and taken into custody to local jails or lockups? These and similar questions will be examined here.

Since there have been several significant changes in state and federal laws during the last few decades concerning how juvenile offenders are defined and should be processed, police procedures involving juveniles have been modified greatly. Certain classes of juvenile offenders have been reclassified by law. Most notably, a clear distinction exists between status offenders and delinquent offenders in every jurisdiction. However, police officers are those who interface most often with juveniles on the streets. Because many of these police officer/juvenile encounters are diffuse and it is unclear whether any criminal laws have been violated, police officers must use their discretion when interpreting each situation and the events observed. What is the nature of police response to changing procedures about how certain types of juveniles should be processed? Do police officers generally follow procedure and make the same distinctions between juveniles as the law requires? The implications of deinstitutionalizing status offenders (DSO) for influencing police discretion and conduct will be examined.

POLICE DISCRETION: USE AND ABUSE

Few will contest the idea that police officers make up the front line or first line of defense in the prevention and/or control of street crime, although the effectiveness of this line in crime control continues to be questioned (Prenzler and Hayes 1999). Police officers are vested with considerable **discretionary powers,** depending upon the circumstances, ranging from verbal warnings in confrontations with the public to the application of deadly force (*Tennessee v. Garner*

1985). Police discretion is the range of behavioral choices police officers have within the limits of their power (American Bar Association 1997). Beyond the formal training police officers receive from law enforcement agency training academies, police discretion is influenced by many other factors, including the situation, as well as the race, ethnicity, gender, socioeconomic status, and age of those confronted. Many of those stopped by police, questioned, and subsequently arrested and detained in jails or other lockup facilities, even for short periods, are juveniles.

The Diffuseness of Police Officer Roles

The public tends to define the police role diffusely, where police are expected to address a wide variety of human problems. The nature of this police intervention is that the police will intervene in various situations and ensure that matters do not get worse (Worrall and Marenin 1998). Thus, police training in various jurisdictions is geared to reflect this broad public expectation of the police role. Training manuals for police officers include numerous examples of field situations, including how to deal with domestic disturbances, traffic violations, narcotics, civil disorders, vice, drunkenness, federal offenses, and juveniles (Hoath, Schneider, and Starr 1998).

Much of this **situationally based discretion** in confronting crime in the streets and the public is covert. Most of what transpires in the interaction between police officers and suspects is known only to these actors. Thus, it is often difficult to enforce consistently high standards of accountability for police to observe in their diverse public encounters (Worrall and Marenin 1998). In short, police officers make on-the-spot decisions about whether to move beyond simple verbal warnings or reprimands to more formal actions against those stopped and questioned on suspicion. Considering the circumstances or situation, law enforcement officers may be more or less aggressive.

Contributing to the diffuseness of police officer roles in communities is a relatively recent phenomenon known as **community policing.** Community policing is a major policing reform that broadens the police mission from a narrow focus on crime to a mandate that encourages the police to explore creative solutions for a host of community concerns, including crime, fear of crime, disorder, and neighborhood decay. It rests on the belief that only by working together will people and the police be able to improve the quality of life in the community, with the police not only as enforcers, but also as advisors, facilitators, and supporters of new community-based police-supervised initiatives (Udeshi 1998).

One immediate effect of community policing in many neighborhoods is to place greater discretionary power in the hands of police officers, whether they are on foot or in cruisers. An implicit consequence of community policing is to create better relations between the police department and the community, in order for community residents to place greater trust in the police rather than to fear them (Guarino-Ghezzi and Carr 1996). In communities where such discretionary power shifts occur through planning, police officers may be expected by higher-ups to take a greater interest in youths, even where petty infractions are involved. Police officers may be punished for failing to take seriously minor infractions and for not intervening when necessary. Thus, they are in a dilemma about whether to get involved in the activities of minor offenders. In more sensitive settings, where ethnicity may play an important role, law enforcement officers may be criticized unfairly by citizens for simply doing their jobs (Hoath, Schneider, and Starr 1998).

For many police officers, stopping and detaining juveniles is not a particularly popular activity. One reason is that juvenile court judges are inclined to be quite lenient with juvenile first offenders or minor offenders (Leiber, Nalla, and Farnworth 1998). Many juvenile courts consider youths chronic offenders only after they have been adjudicated as delinquents five or six times (Snyder and Sickmund 1995). Thus, the considerable time police officers spend by taking youths into custody and filling out extensive paperwork seems like so much wasted time when these youths are released later with only verbal warnings from judges. There are also additional regulations governing how juveniles should be processed and detained when brought to jails following their encounters with police officers. These increasingly complex procedures for juvenile offender processing discourage police–juvenile interaction except under the most serious circumstances and where serious crimes have been committed.

Nevertheless, police officers in every jurisdiction encounter large numbers of juveniles annually during their patrols or **beats.** Because of the informal nature of many of these police officer/juvenile encounters, the *UCR* and other official sources for arrest information fail to disclose the true incidence of all juvenile contacts with the law. In 2000 there were over 2 million juvenile arrests, about half of which were petitioned to juvenile courts for further action (Maguire and Pastore 2002). Furthermore, self-reports from juveniles in elementary schools and high schools suggest considerably greater delinquent activity as well as contacts with police that do not necessarily result in arrests or being taken into custody for brief periods (Maguire and Pastore 2002).

Juvenile Gang Units in Police Departments

In the early years of police-juvenile encounters, police departments operated under a type of siege mentality. In Los Angeles, for example, the zoot suit riots of 1943 involved a ten-day attack by civilians on alleged Mexican American youth gang members. Extraordinarily repressive police policies were implemented at that time, and police–juvenile relations were strained for many decades (Appier 1990). Subsequently, police departments throughout the nation, particularly larger municipal police departments with 200 or more officers, established specialized juvenile units as a part of their organizational structure to deal with different types of offenders. Even relatively small departments in remote geographical areas have at least one juvenile officer who deals exclusively with juvenile affairs. Despite this specialization, however, every police officer who encounters juveniles while policing temporarily becomes a juvenile officer (Wright 1997). Not all of the police activities in these juvenile units have been directed at gang violence or violent offenses committed by juveniles, however. Those targeted for active police intervention and assistance have included truants, runaways and missing children, property offenders and those who commit vehicular theft, curfew violators, and school-related offenders (Virginia Commission on Youth 1998). Police interest in gangs is most often focused upon understanding and prevention rather than retaliation (Gaffney et al. 1997). Prevention measures by police include profiling gang members, learning the methods used by gangs to recruit new members, identifying the neighborhood roots that spawn and perpetuate gang activity, understanding the influence and presence of gang members in prison settings, providing materials and strategies for parents and school authorities to use for coping with gang activities, and examining gang structure (Carstarphen and Shapiro 1997; Howell 1998).

In Cleveland, Ohio, for example, a study of youth gangs identified denial as a typical official response of law enforcement to the presence of youth gangs (Torok and Trump 1994, 13). One consequence was that many Ohio youths interpreted this police denial of their existence as tacit approval for their operation in virtually any Ohio city, with impunity. Victimization of community residents is promoted as one result of this unbridled gang activity. However, in 1990 a Youth/Gang Unit was established by the Cleveland Police Department. The Youth component of this Unit investigates nongang-related crimes, which are not normally investigated by detectives. However, members of the Gang Unit conduct in-depth investigations to identify gang members and obtain information about gang territories, activities, and methods of operation in order to ensure successful prosecution of gang members. They supplement their activities with aggressive street enforcement. One innovation is that the Youth Gang Unit has collaborated with school authorities to establish Youth Gang Units within the Division of Safety and Security, which is a part of the public school system. This Youth Gang Unit addresses gang crimes and school rule violations. It consists of four school security officers and a unit coordinator and serves 127 schools and over 73,000 students (Torok and Trump 1994, 14). During the first year of this unit's operation, unit personnel investigated 400 gang-related school incidents, identified over 1,000 gang members, and trained 7,000 staff members, parents, and youth service providers to recognize and intervene in gang problems. With increased violence occurring in the nation's schools, greater attention is directed to school crime and safety (Kaufman et al. 1998).

By 1997, all fifty-one jurisdictions in the United States had made extensive changes in their laws concerning juveniles who commit violent or serious crimes (Torbet and Szymanski 1998). In turn, these legislative changes have caused numerous police departments to implement programs that will achieve certain delinquency prevention objectives contemplated by these changes.

Actually, the activities of juvenile units or **youth squads** are largely directed toward delinquency prevention (Joe 1995). These units tend to be **reactive units,** in that they respond to public requests for intervention and assistance whenever offenses committed by juveniles are reported. That is, these officers react to calls from others about crimes that have already been committed or are in progress. Gang fights or break-ins involving youths would activate these juvenile units. In contrast, police officers who patrol city streets are most often **proactive units** involved in contacts with juveniles who may or may not be offenders and/or law violators. These officers are almost constantly on the lookout for suspicious activities. They monitor the streets and investigate potentially troublesome situations (Howell and Decker 1999).

Proactive Restorative Policing

In Bethlehem, Pennsylvania, a Police Family Group Conference Project (FGC) was established in the mid-1990s and coordinated by the Bethlehem Police Department (McCold and Wachtel 1998). First-time moderately serious juvenile offenders were randomly assigned either to formal adjudication in juvenile court or to a diversionary **restorative policing** process involving family group conference. Police-based family group conferencing uses trained police officers to facilitate meetings attended by juvenile offenders, their victims, and their families and/or friends to discuss the harm caused by the offender's action and to create an agreement to repair the harm. Data were obtained and analyzed for 80 FGC participants, 180 victims, and 169 parents. These data were compared with control groups with similar characteristics. The FGC participation rate was 42 percent; 100 percent of the conferences produced an agreement on restorative actions; and 94 percent of all offenders were in full compliance with the agreements. The FGC seemed to produce lower rearrest rates among participants, and perceptions of fairness were as high as 96 percent for all participants. Researchers concluded that the Bethlehem Police Department was able to reduce recidivism substantially among FGC participants while avoiding net-widening. It was also demonstrated that police officers were able to conduct FGCs successfully and without special training. Thus the potential for applying FGCs in other jurisdictions was demonstrated.

Youth Gangs, Minority Status, and Gender

Types and Numbers of Gangs.   The increased visibility of delinquent gangs organized along ethnic and racial lines in many cities and the violence such gangs manifest have caused police departments to establish task forces of special police officers who do nothing but monitor and investigate gang activities (Howell and Decker 1999). Some writers have classified these gangs as **scavenger gangs, territorial gangs,** and **corporate gangs** (Shelden, Tracy, and Brown 2001). Scavenger gangs form primarily as a means of socializing and for mutual protection. Territorial gangs are organized for the purpose of preserving a fixed amount of territory, such as several city blocks. They maintain control over these geographical areas and repel efforts by other gangs to invade their territory or turf. The most violent gangs are corporate gangs. These types of gangs emulate organized crime syndicates. While all types of gangs pose dangers to the public, corporate gangs are more profit-motivated and rely on illicit activities such as drug trafficking to further their profit interests. Thus, corporate gangs are more dangerous than scavenger or territorial gangs. Corporate gangs use excessive violence, including murder, to carry out their goals. Often, innocent bystanders are gunned down as victims of gang retaliation against rival gangs and gang members.

Less conventional gangs, such as the Skinheads, have been targeted by some youth gang bureaus and other police agencies within departments. For example, Skinheads claimed at least 70,000 members worldwide in 1995. They have a cumulative record of gang violence involving weapons. And it is not always cities with large populations where police gang units are deployed. In Alabama, for instance, law enforcement agencies in forty-six cities with populations of 10,000 or more have reported substantial gang activities in their jurisdictions (Armor and Jackson 1995). Alabama officials report that their gang visibility is comparable to that reported by larger cities, especially concerning the amount of female involvement or participation in gangs, the trappings of gang culture, and other critical gang elements. Officials in other jurisdictions have reported similar gang presence and activity (Gullotta, Adams, and Montemayor 1998).

In 1995, the National Youth Gang Center (NYGC) conducted an extensive survey that became known as the **National Youth Gang Survey (NYGS)** (Wilson

 **BOX 6.1**

DETROIT TEEN GANG PUTS GIRLS INTO PROSTITUTION

The Asian King Posse Gang

It happened in St. Paul, Minnesota. Two girls, ages 11 and 13, ran away from a shelter in February 1999. Then they met Kong Meng Kue, 24, leader of an Asian gang known as the Asian King Posse. The girls were kidnapped and taken to Detroit, Michigan. Kue forced the two girls to have sex with several men and forced them into prostitution. Both girls were later taken to Indiana where they later escaped. Authorities there sent them back to Minnesota, where police investigated their kidnapping. A police investigation led to the arrest of Kue on charges of kidnapping and rape. An informant told investigators that Kue was an original member of the Asian King Posse and that his role is to lure young, female Asian runaways to go with him to Detroit, where they are forced into prostitution. The Asian King Posse is a dominant gang in the greater Detroit area, and only recently has the gang had a presence in St. Paul. Kue was being held in lieu of $1 million bond. Kue moved to Minnesota from Michigan in August 1999. Since Kue transported the girls across state lines for the purpose of prostitution, there was a chance that he could face federal charges. In October 1999 five boys and men were charged with rape in Detroit after three Hmong teenage girls said they were lured from a party in Sheboygan, Wisconsin, taken to Detroit, and repeatedly raped. That case was linked to a gang known as the Bloods 116. The Minnesota Gang Strike Force was investigating the activities of several gangs known to be active in the St. Paul area.

What should be the punishment for Kue if he is convicted of kidnapping and prostitution? Should the juvenile gang somehow be penalized for engaging in illicit activities such as organized prostitution? What do you think?

Source: Adapted from the Associated Press, "Reputed Detroit Gang Member Charged with Kidnapping St. Paul Girls." November 8, 1999.

2001, xiii). Subsequently, the NYSG has been conducted annually to track gang activities and describe critical gang components and characteristics. At least nine types of gangs were identified in the original survey: (1) juvenile gangs, (2) street gangs, (3) taggers, (4) drug gangs, (5) satanic groups, (6) posses, (7) crews, (8) stoners, and (9) terrorist groups. Traditionally, gangs were formed by racial, ethnic, or religious groups. Gangs of today are based on needs to identify with a group. However, not all gangs today are limited to youths. Increasing numbers of youth gangs have adults as members. On the basis of the 1998 NYGS, it is estimated that there were over 28,700 gangs with a membership in excess of 780,000 (Wilson 2001, 13).

Myths and Truths about Gangs

Joan Moore (1993, 28–29) has described several stereotypes of gangs that are not true. These include:

1. Gangs are exclusively males who are violent, addicted to drugs and alcohol, sexually hyperactive, unpredictable, and confrontational.

2. They are either all African American or all Hispanic.

3. They thrive in inner-city neighborhoods, where they dominate, intimidate, and prey upon innocent citizens.

4. They all deal heavily in drugs, especially crack cocaine.

5. All gangs are alike.

6. There is no good in gangs; it is all bad.

7. Gangs are basically criminal enterprises and youths start gangs in order to collectively commit crimes.

Findings that challenge these erroneous and stereotypical gang characteristics are:

1. Gangs, drugs, and violence appear to apply more to adult drug and criminal gangs than to youth gangs.

2. The connection between gangs, drugs, and violence is not as strong as it has been believed.

3. More young adult males than juveniles are involved in most criminal youth gangs, and they appear to be disproportionately involved in serious and violent crimes.

4. It is not as difficult for adolescents to resist gang pressures as was commonly believed. Youths can refuse to join gangs without reprisals.

5. Gang members can usually leave their gangs without serious consequences.

6. Modern gangs make less use of gang symbols and rites than gangs of the past.

7. Modern youth gangs are based less on territory than in the past.

8. More adolescents are gang members than in past years.

9. More gangs are in suburban areas, small towns, and rural areas than in the past.

10. There is more gang presence in the schools than in the 1980s and 1990s.

11. White gang members are more prevalent in adolescent gangs than in the past.

12. Females are more prevalent in adolescent gangs than previously reported.

13. Gangs in rural and sparsely populated areas are quite different from city gangs (Wilson 2001, 49–50).

The fact of racial and ethnic disproportionality in the juvenile justice system is underscored by a study undertaken by Darlene Conley in 1994. The juvenile justice system of a western state was investigated. Juvenile courts in six counties were selected as the target for her research. A representative sample of 1,777 juvenile cases was drawn, together with 170 in-depth interviews with court personnel, community leaders, defense attorneys, prosecutors, law enforcement officers, parents, youths and others. The study also included 65 hours of participant observation covering court proceedings and plea bargaining involving adjudicated juveniles. Focus group interviews with juveniles were also conducted. It was found that blacks were twice as likely than whites

BOX 6.2

Eric Frederic
Police Officer, Fremont, California, Police Department

Statistics:

B.A. (Spanish, business), Brigham Young University; M.A. (criminal justice administration and management), University of Alaska–Fairbanks

Background and Interests:

I started my career in police work at the age of 14 with the Police Explorers in a small town called Palos Verdes Estates (PVE) in Southern California. I went through the Explorer Academy and started working at the PVE Police Department filing citations, learning dispatch and jail, and riding with the officers. I continued riding with the officers and learning what they do. By the time I was graduating from high school, everyone knew I worked for the police department and made sure they didn't offer me any drugs at parties. When I turned 18, I was hired full-time as a dispatcher and jailer. I continued my education at the local community college, getting my general education classes out of the way.

By that time, I had decided that I wanted to be a police officer, and so I put in an application for the Reserve Program when I was 20. The chief told me to wait a little longer, and then he announced that he was going to hire another police officer. He encouraged me to put in an application, and so I did. I placed number two on the list and when the number one candidate had a problem, I was given the job.

I went through the Los Angeles Sheriff's Academy in 1989 and graduated. I returned to PVE and went through the Field Training Officer (FTO) program they had just developed. I completed probation and started working on my own there. Luckily, I was born and raised there, and so I knew the area and clientele. The city was a predominantly upper-class bedroom community that wanted to be treated as such. The chief asked us not to write citizens of the city tickets, but rather, he demanded that we write several tickets a day to outsiders. It was not a big deal, but I did not like the idea of ticket quotas. The chief also had some other peculiar ideas and I became disenchanted with the job. In the summer of 1991, I quit the department.

Next, I served a mission for my church, which took me to the Dominican Republic for two years. There, I learned Spanish and how to live in an underprivileged society. I came back from my mission a changed man. I then attended Brigham Young University and graduated with my B.A. in Spanish. I got married and then moved back to California, where my wife attended San Jose State University for her master's degree. I decided to get back into police work at that time.

Because several years had past since I quit police officer work, my basic POST (Police Officer Selection Test) certificate had expired. I put myself through a refresher course and then applied to local law enforcement agencies. The Fremont, California, Police Department hired me in 1996. I started working patrol and learned more in the first month than all of the years I had spent at PVE. Fremont is a large city with a population of 210,000, and a very diverse ethnic population. I had to learn to do police work all over again. In Fremont, we are expected to do our own follow-ups, from conducting photo line-ups to interviewing suspects in murder cases. In PVE, the biggest thing I had to do was tell the owner of a barking dog to keep his dog quiet. The detectives did all of the follow-ups there in PVE.

After I completed a two-year probationary period in Fremont, I started applying for specific jobs. I became a member of the bicycle patrol team, a firearms instructor, a CPR/First Aid Instructor, and a member of several committees for improving the police department. I also applied for the position of School Resource Officer (SRO) and received the position at one of the five high schools in Fremont. I have been a SRO for the past four years and have loved it. I volunteered my time as a football coach for the school and had the opportunity to meet the students in a different light. The students got to know me as a regular guy and not just as a cop. The job was demanding, stretching my knowledge and abilities beyond what I had previously been able to do (you wouldn't believe some of the stupid things kids do). Unfortunately, my time at the school is over, and I am due to rotate back out to patrol in a few months. I have learned quite a bit though, and I am a much more well-rounded individual for all of my experiences.

Most of the issues I have dealt with at school are pretty routine. I say "routine" because I deal with them all of the time. But when I tell other patrol officers about them, they usually thank the powers-that-be that they don't have to work in the schools. Just last week, I had a student come into my office to tell me that her father had been molesting her. I conducted an in-depth interview and learned that her father had been having sexual intercourse with her for the past several years. We attempted to locate the father but were unable to do so. I eventually walked the case to the district attorney and then spoke with the judge. I was able to get a warrant for $250,000 for the father. We served him that night and threw him in jail.

He knew he was busted, because as soon as he saw us, he said he wanted his lawyer.

In another case, a Caucasian girl got into a fight with another student during lunch at a local shopping center. One of the store owners, an Oriental man, broke up the fight and got a little rough with one of the students. The student claimed that the store owner was prejudiced and that he was too rough because of it. What's funny about this incident is that just after the September 11, 2001, New York World Trade Center disaster, I had arrested this same juvenile for doing the same thing. He made some comments to a boy from the Middle East, accusing him of being involved in the attacks. Then he beat up the boy. The youthful victim didn't understand English and was simply trying to walk away. I arrested the Caucasian youth on a hate crime charge, and it made the papers because of the attention received by the September 11th terrorist incident. Other issues I deal with frequently at the schools include drugs (mostly marijuana, but a little sprinkling of ecstasy, LSD, GHB, and methamphetamines), thefts, and fights.

Advice to Students:

Get your degree in something you enjoy. Several of my friends have been injured on the job and cannot continue as police officers. They now have to find something else to do. Those who had a degree in something other than police-related fields were able to support their families by choosing alternative careers. Most departments will give you an educational incentive, regardless of any degrees you possess. Make sure you learn something from every situation you encounter, and don't take things personally. It's a job—a great, fun, active job, but still a job.

to be arrested, five times more likely to be referred to juvenile court, five times more likely to be detained, three times more likely to be charged, two and half times more likely to be adjudicated delinquent; and eleven times more likely to be placed in secure confinement for a lengthy period. Hispanics were also overrepresented in the same counties, although they were not processed as extensively as blacks. Similar findings relative to dissimilar treatment of minority juveniles have been reported elsewhere (Guarino-Ghezzi 1994).

Female Gangs

How prevalent are female gangs in the United States? Do female gangs commit similar types of offenses compared with male gangs? In 1998 there were 80,000 female gang members in the United States, accounting for about 10 percent of all gang membership (Wilson 2001, 19). Contemporary descriptions of female gang members suggest that they typically lack a formal education; have violent experiences at their schools; have seriously dysfunctional family lives; and have social problems including poverty, substance abuse, and gang violence (Molidor 1996). Interviews with a sample of Texas female gang members indicated that they often join gangs to achieve power and protection, engendering respect from others based upon fear, and they often resort to more serious criminal conduct (Dukes, Martinez, and Stein 1997). Often, membership in female gangs is contingent upon one's ethnic or racial status. Family disintegration and community deterioration often lead female gang members to create their own subculture where recognition can more easily be attained (Bankston and Caldas 1996). Another factor is the lack of appropriate intervention, diversion, and treatment alternatives available to female juveniles compared with their male counterparts. With the presence of such gender inequities, young female involvement in delinquent behavior is more easily explained (American Bar Association 2001).

Rosenbaum (1996) studied female gang members who had earlier been committed to the California Youth Authority in 1990. She studied a sample of 70 girls with known gang affiliations. Almost all the girls studied by Rosenbaum had records of violent offending. The girls averaged 4 arrests, and 62 percent of their commitment offenses were committed with other female gang members. Rosenbaum found that many of these girls joined gangs initially to satisfy needs that they could not satisfy from their home environments. Gang affiliation gave these girls loyalty to friends, fun, and excitement. Furthermore, many of these female gang members were of minority status and resented the white, blond "California girl" image that is often unattainable by minority girls. Thus, female gang criminality, at least in Southern California, appeared to be similar to male gang criminality in both the level and nature of violence. Offense similarities between female and male gang members have been reported in other jurisdictions (Esbensen and Winfree 1998).

Profiling of female gang members has been limited, in part because of inaccessibility by researchers. However, interviews have been conducted with female gang members who are or have been incarcerated in juvenile facilities. A large-scale study was conducted by the National Gang Crime Research Center. Data were gathered from 17 states and 85 correctional facilities, including boot camps and juvenile institutions. The sample comprised 10,166 offenders of whom 4,140 were self-reported gang members. Over 1,000 of these gang members were female. On the basis of reported information, females were more likely than males to have been sexually abused, grown up in a father-only household, stopped committing violent crimes if they were juveniles tried as adults, and joined gangs while incarcerated. Female gang members compared with male gang members were less likely to have fired a gun at a police officer, held rank or any leadership position in a gang, and engaged in physical fights with other rival gang members while incarcerated. The implication from this research is that at least for these females studied, they were generally less violent in their offending compared with their male counterparts, although violence differences between male and female gang members are gradually diminishing (National Gang Crime Research Center 1997, 2000). However, the research is persuasive in that the nature and seriousness of female offending is increasingly matching male offending patterns and frequency (Curry 1998; Winokur 1999). It is too early to make sweeping generalizations about female delinquents and whether they are becoming more violent. More attention needs to be directed toward understanding their interpersonal behaviors as well as certain institutionalized patterns of a patriarchal society (Chesney-Lind and Paramore 2001).

Juvenile Response to Police Officer Contacts

Police officers who observe juveniles in pairs or larger groupings, particularly in areas known to be gang-dominated, may assume that these youths are gang-related, and this observation may heighten police officer interest in and activity against them (Bankston 1998). The nature of this heightened interest and activity may result in more frequent stopping and questioning certain juveniles on the basis of their appearance and geographical location and whether they are minority youths. The precise impact of police–gang interactions is unclear, although in some jurisdictions, proactive policing against gang members has created sufficient conflict necessary to unify and perpetuate some gangs (Miller, Ruefle, and Wright 1997).

While some investigators question whether police officers discriminate against certain youths or single them out for stopping and questioning on the basis of racial or ethnic factors, other researchers have found patterns of police behavior that appear discriminatory on racial or ethnic grounds (Blakemore and Blakemore 1998). At least in some jurisdictions, minority youth stops, arrest rates, and detentions are at least three times as high as those for white youths (Jackson 1998).

However, much police officer activity is centered in high-crime areas that also tend to be areas inhabited by large numbers of persons of lower socioeconomic statuses (SES). And those areas with larger numbers of persons in the lower socioeconomic statuses are also those that contain larger concentrations of minorities (Hazlehurst and Hazlehurst 1998). Thus, some selectivity regulates where police officers will concentrate their patrol efforts as well as those youths they target for questioning and those they choose to ignore. Some observers believe that this opens the door to allegations of police officer harassment against certain classes of juvenile offenders on the basis of subjectively determined stereotypical features such as a youth's appearance (Hagedorn 1998).

Interestingly, how youths behave toward police officers whenever juveniles are stopped and questioned by them seems to make an important difference about what the officers will eventually do. Research about the appearance and demeanor of youths stopped by police officers and their subsequent actions indicates that youths who were poorly dressed and/or behaved defiantly and belligerently toward police were more likely to be harassed, possibly arrested (Curry and Decker 1998). Subsequent research is consistent with these early findings and suggests that cooperative, neatly dressed youths stand a better chance of avoiding being stopped, questioned, or arrested by police (Shelden, Tracy, and Brown 2001).

In fact, some police officers insist that a youth's demeanor when responding to police questioning on the street is crucial to whether the youth will be taken into custody, even if temporarily. Therefore, if youths do not display the proper amount of deference toward police officers whenever those youths are stopped and questioned, the youths stand a good chance of being taken to the police station for further questioning (Reynolds, Seydlitz, and Jenkins 2000). Interestingly, youths also may be too polite and arouse the suspicions of police officers. Thus, there is an elusive range of politeness that minimizes a youth's chances of being taken into custody. It is possible to be too polite or not polite enough so that police officers are sufficiently aggravated or motivated to act. According to some persons, police officer discretionary abuse occurs when "juveniles are detained when there is little or no evidence that incarceration is necessary or desirable to meet the generally accepted goals of detention" (Roberts 1989, 150). Despite statutory safeguards about detaining youths in adult jails for long periods and the division of labor relating to youthful offender processing in any jurisdiction, police officers are free to do pretty much whatever they want relative to juveniles they question and who are either acting suspiciously or belligerently. If any pretext exists for assuming that certain youths have been or are engaging in delinquent acts, they are subject to temporary detention by police officers. In many instances, these detention decisions by police are purely arbitrary (Neely 1997).

The following is a listing of discretionary actions that may be taken by police officers when encountering youths on the street:

1. Police officers may ignore the behaviors of youths they observe in the absence of citizen complaints. The most frequent types of encounters police officers have with juveniles do not stem from complaints filed by others. Rather, police officers observe youths under a wide variety of circumstances. The situation and circumstances are important, since youths walking down a street in pairs during daylight hours would not attract the same kind of attention as pairs of youths walking the streets late at night. Depending upon what the officers regard as serious behaviors, if youths are on skateboards on the sidewalks of the main street of a local community, they may or may not be posing risks to other pedestrians. If youths are playing ball on a vacant lot near other homes in a neighborhood, they may or may not be disturbing others. Police action in each case is probably unwarranted.

2. Police officers may act passively on someone's complaint about juvenile behaviors. If a store owner complains that youths are jeopardizing the safety of store customers by riding their skateboards down crowded city streets, police officers may respond by directing youths to other streets for their skateboarding. If neighbors complain that youths are making too much noise playing in a nearby vacant lot, police officers may appear and advise youths to play elsewhere. The intent of police officers in these situations is twofold. First, they want citizens to know they are there doing something. Second, they want citizens to know action has been taken and the problem no longer exists. Police officers continue to view the behaviors they observe as not especially serious. In these instances, police warnings are ordinarily sufficient to satisfy complainants. Since complaints were made by complainants, dispositions of those complaints are usually logged officially. Police officers may or may not choose to name those

youths warned. Rather, they may file a generalized report briefly describing their action taken.

3. Police officers may take youths into custody and release them to parents or guardians without incident. Those youths who may be acting suspiciously or who are in places where their presence might indicate an intent to do something unlawful (e.g., the youths who were in the uninhabited house to crash after their party) are likely to be taken into custody for more extensive questioning. In many instances, these **stationhouse adjustments** may result in their release to parents with warnings from police about refraining from suspicious conduct in the future. While these actions are official in the sense that police officers actually took youths into custody for a brief period and made records of these temporary detentions, they do not result in official action or intervention by intake officers or juvenile courts.

4. Police officers may take youths into custody and refer them officially to community service agencies for assistance or treatment. Sometimes youths appear to police to be under the influence of drugs or alcohol when they are stopped and questioned. Other youths may not have parents or guardians responsible for their conduct. They may be classified by police officers as runaways. In these cases, police officers arrange for various community services to take custody of these juveniles for treatment or assistance. These youths will be under agency care until arrangements can be made for their placement with relatives or in foster homes. Those youths with chemical dependencies may undergo medical treatment and therapy. In either case, juvenile courts are avoided.

5. Police officers may take youths into custody, file specific charges against them, and refer them to juvenile intake where they may or may not be detained. Only a small percentage of all juveniles detained by police will subsequently be charged with offenses. Conservatively, probably less than 10 percent of all juveniles who have contact with police officers annually engage in serious violent or property offenses (Snyder, Sickmund, and Poe-Yamagata 1996). Therefore, many youths are taken into custody for minor infractions, and their referrals to juvenile intake may or may not result in short- or long-term confinement. The discretion shifts from police officers to intake officers whether to process certain juveniles further into the juvenile justice system. Those juveniles who are deemed dangerous, violent, or persistent-nonviolent are most likely to be subject to detention until adjudication by a juvenile court. Police officers may respond to citizen complaints or actually observe juveniles engaging in illegal conduct. Their likelihood of taking these youths into custody for such wrongdoings alleged or observed is increased accordingly.

6. Police officers may take youths into custody, file criminal charges against them, and statutorily place them in jails pending their initial appearance, a preliminary hearing, and a subsequent trial. Some juveniles may be classified as adults for the purpose of transferring them to criminal courts where they might receive harsher punishments. Jurisdictions such as Illinois, Washington, DC, New York, and California are a few of many places where **automatic transfer laws** exist and where some juveniles are automatically placed within the power of criminal courts rather than juvenile courts. Therefore, police officers *must* act in accordance with certain statutory provisions when handling certain juvenile offenders, whenever they effect

arrests of youthful suspects. Often, they have no choice in the matter. Changing get-tough policies toward violent or serious juvenile offenders are making it more difficult for police to be lenient when confronting juveniles on city streets (Torbet et al. 1996).

Therefore, police discretion is exercised the most during the normal course of police patrols. Those youths who stand the best chance of being targeted for special police attention include minorities who are acting suspiciously and living in high-crime neighborhoods known as gang territories. Also increasing the likelihood of being taken into custody is the demeanor or behaviors exhibited by youths, whether they are polite or impolite to police officers. Short of any illicit conduct actually observed by or reported to police officers, a youth's appearance and behaviors are key considerations in whether he or she will be harassed and/or detained temporarily by police. However, comparatively few youths are actually arrested in relation to the actual number of police officer/juvenile encounters on city streets.

ARRESTS OF JUVENILES

Police officers need little, if any, provocation to bring juveniles into custody (Mendel 1995). Arrests of juveniles are, by degree, more serious than acts of bringing them into custody. Since any juvenile may be taken into custody for suspicious behavior or on any other pretext, all types of juveniles may be detained at police headquarters or at a sheriff's station, department, or jail temporarily. Suspected runaways, truants, or curfew violators may be taken into custody for their own welfare or protection, not necessarily for the purpose of facing subsequent offenses. It is standard policy in most jurisdictions, considering the sophistication of available social services, for police officers and jailers to turn over juveniles to the appropriate agencies as soon as possible after these youths have been apprehended or taken into custody (Guarino-Ghezzi 1994).

Before police officers turn juveniles over to intake officials or juvenile probation officers for further processing, they ordinarily complete an arrest report, noting the youth's name; address; parent's or guardian's name and address; offenses alleged; circumstances; whether other juveniles were involved and apprehended; the juvenile's prior record, if any; height; weight; age; and other classificatory information. If immediate action against the juvenile is warranted, the police officer may complete and file an application for filing of a juvenile court petition. An affidavit and application used by San Diego County, California, is shown in Figure 6.1.

Juvenile-Adult Distinctions

According to the Juvenile Justice and Delinquency Prevention Act of 1974 and its subsequent amendments, juveniles must be separated from adults, both by sight and sound, and treated as juveniles as soon as possible following their apprehension. If juveniles are brought into custody and charged with offenses that might be either felonies or misdemeanors if committed by adults, they may be clearly distinguishable as juveniles. It would be difficult to conclude that an 8-, 9-, or 10-year-old could pass for 18 or older. But many juveniles who are taken

Affidavit and Application for Filing of Juvenile Court Petition
(Welfare and Institutions Code Section 653)

I,_____
    Officer's/Citizen's Name

_____hereby state that
Officer's Agency & Duty Station or Citizen's Address

_____a   minor,   DOB_____

_____is within San Diego County   _____resides within San Diego County
_____was within San Diego County   _____committed an offense described within sec-
                                             tions 601/602 within San Diego County

and that said minor comes within the provisions of sections 601/602 of the Welfare and Institutions Code of the State of California as evidenced by the case reports dated _____ and consisting of _____ pages, which are attached hereto and incorporated by reference herein. On the basis of this information, the undersigned requests that a Juvenile Court Petition be filed on the above named minor for the offense(s) of

_____
(State the name of the offense and the appropriate statutory authority)

I declare under penalty of perjury that the facts set forth in this affidavit and its attachments are true and correct to the best of my knowledge.

Dated: _____   Signed:_____

Companions referred_____

Companions not referred_____

REPORT OF ACTION AND ENDORSEMENT

The following action was taken on this application: _____
                                                           (JDA No. or Misd. No.)

_____Petition requested under section(s)_____
_____D.A. reject
_____Referred to Traffic Court
_____Referral recorded and handled informally**

_____Active delinquent ward (602 W&I)/Offense reported to Juvenile Court**
_____6 Months' Probation Supervision (654 W&I)**

**Reasons(s):
_____Active to another jurisdiction   _____Family moving
_____Active dependent ward (300 W&I) _____Referred to community agency
_____Minor offense   _____PC 26 problem
_____No prior referral   _____Administrative exception
_____No prior arrests (2 yr. period)   _____Minor cannot be located
_____Transient   _____Parents handling appropriately
_____Restitution paid/property recovered _____Low maturity/intellectual level

Other reasons/Additional information (if any):_____
_____
_____

_____   _____   _____   _____
(Date)   (Please Print)   (Deputy Probation Officer)   (Phone No.)

Prob. 419 (8-87)   Dist: White-Ref.Agency   Canary-Prob. Clerk   Pink-Prob.File

FIGURE 6.1   Affidavit and application used by San Diego County, California

into custody may or may not be under 18. Their appearance is deceptive, and if they deliberately wish to conceal information about their identity or age from officers, it is relatively easy for them to do so. This is a common occurrence, since many juveniles are afraid that police will notify their parents. Fear of parental reaction may sometimes be more compelling than the fear youths may have of police officers and possible confinement in a jail.

Because juveniles generally have less understanding of the law compared with adults, especially those who make careers out of crime, they may believe that they will fare better if officers believe that they are adults and not juvenile offenders (Guarino-Ghezzi 1994). Perhaps there is a chance they might be released after spending a few hours or even a day or two confined in a jail cell. However, if they are identified positively as juveniles, then parents will invariably be notified of their arrest. But these youths often underestimate the resources police have at their disposal to verify information received from those booked after arrests. With proper identification, adults are ordinarily entitled to make bail and obtain early temporary release from jail. If fake IDs are used by these juveniles, however, this phony information is easily detected and arouses police officer suspicions and interest in these youths. They will likely be detained as long as it takes to establish their true identities and ages. Furnishing police officers with false information is a rapid way to be placed in preventive detention for an indefinite period. And police officers are entitled to use preventive detention lawfully in such cases (*Schall v. Martin* 1984).

The Ambiguity of Juvenile Arrests

Little uniformity exists among jurisdictions about how an arrest is defined. There is even greater ambiguity about what constitutes a juvenile arrest (McDowall, Loftin, and Wiersema 2000). Technically, an arrest is the legal detainment of a person to answer for criminal charges or (infrequently at present) civil demands (Black 1990). Available evidence suggests that increasing numbers of police departments are proactively changing their police–juvenile policies so that decision making regarding juvenile processing will be more rational and effective (U.S. National Institute of Justice 1998).

Early research by Klein, Rosenzweig, and Bates (1975) focused upon juvenile arrest procedures followed by forty-nine suburban and urban police departments in a large metropolitan county. Over 250 police chiefs and juvenile officers and their supervisors were surveyed, some of whom participated in follow-up, in-depth interviews about juvenile arrests and processing. Among police chiefs, for example, fewer than 50 percent were in agreement that booking juvenile suspects was the equivalent of arresting them. Further, respondents variously believed that arrests involved simple police contact with juveniles and cautioning behavior. Others believed that taking youths into custody and releasing them to parents constituted an arrest. Less than half of those surveyed appeared thoroughly familiar with juvenile rights under the law and the different restrictions applicable to their processing by police officers. Record-keeping and other activities related to juvenile processing by police have not changed much in subsequent years (Bilchik 1998).

Booking, Fingerprinting, and Photographing Juvenile Suspects

Under the Juvenile Justice and Delinquency Prevention Act of 1974, its subsequent revisions, and recommendations from the National Advisory Committee on Criminal Justice Standards and Goals in 1976, significant restrictions were placed on law enforcement agencies concerning how juveniles should be processed and the nature and types of records that may be maintained relating to such processing. Under the 1974 Act, for instance, status offenders were separated from delinquent offenders through deinstitutionalization or DSO. According to the 1974 Act, status offenders should not be taken to jails for temporary detention. Rather, they should be taken to social service agencies for less formal dispositions. One intent of the Act was to minimize the adverse impact and labeling influence associated with jails (Fendrich and Xu 1994). While DSO is fairly common in most jurisdictions, police officer discretion causes a significant proportion of status offenders to be processed as delinquent anyway. Thus, some status offenders fall through the cracks and continue to be placed in U.S. jails annually, even though such housing is only for a few hours.

Since most juveniles are under the jurisdiction of juvenile courts, extensions of civil authority, procedural safeguards for juveniles are in place to prescribe conduct for both police and jail officers in their dealings with juveniles (Miller 1995). For example, it is common practice for jail officers to photograph and fingerprint adult offenders. This is basic booking procedure. However, juveniles are often processed differently at the point of booking. Most jurisdictions have restricted photographing and fingerprinting juveniles for purposes related solely to their identification and eventual placement with parents or guardians. Fingerprinting is also useful if property crimes have been committed and fingerprints have been left at crime scenes (Florida Advisory Council on Intergovernmental Relations 1994).

Interrogations of Juvenile Suspects

Until 1966, custodial interrogations of criminal suspects by police were largely unregulated. Many of these custodial interrogations involved police brutality against particular suspects who were believed guilty of certain crimes. Suspects were denied access to defense counsel, and they were interrogated for many hours at a time, often without food, water, or rest. More than a few suspects confessed to crimes they didn't commit simply to end these brutal interrogations. However, in 1966 the U.S. Supreme Court heard the case of *Miranda v. Arizona*. Miranda was arrested on suspicion of rape and kidnapping. He was not permitted to talk to an attorney, nor was he advised of his right to one. He was interrogated by police for several hours, eventually confessing and signing a written confession. He was convicted. Miranda appealed, contending that his right to due process had been violated because he had not first been advised of his right to remain silent and to have an attorney present during a custodial interrogation. The U.S. Supreme Court agreed and set forth what later became known as the Miranda warning. This monumental decision provided that confessions made by suspects who were not notified of their due-process rights cannot be admitted as evidence. Suspects must be advised of certain rights before they are questioned by police; these rights include the right to remain silent, the right to counsel, the right to free counsel if suspects cannot afford one, and the right to terminate questioning at any time.

When the Miranda warning became official policy for police officers when arresting criminal suspects, the warning and accompanying constitutional safeguards were not believed by police to be applicable to juveniles. Thus, law enforcement officers continued to question youths about crimes during several post–Miranda years. Since it is generally accepted that a juvenile's understanding of the law is poor, it might be further assumed that juveniles might be more easily manipulated by law enforcement authorities.

A decision to protect juveniles from themselves by making incriminating Fifth Amendment–type statements was made by the U.S. Supreme Court in 1979. In that year, the U.S. Supreme Court decided the case of *Fare v. Michael C.* Michael C. was a juvenile charged with murder. During a preliminary interrogation, Michael C. was alone with police officers and detectives. Neither his parents nor an attorney were present. Michael C. asked to see his probation officer, but the interrogating detectives denied this request, since a probation officer is not an attorney and cannot be permitted to function as defense counsel under these circumstances. Subsequently, Michael C. waived his right to counsel and answered police questions. He was convicted of murder and appealed, alleging that his right to counsel was violated when he asked to see his probation officer and his request had been denied by the investigating officers. The court considered Michael C.'s case and determined that Michael C. had, indeed, made an intelligent, understanding, and voluntary waiver of his rights. The standard devised by the U.S. Supreme Court was the **totality of circumstances** test, which was essentially a standard they had adopted earlier in a criminal case involving an adult offender. Thus, the U.S. Supreme Court said that juvenile rights waivers should not be based on one sole characteristic or procedure, but rather, on all of the relevant circumstances of the case.

This case involved a juvenile who waived his constitutional right to be questioned by police about his involvement in a crime. The Court ruled that the totality of circumstances test should govern whether juveniles intelligently and knowingly waive their right to be questioned by police about crimes, and whether it is necessary first to obtain parental consent. Undoubtedly, this decision had led many states to enact statutes that specifically render inadmissible any admissions juveniles might make to police in the absence of parental guidance or consent (del Carmen, Parker, and Reddington 1998).

Expungement and Sealing Policies

Historically, once photographs and fingerprints have been taken, they have been destroyed as soon as possible following their use by police (Torbet et al. 1996, xiv). If such records exist in police department files after juveniles have reached the age of their majority, they may have their records expunged or sealed through **expungement orders.** Expungement orders are usually issued from judges to police departments and juvenile agencies to destroy any file material relating to one's juvenile offense history. Policies relating to records expungements vary among jurisdictions. Expunging one's juvenile record, sometimes known as **sealing records of juveniles,** is a means of preserving and insuring confidentiality of information that might otherwise prove harmful to adults if disclosed to others such as employers (Funk 1996).

Theoretically, sealing of records is intended as a rehabilitative device, although not all juvenile justice professionals believe that sealing one's records and enforcing the confidentiality about one's juvenile past through expungement is always beneficial to the general public. Investigations of state policies about police fingerprinting of juvenile suspects have indicated that these policies are diverse and inconsistent among jurisdictions (Funk 1996). Further, there continues to be considerable disagreement about how such fingerprint and related information should be used by either juvenile or criminal courts in their subsequent processing of youthful offenders (Miller 1995). In 1997, forty-seven states permitted fingerprinting of juveniles, while forty-six states allowed photographing of them for law enforcement purposes.

By 1997, many jurisdictions extended the time interval for sealing or expunging one's juvenile record. Most states have increased the number of years that must pass before one's juvenile record can be expunged. Thus, one's juvenile record may not be expunged for several years after a person has become an adult. In fact, in 1997, twenty-five states specified that if any juvenile has committed a violent or other serious felony, his or her juvenile record cannot be sealed or expunged (Torbet and Szymanski 1998). Indications are that more states will adopt similar policies in the immediate future.

By 1997, thirty states had mandated open proceedings and the release of juvenile records to the public, particularly where serious offenses are involved (Torbet and Szymanski 1998). Furthermore, many states now expose juvenile court records to school officials or require that schools be notified whenever a juvenile is taken into custody for a crime of violence or when a deadly weapon is used. Another widely adopted policy change is that forty-four states have lowered the age at which juvenile court records may be made available to the public. Also, these states have established statewide repositories of information about violent and serious juveniles.

STATUS OFFENDERS AND JUVENILE DELINQUENTS

One of the more controversial issues in juvenile justice is how status offenders should be classified and managed. The fact that status offenders are labeled as status offenders contributes significantly to this controversy (Hil and McMahon 2001). Such a label implies that all status offenders are somehow alike and should be treated similarly in all jurisdictions. But this implication is about as valid as assuming that all juvenile delinquents are alike and should be treated similarly. If we think about the etiology of runaway behavior compared with the respective etiologies of curfew violation, truancy, incorrigibility, liquor law violation, and sex offenses, it is likely that different sets of explanatory factors account for each type of deviant conduct (Hoge 2001). Thus, different treatments, remedies, or solutions would be required for dealing with each effectively.

In 1974, the Juvenile Justice and Delinquency Prevention Act acknowledged some major differences between status offenders and delinquents by mandating that status offenders should not be institutionalized as though they had committed crimes. Rather, they should be diverted away from the trappings of juvenile courts that seemingly criminalize their behaviors. By managing status offenders less formally and dealing with their behaviors largely through counseling and assistance provided through community-based services, it was reasoned that they would be less likely to define themselves as delinquent and that others would be less likely to define them as delinquent as well. The long-range implication of such differential treatment is that status offenders will not be inclined to progress or escalate to more serious types of offenses compared with those more serious delinquent offenders who are exposed to the **criminogenic environment** of the juvenile courtroom (Hoge 2001; Toombs, Benda, and Corwyn 2000).

Between the time the 1974 Act was implemented and individual states adopted policies to desinstitutionalize status offenders, there was a 95 percent

BOX 6.3

PUDDLE PRANK GETS BOY IN TROUBLE

Kyle Fredrikson, 12

Imagine this. You are walking back from lunch across the Inverness Middle School in Inverness, Florida. Suddenly, a boy purposely stomps water on you from a nearby puddle. You are drenched in muddy water and you stand there, wondering what recourse you have against the unruly youth. A police arrest? Hardly. But that's what happened to Kyle Fredrikson, 12. Investigating authorities said that Kyle Fredrikson was walking back to class from lunch when he decided to purposely stomp water on some friends, including a teacher. This was after he had been told numerous times by the teacher to keep with the group and stay out of the rain and puddles. At that point, a sheriff's deputy who was nearby took the sixth grader to the school office, where Fredrikson was cuffed, placed in a patrol car, and taken to jail. After being detained in a holding room for two hours, Fredrikson was eventually released to the custody of his mother and grandmother. The incident provoked outrage from the parents, Chuck and Brenda Fredrikson. The father said,

"The inmates had access to him. Can you imagine that for stomping in a mud puddle?" Lt. James Martone, who oversees the school resource officer program of which the deputy, Tim Langer, is a part, said that Langer had made a proper arrest. The situation was discussed with Inverness Middle School Principal Cindy Staten and she and sheriff's officials decided that the arrest would be appropriate under the circumstances. In his defense, Kyle's family said that he has a hyperactive disorder and is in a class with similar children. According to the family, Deputy Langer should have taken that into account before arresting him.

Do you think this incident is too trivial to merit an arrest and a two-hour jail detention? What would you do to sanction a youth for misbehaving in such a way on the school playground, especially after being warned numerous times to refrain from such conduct? Should there be a juvenile court disposition of the matter? If you were the juvenile court judge, how would you punish Fredrikson? What do you think?

Source: Adapted from the Associated Press, "Puddle Prank Gets Boy in Trouble," December 9, 1999.

reduction in the number of status offenders who are placed in some type of secure confinement (U.S. General Accounting Office 1996b). However, a portion of those detained consisted of status offenders who violated court orders, or one or more conditions imposed by juvenile court judges at the time of their status offender adjudications. Status offenders tend to exhibit less recidivism compared with those referred to juvenile court for delinquent acts. Further, the earlier juveniles are referred to juvenile court, for whatever reason, the more likely they will be to reoffend and reappear in juvenile courts (Snyder, Sickmund, and Poe-Yamagata 1996). Therefore, diversionary procedures employed by police officers at their discretion when confronting extremely youthful offenders or those who are not doing anything particularly unlawful would seem to be justified on the basis of existing research evidence (Hoge 2001).

But deinstitutionalizing status offenders is seen by some persons as tantamount to relinquishing juvenile court control over them, and not all persons favor this particular maneuver. A strong undercurrent of *parens patriae* persists, especially pertaining to those status offenders who need supervision and guidance from caring adults. Retaining control over status offenders is one means whereby the juvenile court can compel them to receive needed assistance and/or appropriate treatment (Hoge 2001). But disagreement exists about the most effective forms of intervention to be provided status offenders. One problem experienced by more than a few juvenile justice systems is inadequate resources for status offenders and others requiring less drastic interventions as alternatives to incarceration.

DIVESTITURE AND ITS IMPLICATIONS: NET-WIDENING

Divestiture means that juvenile courts relinquish their jurisdiction or authority over certain types of offenders, such as status offenders. Thus, if a juvenile court in Kansas or Colorado were to divest itself of authority over status offenders or children in need of supervision, then those processing status offenders, such as police officers, would probably take such offenders to social service agencies or other community organizations designed to deal with these youths. But it doesn't always work this way in some jurisdictions (Castellano 1986).

Under divestiture provisions, status offenses are simply removed from the jurisdiction of juvenile courts. Various community agencies and social service organizations take over the responsibility for insuring that status offenders will receive proper assistance and treatment. Referrals to juvenile court, incarceration, and the imposition of formal sanctions are no longer justified on the basis that one is a status offender and should suffer this processing and these punishments.

Relabeling Status Offenses as Delinquent Offenses

Because of police discretion, curfew violation, runaway behavior, and truancy can easily be reinterpreted or relabeled as attempted burglary or attempted larceny. Hanging out or common loitering may be defined by police as behaviors associated with casing homes, businesses, and automobiles as future targets for burglary and theft. And these acts are sufficiently serious and provocative to bring more juveniles into the juvenile justice system, thereby widening the net. Widening the net occurs whenever juveniles who would ordinarily have been dealt with by police differently prior to divestiture are brought into the juvenile justice system (Mears 2000). Prior to divestiture, many status offenders would have received wrist-slaps and verbal warnings by police instead of being taken into custody. However, when police officers resort to relabeling status offenses as conceivably criminal actions, greater rather than fewer numbers of juveniles will be netted into the juvenile justice system in the postdivestiture period than was the case in the predivestiture period.

In the Washington cities of Yakima and Seattle, police officers were not particularly receptive to the idea that their discretion in certain juvenile matters was abolished by legislative mandate in the late 1970s. In effect, the police officers in these cities literally created a fictitious juvenile delinquency wave in the postdivestiture period, where the rate of delinquency appeared to double over night. Such an artificial wave was easily accomplished, since these front-line officers merely defined juvenile behaviors differently according to their unchecked discretion. A similar phenomenon occurred in Connecticut during approximately the same period (Logan and Rausch 1985). The primary implication of their actions seems to be that they perceived divestiture as a criticism of their integrity and discretionary quality in dealing with juvenile matters rather than as a positive move to assist certain youths in avoiding the delinquency label (Lieb, Fish, and Crosby 1994).

An ambitious DSO provision was implemented in California on a statewide basis. Again, like Washington, DSO did not necessarily deliver what was intended by deinstitutionalization and divestiture. For example, a study of San Bernardino County by Krause and McShane (1994) examined 123 youths who had had previous involvement with the juvenile justice system and 493 youths who had no prior involvement with it. Both groups of juveniles consisted of nonserious youths who were largely from dysfunctional families. Prior to DSO many of these youths would simply be diverted from the juvenile justice system and subjected to family counseling outside of any custodial setting. However, following DSO in San Bernardino County, many of the youths who normally would have been given diversion and family counseling were relabeled, placed in custody in juvenile hall, and placed outside their parents' homes in foster care or group homes. Krause and McShane strongly recommended that San Bernardino County juvenile authorities should seriously reexamine their institutionalization criteria and invoke more effective screening mechanisms to avoid the practice of detaining for prolonged periods those youths who deserve to be diverted instead.

Protecting Status Offenders from Themselves

Many runaways and truants may have certain mental health or educational needs that can only be met through mandatory participation in a mental health therapy program or educational intervention (Kingree, Braithwaite, and Woodring 2001). Court intervention may be necessary to insure that juveniles take advantage of these services. Informal dispositions of status offense cases may not have the legal coercion of a juvenile court order. Thus, one's participation in various assistance programs is either voluntary or strongly recommended. However, agency response in accommodating youths with various problems seems selective and discriminatory. Often, those youths most in need of certain agency services are turned away as unqualified. Thus, status offender referrals to certain agencies may be unproductive, particularly if the status offenders are psychotic, violent, or drug/alcohol dependent (Little Hoover Commission 1990).

Parens Patriae versus Due Process

The *parens patriae* philosophy is in increasing conflict with the due process orientation that typifies most juvenile court procedures today. Status offenders represent a juvenile offender class clearly in the middle of this conflict. Reducing admissions of status offenders to various detention centers and treatment facilities is seen by some persons as a reversal of the hardening effect of custodial confinement on these youths (U.S. General Accounting Office 1991).

Gender Stereotyping and DSO

A continuing problem of DSO in any jurisdiction is how male and female status offenders are differentially treated by juvenile court judges. For instance, in a survey of 87 juvenile probation officers in a large metropolitan county of a southwestern state, it has been found that female juveniles tend to receive relatively punitive protection from juvenile court judges (Reese and Curtis 1991). In fact, this differential treatment of females by juvenile courts seems fairly routinized and institutionalized. DSO has failed to change how juvenile court judges dispose of female status offense cases compared with how cases were disposed prior to DSO. It has been suggested that judicial stereotyping of female status offenders is such that many judges act to protect females from the system and society by placing them in restrictive circumstances such as secure confinement, even if their offenses do not warrant such placement. Thus, a double standard continues to be applied, despite the best intentions of DSO.

Race and Ethnicity

Do juvenile court judges stereotype status offenders on other factors besides gender? Some jurisdictions report that disproportionately high numbers of black youths are represented in their juvenile justice system (Adams, Johnson, and Evans 1998). In Georgia, for instance, a youth's race has had a direct impact upon disposition decision making, as well as at the law enforcement, intake, and adjudication decision points (Brooks and Jeon 2001). Closely related to the race variable was socioeconomic status. Thus, race and socioeconomic status operated in this instance to predict correctly more adverse consequences for youths who were black compared with other youths who had committed similar offenses, had similar delinquency histories, but were white.

A study prepared for the Virginia Department of Criminal Justice Services investigated 1,256 youths processed in Fairfax County, Virginia, in the early 1990s. Race was studied as it contributed to disparities in treatment of various juvenile offenders at different stages of juvenile justice processing (Williams and Cohen 1993). Generally, race did not seem to impact whether incarceration was imposed for youths charged with serious crimes in the initial stages of their processing. If the nature of the offense was serious enough, then youths were detained. For those youths charged with felonies, minority incarcerations were significantly higher than incarcerations of white juveniles. Later in their processing, black youths were more likely to have court-appointed counsel or no counsel, while white youths tended to have private counsel. Black male juveniles tended to be adjudicated delinquent more frequently and to receive longer incarcerative terms compared with white offenders, controlling for adjudication offense and prior record.

Presently, juvenile justice policy statements have been made declaring differential treatment on the basis of race/ethnicity, gender, and socioeconomic status to be illegal, immoral, and inadvisable. Such extralegal factors should have no place in determining one's chances in the juvenile justice system, whether one is a delinquent or a status offender (Bruce 2000; McCord, Widom, and Crowell 2001).

REDEFINING DELINQUENCY

Police officers might consider taking a more proactive role as interventionists in the lives of juvenile offenders encountered on the street. For instance, Trojanowicz and Bucqueroux (1990, 238) say that

> young people do not launch long-term criminal careers with a daring bank robbery, an elaborate kidnapping scheme, or a million-dollar dope deal. Yet the traditional police delivery system does not want officers 'wasting' much time tracking down the kid who may have thrown rocks through a few windows at school. Narcotics officers on their way to bust Mr. Big at the dope house cruise right by those fleet-footed 10-year-old lookouts. And a call about a botched attempt by a youngster to hotwire a car would not be much of a priority, especially where far more serious crimes occur every day.

These criminologists indicate that officers should be encouraged to intervene and to take these petty offenses and juvenile infractions seriously. It is possible for police officers to identify those youngsters most at risk in particular neighborhoods and perhaps do something to assist them to refrain from future lives of crime.

But the nature of systems is such that the actions of particular parts of the system may not function properly or be permitted to function properly in relation to other systemic parts (Guarino-Ghezzi 1994). This was especially the case when divestiture of jurisdiction was implemented in Yakima and Seattle, Washington, during the 1980s and status offenders were removed from the jurisdiction of the juvenile courts. Whether or not Yakima or Seattle police officers were justified in doing so, they intervened in the lives of numerous status offenders after divestiture was enacted and relabeled status offenses as delinquent offenses. This intervention was contrary to the spirit of intervention explicitly outlined by Trojanowicz and Bucqueroux in their description of police actions under community policing policies. More status offenders and petty offenders on the streets of Yakima and Seattle were taken to jails and juvenile halls following divestiture than in previous years. This is quite different from officers acting as interventionists in positive ways and doing things for youths rather than against them.

There are obvious gaps between different contact points in the juvenile justice system. It is one thing to legislate change and remove status offenders from the jurisdiction of juvenile court judges and police officers. It is quite another thing to expect that juvenile court judges and police officers will automatically relinquish their powers over status offenders. While many juvenile court judges and police officers won't admit it to others, they do not like having their discretionary powers limited or undermined by legislatures (U.S. General Accounting Office 1995b).

Some observers have recommended that police departments should have separate units to interface with juveniles and manage them. This has already been accomplished in many of the larger city police departments throughout the United States (Brantley and DiRosa 1994). However, many smaller police departments and sheriff's offices simply lack the staff or facilities to accommodate such special youth units. These luxuries are usually enjoyed only by larger departments. Smaller departments must be content with individual officers who assume responsibilities for managing juvenile offenders and perform related tasks. The majority of initial contacts with juveniles who engage in unacceptable behaviors continue to be made by uniformed police officers while on patrol (Sealock and Simpson 1998).

Police officers will continue to exhibit interest in those juveniles who violate criminal laws. Offense seriousness and the totality of circumstances will usually dictate their reactions in street encounters with these youths. But most juveniles who are the subjects of police-initiated contacts have committed no crimes. These may be status offenders or those reported to police as **children in need of supervision (CHINS)** (Mentaberry 1999). The wise use of discretion by police officers is especially crucial in dealing with status offenders. Fine lines may be drawn by academicians and others to distinguish between offender arrests and temporary detentions resulting from being taken into custody, but the bottom line is usually a record of the contact being entered in a juvenile file. One increasingly important buffer between police actions against status offenders and less serious delinquents is to divert certain juveniles to alternative and informal mechanisms where their cases can be disposed of with little, if any, visibility (Harrison, Maupin, and Mays 2001). In later chapters, various alternatives to the formality of juvenile court proceedings will be described.

SUMMARY

Police officers are the primary means whereby juveniles are brought into the juvenile justice system. Much of this action depends upon police discretion, or the range of behavioral choices police have within the limits of their power. Police officers perform diffuse roles, where much is expected of them from the public. They are expected to resolve disputes and to investigate any citizen complaints. These complaints may sometimes involve juveniles who may or may not be violating criminal laws. Officers who encounter youths must define their behaviors, largely on situational factors. Such situationally based discretion is believed by some experts to be discriminatory and unfair.

Juveniles may only be fingerprinted and photographed if such measures are to determine their identity, age, and relation to any ongoing criminal investigation. Their photographs and fingerprints are usually destroyed soon after their identity has been established or the investigation has been completed by police. Juveniles brought to jails or comparable facilities are usually booked, and records are maintained of these incidents until juveniles reach the age of their majority. At such time, juveniles may have their records as juveniles expunged and/or sealed as a means of constitutionally protecting their privacy and other rights. The question of whether juvenile courts should retain control over certain types of juvenile offenders continues to be debated. Little agreement exists about whether the *parens patriae* doctrine should be abandoned in favor of the due-process doctrine, where juveniles are vested with increasing numbers of rights commensurate with adults.

Police officers are encouraged by some experts to become more actively involved in preventing delinquency through creative solutions to juvenile problems. Therefore, police officers may take a more proactive role as interventionists for the purpose of identifying and doing something about children at risk. However, police behaviors in the context of community policing may be frustrated to a degree by a get-tough policy toward juveniles that is prevalent throughout the juvenile justice system. Influencing a police officer's discretion to take youths into custody is their appearance and demeanor. Youths who are of minority status, in the lower socioeconomic statuses, who dress poorly, or who do not show police officers the proper amount of deference stand a good chance of being taken into custody compared with those with opposite characteristics.

QUESTIONS FOR REVIEW

1. What is meant by police discretion? In what respects is it both used and abused?
2. How are police officer roles considered diffuse regarding interactions with juveniles?
3. What are youth squads and gang units? What are their functions?
4. What is meant by proactive restorative policing?
5. What are several myths and truths about juvenile gangs and their membership?
6. What proportion of gangs in the United States are female gangs? What are some general characteristics of female gang members?
7. What are four different discretionary actions police officers can take in relation to juveniles they encounter?
8. Why are arrests of juveniles sometimes ambiguous?
9. Under what circumstances can police officers book, fingerprint, and photograph juvenile suspects?
10. What is meant by expungement or sealing records? How does divestiture of jurisdiction lead to net widening?

SUGGESTED READINGS

Bauer, Robert et al. 2000. *Juvenile crime and justice activities in Illinois: An overview of trends.* Chicago: Illinois Criminal Justice Information Authority.

Hoge, Robert D. 2001. *The juvenile offender: Theory, research, and applications.* Boston: Kluwer Academic Publishers.

McCord, Joan, Cathy Spatz Widom, and Nancy A. Crowell, eds. 2001. *Juvenile crime, juvenile justice.* Washington, DC: National Academy Press.

INTERNET CONNECTIONS

Federal Gang Violence Act
http://www.senate.gov/member/ca/feinstein/general/gangs.html

Fight Crime, Invest in Kids
http://www.fightcrime.org/

Gangs: A Bibliography
http://www-lib.usc.edu/~anthonya.gang.htm

Gangs in the Schools
http://www.eric-web.tc.columbia.edu/alerts/ia46.html

Juvenile Justice Information Center
http://www.jjic.org/

Juvenile Law Center
http://www.jlc.org/

National Youth Gang Center
http://www.iir.com/nygc

REALJUSTICE
http://www.realjustice.org/

Schools, Not Jails
http://www.schoolsnotjails.com/

Urban Institute
http://www.urban.org/

Youth Gangs—Out of Control
http://www.townhall.com/frc

Chapter Outline

Key Terms
Chapter Objectives
Introduction
What Is Intake?
Intake Proceedings: Where Do
   We Go from Here?
Legal Factors: Crime Seriousness,
   Type of Crime Committed,
   Evidence, and Prior Record

Extralegal Factors: Age, Gender,
   Race/Ethnicity, and Socio-
   economic Status of Juvenile
   Offenders
Preliminary Decision Making:
   Diversion and Other Options
Assessment of Guardianship

Summary
Questions for Review
Suggested Readings
Internet Connections

Key Terms

Assessment centers
Due process
Extralegal factors
Interagency Agreement Plan

Legal factors
Recidivism
Socioeconomic status (SES)

Stop Assaultive Children (SAC)
   Program
Strategic leniency

> ## Chapter Objectives
>
> *As a result of reading this chapter, you should realize the following objectives:*
>
> 1. Understand the intake process.
> 2. Learn about the roles of juvenile intake officers and the screening decisions they make.
> 3. Understand different models for dealing with juvenile offenders.
> 4. Distinguish between and learn about several important legal and extralegal factors that affect how juveniles are processed and treated within the juvenile justice system.
> 5. Describe several preliminary options available for juvenile offenders in lieu of formal juvenile court processing.

INTRODUCTION

• *The Detroit intake officer listened while the 14-year-old youth, Bobby Z., sobbed and told his version of why he had "tagged" his school with a can of spray paint. He said there was a gang called the Hard Riders, and he wanted to be a member of it. He had seen signs of their presence around his neighborhood, their graffiti, and he wanted to let them know he could do it at his school. Unfortunately for Bobby Z., a teacher was glancing out of her classroom at the time of the tagging. She caught Bobby Z. in the act. The intake officer, together with Bobby Z.'s mother and father, listened to this gang "wannabe" tell his sad tale. At the end of the session, the intake officer advised the parents that the school would have to repaint the portion of the wall tagged by Bobby Z., and that the expense would have to be paid by them. However, he told Bobby Z. that if he wanted to avoid further involvement with the juvenile justice system, he could pay his parents for the expense by working at different jobs at home. This was agreeable to all. The parents signed an informal agreement with the intake officer, a juvenile probation officer, and the school wall was subsequently repainted. The parents reimbursed the school for the expense of the repairs, and Bobby Z. repaid his parents over the next six months from monies earned from household chores.* [Adapted from the Associated Press, "Informal Solutions to Serious Gang Problems in Detroit." September 30, 2002].

• *James B., 12, sat in front of the Chicago intake officer with a smug look on his face. His mother sat at his side. He was being screened for possible future legal action by the juvenile court for his role in the theft of money and property from the burglary of a neighbor's home. The intake officer examined some documents indicating that James B. had been in trouble with the law on several prior occasions. In fact, James B. had been adjudicated delinquent on two prior occasions and given probation. Both incidents involved petty theft. The intake officer asked James B. if he had learned anything from the probation he had been given previously. James B. gave the intake officer all of the ammunition he needed to send the youth further into the system. James B. said, "Nobody cares about me. Me and my friends do this stuff [the burglaries and thefts] because we like to. We're gettin' probation anyway, so why quit? We're just kids and the cops can't do anything to us." The intake officer advised the parents that he was recommending further action by the juvenile court prosecutor and that James B. would likely face the juvenile court judge in an adjudicatory proceeding. Subsequently, the juvenile court judge adjudicated James B. delinquent and ordered him confined to a state industrial school for six months.* [Adapted from the Associated Press, "How Many Repeat Offenders Are There Among Chicago's Youth?" March 1, 2002].

• *Daryl K., 15, sat before the Jacksonville, Florida, intake officer on charges of lewd conduct. He had exposed himself to a girl at school the week before. Daryl's father and mother accompanied him to the intake hearing, and the intake officer wanted to know why Daryl K. did what he had done. He had no particular explanation, although he did admit that he had exposed himself to other girls in the past without consequence. The intake officer advised the parents that he was recommending a psychiatric evaluation for Daryl K. and sex offender counseling at a nearby social services clinic. He said that if Daryl K. would undergo the psychiatric evaluation and participate in the sex offender counseling for three months, he would consider terminating the case. The parents and Daryl K. agreed to the psychiatric evaluation and counseling. Three months later, Daryl K. returned to face the intake officer once again, this time with a favorable report from the social services clinic about Daryl K.'s progress. A follow-up by the intake officer six months later disclosed that Daryl K. had been law-abiding and had controlled his sexual urges.* [Adapted from the Associated Press, "Sex Offender Therapy Works for Teens in Florida." July 1, 2002].

This chapter is about the intake process. Intake officers encounter virtually every sort of juvenile offender imaginable. They must assess the circumstances and make fairly rapid decisions about whether to advance certain youths further into the juvenile justice system. The circumstances are not limited to the allegations or infractions. Rather, they encompass numerous dimensions, including age of offender, gender, ethnicity or race, type and seriousness of offenses alleged, school records, parental behaviors, and prior records of juveniles, if any. Did the juvenile act alone or in concert with others? Were there victims? Was anyone killed or seriously injured?

Because of the differential training juvenile probation officers receive and the individual orientations they manifest, their behaviors as intake officers may be better understood by paying attention to certain models that are commonly used in dealing with juvenile offenders. Several popular treatment models and orientations will be described and discussed. Many of those youths appearing before intake officers are first offenders. Because of the continuing belief by many persons that one major function of juvenile justice is to rehabilitate and redirect one's deviant behaviors toward more legitimate and proper conduct, intake officers give serious consideration to diversion as a nonpunitive option. Several forms of diversion will be described.

Intake also functions as one of the first screening mechanisms for filtering only the most serious offenders further into the system and diverting the least serious youths away from it. A major consideration in the diversion decision, therefore, is whether responsible guardianship exists for managing youthful offenders. The importance of this consideration will be discussed, and various juvenile offender implications will be assessed.

WHAT IS INTAKE?

Intake or an intake screening is the second major step in the juvenile justice process. Intake is a more or less informally conducted screening procedure whereby intake probation officers or other juvenile court functionaries decide whether detained juveniles should be (1) unconditionally released from the juvenile justice system, (2) released to parents or guardians subject to a subsequent juvenile court appearance, (3) released or referred to one or more community-based services or resources, (4) placed in secure confinement subject to a subsequent juvenile court appearance, or (5) waived or transferred to the jurisdiction of criminal courts. Many jurisdictions are currently reevaluating the intake process and whether it should be modified (Feld 2000).

Intake usually occurs in the office of a juvenile probation officer away from the formal juvenile court area. The juvenile probation officer, or intake officer, schedules an appointment with the juvenile and the juvenile's parents to consider the allegations made against the juvenile. The meeting is informal. An attorney representing the juvenile's interests may attend, although the primary purpose of the intake hearing is to screen juveniles and determine which ones are deserving of further attention from the juvenile justice system. Juvenile probation officers are vested with limited powers, but they do not have full adjudicatory authority possessed by juvenile court judges. Especially for petty offending, intake officers can divert a case to social services, or they can recommend a full-fledged juvenile prosecution.

The Discretionary Powers of Intake Officers

The pivotal role played by intake probation officers cannot be underestimated. While police officers are often guided by rules and regulations that require specific actions such as taking juveniles into custody when certain events are observed or reported, the guidelines governing intake actions and decision making are less clear-cut. In most jurisdictions, intake proceedings are not open to the public, involve few participants, and do not presume the existence of the full range of a juvenile's constitutional rights. This is not meant to imply that juveniles may not exercise one or more of their constitutional rights during an intake hearing or proceeding, but rather, the informal nature of many intake proceedings is such that one's constitutional rights are not usually the primary issue. The primary formality of these proceedings consists of information compiled by intake officers during their interviews with juvenile arrestees. The long-range effects of intake decision making are often serious and have profound implications for juvenile offenders once they reach adulthood (Glaser et al. 2001).

Intake officers must often rely on their own powers of observation, feelings, and past experiences rather than a list of specific decision-making criteria in order to determine what they believe is best for each juvenile. Each juvenile's case is different from all others, despite the fact that several types of offenses occur with great frequency (e.g., shoplifting and theft, burglary, and other property crimes). Some juveniles have lengthy records of delinquent conduct, while others are first-time offenders. Many jurisdictions have standard forms completed by probation officers during intake interviews. One of these forms is a Social History Report illustrated in Figure 7.1.

Sometimes intake officers will have access to several alternative indicators of a juvenile's behavior, both past and future, through the administration of paper–pencil instruments that purportedly measure one's risk or likelihood of reoffending. Armed with this information, intake officers attempt to make important decisions about what should be done with and for juveniles who appear before them.

Various studies of intake officers have been conducted in an effort to determine the successfulness of their actions in influencing the lives of those they screen. For instance, during the period 1986–1987, 81 juvenile male offenders were court-referred to Lakeside Center, a residential treatment center in St.

Social History Report

Routing Information			Case Identification	

TO: _____   CASE NAME: _____

FROM: _____ DATE: _____   SERIAL: _____   STATUS: _____

AREA: _____ OFFICE: _____   BIRTH DATE: _____ SEX: ___ RACE: _____

REPORT REQUESTED BY: _____   JPC ASSIGNED CASE: _____

1. IDENTIFYING DATA
    a.   Youth's birthplace:
    b.   Youth's birth status:
    c.   Other names used:
    d.   Youth's address at time of commitment:
    e.   With whom living at time of commitment:
    f.   Family's relationship to youth:
    g.   Legal guardian:
    h.   Social security number: Youth: Father: Mother:

2. PERSONS AND AGENCIES INTERVIEWED

3. AGENCIES THAT HAVE WORKED WITH YOUTH AND FAMILY

4. DELINQUENCY HISTORY (USE ONLY AS SUPPLEMENTAL TO COURT REPORT. IDENTIFY ANY PARTICULAR CHRONIC AND/OR PECULIAR PROBLEMS.)

5. DEVELOPMENTAL HISTORY
    a.   Early history (Use only when obvious value in detailing youth's problems.)
    b.   Medical history (Detail only if pertinent.)
    c.   Description of youth (How parents perceive youth, attitudes, and behavior patterns.)

6. FAMILY HISTORY—REVISED
    a.   Marital history and youth's previous living situations
    b.   Father
    c.   Mother
    d.   Siblings
    e.   Family income
    f.   Parents' perception of problem
    g.   Impression of family functioning
        (1)   How parents relate to youth
        (2)   Parents' concept of discipline
        (3)   Evaluation of parent role (how they should/do perform as parents)
        (4)   JPC's impression of performance and evaluation (identify strengths and weaknesses)
        (5)   Family's financial resources, including benefits, veterans, social security, welfare, etc., medical/hospital insurance (Note: Income is reported elsewhere—preadmission history.)

7. COMMUNITY INFORMATION
    a.   Placement possibilities, including own home. (Note attitudes, family structural compatibility, and other placement considerations.)
    b.   Community attitudes toward placement
        (1)   Neighbors
        (2)   School officials

8. SCHOOL AND VOCATIONAL HISTORY
    a.   School performance
        (1)   Last school attended and grade completed
        (2)   Level of scholastic performance
    b.   Vocational history
        (1)   Part-time or full-time jobs held
        (2)   Performance evaluation

9. IMPRESSIONS AND RECOMMENDATIONS
    a.   Overall evaluation by JPC
    b.   Family's willingness to become involved and cooperate
    c.   Problem list (JPC's perception of specific problems)
    d.   Strengths and assets of family and youth which can be used in dealing with problems.

FIGURE 7.1   Social history report
Source: From Thomas G. Pinnock, *Necessary Information for Diagnosis* (Olympia, VA: Bureau of Juvenile Rehabilitation, Department of Social and Health Services, 1976), p. 11.

Louis, Missouri. Previously, these juveniles had been rated and evaluated by intake officers. The officers reviewed social and referral history information, and they conducted an admission interview with each youth. The intake officers rated these juveniles as "good," "fair," or "poor" in terms of their prognosis for whether each juvenile would reoffend. Later, after the juveniles had attended the Lakeside Center for a period of time, a majority successfully completed the program, while 27 percent failed to complete it. Those who completed the program were far less likely to reoffend later when follow-ups were conducted. However, specific juveniles who were rated earlier by intake officers as having a "fair" or "poor" prognosis reoffended at a much higher rate compared with those rated by these officers as "good." Researchers concluded that intake officer assessments of the future conduct of juveniles they screened were highly reliable, especially when accompanied by an independent risk assessment device to measure their propensity to reoffend (Sawicki, Schaeffer, and Thies 1999).

The process of intake is far from uniform throughout all U.S. jurisdictions. Often, intake officers do not believe that a comprehensive assessment of all juveniles is necessary at the point of intake (Mears and Kelly 1999). Juvenile probation office policies may not be clearly articulated, thus causing some confusion among intake officers about how intake screenings should be conducted and which variables should be considered most crucial in intake decision making. A wide variety of early interventions suggests a lack of consistency among jurisdictions and how effectively intake officers perform their jobs (Castellano and Ferguson 1998; Glaser et al. 2001). Furthermore, some evidence suggests that certain minorities, especially black youths, are overrepresented at intake proceedings compared with the entire juvenile offending population in some jurisdictions, such as North Carolina (Dean, Hirschel, and Brame 1996). One possible remedy for inequities in juvenile processing and inconsistent policy decision making is the establishment of assessment centers.

Florida Assessment Centers

In Florida, juvenile **assessment centers** have been established as processing points for juveniles who have been taken into custody or arrested. These centers provide comprehensive screenings and assessments of youths to match var-

Youths often appear at intake hearings with one or both parents and an attorney.

ious available services to client needs, promote interagency coordination, and to generate data relevant to resource investment and treatment outcomes (Dembo et al. 2000a). Florida intake officers conduct clinical screenings, recommend confinement, make provisions for youth custody and supervision, arrange transportation, and track juveniles as they move throughout the juvenile justice system.

The U.S. Supreme Court has rejected attempts by various interests to extend the full range of **due-process** guarantees for juveniles to intake proceedings, largely because of the informal nature of them (Butts et al. 1996, 8). Thus, there are numerous interjurisdictional variations concerning the intake process and the extent to which one's constitutional rights are safeguarded or protected (del Carmen, Parker, and Reddington 1998). Generally, these proceedings are conducted informally, without court reporters and other personnel who are normally equated with formal court decorum. A casually dressed, folksy juvenile probation officer sits at a desk with the juvenile accused of some infraction or crime or alleged to be in need of some special supervision or care. One or both parents may be present at this informal hearing, although it is not unusual for parents or guardians to be absent from such proceedings. Victims may or may not attend, again depending upon the jurisdiction.

 **BOX 7.1**

A DIFFERENT KIND OF SCHOOL DISCIPLINE

Maxie Rivers, Hillcrest School

It happened in Franklin Township, New Jersey, at the Hillcrest School. An 11-year-old, Aaron Lawton, missed a homework assignment, failing to turn it in. The teacher, Maxie Rivers, wanted to teach Aaron and other students a lesson so that they wouldn't turn in any more late papers. His idea was as follows. Maxie told his sixth-grade class, "How about we make a bet? If you miss an assignment, the whole class gets to deck you." When Aaron Lawton heard this, he thought the teacher was joking. No joke. The very next time Aaron failed to turn in an assignment, Rivers told him to put his arms up and boys and girls stood in line and punched him. Aaron said, "Some of the punches were hard, some were soft, and some were in between." Aaron's father, who heard about the incident later, said, "That's like telling kids: 'Let's settle disputes with violence.' I mean, push-ups I could understand, but this?"

Aaron Lawton was taken to a hospital and examined for injuries later. A doctor said that he suffered some bruises. Maxie Rivers was suspended with pay while Hillcrest School officials continued to investigate the incident. Michael Barrett, an attorney for Rivers, said, "Mr. Rivers sees in retrospect that this wasn't the best way to reinforce the lesson. The May 16th incident was 'lighthearted,' and the other youngsters merely 'tapped' him kiddingly. Only his best friend—as best friends will—punched him."

What restrictions should be placed on teachers about how they convey object lessons to their pupils? Is physical punishment ever justified in the classroom for failure to turn in homework? How should Rivers himself be disciplined in this incident? What type of lesson do you think the children learned from this incident? What do you think?

Source: Adapted from the Associated Press, "Teacher Let Kids Hit Student." May 28, 2000.

The Increasing Formalization of Intake

Intake is such an important stage of a juvenile's processing that it must be scrupulously monitored so that fairness and equitable treatment of juveniles by intake officers is preserved. Both legal and extralegal factors have been found to influence intake decision making in various jurisdictions. For instance, a study of the intake process in Iowa provides information about intake proceedings suggesting that extralegal factors are often at work to influence intake officer decision making. Leiber (1995) investigated a random sample of referrals to juvenile courts in Iowa during the period 1980–1991. Included in his study were 3,437 white juveniles, 2,784 black juveniles, and 350 Hispanic juveniles. Agency records provided detailed information about how the cases were disposed and processed at different stages, commencing with intake. Leiber found that the ultimate case outcome was influenced mostly by legal factors, such as offense seriousness, prior record of offending, and one's age. However, he found compelling evidence of discrimination in offender processing at the intake stage. Black juveniles tended to receive a larger proportion of recommendations from intake officers for further proceedings in the juvenile justice system. Black juveniles were also far less likely than whites and Hispanics to receive diversion or other lenient outcomes from the intake proceeding.

Often, these disparities in processing juveniles at the intake stage are attributable to the subjective impressions of intake officers. While most of these officers are perhaps well-intentioned in their individualization of juvenile treatment, there is some general bias inherent in such individualization. This bias occurs most likely as the result of gender, race/ethnicity, and socioeconomic factors (Dean, Hirschel, and Brame 1996). Adding fuel to the charge that the intake process is often discriminatory according to race/ethnicity, gender, and socioeconomic status, a study of 1,256 youths was undertaken in Fairfax County, Virginia, in the early 1990s (Williams and Cohen 1993). It was determined that disproportionately more black youths were processed at the point of intake compared with youths of other races/ethnicities. While secure confinement was almost always used for those juveniles where serious offenses were alleged, disproportionately more minority offenders were placed in secure confinement, even controlling for type of offense and prior juvenile record. Further, blacks were less likely than whites to receive lenient dispositions and treatment. Disproportionately lower numbers of blacks were likely to have hearings compared with whites, and more minorities used public defenders. Thus, minorities, especially black males, received adverse treatment at the early stages of their processing. All of this adverse treatment had the cumulative effect of maximizing the harshness of their dispositions at later stages (Kurtz, Giddings, and Sutphen 1993).

Regardless of whether any particular jurisdiction exhibits differential, preferential, or discriminatory treatment toward juvenile offenders at *any* stage of their processing, there are those who believe that increased defense attorney involvement for at least the most serious juveniles is a necessity (Burruss and Kempf-Leonard 2002). The primary reason for the presence of defense attorney involvement in the early stages of a juvenile's processing is to ensure that the juvenile's due-process rights are observed. If there are extralegal factors at work that somehow influence an intake officer's view of a particular juvenile's case, then the impact of these extralegal factors can be diffused or at least minimized by the presence of someone who knows the law—a defense attorney. During the 1980s where data were available from reporting states, the amount of attorney use in juvenile proceedings increased substantially (Champion 1992). Specific states involved in a ten-year examination of juvenile attorney use trends were California, Montana, Nebraska, North Dakota, and Pennsylvania. Attorney use increased systematically during this decade.

The increased presence of counsel in juvenile proceedings at virtually any stage may have both positive and negative effects (Feld 1995). An attorney's presence can preserve due process. Intake officers and other juvenile court actors, including judges, are inclined to apply juvenile law more precisely than under circumstances where defense counsel are not present to represent youthful offenders. Where defense counsel are not present, however, the law might be relaxed to the point where some juveniles' rights are ignored or trivialized. But an attorney's presence in juvenile proceedings criminalizes these proceedings to a degree. The fact of needing an attorney for one's defense in juvenile court is suggestive of criminal proceedings and ensuring a criminal defendant's right to due process. In circumstances where defense counsel and prosecutors argue the facts of particular cases, juveniles cannot help but be influenced by this adversarial event.

This experience is sometimes so traumatic that juveniles come to identify with criminals who go through essentially the same process. Many persons believe that youths who identify with criminals will eventually label themselves as criminal or delinquent, and thus they will be harmed from the experience. This is consistent with labeling theory, where self-definitions of particular types of persons are acquired by others, such as juveniles identifying with criminals on the basis of how they, the juveniles themselves, are treated and defined by others (Lemert 1951, 1967a). To the extent that labeling theory adversely influences youths who are either first offenders or have only committed minor infractions, including status offenses, then some thought ought to be given to maintaining a degree of informality in intake proceedings. Nevertheless, it is important to emphasize a youth's accountability at all stages of juvenile justice processing (Hornick and Rodal 1995).

The Need for Greater Accountability

More than a few persons seek greater accountability from those who work with juvenile offenders from intake through adjudication and disposition (Feld 2000). Presently, there is much variation among juvenile justice systems throughout the United States. Different types of family courts attempt to apply juvenile law in resolving a wide assortment of familial disputes and juvenile matters. Juvenile courts are increasingly seeking new methods and techniques, such as expanded intake functions and nonadversarial resolution of disputes, not only to create smoother case processing for juvenile courts, but also to provide more efficient, just, and enforceable social solutions to diverse juvenile problems. Accountability for judicial power requires that the court act comprehensively in providing social services either directly or by way of referral. This accountability involves not only the enforcement of dispositional orders requiring the parties and families to respond, but also the agencies and service providers to function effectively and the court to hold itself responsible for its case processing and management systems (Page 1993).

INTAKE PROCEEDINGS: WHERE DO WE GO FROM HERE?

Intake Compared with Plea Bargaining

A parallel has been drawn between what goes on in juvenile intake hearings and criminal plea bargaining (Dougherty 1988). In plea bargaining, prosecutors and defense attorneys will negotiate a guilty plea and a punishment that are acceptable to both parties. Ordinarily, plea bargaining occurs before any formal disposition or trial. Thus, the accused waives certain constitutional rights, including the right to a trial by jury, the right to confront and cross-examine witnesses, and the right against self-incrimination. A plea bargain is an admission of guilt to one or more criminal charges, and it is anticipated by those entering guilty pleas that leniency will be extended to them in exchange for their guilty pleas. The theory is that the accused will save the state considerable time and expense otherwise allocated to trials as well as the important prosecutorial burden of proving the defendant's guilt beyond a reasonable doubt. Although some jurisdictions prohibit plea bargaining (e.g., Alaska and selected counties throughout the United States), the U.S. Supreme Court has ruled that plea bargaining is constitutional in any jurisdiction that wishes to use it (*Brady v. United States* 1970).

For many cases, this exchange is a reasonable one. In adult cases, crime for crime, other factors being reasonably equal, convicted offenders who plea bargain receive more lenient treatment compared with those who subject the state to the time and expense of jury trials (Champion and Mays 1991). Plea bargaining is favored by those who believe that it accelerates the criminal justice process.

During intake hearings, intake probation officers have almost unlimited discretion regarding specific outcomes for youths, especially those where minor offending is alleged. Apart from certain state-mandated hearings that must precede formal adjudicatory proceedings by juvenile court judges, no constitutional provisions require states to conduct such hearings (del Carmen, Parker, and Reddington 1998). Intake officers seldom hear legal arguments or evaluate the sufficiency of evidence on behalf of or against youths sitting before them. These proceedings, which most often are informally conducted, usually result in adjustments, where intake officers adjust disputes or allegations informally. Thus, parents and youths are sometimes deliberately discouraged from having legal counsel to assist them at this critical screening stage (U.S. General Accounting Office 1995a).

Intake officers, then, are in the business of behavioral prediction. They must make important predictions about what they believe will be the future conduct of each juvenile, depending upon their decision. Sometimes personality tests are administered to certain youths in order to determine their degree of social or psychological adjustment or aptitude. Those considered dangerous, either to themselves or to others, are detained at youth centers or other juvenile custodial facilities until a detention hearing is conducted. Florida Juvenile Assessment Centers administer a battery of tests to juveniles during intake, including clinical screenings by psychiatric professionals (Dembo et al. 2000b). For sex offenders in some jurisdictions, other psychological assessments are made and inventories administered, such as the Tennessee Self-Concept Scale, Beck Depression Inventory, the Rape-Myth Acceptance Scale, the Adversarial

Sexual Attitudes Scale, and the Assessing Environments Scale, the Buss-Durkee Hostility Inventory, and the Youth Self-Report (Worling 1995). On the basis of these and other criteria, decisions are made by intake officers about whether additional steps are necessary in juvenile offender processing.

Intake officers may decide to refer juveniles to community-based services or agencies where they can receive needed treatment in cases such as alcohol or drug dependency. They may decide that certain juveniles should be detained in secure facilities to await a subsequent adjudication of their cases by juvenile court judges (Schwartz and Barton 1994). Therefore, any action they take, other than outright dismissal of charges, that requires juveniles to fulfill certain conditions (e.g., attend special classes or receive therapy from some community agency or mental health facility) is based upon their presumption that the juvenile is guilty of the acts alleged by complainants.

If parents or guardians or the juveniles themselves insist that the intervention of an attorney is necessary during such informal proceedings, this effectively eliminates the informality and places certain constraints on intake officers. The coercive nature of their position is such that they may compel youths to receive therapy, make restitution, or comply with any number of other conditions to avoid further involvement in the juvenile justice process. It is relatively easy to file petitions against juveniles and compel them to face juvenile court judges (Leiber 1995).

There are some adverse consequences of plea bargaining for juveniles, however. In some jurisdictions at least, it has been found that if juveniles admit to their crimes, they are treated more severely than juveniles who denied committing their crimes (Ruback and Vardaman 1997). For instance, researchers studied 2,043 adjudication decisions in sixteen Georgia counties. Compared with juveniles who denied committing a crime but were adjudicated delinquent anyway, those youths who admitted their crimes to juvenile court judges received harsher dispositions in terms of longer terms of probation, longer incarcerative dispositions, and a greater proportion of more severe dispositions generally. Investigators found that race had no effect on judicial decision making. This study suggests that juvenile plea bargaining may not work the same way as it usually does for adults.

Parens Patriae Perpetuated

Some evidence indicates that intake probation officers in many jurisdictions are perpetuating the *parens patriae* philosophy. For example, a study of intake probation officers in a southwestern U.S. metropolitan jurisdiction revealed that probation officers believed that they were the primary source of their juvenile clients' understanding of their legal rights, although these same probation officers did not themselves appear to have a sound grasp or understanding of these same juvenile rights (Lawrence 1984). In this same jurisdiction, juveniles believed that they clearly understood their legal rights. However, interview data from them suggested that, in general, they tended to have a very poor understanding of their rights. Emerging from this study was a general recommendation that probation officers who perform intake functions should receive more training and preparation for these important roles.

Juvenile court judges have been criticized for ineffective decision making about the conditions of one's probation and the social and community services they should receive. In more than a few instances, judges are limited primarily because there are limited social services available in their communities. Thus, even if judges wanted to maximize their effectiveness in placing youths in treatment programs that could help them, their actions would be frustrated by an absence of such programs (Ellsworth, Kinsella, and Massin 1992).

Studies of intake dispositions in several jurisdictions have found that most intake dispositions tend to be influenced by extralegal factors, such as family, school, and employment (Wordes, Bynum, and Corley 1994). The preoccupation of intake probation officers in this jurisdiction with social adjustment factors rather than legalistic ones reflected a strong paternalistic orientation in dispositional decision making. Many intake officers dispose of cases according to what they perceived to be in the best interests of the children involved, rather than according to legalistic criteria, such as witness credibility, tangible evidence, and one's prior offending record (Holsinger and Latessa 1999).

Intake probation officers are not inundated exclusively with cases that require fine judgment calls and discretionary hair-splitting. Many youths appearing before intake officers are hard-core offenders and recidivists who have been there before (Menon and Jordan 1997). Also, evidentiary information presented by arresting officers is overwhelming in many cases, and a large portion of these cases tend to be rather serious. Therefore, intake officers will send many of these juveniles to juvenile court and/or arrange for a detention hearing so that they may be confined for their own safety as well as for the safety of others. Increasingly, serious juvenile offenders will be referred to juvenile prosecutors with recommendations that these juveniles should be transferred to the jurisdiction of criminal courts. The theory for this measure is that juveniles who are transferred to criminal courts will be amenable to more severe punishments normally meted out to adult offenders. However, it is questionable at present whether those who are transferred to criminal courts actually receive punishments that are more severe than they would otherwise receive if their cases were adjudicated in juvenile courts (Champion and Mays 1991).

Thus, intake is a screening mechanism designed to separate the more serious cases from the less serious ones as juveniles are processed by the system. Intake officers perform classificatory functions, where they attempt to classify informally large numbers of juveniles according to abstract criteria. Clearly, intake is not an infallible process. Much depends upon the particular experience and training of individual intake probation officers, juvenile court caseloads, and the nature of cases subject to intake decision making.

The discretionary powers of intake probation officers are in some ways equivalent to prosecutors in criminal courts. Intake officers may direct cases further into the system, they may defer certain cases pending some fulfillment of conditions, or they may abandon cases altogether and dismiss them from further processing. This powerful discretion can be used in both positive and negative ways, however. In response to a growing demand for juvenile justice reforms, numerous juvenile court judges have urged that more objective criteria be used for evaluating youthful offenders in the early stages of their processing, particularly at intake (McCarter 1997; Podkopacz 1996).

 **BOX 7.2**

ANOTHER SCHOOL TRAGEDY IN LAKE WORTH, FLORIDA

Lake Worth Community Middle School and 13-Year-Old Nathaniel Brazill

Lake Worth, Florida is a nice community. You don't associate violence with Lake Worth. However, on May 26, 2000, a 13-year-old student came to the Lake Worth Community Middle School he attended and fatally shot a teacher with a semiautomatic pistol. How did it happen and what led up to the fatality? The student, Nathaniel Brazill, 13, had recently been suspended from the school for throwing water balloons on the last day of classes. During the early afternoon of his suspension, Brazill went to the home of his grandmother, Eberlena Josey. He asked her for a key to his house, since his parents were not at home. Josey said that her daughter had called earlier in the day and said that Nathaniel had been suspended and that he was going to have to walk home. Josey gave Nathaniel the key and he left for his own home. Shortly before 3:30 that same afternoon, Nathaniel Brazill, an honors student, returned to the middle school to see some of his friends. They were congregating outside of the classroom of a teacher, 35-year-old language arts teacher Barry Grunow. Grunow was one of Brazill's teachers, but he wasn't the teacher who got Brazill suspended for the water balloon incident.

Grunow, a native of Lake Worth, was standing in the hallway talking with other students when he saw Brazill. Grunow asked everyone to get back into class, since it was too early to be dismissed. Grunow asked Brazill to leave the classroom. Shortly thereafter, Brazill pulled out a semiautomatic pistol and shot Grunow point blank in the face, killing him instantly. Brazill left the campus, riding away on his bicycle. Later, Brazill flagged down a police officer about a quarter mile from the school and surrendered. He was questioned by police later. It seems Brazill had stolen the gun from his grandfather's dresser drawer one week earlier. The gun was a compact, 5-inch

model called a Raven that was loaded with four bullets. A witness to the murder, 13-year-old Amanda Grunwald, said that Brazill calmly pulled out the pistol and shot Grunow in the face with one shot. "He was standing out in the hall, telling everybody to back into class because it wasn't time to be dismissed. Five seconds later, he was shot," said Amanda. Grunow was the father of two and had worked at the school for seven years. Brazill said he "liked the teacher."

Brazill Changes His Story

In a subsequent development, Brazill gave an interview to the press of the *Miami Herald.* Brazill said that "I wasn't thinking clearly when I took the gun to school on that day. I was too upset. I had the gun hidden in my dresser because I was going to ask my uncle in the Army to teach me how to use it for my future career in the military or law enforcement. I don't know how or why it happened the way it did." Brazill said that he went to Grunow's class to talk to a girl and tell her to have a good summer. Brazill said that Grunow told him that he couldn't talk with the girl, and that then, Brazill pulled the loaded gun out of his pocket, pointed it at the teacher, and fired point blank in the teacher's face. Brazill said, "I smiled at Mr. Grunow and he smiled at me. He pushed the gun away like he thought it was a fake. It was kind of like a joke—the kind of joke we always had between us. Then the gun went off. I don't know how it happened." Brazill, who is an honor student who had ambitions to become a Secret Service agent, said he was upset over his ten-day suspension from school. He said, "I thought I'd never catch up at the beginning of the next year. All of my friends would leave me behind. I thought my future was ruined." Actually, Brazill's statements to the press may ultimately seal his fate. By going to his home, retrieving a pistol, returning to school, and shooting a teacher, it was fairly clear that Brazill had more than friendly banter on his mind when he confronted the teacher in the hallway. In May 2001, Brazill was convicted of second-degree murder. He faced a sentence of 20 years or more for this crime.

What type of security should middle schools have to prevent students from bringing dangerous weapons to the campus? Are metal detectors at the front doors of schools the answer? How can future situations such as this be prevented if at all? How should Nathaniel Brazill be punished? Should he be tried as an adult? What do you think?

Source: Adapted from the Associated Press, "Student Shoots, Kills Teacher." May 27, 2000, A3; Associated Press, "Slain Teacher Mourned: Flowers, Notes at School Where Popular Teacher Fatally Shot." May 28, 2000; Adapted from the Associated Press, "13-Year-Old Indicted as Adult in Slaying." June 13, 2000; Adapted from the Associated Press, "Boy in Teaching Shooting Death Said He 'Wasn't Thinking Clearly.'" September 12, 2000; Adapted from the Associated Press, "Brazill Convicted." May 20, 2001.

LEGAL FACTORS: CRIME SERIOUSNESS, TYPE OF CRIME COMMITTED, EVIDENCE, AND PRIOR RECORD

A distinction is made between **legal factors** and **extralegal factors** that relate to intake decision making, as well as at other stages of the juvenile justice process. Legal factors relate to purely factual information about the offenses alleged, such as crime seriousness, the type of crime committed, any inculpatory (incriminating) or exculpatory (exonerating) evidence against offending juveniles, and the existence or absence of prior juvenile records or delinquency adjudications. Extralegal factors include, but are not limited to, juvenile offender attitudes, school grades and standing, gender, race or ethnicity, socioeconomic status, and age. Age also functions as a legal factor for certain types of offenses. Specific legal variables examined here include (1) offense seriousness, (2) type of crime committed, (3) inculpatory or exculpatory evidence, and (4) prior record.

Offense Seriousness

Offense or crime seriousness pertains to whether bodily harm was inflicted or death resulted from the youth's act. Those offenses considered as serious include forcible rape, aggravated assault, robbery, and homicide. These are crimes against persons or violent crimes. By degree, they are more serious than the conglomerate of property offenses, including vehicular theft, larceny, and burglary. In recent years, drug use has escalated among youths and adults in the United States and is considered as one of the most serious of the nation's crime problems. One general deterrent in every jurisdiction has been the imposition of stiff sentences and fines on those who sell drugs to others, and lesser punishments imposed on those who possess drugs for personal use. All large cities in the United States today have numerous youth gangs, many of which are involved rather heavily in drug trafficking (Wilson 2001). One result of such widespread drug trafficking among youths is the provision in most juvenile courts for more stringent penalties to be imposed for drug sales and possession. Thus, crimes don't always have to be violent in order to be considered serious.

Type of Crime Committed

Another key factor in screening cases for possible subsequent processing by the juvenile justice system is the type of crime or offense committed (Holsinger and Latessa 1999). Is the offense property-related or violent? Was the act either a felony or a misdemeanor? Were there victims with apparent injuries? Did the youths act alone or in concert with others, and what was the nature of their role in the offense? Were they initiators or leaders, and did they encourage or incite others to offend? Intake officers are more likely to refer cases to juvenile prosecutors where juveniles are older (i.e., 16 years of age and over), and where the offenses alleged are especially serious, compared with referring younger, petty, first offenders to prosecutors for additional processing (Schwartz and Barton 1994).

One implication of these findings for juvenile justice policy is that generally, leniency with many offenders, particularly first offenders, is accompanied by less recidivism. However, this conclusion may be premature and misleading (Niarhos and Routh 1992). Shay Bilchik has noted that greater intrusion into the juvenile justice system characterizes more serious offenders, probably meaning more chronic, persistent, dangerous, or habitual offenders—precisely the category of youthful offenders who are more likely to reoffend anyway (Bilchik 1996). Perhaps the term **strategic leniency** is appropriate here. The implication is that at least some punishment, properly administered, appears to

 **BOX 7.3**

 **PERSONALITY HIGHLIGHT**

Terry A. Snow
Superintendent, Burnett-Bayland Reception Center, Harris County Juvenile Probation, Houston, Texas

Statistics:

B.A. (criminal justice), University of Dayton (OH); M.A. (clinical psychology), Texas Southern University; Ph.D. (juvenile justice), Prairie View A & M University

Background and Interests:

Presently, I am the Superintendent of Burnett-Bayland Reception Center, the first facility in Texas to combine assessment and the treatment of 144 adjudicated delinquents under one roof. I have been with the Harris County Juvenile Probation Department for seventeen years, enjoying working with the fourth largest probation department in the United States. Burnett-Bayland Reception Center (BBRC) is novel in that the

concept was developed and completed in a joint collaboration between the state and county. The state provided the initial funding to build BBRC, and the County Commissioner's Office completed the process with additional building and employee funding.

Born in Bermuda but reared in Ohio, I was instilled with an ethic of working hard, a gift from God to work with juveniles, and the passion to work with children. After graduating from the University of Dayton, I moved to Texas to seek warm weather and new experiences. I have found both in this move. Starting from the ground up, this experience has allowed me to have the perspective from a variety of viewpoints. I have worked as a security officer, child-care worker, institutional officer, juvenile probation officer, supervisor, administrator, assistant superintendent, and now superintendent. All of these positions have allowed me to develop some insight into how a 144-bed secure facility ought to be run.

My two most insightful positions were as an institutional officer and juvenile probation officer. As an institutional officer, I was charged with the daily direct care of juveniles. This position allowed me to see all facets of the juvenile and demanded that I find a variety of ways to address each juvenile's individual and unique circumstances. With juveniles, one size does not fit all, and an institutional officer must find the way to reach each child and maintain his or her own emotional and physical safety at the same time. This position helped me to understand that the dynamics of a child's youth can impact their behavior, but the work that an institutional officer can provide can help to change that negative behavior and outlook. And the opposite is also true. An institutional officer who is neither invested in juveniles nor in their future can do additional harm if not properly trained.

As a juvenile probation officer, I was allowed to go directly into a child's environment, which included the home, school, job, and community. I saw the effects of all of the surrounding circumstances a juvenile is faced with on a daily and consistent basis. It was in this position as a juvenile probation officer that I had to take off my rose-colored glasses.

What I had previously imagined was so far from the actual reality. I saw more than I ever wanted to see or know. I saw the deplorable living conditions. When I walked into a home infested with rats and roaches, I had to maintain my composure as if nothing was offensive or unseemly. I then had to change my philosophy and understand that not everyone is blessed with the gift of exposure, environmental security, or adequate living conditions. Now I was able

to equip youth and tell them, "I have seen where you live and what you are facing, and this is what you can do to change your future." I did not accept their excuses, but I encouraged them to continue with their education, as that held the key for them changing their environment and life.

As a superintendent, I am able to relate to the institutional officers, probation officers, as well as the juveniles. BBRC has a specialized certified sex offender program, drug treatment program, and a mental health unit. When dealing with these diverse populations, every position in the building is tandem to the juveniles' success once released. A strong working relationship must be in place for everyone working with the juvenile. Therefore, the juvenile probation officer and institutional officer work side by side with the treatment team to ensure complete uniformity and a consistent approach in providing daily care and treatment. Teaching and training are the cornerstones in attempting to provide the juvenile with making different choices once they are returned home. Being superintendent charged with opening, running, and coordinating BBRC has afforded me the opportunity to build and shape the concept of teamwork and provide the optimal circumstances for effective treatment. The old saying about "being as good as the people you surround yourself with" is correct. We have been so fortunate to have a phenomenal administrative, casework, medical, and therapeutic team.

Advice to Students:

The segment of advice I would like to share with anyone considering the field of working with juveniles in any capacity is to *have the desire.* Regardless of what position you occupy, know that you will have an impact. Take that challenge seriously because your deeds and words can make a difference. My goal has never been to change a juvenile, only to make him or her more responsible and accountable for the choices he or she makes. Keep in mind that not only do you work with the juveniles, you must also work in accord with the families and the communities where they live.

have therapeutic value for many juvenile offenders compared with no punishment.

Inculpatory or Exculpatory Evidence

Offense seriousness and type of crime are considered quite influential at intake hearings, but some attention is also given by intake officers to the evidence police officers and others have acquired to show the offender's guilt. Direct evidence, such as eyewitness accounts of the youth's behavior, tangible objects such as weapons, and the totality of circumstances give the intake officer a reasonably good idea of where the case would end eventually if it reached the adjudicatory stage in a juvenile court.

Also, intake officers can consider exculpatory evidence or materials and testimony from others informally that provide alibis for juveniles or mitigate the seriousness of their offenses. Evidentiary factors are important in establishing one's guilt or innocence, but referrals of juveniles by police officers to intake usually is indicative of the fact that the officers were persuaded to act in accordance with the situation they confronted. It is extraordinary for officers to pursue juvenile cases to the intake stage purely on the basis of whim, although some officers do so as a means of punishing certain juvenile offenders with poor attitudes. Most intake officers screen the least serious cases quickly at intake or provide dispositions for juveniles other than formal ones.

Prior Record

Intake officers use prior records of delinquency adjudications and factor this data into their decisions. In other jurisdictions, even jurisdictions in other countries such as Canada, prior records strongly suggest that prior treatments and/or punishments were apparently ineffective at curbing offender recidivism (Kowalski and Caputo 1999). It would be logical to suspect that intake officers would deal more harshly with those having prior records of delinquency adjudications. One's prior record of juvenile offenses would suggest persistence and chronicity, perhaps a rejection of and resistance to prior attempts at intervention and treatment. And in some of these cases, harsher punishments and dispositions have been observed. However, this is not a blanket generalization designed to cover all offense categories. Some offense categories have greater priority over others for many intake officers (Wordes, Bynum, and Corley 1994).

Also, the previous disposition of a particular juvenile's case seems to be a good predictor of subsequent case dispositions for that same offender. For example, a study of the influence of prior records and prior adjudications on instant offense dispositions has shown that dispositions for prior offenses have a significant impact on current dispositions for those very same offenses, regardless of the type or seriousness of the offense. Thus, if a juvenile has formerly been adjudicated delinquent on a burglary charge and probation for six months was imposed as the punishment, a new burglary charge against that same juvenile will likely result in the same probationary punishment for six months (Snyder and Sickmund 1995).

EXTRALEGAL FACTORS: AGE, GENDER, RACE/ETHNICITY, AND SOCIOECONOMIC STATUS OF JUVENILE OFFENDERS

Most intake officers have vested interests in the decisions they make during screening hearings. They want to be fair to all juveniles, but at the same time, they are interested in individualizing their decision making according to each juvenile case. This means that they must balance their interests and objectives to achieve multiple goals, some of which may be in conflict. Furthermore, in recent years, greater pressure has been exerted on all juvenile justice components to implement those policies and procedures that will increase offender accountability at all stages of processing. Thus, a balanced approach has been suggested (Seyko 2001). Three major goals of the balanced approach for probation officers serving in various capacities in relation to their clients include: (1) protecting the community, (2) imposing accountability for offenses, and (3) equipping juvenile offenders with competencies to live productively and responsibly in the community.

Ideally, each of these goals is equal. These researchers say that such balanced objectives have been used by probation officers in Deschutes County, Oregon, Austin, Texas, and the Menominee Indian Reservation in Wisconsin. Individuality in decision making, where all three goals can be assessed for each juvenile offender, is sought. However, these three goals may have variable importance to probation officers performing intake functions in other jurisdictions. Depending upon their orientation, some intake officers may emphasize their community protection function, while others may emphasize juvenile offender accountability. Those officers with rehabilitative interests would tend to promote educational programs that would enable youths to operate productively in their respective communities.

In the context of attempting to achieve these three objectives and balance them, several extralegal characteristics of juvenile offenders have emerged to influence adversely the equality of treatment these youths may receive from probation officers at intake: (1) age, (2) gender, (3) race/ethnicity, and (4) socioeconomic status.

Age

Age is both a legal and an extralegal factor in the juvenile justice system. Age is legally relevant in decisions about waivers to criminal court jurisdiction. Waivers of juveniles under the age of 16 to criminal courts are relatively rare, for example (Champion and Mays 1991). Also, age has extralegal relevance. Older youths perhaps are assumed to be more responsible for their actions compared with younger youths, and they are often treated accordingly. Also, older youths are more likely to have prior records as juvenile offenders, be more resistant to or unwilling to accept intervention, and manifest greater adult-like self-reliance (Kowalski and Caputo 1999). Further, arrest data show that the peak ages of criminality lie between the sixteenth and twentieth birthdays (Maguire and Pastore 2002). Perhaps some intake officers believe that more aggressiveness in their decision making should be directed against older juveniles than against the younger ones.

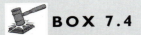 **BOX 7.4**

ARE SCHOOL SHOOTINGS AN EXCLUSIVELY U.S. PHENOMENON?

In Upper Nazareth

The boy charged toward the other boys who were hanging out at a bus stop. They had called him names and taunted him. He had a knife and stabbed one boy to death. In a nearby city, a 15-year-old boy was killed by five of his schoolmates who were armed with knives and a baseball bat in a public park after the victim was accused of name calling. Inner-city Chicago? Downtown Detroit? New York City slums? No. All of the above happened in Jerusalem and Upper Nazareth, Israel. According to Israeli officials, the Upper Nazareth killing took place on June 3, 1999 in the town of 45,000. It began during a break at Yigal Alon High School. A group of boys was standing in the yard and one asked another for a lick of his ice cream. Ninth-grader Yevgeny Yakobovich, whose parents immigrated from Belarus in 1995, quipped that the boy with the ice cream wouldn't share because "he is fat and a miser." The boy teased by Yakobovich decided to take revenge and rallied four friends. The five went home after school and picked up knives, a baseball bat, and brass knuckles. Then they headed back to the park. They stabbed, beat, and kicked Yakobovich until he slumped to the ground, then they walked away. The suspects then returned to their homes as though nothing had ever happened. Israeli officers blame violent TV shows and computer games originating from the United States on the present rash of Israel's juvenile violence. "To my great sorrow, we import many things from the United States, and it seems we are also importing some violence from there," according to Education Minister Yitzhah Levy, who has ordered teachers to discuss the stabbings with their students. Many others say the violence among teens should come as no surprise. Israeli society is becoming increasingly divided, pitting immigrants against veteran Israelis, religious against secular, and Arabs against Jews. The public discourse has become so shrill that the attorney general has pleaded with newly elected legislators to tone down their rhetoric. "Will school shootings be next?" asked Prime Minister Ehud Barak, echoing widespread concern among Israeli families.

Is youth violence largely a U.S. phenomenon? Are U.S. manufacturers of videogames to blame for violence among youths in other countries? What do you think?

Source: Adapted from the Associated Press, "Israelis Shocked by Teen Killings." June 12, 1999.

However, the earlier the onset of a juvenile's contact with the juvenile justice system and police, the more serious the problem (Pallone 1994). Thus, younger offenders rather than older offenders are often treated with greater interest and attention. This is supported by the array of risk assessment instruments used by both juvenile and adult corrections departments throughout the United States today (Jones et al. 2001). Almost every one of these instruments uses age as an important component in arriving at one's degree of risk or dangerousness. The younger the offender, the greater weight is assigned. This means that if youths become involved with delinquent acts at earlier ages, then greater weight is given and the youth's dangerousness score increases (Champion 1994). This evidences the seriousness with which age is regarded as a predictor of chronic and persistent recidivism, whether property or violent offending is involved. Some studies also imply that the earlier the onset of delinquency, the more likely it will be that these youthful offenders will be arrested and incarcerated for crimes committed as adults (Kapp, Schwartz, and Epstein 1994).

For many intake officers, the age factor appears to function in much the same fashion in influencing their intake decision making as it does when prosecutors assess the seriousness of identical offenses committed by both youths and adult offenders (Harris 1988). For an assortment of nonrational reasons, armed robbery is not as serious for some prosecutors when committed by a 12-year-old as it is when it is committed by a 21-year-old. Applied to intake decision making, probation officers may regard certain serious offenses as less serious when committed by those 13 and under, while 14-year-olds and older youths may have those same offenses judged as more serious. There are no precise age divisions that separate younger from older youthful offenders when one's age is functioning as an extralegal factor.

Gender

Generally, traditional patterns of female delinquency have persisted over the years. Because there are so few female juvenile offenders compared with their male counterparts, the influence of gender on intake decision making and at other stages of the juvenile justice process has not been investigated extensively. Juvenile females make up approximately 14 percent of the juvenile incarcerative population in the United States annually (American Correctional Association 2002). Females are only slightly more represented proportionately among those on probation or involved in assorted public and private aftercare services. Explanations for gender differences in their comparative rate of offending have ranged from different socialization experiences to different testosterone levels and genetic compositions (DeZolt, Schmidt, and Gilcher 1996).

Differential treatment of males and females in both the juvenile and criminal justice systems is well documented. However, some of the traditional reasons given for such differential treatment, especially about female juveniles and their delinquency patterns, appear to be misconceived or have no basis in fact. Selected assessments of the impact of gender on intake decision making show that it is only moderately related to dispositions, consistent with intake guidelines in selected jurisdictions such as Arizona and Florida (Coffey 1995; University of New Mexico 1996). Investigations of other jurisdictions as well as analyses of national figures show generally that female juveniles seem to be detained less often than male juveniles, and/or they are returned to the community at a greater rate than males, and/or they are committed to secure confinement at a much lower rate than males (Hodges and Kim 2000).

Within the just-deserts, justice, or crime control frameworks, the attention of those interested in the juvenile justice system is focused upon the act more than upon the juveniles committing the act or their physical or social characteristics. Thus, gender differences leading to differential treatment of offenders who behave similarly would not be acceptable. However, the differential treatment of male and female juveniles in the United States and other countries persists (U.S. General Accounting Office 1995a).

A strong contributing factor is the paternalistic view of juvenile court judges and others in the juvenile justice system that has persisted over time in the aftermath and influence of *parens patriae*. Differences between the arrest rates of female and male juveniles and the proportion of females to males who are subsequently adjudicated as delinquent suggests that the case attrition rate for females is significantly higher at intake than it is for male juveniles (Rowe, Vazsonyi, and Flannery 1995). Specific studies of intake decision making have disclosed, however, that gender exerts only an indirect impact on such decision making by officers (Hsieh 1993). Paradoxically, female juveniles with prior referrals to juvenile court seem to be treated more harshly than male offenders with prior referrals, especially for committing one of several index violent offenses. Based upon his analysis of the juvenile court careers of 69,504 juvenile offenders in Arizona and Utah, Snyder (1988) calculated probabilities of being referred to juvenile court for an index violent offense, where both male and female juveniles had similar numbers of prior court referrals. He found that males with eight prior referrals were more than three times as likely to be referred to juvenile court for an index violent offense than a male with only one previous referral, and more than twice as likely as a male with two prior referrals. However, females with eight prior referrals were six times as likely to be referred to juvenile court for an index violent offense compared with females who had only one prior referral, and three times as likely to be referred compared with females with two prior referrals (1988, 44–45). There were negligible differences between male and female juvenile offenders relating to referrals for property crimes.

Thus, it would seem that first-offender females are more likely to experience favorable differential treatment from the juvenile justice system compared with those females with records of prior referrals (Triplett and Myers 1995). In Howard Snyder's study, for instance, the great differential referral rate between male and female juveniles may have been the result of a backlash phenomenon, where females were being unduly penalized later for the greater leniency extended toward them earlier by juvenile justice authorities.

In some intervention projects designed to decrease or eliminate female gang delinquency, researchers have attempted to undermine the normative group functions served by gangs (Wang 2000). In one intervention project known as the Tabula Rasa Intervention Project for Delinquent Gang-Involved Females in Ohio, a sample of female gang members was targeted for intervention. The nature of the intervention consisted of several components. These were (1) an educational component, (2) a wellness component, and (3) a job skills and vocational component. Many female gang members lacked formal education and coping skills. Also, they lacked various skills that would make them employable. Each participant was obligated to develop specific goals within each of these components and strive to achieve them with interventionist assistance. The objective of the intervention was to interrupt the influence of gang membership and to divert these girls' interests in more productive directions. Early results of the intervention program for the participating females were regarded as successful (DeZolt, Schmidt, and Gilcher 1996).

Race and Ethnicity

More important as predictors of decision making at virtually every stage of the juvenile justice process are race and ethnicity. Race and ethnicity appear to be significant predictor variables in arrest and detention discretion as well as referrals (Schafer 1998). For instance, Bishop and Frazier (1996) have found clear evidence of racial disparities in juvenile justice processing at the point of intake and at other stages. Generally, the effect of race was disadvantageous to those juveniles processed. They studied 161,369 youths processed by the Florida Department of Health and Rehabilitative Services in 1987. Further, they interviewed 34 juvenile justice officials. Most affected by racial factors were delinquent offenders compared with status offenders. Blacks, Hispanics, and other minorities tended to be advanced further into the juvenile justice system by intake officers. However, white status offenders were penalized more harshly than minority status offenders. In fact, white status offenders were more likely to be incarcerated more often than minority status offenders. Thus, at least for Florida during the year examined, racial factors were at work in different ways to influence how youths were processed, either as delinquents or status offenders.

Minority overrepresentation throughout the juvenile justice process has been reported in a study of North Carolina juveniles. Data were obtained from case files of all juveniles processed through intake during 1993 in ten North Carolina counties (Dean, Hirschel, and Brame 1996). While black juveniles accounted for substantially less than half of the delinquency in these counties, half of the juveniles referred to intake were black. Interestingly, blacks comprised only about one-fourth of the entire juvenile population for these counties. Furthermore, half of those adjudicated delinquent were black, while two-thirds of those committed to secure confinement were black. The use of other control variables failed to reveal any other critical operating factor besides race in this disproportionate offender processing. Absent any other reason for such disparate treatment of these juveniles, we may conclude that at least in this study, race was a crucial intervening variable influencing juvenile case outcomes, even though it is an extralegal factor.

Socioeconomic Status

Closely related to racial and ethnic factors as extralegal considerations in intake decision making is the **socioeconomic status (SES)** of juvenile offenders. It has been found that, generally, the poor as well as racial and ethnic minorities are disenfranchised by the juvenile justice system at various stages (U.S. General Accounting Office 1995a). One explanation for this alleged disenfranchisement is more limited access to economic resources among the poor and minorities. More restricted economic resources reduces the quality of legal defenses that may be accessed by the socioeconomically disadvantaged. Greater reliance on public defenders is observed among the poor compared with those who are financially advantaged (Leiber and Stairs 1999).

A greater proportion of the socioeconomically disadvantaged tend to acquiesce and quietly accept systemic sanctions that accompany charges of wrongdoing rather than acquire counsel and contest the charges formally in court. But not all investigators believe that the relation between SES and delinquency is necessarily strong or negative. For instance, Leona Lee (1995) studied 3,520 youths who were charged with delinquent offenses between 1977 and 1986 and had ten or fewer referrals. She found that intake disposition was determined primarily by the type of prior disposition rather than by the seriousness of the current offense or the socioeconomic background of juveniles.

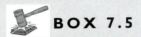 **BOX 7.5**

Irma Roxana Ponce
Case Manager, Communities in Schools

Statistics:

A.S., Laredo Community College; B.A. (psychology), Texas A & M International University; M.S. (criminal justice), Texas A & M International University

Background and Work Experience:

Originally, I had planned a career in the medical field, and so I pursued an undergraduate degree in psychology because I believed that this would prove beneficial for my graduate studies. It was at this time that I enrolled in a criminal justice course as an elective. The course proved to be quite interesting and challenging. I continued to enroll in criminal justice courses in order to learn more about our criminal justice system. I became so intrigued by the system and how it works that upon graduation, instead of pursuing a career in physical therapy as I had planned, I opted to pursue a master's degree in criminal justice.

Presently, I am employed as a case manager for Communities in Schools, a prevention and early intervention program. This program is aimed at helping students stay in school while preparing them for the future. As a case manager, I work with high school students, ages 14 to 18. I must admit that working with this age group has been quite an experience. After all, this is the age when many youths become confused and are in need of guidance. Every day presents a new challenge, but at the end of each day, I can go home with the satisfaction that I made a positive impact on a student's life. I don't think anything can be more rewarding than having someone thank you for making a difference in their life or for simply being there when they needed you the most.

Although I enjoy working with students, I would like to make a transition into the area of probation. Given my experience with teenagers, I have considered juvenile probation. Ultimately, however, I would like to be employed as a federal probation officer.

Advice to Students:

It's never too late to change your mind. Suddenly, if you feel the need to change career paths, don't be afraid to do so. The most important thing to remember is that it's your future, and you're the only one who knows what's best for you!

PRELIMINARY DECISION MAKING: DIVERSION AND OTHER OPTIONS

Diverting Certain Juveniles from the System

A long-range interest of most, if not all, intake officers is minimizing recidivism among those diverted from the system at the time of an intake hearing. **Recidivism** is also a commonly used measure of program effectiveness in both adult and juvenile offender treatment and sanctioning schemes (Hodges and Kim 2000). Because of the fragmented nature of the juvenile justice systems throughout the United States, it is extremely difficult to compile reliable, accurate information about the extent of juvenile delinquent recidivism. However, criminal justice practitioners estimate that the rate of recidivism among juveniles is similar to that for adult criminal offenders (Smith and Aloisi 1999). In a government-sponsored study of 272,111 former state prison inmates released in 1994, for instance, inmates were tracked for three years. Sixty-seven percent were rearrested for a new crime within this three-year period, while 46.9 were reconvicted for a new offense (Langan and Levin 2002, 1). For those inmates age 17 or younger who were released, 82.1 percent were rearrested within three years, while 55.7 percent were reconvicted for a new offense. To the extent that juvenile recidivism figures parallel these findings, the problem of juvenile offender recidivism is a potentially serious one.

Intake officer interest in the type of offense committed is triggered not only by the seriousness of the act itself and what should be done about it, but by evidence from various jurisdictions that suggests that recidivism rates vary substantially for different types of juvenile offenders. For example, studies of violent and nonviolent and chronic and nonchronic juvenile recidivists suggest that greater proportions of chronic offenders repeat violent offenses than nonchronic offenders. However, chronic offenders also commit subsequent nonviolent acts as well as violent ones. Despite increasing juvenile violence, it remains the case that only a small proportion of youths accounts for a majority of the violent crimes committed (Jones and Krisberg 1994).

How Should We Deal with Chronic Violent Offenders?

Closely associated with recidivism among chronic violent offenders in certain jurisdictions are predictor variables such as whether the delinquent has delinquent siblings and/or significant others as associates, whether the delinquent has school problems, and whether the acts committed were misdemeanors or felonies (U.S. General Accounting Office 1995a). Some jurisdictions, such as San Diego County, California, attempt to divert and process informally nonserious and first offenders through an **Interagency Agreement Plan.** This plan seems to be modestly successful at reducing recidivism (Pennell, Curtis, and Scheck 1990). For more serious offenders designated as chronic, violent, aggressive, or persistent, various types of mandatory group therapy have been regarded as successful interventions in past years (Hodges and Kim 2000).

In growing numbers of jurisdictions, chronic violent or serious offenders and other aggressive youths have been targeted for priority processing at intake and other stages (U.S. House of Representatives 1995). Harsher measures, including rapid identification of youths, expedited hearings, close monitoring of their cases, and their segregation from other, less serious offenders, have been employed by different Hawaiian juvenile justice units as a means of crime control. Continuous counseling, placement in long-term secure confinement facilities, extended court jurisdiction, and the revelation of these youths' identities to the public seem effective at curbing recidivism among these hardcore offenders. Several constitutional issues that must be resolved concern the identities of juvenile offenders and the publication of information about them made available to others.

The Inadequacy of Treatment and Community Services

Also, many jurisdictions are hard pressed to provide adequate treatment facilities and interventions that contain the ingredients for effectiveness. Some programs might have security without a jail-like atmosphere, close coordination and cooperation between the community and the criminal justice system, paraprofessional staffs, and provisions for remedial education and job training for these youths. But existing limited budgets and other priorities in many jurisdictions prevent the development of such sophisticated interventions. Yet other persons believe that interventions should be aimed at modifying one's social and psychological environment that fostered such violence and chronicity originally (Smith, Aloisi, and Goldstein 1996).

Intake officers are also influenced by existing services and programs, especially in their decisions about violent offenders. In Tucson, Arizona, for example, a **Stop Assaultive Children (SAC) Program** was created in the late 1980s and designed especially for those youths who have committed family violence (Zaslaw 1989). In this SAC program, the child is usually detained or locked up in a juvenile detention center for one day, and release from detention is contingent upon the youth's attendance at school, abiding by a curfew, refraining from committing future delinquent acts or violence, and an agreement by the youth to be interviewed by the intake officer. Children in the SAC program are ordered to reappear within two weeks, at which time their prosecution is deferred for three months, provided that they are accepted into SAC. All SAC participants must sign a contract acknowledging responsibility for their acts, agreeing further to participate in counseling and/or volunteer work, or to make a donation to a domestic violence service or agency. If the contract is unfulfilled for any reason, the juvenile is subsequently prosecuted.

Parents are also obligated to sign the contract and to enforce its conditions. The primary result of the successful completion of the SAC program is a dismissal of all charges against the juvenile. Zaslaw (1989) reports favorably that the SAC program has had a recidivism rate of only 9.6 percent compared with a recidivism rate of 48.7 percent among a control group of assaultive delinquent nonprogram participants in the same jurisdiction. But while Tucson may be able to operate such programs successfully, other jurisdictions may not be as fortunate, or intake officers elsewhere may believe their own plans for intervention are more effective.

Getting Tough with Persistent Offenders

For persistent offenders and otherwise hardcore violent recidivists, even for some violent first offenders, the strategy employed at intake may be a waiver of jurisdiction to criminal courts (Champion and Mays 1991). Some jurisdictions, such as New York, Washington, and Illinois, have automatic transfer laws that compel juvenile authorities to send certain types of juvenile offenders in a particular age range (normally 16 or 17 years of age) directly to criminal court to be processed as adults. The manifest intent of such waivers to criminal court is for harsher punishments to be imposed on these youthful offenders beyond those that can ordinarily be administered within the power of juvenile court judges.

The get-tough movement clearly has incarceration in mind for those youths who have been adjudicated delinquent for violent offenses. Anything less than secure confinement for such youths adjudicated for aggravated assault, rape, robbery, or homicide is considered as too lenient. However, some juvenile justice observers argue that there is presently too much incarceration, that incarceration is overdone, and that many youths can remain in their communities under close supervision, participating in productive self-improvement and rehabilitative programs (Benda 1999).

Is There Too Much Juvenile Incarceration?

Several alternatives to confinement have been investigated in Delaware (Brandau 1992). In 1987 the Delaware Plan was established, whereby certain community programs were established as alternatives to incarcerating certain types of delinquent offenders. Brandau found that over time, a sample of 363 youths adjudicated for various serious delinquency offenses were assigned randomly to either reform school, placed on probation, or sent to the Delaware Bay Marine Institute (DBMI). The DBMI was a community-based program designed to equip certain youths with coping skills and other useful experiences. Legal, social, and demographic variables were controlled, and all youths were evaluated according to whether they were more likely to be assigned to the reform school following their delinquency adjudications. Subsequently, recidivism information was compiled for all youths to determine the influence of the different experiences on them. Youths in the DBMI program had recidivism rates similar to those placed on straight probation and those placed in reform schools. This finding is significant because it shows in this instance, at least, that the DBMI program was about as effective as incarceration or probation for decreasing one's likelihood of recidivating. Since incarcerating juveniles is more expensive than placing them on probation or in the DBMI program, it is suggested that nonincarcerative community-based alternatives should be used more frequently, even for serious offenders.

Some criminologists argue that secure confinement is overused in many instances where juveniles have been adjudicated (Jones and Krisberg 1994). For instance, several general trends in juvenile justice and juvenile justice reform during the period 1982–1992 were examined, and it was found that many incarcerated youths did not need to be incarcerated. Over a third of those youths in state training schools belonged in less secure settings. Interestingly, the researchers found that most incarcerated youths had committed nonviolent property offenses rather than violent offenses (Jones and Krisberg 1994). This suggests strongly that in many jurisdictions, juvenile court judges are exercising a rather heavy hand when meting out punishments and disposing of cases through secure custody rather than imposing alternative community-based punishments. Increasingly emphasized—particularly as a cost-cutting measure—is focusing attention on methods or interventions that will reduce the recidivism rates of previously committed youth (Florida Department of Juvenile Justice Bureau of Data and Research 2000).

ASSESSMENT OF GUARDIANSHIP

While most cases that are furthered to the intake stage of the juvenile justice process involve some type of juvenile offending, criminal or otherwise, intake officers are often confronted with cases that require assessments of a youth's parents or guardians and the general sociocultural environment. Ordinarily, children in need of supervision (CHINS), including unruly or incorrigible youths, dependent and/or neglected youths, and abused children, are channeled by police officers to certain community agencies for special services and placement. Departments of Health and Human Services, social welfare agencies, and family crisis or intervention centers are frequently contacted and receive youths for further processing. However, if some youths in need of supervision are eventually subject to intake screenings, probation officers must evaluate the nature of one's needs and the seriousness of the situation before a disposition of the case is made. Beyond the broad classification of CHINS, many youths may have chemical dependencies that precipitated their delinquent conduct and require medical attention rather than punishment.

Examples of such youths include youthful male and female prostitutes who originally may have been runaways and/or incorrigible, alcohol- or drug-dependent youths who have turned to burglary and petty theft to support their dependencies, psychologically disturbed or mentally retarded juveniles, and sexually exploited children. If the facts disclosed at intake enable probation officers to make the strong presumption that certain youths should be diverted to human services shelters or community welfare agencies for treatment or temporary management, then this conditional disposition can be made of the case. This decision is often predicated upon the belief that a strong connection exists between the child's delinquency and physical, psychological, or sexual abuse received from adults or significant others. Thus, it is imperative that early interventions be attempted with those considered to be at the greatest risk of chronic offending (Lynam 1996).

SUMMARY

This chapter has examined a crucial phase of the juvenile justice process known as intake. Intake is a screening mechanism designed to separate more serious juvenile offenders from less serious ones. Intake proceedings are generally informal, and although juveniles interviewed during intake may have counsel present, the usual rules and constitutional provisions that govern juvenile court proceedings and matters of an evidentiary nature are not normally observed. In fact, the presence of defense counsel may prejudice cases adversely against juveniles. In some respects, intake for juveniles is similar to plea bargaining for adults.

Functioning as considerations in disposing of cases at intake are both legal and extralegal factors. Legal factors pertain to strictly factual information about crimes or offenses alleged. These include crime seriousness, type of offense, prior record, if any, age of offenders, and the existence of either exculpatory or inculpatory evidence. Extralegal factors pertain to the characteristics of juveniles themselves that are extraneous to the formal intake decision, but nevertheless are believed to have significant impacts on it. These include age, race, ethnicity, gender, and socioeconomic status. Age plays a dual role as a legal and an extralegal factor, especially as it is relevant for waiver decisions. As an extralegal factor, it may influence the harshness or leniency of dispositions made by intake officers.

Intake officers are encouraged to adopt a balanced approach that includes the goals of protecting society, making youths increasingly accountable for their actions, and providing juveniles with worthwhile activities and skills that will assist them in becoming more productive citizens of their communities. While most youths reaching the intake stage have been accused of one type of offense or another, some youths are in need of supervision by various community-based agencies and organizations. One's training and educational background are helpful in judging the familial and other social and psychological circumstances of youths if they were to be released to parental custody. The quality of existing community services also influences their release and diversion decisions.

QUESTIONS FOR REVIEW

1. What is meant by intake? Who performs intake functions and why?

2. What are the discretionary powers of intake officers?

3. What is meant by an assessment center? What are some purposes of the Florida Assessment Center?

4. In what respects has intake become increasingly formalized?

5. How does intake compare with plea bargaining? How is the doctrine of *parens patriae* perpetuated through the intake process?

6. What are three legal factors and how are they used in intake decision making?

7. What are three extralegal factors and what is their influence on the intake process?

8. What types of juvenile offenders should be diverted from the juvenile justice system? Why?

9. How should we deal with chronic and violent juvenile offenders?

10. Do we use incarceration too much for punishing juvenile offenders? Under what circumstances should incarceration be used? Which factors should determine whether a particular juvenile should be confined to an industrial school?

SUGGESTED READINGS

Dembo, Richard, ed. 2001. Family empowerment as an intervention strategy in juvenile delinquency. *Journal of Offender Rehabilitation* 33:1–109.

Glaser, Brian A. et al. 2001. Multi-observer assessment of problem behavior in adjudicated youths: Patterns of discrepancies. *Child and Family Behavior Therapy* 23:33–45.

Seyko, Ronald J. 2001. Balanced approach and restorative justice efforts in Allegheny County, Pennsylvania. *Prison Journal* 81:187–205.

INTERNET CONNECTIONS

National Council on Juvenile and Family Court Judges
http://www.ncjfcj.org/

Peacefire.org
http://www.peacefire.org/

Safe and Responsive Schools Project
http://www.indiana.edu~safeschl/

Teens, Crime, and the Community
http://www.nationalaltcc.org/

Unusual Suspects Theatre Company
http://www.theunusualsuspects.org/index.html

CHAPTER 8 | *Prosecutorial Decision Making in Juvenile Justice*

Chapter Outline

Key Terms
Chapter Objectives
Introduction
The Changing Prosecutorial Role
  in Juvenile Matters

Public Defenders for Juveniles
The Speedy Trial Rights
  of Juveniles
The Advocacy Role of Defense
  Attorneys

Summary
Questions for Review
Suggested Readings
Internet Connections

Key Terms

Barker balancing test
Confidentiality privilege

Guardians ad litem
Statute of limitations

With prejudice
Without prejudice

Chapter Objectives

As a result of reading this chapter, you will realize the following objectives:

1. Understand the importance of defense counsels for juveniles charged with crimes.
2. Learn about the changing prosecutorial role relative to juvenile offenders.
3. Learn about important procedural safeguards to protect the privacy of juveniles, including rules governing photographing and fingerprinting juveniles, and making juvenile records accessible to the public.
4. Learn about the time restrictions governing juvenile offender processing.
5. Understand the speedy trial rights for juvenile offenders.
6. Understand the growing formality of juvenile offender processing and the greater adversarial nature of juvenile court proceedings.
7. Understand the importance of plea bargaining in juvenile cases.

INTRODUCTION

• *It happened in Pensacola, Florida. Alex King, 12, and his brother Derek, 13, confessed that they hit their father ten times or more with a baseball bat while he sat asleep in a chair. Then the boys set fire to the home in an attempt to destroy evidence of the crime. Firefighters responded to the fire at the home of Terry Lee King, where they put out the fire before it consumed the house. They found a broken aluminum baseball bat, which they turned over to police. Before the young boys confessed to their father's murder, they had fled their home and were temporarily hidden by a child molester, Marvin Chavis, 40, of Pensacola. Subsequently, the boys turned themselves over to police where they gave confessions. They claimed that their father had both psychologically and sexually abused them. Investigators found a note written by Alex King that his life was cloudy and confused without goals, and that he was uncertain whether he wanted to be a teacher, governor, or president—until Chavis befriended him. Alex wrote that "Rick let me see what I don't understand. Life isn't about having a job. Life isn't about importance. Fame. My ultimate goal in life now is what his is. It is about sharing your life with someone else's. Before I met Rick, I was straight; but now I am gay." Investigators said that the boys had given deceptive statements to police when they were initially interrogated. When the boys confessed, they said that they were worried that they were going to be spanked for running away, and that their father had gotten physical with them. According to the prosecution, Chavis had convinced the boys that their father had been mentally abusing them. Chavis himself had been convicted in 1984 of lewd and lascivious conduct with two boys. He also gave conflicting statements when talking to police. Chavis was charged with being an accessory after the fact of murder. Is mental abuse a viable defense for what these boys did to their father?* [Adapted from Bill Kaczor and the Associated Press, "Boy Accused of Father's Murder Wrote of Molestation." December 30, 2001].

• *Laurie Show, 17, was slashed to death with a butcher knife on December 20, 1991, by Lisa Michelle Lambert. According to police reports and a confession by Lambert, 19, she was living with her boyfriend, Lawrence Yunkin, 20, when she learned that Yunkin had previously dated Laurie Show. The liaison enraged Lambert. She lured Show's mother away from the condominium they shared in East Lampeter Township near Lancaster, Pennsylvania. Then she and a friend, Tabitha Buck, 18, entered the home while Yunkin*

waited in a getaway car. Show was stabbed several times and her throat was slashed. Subsequently, police investigators obtained a confession from Lambert, indicating that she accompanied Buck into the apartment. She said she only intended to play a prank on Show by tying her up and cutting off her hair. She said that things got out of hand, that Laurie became hysterical, and that she [Michelle] stabbed her [Laurie] to "quiet her down." Later, Hazel Show, Michelle's mother, returned to her apartment and found her daughter dying. Laurie's last words to her mother were, "Michelle did it." Despite the confession, which Michelle later recanted, Michelle was tried for Laurie Show's murder and convicted. [Adapted from Timothy D. May and the Associated Press, "Family Satisfied with Guilty Verdict in Daughter's Death." December 10, 2001].

One important result of the U.S. Supreme Court decision in *Gault* for youths to be represented by counsel in juvenile court was the immediate transition of juvenile proceedings from unilateral hearings into adversarial proceedings, with much higher levels of procedural formality. The adversarial system has long been a feature of U.S. courts for adults, where plaintiffs and defendants litigate cases civilly for damages and where prosecutors and defense attorneys respectively attempt to convince judges or juries of the guilt or innocence of criminal defendants and seek either their incarceration or exoneration.

In juvenile courts, prosecutors are taking on greater significance in juvenile courts commensurate with the more limited role and jurisdiction of juvenile court judges. As is the case in the criminal justice system in response to get-tough criminal justice reforms, many of the juvenile reforms that have occurred in recent decades have shifted much of the discretionary power backward in the juvenile justice system, toward prosecutors, intake officers, and law enforcement officers. In part because of the divestiture of jurisdiction of juvenile court judges over status offenders, prosecutors are confronted with more serious youthful offenders. Their tasks are made more complex because of the increased prominence given to defense attorneys in juvenile court proceedings by the U.S. Supreme Court. The nature of the changing roles of prosecutors relating to juveniles will be examined.

The juvenile court itself has gradually transformed over the last several decades. As the due-process emphasis has increased, juvenile accountability for their actions has been heightened. One way of heightening juvenile accountability is to open juvenile courts to greater public scrutiny. While many protective confidentiality safeguards remain in place for juveniles in various states, there is a growing trend toward eliminating the confidentiality of these proceedings as well as making juvenile records available to the public. One reason for preserving the confidentiality of juvenile matters has been that juvenile courts are civil rather than criminal. However, the get-tough movement is pushing for greater accountability for juvenile offenders by removing this confidentiality. One implication of eliminating the confidentiality of information about juveniles is greater information sharing and exchange between juvenile justice systems in different jurisdictions. All too often, juveniles who are chronic, persistent, and violent offenders have become first offenders by the simple act of moving from one location to another. It is becoming more difficult for juveniles to jettison their delinquent histories by changing jurisdictions. The implications for juveniles of changing confidentiality laws will be examined.

Furthermore, the time standards governing prosecutions against juveniles have been accelerated. In some respects, these changing and accelerated time standards are similar to the speedy trial rights of adult criminal defendants. One explanation for accelerating the juvenile justice process is that in order for juveniles to appreciate the consequences of whatever they have done, a shorter time interval should exist between the delinquent acts alleged and the adjudicatory proceedings to determine their guilt or innocence and an appropriate punishment. Time standards governing juvenile processing vary considerably among the different juvenile justice systems. These time standards will be described and discussed.

Increasingly, juvenile courts are viewed as due-process courts rather than traditional courts. Traditional courts are characterized as less formal, with primary consideration given to the individual needs of juvenile offenders. A key goal of such courts is rehabilitation. Due-process juvenile courts are characterized by more formal procedures, greater emphasis upon juvenile rights, and greater importance attached to offense characteristics and seriousness. Key goals sought in due-process juvenile courts are just deserts and justice, heightening offender accountability, and ensuring equitable treatment. Therefore, the role of defense counsel has become increasingly important as a means of safeguarding the due-process rights of juvenile defendants. Their presence has elevated these proceedings to new levels of formality. The role and functions of defense counsel in juvenile matters will be described and explained.

As the presence of defense counsel for juveniles in juvenile courts has increased over the past several decades, several questions have arisen concerning their effectiveness in case resolutions and outcomes. Do defense counsels make a significant difference for juveniles in their case dispositions? As in criminal matters, defense counsel for juveniles negotiate plea bargains or agreements with juvenile court prosecutors. Greater numbers of cases against juveniles are settled through plea bargains concluded between defense counsel and prosecutors. The nature and extent of such plea bargaining will be described.

THE CHANGING PROSECUTORIAL ROLE IN JUVENILE MATTERS

Juvenile court prosecutors have had to make several adjustments in their orientation toward and treatment of juvenile defendants during the last several decades (DeFrances and Steadman 1998). As juveniles acquire more legal rights, prosecutors must be increasingly sensitive to these rights and constitutional safeguards and ensure that they are not violated. Constitutional rights violations can and will be challenged in the event of unfavorable juvenile court adjudications and/or sentences (Wilson and Petersilia 2002).

For example, the standard of proof in juvenile proceedings, as well as the introduction of evidence against youths, is currently different compared with pre-*Gault* years. Defense counsel may now aggressively challenge the quality of evidence against youths and how it was obtained, the accuracy of confessions or other incriminating utterances made by youths while in custody and under interrogation, the veracity of witnesses, and whether juveniles understand the rights they are asked to waive by law enforcement officers and others (del Carmen, Parker, and Reddington 1998).

Modifying Prosecutorial Roles by Changing the Standard of Proof in Juvenile Proceedings

Regarding the standard of proof in juvenile courts prior to 1970, it was customary to use the preponderance of the evidence standard in determining whether a juvenile was delinquent. This was a far less stringent standard compared with criminal court proceedings, where the standard of proof used to determine a defendant's guilt is "beyond a reasonable doubt." On the basis of using the preponderance of evidence standard, juvenile court judges could find juveniles delinquent and order them incarcerated in industrial schools or detention facilities for more or less long periods. Thus, a loss of a juvenile's liberty rested on a finding by the juvenile court judge based upon a relatively weak civil evidentiary standard.

However, the case of *In re Winship* (1970) resulted in the U.S. Supreme Court decision to require the beyond a reasonable doubt standard in all juvenile court cases where the juvenile was in danger of losing his or her liberty. Although every juvenile court jurisdiction continues to use the preponderance of evidence standard for certain juvenile proceedings currently, these jurisdictions are required to use the criminal standard of beyond a reasonable doubt whenever an adjudication of delinquency can result in confinement or a loss of liberty (del Carmen, Parker, and Reddington 1998).

Juveniles have benefited in at least one respect as the result of these new rights and standards of proof. These changed conditions have forced law enforcement officers, prosecutors, and judges to be more careful and discriminating when charging juveniles with certain offenses. However, changing the technical ground rules for proceeding against juveniles has not necessarily resulted in substantial changes in police officer discretion, prosecutorial discretion, or judicial discretion (Goldkamp et al. 1999). Juveniles remain second-class citizens, in a sense, since they continue to be subject to street-level justice by police officers.

Despite the increased bureaucratization of juvenile courts, these courts continue to exhibit some of the traditionalism of the pre-*Gault* years (Johnston and Secret 1995). This means that relatively little change has occurred in the nature of juvenile adjudications. Juvenile court judges, with the exception of those few jurisdictions that provide jury trials for serious juvenile cases, continue to make adjudicatory decisions as they did prior to *In re Winship* (1970) (Secret and Johnston 1996). Regardless of new evidentiary standards and proof of guilt requirements, these judges continue to exercise their individual discretion and decide whether a youth's guilt or delinquency has been established beyond a reasonable doubt. The fact is that nearly 80 percent of all states do not provide jury trials for juveniles in juvenile courts. Therefore, bench trials, where the judge decides each case, are used. We don't know how many judges are or are not complying with the beyond a reasonable doubt standard, since these judges are exclusively the finders of fact. In one respect, at least, the *In re Winship* case was a somewhat hollow victory for juveniles in jeopardy of losing their liberty. The beyond a reasonable doubt standard was established, but its use is dependent upon the subjective judgments of juvenile court judges.

For juvenile court prosecutors, changing the standard of proof to beyond a reasonable doubt made their cases harder to prove, even under bench trial conditions compared with jury trial conditions. Thus, the stage was set for greater use of plea bargaining in juvenile cases, especially when the evidence was weak and not particularly compelling. One important reason for weak evidence in juvenile cases is that in many jurisdictions, police officers do not regard juvenile offending as serious as adult offending. Therefore, evidence-gathering procedures relating to delinquent acts may not be as aggressive as evidence-gathering procedures relating to serious adult crimes. Lackluster evidence-gathering by police in juvenile delinquency cases may be explained by the fact that juvenile courts have exhibited extraordinary leniency toward juveniles, even where serious crimes were alleged and the evidence was strong. It is discouraging for police officers to see their best evidence-gathering efforts wasted when a juvenile court judge disposes an adjudicated juvenile delinquent to probation or some other lenient punishment.

For the most part, however, juvenile court prosecutors have adapted well to their changing roles as the juvenile court has gradually transformed (Massachusetts Statistical Analysis Center 2001). The due process emphasis has prompted many prosecutors to prioritize their prosecutorial discretion according to a juvenile's offense history and crime seriousness (Snyder, Sickmund, and Poe-Yamagata 2000). Nevertheless, this priority shift has not caused prosecutors to ignore potentially mitigating factors in individual juvenile cases, such as undue exposure to violence and domestic abuse (Jacobson 2000).

Eliminating the Confidentiality of Juvenile Court Proceedings and Record-Keeping

Enhancing the accountability of juvenile courts is greater public access to them under the provisions of the First Amendment. This also applies to interjurisdictional requests for juvenile information among the states (Musser 2001). During the 1990s, considerable changes have occurred regarding the confidentiality of juvenile court matters as well as juvenile records. Table 8.1 shows a summary of confidentiality provisions of the various states for 1996–1997.

In 1997, for instance, thirty states had provisions for open hearings in juvenile or family court proceedings. Only eight states did not provide for the release of the names of those juveniles charged with serious offenses. Only two states did not permit court record releases to interested parties. In fact, all states currently make available juvenile court records to any party showing a legitimate interest. In such cases, information is ordinarily obtained through a court order. Fingerprinting and photographing of juveniles is conducted routinely in most states. Half the states require registration of all juvenile offenders when they enter new jurisdictions. Also, most states presently have state repositories of juvenile records and other relevant information about juvenile offending. Seventeen states prohibited sealing or expunging juvenile court records after certain dates, such as one's age of majority or adulthood (Bilchik 1996, 37–38). Therefore, juveniles today are considerably more likely to have their offenses known to the public. Open-records policies are increasingly favored by the public and juvenile justice professionals (Chambliss, Dohrn, and Drizin 2000).

Kansas is an example of a state that made substantial changes in its confidentiality provisions governing juvenile offenders. The juvenile crime rate rose nationwide during the 1990s, and Kansas juvenile crime escalated accordingly during this same time interval. In an effort to hold juveniles more accountable for their actions, the Kansas State Legislature demanded a more open juvenile justice system. Several measures to enhance accountability were established:

TABLE 8.1

Summary of Provisions Limiting Confidentiality for Serious and Violent Juvenile Offenders, 1997

State	Open Hearing	Release of Name	Release of Court Record[a]	Statewide Repository[b]	Finger-printing	Photo-graphing	Offender Registration	Seal/Expunge Records Prohibited
Totals:	30	42	48	44	47	46	39	25
Alabama			•	•	•	•	•	
Alaska	•	•	•	•	•	•	•	•
Arizona	•	•	•	•	•	•	•	
Arkansas		•	•	•	•	•	•	
California	•	•	•	•	•	•	•	•
Colorado	•	•	•	•	•	•	•	
Connecticut			•	•				
Delaware	•	•	•	•	•	•	•	
Dist. of Columbia			•		•	•		
Florida	•	•	•	•	•	•	•	•
Georgia	•	•	•		•	•	•	•
Hawaii	•	•	•				•	
Idaho	•	•	•		•	•	•	
Illinois		•	•		•	•	•	
Indiana	•	•	•	•	•	•	•	
Iowa	•	•	•	•	•	•	•	•
Kansas	•	•	•	•	•	•	•	•
Kentucky		•	•	•	•	•	•	•
Louisiana	•	•	•	•	•	•	•	•
Maine	•	•	•				•	
Maryland	•		•			•		
Massachusetts	•	•	•		•	•	•	
Michigan	•	•	•	•	•	•	•	•
Minnesota	•	•	•	•	•	•	•	
Mississippi		•		•			•	
Missouri	•	•	•	•	•	•	•	
Montana	•	•	•	•	•	•	•	•
Nebraska		•	•	•	•			
Nevada	•	•	•		•	•	•	•
New Hampshire		•	•			•	•	
New Jersey		•	•	•	•	•	•	
New Mexico	•							
New York		•	•					
North Carolina			•				•	•
North Dakota		•	•	•	•	•		
Ohio				•	•	•	•	
Oklahoma	•	•	•	•	•	•	•	•
Oregon		•	•	•	•	•	•	•
Pennsylvania	•	•	•	•	•	•	•	•
Rhode Island		•	•	•	•	•	•	
South Carolina		•	•	•	•	•	•	•
South Dakota		•	•	•	•	•	•	

TABLE 8.1 (CONTINUED)

Summary of Provisions Limiting Confidentiality for Serious and Violent Juvenile Offenders, 1997

State	Open Hearing	Release of Name	Release of Court Record[a]	Statewide Repository[b]	Finger-printing	Photo-graphing	Offender Registration	Seal/Expunge Records Prohibited
Tennessee		•	•	•	•	•	•	
Texas	•	•	•	•	•	•	•	•
Utah	•	•	•	•	•	•	•	•
Vermont					•	•		
Virginia	•			•	•	•	•	
Washington	•	•	•	•	•	•	•	•
West Virginia		•	•		•			•
Wisconsin	•	•	•	•			•	
Wyoming		•	•	•	•	•	•	•

Legend: • indicates the provision(s) allowed by each state as of the end of the 1997 legislative session.

[a]In this category, • indicates a provision for juvenile court records to be specifically released to at least one of the following parties: the public, the victims(s), the school(s), the prosecutor, law enforcement, or social agency; however, all states allow records to be released to any party who can show a legitimate interest, typically by court order.

[b]In this category, • indicates a provision for fingerprints to be part of a separate juvenile or adult criminal history repository.

Source: Patricia Torbet and Linda Szymanski, *State Legislative Responses to Violent Juvenile Crime: 1996–1997 Update.* Washington, DC: U.S. Department of Justice, 1998:10.

1. Parents of offenders younger than 18 now may be assessed the cost of certain services, such as probation and out-of-home placement services; juvenile offenders 18 and older can be assessed the costs.

2. Courts now may order families to attend counseling together.

3. Parents' health insurance policies now may be accessed to pay for their child's care while in state custody. Kansas previously paid for drug treatment and medical care expenses for juvenile offenders because most insurance policies did not cover these costs while a juvenile offender was in state custody.

4. Hearings for juvenile offenders 16 and older are open to the public.

5. Official file records for juvenile offenders are open to the public (Musser 2001, 112–113).

The Kansas law now states that the official file shall be open for public inspection as to any juvenile 14 or more years of age at the time any act is alleged to have been committed or as to any juvenile less than 14 years of age at the time any act is alleged to have been committed except if the judge determines that opening the official file for public inspection is not in the best interest of such juvenile who is less than 14 years of age. Not all records are open. Personal history files, including reports and information the court receives, are privileged and only may be seen by the parties' attorneys and juvenile intake and assessment staff or by order of a district court judge. Between 1995 and 2001, the Office of Juvenile Justice and Delinquency Prevention has noted that more states have made substantial changes with juvenile records, such as greater identification of juveniles, while others are considering making juvenile records available to the public (Musser 2001, 113). This means that the **confidentiality privilege** that juveniles have enjoyed for many decades is rapidly disappearing.

Open Juvenile Proceedings and Changing Judicial Conduct

The greater formality of juvenile proceedings as well as their openness to others may restrict the discretion of juvenile court judges, although this limitation is not particularly an undesirable one (Steinhart 1994). Juvenile court judges have been known to make decisions that only incidentally related to one's alleged offense. For instance, Emerson (1969, 88–89) reported that a juvenile court judge once ordered physical examinations for two 15-year-old girls who had been arrested for shoplifting [clothes] in a department store. Among other things, he wished to determine whether they had been sexually active. His motives were patently unclear, since knowing whether the girls had been sexually active is wholly unrelated to shoplifting. Nevertheless, the physicals were conducted, although it is unknown what the judge did with this information or how it was used in their adjudications and dispositions. Today, it is doubtful that many juvenile court judges would be able to get away with irrelevant and demeaning requests such as the one described by Emerson. The presence of a defense counsel representing the juvenile's interests and promoting due process would tend to deter judges from such conduct.

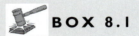

BOX 8.1

THE TWELVE-YEAR-OLD MURDERER

11-Year-Old Enrique Guerra, Jr., Victim

Two weeks before his twelfth birthday, 11-year-old Enrique Guerra, Jr. was playing down the street with some friends. They were playing with different weapons, including a BB gun and a pellet gun. The play was rough, as the boys pointed the guns at each other, pretending to fire them. At one point, a 12-year-old boy pointed a pellet gun at Enrique Guerra and fired it. The pellet struck Guerra in the chest. Guerra began walking back toward his house and suddenly collapsed. He died shortly thereafter. Guerra's father, who was unaware that his son had been shot, heard the commotion outside and went to investigate. He couldn't believe what he saw. His son was rushed to the hospital but was dead on arrival. The pellet had pierced his heart.

Subsequently, the 12-year-old was taken into custody and charged with manslaughter. If he is found guilty of manslaughter, he could be held in a juvenile detention center until age 18. He has no prior history of drugs of acts of violence. Some persons who witnessed the shooting said it was an accident.

How would you punish a 12-year-old for shooting another boy with a pellet gun? Should pellet guns be prohibited or restricted like other types of firearms?

Source: Adapted from Diana De La Garza and the Associated Press, "12-Year-Old Detained for Pellet Gun Killing." December 1, 2001.

The Prosecution Decision beyond 2000

The juvenile justice system has been notoriously slow in its case processing of juvenile offenders (Knepper and Barton 1996). In fact, delays in filing charges against juveniles and the eventual adjudicatory hearing are chronic in many jurisdictions. Juveniles arrested for various types of offenses may wait a year or longer in some jurisdictions before their cases are heard by juvenile court judges. Juvenile court prosecutors may delay filing charges against particular juveniles for a variety of reasons. The most obvious reasons for delays—court caseload backlogs, crowded court dockets, insufficient prosecutorial staff, too much paperwork—are not always valid reasons. In many instances, the actors themselves are at fault. In short, prosecutors and judges may simply be plodding along at a slow pace, because of their own personal dispositions and work habits. It has been illustrated that in many jurisdictions where prosecutors and judges have aggressively tackled their caseload problems and forced functionaries to work faster, juvenile caseload processing has been greatly accelerated. Thus, the time between a juvenile's arrest and disposition has been greatly shortened because of individual decision making and not because of any organizational constraints or overwork (Butts and Halemba 1996, 73–91).

Another factor contributing to juvenile court delays is the sizable increase in juvenile court caseloads. In 1988, for example, juvenile courts processed 3,200 delinquency cases per day. By 1997 these same courts were processing 4,800 delinquency cases per day (Sickmund 2000, 2). Many of these cases involved serious and violent offenses, as well as an ever-expanding number of drug offenses. In fact, the number of juvenile court cases involving drug offenses more than doubled between 1993 and 1998 (Stahl 2001, 1). For instance, drug offense cases accounted for 11 percent of all delinquency cases in 1998, compared with only 8 percent of all cases in 1994. The proportionate female juvenile involvement in drug cases increased from 14 to 16 percent between 1994 and 1998 as well. These types of cases take more time to resolve, simply because of their greater complexity. The juvenile courts have simply failed to keep pace with the growth of juvenile crime over the last few decades.

In 1997, juvenile court prosecutors in thirty states were at liberty to file charges against juvenile offenders whenever they decided. No binding legislative provisions were applicable to these actors to force them to act promptly and bring a youth's case before the juvenile court. Since that time, twenty states have established time limits that cannot be exceeded between the time of a juvenile's court referral and the filing of charges by prosecutors. Table 8.2 shows various time limits imposed by various states for juvenile court adjudication and disposition of cases. For instance, in Minnesota, juvenile court prosecutors must file charges against juveniles within 30 days of their referral to juvenile court by police, if such juveniles are placed in secure confinement. These same prosecutors must file charges against undetained juveniles within 60 days following the juvenile's referral to juvenile court by police. In Maryland, prosecutors have 60 days to file charges against either detained or undetained juveniles following their court referrals. And in Georgia and Ohio, prosecutors must file charges within 10 days if juveniles are being detained. A failure to file charges against juveniles in these jurisdictions within the time periods specified results in a dismissal of their cases **with prejudice,** meaning that the prosecutors cannot refile charges again at a later date against the same offenders (Butts and Sanborn 1999).

TABLE 8.2

Time Limits (in Days) for Juvenile Court Adjudication and Disposition Hearings, in Cases *Not* Involving Proceedings for Transfer to Criminal Court[a]

State	Court Referral	Start of Adjudication Deadline				Start of Disposition Deadline	
		Filing of Charges (det/ not det)	Preliminary Hearing (det/ not det)	Detention Admission	Detention Hearing	Filing of Charges (det/ not det)	Adjudication (det/ not det)
Alaska							Immed.[b]
Arizona			30/60				30/45
Arkansas					14		14/—
California	30	30[b]		15			
Delaware				30[c]			
Florida		21/90[c]					15/—
Georgia		10/60					30/—
Illinois		120[b,c]		10[c]			
Iowa		60[b,d]					ASAP[b]
Louisiana			30/90				30[b]
Maryland		60[b]		30			30[b]
Massachusetts	60						
Michigan		180[b]		63			35/—
Minnesota		30/60					15[c]/45[c]
Mississippi		90/—		21			14/—
Montana							ASAP[b]
Nebraska		180/—				180[c]	
New Hampshire		21/30					21/30
New Jersey				30			30/60
New Mexico							20/—
New York			14/60				10/50
North Dakota		30[b]		14			
Ohio		10/—					Immed.[b]
Oregon	56			28			28[c]
Pennsylvania		10/—					20/—
Rhode Island				7			
South Carolina		40[b]					
Tennessee		—/90		30			15/90
Texas		10/—					
Vermont		15/—					30[b]
Virginia		—/120		21			30/—
Washington		30[b]/60[b]					14/21
Wisconsin			20[e]/30[e]			10[e]/30[e]	10/30
Wyoming					60		

[a]Twenty states did not have time limits for adjudication as of 1993: AL, AK, CO, CT, DC, HI, ID, IN, KS, KY, ME, MO, MT, NV, NM, NC, OK, SD, UT, and WV. Twenty-six states did not have time limits for dispositions: AL, CA, CO, CT, DE, DC, HI, ID, IL, IN, KS, KY, ME, MA, MO, NV, NC, ND, OK, RI, SC, SD, TX, UT, WV, and WY.
[b]Statute did not distinguish detention status.
[c]Extensions are possible.
[d]If statutory right to speedy trial is waived.
[e]Statute-specified time from "plea hearing."
Source: Butts, 1996b: 557–558. Data source: analysis by the National Center for Juvenile Justice. Reprinted by permission, of the American Journal of Criminal Law and the authors.

Time Standards in Juvenile Court for Prosecutors and Other Actors

Establishing time standards for accomplishing various procedures within the juvenile justice process are not new. As early as 1971, various organizations were at work to encourage the juvenile justice system to process cases more quickly. It was believed at the time that only legislatively created time standards would cause police, intake officers, prosecutors, and judges to take faster action in processing juvenile offenders.

Butts (1996b, 544–547) notes, for instance, that the Joint Commission on Juvenile Justice Standards led the way in 1971 with early time standards for juvenile processing. A product of the Institute of Judicial Administration (IJA) and the American Bar Association (ABA), the IJA/ABA Project convened periodically over the next several years and issued 27 different volumes during the years 1977 through 1980. The standards promulgated by the IJA/ABA Project were intended as guidelines for juvenile courts and the juvenile justice system generally. The Commission formed through the IJA/ABA Project was guided by the principle that juvenile court cases should always be processed without unnecessary delay (Butts 1996a, 545).

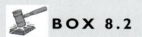 **BOX 8.2**  **PERSONALITY HIGHLIGHT**

Donald B. Hale
Investigator, Webb County, Texas, Attorney's Office

Statistics:

Associates of Applied Science (criminal justice), Laredo Community College; B.S. cum laude (criminal justice, sociology), Texas A & M International University; M.S. (in progress), Texas A & M International University; Master Peace Officer and Instructor, Texas Commission of Law Enforcement

Background and Interests:

Presently, I am investigator with the Webb County Attorney's Office in Laredo, Texas. Our office is responsible for the prosecution of juvenile offenders, as well as all civil litigation in Webb County. I am tasked with assisting the County Attorneys with follow-up investigations and case analyses involving juvenile offenders. As an Investigator, I must interview witnesses, obtain lab reports, and assess the vitality of the evidence for prosecutors. Some of the criminal acts that are committed are so heinous that juvenile offenders may be certified as adults. After certification, the offender may be prosecuted and adjudicated through the adult system, resulting in stiffer penalties. I also spearhead the code enforcement division where the office initiates and investigates illegal dumping and environmental crimes.

Furthermore, I am employed as an adjunct faculty member at the Laredo Community College Regional Police Academy. I serve as an Instructor under Raymond E. Garner, Police Academy Director, and retired Sergeant, Texas Department of Public Safety. I have had the opportunity to be included in numerous parts of the curriculum

(continued)

BOX 8.2 (*Continued*)

that include patrol procedures, defense tactics, constitutional law, search and seizure, firearms, and special investigative topics.

Prior to this position, I was employed with the Webb County Sheriff's Department for nearly twelve years. While employed in this department, I had the opportunity to work in numerous capacities. I started as a correctional officer and ended my tenure in the patrol division. I had the opportunity to diversify my experience by obtaining a position on a Federal Drug Task Force for three years. I also served as a member of the Sheriff's S.W.A.T. team, ultimately obtaining the position of Assistant Commander. My tenure and experiences with the Sheriff's Department have left me with lifetime friendships and memories.

Experiences:

Throughout my career, I have had the opportunity to be involved in many perilous situations and assignments. There is one particular incident that has been unforgettable. In 1993, I was patrolling a rural area in Webb County with Homero "Ranger" Rangel, who was recently assigned to the division. I had been with the patrol division for about eight months and was considered a rookie myself. During this time, the Sheriff's Department was extremely understaffed. My partner and I were covering the southern part of Webb County.

Our supervisor, Lt. Manuel Gomez, was also in the area. I don't know if he was checking the area, or assuring that the rookies were O.K. My partner and I were dispatched to a burglary report. We arrived at the location and began the paperwork and interview process. Shortly thereafter, we heard a call over the radio with a complaint of loud music in the adjacent city. Lt. Gomez intervened and advised that he would handle the call. We continued to take the burglary report. Lt. Gomez arrived and could not be reached over the radio after a

couple of minutes. I immediately advised my partner to stop writing the report and advise the complainant that we would return to finish the report. I had the distinct feeling that something was terribly wrong. I took the car keys from my partner and drove code-3 (with emergency lights and siren) toward the location where Lt. Gomez was, and continued to attempt to contact him, but there was no response. Within minutes, we arrived at the location and saw a crowd of approximately thirty teenagers. Lt. Gomez's unit was parked in front with no one in sight. Homero and I rushed out of the patrol car towards the teen crowd and located Lt. Gomez scuffling on the ground with two male subjects. The crowd was very aggressive; they were throwing beer bottles and attempting to disarm my supervisor. It was a very volatile situation that continued to escalate. I felt that I would have exacerbated the situation by attempting an immediate arrest and apprehension. We were unequivocally outnumbered by a group of intoxicated teens. There was a brief period of despondency, but we were able to prevail unscathed. Ultimately, we were able to disperse the crowd and arrested the suspect who attempted to disarm my supervisor. To everyone's disbelief, the suspect turned out to be a juvenile who was high on drugs. After this day, we were no longer considered as rookies, and we garnered the respect from the senior officers.

Advice to Students:

The best advice I could give any student is to continue your education, regardless of the circumstances or situation. Education will enhance your professionalism and allow you to diversify your knowledge in every aspect of society. Education is part of the conceptual framework for advancement in every field of law enforcement. As one of my undergraduate professors has stated, "Education is a necessity, not a luxury."

The IJA/ABA standards relating to processing juveniles were as follows (Butts 1996a, 546):

Time	Action
2 hours	Between police referral and the decision to detain
24 hours	Between detention and a petition justifying further detention
15 days	Between police referral and adjudication (if youth is detained)
30 days	Between police referral and adjudication (if youth is not detained)
15 days	Between adjudication and final disposition (if youth is detained)
30 days	Between adjudication and final disposition (if youth is not detained)

Notice that in these time guidelines, law enforcement officers are not given much time to detain youths once they have been taken into custody. Once police officers have referred a youth to juvenile court, only 2 hours is recommended in order for a decision to be made about detaining the youth. If a youth is detained, then only 24 hours are allowed between the start of one's detention and filing a petition to justify further detention. And depending upon whether youths are detained or undetained, the time limits recommended are either 15 or 30 days respectively between detention and adjudication. These guidelines are rather rigorous compared with the traditional sluggishness of juvenile offender processing. Table 8.2 shows that only a handful of states thus far have adopted these or more rigorous standards for filing charges against juveniles (Georgia, Ohio, Pennsylvania, Texas, and Vermont).

Butts (1996b, 547) also notes that similar time limits for juvenile processing were recommended contemporaneously by the National Advisory Committee for Juvenile Justice and Delinquency Prevention in 1980. These limits are shown below (Butts 1996b, 546–547):

Time	Action
24 hours	Between police referral and the report of intake decision (if youth is detained)
30 days	Between police referral and the report of intake decision (if youth is not detained)
24 hours	Between detention and detention hearing
2 days	Between intake report and the filing of a petition by the prosecutor (if detained)
5 days	Between intake report and the filing of a petition by the prosecutor (if not detained)
5 days	Between filing of the petition and the initial arraignment hearing
15 days	Between filing of the petition and adjudication (if detained)
30 days	Between filing of the petition and adjudication (if not detained)
15 days	Between adjudication and final disposition.

Again, the National Advisory Committee gave little latitude to juvenile court prosecutors in dispatching juvenile cases. In this particular arrangement of scenarios, however, the intake stage was addressed, and rather strongly. Not only were prosecutors obligated to file petitions against specified juveniles more quickly following intake, but intake officers were required to make their assessments of juveniles and file reports of these assessments within a two-day period. One major difference in the National Advisory Committee recommendations and guidelines was the fact that if certain actors in the juvenile justice system did not comply with these time standards, then cases against certain juveniles could be dismissed, but **without prejudice.** This meant that juvenile court prosecutors could resurrect the original charges and refile them with the juvenile court at a later date. Thus, no particularly compelling constraints were placed on either intake officers or prosecutors to act in a timely manner, according to this second set of standards. However, we must recognize that neither the IJA/ABA time guidelines nor the National Advisory Committee guidelines are binding on any state jurisdiction. They are set forth as strongly recommended guidelines for juvenile court officials to follow.

Why Should the Juvenile Justice Process Be Accelerated?

Several compelling arguments are made for why juvenile justice should be applied quickly. Butts (1996b, 525–526) and others (New York Commission 1994; Towberman 1992) make compelling arguments that adolescence is a critical period wherein youths undergo many changes. Maturational factors seem especially accelerated, while one's personality and response to peer pressures are modified and enhanced in diverse ways. A month may seem like a year to most adolescents. Secure confinement of 24 hours is a serious deprivation of one's freedom. When some juvenile cases undergo protracted delays of up to a year or longer, it is difficult for many youths to accept their subsequent punishment for something they did long ago. More than a few juveniles have grown out of delinquency by the time their cases come before the juvenile court, and they wonder why they now being punished for something they did when they were younger.

Studies of juvenile justice system delays disclose that the size of a jurisdiction plays an important part in how fast juvenile cases are concluded. In 1985, for example, the median number of days it took to process juvenile cases in a large sample of U.S. county jurisdictions was about 44 days. By 1994, the median processing time in these same counties was 92 days (Butts and Halemba 1996, 131). For smaller jurisdictions with fewer and presumably less serious cases to process, case processing time ranged from 34 to 83 days in 1994, while larger counties took from 59 to 110 days to complete juvenile case processing.

These juvenile justice processing delays parallel criminal court processing of adult defendants. We might be inclined to accept these long juvenile justice delays if the cases processed were sufficiently serious to warrant more court time. However, only about 17 percent of all cases handled by both small and large county jurisdictions involved serious or person offenses in 1994 (Butts and Halemba 1996, 129).

Therefore, it has been recommended that juvenile justice case processing time should be decreased so as to move the disposition closer to the time when the offense was committed. Juveniles should be able to relate whatever happens to them in court later to the offense they committed earlier. In more than a few instances, juveniles awaiting trial on one charge have had subsequent opportunities to reoffend. When they are arrested for new offenses before being adjudicated for earlier offenses, their cognitive development may inhibit their understanding of the process and their disposition (Butts 1996b, 525).

Shine and Price (1992) provide two important reasons for why juvenile cases should be processed quickly. These reasons are:

1. In order to maximize the impact upon the juvenile that he or she has been caught in a criminal act, that he or she will be held accountable for what he or she has done, and that there will be consequences for this action, it is important that the case be resolved quickly. If the case continues too long, the impact of the message is diluted, either because the juvenile has been subsequently arrested for other offenses and loses track of just what it is that he or she is being prosecuted for or because the juvenile has not engaged in any further delinquent acts and feels that any consequences for the past offense are unfair.

2. If there are victims, then unwarranted delays in juvenile case processing are unfair and damaging to victims. Many victims suffer some type of financial loss or physical injury. Expenses are incurred. Faster resolutions of juvenile court cases can lead to more rapid compensation and victim restitution plans imposed by the court. Such compensation of victim restitution can do much to alleviate any continued suffering victims may endure.

PUBLIC DEFENDERS FOR JUVENILES

Greater procedural formality in the juvenile justice system has been occurred with respect to the appointment of public defenders for juveniles who are indigent. Every juvenile court jurisdiction provides public defenders for juveniles and their families who cannot afford to appoint private counsel, especially in more serious cases where incarceration in secure confinement facilities is a strong possibility (Eskridge 1996). Formerly, defense counsels for juveniles often were the juvenile's probation officer or a social caseworker with a vested interest in the case. It is not entirely clear how these officers and workers were able to separate their law enforcement and defense functions to avoid allegations of conflicts of interest. But little interest in the quality of defense of juvenile cases was exhibited by the public in previous years anyway. While some persons believe that juveniles are now insulated to some extent from the whims of juvenile court prosecutors and judges, others suspect that defense attorneys have in some instances made it more difficult for juveniles to receive fair treatment.

During intake, it has been found that the presence of attorneys, who represent juveniles' interests and attempt to protect them so that their full range of constitutional rights are observed at each stage of the juvenile justice process, actually detract from the informal nature of intake. Intake officers change these proceedings into formal hearings, and recommendations for subsequent dispositions might be more severe than if defense attorneys were not present. In fact, intake officers have openly discouraged juveniles and their parents from availing themselves of an attorneys' services at this stage, since their presence hampers informal adjustments of cases and limits a youth's informal compliance with informal probationary conditions. In some cases, intake officers consider themselves the primary source of a youth's understanding of legal rights, although a recommendation that these officers receive more training and preparation in law and juvenile rights suggests that their own understanding of the law merits improvement (Towberman 1992).

In a growing number of instances, many cases are being diverted to victim–offender mediation, where various nonprofit, private organizations receive referrals from juvenile courts. The intent of such victim–offender mediation is to reach a resolution of differences between victims and offenders without subjecting offenders to juvenile court and its adverse labeling impact. In those communities with mediation programs, there is support from community residents. Financial support in the form of grants is provided from local, state and federal grants. Mediators may be interested citizens, retired judges, community leaders, or even intake officers who undertake these tasks during nonworking hours (Hughes and Schneider 1989).

Despite these alternatives to juvenile court action, it is true that juvenile court proceedings have become increasingly formalized (Feld 1993a). Further, public access to these proceedings in most jurisdictions is increasing (Bilchik 1996). Thus, the presence of defense counsel, an adversarial scenario, a trial-like atmosphere where witnesses testify for and against juvenile defendants, and adherence to Rules of Procedure for Juvenile Courts are clear indicators of greater formalization, bureaucratization, and criminalization, as Feld (1995) and others have suggested.

Two problems have been highlighted relating to the use of public defenders in juvenile courts. These problems include the limited resources and growing caseloads of public defenders for juveniles in many jurisdictions. A study examined the access to counsel in selected states and local juvenile delinquency proceedings (U.S. General Accounting Office 1995b). Data sources were relevant state statutes, state administrative procedures, and case law in fifteen states; National Council on Juvenile Justice statistics for three states; national surveys of county prosecutors and public defenders; telephone interviews with selected state and local judges in eight states; and site visits to juvenile justice officials in four states. Statutes guaranteeing a juvenile's right to counsel were found in all fifteen states examined. Overall, the rate of defense counsel representation for juveniles varied from 65 percent in Nebraska to 97 percent in California. Representation by offense category varied, as did the overall impact of representation on case outcomes. In most cases where juveniles were not represented by counsel, juveniles were less likely to receive out-of-home placements, such as a disposition to an industrial school. This shouldn't be interpreted to mean that defense counsel cause more juveniles to receive out-of-home placements. Rather, a better explanation is that defense counsel were not used in the least serious cases, those that didn't merit placement in an institution anyway. Prosecutors and juvenile justice officials were generally pleased with the quality of counsel provided to juveniles, apart from their concerns about scarce resources and growing caseloads (U.S. General Accounting Office 1995b).

THE SPEEDY TRIAL RIGHTS OF JUVENILES

Juveniles have no federal constitutional right to a speedy trial (del Carmen, Parker, and Reddington 1998). The U.S. Supreme Court has not decided any juvenile case that would entitle a juvenile to a speedy trial commensurate with adults in criminal courts. Criminal defendants are assured a speedy trial through the Sixth Amendment and the leading 1972 case of *Barker v. Wingo* [see Box 8.3]. This case led to the establishment of the **Barker balancing test.** Each state and the federal government has established speedy trial procedures that establish time standards between different events, such as between the time of arrest and initial appearance, between one's initial appearance and arraignment, and between one's arraignment and trial. The federal government uses a 100-day standard. New Mexico is perhaps the most liberal, providing a 180-day period. Many states have adopted the federal standard.

For juveniles, standards vary among jurisdictions between comparable stages of juvenile justice processing, such as between arrest and intake, between intake and prosecutorial decision making and case filing, between case filing and adjudication, and between adjudication and disposition. However, some state legislatures have provided time standards that proscribe different maximum time limits between each of these events. As of 1993, for instance, thirty states provided some form of time limit for adjudications following arrests. Twenty-six states did not have time limits between adjudications and dispositions of juveniles. And only a handful of state courts have recognized some form of speedy trial rights for accused juveniles (Butts 1996b, 553, 558).

Jeffrey Butts (1996b, 554) recommends that youths facing adjudication for delinquent offenses should be vested with the same speedy trial rights as adults. Thus, a federal constitutional right to a speedy trial for juvenile defen-

---

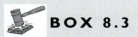 **BOX 8.3**

DO JUVENILES HAVE A RIGHT TO A SPEEDY TRIAL?

The Case of Barker v. Wingo

Barker and another person were alleged to have shot an elderly couple in July 1958. They were arrested later and a grand jury indicted them in September 1958. Kentucky prosecutors sought 16 continuances to prolong the trial of Barker. Barker's companion, Manning, was subjected to five different trials, where a hung jury was found except in the fifth trial, where Manning was convicted. Then, Barker's trial was scheduled. During these five trials, Barker made no attempt to protest or to encourage a trial on his own behalf. After scheduling and postponing Barker's trial for various reasons, his trial was finally held in October 1963, and he was convicted. He appealed, alleging a violation of his right to a speedy trial. The U.S. Supreme Court heard the case and declared that since from every apparent factor, Barker did not want a speedy trial, he was not entitled to one. The case significance is that if you want a speedy trial, you must assert your privilege to have

one. Defendants must assert their desire to have a speedy trial in order for the speedy trial provision to be invoked and for Amendment rights to be enforceable. In Barker's case, the U.S. Supreme Court said that Barker was not deprived of his due process right to a speedy trial, largely because the defendant did not desire one (at 2195).

The present standard, known as the Barker balancing test, consists of four factors. These are:

1. The length of the delay between charging the defendant and the defendant's trial.
2. The reason for the delay.
3. The defendant's assertion of his or her due process right to a speedy trial.
4. The existence of prejudice to the defendant by prosecutorial and/or judicial actions.

Source: Barker v. Wingo, 407 U.S. 514, 92 S.Ct. 2182 (1972).

dants would send the message that efficient case processing is an essential element in the overall effectiveness of the juvenile justice system. Often, juvenile court actors themselves can greatly enhance juvenile case processing by their own behaviors. Juvenile court judges are particularly powerful entities, and their decision making can be far-reaching, extending back to the time of juvenile arrests and intake proceedings, as well as forward to prosecutorial filings, adjudicatory proceedings, and disposition hearings.

The findings of researchers suggest that the longer juveniles remain within the juvenile justice system, the more adverse the consequences for their subsequent recidivism and seriousness of offending (Butts and Gable 1992). One reason juvenile case processing has been sluggish is that the doctrine of *parens patriae* has been pervasive, suggesting rehabilitation over other themes, such as punishment, crime control or due process. According to the *parens patriae* concept, juvenile courts need a certain amount of time to provide for the needs of youths drawn into the system. If insufficient time is allocated for rehabilitation, then rehabilitation will not occur. However, the U.S. Supreme Court has characterized the doctrine of *parens patriae* as "murky" and of "dubious historical relevance" in the case of *In re Gault* (1967). The U.S. Supreme Court also declared in *Gault* that juveniles do not need to give up their due process rights under the Fourteenth Amendment in order to derive juvenile justice system benefits because of their status as juvenile offenders, such as the greater concern for their well-being supposedly inherent in juvenile court proceedings (Butts 1996b, 538). Instead, the U.S. Supreme Court suggested the due process principles of fairness, impartiality, and orderliness were of paramount importance in contrast with the *parens patriae* philosophy. Essentially the U.S. Supreme Court has acted to bring the juvenile court system under constitutional control (Manfredi 1998).

Examinations of juvenile court prosecutorial opinions about the effectiveness of juvenile court processing indicate that in at least some jurisdictions, such as Illinois, prosecutors perceive juvenile courts to be relatively ineffective at rehabilitating juveniles (Ellsworth, Kinsella, and Massin 1992). These prosecutors believe that probation services are most vital to a youth's rehabilitation and that specific community programs and services intended to prevent delinquency are either inadequate, nonexistent, or ineffective. Specific sectors of the community were targeted as most important by these prosecutors. They believe that greater juvenile court intervention should occur in school matters. All things considered, however, these prosecutors believe that their rehabilitative impact in specific juvenile cases becomes less effective as their involvement in such cases increases. Again, this suggests moving youths through the system more quickly to minimize their exposure to the process.

THE ADVOCACY ROLE OF DEFENSE ATTORNEYS

For especially serious juvenile offender cases, defense attorneys are increasingly useful and necessary as a means of safeguarding juvenile rights and holding the juvenile justice system more accountable regarding its treatment of juvenile offenders. For instance, it is important for defense counsel to advise their clients about the **statute of limitations** associated with various offenses, where the government can bring charges within specified time periods following the crime's occurrence. Some crimes, like murder, have no statute of limitations, and thus there is an indefinite period of time when the state can bring charges against a potential defendant (see Box 8.4). Widespread abuse of discretion by various actors throughout all stages of the juvenile justice process is well documented. The intrusion of defense attorneys into the juvenile justice process, under a new due process framework, is anticipated as a logical consequence of the rights juveniles have obtained from the U.S. Supreme Court (DeFrances and Strom 1997).

BOX 8.4

ON THE STATUTE OF LIMITATIONS FOR MURDER

Michael Skakel, 39

It happened in Greenwich, Connecticut, in 1975. A 15-year-old girl, Martha Moxley, was bludgeoned to death with a golf club. The case remained unsolved for twenty-five years, until a tip revealed the possible involvement of a 39-year-old nephew of Robert F. Kennedy, Michael Skakel. Skakel's involvement in Moxley's murder apparently showed his culpability at age 15. Moxley was a neighbor and childhood friend of Skakel's. But there are several potentially unresolvable wrinkles that could complicate how Skakel is processed. Since Skakel was 15 when Moxley's murder occurred, the case is within the jurisdiction of the juvenile court in Connecticut. When the murder occurred in 1975, 1975 law provided that if a juvenile were found guilty of murder in juvenile court, he would face a maximum of only 4 years if he was tried as a juvenile. If he were tried as an adult, he would get from 25 years to life. Most legal experts interviewed at the time said that Skakel will be subject to the laws that prevailed in 1975 when the murder was alleged. In 1975 prosecutors were required to present evidence at a hearing to convince a judge that the case should be transferred to adult court. Under current law, murder cases are automatically transferred to adult court. While it was unlikely that Skakel's case would remain in juvenile court, there were several legal hurdles that prosecutors must overcome. One Yale Law School professor, David Rosen, said it was entirely possible for Skakel to be found guilty and receive virtually no punishment for the offense. Rosen said that "the juvenile court, under the 1975 law, did not have the authority to send him to an adult facility. Therefore, he might not be subject to punishment decades later for crimes committed as a child—no matter how terrible the crime." There is also the question as to whether the adult courts can punish him, even if the case is transferred to them. Rosen added, "The adult court doesn't have authority over him unless the juvenile court is allowed to transfer him, but it's only allowed to transfer him, it seems to me, if he's a child. The reason we're going around in circles is that the law at that time was designed for the protection and correction of children so that they would not become criminals in their adult years. It was designed for rehabilitation, not punishment." Skakel was processed at the Greenwich Police Department, where he surrendered on January 19, 2000. Skakel became the oldest person ever to be treated as a juvenile in Connecticut courts. The notion of a person pushing 40 appearing in juvenile court next to teenagers has prompted some chuckling in Connecticut legal circles. Hillary Barger, a juvenile prosecutor in Bridgeport, said that Skakel's lawyers could keep the case in juvenile court for a year or more if they fight the transfer to adult court. She said, "The situation of a 40-year-old was never anticipated by the law. This could take a very long time to resolve."

In a follow-up, Skakel was subsequently tried as an adult in criminal court for the murder and convicted. In 2002 he had launched an appeal.

Source: Adapted from the Associated Press, "Trying an Adult as a Child: 39-Year-Old Defendant in Greenwich Murder Is Headed for Juvenile Court." January 21, 2000.

Attorneys for Juveniles as a Matter of Right

Although juveniles are entitled to the services of attorneys at all stages of juvenile proceedings, some investigators have shown that about half of all youths processed in the juvenile justice system are not represented by counsel (Feld 1988a). Shortly after the *Gault* decision in 1967, the Minnesota legislature mandated the assistance of counsel for all juveniles in delinquency proceedings. It was believed that making provisions for defense counsel would maximize the equitable treatment of youths by Minnesota juvenile courts. However, Feld's (1988b) analysis of 17,195 cases involving adjudications of delinquency in 1986 found that only about half of all juveniles adjudicated delinquent in these Minnesota juvenile courts had attorneys to represent them.

Analyzing adjudication data from an earlier period in five other jurisdictions besides Minnesota, Feld (1988b) discovered similar figures. Roughly half of all juveniles adjudicated delinquent in these state juvenile courts had legal representation at the time of their adjudications. It is unclear whether the juveniles who did not have defense counsel also did not request defense counsel. It would have been inconsistent with *Gault* as well as unconstitutional if these juveniles had requested defense counsel and been denied it in those jurisdictions. But Feld may have provided at least two plausible explanations for this finding. He found that juveniles who were represented by attorneys in each of these jurisdictions, and who were also adjudicated as delinquent, tended to receive harsher sentences and dispositions from juvenile court judges compared with those juveniles who did not have defense counsel to represent them. Thus, it would seem that the presence of defense counsel in juvenile courts, at least in those jurisdictions examined by Feld, actually aggravated the dispositional outcome rather than mitigated it. An alternative explanation is that the more serious offenders in those jurisdictions were more likely to acquire counsel. Thus, they would logically receive harsher sentences compared with less serious offenders, if they were ultimately adjudicated as delinquents.

Subsequent to Feld's research, the presence of defense counsel in juvenile proceedings has escalated dramatically (U.S. General Accounting Office 1995b). Although there continue to be regional variations in the proportionate representation of juveniles by defense counsel, especially rural areas contrasted with urban areas, the overall trend has been toward increased attorney representation. With the presence of defense counsel in juvenile proceedings becoming increasingly commonplace, it is also likely that the adverse impact of defense attorneys on the outcomes of these proceedings has lessened accordingly (Eskridge 1996).

Defense Counsel and Ensuring Due Process Rights for Juveniles

The manifest function of defense attorneys in juvenile courts is to ensure that due process is fulfilled by all participants. Defense attorneys are the primary advocates of fairness for juveniles who are charged with crimes or other types of offenses. Minors, particularly very young youths, are more susceptible to the persuasiveness of adults. Law enforcement officers, intake officers, and prosecutors might extract incriminating evidence from juveniles in much the same way as police officers and prosecutors might extract inculpatory information from suspects in criminal cases, provided that certain constitutional safeguards were not in place. For adults, a major constitutional safeguard is the Miranda warning, which, among other things, advises those arrested for crimes of their right to an attorney, their right to terminate police interrogations whenever they wish and remain silent, their right to have their attorneys present during questioning, and the right to have an attorney appointed for them if they cannot afford one (Sanborn 1994).

BOX 8.5

SHOULD JUVENILES BE ENTITLED TO CONFIDENTIALITY IF THEY COMMIT CRIMES?

News Media Attempt to Protect Identities of Juvenile Suspects

Under Texas law, the names of juveniles may be included in any news source whenever they are charged with crimes. This includes newspapers, radio reports, and televised news programs. But juvenile court documents and corresponding police reports about juveniles are confidential and not disclosed to the public. However, other states, such as Florida, permit disclosures of this information. Which should it be as a general policy throughout the United States? This is currently a dilemma for more than a few jurisdictions. In May 2000 two 12-year-old boys were arrested for carrying dangerous firearms to Irving Middle School in San Antonio, Texas. While their identities were known to other students, the newscasts about this event did not disclose their names or addresses, only their genders and ages. There are differing points of view about how much information should be disclosed to the public, if at all, about juveniles who commit crimes. In Texas, television stations will do various things to obscure identities of juveniles. Some newspapers and television stations will offer portions of names or run images at strange angles to show bodies from the shoulders down. While the media are legally free to run the names of juveniles charged with crimes, journalists most often take great pains to afford children protections rarely given to adults. The thinking seems to be that this protection will avoid branding children for the rest of their lives. Some critics think some juveniles need branding.

A juvenile court judge has raised an interesting point. Judge Carmen Kelsey says that anyone who wants to come to juvenile court and sit in on court proceedings can find out the names and addresses of any juvenile charged with any offense. The court is open to the public and never closed. "You don't get written information, but you get the next best thing. You get their names and you can see who they are," says Kelsey. "On the one hand, you don't want a secret hearing where someone's rights can be violated, but at the same time, you want to be protective of juveniles," he adds. In the San Antonio case, the two 12-year-olds were armed with a .22 caliber rifle and a .25 caliber handgun with which they planned to kill two fellow students. Juan Perez, 42, a systems engineer, says he's thankful that the Irving Middle School boys were caught, but he still wants to know who they are, regardless of whether they are ever convicted. "If I do something wrong, I will be published and I will be embarrassed," he said. "You should not have amnesty just because you are a kid," he added. In 1999 Florida enacted new rules that made a wealth of information about juvenile criminals available to the public. A New Mexico judge ruled in early 2000 that the names of juveniles who are arrested will have their names published as a matter of public record.

Should there be a national policy about disclosing the identities of juveniles who are accused of committing crimes? Should the press print faces and names of juveniles accused of crimes? How much confidentiality should juveniles be permitted? What do you think?

Source: Adapted from Dane Schiller and the Associated Press, "Kids' Names Often Withheld." May 25, 2000.

Some persons believe that the U.S. Supreme Court has always supported the *parens patriae* nature of juvenile courts and that their purportedly liberal decisions about juvenile constitutional guarantees have been intended only to provide minimal procedural protections. Nevertheless, the possibilities of incarceration in secure juvenile incarcerative facilities and/or transfer to criminal court jurisdiction where harsher penalties may be administered are sufficient to warrant the intervention of defense counsel in many juvenile cases (Feld 1993b). At the very least, defense counsel may prevent some youths from being railroaded into accepting unnecessary conditional interventions from intake officers or juvenile court judges. It is not the intention of defense attorneys to aggravate matters and cause their juvenile clients to receive harsher punishments than they would normally receive from the same judges if defense counsel weren't present. But it is a curious paradox that those seeking justice and due process and who exercise their rights for these aims are often penalized for exercising these rights.

In many respects, this paradox is similar to the disparity in sentencing among those who have similar criminal histories and are convicted for the same offenses, but who receive widely disparate sentences depending upon whether their convictions are obtained through plea bargaining or a jury verdict in a criminal trial. There is no particular reason for judges to impose harsher punishments on convicted offenders who exercise their right to a jury trial compared with those who enter into plea agreements and plead guilty, but differential punishments are frequently administered (Wu, Cernkovich, and Dunn 1997). One explanation, an extralegal and nonlegal one, is that the extra punishment is the penalty for obligating the state to prove its case against the defendant in open court. Being aware of this type of sentencing disparity, many defense attorneys counsel their clients, especially where there is strong inculpatory evidence, to plead guilty to lesser charges and accept a lesser penalty to avoid more severe punishments that judges almost certainly will impose upon conviction through a trial. It would appear from the available evidence that juvenile court judges may be guilty of the same behavior when relating to juvenile clients who are represented by counsel and those who are not. For the present, anyway, being represented by counsel in juvenile court seems more of a liability than an asset.

Are Attorneys Being Used More Frequently by Juvenile Defendants?

Yes. At least a survey of five states during the 1980–1995 period (California, Montana, Nebraska, North Dakota, and Pennsylvania) found that attorney use by juvenile offenders increased systematically across these years (Champion 1999). Attorney use varies by jurisdiction, however. In the mid-1990s, over 90 percent of all California juvenile cases involved either private or publicly appointed defense counsel. However, in states such as Nebraska and North Dakota, attorney use by juveniles occurred in about 60 percent of the cases.

It may seem that whenever youths invoke their right to an attorney, it would be under circumstances where the offenses alleged are serious or violent. While it is true that attorney use was more prevalent in these states where serious and violent offenses were alleged, it is also true that attorney use increased during the ten-year period for status offenders and those charged with public order, property, and drug offenses as well. The primary implication of this research is that juvenile courts are experiencing greater defense attorney involvement each year. If these states are representative of all U.S. jurisdictions, then the formalization of juvenile courtrooms is definitely increasing with greater involvement of defense counsel in juvenile cases.

Do Defense Counsel for Juveniles Make a Difference in Their Case Dispositions?

The use of defense counsel by juveniles results in mixed outcomes (U.S. General Accounting Office 1995b). In some instances, because of the greater formality of the proceeding because defense counsel are present, outcomes occur that may be unfavorable to juvenile defendants. For instance, if an intake officer would be inclined to divert a particular case from the juvenile justice system because of his or her judgment that the youth will probably not reoffend, this diversion decision may not be made if an attorney is present to represent the juvenile's interests. The intake officer may feel that a higher authority should decide the case. The defense counsel may be intimidating. In an otherwise attorney-free environment, the intake officer would act differently. Thus, different actions by different actors in the system may be anticipated, depending upon the presence or absence of an attorney.

In cases adjudicated before juvenile court judges, a defense counsel's presence seems to work for the juvenile's benefit. Judicial discretion is affected to the extent that stricter or less strict adherence to juvenile laws is affected. There seems to be a tendency for juvenile court judges to be more lenient with juveniles who are represented by defense counsel compared with those juvenile defendants who are not represented by defense counsel. This leniency manifests itself in various ways. For instance, juvenile court judges may impose probation more often than incarceration where juveniles are represented by counsel. Represented juveniles who are disposed to a secure facility for a period of months may serve shorter incarcerative terms compared with those juveniles sent to these same secure facilities but who were not represented by counsel. More frequent granting of juvenile parole occurs among those youths represented by counsel compared with those youths not represented by counsel. Little data are available among the states concerning the frequency with which leniency is dispensed where attorneys are either present or absent in juvenile cases. However, the general impression from the literature is that defense counsel are of greater benefit to juvenile offenders than a total absence of counsel (Puritz et al. 1995).

Comparative research studying the effects of counsel on juvenile court dispositions has been conducted in Australia and Canada. In Canada, for instance, an examination was made of 2,000 juvenile delinquent cases during 1981 (Carrington and Moyer 1990). Most juveniles had some type of legal representation at some point during their juvenile justice system processing. It was found that for those accused juveniles with legal representation, they generally had lower rates of conviction, mainly because of the greater use of not-guilty pleas. Despite the lower rates of conviction, these researchers believed that the ultimate impact of legal representation on juvenile adjudication rates was rather small.

In Australia, it has been found that a considerable gap exists between the philosophical role intended for defense counsel in juvenile cases and what actually happens in practice. Sixteen lawyers were surveyed in 1989 to determine how they viewed their roles and effectiveness in juvenile matters. Most lawyers revealed that their impact upon the legal process was that they facilitated plea bargaining for their youthful clients. In practice, they obtained for their clients the best possible deals in the short time provided for their interactions with juvenile courts and prosecutors. These informal agreements and legal shortcuts were neither contemplated nor intended by the Australian legislature. In fact, the intended function of greater attorney involvement in juvenile matters, according to the Australian legislature, was to ensure greater fundamental fairness in juvenile case processing. It would seem that more frequent plea bargaining and deal-cutting were the more realistic outcomes of defense counsel involvement in the cases surveyed here (Naffine and Wundersitz 1991).

Defense Counsel as *Guardians Ad Litem*

In some juvenile cases, child abuse has been alleged. Thus, defense counsel perform additional responsibilities as they attempt to ensure that the best interests of their clients are served in ways that will protect children from parents who abuse them (Keilitz et al. 1997; Minnesota Office of the Legislative Auditor 1995). ***Guardians ad litem*** are special guardians appointed by the court in which a particular litigation is pending to represent a youth, ward, or unborn person in that particular litigation (Black 1990, 706). Most juvenile court jurisdictions have *guardian ad litem* programs, where interested persons serve in this capacity. In some cases, defense counsel for youths perform the dual role of defense counsel and the youth's *guardian ad litem* (Dalley 1997). *Guardians ad litem* are supposed to work in ways that will benefit those they represent, and such guardians provide legal protection from others. Defense counsel working as *guardians ad litem* may act to further the child's best interests, despite a child's contrary requests or demands. Thus, this is a different type of nonadversarial role performed by some defense counsel (Eltringham and Aldridge 2000).

Juvenile Offender Plea Bargaining and the Role of Defense Counsel

Often, we think that plea bargaining occurs only within the criminal justice system. The fact is that juveniles enter into plea agreements with juvenile court prosecutors with great frequency (Sanborn 1993b). Sanborn says that plea bargaining is an invaluable tool with which to eliminate case backlogs that might occur in some of the larger juvenile courts. Sanborn gathered data from 100 juvenile court officers in 1988. Specifically, Sanborn wanted to know whether plea bargaining was consistent with the guiding doctrine of *parens patriae* that characterized juvenile courts at that time. Most of those surveyed believed that plea bargaining was used solely to help those youths in need of social services or other forms of assistance. Defense counsel entering into plea agreements with juvenile court prosecutors wanted the least restrictive option imposed on their juvenile clients. Most frequently sought by defense counsel were charge reductions against their clients by prosecutors. Defense counsel were interested in reducing the stigma of a serious, negative juvenile court profile of their youthful clients by seeking reduced charges from prosecutors. Prosecutors would benefit in that plea agreements would speed up case processing and save them time from having to prove critical elements of crimes against juvenile defendants. Both actors, prosecutors and defense attorneys, sought personal goals instead of pursuing some type of *parens patriae* objective. The former were interested in concluding adjudications with sanctions, while the latter were interested in protecting their clients from more serious charges that could influence their future lives.

The degree to which *parens patriae* is alive and well depends on how much a particular court has accepted and furthered the due process renovation created by *Gault* (Sanborn 1994). If fairness is to be realized in the adjudicatory hearing of juveniles, judges and defense attorneys should know the rules of criminal procedure and evidence, and they must be made aware that adjudications are serious for youths. Defense lawyers should also be reminded that appellate review is both a necessary and valuable weapon, although few juvenile court decisions are ever appealed (Puritz et al. 1995). However, one continuing and troublesome aspect of plea bargaining in the juvenile justice system is that admissions of guilt are elicited from juveniles without benefit of a trial.

Parental Intrusion in Juvenile Courts Is Often More Damaging Than Attorney Involvement

The impact of the parents of juveniles who appear in juvenile courts has been investigated (Sanborn 1995). The attitudes and opinions of various juvenile justice actors, such as judges, prosecutors, defense attorneys, and probation officers have been investigated. In more than a few instances, parents of processed juveniles tend to make matters for their children worse by their own actions. Some parents threaten intake officers, prosecutors, and/or judges. Many of those surveyed viewed the interventions of parents in juvenile proceedings as primarily negative. Some of their negative behaviors might be due to a basic misunderstanding of the due process rights of their children. Other parents may feel that the juvenile court is not a formally contrived proceeding with legal powers. As some parents attempt to intervene and circumvent procedural matters before the juvenile court, all actors, including defense counsel, become exasperated and tend to impose harsher sanctions than would otherwise be imposed if the parents were not there. However, parental involvement in juvenile matters is often required according to court or procedural rules.

It is clear from juvenile justice trends observed in most states thus far that defense counsel are increasingly present during all stages of juvenile processing. This increased involvement of defense counsel is intended to ensure that a juvenile's constitutional rights are observed. Another intention of counsel is to ensure the best dispositional outcome for their youthful clients. This usually means some form of lenient treatment from the system. We have seen that attorney involvement does preserve one's rights at different processing stages; however, it is not yet clear whether a defense counsel's presence is totally beneficial to juvenile clients at all times. Too much formalization may cause various actors (e.g., intake officers, prosecutors, judges) to act differently when others are present who can monitor their actions. The traditional view of juvenile courts is that whatever is done to and for the juvenile will be in the youth's best interests. Sometimes, this means making one type of decision for one offender and a different type of decision for another offender, even when the offenders share similar background characteristics and have committed similar offenses.

Extralegal factors, such as race/ethnicity, socioeconomic status, gender, age, and a youth's demeanor all contribute to decision making at different processing stages (Leonard, Pope, and Feyerherm 1995). Ideally, these criteria should not be considered when making decisions about juvenile offenders. But sometimes judges and others will respond and make decisions about some youths based upon these and other variables (Wu, Cernkovich, and Dunn 1997). In many cases, these decisions are favorable for the youths involved, but outsiders may perceive this differential treatment to be inherently unequal treatment. Thus, questions arise about one's equal protection rights as set forth in the Fourteenth Amendment. In the name of equal protection, therefore, judges and others may tend to deal with some offenders more severely, simply to preserve due process (Gottfredson and Uihlein 1992). And this greater harshness is sometimes the result of a defense attorney's presence.

Consider the following scenario. Two 12-year-old youths have been taken into custody for theft. One boy stole some candy from a grocery store, while the other boy stole some pencils from a convenience store. Both boys have no prior juvenile records. One boy is Hispanic, while the other is Asian. The intake officer, who is black, sees both boys and their families, with no defense counsel present. The Hispanic boy utters various obscenities at the intake officer. The Asian boy sits calmly and responds politely to questions asked. The intake officer might be inclined to recommend further juvenile justice processing for the Hispanic juvenile, while he might be inclined to divert the Asian juvenile from the system. Is this decision motivated by prejudice? Or is the decision motivated by the attitude or demeanor displayed by each youth? If, in fact, these different decisions are made, the Hispanic boy is adversely affected by the intake officer's decision. But the Asian boy benefits from the informal handling of his case by the intake officer.

Now let's consider these same scenarios, but in each case, we will place in the room defense counsel for both youths. Whether the defense counsel are privately retained or publicly appointed, they are interested in justice for their respective clients. Because of the presence of an attorney in each of the cases, the intake officer decides to apply standard decision-making criteria. Both of these boys have committed theft, at least a misdemeanor if an adult committed these acts. Thus, the intake officer moves both boys further into the system, so that a juvenile court prosecutor can take over from there. In the Hispanic boy's case, the presence of his defense counsel merely gave credence to the intake officer's decision to move the boy further into the system. The boy's demeanor or attitude didn't help matters, but the intake officer is merely following the rules. The letter of the law is applied. In the Asian youth's situation, the intake officer moves the boy further into the system, even though he believes this decision is *not* in the boy's best interests. But the intake officer is treating both boys equally, thus ensuring their due process and equal protection rights under the Fourteenth Amendment. The presence of defense counsel explains the consistency of the intake officer's conduct in both cases.

Some get-tough observers may say, so what? The boys stole something of value and they must learn not to steal. If we excuse the Asian boy from the system without punishing him, he will learn contempt for the system because the system is lenient and tolerates theft. The due-process view is that both boys need to be punished equally, because they have equal background characteristics and have committed commensurate offenses. Should they be punished equally? At the other end of the spectrum are those who wish to preserve the *parens patriae* concept of juvenile courts. Doing things that are in a youth's best interests may involve making decisions that may be inherently discriminatory. Should we punish one's demeanor or attitude, which varies greatly from youth to youth, or should we punish the same delinquent acts in the same ways? This hypothetical example shows both the good and bad stemming from greater attorney involvement in juvenile proceedings at any stage.

SUMMARY

Early juvenile proceedings were guided by the principle of *parens patriae*, and decisions were made by judges and others presumably for the benefit of affected juveniles. The frequent arbitrariness of these decisions prompted allegations of unfairness and inequitable treatment. In time, the juvenile court became an adversarial system, where prosecutors and defense attorneys would respectively prosecute and defend juvenile clients accused of crimes.

Juvenile court prosecutors are making increasingly important decisions about juvenile defendants. Prosecutors are expected to pursue charges against juveniles, especially where serious offenses are alleged. In a growing number of jurisdictions, prosecutors may decide to charge certain juveniles as adults and recommend their cases to the criminal courts. Where juvenile courts retain jurisdiction over youths, the standard of proof has changed to beyond a reasonable doubt, especially in those cases where a juvenile's liberty is at stake. In view of the criminal standard of beyond a reasonable doubt, this means that prosecutors must build more compelling cases against alleged juvenile offenders. The evidentiary standards are increasingly rigorous, and the greater involvement of defense counsels in juvenile cases holds juvenile court prosecutors to a higher standard.

Significant changes have occurred relating to the time standards governing legal actions against juveniles. While juveniles are not entitled to the same speedy trial rights as adults in criminal courts, the juvenile justice system is nevertheless obligated to observe more stringent timelines for pursuing their cases against juvenile suspects. Juveniles enjoy a broader range of due process rights. But with greater rights comes greater accountability. One important dimension of heightening the accountability of juveniles is accelerating the juvenile justice process. Accelerating juvenile offender case processing is one means of bringing the subsequent punishment closer to the time when the offense was committed. This feature is especially important for juvenile offenders, who generally have a different conceptual appreciation of time compared with adult offenders. Another dimension is removing the cloak of confidentiality from juvenile court proceedings and opening these proceedings to the public. Less confidentiality is associated with juvenile record-keeping, and allowing greater public access to juvenile files.

As juveniles have acquired greater legal rights, there has been an increased need for legal representation in juvenile courts. Juveniles are entitled to an attorney as a matter of right whenever they are referred to juvenile court for adjudicatory proceedings. In almost every urban jurisdiction today, juveniles are represented by defense counsel in over 90 percent of all juvenile court cases. In rural jurisidictions, defense attorney use is not as high, although it is increasing steadily each year. The roles of defense counsels in juvenile court proceedings should not be underestimated. Defense counsels insure that a juvenile's rights are protected, and they strive to make a difference in their clients' case dispositions. If private counsels cannot be afforded by juveniles and their families, public defenders are appointed to represent juveniles in almost every jurisdiction. As in the criminal justice system, defense counsels for juvenile clients engage in plea bargaining to minimize the severity of offender punishment.

QUESTIONS FOR REVIEW

1. What is meant by an adversarial proceeding? How has the prosecutorial role in juvenile courts changed?

2. In what respects has the standard of proof, beyond a reasonable doubt, modified the prosecutorial role?

3. Should confidentiality of juvenile records be maintained? Why or why not?

4. What are some reasons for removing confidentiality surrounding juvenile records and opening juvenile courts to the general public?

5. What kinds of time standards govern prosecutorial decision making in the juvenile justice system? Are these time standards uniform for all jurisdictions?

6. What are some reasons for accelerating the time interval between when a juvenile is charged with a delinquent act and an adjudicatory hearing?

7. Under what circumstances are public defenders appointed for juveniles? Are all juveniles entitled to an attorney in juvenile court? Why or why not?

8. What are the speedy trial rights of juvenile offenders?

9. What is the significance of the *Barker v. Wingo* case? In what respects does it apply to juveniles, if at all?

10. How do defense counsels insure that a juvenile's due process rights are preserved? What are *guardians ad litem* and what are their functions?

SUGGESTED READINGS

Eltringham, Simon and Jan Aldridge. 2000. The extent of children's knowledge of court as estimated by *guardians ad litem. Child Abuse Review* 9:275–286.

Jacobson, Wendy B. 2000. *Safe from the start: Taking action on children exposed to violence.* Washington, DC: Office of Juvenile Justice and Delinquency Prevention.

Massachusetts Statistical Analysis Center. 2001. *Implementation of the Juvenile Justice Reform Act: Youthful offenders in Massachusetts.* Boston: Massachusetts Statistical Analysis Center.

INTERNET CONNECTIONS

Action without Borders
http://www.idealist.org/

Teenage CURFEW
http://www.webspan.net/S~byrne/curfew.html

Victim-Offender Mediation Association
http://www.igc.org/voma

Youth Law Center
http://www.youthlawcenter.com/

Youth on Trial: A Developmental Perspective on Juvenile Justice
http://www.macadoldev-juvjustice.org/

Chapter Outline

Key Terms

Acceptance of responsibility
Blended sentencing
Capital punishment
Certification
Concurrent jurisdiction
Contempt of court
Criminal-exclusive blend
Criminal-inclusive blend
Death penalty
Demand waiver
Direct file
Discretionary waivers

Judicial waivers
Juvenile-contiguous blend
Juvenile court records
Juvenile-exclusive blend
Juvenile-inclusive blend
Legislative waiver
Life-without-parole
Mandatory waiver
Nolle prosequi
Once an adult/always an adult
    provision
Placed

Placement
Presumptive waiver
Reverse waiver
Reverse waiver hearings, reverse
    waiver actions
Statutory exclusion
Sustained petitions
Transfer hearings
Transfers
Waiver
Waiver hearing
Waiver motion

Chapter Objectives

As a result of reading this chapter, you will have accomplished the following objectives:

1. Distinguish between different types of offenses in terms of their seriousness.
2. Understand the criminal justice and juvenile justice system responses to juvenile violence.
3. Understand the get-tough movement and the policies advocated toward violent juveniles.
4. Understand the meaning of juvenile transfers, waivers, and certifications.
5. Understand different types of waiver actions and their implications for juvenile offenders.
6. Learn about the ages at which juveniles may be transferred to criminal court for processing.
7. Understand the importance of waiver hearings for juveniles.
8. Become familiar with important case law governing juvenile transfers or waivers.
9. Understand blended sentencing statutes as emerging optional punishments for juveniles who commit serious crimes.

INTRODUCTION

• *It happened in Chicago, Illinois on January 9, 1997. A 10-year-old girl, known only as Girl X to protect her identity, was found dumped in a stairwell in the blighted Cabrini-Green public housing project. Roach killer had been sprayed down her throat and she had been severely beaten and sexually assaulted. Authorities say that the 4'8" girl has made remarkable progress since the beating. They cannot determine whether she will ever see or talk again. She is communicative and is able to express her needs, according to hospital officials. Authorities have determined that the perpetrators were three youths, probably in their early teens. Dr. Gayle Spill of the Schwab Rehabilitation Hospital, said that Girl X is unable to walk, speak, or see. However, she uses hand signals and gestures to communicate with hospital staff. "She hates vegetables and loves pizza," says Dr. Spill. "She has an excellent sense of humor and often teases family and staff." What type of punishment would you impose, provided the perpetrator is apprehended? Would the age of the attacker make any difference in the punishment you might suggest? Why or why not? [Adapted from the Associated Press, "Beating Victim Making Progress." June 14, 1997.]*

• *How could it happen? On Tuesday, March 29, 2000, a 6-year-old boy went to school armed with a loaded .32 caliber pistol. He shot and killed another 6-year-old female classmate, Kayla Rolland. Police were perplexed about where the boy could have obtained the weapon. Subsequent investigation led to the discovery that the boy had retrieved the weapon from under the bed blankets of Jamelle James, 19, who lived in a flophouse where the 6-year-old resided with his mother and uncle. Originally, police searched the boy's house and determined that it was frequented by strangers. The boy had been staying with his mother, Tamarla Owens, 29, and an uncle, Sir Marcus B. Winfrey, 21. The search of the home uncovered some stolen property, and Winfrey was ar-*

rested by police later on charges of receiving stolen property. It was also determined that the boy's father was in prison and that the house was known as a place where people could trade crack for guns. Dedric Owens, the boy's father, was in prison on a parole violation related to 1995 drug and burglary charges. When Owens was interviewed by reporters in prison, he apologized for the shooting but said that neither he nor the boy should be held responsible. "The only thing I feel responsible for is not being there in his life like I'm supposed to be like a father, every day." Reports by independent investigators indicated that two of the boy's classmates told police that they had seen guns at the house where the boy was staying on previous occasions. Marijuana was also smoked regularly at the home by different individuals. Regarding the subsequent arrest of 19-year-old Jamelle James, owner of the gun that killed Kayla Rolland, Genessee County Prosecutor Arthur Busch said, "We're not looking for a scapegoat in this case; we're just looking for justice for Kayla." James was arraigned on March 1, 2000, and bond was set at $100,000. When Judge Richard L. Hughes set the bond, James made an obscene gesture at reporter cameras as he was led from the courthouse. Earlier, the judge had asked James if he understood the charges against him and that the manslaughter charge carries a possible 15-year sentence. James replied "Yes," when the judge asked him the question. James's lawyer, Jeffrey Skinner, said after the arraignment that the $100,000 bond was excessive. In the complaint against James, prosecutors allege that James kept the pistol loaded, had twirled it in front of the boy, failed to keep the gun secure, and created an atmosphere of reckless circumstances. Busch said, "I hope this prosecution sends a message to America that those guns that you think can make you safer can make our community more dangerous." The charge requires prosecutors to show gross negligence that gave the boy access to the gun. Busch said that he would allege that James contributed to the delinquency of a minor. Should the 6-year-old bear any type of responsibility in the matter? It is a matter of law that youths under the age of 7 are presumed incapable of formulating criminal intent. What if the youth had been 7 years of age? Would this one-year difference had mattered in this case? What do you think? [Adapted from the Associated Press, "Prosecutors in Michigan Shooting File Manslaughter Charges over Gun." March 3, 2000.]

• It seems to be happening with increasing frequency. Motorists will get mad over another's driving and do something violent about it. In Glendale, Arizona, a 15-year-old was killed as the result of what has become known as "road rage." Two cars of teenagers were parallel at a traffic light. Suddenly, one car spurted away from the stop light, closely followed by the other car. The cars reached speeds of 90 mph, through residential neighborhoods, until the eluding vehicle wrecked. The pursuers got out of their car and proceeded to beat up the occupants of the other car. When the beatings ceased, the attackers fled. Marco Rubalcalvas, 15, was beaten to death. No suspects were arrested. Witnesses said that an argument had erupted between the two cars' teen occupants. Then the chase ensued. The eluding car contained three teenagers, including Marco. When their car ran through a fence and overturned, at least two of the pursuers got out and beat Rubalcalvas and his friends with aluminum baseball bats. The other companions of Rubalcalvas were in critical condition, but they survived the assault. This was the second such incident in two weeks in Glendale. What should be done to the youthful perpetrators of this road rage if apprehended? Should they be prosecuted as adults in criminal court? [Adapted from the Associated Press, "Road Rage Leads to Beating, Death." May 27, 1998.]

Juvenile arrest rates for violent crimes began to increase in the late 1980s. The juvenile violent crime rate soared by more than 180 percent between 1988 and 1994 after more than a decade of relative stability (Bilchik 1996, 1). Much of this violence was strongly associated with drugs and alcohol (Shannon 1998). In the late 1990s juvenile violence decreased slightly, although juvenile violent crime arrests were 60 percent higher in 1996 than they were in 1987 (Torbet and Szymanski 1998, 2). In 2000, 2.1 million youths under age 18 had been arrested for various crimes. There were 3,182 youths arrested for rape; 919 for murder or nonnegligent manslaughter; 18,735 for robbery; and 45,080 for aggravated assault (Maguire and Pastore 2002).

What responses to these offenses should be made by the juvenile justice system? What are the limits of sanctions to be imposed by juvenile courts? Should some youths be held more accountable than others, in view of the crimes they commit? Are some youths more amenable to criminal punishments than others? Where should the line be drawn about who should receive criminal penalties and who should not receive them? How should legal and extralegal factors influence whether juveniles should be treated as adults (Sealock and Simpson 1998)?

This chapter examines waiver decision making. Waivers, also known as transfers and certifications, are transferrals or shifts of jurisdiction over certain types of cases from the authority of juvenile courts to the authority of criminal courts. These terms will be used throughout this and other chapters interchangeably. Youths who are subjected to waivers are not tried as juveniles in juvenile courts. Rather, they are redefined and classified as adults and eventually tried in criminal courts. Only a small proportion of juveniles are subject to criminal court transfers annually. Preliminary determinations are made of crime seriousness, the youth's characteristics, such as age and other factors associated with the type of crime committed, and the amount or degree of victim injuries inflicted. This process will be described.

Several types of waivers may be exercised by either judges or juvenile prosecutors, depending upon the jurisdiction. In some jurisdictions, provisions exist for the automatic transfer of certain juvenile offenders to criminal court. These variations in waiver procedures will be outlined and discussed. Because of the potentially serious nature of penalties that criminal courts may impose if youths are eventually found guilty through bench or jury trials or plea bargaining, several implications of waivers for affected juveniles will be examined. Waivers may be contested, and these occasions are known as waiver hearings. In those jurisdictions with statutory automatic transfer provisions, juveniles are entitled to reverse waiver hearings. Both options have strengths and weaknesses, benefits and disadvantages for youths charged with crimes. These will be described. Because waivers of juveniles to criminal court may be made at several junctures in the juvenile justice process (e.g., automatically by statute, before or after intake, at the prosecution stage, or at adjudication in juvenile court), it was believed important to discuss this event now rather than in a later chapter. Subsequently, we can see how waivers function as options for various actors in the juvenile justice system, and we can understand and appreciate the significance of them as well as their several implications for affected juveniles.

An integral feature of the juvenile justice process is the adversarial relation between defense counsel and prosecutors. Both of these roles will be examined as they relate to waiver decisions. Finally, a get-tough movement has been observed over the last few decades, within both the criminal and juvenile justice systems. For criminals, getting tough means stiffer sentences and heavier fines, fewer loopholes that may be used to elude convictions for crimes, and less prosecutorial and judicial discretion relating to minimizing charges filed and penalties assessed. For juveniles, get-tough means moving away from the traditional rehabilitative orientation that characterized early juvenile court processes and decision making and toward more punitive sanctions, greater use of incarceration, especially for more serious youthful offenders, obligating more youths to be held accountable for their actions, and more liberal use of waivers to criminal courts for the most serious offenders. Waivers represent a hard line against selected juvenile offenders. Contemporary waiver patterns among the states will be illustrated and waiver trends described.

SERIOUSNESS OF THE OFFENSE AND WAIVER DECISION MAKING

Seriousness of the Offense

Investigations of the nature and seriousness of violent juvenile offending have been conducted by several researchers. Some researchers have concluded that today's juveniles do not commit more acts of violence than did juveniles in previous generations, but more juveniles are violent (Zimring 1998). However, in a comparison of mid-1990s juvenile offending with the nature and type of juvenile offending in 1980, it was found that about the same proportion of youths commit serious violent offenses in 1994 as they did in 1980. However, the violent acts committed in the 1990s are more lethal, with larger proportions of these violent acts likely to result in either serious injury or death. It has been found that the peak years of committing violent acts among juveniles are between the ages of 15 and 16. Also, the major causes of juvenile violence tend to be poor family relations, socioeconomically disadvantaged neighborhoods, poor school adjustments, peer pressure, greater availability of firearms, and greater dependence on alcohol or drugs (Elliott 1994a, 1994b).

Separating Status Offenders from Delinquent Offenders

One of the first steps taken to separate juveniles into different offending categories was the deinstitutionalization of status offenses or DSO. Also including divestiture, this major juvenile justice system reform was calculated to remove the least serious and noncriminal offenders from the jurisdiction of juvenile courts in every jurisdiction. Presumably and ideally, after DSO has occurred, only those juveniles who are charged with felonies and/or misdemeanors—delinquents—will be brought into the juvenile justice process and formally adjudicated in juvenile courts. These courts would also retain supervisory control over children in need of supervision, abused children, or neglected children. In reality, events have not turned out as legislators had originally anticipated or intended. Many status offenders continue to filter into the juvenile justice system in most jurisdictions.

When DSO occurred on a large scale throughout the United States during the late 1970s, several jurisdictions, including West Virginia, made policy decisions about how both nonserious and serious offenders would henceforth be treated by their juvenile justice systems. In West Virginia, for instance, the Supreme Court of Appeals ruled in 1977 that an adjudicated delinquent was constitutionally entitled to receive the least restrictive alternative treatment consistent with his or her rehabilitative needs (*State ex rel. Harris v. Calendine,*

BOX 9.1

SEPARATING JUVENILES FROM ADULTS IN JAILS BY SIGHT AND SOUND

The Ward County, North Dakota Jail

A continuing problem of small jails is what to do with juveniles taken into custody by police. A majority of jails in the United States are small, housing fewer than 100 inmates. When juveniles are arrested in certain areas, there is no place other than a jail to accommodate them. The federal government and most states have provisions that require separate areas for juveniles and adults, if juveniles are to be housed in jails for short periods. The provision calls for "sight-and-sound" separation of juveniles from adults. Juveniles must be maintained in areas that are separated by sight and sound from adult inmates.

In Ward County, North Dakota, the county jail is being renovated in order to comply with the sight-and-sound provision of federal and state mandates. The cost of renovation is staggering. For instance, a proposed remodeling of an unused jail kitchen into a juvenile detention facility is estimated to cost from $270,000 to $403,000. State and county officials have explored different options related to remodeling costs. Ward County Sheriff Vern Erck said that a committee is looking at renovating existing

jail cell space to save the county at least $60,000. A proposal is to use existing cell space differently and to process juvenile offenders through the same entrances used by adult offenders. Sheriff Erck said that "We can take them (juveniles) in (to the jail) the normal way if there are no adult prisoners around. Once they are in the cells we have designated, they will be separated from adults by sight and sound." Thus, some coordination must exist to ensure that adult offenders are not being processed at the same time that juvenile offenders are brought in for temporary detention. There are several purposes for short-term detention of juveniles at the jail. In 1998 there were no community facilities to house juveniles. Juveniles must be held until their parents are notified and they can come to the jail and claim their children.

Should communities establish separate facilities for housing juveniles apart from existing jails? Who should staff these facilities? What qualifications should persons have who administer juvenile detention centers? What do you think?

Source: Adapted from the Associated Press, "Committee Drafts Plan for Jail Renovation." June 4, 1998.

[1977]). While this decision didn't eliminate institutionalizing more serious or violent juveniles, it did encourage juvenile court judges to consider seriously various alternatives to incarceration as punishments for youthful offenders. Relating to DSO, the Court also prohibited the commingling of adjudicated status offenders and adjudicated delinquent offenders in secure, prison-like facilities (Mones 1984). Again, the court didn't necessarily rule out the secure confinement, long-term or otherwise, of status offenders as a possible sanction by juvenile court judges, despite encouragement by the Court for judges first to attempt to apply nonincarcerative sanctions before imposing incarcerative penalties.

These mixed messages sent by the West Virginia Supreme Court of Appeals did little, if anything, to restrict the discretionary powers of juvenile court judges. The Court's emphasis on rehabilitation and alternative treatments to be considered by juvenile court judges reinforced the traditional concept of juvenile courts as rehabilitative rather than punitive sanctioning bodies. However, the Court's ruling led to a substantial overhaul of the West Virginia juvenile code as well as a substantial drop in the incarcerated juvenile offender population in state-operated correctional facilities.

Juvenile Court Adjudications for Status Offenders

In many jurisdictions, DSO has reduced the volume of juvenile court cases over the years, but it has not prevented juvenile courts from continuing to adjudicate large numbers of status offenders annually (Holden and Kapler 1995). A comprehensive study of U.S. juvenile courts between 1990 and 1997 shows systematic increases in the absolute numbers of status offenders adjudicated across all status offense categories (National Center for Juvenile Justice 2001). In 1997 an estimated 158,500 status offense cases were formally processed by juvenile courts through referrals and subsequent status offender petitions. These represent about a fifth of all status offense cases that came to the attention of juvenile courts (782,500) in 1997. Proportionately, status offense cases processed formally by juvenile courts comprised only 14 percent of the entire delinquency and status offense court caseload. In 1997, juvenile courts formally processed approximately 24,000 runaway cases; 40,500 truancy cases; 21,300 ungovernability cases; 40,700 status liquor law violation cases; and 32,100 other miscellaneous status offense cases. Thus, truancy and liquor law violations were most often referred to juvenile courts for some type of action. About half of these referrals were made by police officers. About 52 percent of all of these cases were adjudicated as status offenders (National Center for Juvenile Justice 2001). Among those status offense cases that were not adjudicated, 67 percent were dismissed, 23 percent resulted in informal sanctions other than probation or out-of-home placement (e.g., fines, community service, restitution, or referrals to other community agencies for services), 10 percent resulted in informal probation, and less than 1 percent resulted in placement. **Placement** refers to out-of-home placement, such as a group home or foster care. Seldom does placement mean secure confinement for status offenders in a state industrial school or reform school. Thus, juveniles who are subjected to these dispositional options are considered **placed.**

Formal adjudications become an official part of a juvenile's record. For offenders who are nonadjudicated, a formal decision is not rendered; rather, an informal declaration is made by the judge to dispose of these cases with minimal intrusion into the families and lives of those affected by the court decision.

The Use of Contempt Power to Incarcerate Nondelinquent Youths

While most adjudicated status offenders are not sent to industrial schools or directed to alternative out-of-home placements, it is the case that juvenile court judges wield considerable power to make status offenders comply with routine court directives (Beger 1994). Truants may be ordered by the judge to attend school. Incorrigible youths may be ordered to obey their parents and remain law-abiding. Runaways may be ordered to participate in group counseling. Those youths with alcohol or drug dependencies may be ordered to attend individual counseling and alcohol/drug education sessions on a regular basis. If certain status offenders fail to obey these judicial directives in any way, they are at risk of being cited for **contempt of court.** A contempt-of-court citation is a misdemeanor, and juvenile court judges can use their contempt power to incarcerate any status offenders who do not comply with their orders. This judicial contempt power is unlimited.

Some observers believe that the use of contempt power by juvenile court judges is an abuse of judicial discretion. This is because some juvenile court judges hold juveniles accountable for their actions and consider them like adults in terms of their understanding of the law. Also, contempt power allows judges to circumvent and suspend procedural protections provided under state juvenile court acts. Further, incarcerating status offenders as a punishment for contempt of court is inconsistent with legislative priorities. Thus, citing and incarcerating status offenders for contempt has created a dual system in which judges are free to uphold protective provisions of the act or ignore them in favor of punishment by invoking contempt power (Beger 1994). Therefore, status offenders are not fully insulated from incarceration as a punishment, despite the prevalence of DSO throughout the United States.

Delinquent Offenders and Juvenile Court Dispositions

Assuming that for the majority of jurisdictions juvenile courts have effectively weeded out the bulk of the nonserious, nondelinquent cases, the remainder should theoretically consist of those charged with delinquent offenses or acts that would be criminal if adults committed them. Juvenile courts in the United States processed nearly 1.8 million delinquency cases in 1997 (National Center for Juvenile Justice 2001). This number represents a 48 percent increase over the number of delinquency cases handled in 1988. About 60 percent of all cases processed in 1997 were handled formally, where a petition was filed requesting an adjudicatory hearing. Furthermore, about 60 percent of these formally processed cases resulted in delinquency adjudications. About half of all adjudicated delinquents received probation or some other conditional release. About 30 percent of those adjudicated delinquent were ordered placed in a residential facility, such as a group home or a foster home. Approximately 19 percent of all adjudicated delinquency cases resulted in placement in secure detention facilities, such as industrial schools. The juvenile courts waived jurisdiction and transferred youths to criminal courts in 1 percent of all formally handled cases (National Center for Juvenile Justice 2001).

Between 1972 and 2000, several significant trends have occurred with respect to juveniles who have been arrested or taken into police custody. Table 9.1 shows the percent distribution of juveniles taken into police custody during this time interval, the referrals of juveniles to juvenile court, those cases handled within the department and released, and several other interesting outcomes. In 1972, for instance, 50.8 percent of all juveniles taken into police custody were referred to juvenile courts, whereas 48 percent of these cases were handled within the department and subsequently released. However, during the next twenty-eight years, the percentage of referrals to juvenile court systematically increased so that by 2000, 70.8 percent of all juveniles taken into custody by police were referred to juvenile court. Only 20.3 percent were handled within police departments and released through stationhouse adjustments (Maguire and Pastore 2002).

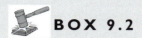

BOX 9.2

PERSONALITY HIGHLIGHT

Rosario Molina
Probation Officer, Webb County Juvenile Department

Statistics:

B.S. (criminal justice), Laredo State University

Background and Experience:

In 1993, after receiving a B.S. degree in criminal justice, I embarked on a rewarding, and may I say, often challenging, career as a juvenile probation officer. During my college years, I never really gave much thought to juvenile justice, choosing to concentrate mainly on a possible career as a federal law enforcement agent. That all changed when, during my senior year, I enrolled in an internship at a local residential drug treatment center for troubled youths. I have to admit that for the first time in my life, I began to understand the tremendous impact that drugs have on our community, families, and children, as well as on our future. I can't say with certainty, or specify at what exact moment I decided that working with children was my calling, but nonetheless, I decided to make it my career.

My first exposure to the juvenile justice system came when I was hired to work as a childcare worker by the Webb County Juvenile Detention Center. My job duties included, but were not limited to, providing security, supervision, and guidance to youth in secure custody. I have to be honest and say the following: There isn't a textbook in the world that can prepare you for dealing one-on-one with children who are detained for crimes ranging from petty offenses to capital murder. This, I would later learn, comes through on-the-job experience. And, as I would also learn, juvenile delinquency is not specific to any racial group, social status, or gender. Despite many of the popular misconceptions about juvenile delinquency, including the belief that it goes hand-in-hand with poverty, the truth is that I have seen children from all walks of life come through our in-

take (booking) area. What I also saw were many disappointed and angry parents. Many were angered at the system for ensnaring their children unjustly, and others were visibly disappointed, as though they were seeing their life's work dissolve before their eyes. And perhaps most disturbing were parents who had given up. Frustrated, disappointed, and without any answers, these parents appeared willing to relinquish their parental responsibilities to the juvenile justice system.

After two years of working as a child-care worker, I decided that I had learned all I could in that specific area and applied for the position of Juvenile Probation Officer. Fortunately for me, there was a vacancy at the time and I was immediately hired. Finally, I could see the whole picture. For the past two years I had seen the end result, but not the different circumstances and incidents that had landed many of the juveniles that I had worked with in the detention facility. I soon discovered that juvenile delinquency is caused by many different variables, many easy to resolve, and others complete impossibilities. Lack of family structure, peer pressure, and a lack of interest in school lead many of these children to a life of delinquency, and in many cases, into a life of crime.

Advice to Students:

My advice to students seeking a career in criminal justice is to pursue your interests to their fullest. Remember, criminal justice is not a very lucrative field, monetarily, that is. Yet, if you're looking for a challenging career where you are constantly growing as an individual and are motivated by serving your community, then you can't go wrong. And you can take that to the bank!

TABLE 9.1

Percent Distribution of Juveniles Taken into Police Custody By Method of Disposition, United States, 1972–2000[a]

	Referred to Juvenile Court Jurisdiction	Handled Within Department and Released	Referred to Criminal or Adult Court	Referred to Other Police Agency	Referred to Welfare Agency
1972	50.8%	45.0%	1.3%	1.6%	1.3%
1973	49.5	45.2	1.5	2.3	1.4
1974	47.0	44.4	3.7	2.4	2.5
1975	52.7	41.6	2.3	1.9	1.4
1976	53.4	39.0	4.4	1.7	1.6
1977	53.2	38.1	3.9	1.8	3.0
1978	55.9	36.6	3.8	1.8	1.9
1979	57.3	34.6	4.8	1.7	1.6
1980	58.1	33.8	4.8	1.7	1.6
1981	58.0	33.8	5.1	1.6	1.5
1982	58.9	32.5	5.4	1.5	1.6
1983	57.5	32.8	4.8	1.7	3.1
1984	60.0	31.5	5.2	1.3	2.0
1985	61.8	30.7	4.4	1.2	1.9
1986	61.7	29.9	5.5	1.1	1.8
1987	62.0	30.3	5.2	1.0	1.4
1988	63.1	29.1	4.7	1.1	1.9
1989	63.9	28.7	4.5	1.2	1.7
1990	64.5	28.3	4.5	1.1	1.6
1991	64.2	28.1	5.0	1.0	1.7
1992	62.5	30.1	4.7	1.1	1.7
1993	67.3	25.6	4.8	0.9	1.5
1994	63.2	29.5	4.7	1.0	1.7
1995	65.7	28.4	3.3	0.9	1.7
1996	68.6	23.3	6.2	0.9	0.9
1997	66.9	24.6	6.6	0.8	1.1
1998	69.2	22.2	6.8	0.9	1.0
1999	69.2	22.5	6.4	1.0	0.8
2000	70.8	20.3	7.0	1.1	0.8

Note: See *Notes*, tables 4.1 and 4.2. These data include all offenses except traffic and neglect cases.
[a]Because of rounding, percents may not add to 100.
Source: U.S. Department of Justice, Federal Bureau of Investigation, *Crime in the United States, 1972*, p. 116; *1973*, p. 119; *1974*, p. 177; *1975*, p. 177; *1976*, p. 220; *1977*, p. 219; *1978*, p. 228; *1979*, p. 230; *1980*, p. 258; *1961*, p. 233; *1982*, p. 242; *1983*, p. 245; *1984*, p. 238; *1985*, p. 240; *1986*, p. 240; *1987*, p. 225; *1988*, p. 229; *1989*, p. 233; *1990*, p. 235; *1991*, p. 278; *1992*, p. 282; *1993*, p. 282; *1994*, p. 282; *1995*, p. 265; *1996*, p. 271; *1997*, p. 279; *1998*, p. 267; *1999*, p. 269; *2000*, p. 273 (Washington, DC: USGPO).

From Table 9.1 it can also be determined that only 1.6 percent of all juveniles taken into police custody in 1972 were referred to criminal or adult court. However, this percentage gradually increased over time so that in 2000, 7 percent of all juvenile arrestees were referred to criminal courts for further action. It is interesting to note that the percentage of cases referred to other police agencies did not change much during the period 1972–2000. The percentage of referrals to other police agencies varied between 1 and 2 percent.

One especially significant disclosure from Table 9.1 is the change in the percentage of referrals to welfare agencies or social service organizations within the community. It is presumed that as the result of DSO, police officers would be more inclined to refer a larger proportion of youths taken into custody to social service agencies or welfare agencies. This outcome would be expected, considering the impact of the Juvenile Justice and Delinquency Prevention Act of 1974 (JJDPA) and its subsequent amendments. Not only was decarceration of status offenders mandated, but divestiture of juvenile court jurisdiction over such offenders was also encouraged. These events would translate into greater use of social service organizations and welfare agencies in the processing of less serious status and delinquent offenders. Indeed, an inspection of Table 9.1 for the years immediately preceding and following the JJDPA in 1974 shows that referrals of juveniles taken into custody by police to welfare agencies increased from 1.3 percent in 1972 to 3 percent in 1977. This percentage peaked in 1983, when 3.1 percent of juvenile referrals were to welfare agencies. However, this figure declined significantly subsequent to 1983 so that by 2000, only .8 percent of all juvenile arrestees were referred to social services in communities (Maguire and Pastore 2002). This trend is perplexing, especially in view of the sizable numbers of status offense cases that juvenile courts continue to process (Beyer, Grisso, and Young 1997). Ideally, at least, there should be more social service agency referrals than fewer referrals across these years. This event has not occurred.

As was indicated earlier, less than 1 percent of all juvenile cases are transferred annually from the jurisdiction of juvenile courts to the jurisdiction of criminal courts. At the end of the 1999 legislative sessions of all states, forty-seven state jurisdictions and the District of Columbia gave juvenile court judges the power to waive their jurisdiction over certain juveniles so that they could be transferred to criminal court. However, in 1999 all states had some type of mechanism in place so that specific juvenile offenders could be treated as adults for the purpose of a prosecution in criminal courts (Griffin 2000, 1).

Transfers, Waivers, and Certifications

What are Transfers?   **Transfers** refer to changing the jurisdiction over certain juvenile offenders to another jurisdiction, usually from juvenile court jurisdiction to criminal court jurisdiction (Massachusetts Statistical Analysis Center 2001). Transfers are also known as waivers, referring to a **waiver** or change of jurisdiction from the authority of juvenile court judges to criminal court judges. Prosecutors or juvenile court judges decide that in some cases, juveniles should be waived or transferred to the jurisdiction of criminal courts. Presumably, those cases that are waived or transferred are the most serious cases, involving violent or serious offenses, such as homicide, aggravated assault, forcible rape, robbery, or drug-dealing activities (Bishop 2000). These jurisdictions conduct **transfer hearings.**

In some jurisdictions, such as Texas and Utah, juveniles are waived or transferred to criminal courts through a process known as **certification** (Arrigona, Hodgson, and Reed 1999). A certification is a formal procedure whereby the state declares the juvenile to be an adult for the purpose of a criminal prosecution in a criminal court (Torbet et al. 2000). The results of certifications are the same as for waivers or transfers. Thus, certifications, waivers, and transfers result in juvenile offenders being subject to the jurisdiction of criminal courts where they can be prosecuted as though they were adult offenders. A 14-year-old murderer, for instance, might be transferred to criminal court for a criminal prosecution on the murder charge. In criminal court, the juvenile, now being treated as though he were an adult, can be convicted of the murder and sentenced to a prison term for one or more years. If the juvenile is charged with capital murder, is 16 or older, and lives in a state where the death penalty is administered to those convicted of capital murder, then he or she can potentially receive the death penalty as the maximum punishment for that offense, provided there is a capital murder conviction (Cothern 2000). Or criminal court judges might impose life-without-parole sentences on these convicted 16- or 17-year-olds. Imposing life-without-parole sentences or the death penalty are *not* within the jurisdiction of juvenile court judges. Their jurisdiction ends when an offender becomes an adult. Thus, a delinquency adjudication on capital murder charges in juvenile court might result in a juvenile being placed in the state industrial school until he is 18 or 21, depending upon whichever is the age of majority or adulthood.

The actual numbers of juveniles waived to the jurisdiction of criminal courts annually has fluctuated between 6,700 in 1988 to 11,700 in 1994. Waivers declined by 1997 to 8,400 juveniles. Overall, between 1988 and 1997, there was a 74 percent increase in the use of waivers by U.S. juvenile courts (Sickmund 2000, 11).

The Rationale for Using Transfers, Waivers, or Certifications. The basic rationale underlying the use of waivers is that the most serious juvenile offenders will be transferred to the jurisdiction of criminal courts where the harshest punishments, including capital punishment, may be imposed as sanctions (Bishop et al. 1996). Since juvenile courts lack the jurisdiction and decision-making power to impose anything harsher than secure confinement dispositions of limited duration in industrial or reform schools, it would seem that the waiver would be an ideal way to impose the most severe punishments on those juveniles who commit the most violent acts (Puzzanchera 2000). A list of reasons for using transfers, waivers or certifications are as follows:

1. To make it possible for harsher punishments to be imposed.
2. To provide just-deserts and proportionately severe punishments on those juveniles who deserve such punishments by their more violent actions.
3. To foster fairness in administering punishments according to one's serious offending.
4. To hold serious or violent offenders more accountable for what they have done.
5. To show other juveniles who contemplate committing serious offenses that the system works and that harsh punishments can be expected if serious offenses are committed.
6. To provide a deterrent to decrease juvenile violence.
7. To overcome the traditional leniency of juvenile courts and provide more realistic sanctions.
8. To make youths realize the seriousness of their offending and induce remorse and **acceptance of responsibility.**

Ideal Offender Characteristics for Justifying Transfers to Criminal Courts.

Those designated for transfer or waiver by various participants in the juvenile justice process should exhibit certain consistent characteristics (Bishop et al. 2001; Puzzanchera 2000). Age, offense seriousness, and prior record (including previous referrals to juvenile court, intake proceedings and dispositions, or juvenile court delinquency adjudications) are some of these characteristics.

Juvenile offenders most in need of processing by criminal courts should be chronic, persistent, and violent offenders. Person offenses, such as rape, murder, robbery, and aggravated assault, should top the list of those who merit transfer from the jurisdiction of juvenile courts to criminal courts for criminal prosecutions (Bishop 2000). Because of the therapeutic environment generated by juvenile courts and their emphasis upon rehabilitation, treatment, and reform, less serious property and drug offenders, a largely nonviolent class, might benefit more from juvenile court processing (Beyer, Grisso, and Young 1997; Griffin, Torbet, and Szymanski 1998). Therefore, we would expect to see almost all transferred cases to criminal court typified by person or violent offenders, clearly the most serious and dangerous juvenile offender class (Maine Legislative Office of Policy and Legal Analysis 2000; Myers 2001).

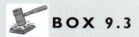

BOX 9.3

JUVENILE CERTIFIED AS AN ADULT IN DRIVE-BY SHOOTING

Holkon Rodriguez Garza, 17

In Laredo, Texas, a teenager was certified as an adult by the juvenile court on charges of murder, felony one, and aggravated assault with a deadly weapon. According to police sources, Jose Ortiz Jr., 16, was shot and killed during a drive-by shooting that occurred on December 14, 2001. The shooting occurred in front of a residence where a party was in progress. Vehicle occupants were described by witnesses who said that the passing Honda drove by and one or more persons opened fire. Ortiz was shot in the head and died instantly. Another person, Bernardo Jimenez, received a gunshot would to one of his legs.

Subsequently, the identity of the shooter became known. Police arrested Holkon Rodriguez Garza, 16, who was a pas-senger in the Honda and who fired the weapon that killed Ortiz. After Garza was certified as an adult, he was transferred to the Webb County Jail where he remained under $50,000 bond. The certification process is complex. However, once it is completed, juveniles are treated as adults for purposes of prosecutions in criminal court. Garza faced the possibility of the death penalty, since he was 16 at the time he allegedly shot Ortiz.

Should 16-year-olds be treated like adults for purposes of criminal prosecutions? What should be the youngest age at which juveniles can be certified as adults and tried in criminal courts? What do you think?

Source: Adapted from the Associated Press, "Teen Certified an Adult in Drive-By Shooting Case." April 18, 2002.

TABLE 9.2

The Characteristics of Waived Cases Changed between 1989 and 1998

	1989	*1994*	*1998*
Total cases waived	8,000	12,100	8,100
Most serious offense			
Person	28%	43%	36%
Property	48	37	40
Drug	16	11	16
Public order	7	8	8
Gender			
Male	95%	95%	93%
Female	5	5	7
Age (years) at time of referral			
Under 16	11%	13%	13%
16 or older	89	87	87
Race/ethnicity			
White	49%	51%	55%
Black	50	45	42
Other	2	4	3
Predisposition detention			
Detained	59%	56%	50%
Not detained	41	44	50

Note: Detail may not equal 100% due to rounding.
Source: Charles M. Puzzanchera (2001), *Delinquency Cases Waived to Criminal Court, 1989–1998.* Washington, DC: U.S. Department of Justice.

Actual Characteristics of Transferred Juveniles. Are the most serious juveniles actually transferred to criminal courts for processing? No. Table 9.2 shows a comparison of the characteristics of waived juvenile cases for the years 1989, 1994, and 1998. First, Table 9.2 shows that the numbers of waived cases fluctuated during these years, from 8,000 in 1989 to 8,100 in 1998. The peak year was 1994 and involved 12,100 transfers. It is clear from the figures in Table 9.2 that person offenses, the most serious offender class, did not represent the bulk of transferred cases. In fact, in 1989, property offenses accounted for 48 percent of all transferred cases, followed by person offenses (28 percent), drug offenses (16 percent), and public order offenses (7 percent) (Puzzanchera 2001, 2).

In 1994, transfers of person or violent juvenile offenders increased to 43 percent, and property offenders represented 37 percent of those transferred. Drugs and public order offenses accounted for the remaining 19 percent. By 1998, however, person offenders represented only 36 percent of all transferred youths. Those juveniles charged with various drug offenses represented 16 percent of all transferred youths. Those charged with public order offenses represented 8 percent of those transferred. Therefore, if we combine the nonviolent categories of property offending, drug offending, and public order offending, they account for 60 percent of all transferred youths in 1998. Clearly, the most violent person offenders are not being targeted for transfer to criminal courts. Juvenile court judges ought to be concerned about these alarming figures (Myers 1999; Torbet et al. 2000).

Figure 9.1 provides us with a graphic portrayal of the profile of transferred youths by offense across the years 1989–1998. These figures reflect the fact that although the number of juveniles alleged to have committed person offenses actually increased during the period 1989–1994, there was a substantial decline of transfers of such juveniles by 1998. It is also noteworthy to recognize the abrupt increase in transfers of juveniles charged with various drug crimes in 1991. This increase in the representation of drug offenders in criminal courts reflects various federal and state initiatives to treat drug offenders more harshly and subject them to greater punishments.

Returning to Table 9.2, there are some other interesting disclosures. Despite earlier references to more extensive and violent female juvenile offending, female juveniles transferred to criminal court increased from 5 percent in 1989 to 7 percent in 1998. It is also significant to note that youths under age 16 are being transferred to a greater degree in 1998 compared with 1989. In 1989, for instance, only 11 percent of those transferred to criminal court were under age 16. In 1998, however, this figure had grown to 13 percent. This is likely reflective of the get-tough movement reaction toward more violent crimes committed by younger youths. Regarding race/ethnicity, the percentage of white youths transferred to criminal courts increased from 49 percent in 1989 to 55 percent in 1998, whereas the percentage of black youths declined from 50 percent to 42 percent during the same time interval (Puzzanchera 2001, 2). The disproportionate representation of blacks transferred to criminal courts has drawn criticism from various observers (Fagan and Zimring 2000; Griffin, Torbet, and Szymanski 1998).

Table 9.3 shows the youngest ages at which juveniles could be transferred or waived to criminal courts in all U.S. jurisdictions in 1997 (Torbet and Szymanski 1998).

In 1997, eighteen states and all federal districts indicated no specified age for transferring juveniles to criminal courts for processing. Two states, Vermont and Wisconsin, specified age 10 as the minimum age at which a juvenile could be waived. Colorado, Missouri, Montana, and Oregon established age 12 as the

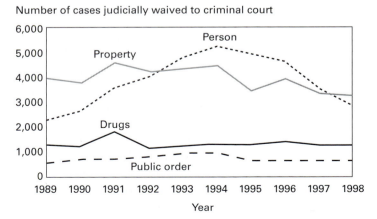

From 1993 to 1997, more person offense than property offense cases were judicially waived

FIGURE 9.1 Number of Cases Judicially Waived to Criminal Court, by Type of Offense

Source: Charles M. Puzzanchera (2001). *Delinquency Cases Waived to Criminal Court, 1989–1998.* Washington, DC: U.S. Department of Justice. p. 1.

TABLE 9.3

Minimum Age for Transferring Juveniles to Adult Court

Minimum Age	States
None	Arizona, Florida, Georgia, Indiana, Maine, Maryland, Nebraska, Nevada, New Hampshire, Oklahoma, Pennsylvania, Rhode Island, South Carolina, South Dakota, Tennessee, Washington, West Virginia
10	Vermont, Wisconsin
12	Colorado, Missouri, Montana, Oregon
13	Illinois, Mississippi, New York, North Carolina, Wyoming
14	Alabama, Arkansas, California, Connecticut, Iowa, Kansas, Kentucky, Louisiana, Massachusetts, Michigan, Minnesota, New Jersey, New Mexico, North Dakota, Ohio, Texas, Utah, Virginia
15	District of Columbia
16	Hawaii

earliest age for a juvenile waiver. Eighteen states used age 14 as the youngest transfer age, while the District of Columbia set the minimum transfer age at 15, and one state, Hawaii, used the minimum transfer age of 16. Thus, since 1987 a majority of states reduced substantially the age at which juveniles could be tried as adults in criminal courts.

Some idea of the aggressiveness of state governments and public policies directed toward getting tough toward violent juvenile offending is provided by Table 9.4. Table 9.4 shows the various states that have modified or enacted changes in their transfer provisions for juveniles during the 1996–1997 period.

Inspecting Table 9.4, we can see that under judicial waiver modifications, four states lowered the age limit at which juveniles can be transferred to criminal court. One example of a significant age modification is Missouri, where the minimum age for juvenile transfers was lowered from 14 to 12 for any felony. In the case of Texas, the minimum transfer age was lowered from 15 to 10. Virginia lowered the transfer age from 15 to 14. Table 9.4 also shows that other modifications were made to get tough toward juvenile offenders. Ten states added crimes to the list of those qualifying youths for transfer to criminal courts. In six states, the age of criminal accountability was lowered, while twenty-four states authorized additional crimes to be included that would automatically direct that the criminal court would have jurisdiction rather than the juvenile court.

Waiver Decision Making

Organizational and political factors are at work to influence the upward trend in the use of transfers. Politicians wish to present a get-tough facade to the public by citing waiver statistics and showing their increased use is the political response to the rise in serious youth crime. Despite political rhetoric, there has been an increase in the use of waivers. Between 1989 and 1993, for instance,

TABLE 9.4

States Modifying or Enacting Transfer Provisions, 1996–1997

Type of Transfer Provision	Action Taken (Number of States)	States Making Changes	Examples
Discretionary Waiver	Added crimes (7 states)	DE, KY, LA, MT, NV, RI, WA	Kentucky: 1996 provision permits the juvenile court to transfer a juvenile to criminal court if 14 years old and charged with a felony with a firearm.
	Lowered age limit (4 states)	CO, DE, HI, VA	Hawaii: 1997 provision adds language that allows waiver of a minor at any age (previously 16) if charged with first- or second-degree murder (or attempts) and there is no evidence that the person is committable to an institution for the mentally defective or mentally ill.
	Added or modified prior record provisions (4 states)	FL, HI, IN, KY	Florida: 1997 legislation requires that if the juvenile is 14 at the time of a fourth felony, and certain conditions apply, the State's attorney must ask the court to transfer him or her and certify the child as an adult or must provide written reasons for not making such a request.
Presumptive Waiver	Enacted provisions (2 states)	KS, UT	Kansas: 1996 legislation shifts the burden of proof to the child to rebut the presumption that the child is an adult.
Direct File	Enacted or modified (8 states)	AR, AZ, CO, FL, GA, MA, MT, OK	Colorado: 1996 legislation adds vehicular homicide, vehicular assault, and felonious arson to direct file statute.
Statutory Exclusion	Enacted provision (2 states)	AZ, MA	Arizona: 1997 legislation establishes exclusion for 15- to 17-year-olds charged with certain violent felonies.
	Added crimes (12 states)	AL, AK, DE, GA, IL, IN, OK, OR, SC, SD, UT, WA	Georgia: 1997 legislation adds crime of battery if victim is a teacher or other school personnel to list of designated felonies.
	Lowered age limit (1 state)	DE	Delaware: 1996 legislation lowers from 16 to 15 the age for which the offense of possession of a firearm during the commission of a felony is automatically prosecuted in criminal court.
	Added lesser-included offense (1 state)	IN	Indiana: 1997 legislation lists exclusion offenses, including any offense that may be joined with the listed offenses.

Source: Patricia Torbet and Linda Szymanski, *State Legislative Responses to Violent Juvenile Crime: 1996–1997 Update.* Washington, DC: U.S. Department of Justice, 1998:5.

BOX 9.4

The Case of Samuel Sheinbein, 19

It happened in Aspen Hill, Maryland, on September 16, 1997. Samuel Sheinbein, 17, choked to death 19-year-old Alfred Tello Jr. with a rope and hit him several times with a sharp object. Sheinbein then dismembered Tello's body with an electric saw and burned it. Another boy believed to be involved in the murder and mutilation, Aaron Needle, was arrested and subsequently killed himself while being held in detention. Sheinbein fled to Israel shortly thereafter, escaping prosecution for the Maryland murder. Sheinbein picked Israel because that was the birthplace of his father. Sheinbein also believed that he could successfully avoid prosecution for murder in Maryland by fighting extradition back to the United States. When Maryland authorities learned that Sheinbein had fled to Israel, they immediately sought to extradite him. But Israeli authorities refused to release him to U.S. authorities. Subsequently, a plea bargain was worked out where Sheinbein would be tried as a juvenile in Israel and sentenced to the maximum sentence under Israeli law. In this case, Sheinbein received a 24-year term for his role in the murder of Alfred Tello. This is the toughest sentence ever imposed on a juvenile by an Israeli court. But Sheinbein is eligible for 24-hour furloughs within four years. He is also eligible for parole after serving 16 years of the 24-year sentence. The right against double jeopardy does not apply to convictions outside of the United States. Thus, it is entirely possible that some time in the future, Sheinbein may in fact be tried in Maryland for murder. Sheinbein successfully sought refuge in Israel under a law that prevented the extradition of Israeli citizens to foreign courts. Israel's refusal to release Sheinbein to the United States prompted several Congressmen to threaten to cut off foreign aid to Israel. Sheinbein's mother thought her son's sentence was "unfair." "It couldn't have happened to a better kid," she said as her son was led away. Victoria Sheinbein defended her son despite the inculpatory evidence and his own confession.

If Sheinbein ever returns to the United States, should he be prosecuted for the murder-mutilation? What punishment should the Israeli court have imposed for the brutal murder? Do you think Sheinbein was given an appropriate sentence in view of what others receive for murder convictions in the United States? What do you think?

Source: Adapted from the Associated Press, "Judge Sentences Maryland Teen-Ager to 24 Years for Murder." October 25, 1999.

the use of transfers increased by 41 percent (Bilchik 1996, 13). A majority of those transferred were charged with felonies (Ruddell, Mays, and Giever 1998).

As will be seen in the following section, there are several types of waivers that can be used to negotiate transfers of jurisdiction from juvenile to criminal courts. One of these is the automatic transfer or automatic waiver, which several jurisdictions currently employ. This means that if youthful offenders are within a particular age range, such as ages 16 or 17, and if they are charged with specific types of offenses (usually murder, robbery, rape, aggravated assault, and other violent crimes), they will be transferred automatically to criminal courts. These types of waivers, also known as legislative waivers because they were mandated by legislative bodies in various states and carry the weight of statutory authority, involve no discretionary action among prosecutors or judges (Bilchik 1996). For other types of waivers, the decision-making process is largely discretionary (Torbet and Szymanski 1998).

Because of the discretionary nature of the waiver process, large numbers of the wrong types of juveniles are transferred to criminal courts. The wrong types of juveniles are wrong because they are not those originally targeted by juvenile justice professionals and reformers to be the primary candidates for transfers. The primary targets of waivers are intended to be the most serious, violent, and dangerous juveniles who also the most likely to deserve more serious sanctions that criminal courts can impose. But there is a serious credibility gap between the types of juveniles who are actually transferred each year and those who should be transferred. In 1994, for instance, we have already seen that nearly half (45 percent) of all youths transferred to criminal court were charged with property or public order offenses. These types of offenses include theft, burglary, petty larceny, and disturbing the peace. Only 44 percent of those transferred in 1994 were charged with person offenses or violent crimes. If transfers, waivers, or certifications were applied as they should be applied, 100 percent of those transferred annually would be serious, violent offenders. Juvenile courts would handle all of the other cases.

Why Do Property and Public Order Offenders Get Transferred to Criminal Court?   An interested public wants to know why juvenile courts would send property offenders or public order offenders to criminal courts for processing. After all, these are the least serious offenders compared with those committing aggravated assault, attempted murder, homicide, forcible rape, and armed robbery. Studies of juvenile court judges disclose that often, persistent nonserious offenders are transferred from juvenile courts because juvenile court judges are tired of seeing these same offenders in their courts. They believe that if such persistent offenders are sent to criminal courts, this will be a better deterrent to their future offending (Champion and Mays 1991). What these judges do not understand is that criminal court prosecutors and judges often tend to downplay the significance of these small-time offenders. At least half of these nonserious property offenders will have their cases dismissed, diverted, or down-

Michael Carneal, 14, was tried as an adult for shooting to death several students at a Paducah, Kentucky high school in January, 1998.

graded (Jensen and Metsger 1994). Another 40 percent will enter plea bargains and receive probation from criminal court judges. Most criminal court judges do not want to put 14-year-old property offenders or public order offenders in adult prisons, where chronic overcrowding and the potential for sexual exploitation are pervasive. Thus, only about 10 percent of those nonserious offenders who are transferred annually will be placed in confinement for a term of months or years. About 90 percent will return to their neighborhoods and continue to reoffend (Champion and Mays 1991).

A list of some of the factors cited by juvenile court judges that result in the transfer of nonserious property, public order, or drug offenders to criminal court are:

1. Although property offenders aren't especially serious or violent, their persistence in offending causes juvenile court judges to tire of their frequent appearances; transfers of these offenders to criminal court will "teach them a lesson."

2. Some jurisdictions mandate transfers to criminal court of those offenders who exceed some previously determined maximum of juvenile court adjudications; these may include property or public order offenders.

3. Individual differences among juvenile court judges will dictate which juveniles are transferred, despite the seriousness of their offense; if the judge doesn't like a particular youth's attitude, the youth will be transferred.

4. Any kind of drug offense should be dealt with by criminal courts; thus, a simple "possession of a controlled substance" charge (e.g., prescription medicine) may be sufficient to qualify a juvenile for a criminal court transfer.

5. What is a serious or violent offense in one juvenile court jurisdiction may not be considered serious or violent in another jurisdiction; thus, different standards are applied to the same types of juveniles in different jurisdictions.

In 1997 there was a continuing pattern of transferring mostly property, public order, and drug offenders to criminal courts, despite major changes in state and federal transfer policies. Thus far, it is questionable whether waivers have functioned as effective deterrents to future juvenile offending. For example, a study of waived youths in Idaho between 1976 and 1986 found that numerous youths were transferred to criminal courts for processing. These youths ranged in age from 14 to 18. Once processed, a majority of these youths continued to reoffend in later years. This was attributed to prosecutorial leniency, whereby more serious offenses charged against juveniles were downgraded to less serious ones before being concluded with diversion or probation (Jensen and Metsger 1994). Also cited were the facts that juveniles don't always know that when they commit certain acts, they will be transferred to criminal court; one's youthfulness also often functions as a mitigating factor, causing charge reductions or dismissals.

In some jurisdictions where gang presence is strong, local task forces have targeted gangs for harsher treatment, including the greater likelihood of being transferred to criminal court. A study of thirty-eight state jurisdictions disclosed, however, that most prosecutors had no specific plans relating to dealing with gang members when they were transferred to criminal courts. Further, specialized gang prosecution units were rare (5 percent), even though it was believed that tougher juvenile laws would help combat the gang problem (Knox, Martin, and Tromanhauser 1995). Most jurisdictions continue to experiment with various strategies that will target the most serious offenders for criminal prosecutions (Macallair and Courtney 1995).

TYPES OF WAIVERS

There are four types of waiver actions. These include (1) judicial waivers, (2) direct file, (3) statutory exclusion, and (4) demand waivers.

Judicial Waivers

The largest numbers of waivers from juvenile to criminal court annually come about as the result of direct judicial action. **Judicial waivers** give the juvenile court judge the authority to decide whether to waive jurisdiction and transfer the case to criminal court (Myers 2001). There are three kinds of judicial waivers: (1) discretionary, (2) mandatory, and (3) presumptive.

Discretionary waivers. **Discretionary waivers** empower the judge to waive jurisdiction over the juvenile and transfer the case to criminal court. Because of this type of waiver, judicial waivers are sometimes known as discretionary waivers. This is because the judge may or may not decide to waive particular youths to criminal courts for processing (Robinson 1991).

Mandatory waivers. In the case of a **mandatory waiver,** the juvenile court judge *must* waive jurisdiction over the juvenile to criminal court if probable cause exists that the juvenile committed the alleged offense.

Presumptive waivers. Under the **presumptive waiver** scenario, judges still decide to transfer youths to criminal courts. However, the burden of proof concerning a transfer decision is shifted from the state to the juvenile. It requires that certain juveniles shall be waived to criminal court unless they can prove that they are suited for juvenile rehabilitation. In this respect, at least, they are similar to mandatory waivers. Defense counsels who wish to keep their juvenile clients within the jurisdiction of the juvenile court have a relatively difficult time arguing that their clients deserve a juvenile court adjudicatory hearing instead of prosecution in criminal court.

Table 9.5 shows the minimum ages for judicial waivers among the states and the District of Columbia for 1997. Judicial waivers are often criticized because of their subjectivity. Two different youths charged with identical offenses may appear at different times before the same judge. On the basis of impressions formed about the youths, the judge may decide to transfer one youth to criminal court and adjudicate the other youth in juvenile court. Obviously, the intrusion of extralegal factors into this important action generates a degree of unfairness and inequality. A youth's appearance and attitude emerge as significant factors that will either make or break the offender in the eyes of the judge. These socioeconomic and behavioral criteria often overshadow the seriousness or pettiness of offenses alleged. In the context of this particular type of transfer,

TABLE 9.5

Minimum Ages for Judicial Waivers, by Offense Category, 1997

Judicial Waiver Offense and Minimum Age Criteria, 1997

States	Minimum Age for Judicial Waiver	Any Criminal Offense	Certain Felonies	Capital Crimes	Murder	Certain Person Offenses	Certain Property Offenses	Certain Drug Offenses	Certain Weapon Offenses
Alabama	14*	14							
Alaska	NS*	NS				NS			
Arizona	NS		NS						
Arkansas	14		14	14	14	14			14
California	14	16	16		14	14	14	14	
Colorado	12	12			12	12			
Connecticut	14		14	14	14				
Delaware	NS	NS	15[a]		NS	NS	16[b]	16[b]	
District of Columbia	NS	15	15		15	15	15		NS
Florida	14	14							
Georgia	13	15		13	14[c]	14[c]	15[b]		
Hawaii	NS		14		NS	NS			
Idaho	NS	14	NS		NS	NS	NS	NS	
Illinois	13	13	15						
Indiana	NS	14	NS[b]		10			16	
Iowa	14	14	15						
Kansas	10	10	14			14		14	
Kentucky	14		14	14					
Louisiana	14				14	14			
Maine	NS		NS		NS				
Maryland	NS	15		NS					
Michigan	14	14							
Minnesota	14		14						
Mississippi	13	13							
Missouri	12	12							
Montana	NS	NS							
Nevada	14	14	14			14			
New Hampshire	13		15		13	13		15	
New Jersey	14	14[b]			14	14	14	14	14
North Carolina	13		13	13					
North Dakota	14	16	14[b]		14	14		14	
Ohio	14		14		14	14	16		
Oklahoma	NS		NS						
Oregon	NS		15		NS	NS	15		
Pennsylvania	14		14		15	15			
Rhode Island	NS		16	NS	17	17			
South Carolina	NS	16	14		NS	NS		14	14
South Dakota	NS		NS						
Tennessee	NS	16			NS	NS			
Texas	14		14	14				14	
Utah	14		14			16	16		16
Vermont	10				10	10	10		
Virginia	14		14		14	14			
Washington	NS	NS							
West Virginia	NS		NS		NS	NS	NS	NS	
Wisconsin	14	15	14		14	14	14	14	
Wyoming	13	13							

Examples: Alabama allows waiver for any delinquency (criminal) offense involving a juvenile age 14 or older. Arizona allows waiver for any juvenile charged with a felony. New Jersey allows waiver for juveniles age 14 or older who are charged with murder or certain person, property, drug, or weapon offenses. In New Jersey, juveniles age 14 or older who have prior adjudications or convictions for certain offenses can be waived regardless of the current offense.

Note: Ages in minimum age column may not apply to all offense restrictions but represent the youngest possible age at which a juvenile may be judicially waived to criminal court.

*"NS" indicates that in at least one of the offense restrictions indicated, no minimum age is specified.

[a]Only if committed while escaping from specified juvenile facilities.

[b]Requires prior adjudication(s) or conviction(s), which may be required to have been for the same or a more serious offense type.

[c]Only if committed while in custody.

Source: Adapted from Snyder, H., and Sickmund, M. 1999. *Juvenile Offenders and Victims: 1999 National Report.* Washington, DC: U.S. Department of Justice. Office of Justice Programs, Office of Juvenile Justice and Delinquency Prevention.

it is easy to see how some persistent, nonviolent offenders may suffer waiver to criminal court. This is an easy way for the judge to get rid of them.

Although judges have this discretionary power in most jurisdictions, youths are still entitled to a hearing where they can protest the waiver action (Myers 1999). While it is true that the criminal court poses risks to juveniles in terms of potentially harsher penalties, it is also true that being tried as an adult entitles youths to all of the adult constitutional safeguards, including the right to a trial by jury. In a later section of this chapter, we will examine closely this and other options that may be of benefit to certain juveniles. Thus, some juveniles may not want to fight waiver or transfer actions, largely because they may be treated more leniently by criminal courts.

Direct File

Whenever offenders are screened at intake and referred to the juvenile court for possible prosecution, prosecutors in various jurisdictions will conduct further screenings of these youths. They determine which cases merit further action and formal adjudication by judges. Not all cases sent to prosecutors by intake officers automatically result in subsequent formal juvenile court action. Prosecutors may decline to prosecute certain cases, particularly if there are problems with witnesses who are either missing or who refuse to testify, if there are evidentiary issues, or if there are overloaded juvenile court dockets. A relatively small proportion of cases may warrant waivers to criminal courts (Feld 2001). Table 9.6 shows the states that had direct file or concurrent jurisdiction provisions in 1997.

Under **direct file,** the prosecutor has the sole authority to decide whether any given juvenile case will be heard in criminal court or juvenile court. Essentially, the prosecutor decides which court should have jurisdiction over the juvenile. Prosecutors with direct file power are said to have **concurrent jurisdiction.** This is another name for direct file. In Florida, for example, prosecutors have concurrent jurisdiction. They may file extremely serious charges (e.g., murder, rape, aggravated assault, robbery) against youths in criminal courts and present cases to grand juries for indictment action. Or prosecutors may decide to file the same cases in the juvenile court (Griffin, Torbet, and Szymanski 1998).

Statutory Exclusion

Statutory exclusion means that certain juvenile offenders are automatically excluded from the juvenile court's original jurisdiction (Ziedenberg et al. 2001). Legislatures of various states declare a particular list of offenses to be excluded from the jurisdiction of juvenile courts. Added to this list of excluded offenses is a particular age range. Thus, in Illinois, if a 16-year-old juvenile is charged with murder, rape, or aggravated assault, this particular juvenile is automatically excluded from the jurisdiction of the juvenile court. Instead, the case will be heard in criminal court (DeFrances and Strom 1997). In 1997, twenty-eight states had statutory exclusion provisions and excluded certain types of offenders from juvenile court jurisdiction (Snyder, Sickmund, and Poe-Yamagata 2000). Table 9.7 shows the states that use statutory exclusion, by minimum age and offense for 1997.

TABLE 9.6

States with Concurrent Jurisdiction and Direct File Provisions, by Offense, 1997.

Concurrent Jurisdiction Offense and Minimum Age Criteria, 1997

States	Minimum Age for Concurrent Jurisdiction	Any Criminal Offense	Certain Felonies	Capital Crimes	Murder	Certain Offenses			
						Person Offenses	Property Offenses	Drug Offenses	Weapon Offenses
Arizona	14		14						
Arkansas	14		14	14	14	14			14
Colorado	14		14		14	14	14		14
District of Columbia	16				16	16	16		
Florida	NS*	16[a]	16	NS[b]	14	14	14		14
Georgia	NS			NS					
Louisiana	15				15	15	15	15	
Massachusetts	14		14			14			14
Michigan	14		14		14	14	14	14	
Montana	12				12	12	16	16	16
Nebraska	NS	16[c]	NS						
Oklahoma	15				15	15	15	16	16
Vermont	16	16							
Virginia	14				14	14			
Wyoming	14	17	14						

Examples: In Arizona, prosecutors have discretion to file directly in criminal court those cases involving juveniles age 14 or older charged with certain felonies (defined in State statutes). In Florida, prosecutors may "direct file" cases involving juveniles age 16 or older charged with a misdemeanor (if they have a prior adjudication) or a felony offense and those age 14 or older charged with murder or certain person, property, or weapon offenses; no minimum age is specified for cases in which a grand jury indicts a juvenile for a capital offense.

Note: Ages in minimum age column may not apply to all offense restrictions but represent the youngest possible age at which a juvenile's case may be filed directly in criminal court.

*"NS" indicates that in at least one of the offense restrictions indicated, no minimum age is specified.

[a]Applies to misdemeanors and requires prior adjudication(s), which may be required to have been for the same or a more serious offense type.

[b]Requires grand jury indictment.

[c]Applies to misdemeanors.

Source: Adapted from Snyder, H., and Sickmund, M. 1999. *Juvenile Offenders and Victims: 1999 National Report.* Washington, DC: U.S. Department of Justice, Office of Justice Programs, Office of Juvenile Justice and Delinquency Prevention.

Because state legislatures created statutory exclusion provisions, this waiver action is sometimes known as a **legislative waiver** (Myers 2001). And because these provisions mandate the automatic waiver of juveniles to criminal court, they are also known as automatic waivers.

Demand Waivers

Under certain conditions and in selected jurisdictions, juveniles may submit motions for **demand waiver** actions. Demand waiver actions are requests or motions filed by juveniles and their attorneys to have their cases transferred from

TABLE 9.7

States with Statutory Exclusion by Offense and Minimum Age, 1997

Statutory Exclusion Offense and Minimum Age Criteria, 1997

| States | Minimum Age for Concurrent Jurisdiction | Any Criminal Offense | Certain Felonies | Capital Crimes | Murder | Certain Offenses | | | |
						Person Offenses	Property Offenses	Drug Offenses	Weapon Offenses
Alabama	16		16	16				16	
Alaska	16					16	16		
Arizona	15		15ᵃ		15	15			
Delaware	15		15						
Florida	NS*	NSᵃ				NS			
Georgia	13				13	13			
Idaho	14				14	14	14	14	
Illinois	13		15ᵇ		13	15		15	15
Indiana	16		16		16	16		16	16
Iowa	16		16					16	16
Louisiana	15				15	15			
Maryland	14			14	16	16			16
Massachusetts	14				14				
Minnesota	16				16				
Mississippi	13		13	13					
Montana	17				17	17	17	17	17
Nevada	NS	NSᵃ			NS	16ᵃ			
New Mexico	15				15ᶜ				
New York	13				13	14	14		
Oklahoma	13				13				
Oregon	15				15	15			
Pennsylvania	NS				NS	15			
South Carolina	16		16						
South Dakota	16		16						
Utah	16		16ᵈ		16				
Vermont	14				14	14	14		
Washington	16				16	16	16		
Wisconsin	NS				10	NSᵉ			

Examples: In Delaware, juveniles age 15 or older charged with certain felonies must be tried in criminal court. In Arizona, juveniles age 15 or older must be tried in criminal court if they are charged with murder or certain person offenses or if they have prior felony adjudications and are charged with a felony.

Note: Ages in minimum age column may not apply to all offense restrictions but represent the youngest possible age at which a juvenile's case may be excluded from juvenile court.

*"NS" indicates that in at least one of the offense restrictions indicated, no minimum age is specified.

ᵃRequires prior adjudication(s), or conviction(s), which may be required to have been for the same or a more serious offense type.

ᵇOnly escape or bail violation while subject to prosecution in criminal court.

ᶜRequires grand jury indictment.

ᵈRequires prior commitment in a secure facility.

ᵉOnly if charged while confined or on probation or parole.

Source: Adapted from Snyder, H., and Sickmund, M. 1999. *Juvenile Offenders and Victims: 1999 National Report.* Washington, DC: U.S. Department of Justice, Office of Justice Programs, Office of Juvenile Justice and Delinquency Prevention.

juvenile courts to criminal courts (Teitelbaum et al. 1980). Why would juveniles want to have their cases transferred to criminal courts?

One reason is that most U.S. jurisdictions do not provide jury trials for juveniles in juvenile courts as a matter of right (*McKeiver v. Pennsylvania* 1971). However, about a fifth of the states have established provisions for jury trials for juveniles at their request and depending upon the nature of the charges against them. In the remainder of the states, jury trials for juveniles are granted only at the discretion of the juvenile court judge. Most juvenile court judges are not inclined to grant jury trials to juveniles. Thus, if juveniles are (1) in a jurisdiction where they are not entitled to a jury trial even if they request one from the juvenile court judge, (2) face serious charges, and (3) believe that their cases would receive greater impartiality from a jury in a criminal courtroom, they may seek a demand waiver in order to have their cases transferred to criminal court. Florida permits demand waivers as one of several waiver options (Bilchik 1996, 3).

Other Types of Waivers

Reverse Waivers   A **reverse waiver** is an action by the criminal court to transfer direct file or statutory exclusion cases from criminal court back to juvenile court, usually at the recommendation of the prosecutor (Bilchik 1996, 4). Typically, juveniles who would be involved in these reverse waiver hearings would be those who were automatically sent to criminal court because of statutory exclusion. Thus, criminal court judges can send at least some of these juveniles back to the jurisdiction of the juvenile court. Reverse waiver actions may also be instigated by defense counsels on behalf of their clients.

Once an Adult/Always an Adult. The **once an adult/always an adult provision** is perhaps the most serious and long-lasting for affected juvenile offenders. This provision means that once juveniles have been convicted in criminal court, they are forever after considered adults for the purpose of criminal prosecutions. For instance, suppose a 12-year-old is transferred to criminal court in Vermont and subsequently convicted of a crime. Subsequently, at age 15, if the same juvenile commits another crime, such as vehicular theft, he would be subject to prosecution in criminal court. Thus, the fact of a criminal court conviction means that the juvenile permanently loses his or her access to the juvenile court. In 1997, thirty-one states had once an adult/always an adult provisions (Snyder and Sickmund 1999).

Interestingly, the once an adult/always an adult provision is not as ominous as it appears. It requires that particular jurisdictions keep track of each juvenile offender previously convicted of a crime. This record-keeping is not particularly sophisticated in different jurisdictions. Some juveniles may simply move away from the jurisdiction where they were originally convicted. Fourteen-year-old juveniles who are convicted of a crime in California may move to North Dakota or Vermont, where they may be treated as first offenders in those juvenile courts. How are North Dakota and Vermont juvenile courts supposed to know that a particular 14-year-old has a criminal conviction in California? Information sharing among juvenile courts throughout the United States is very limited or nonexistent. Thus, the intent of the once an adult/always an adult provision can often be defeated simply by relocating and moving to another jurisdiction. This is true also of juvenile court jurisdictions within the same state. In California, for instance, a state with the once an adult/always an adult provision, if a juvenile has been transferred to a criminal court for prosecution in Long Beach, California, and moves to Bellflower, Carson, Paramount, or Pomona, other California cities, it is very likely that the juvenile courts in those cities will be unaware of the fact that the juvenile was treated as an adult for purposes of a criminal prosecution in Long Beach. Such is the state of the art regarding juvenile record information-sharing among California juvenile courts.

The fact is that most states have a combination of various transfer or waiver provisions. Table 9.8 shows all states according to the types of transfer provisions they have enacted as of 1997.

The most popular type of waiver action is the judicial waiver, where forty-six states and the District of Columbia had judicial waiver provisions in 1997 (Snyder and Sickmund 1999). Over half of all states (28) had statutory exclusion provisions in 1997. Reverse waivers, which result from automatic or legislative waivers, were used in twenty-three states in 1997. Also, thirty-one states enacted the once an adult/always an adult provision. Fifteen states had concurrent jurisdiction or direct file provisions.

WAIVER AND REVERSE WAIVER HEARINGS

Waiver Hearings

All juveniles who are waived to criminal court for processing are entitled to a hearing on the waiver if they request one (Massachusetts Statistical Analysis Center 2001). A **waiver hearing** is a formal proceeding designed to determine whether the waiver action taken by the judge or prosecutor is the correct action and that the juvenile should be transferred to criminal court. Waiver hearings are normally conducted before the juvenile court judge. Waiver hearings are initiated through a **waiver motion,** where the prosecutor usually requests the judge to send the case to criminal court. These hearings are to some extent evidentiary, since a case must be made for why criminal courts should have jurisdiction in any specific instance. Usually, juveniles with lengthy prior records, several previous referrals, and/or one or more previous adjudications as delinquent are more susceptible to being transferred. While the offenses alleged are most often crimes, it is not always the case that the crimes are the most serious ones. Depending upon the jurisdiction, the seriousness of crimes associated with transferred cases varies. As has been shown by previous research, large numbers of cases involving property crimes are transferred to criminal courts for processing. In some instances, chronic, persistent, or habitual status offenders have been transferred, particularly if they have violated specific court orders to attend school, participate in therapeutic programs, perform community service work, make restitution, or engage in some other constructive enterprise.

If waivers are to be fully effective, then only those most serious offenders should be targeted for transfer. Transferring less serious and petty offenders accomplishes little in the way of enhanced punishments for these offenders. Criminal courts often regard transfers of such cases as nuisances, and it is not uncommon to see the widespread use of probation or diversion here. Criminal court prosecutors may **_nolle prosequi_** many of these cases before they reach the trial stage. In a significant number of other cases, plea bargaining agreements are concluded that result in substantially more lenient penalties (Jensen and Metsger 1994).

TABLE 9.8

Juvenile Transfer Provisions for All States, 1997

State	Judicial Waiver			Concurrent Jurisdiction	Statutory Exclusion	Reverse Waiver	Once an Adult Always an Adult
	Discretionary	Presumptive	Mandatory				
Total Number of States	46	15	14	15	28	23	31
Alabama	•				•		•
Alaska	•		•		•		
Arizona	•		•	•	•	•	•
Arkansas	•			•		•	
California	•	•					
Colorado	•					•	
Connecticut				•		•	
Delaware	•			•	•	•	•
District of Columbia	•	•			•		•
Florida	•			•	•		•
Georgia	•		•	•	•	•	
Hawaii	•						•
Idaho	•				•		•
Illinois	•	•		•	•		•
Indiana	•		•		•		•
Iowa	•				•	•	•
Kansas	•	•			•		•
Kentucky	•			•		•	
Louisiana	•			•	•		
Maine	•				•		
Maryland	•				•	•	
Massachusetts				•	•		
Michigan	•			•			•
Minnesota	•	•			•		•
Mississippi	•				•		•
Missouri	•				•		•
Montana	•			•	•		
Nebraska				•		•	
Nevada	•	•			•	•	•
New Hampshire	•	•					•
New Jersey	•	•					
New Mexico					•		
New York					•	•	
North Carolina	•			•			
North Dakota	•		•	•			•
Ohio	•						•
Oklahoma	•			•	•	•	•
Oregon	•				•	•	•
Pennsylvania	•	•			•	•	•
Rhode Island	•	•		•			•
South Carolina	•		•	•	•		
South Dakota	•				•		•
Tennessee	•					•	•
Texas	•						•
Utah	•	•			•		•
Vermont	•			•		•	
Virginia	•		•	•	•	•	•
Washington	•				•		•
West Virginia	•		•				
Wisconsin	•				•	•	•
Wyoming	•			•			

Note: In States with a combination of transfer mechanisms, the exclusion, mandatory waiver, or concurrent jurisdiction provisions generally target the oldest juveniles and/or those charged with the most serious offenses, while those charged with relatively less serious offenses and/or younger juveniles may be eligible for discretionary waiver.

Source: Adapted from Snyder, H., and Sickmund, M. 1999. *Juvenile Offenders and Victims: 1999 National Report.* Washington, DC: U.S. Department of Justice, Office of Justice Programs, Office of Juvenile Justice and Delinquency Prevention.

Reverse Waiver Hearings

In those jurisdictions with direct file or statutory exclusion provisions, juveniles and their attorneys may contest these waiver actions through **reverse waiver hearings** or **reverse waiver actions.** Reverse waiver hearings are conducted before criminal court judges to determine whether to send the juvenile's case back to juvenile court (Virginia Commission on Youth 1993). For both waiver and reverse waiver hearings, defense counsel and the prosecution attempt to make a case for their desired action. In many respects, these hearings are similar to preliminary hearings or preliminary examinations conducted within the criminal justice framework. Some evidence and testimony are permitted, and arguments for both sides are heard. Once all arguments have been presented and each side has had a chance to rebut the opponents' arguments, the judge decides the matter.

Time Standards Governing Waiver Decisions

Although only less than 1 percent of all juveniles processed by the juvenile justice system annually are transferred to criminal courts for processing as adults, only eight states had time limits governing transfer provisions for juveniles as of 1993 (Butts 1996b, 559). These states included Arizona, Indiana, Iowa, Maryland, Massachusetts, Michigan, Minnesota, New Mexico, and Virginia. Table 9.9 shows the time limits that govern juvenile court handling of delinquency cases considered for transfer to criminal court.

We can see from Table 9.9 that for Maryland, as an example, a 30-day maximum time limit exists between one's detention and the transfer hearing. If the transfer hearing results in a denial of the transfer, then there is a 30-day maximum between the denial of the transfer and the juvenile court adjudication. In contrast, Minnesota provides only a 1-day maximum between placing youths in adult jails and filing transfer motions by juvenile court prosecutors. New Mexico's provisions are similar to those of Maryland.

IMPLICATIONS OF WAIVER HEARINGS FOR JUVENILES

Those juveniles who contest or fight their transfers to criminal courts or attempt to obtain a reverse waiver wish to remain within the juvenile justice system, be treated as juveniles, and be adjudicated by juvenile court judges. But not all juveniles who are the subject of transfer are eager to contest the transfer. There are several important implications for youths, depending upon the nature of their offenses, their prior records, and the potential penalties the respective courts may impose. Under the right circumstances, having one's case transferred to criminal court may offer juvenile defendants considerable advantages not normally enjoyed if their cases were to remain in the juvenile court. In the following discussion, some of the major advantages of disadvantages of being transferred will be examined.

TABLE 9.9

Time Limits on Juvenile Court Handling of Delinquency Cases Considered for Transfer to Criminal Court[a]

State	Limits
Arizona	• 30-day maximum between motion for transfer and transfer hearing • 30-day maximum between denial of transfer and juvenile court adjudication
Indiana	• 20-day maximum between case referral and transfer hearing if youth is detained (otherwise, 60 days maximum)
Iowa	• 40-day maximum between case referral and transfer hearing
Maryland	• 30-day maximum between time of detention and transfer hearing • 30-day maximum between denial of transfer and juvenile court adjudication
Massachusetts	• 30-day maximum between case referral and part A of transfer hearing • 45-day maximum between parts A and B of transfer hearing • 21-day maximum between denial of transfer and juvenile court adjudication if youth is detained (otherwise, 30 days maximum)
Michigan	• 28-day maximum between case referral and phase 1 of transfer hearing • 35-day maximum between case referral and phase 2 of transfer hearing • 28-day maximum between phases 1 and 2 of transfer hearing • 28-day maximum between denial of transfer and juvenile court adjudication if detained
Minnesota	• 1-day maximum between placement of youth in adult jail and filing of transfer motion
New Mexico	• 30-day maximum between motion of transfer and transfer hearing if youth is detained (otherwise, 90 days) • 30-day maximum between denial of transfer and juvenile court adjudication if youth is detained (otherwise, 90 days)
Virginia	• 21-day maximum between time of detention and *either* transfer hearing or adjudication • 30-day maximum between denial of transfer and juvenile court disposition if detained

[a]Forty-two states (and the District of Columbia) did not have time limits for transfer cases as of 1993.
Source: Butts, 1996b: 559–560. Data source: Analysis by the National Center for Juvenile Justice. Reprinted with the permission of the American Journal of Criminal Law and the authors.

Positive Benefits Resulting from Juvenile Court Adjudications

Among the positive benefits of having one's case heard in juvenile court are that

1. Juvenile court proceedings are civil, not criminal; thus, juveniles do not acquire criminal records.

2. Juveniles are less likely to receive sentences of incarceration.

3. Compared with criminal court judges, juvenile court judges have considerably more discretion in influencing a youth's life chances prior to or at the time of adjudication.

4. Juvenile courts are traditionally more lenient than criminal courts.

5. There is considerably more public sympathy extended to those who are processed in the juvenile justice system, despite the general public advocacy for a greater get-tough policy.

6. Compared with criminal courts, juvenile courts do not have as elaborate an information-exchange apparatus to determine whether certain juveniles have been adjudicated delinquent by juvenile courts in other jurisdictions.

7. Life imprisonment and the death penalty lie beyond the jurisdiction of juvenile judges, and they cannot impose these harsh sentences.

First, since juvenile courts are civil bodies, records of juvenile adjudications are suppressed, expunged, or otherwise deleted when these adjudicated juveniles reach adulthood (Clarke 1994). Also, juvenile court judges often act compassionately by sentencing youthful offenders to probation, issuing verbal warnings or reprimands, or imposing nonincarcerative, nonfine alternatives as sanctions.

A fourth advantage is that juvenile courts are traditionally noted for their lenient treatment of juveniles. This seems to be more a function of the influence of priorities in dealing with juvenile offenders rather than some immovable policy that might impose standard punishments of incarceration as penalties. For example, a national conference of juvenile justice researchers in New Orleans, Louisiana recommended that juvenile courts should emphasize three general goals in their adjudication decisions: (1) protection of the community, (2) imposing accountability, and (3) helping juveniles and equipping them to live productively and responsibly in the community (Maloney, Romig, and Armstrong 1988). This balanced approach is largely constructive in that it heavily emphasizes those skills that lead to the rehabilitation of youthful offenders. And in the minds of many citizens, rehabilitation is equated with leniency. Increasingly used, however, are residential placement facilities in various jurisdictions, where the rate of recidivism among juveniles is relatively low compared with those offenders with more extensive histories of delinquent conduct.

A fifth advantage of juvenile court processing is that sympathy for youths who commit offenses is easier to extend in sentencing. Many juveniles get into trouble because of sociocultural circumstances. Individualized treatment may be necessary, perhaps administered through appropriate community-based facilities, in order to promote greater respect for the law as well as to provide needed services (Coalition for Juvenile Justice 1994). Mandatory diversion policies have received some public support in various jurisdictions, especially where less serious youthful offenders are involved and they are charged with nonviolent, petty crimes (Poulos and Orchowsky 1994). Many of these juveniles may not require intensive supervised probation or incarceration, but rather, they require responsible supervision to guide them toward and assist them in various services and treatment-oriented agencies.

Juvenile courts do not ordinarily exchange information with most other juvenile courts in a massive national communication network. Local control over youthful offenders accomplishes only this limited objective—local control. Thus, juveniles might migrate to other jurisdictions and offend repeatedly, where getting caught in those alternative jurisdictions would not be treated as recidivism in the original jurisdiction. This is beneficial for juveniles who might seek to commit numerous offenses in a broad range of contiguous jurisdictions. The probability that their acts in one jurisdiction would come to the attention of juvenile officials in their own jurisdiction is often remote.

Furthermore, juveniles in certain jurisdictions may reappear before the same juvenile court judge frequently. Multiple adjudications for serious offenses do not mean automatically that these youths will be placed in juvenile detention or transferred to criminal court (Butts et al. 1996). Even those who reappear before the same juvenile court judge may be adjudicated repeatedly without significant effect. In one investigation, it was found that a sample of serious juvenile offenders had been adjudicated in the same jurisdiction an average of ten times (Snyder, Sickmund, and Poe-Yamagata 1996). Thus, juvenile court judges may give juveniles the "benefit of the doubt" and impose nondetention alternatives. Nondetention alternatives as sentences are influenced significantly by the degree of overcrowding in secure juvenile facilities. Thus, leniency displayed by juvenile court judges may really be due to necessity rather than because of some personal belief that incarceration should be avoided.

Finally, it is beyond the jurisdiction of juvenile court judges to impose life imprisonment and/or the death penalty, despite the potential for jury trials in some juvenile court jurisdictions (Bilchik 1996). Thus, if offenders come before a juvenile court judge for processing and have committed especially aggravated violent or capital offenses, the juvenile court judge's options are limited. Incarceration in a juvenile facility, possibly for a prolonged period, is the most powerful sanction available to these judges. However, if waiver actions are successful, the road is paved for the possible application of such punishments in criminal courts.

Unfavorable Implications of Juvenile Court Adjudications

Juvenile courts are not perfect, however, and they may be disadvantageous to youthful many offenders. Some of their major limitations are that

1. Juvenile court judges have the power to administer lengthy sentences of incarceration, not only for serious and dangerous offenders, but for status offenders as well.
2. In most states, juvenile courts are not required to provide juveniles with a trial by jury.
3. Because of their wide discretion in handling juveniles, judges may underpenalize a large number of those appearing before them on various charges.
4. Juveniles do not enjoy the same range of constitutional rights as adults in criminal courts.

Adverse to juveniles, juvenile court judges may impose short- or long-term secure confinement on offenders, regardless of the nonseriousness or pettiness of their offenses. The case of *In re Gault* (1967) makes it abundantly clear that juvenile court judges can impose lengthy custodial dispositions for youths adjudicated delinquent for relative minor offending. For committing the same offense, an adult would have been fined $50 and may have served up to 30 days in a local jail. As we learned in Gault's case, the disposition to an industrial school for nearly six years was excessive, and there were constitutional irregularities. This unusual incarcerative sentence was subsequently overturned by the U.S. Supreme Court on several important constitutional grounds. However, juvenile court judges continue to have broad discretionary powers and may impose similar sentences, provided that the constitutional guarantees assured by the *Gault* decision are present in any subsequent case.

The case of *Gault* is not an isolated instance of disposing of youths who have committed petty offenses with long periods of secure confinement. For instance, in Hennepin County, Minnesota, 330 transfer motions between 1986 and 1992 were studied by Podkopacz and Feld (1996). These researchers found that when juveniles were transferred to criminal courts for various crimes, those charged with violent offenses tended to serve longer prison terms than the periods of incarceration imposed on juveniles who committed the same types of offenses, but who had their cases adjudicated in juvenile courts. However, juvenile court judges typically imposed *longer* incarcerative sentences on property offenders compared with how criminal courts sentenced convicted juvenile property offenders who had been transferred to criminal court jurisdiction. Thus, these researchers question existing juvenile court policies about the nature and types of dispositions imposed on adjudicated juvenile offenders. Presently, there is great diversity among juvenile court judges in different states about the nature and types of dispositions they impose on juveniles adjudicated for similar offenses.

Another disadvantage of juvenile courts is that granting any juvenile a jury trial is mostly the discretion of prosecutors and juvenile court judges. If the judge approves, the juvenile may receive a jury trial in selected jurisdictions, if a jury trial is requested. This practice typifies juvenile courts in thirty-eight states. In the remaining states, juveniles may request and receive trials under certain circumstances. In other words, the state legislatures of at least twelve states have made it possible for juveniles to receive jury trials upon request, although the circumstances for such jury trial requests parallel closely the jury trial requests of defendants in criminal courts. Again, we must consider the civil–criminal distinction that adheres respectively to juvenile and criminal court proceedings. Jury trials in juvenile courts retain the civil connotation, without juveniles' acquiring criminal records. However, jury trials in adult criminal courts, upon the defendant's conviction, result in the offender's acquisition of a criminal record.

A third limitation of juvenile proceedings is that the wide discretion enjoyed by most juvenile court judges is often abused (Virginia Commission on Youth 1994a). This abuse is largely in the form of excessive leniency, and it doesn't occur exclusively at the adjudicatory stage of juvenile processing. Because of this leniency and wide discretionary power, many juvenile courts have drawn criticisms from both the public and juvenile justice professionals. A common criticism is that juvenile courts neglect the accountability issue through the excessive use of probation or diversion (Bilchik 1996).

Another criticism of these courts is that juveniles do not enjoy the full range of constitutional rights that apply to adults in criminal courts (Snyder, Sickmund, and Poe-Yamagata 2000). In many jurisdictions, transcripts of proceedings are not made or retained for juveniles where serious charges are alleged, unless special arrangements are made beforehand. Thus, when juveniles in these jurisdictions appeal their adjudications to higher courts, they may or may not have the written record to rely upon when lodging appeals with appellate courts.

DEFENSE AND PROSECUTORIAL CONSIDERATIONS RELATING TO WAIVERS

Juvenile Trial Options: Interstate Variations

Juveniles are only infrequently given a jury trial if their cases are adjudicated by juvenile courts. Table 9.10 shows the interstate variation in jury trials for juveniles in juvenile courts in 1997. In nearly 80 percent of all state juvenile courts, jury trials for juveniles are denied. There is a great deal of variation among jurisdictions relating to trying and disposing of juvenile offenders (Klug 2001).

Implications of Criminal Court Processing

When juveniles are waived to criminal court, then the full range of constitutional guarantees for adults also attaches for them (DeFrances and Strom 1997). We have already examined the advantages of permitting or petitioning the juvenile court to retain jurisdiction in certain cases. An absence of a criminal record, limited punishments, extensive leniency, and a greater variety of discre-

---

TABLE 9.10

Interstate Variation in Jury Trials for Juveniles, 1997

Provision	States
Jury trial granted upon request by juvenile	Alaska, California, Kansas, Massachusetts, Michigan, Minnesota, New Mexico, Oklahoma, Texas, West Virginia, Wisconsin, Wyoming
Juvenile denied right to trial by jury	Alabama, Florida, Georgia, Hawaii, Indiana, Iowa, Louisiana, Maine, Maryland, Mississippi, Nebraska, Nevada, New Jersey, North Carolina, North Dakota, Ohio, Oregon, Pennsylvania, South Carolina, Tennessee, Utah, Vermont, Washington
No mention	Alaska, Arizona, California, Connecticut, Colorado, Idaho, Illinois, Missouri, New Hampshire, New Mexico, New York, Virginia
By court order	South Dakota

Source: Patricia Torbet and Linda Szymanski, *State Legislative Responses to Violent Juvenile Crime: 1996–1997 Update.* Washington, DC: U.S. Department of Justice, 1998.

tionary options on the part of juvenile court judges make juvenile courts an attractive adjudicatory medium, if the juvenile has a choice. Of course, even if the crimes alleged are serious, leniency may assume the form of a dismissal of charges, charge reductions, warnings, and other nonadjudicatory penalties.

The primary implications for juveniles of being processed through the criminal justice system are several, and they are quite important. First, depending upon the seriousness of the offenses alleged, a jury trial may be a matter of right. Second, periods of lengthy incarceration in minimum, medium, and maximum security facilities with adults becomes a real possibility (Merlo, Benekos, and Cook 1997). Third, criminal courts in a majority of state jurisdictions may impose the death penalty in capital cases. A sensitive subject with most citizens is whether juveniles should receive the death penalty if convicted of capital crimes. In recent years, the U.S. Supreme Court has addressed this issue specifically and ruled that in those states where the death penalty is imposed, the death penalty may be imposed as a punishment on any juvenile who was age 16 or older at the time the capital offense was committed (*Stanford v. Kentucky* 1989; *Wilkins v. Missouri* 1989).

Jury Trials as a Matter of Right for Serious Offenses

A primary benefit of a transfer to criminal court is the absolute right to a jury trial (Fritsch and Hemmens 1995). This is conditional, however, and depends upon the minimum incarcerative period associated with one or more criminal charges filed against defendants. In only twelve state jurisdictions, juveniles have a jury trial right granted through legislative action (Torbet and Szymanski 1998). However, when juveniles reach criminal courts, certain constitutional provisions apply to them as well as to adults. First, anyone charged with a crime where the possible sentence is six months' incarceration or more, with exceptions, is entitled to a jury trial if one is requested (*Baldwin v. New York* 1970). Therefore, jury trials are not discretionary matters for judges to decide. Any defendant who may be subject to more than six months' incarceration in a jail or prison as the prescribed statutory punishment associated with the criminal offenses alleged may request and receive a jury trial from any U.S. judge, in either state or federal courts.

Juveniles who are charged with particularly serious crimes, and where several aggravating circumstances are apparent, stand a good chance of receiving favorable treatment from juries. Aggravating circumstances include a victim's death or the infliction of serious bodily injuries, committing an offense while on bail for another offense or on probation or parole, use of extreme cruelty in the commission of the crime, use of a dangerous weapon in the commission of a crime, a prior record, and leadership in the commission of offenses alleged. However, mitigating circumstances, those factors that tend to lessen the severity of sentencing, include duress or extreme provocation, mental incapacitation, motivation to provide necessities, youthfulness or old age, and no previous criminal record.

Among the several aggravating and mitigating circumstances listed above, having a prior record or being a first offender becomes an important consideration. Youths who are transferred to criminal courts sometimes do not have previous criminal records. This doesn't mean that they haven't committed earlier crimes, but rather, that their records are **juvenile court records.** Juveniles may

 **BOX 9.5**

Teens Torture and Murder Other Teen

It happened in Atlanta, Georgia. Seventeen-year-old Krystal Archer was with her boyfriend and three other youths, including another female. They were Timothy Cole, 21 and Christopher Teal, 19, of Covington, and Danielle Hubbard, 18, of Athens. One night in October 1999, the four were in the woods outside of Atlanta. An argument erupted between Krystal and Danielle involving the respective boyfriends. Archer thought that Hubbard was "eyeing her boyfriend." A fight broke out between the two girls. Eventually, the two males became involved and the fighting intensified. Then things got ugly. Krystal Archer was forced to strip and commit various sex acts, some acts performed on her own body. The other three youths hit her with rocks and sticks. Then three times they threw her down into a ravine that contained about 2 feet of water. They tied her to a small tree. She begged them to leave her alone. Then one of them walked up and set her hair on fire. She passed out. They left her tied to the tree, bleeding and unconscious. They returned

the next day and found her alive but unconscious. They beat her again with sticks and rocks and piled brush on top of her so that she wouldn't be found. When they returned to the site the third day, they found her still alive. They tried to hit her on the head with large rocks to "finish her off." On the fourth day, they returned again and found that Krystal had crawled about 15 yards and propped herself up against a tree. This time they had a butcher knife and stabbed her five or six times in the chest and neck. Then they slit her throat and she died. Expressing no remorse, the three attackers confessed to police who investigated when Krystal's boyfriend, Timothy Cole, led police to her body. The three were charged with felony murder and aggravated assault.

What should be the punishment for such a heinous crime? What would cause teenagers to attack another teen in such a brutal fashion? Should this be a first-degree murder charge instead of felony murder? What do you think?

Source: Adapted from the Associated Press, "Male Suspect Admits to Killing Teen-Ager After Four Days of Torture." September 3, 1999.

have **sustained petitions,** where the facts alleged against them have been determined to be true by the juvenile court judge. However, this adjudication hearing is a civil proceeding. As such, technically, these youths do not bring prior criminal records into the criminal courtroom. This is a favorable factor for juveniles to consider when deciding whether to challenge transfers or have their automatic waivers reversed. However, changes in state laws regarding the confidentiality of juvenile court records have been made so that greater access to such records is available to others and for longer periods beyond one's adulthood (Bilchik 1996). Increasingly, one's juvenile past may affect one's criminal court trial outcome and sentencing.

Another important factor relative to having access to a jury trial is that prosecutors often try to avoid them, opting for a simple plea bargain agreement instead. Plea bargaining or plea negotiating is a preconviction bargain between the state and the defendant where the defendant enters a guilty plea in exchange for leniency in the form of reduced charges or less harsh treatment at the time of sentencing. It is well known that plea bargaining in the United States accounts for approximately 90 percent of all criminal convictions. But plea bargaining also involves an admission of guilt without benefit of a trial. For this reason, plea bargaining is often criticized.

Jury trials are costly and the results of jury deliberations are unpredictable. If prosecutors can obtain guilty pleas from transferred juveniles, they assist the state and themselves, both in terms of the costs of prosecution and avoidance of jury whims in youthful offender cases. Also, plea bargaining in transferred juvenile cases often results in convictions on lesser charges, specifically charges that would not have prompted the transfer or waiver from juvenile courts initially. However, this is a bit ironic, since it suggests that the criminal justice system is inadvertently sabotaging the primary purpose of juvenile transfers through plea bargaining arrangements that are otherwise commonplace for adult criminals. Furthermore, when prosecutors decide to file charges, sufficient evidence should exist to increase the chances of a successful prosecution.

Also, the charges alleged should be serious ones. But many transferred juveniles are not necessarily the most serious youthful offenders, and the standard of evidence in juvenile courts is sometimes not as rigorous as it is in criminal courts. Thus, many transferred juvenile cases fail from the outset and are dismissed by the prosecutors themselves, often because of inadequate or poor evidence.

Closely associated with prosecutorial reluctance to prosecute many of these transferred juveniles is the fact that a majority of those transferred are charged with property crimes (Bilchik 1996). While these cases may stand out from other cases coming before juvenile court judges, prosecutors and criminal court judges might regard them as insignificant. Thus, juveniles enter the adult system from juvenile courts, where their offenses set them apart from most other juvenile offenders. But alongside adults in criminal courts, they become one of many property offenders who face criminal processing. Their youthful age works in their behalf to improve the chances of having their cases dismissed or of being acquitted by juries. Most prosecutors wish to reserve jury trials for only the most serious offenders. Therefore, their general inclination is to treat youthful property offenders with greater leniency, unless they elect to *nolle prosequi* outright.

The Potential for Capital Punishment

The most important implication for juveniles transferred to criminal courts is the potential imposition of the **death penalty** upon their conviction for a capital crime. About two-thirds of the states use **capital punishment** for prescribed offenses that are especially aggravated. For youths who are age 16 or older at the time they committed a capital offense and who live in a state that has the death penalty, they are in jeopardy of being sentenced to death (*Stanford v. Kentucky* 1989; *Wilkins v. Missouri* 1989).

An alternative to the death penalty applied to juveniles is the life-without-parole option. In 1999, forty states had **life-without-parole** provisions for capital murder statutes, including aggravated homicide as well as for habitual or career offenders (Snell 2001). Thus, it is possible for youths to be sentenced to life without the possibility of parole if they are convicted of a capital offense in a state with or without the death penalty (Moon et al. 2000). In these instances, juveniles take their chances in criminal courts, often not knowing what outcome can be expected.

BLENDED SENTENCING STATUTES

In recent years, many states have legislatively redefined the juvenile court's purpose and role by diminishing the role of rehabilitation and heightening the importance of public safety, punishment, and accountability in the juvenile justice system (Feld 1995). One of the most dramatic changes in the dispositional/sentencing options available to juvenile court judges is **blended sentencing.** Blended-sentencing statutes represent a dramatic change in dispositional/sentencing options available to judges. Blended sentencing refers to the imposition of juvenile and/or adult correctional sanctions on serious and violent juvenile offenders who have been adjudicated in juvenile court or convicted in criminal court (Torbet and Szymanski 1998, 6). Blended sentencing options are usually based upon age or upon a combination of age and offense (Bilchik 1996, 11).

There are five blended sentencing models. Figure 9.3 shows these five models. These include (1) juvenile-exclusive blend, (2) juvenile-inclusive blend, (3) juvenile-contiguous blend, (4) criminal-exclusive blend, and (5) criminal-inclusive blend.

The Juvenile-Exclusive Blend

The **juvenile-exclusive blend** involves a disposition by the juvenile court judge that is either a disposition to the juvenile correctional system or to the adult correctional system, but not both. Thus, a judge might order a juvenile adjudicated delinquent for aggravated assault to serve 3 years in a juvenile industrial school, or the judge may order the adjudicated delinquent to serve 3 years in a prison for adults. The judge cannot impose *both* types of punishment under this model, however. In 1996, only one state, New Mexico, provided such a sentencing option for its juvenile court judges.

The Juvenile-Inclusive Blend

The **juvenile-inclusive blend** involves a disposition by the juvenile court judge that is both a juvenile correctional sanction and an adult correctional sanction. In cases such as this, suppose the judge had adjudicated a 15-year-old juvenile delinquent on a charge of vehicular theft. The judge might impose a disposition of 2 years in a juvenile industrial school or reform school. Further, the judge might impose a sentence of 3 additional years in an adult penitentiary. However, the second sentence to the adult prison would typically be suspended, unless the juvenile violated one or more conditions of his or her original disposition and any conditions accompanying the disposition. Usually, this suspension period would run until the youth reaches age 18 or 21. If the offender were to commit a new offense or violate one or more program conditions, he or she would immediately be placed in the adult prison to serve the second sentence originally imposed.

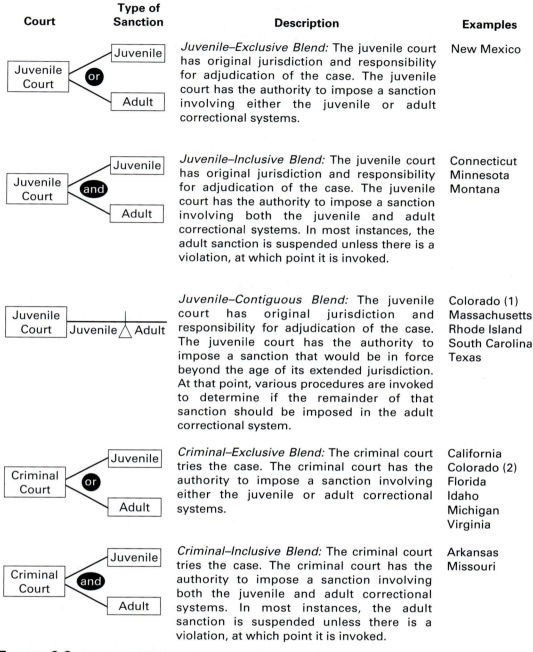

FIGURE 9.2 "Models of 'Blended Sentencing' Statutes" (Bilchik, 1996:13)

The Juvenile-Contiguous Blend

The **juvenile-contiguous blend** involves a disposition by a juvenile court judge that may extend beyond the jurisdictional age limit of the offender. When the age limit of the juvenile court jurisdiction is reached, various procedures may be invoked to transfer the case to the jurisdiction of adult corrections. States with this juvenile-contiguous blend include Colorado, Massachusetts, Rhode Island, South Carolina, and Texas. In 1987 the Texas legislature enacted a determinate sentencing law that is an example of the juvenile-contiguous blended sentencing model, whereby for certain offenses the juvenile court may impose a sentence that may remain in effect beyond its extended jurisdiction (Torbet and Szymanski 1998, 7). In Texas, for example, a 15-year-old youth who has been adjudicated delinquent on a murder charge can be given a determinate sentence of from 1 to 30 years. At the time of the disposition in juvenile court, the youth is sent to the Texas Youth Commission and incarcerated in one of its facilities (similar to reform or industrial schools). By the time the youth reaches age 17½, the juvenile court must conduct a hearing to determine whether the youth should be sent to the Texas Department of Corrections to serve some or all of the remaining sentence. At this hearing, the youth may present evidence in his or her favor to show why he or she has become rehabilitated and no longer should be confined. However, evidence of institutional misconduct may be presented by the prosecutor to show why the youth should be incarcerated for more years in a Texas prison. This hearing functions as an incentive for the youth to behave and try to improve his or her behavior while confined in the juvenile facility. Some persons believe that this particular sentencing blend is the most effective at punishing serious and violent offenders while providing them with a final chance to access certain provided Texas rehabilitative programs (Dawson 1995).

On February 16, 1997, a 12-year-old Austin, Texas, girl was convicted and sentenced by a juvenile court judge to 25 years imprisonment. She had beaten a 2½-year-old toddler, Jayla Belton, to death in her grandmother's unlicensed day care center. In May 1996, she had been found guilty of the toddler's murder and given a 40-year sentence. Her first conviction was thrown out, however, since the court found that she was not adequately defended. In her first conviction when she was 11, the girl could have been released by age 16 or transferred to an adult prison, where she would serve out the remaining years of her original sentence. Prosecutors said that the girl kicked and beat Jayla Belton because she was angry about being left to babysit the toddler. The child died of a ruptured liver. In the sentencing scheme used by the judge, the girl's case would be reviewed before she became an adult. If her conduct while confined as a juvenile is poor, then there is a good likelihood that the results of a hearing will result in the girl being transferred to the Texas Department of Corrections to serve more time for her crime as an adult (Associated Press 1997, A2).

In 1995 the Texas legislature expanded the number of offenses that qualify for the most severe sentences, and it added an additional crime in 1997. The Texas legislature also established a seven-level system of progressive sanctions to be used by juvenile court judges, with determinate sentences acquiring the status of the most severe tier (Torbet and Szymanski 1998, 7). In October 1997, the Texas Criminal Justice Policy Council issued a report that profiled the offenders disposed by juvenile courts under the determinate sentencing procedure. Between 1990 and 1996, the number of juveniles committed to the Texas Youth Commission with determinate sentences more than quadrupled from 48 to 207, representing 8 percent of all commitments compared with 2 percent in 1990 (Torbet and Szymanski 1998, 7).

The Criminal-Exclusive Blend

The **criminal-exclusive blend** involves a decision by a criminal court judge to impose either a juvenile court sanction or a criminal court sanction, but not both. For example, a criminal court judge may hear the case of a 15-year-old youth who has been transferred to criminal court on a rape charge. The youth is convicted in a jury trial in criminal court. At this point, the judge has two options: The judge can sentence the offender to a prison term in an adult correctional facility, or the judge can impose an incarcerative sentence for the youth to serve in a juvenile facility. The judge may believe that the 15-year-old would be better off in a juvenile industrial school rather than an adult prison. The judge may impose a sentence of adult incarceration, but he or she may be inclined to place the youth in a facility where there are other youths in the offender's age range.

The Criminal-Inclusive Blend

The **criminal-inclusive blend** involves a decision by the criminal court judge to impose both a juvenile penalty and a criminal sentence simultaneously. Again, as in the juvenile-inclusive blend model, the latter criminal sentence may be suspended depending upon the good conduct of the juvenile during the juvenile punishment phase. For example, suppose a 13-year-old boy has been convicted of attempted murder. The boy participated in a drive-by shooting and is a gang member. The criminal court judge sentences the youth to a term of 5 years in a juvenile facility, such as an industrial school. At the same time, the judge imposes a sentence of 20 years on the youth to be spent in an adult correctional facility, following the 5-year sentence in the juvenile facility. However, the adult portion of the sentence may be suspended, depending upon whether the juvenile behaves or misbehaves during his 5-year industrial school incarceration. There is an additional twist to this blend. If the juvenile violates one or more conditions of his confinement in the juvenile facility, the judge has the power to revoke that sentence and invoke the sentence of incarceration in an adult facility. Thus, a powerful incentive is provided for the youth to show evidence that rehabilitation has occurred. It is to the youth's advantage to behave well while confined, since a more ominous sentence of confinement with adult offenders may be imposed at any time. Further, with good behavior, the youth can be free of the system following the period of juvenile confinement; the adult portion of the sentence is suspended if the youth deserves such leniency. One state that has the revocation power and ability to place youths in adult correctional facilities is Arkansas, although this power is rarely used by criminal court judges (Bilchik 1996, 14).

Blended sentencing statutes are intended to provide both juvenile and criminal court judges with a greater range of dispositional and/or sentencing options. In the 1980s and earlier, juvenile courts were notoriously lenient on juvenile offenders. Dispositions of juvenile court judges were mostly nominal or conditional, which usually meant verbal warnings and/or probation. While probation continues to be the sanction of choice in a majority of juvenile courts following delinquency adjudications, many states have armed their juvenile and criminal court judges with greater sanctioning powers. Thus, it is now possible in states such as Colorado, Arkansas, Missouri for juvenile court judges to impose sanctions that extend well beyond their original jurisdictional authority. Juvenile court judges in New Mexico, for instance, can place certain juveniles in either adult or juvenile correctional facilities. Criminal court judges in Florida, Idaho, Michigan, and Missouri can place those convicted of crimes in either juvenile or adult correctional facilities, depending upon the jurisdiction. These are broader and more powerful dispositional and sentencing options to hold youthful offenders more accountable for the serious offenses they commit.

Jury Trials as a Matter of Right in All Juvenile Court Blended Sentencing Proceedings

When juveniles are tried as adults in criminal court, they are entitled to the full range of constitutional rights extended to criminal defendants, including the right to a jury trial. This same provision exists whenever juveniles are tried in juvenile courts and where the juvenile is subject to the application of blended sentencing statutes. All states with either the juvenile-inclusive blend, the juvenile-exclusive blend, or the juvenile-contiguous blend must grant juvenile defendants the right to a jury trial in juvenile court upon request.

If the jury verdict is "guilty," then the juvenile court judge has the right under one of these blended sentencing statutes, depending upon the state jurisdiction, to impose both a juvenile penalty and a criminal penalty, or either a juvenile penalty or a criminal penalty but not both. Thus, juvenile court judges may exercise considerable discretion relating to dispositions and sentencing. If the juvenile court judge is in a state where both juvenile and criminal penalties may be imposed, such as Michigan, he or she may impose both types of penalties on a convicted juvenile or he or she may impose the juvenile penalty but not the criminal penalty. This aspect of blended sentencing is totally discretionary with the judge.

One of the positive aspects of blended sentencing statutes is that the use of transfers or waivers and subsequent waiver hearings are rendered obsolete. By statute, juveniles in one state or another with blended sentencing statutes are either in juvenile or criminal court where the court can exercise one or both types of juvenile and adult sanctions.

Surprisingly, some judges have resisted applying blended sentencing statutes in their jurisdictions, even when they have been authorized to use them. In Michigan, for instance, one juvenile court judge chided the Michigan legislature for passing a blended sentencing statute. When sentencing a juvenile offender who had been convicted of a heinous, premeditated murder, the judge sentenced the juvenile only to the juvenile punishment and did not impose the criminal punishment. He took it upon himself to chastise the Michigan legislature for its abuse of authority in changing the sentencing laws governing youthful offenders.

It is unfortunate that some judges have chosen to view these blended sentencing statutes as somehow incongruous with how juvenile sanctions ought to be imposed. They have overlooked a very important fact that applies to virtually all of these statutes. If a criminal penalty is imposed together with a juvenile penalty, the criminal penalty may be set aside at a later date, provided that the juvenile shows evidence of rehabilitation while confined as a juvenile in an institution.

Suppose a 12-year-old is convicted of murder in Michigan through a jury trial in juvenile court. Suppose the judge were to impose both a juvenile penalty, such as confinement in a secure juvenile facility until the juvenile reaches the age of his or her majority or 21. Further suppose that in addition to this penalty, the judge imposes a sentence of 30 years to life on the juvenile, such sentence to commence upon completion of the juvenile punishment and institutionalization. Provisions are in place in all jurisdictions for a mandatory review of one's juvenile record prior to the age of their majority. Usually, a hearing is set for six months prior to a juvenile's reaching adulthood. The hearing is for the purpose of determining whether the adult portion of the punishment should be imposed. This hearing provides a committee with a unique opportunity to review a youth's prior institutional conduct and determine whether the adult sentence should be set aside. If the juvenile's conduct has been favorable, then it is compelling for the committee to set aside the original adult sentence. The juvenile will be free of the system once he or she becomes an adult. However, suppose that the juvenile has behaved poorly while confined in a juvenile facility. He or she has repeatedly fought with others, been disruptive, and has been resistant to any rehabilitative efforts to improve his or her educational level or receive useful counseling, therapy, or vocational/educational training. For cases such as these, the committee reviewing the juvenile's prior institutional record may be inclined to allow the adult portion of the penalty to resume when the juvenile reaches adulthood. The juvenile will commence a 30-years-to-life sentence upon reaching the age of his or her majority.

The primary positive implication for juveniles sentenced under such blended sentencing statutes is that it provides them with a strong incentive to behave well and to participate in needed counseling, training, or other activities that will improve their skills and psychological and social development. If they know that poor behavior will jeopardize their chances of being released upon reaching adulthood, then they will be motivated to behave in a law-abiding and productive fashion for the period of their confinement in the juvenile facility. The juvenile court judge who fails to recognize the motivational value of these blended sentencing statutes seriously undermines a significant juvenile justice reform.

Judicial resistance to change regarding juvenile sentencing was not anticipated, although Bilchik (1996) has written about his observations and the reactions of both juvenile court and criminal court personnel in those jurisdictions where blended sentencing statutes have been implemented. Bilchik says that there are a number of considerations with respect to the shift toward offense-based sentencing patterns for serious and violent juvenile offenders. Because many of the sentencing options for serious and violent juvenile offenders in juvenile court put the juvenile at risk of an adult sentence or allow that such adjudications will be used in future prosecutions, the right to counsel is a critical concern and has been successfully used to challenge the use of juvenile adjudications in criminal court.

Blended sentencing options demonstrate the ambivalence of what to do about serious and violent juvenile offenders. The creation of middle ground disposition/sentencing and correctional options demonstrates a lack of resolve on two fronts: (1) coming to closure on (i.e., removing) certain juveniles for whom the juvenile justice system is inadequate, or (2) bolstering the resolve and resources of the juvenile justice system to adequately address the needs of these very difficult young offenders. Blended sentencing also creates confusing options for all system actors, including offenders, judges, prosecutors, and corrections administrators. Contact with juvenile and criminal justice personnel across the country revealed that confusion exists about these statutes and the rules and regulations governing them, especially with respect to the juvenile's status during case processing and subsequent placement. This has repercussions on the definition of a juvenile with regard to compliance with the Juvenile Justice and Delinquency Prevention Act mandates (Bilchik 1996, 15). Perhaps in time, the good stemming from the application of these blended sentencing statutes by growing numbers of states will outweigh the negative perceptions of it by various system actors (Torbet et al. 2000).

SUMMARY

Public perceptions of juvenile violence and its supposed increase throughout most U.S. jurisdictions have caused the get-tough movement to permeate the juvenile justice system. Several types of waivers or transfers are used, depending upon the jurisdiction. The most popular waiver, the judicial waiver, is a decision made unilaterally by a juvenile judge that a specific juvenile's case will be heard in criminal court rather than in juvenile court. Several types of judicial waivers include discretionary, mandatory, and presumptive. Prosecutorial waivers are also used, whereby prosecutors may move to transfer certain juveniles from their courts to criminal courts. In many jurisdictions, legislative provisions exist for the automatic transfer of particularly serious cases to criminal court jurisdiction. Illinois and New York are among several states having such automatic transfer provisions, also known as statutory exclusion. Offenses subject to these automatic transfers include, but are not limited to, murder, rape, and robbery. Also, those transferred under such automatic transfer statutes must be either 16 or 17 years of age.

Other options are once an adult/always an adult, meaning that once a juvenile has been tried in criminal court as an adult, that person will forever remain an adult in that jurisdiction for purposes of subsequent criminal prosecutions. Juveniles also have the option to demand being waived to criminal court through exercising a demand waiver motion. Juvenile court judges may grant motions by juveniles and their attorneys to have the juvenile tried in criminal court as an adult. There are advantages and disadvantages associated with these various options. Another type of waiver is direct file, where prosecutors file charges against juvenile offenders in criminal courts rather than in juvenile courts. Also known as concurrent jurisdiction, direct file causes the juvenile to appear before criminal court judges for processing.

The characteristics of those transferred vary widely among jurisdictions. However, most transferred youths have prior records of delinquency, prior adjudications, or some other type of involvement with the juvenile justice system. Many are 16 years of age or older, and the offenses alleged are particularly serious. All juveniles are entitled to a hearing, either before their cases are waived or after they have been waived under automatic transfers. These are known as waiver hearings and reverse waiver hearings. Juveniles who are able to keep their cases within juvenile court jurisdiction generally enjoy a greater degree of leniency than they would otherwise find in criminal courts. Juveniles who are transferred to criminal courts are entitled to jury trials as a matter of right, if their offenses carry incarcerative penalties of six months or more. But in criminal courts, the death penalty may be applied in capital cases.

Waiver patterns and trends are sketchy, since few researchers have studied this phenomenon during the past few decades. An analysis of findings from existing studies suggests inconsistent patterns. However, it is apparent from much research that often, less serious juveniles are transferred to criminal courts rather than more serious ones. Subjective factors, such as one's chronicity or frequent appearances before juvenile judges or rebellious attitudes, often influence judges to transfer such cases out of their jurisdiction, simply to get rid of them. This is not the intended purpose of transfers, which is to provide for harsher penalties to be imposed on the most serious and dangerous juvenile offenders. Some jurisdictions report that this objective is being achieved, although many other jurisdictions report the waivers of large numbers of property and petty offenders. Automatic transfer laws have been enacted to minimize the subjectivity inherent in judicial discretion, but their implementation has been uneven and questionably effective.

Increasingly, blended sentencing statutes have been used by different states to remedy problems encountered by subjective transfer or waiver decision making. Several blended sentencing models were examined, including the juvenile-inclusive blend, the juvenile-exclusive blend, the juvenile-contiguous blend, the criminal-inclusive blend, and the criminal-exclusive blend. Although these blended sentencing statutes have much to offer the juvenile justice systems where they are applied, not everyone is in agreement about their utility or effectiveness. More time is needed in order reach a greater level of acceptance of these relatively new measures as innovative sanctions for serious and violent juvenile offenders.

QUESTIONS FOR REVIEW

1. How does offense serious impact the use of waivers in the juvenile justice system?
2. Why should status offenders be separated from delinquent offenders in juvenile justice system processing?
3. What is meant by the use of contempt power by juvenile court judges? In what ways does the use of contempt power by juvenile court judges influence status offenders?
4. What are transfers, waivers, and certifications? What are their intended objectives? What is the rationale for using transfers?
5. What are some of the ideal characteristics of youths targeted for transfers to criminal courts? What are the actual characteristics of youths who are transferred to criminal courts?
6. What are three types of judicial waivers? What are some major differences between them?
7. What are some contrasts between direct file, legislative waivers, and demand waivers?
8. Under what circumstances are juveniles entitled to hearings on waiver actions?

9. What are some positive and negative implications for juveniles if they have their cases heard in juvenile courts? What are some positive and negative implications for juveniles if they have their cases heard in criminal courts?

10. What are five different kinds of blended sentencing statutes? What are some positive benefits of blended sentencing statutes for serious and violent juvenile offenders?

SUGGESTED READINGS

Austin, James, Kelly Johnson, and Maria Gregoriou. 2000. *Juveniles in adult prisons and jails: A national assessment.* Washington, DC: Bureau of Justice Assistance.

Fagan, Jeffrey and Franklin E. Zimring, eds. 2000. *The changing borders of juvenile justice: Transfers of adolescents to the criminal court.* Chicago: The University of Chicago Press.

Feld, Barry C. 2001. Race, youth violence, and the changing jurisprudence of waiver. *Behavioral Sciences and the Law* 19:3–22.

Snyder, Howard, Melissa Sickmund, and Eileen Poe-Yamagata. 2000. *Juvenile transfers to criminal court in the 1990s: Lessons learned from four studies.* Washington, DC: U.S. Office of Juvenile Justice and Delinquency Prevention.

INTERNET CONNECTIONS

Center on Crime, Communities, and Culture
http://www.soros.org/crime/

Criminal Justice Consortium
http://www.idiom.com/~cjc/

Criminal Justice Policy Foundation
http://www.cjpf.org/

CURE-NY
http://www.users.bestweb.net~cureny/

NetAction
http://www.netaction.org/

CHAPTER 10 | *The Adjudicatory Process: Dispositional Alternatives*

Chapter Outline

Key Terms
Chapter Objectives
Introduction
The Nature of the Offense
First Offender or Repeat
    Offender?

Aggravating and Mitigating Cir-
    cumstances
Juvenile Risk Assessments
    and Predictions
    of Dangerousness

Predisposition Reports
Summary
Questions for Review
Suggested Readings
Internet Connections

Key Terms

Actuarial prediction
Anamnestic prediction
Classification
Clinical prediction
Dangerousness
False negatives
False positives
First offender
Flat time

Needs assessment
Overrides
Prediction
Predictors of dangerousness
    and risk
Predisposition reports
Presentence investigation reports
    (PSIs)
Repeat offender

Risk
Risk/needs assessment instru-
    ments
Selective incapacitation
Victim-impact statement
Violent Juvenile Offender Pro-
    grams (VJOP)

> ### Chapter Objectives
>
> *As a result of reading this chapter, you will realize the following objectives:*
>
> 1. Differentiate between first offenders and repeat offenders.
> 2. Understand the differences between aggravating and mitigating circumstances.
> 3. Learn about juvenile dangerousness and risk, as well as how these phenomena can be assessed.
> 4. Learn about selective incapacitation and how it is used in juvenile cases.
> 5. Learn about anamnestic, actuarial, and clinical prediction, and how each is used to forecast juvenile offender dangerousness.
> 6. Examine several risk instruments, their applications and limitations.
> 7. Understand the importance of victim impact statements in dispositional hearings for juvenile offenders.
> 8. Learn about predispositional reports, who prepares them, and how they are used for sanctioning juveniles.

INTRODUCTION

• *The Oklahoma City bomb that destroyed a large federal building and killed almost 200 persons was homemade out of fertilizer and chemicals. There is greater accessibility to bomb-making technology and the ready availability of bomb materials and components. Bombs can be made out of most household materials. The most commonly made types of bombs are pipe bombs, so-named because a pipe is used and filled with explosive material. Such devices are common tools of the trade for terrorists and others. Homemade bombs are a new fad among U.S. teenagers. Interestingly, the Internet is being blamed for this diffusion of technological know-how about the procedures involved in bomb manufacturing. Authorities suspect that many teenagers have been copying the Unabomber, someone who sent homemade bombs to universities and airlines. Experts say that most homemade bombs are manufactured with no particular human target in mind. The bombmakers simply want to see how easy it is to build a bomb and detonate it. No precise figures are available, but experts say that growing numbers of youths in the 10 to 17 age range are involved in bomb manufacture and use the Internet to acquire the technological information enabling them to put bombs together. Publications are advertised, such as* The Poor Man's James Bond *and* The Anarchist's Cookbook. *These books and others like them describe bombmaking in great detail, indicating major ingredients and proportions to yield desired effects. Several bomb incidents receiving publicity include two teenagers who were arrested in May 1996 for blowing up a baseball dugout with a pipe bomb in Thurmont, Maryland. In February 1996, a 17-year-old was arrested after a 4-inch pipe bomb he built went off, severing telephone lines and punching holes in a garage door. In November 1995, a 14-year-old in Little Rock, Arkansas, blew off his left hand while trying to ignite a pipe bomb. And in Bristol, Connecticut, in September 1995, three teenagers were injured seriously when a homemade pipe bomb made of match heads and copper pipe blew up. Another incident occurred in Pequannock, New Jersey, in May 1995, when a pipe bomb containing gasoline and M-80 firecrackers exploded near a school science laboratory. How serious are youthful bomb makers? What should be their punishments?* [Adapted from Bruce Frankel and Gary Fields, "New Teen Fad: Building Bombs." *USA Today,* May 6, 1996:2A.]

• *It is an old trick. You drive up behind someone stopped at a traffic light, bump him or her with your car, and when the person gets out of his or her automobile to assess the damage, you rob them and steal the car. This is called carjacking, and it is happening in all large cities in the United States. In Miami, Florida, there is a serious car-jacking problem. It is so serious, in fact, that more than a few citizens are driving around the city with firearms for self-protection. On February 26, 2001, two teenage carjackers picked the wrong car to carjack. The pulled up behind an elderly couple stopped at a stop light and bumped their car. The older man behind the wheel of the bumped car didn't move. The teen driver jumped out of his car with a pistol in his hand and charged forward to confront the driver he had just rammed. As he got even with the window, the older man rolled his window down calmly and asked the teen what he wanted. "We want your car, asshole. Get out." At that point, the man raised his own .357 magnum revolver and shot the teen twice in the chest. After seeing his partner fall to the ground, the teen in the other car jumped into the driver's seat and attempted to drive the car away. However, the man with the .357 got out and emptied his gun through the teen's windshield, killing him instantly. The man with the gun turned out to be 72 years of age and a retired security officer. The two dead teens were later identified. They had lengthy prior records of juvenile offending. They were Ramon V., 15, and Hector G., 17. In at least four delinquency adjudications, they both had received probation at the hands of juvenile court judges on charges ranging from aggravated assault to vehicular theft. No charges were placed against the 72-year-old man. Investigators determined that it was simply a case of self-defense.* [Adapted from the Associated Press, "Carjacking Turns Deadly for Carjackers in Miami Incident." August 10, 1999.]

• *What does it take to make money on the Internet? In the case of 11-year-old Jonathan G. Lebed from Cedar Grove, Illinois, all it took was access to a computer, the Internet, and his father's stolen ID. Lebed said that he used to watch CNBC, the television news program that displays the continuously changing prices of stocks. He said, "It intrigued me watching all the numbers go by on television. I've always been interested in business, any kind of politics, finance, anything of that nature." About a year later, when Lebed was 12, he took money from his savings account and began to invest it in stocks over the Internet, pretending to be his father. Eventually, he began to make huge profits by "pumping and dumping." He would buy large blocks of thinly traded stocks, hyping them on financial message boards on the Internet under different false names, and then, within 24 hours, he would dump those same stocks after the price rose. He made at least eleven trades that the Securities and Exchange Commission are aware of. The trades represented only a fraction of the thousands of transactions he made since he was 12. The trades occurred between August 23, 1999 and February 4, 2000. Officials who investigated his transactions said that his parents didn't know what he was doing. His father, Gregory Lebed, said, "He's a good student. They pick on a kid!" The SEC discovered that after the boy had bought a stock, he sent hundreds of identical, false e-mail messages, each under a fictitious name, touting the stock he had just purchased. Others who read these messages would buy up the same stock, causing the price of the stock to rise. When the price was right, Lebed would sell it off, making a sizable profit. Subsequently, Lebed came to the attention of the FBI and the U.S. Department of Justice. An investigation led to his arrest. In a plea bargain agreement worked out in September 2000, Lebed agreed to repay approximately $285,000, which the SEC said represented illegal profits and interest. In exchange, Lebed neither admitted nor denied the allegations, but he agreed to refrain from similar behavior. It is the first time the SEC has brought charges against a minor.* [Adapted from Jeffrey Gold and the Associated Press, "Teen Agrees to Return Stock Profits." September 22, 2000.]

This chapter is about assessing juvenile offenders and making decisions about their prospects for treatment and/or rehabilitation. An important task performed by prosecutors and others at an early stage of the juvenile justice system is to select for prosecution those cases involving the most serious juveniles. Prosecutors must make assessments of probable case outcomes, weighing factors such as the dangerousness of certain youths and the probability of the effectiveness of various kinds of intervention that might be used in their control and management. Forecasts of dangerousness and risk are useful for anticipating the appropriate programs and interventions in diversion and/or probationary decisions with conditions and for making the proper recommendations to juvenile court judges for sanctions. Some of the fairly recent measures of risk assessment and dangerousness predictors will be described. The effectiveness of these measures will also be examined in light of prosecutorial and judicial decision making. Finally, an overview of judicial sentencing options will be presented.

THE NATURE OF THE OFFENSE

In 2000 there were 2 million arrests of youths under age 18 (Maguire and Pastore 2002). About 1.8 million cases were sent to the juvenile justice system for processing. About half of these cases were processed formally. Of the 780,000 petitioned cases that were handled formally, 450,000 juveniles were adjudicated. Of these, about 130,000 were placed in secure institutions, such as industrial schools. About 14,000 cases were recommended for transfer to criminal courts (Maguire and Pastore 2002). Of all arrests of youths under age 18 in 2001, 500,000 were for violent or person offenses, such as aggravated assault, rape, and murder.

During the period 1986–1996, violent crime by juveniles increased by nearly 70 percent nationally (Chesney-Lind et al. 1998). This dramatic increase in juvenile violence has drawn greater public attention to juveniles and to how juvenile courts deal with them. Violence by juveniles is growing at uneven rates among state jurisdictions (Arrigona, Birch, and Dailey 1996). In Hawaii, juvenile arrests for serious crimes of violence increased by over 200 percent during the period 1986–1996 (Chesney-Lind et al. 1998). Referrals to Nebraska juvenile courts for violent offenses increased by over 100 percent during the period 1975–1994 (Nebraska Commission on Law Enforcement and Criminal Justice 1995). Both male and female juveniles are committing violent acts at a greater rate in most jurisdictions, with females outpacing their male counterparts in violence by more than 50 percent. Further, the incidence of violence among younger juveniles is increasing (Poe-Yamagata and Butts 1996).

Adjudicated juveniles are subject to a limited range of juvenile court penalties, from verbal warnings and reprimands to secure confinement in a state industrial school. Delinquent acts involving physical harm to others or the threat of physical harm are considered violent offenses, in contrast with the larger category of property offenses that encompasses vehicular theft, petty larceny, or burglary. Intake officers perform the initial screening function by sending forward only the more serious offenders or those who the intake officers believe should have their cases adjudicated by juvenile court judges.

Juvenile court prosecutors screen those cases further by deciding which cases have the most prosecutive merit. Prosecutors are influenced by numerous factors whether to prosecute juveniles formally. Age, offense seriousness, and previous record often convince prosecutors to move forward with selected cases, whereas they may divert less serious cases to informal arbitration through alternative dispute resolution (Moak and Wallace 2000).

One important consideration is the willingness of juveniles to compensate victims for their monetary losses through a program of restitution. Juries comprised of one's peers may impose restitution as a condition of diversion, and a youth's satisfactory completion of such a diversion program will likely avoid the scars of a formal delinquency adjudication. Juvenile courts continue to view their roles as largely rehabilitative, and judges seek to assist youths in avoiding any negative consequences of secure confinement (Bilchik 1996). Various interventions are believed beneficial to juveniles in lieu of formal adjudicatory actions in juvenile courts.

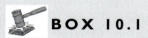 **BOX 10.1**

BRITAIN FREES TWO CHILD MURDERERS

The Murder of 2-Year-Old James Bulger

The crime was especially heinous. Two-year-old James Bulger was in the company of his mother while she shopped in a large Liverpool, England department store in 1991. One second her son, James, was by her side. The next second he was gone. Subsequently, video camera footage revealed that James Bulger was abducted by two young boys. Their identities were subsequently determined and they were apprehended. They were both 10 years old. Their names were Jon Venables and Robert Thompson, and they had been playing hooky from school when they decided to abduct Bulger from the store. Later, they beat Bulger with rocks and mutilated his body. Then they left it on some railroad tracks where a passing train cut it in half. At their trial later in 1993, they described how they abducted James Bulger and killed him. The judge sentenced them to life terms. They were both sent to a juvenile prison. The boys turned 19 in August 2000, and Britain's senior judge, Chief Justice Woolf, ruled that the two boys had been rehabilitated and that the corrosive atmosphere of sending them to prison would do more harm than good.

Britain's national Parole Board considered the case of the two boys in June 2001. They agreed that the boys should be paroled. The boys were released from prison on June 22. Not everyone was happy with this decision. Denise Fergus, James Bulger's mother, is now divorced from James' father and remarried. She said, "I know one day they have got to be released, but I think after eight years, it's too soon for what they have done." The judge banned all media in London from publishing any information about the boys' new identities or addresses for the rest of their lives. The judge said, "These young men are uniquely notorious and are at serious risk of attacks." John Dickinson, the lawyer for Jon Venables, said that Jon was full of remorse about his crime. He said that "All experts have testified about the remorse and changes in these two young men." The teens will first be sent to different halfway houses near their families' new homes. If their rehabilitation continues, they will eventually be permitted to seek work and reenter society under their new identities.

What do you think? Do you think it is too soon to free two young men who committed such a horrible crime in 1991? How do we know they have become rehabilitated? What is the proper punishment for such a brutal murder?

Source: Adapted from the Associated Press, June 23, 2001.

In many jurisdictions, secure confinement is the last resort for judges when disposing serious juvenile offenders (Matese and Tuell 1998). This reluctance to incarcerate juveniles has prompted criticisms that juvenile courts are soft on crime and that present juvenile crime control policies are insufficiently stringent (Coleman Advocates for Children and Youth 1996). Some jurisdictions, such as New York, have established Juvenile Offender laws designed to transfer the most serious juvenile offenders from juvenile court to criminal court. However, such laws have proved ineffective at deterring juvenile violence (Gottfredson, Gottfredson, and Weisman 2001).

Nevertheless, growing rates of violence among juveniles, especially for offenses such as first-degree sexual assault, aggravated robbery, and homicide, and the increasing influence of the get-tough movement in juvenile courts are causing juvenile court judges to impose harsher dispositions for those juveniles who commit more serious offenses. Thus, the nature of the offenses alleged, together with inculpatory evidence against youths charged, weigh heavily in favor of moving certain more serious offenders into the system toward formal adjudication. The rise of youth gangs in large U.S. cities, together with greater involvement in illicit drug trafficking, has done much to place more youths at risk regarding possible incarceration in secure facilities (Howell and Decker 1999).

FIRST OFFENDER OR REPEAT OFFENDER?

Is a juvenile a **first offender** or a **repeat offender?** First offenders have no prior record of delinquency, and it is presumed that their current offense is their first offense. Repeat offenders have prior delinquency or criminal records, either delinquency adjudications or criminal convictions or both. This is a key question raised by prosecutors when examining one's file to determine whether to prosecute the case in court. The overwhelming tendency among prosecutors is either to divert petty first offenders to some conditional program or dismiss these cases outright (Bilchik 1996). Many diversionary programs involve restitution or victim compensation in some form. Contracts are arranged between youths and their victims whereby youths reimburse victims, either partially or completely, for their financial losses. These programs often involve mediators who are responsible for securing agreements between juvenile offenders and their victims. Known as alternative dispute resolution, these mediation programs are believed to be fairly widespread and effective (Smith and Lombardo 2002).

Evidence suggests that prior offenders, even chronic and violent offenders, stand good chances of receiving some nonincarcerative sanction, if they are eventually adjudicated as delinquent (Risler, Sutphen, and Shields 2000). However, chronic juvenile offenders compared with first offenders also have a greater chance of pursuing criminal careers as adults (Lee 1996). Currently, no uniform policies exist among jurisdictions about how chronic offenders should be identified. Because of poor record-keeping and the lack of interjurisdictional record-sharing, many youthful offenders are continually diverted from formal juvenile court processing, despite their chronic recidivism. Some jurisdictions measure whether formal action against juveniles should be taken on the basis of the number of times they have been arrested. After four arrests, youths in some jurisdictions may be considered serious enough to have petitions filed against them as delinquents. During the 1990s, however, the compilation and centralization of state delinquency figures has increased, as well as the openness and availability of this information to the public sector.

Despite the relatively greater seriousness of violent offenses compared with property offenses, property offenders account for nearly two-thirds of all petitioned juveniles annually in most juvenile courts (Bilchik 1996, 9). Substantial numbers of status offenders continue to be processed by the juvenile justice system as well. Thus, it is unclear who is being targeted by get-tough policies nationwide. Ideally, only those most serious chronic and violent juveniles should be targeted for the harshest juvenile court penalties. However, an overwhelming majority of long-term detainees in public and private secure facilities are property offenders, again by a substantial margin of 2 to 1 (Maguire and Pastore 2002). One implication of this finding is that those most likely to be targeted for juvenile court action are persistent or chronic and nonviolent property offenders. They are considered the most troublesome in several respects. They clog juvenile court dockets again and again, and they sluggishly abandon their pattern of delinquent conduct. Further, they consume valuable juvenile court time which costs taxpayers considerable money.

The strong rehabilitative and reintegrative principles upon which the juvenile courts have operated for most of the twentieth century continue to influence how violent juvenile offenders are treated. For instance, various reintegrative programs have been described that are designed especially for violent juvenile offenders, called **Violent Juvenile Offender Programs (VJOP).** These programs provide several positive interventions and treatments (Fagan 1990). Instead of long-term incarceration in secure confinement, many violent juvenile offenders are placed in community-based secure facilities, where they remain for short periods before being reintegrated into their communities. Transitional residential programs include sustained intensive supervision as youths are gradually given freedoms and responsibilities.

The VJOP is based upon a theoretical model integrating strain, control, and learning theories. Four program dimensions include:

1. Social networking: The strengthening of personal bonds (attitudes, commitment, and beliefs) through positive experiences with family members, schools, the workplace, or nondelinquent peers.

2. Provision of opportunities for youths: The strengthening of social bonds (attachment and involvement) through achievement and successful participation in school, workplace, and family activities.

3. Social learning: The process by which personal and social bonds are strengthened and reinforced; strategies include rewards and sanctions for attainment of goals or for contingent behaviors.

4. Goal-oriented behaviors: The linking of specific behaviors to each client's needs and abilities, including problem behaviors and special intervention needs (e.g., substance abuse treatment or psychotherapy) (Fagan 1990, 240).

Violent juvenile offenders who have participated in these programs seem less inclined to recidivate. He believes that "carefully implemented and well-managed intervention programs," those that involve "early reintegration activities preceding release from secure care and intensive supervision in the

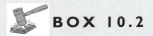

BOX 10.2

STEMMING THE TIDE OF SCHOOL VIOLENCE

New Bedford, Massachusetts

The story was all too familiar. Three teenagers plotted to carry out a massacre at their high school by exploding bombs, shooting other students, and ending their rampage with suicide. Had it not been for a tip from another student who learned about the bombing plans, another Columbine might have occurred. Police acted on the tip and visited the homes of the teenagers involved in the alleged plot. They discovered bomb-making materials, weapons, and a large quantity of ammunition. The three students were charged with conspiracy to commit murder, conspiracy to commit assault and battery with a dangerous weapon, and possession of ammunition. The arrested youths were dressed in Gothic-style clothing and modeled themselves after the shooters at Columbine High School in Colorado.

Police swept the school, the New Bedford High School, and searched all student lockers in an effort to determine whether any other dangerous contraband might be stored there. A janitor found a letter outlining the plans of the youths, which included detonating explosives in the school and then shooting fleeing students. The letter said that the students then planned to kill themselves after authorities arrived. A search of the youths' homes yielded bomb-making instructions, knives, shotgun shells, and pictures of the teenagers holding what appeared to be handguns. The guns were not recovered.

The mothers of two of the arrested youths defended them. "My kids are good kids and this has really been blown out of proportion, and you know, there's just no way anything like that would have happened," said Carol McKeehan, mother of Eric McKeehan, one of the youths taken into custody. Another mother, Susan St. Hilaire, said the charges were based on rumor. "These kids are good kids, all of them," she told reporters outside of the courthouse later. The day following the youths' arrest, many students stayed home from school, fearful for their lives.

In Williamsport, Pennsylvania, another shooting occurred on Wednesday, March 7, 2001. A 14-year-old eighth-grade female walked into a Catholic school, Bishop Neumann Junior-Senior High School, and shot a 13-year-old girl. In this incident, the shooter did not attempt to shoot at other students. She was very focused and went after a specific victim. The victim was Kimberly Marchese, who was shot in the right shoulder and was in stable condition at Geisinger Medical Center in Danville. An administrator disarmed the shooter and she was immediately taken into custody by police. At the time of her interrogation, police didn't know where she got the gun. There were plans to charge the shooter as an adult in a Pennsylvania criminal court. The shooting occurred allegedly as the result of a previous altercation between the two girls.

Are school shootings on the rise again? What more can school officials do to prevent such occurrences? How should school shooters who kill and wound be punished? What do you think?

Source: Adapted from Richard Lewis and the Associated Press. "Students Stay Home in Wake of Death Plot." November 27, 2001; Adapted from Dan Lewerenz and the Associated Press, "Girl Shot in Penn. Catholic School," March 8, 2001.

community, with emphasis on gradual reentry and development of social skills to avoid criminal behavior" do much to "avert the abrupt return to criminality after release from the program" of these youths. Those youths exposed to more conventional and longer secure confinement and treatment appear to recidivate at greater rates and to persist in their delinquent behaviors (Fagan 1990, 258). This view is shared by others (Knight and Tripodi 1996). Therefore, it is difficult to formulate specific guidelines about how violent juvenile offenders ought to be handled in their juvenile court processing. Currently, competing philosophies of rehabilitation and just-deserts recommend polarities in treatments, ranging from total diversion to total secure confinement.

Is the First Offender/Repeat Offender Distinction Relevant? Race, Ethnicity, and Socioeconomic Status Revisited

Juvenile courts are supposed to be objective in their adjudicatory hearings and imposition of sanctions. Legal variables, such as prior record and the seriousness of the current offense, are supposed to be defining criteria for a system of graduated sanctions. Indeed, investigations of selected juvenile courts reveal that current offense seriousness and prior record are the most important variables in determining the dispositions of repeat delinquents (Lee 1996). But juvenile courts in virtually every jurisdiction have drawn criticism that adjudications and dispositions are more a function of race, ethnicity, and socioeconomic status than of offense seriousness and prior record (Arrigona, Birch, and Dailey 1996). This is because of the disproportionately high representation of minorities in juvenile arrests, adjudications, and incarcerative dispositions (Bayens 1999).

In New York, for instance, white juveniles stand a better chance than blacks or Hispanics of not being detained following their arraignment. White juveniles also have a better chance of avoiding incarceration compared with blacks and Hispanics if they are adjudicated delinquent (Liberman, Winterfield, and McElroy 1996). Similar findings were yielded in a study of the Hawaiian juvenile justice system (Chesney-Lind and Matsuo 1995) and research investigations in Iowa (Moore and Kuker 1993), Georgia (Ruback and Vardaman 1997), and North Carolina (Dean, Hirschel, and Brame 1996). This charge against juvenile justice systems in the United States has led to a federal mandate to document the existence and nature of minority overrepresentation and to devise strategies to reduce such overrepresentation. One strategy designed to overcome the prejudicial effects of race, ethnicity, and social class is to establish objective criteria for juvenile justice decision making (Secret and Johnston 1997).

Several objective criteria might be applied to decision making at various points throughout the juvenile justice system. These criteria are found in most state criminal codes and describe various conditions or circumstances that are more or less influential regarding juvenile offender dispositions, regardless of their seriousness. Some of these objective criteria include aggravating and mitigating circumstances.

AGGRAVATING AND MITIGATING CIRCUMSTANCES

Playing an important part in determining how far any particular juvenile moves into the juvenile justice system are various aggravating and mitigating circumstances accompanying their acts. In the early stages of intake and prosecutorial decision making, aggravating and mitigating circumstances are often informally considered, and much depends upon the amount of detail furnished by police officers about the delinquent events. Aggravating circumstances are usually those actions on the part of juveniles that tend to intensify the seriousness of their acts. Accordingly, where aggravating circumstances exist, one's subsequent punishment might be intensified. At the other end of the spectrum are mitigating circumstances, or those factors that might weigh in the juvenile's favor. These circumstances might lessen the seriousness of the act as well as the severity of punishment imposed by juvenile court judges (Sorensen and Wallace 1999). Lists of aggravating and mitigating circumstances are presented below.

Aggravating Circumstances

Aggravating circumstances applicable both to juveniles and adults include:

1. Death or serious bodily injury to one or more victims. The most serious juvenile offenders are those who cause death or serious bodily injury to their victims. Homicide and aggravated assault are those offenses that most directly involve death or serious physical harm to others, although it is possible to inflict serious bodily injury or inflict deep emotional scars through armed robbery and even some property crimes, including burglary (Silver and Miller 2002). The harshest option available to juvenile court judges is direct commitment to secure confinement, such as an industrial school or reform school.

2. An offense committed while the offender is awaiting other delinquency charges. Are juveniles awaiting an intake hearing after being arrested for previous offenses? Many juveniles commit new delinquent acts between the time they are arrested for other offenses and the date of their intake hearing. These offenders are probably good candidates for temporary confinement in secure holding facilities until their cases can be heard by intake officers and delinquency petitions can be filed.

3. An offense committed while the offender is on probation, parole, or work release. Offenders with prior adjudications and who are currently serving their sentences may reoffend during these conditional periods. Usually, a condition of diversionary and probationary programs is that youths refrain from further delinquent activity. Thus, they may be in violation of a program condition. Probation, parole, and work release program violations are separate offenses that are accompanied by harsher penalties. In effect, these are incidents of contempt of court, since they involve violations of direct court-ordered conditional activities. The probation, parole, or work release conditional programs have usually been granted to certain offenders because they have been deemed trustworthy by officials. Therefore, violations of the court's trust are especially serious, and it becomes less likely that these juveniles will be extended such privileges in the future (Kowalski and Caputo 1999).

4. Previous offenses for which the offender has been punished. Having a prior record is a strong indicator of one's chronicity and potential for future offending behavior. Juvenile court judges may be less inclined to be lenient in sentencing those with prior records, especially where serious delinquent acts have been committed. For example, repeat sex offenders are often treated more harshly by juvenile court judges because of their suspected high rate of relapse. Thus, whether the belief that a high rate of relapse among sex offenders is justified, the mere fact of being a sex of-

fender becomes an unofficial aggravating factor for many juvenile court judges (Annon 1996).

5. Leadership in the commission of the delinquent act involving two or more offenders. Especially in gang-related activities, one's leadership role is an aggravating circumstance. Are certain youths gang leaders? Do they incite others to commit delinquent acts? Gang leaders are often targeted for the harshest punishments, since they are most visible to their peers and serve as examples of how the system deals with juvenile offenders. Those playing minor roles in gang-related activity might be treated more leniently by judges.

6. A violent offense involving more than one victim. As the number of victims increases as the result of any delinquent conduct, the potential for physical harm and death rapidly escalates. Robberies of convenience stores and other places where large numbers of customers might be are likely to involve multiple victims. The number of victims or potential victims aggravates the initial delinquent conduct.

7. Extreme cruelty during the commission of the offense. Maiming victims or torturing them during the commission of delinquent acts is considered extreme cruelty and worthy of enhanced punishments by juvenile court judges.

8. Use of a dangerous weapon in the commission of the offense, with high risk to human life. The second and third leading causes of death among juveniles under age 21 are homicides and suicides, and most of these events include the use of firearms (Birkbeck 1998). Using firearms to commit delinquent acts increases greatly the potential harm to victims of such acts. Many states currently have mandatory **flat time** or hard time associated with using firearms during the commission of felonies. This means that if someone uses a dangerous weapon during the commission of a crime, a mandatory sentence enhancement is included, which may be an additional 2- to 5-year sentence in addition to the initial punishment, which might be a 10-year sentence for armed robbery (Sheppard 1999).

Mitigating Circumstances

Mitigating circumstances include the following:

1. No serious bodily injury resulting from the offense. Petty property offenders who do not endanger lives or injure others may have their sentences mitigated as a result. Interestingly, however, property offenders account for a majority of long-term juvenile detainees in industrial schools or secure juvenile facilities.

2. No attempt to inflict serious bodily injury on anyone. Those juveniles who commit theft or burglary usually wish to avoid confrontations with their victims. While some juveniles prepare for such contingencies and therefore pose bodily threats to others, most youthful offenders committing such acts run away from the crime scene if discovered. This is evidence of their desire to avoid inflicting serious bodily harm on their victims.

3. Duress or extreme provocation. A compelling defense used in criminal court cases is that offenders were under duress at the time they committed

their crimes. They may have been forced to act certain ways by others (McCord 1995). Under certain circumstances, youths may plead that they were coerced or were acting under duress when committing delinquent acts in concert with others. Gang membership and gang violence may be precipitated to a degree because of duress. Youths may join gangs for self-protection and to avoid being assaulted by other gang members.

4. Circumstances that justify the conduct. Any circumstance that might justify one's conduct is a mitigating factor. If youths act to protect themselves or others from physical harm, then judges may find these circumstances strong enough to justify whatever conduct was exhibited (Bumby 1994).

5. Mental incapacitation or physical condition that significantly reduced the offender's culpability in the offense. This factor specifies conditions that relate to drug or alcohol dependencies or to mental retardation or mental illness. If youths are suffering from some form of mental illness or are retarded, or if they are alcohol- or drug-dependent, this may limit their capacity to understand the law and interfere with their ability to comply with it (Everle and Maiuro 2001).

6. Cooperation with authorities in apprehending other participants in the act or making restitution to the victims for losses they suffered. Those youths who assist police in apprehending others involved in delinquent acts are credited with these positive deeds. Also, juveniles who make restitution to

BOX 10.3

11-YEAR-OLD MURDERER CONVICTED

Nathaniel Abraham, Pontiac, Michigan

When Nathaniel Abraham was 11 years of age, he shot and killed a stranger outside of a convenience store with a rifle. This wasn't Nathaniel Abraham's first brush with the law. In his earlier years, Abraham had been suspected in over two dozen crimes, including theft, beating two teens with metal pipes, and purse-snatching at gunpoint. David Gorcyca, the prosecutor, said "This case was about intervening on behalf of a troubled and dangerous youth who needed help and didn't get it a long time ago. My whole intent was to not throw away the key on an 11-year-old boy, now 13. My intent was to give him the help he needed." Defense attorney Geoffrey Fiegel said that the verdict was "born out of anger." He added that "I think the rest of the world will scorn us and hold us in contempt" for what was done to Nathaniel Abraham. The facts in the case were in dispute. Prosecutors said that Nathaniel had fired a

Nathaniel Abraham

stolen .22-caliber rifle from about 100 yards away, although later tests placed the distance at 65 yards. Two days after the shooting,

Nathaniel was arrested at his school, his face painted for Halloween. He became the first youngster charged under a 1997 Michigan law allowing adult prosecutions of children of any age for serious crimes. Some law enforcement officials said that Nathaniel's case proved the need to get tough with kids who are a menace to society. But Amnesty International chose his frightened face for the cover of a 1998 report condemning the U.S. criminal justice system as being too harsh with juveniles.

Nathaniel's lawyers argued that Nathaniel was aiming at trees and that the victim was hit by a bullet that ricocheted off a tree. They said that the rifle was defective and couldn't have been aimed with any precision. And they also argued that Nathaniel had the mind of a 6-year-old and could not form the intent to commit murder or understand the charges against him. However, prosecutors contended that Nathaniel's statements to his friends suggested otherwise. He told some of his friends following the shooting, "I shot that nigger." Furthermore, Nathaniel had told a friend that he was going to shoot somebody, practiced his aim on stationary targets, and shot Ronnie Greene, 18, in the head and bragged about it the next day. This case has stirred much debate among criminal justice professionals about how best to deal with violent juvenile offenders. Nathaniel was subsequently acquitted of first-degree murder but convicted of second-degree murder. Under Michigan's new blended sentencing statute, Nathaniel can receive both a juvenile and an adult sentence. This means that he will be incarcerated in a juvenile facility until he is 21. At that time, his case will be reviewed and he will either be released or will have to serve the adult portion of the sentence, which could be life imprisonment. The hearing is to determine whether he had behaved well while incarcerated as a juvenile.

In a follow-up, Nathaniel was given only a juvenile punishment, confinement to a juvenile facility until he reaches the age of his majority or 21. At that time, barring any illegal acts he may commit while confined in the Michigan juvenile facility, Nathaniel will go free. The juvenile court judge rejected the option of imposing an adult sentence for personal reasons.

Should juveniles of any age be eligible for criminal charges? Do you think that Nathaniel's conviction was fair and that second-degree murder was the appropriate conviction offense, especially in view of the fact that he appeared to plan the murder in advance? How do you think we should treat 11-year-old murderers? What is the youngest age someone should be treated as an adult?

Source: Adapted from the Associated Press, "13-Year-Old Boy Is Found Guilty." November 17, 1999; adapted from the Associated Press, "Abraham Sentenced to Juvenile Detention." February 18, 2000.

victims or compensate them in part or in whole for their financial losses stand a good chance of having their cases mitigated through such restitution and good works.

7. No prior record of delinquency. First offender juveniles, particular those under age 16, are especially targeted for more lenient treatment compared with recidivists.

8. Youthfulness. The younger the juvenile, the greater the mitigation. Although youthfulness is not an official mitigating factor under many state statutes, there is considerable support from within the criminal justice community for this circumstance to function as one (Geraghty et al. 1997). As has been shown, under common law, persons who commit crimes and who are under the age of 7 are presumed incapable of formulating criminal intent. However, those who are 8, 9, 10, 11, and 12 years of age are entitled to some mitigation as well, in the opinions of some observers. Not being a fully formed adult renders a juvenile less mature and capable of sound de-

cision making. One line of thought is that it is simply more difficult for juveniles to understand the law and comply with it. Thus, one's youthfulness should be weighed against any aggravating circumstances that might exist.

These lists of aggravating and mitigating circumstances are not exhaustive. Other factors may affect the judicial decision. At each stage of the juvenile justice process, interested officials want to know whether certain offenders will recidivate if they receive leniency. No one knows for sure whether certain offenders will recidivate more frequently than other offenders, although certain factors correlate highly with recidivism. In the following section, we will examine several ways of assessing a juvenile's dangerousness or risk to the community. Such assessments are crucial in many jurisdictions in influencing prosecutorial and judicial decision making.

JUVENILE RISK ASSESSMENTS AND PREDICTIONS OF DANGEROUSNESS

Risk assessment is an element of a classification system and traditionally means the process of determining the probability that an individual will repeat unlawful or destructive behavior (Dillingham et al. 1999). Risk **prediction** takes several forms, including the prediction of violent behavior, predictions of new offenses (recidivism), and the prediction of technical program violations associated with probation and parole. Most states have some semblance of risk assessment of juvenile offenders, but only about half of the states have formal risk assessment instruments (Benda, Corwyn, and Toombs 2001).

Dangerousness and Risk

The concepts of **dangerousness** and **risk** are often used interchangeably. Dangerousness and risk both convey propensities to cause harm to others or oneself. What is the likelihood that any particular offender will be violent toward others? Does an offender pose any risk to public safety? What is the likelihood that any particular offender will commit suicide or attempt it? Risk (or dangerousness) instruments are screening devices intended to distinguish between different types of offenders for purposes of determining initial institutional classification, security placement and inmate management, early release eligibility, and the level of supervision required under conditions of probation or parole. These instruments contain information believed useful in forecasting future delinquent conduct or criminality. This information is collectively referred to as **predictors of dangerousness and risk.** Most state jurisdictions and the federal government regard these measures that forecast future criminality or delinquency as **risk/needs assessment instruments** rather than dangerousness instruments. There is considerable variability among states regarding the format and content of such measures (Risler, Sutphen, and Shields 2000).

Needs Assessment and Its Measurement

Needs assessment instruments are instruments that measure an offender's personal/social skills, health well-being and emotional stability, educational level and vocational strengths and weaknesses, alcohol/drug dependencies, mental ability, and other relevant life factors and that highlight those areas for which services are available and could or should be provided (Benda, Corwyn, and Toombs 2001).

Attempts to forecast juvenile dangerousness/risk and needs are important, because many actors in the juvenile justice system use these predictions or forecasts as the basis for their decision making (Risler, Sutphen, and Shields 2000). Intake officers who initially screen youthful offenders try to decide which offenders are most deserving of leniency and which should be pushed further into the system for formal processing. Prosecutors want to know which juveniles are most receptive to diversion and amenable to change. Thus, they can ensure that only the most serious and chronic offenders will be processed, while the remaining youths will have another chance to live reasonably normal lives in their communities without juvenile justice system supervision. And judges want to know which youths will likely reoffend if returned to their communities through probation or some other nonincarcerative option. Some juvenile offenders may be penalized purely on the basis of their likelihood of future offending. Others may receive leniency because they are considered good probation or parole risks and unlikely to reoffend. Thus, some juveniles are selectively incapacitated. **Selective incapacitation** is confining those who are predicted to pose a risk to others, usually on the basis of their prior record and/or risk score on some risk instrument (Feld 2001; Hayes and Geerken 1997).

Selective Incapacitation

False Positives and False Negatives.   There are at least two major dangers inherent in risk or dangerousness predictions. First, youths who are identified as likely recidivists may receive harsher treatment compared with those who are considered unlikely to reoffend. In fact, many of those youths considered as good risks for probation or diversion may eventually turn out to be dangerous, although predictions of their future conduct gave assurances to the contrary.

It is difficult to predict which youths will be amenable to counseling and other types of delinquency interventions.

Second, those youths who receive harsher punishment and longer confinement because they are believed to be dangerous may not, in fact, be dangerous. Therefore, we risk overpenalizing those who will not be dangerous in the future, although our forecasts suggest they will be dangerous. We also risk underpenalizing those believed by our forecasts not to be dangerous, although a portion will eventually turn out to be dangerous and kill or seriously injure others.

These two scenarios depict **false positives** and **false negatives.** False positives are those persons predicted to be dangerous in the future but who turn out not to be dangerous. False negatives are those persons predicted not to be dangerous in the future but turn out to be dangerous anyway. False positives are those who are unduly punished because of our predictions, while false negatives are those who do not receive needed punishment or future supervision (Smith and Smith 1998). For adult criminals, attempts to forecast criminal behaviors have led to recommendations for selective incapacitation in many jurisdictions. Selective incapacitation involves incarcerating or detaining those persons believed to be likely recidivists on the basis of various behavioral and attitudinal criteria. The theory behind selective incapacitation is that if high-risk offenders can be targeted and controlled through long-term confinement, then their circulation will be limited as well as the potential crimes they might commit (Andersson et al. 1999).

Selective incapacitation is controversial. Samuel Walker (2001) raises five general questions about the usefulness and desirability of selective incapacitation in dealing with offenders in general. They are:

1. Can we correctly estimate the amount of crime reduction?
2. Can we accurately identify chronic offenders and predict their future behavior?
3. Can we afford the monetary costs of implementing selective incapacitation should it involve massive new detention center construction?
4. Can we implement a policy of consistent selective incapacitation without violating constitutional rights?
5. What will be the side effects?

Basically, incapacitation is a strategy for crime control involving the physical isolation of offenders from their communities, usually through incarceration, to prevent them from committing future crimes (Gottfredson and Gottfredson 1990). But Walker's questions are quite important, since there are some important implications of selective incapacitation for youthful offenders. The major harm is penalizing certain youths for acts they haven't yet committed (Danila, Annon, and Anglin 1997). Can we legitimately punish anyone in the United States for suspected future criminality or delinquency? Whatever one's personal feelings in this regard, the answer is that such punishments are imposed each time parole boards deny parole requests or probation recommendations are rejected in favor of incarceration.

Visher (1987, 514–515) describes two types of incapacitation—collective and selective. Under collective incapacitation, crime reduction would be accomplished through traditional offense-based sentencing and incarcerative policies, such as mandatory minimum sentences. Under selective incapacitation, however, those offenders predicted to pose the greatest risk of future crimes would become prime candidates for incarceration and for longer prison sentences. A major problem throughout both the criminal justice system and the juvenile justice system is that no universally acceptable implementation policies have been adopted in most jurisdictions supporting the use of such incapacitation strategies. Further, there are serious problems with many of these instruments because they cannot distinguish adequately between risks posed by male and female juvenile offenders (Loucks and Zamble 1999).

The quality of risk assessment devices is such at present that we cannot depend upon them as absolutely perfect indicators of anyone's future conduct (Champion 1994). One problem is that many risk assessment instruments are almost exclusively tested on adult offenders rather than juvenile offenders. Also, follow-up periods for assessments of predictive effectiveness are often relatively short, thus preventing researchers from validating the predictive utility of these scales over time. Sometimes prediction instruments are better at predicting the future behaviors of low-rate offenders rather than high-rate offenders (Hayes and Geerken 1997). Despite the continuing controversy surrounding the application of risk prediction measures and the criticisms by some researchers that such predictions are either impossible or inappropriate, such predictions continue to be made. Furthermore, several researchers are cautiously optimistic about the predictive utility of the assessment instruments they have devised and used (Benda, Corwyn, and Toombs 2001; Risler, Sutphen, and Shields 2000).

Generally, risk assessment measures are one of the three following categories: (1) anamnestic prediction, (2) actuarial prediction, and (3) clinical prediction.

Anamnestic Prediction. **Anamnestic prediction** uses past sets of circumstances to predict future behaviors. If the current circumstances are similar to past circumstances, where previous offense behaviors were observed, then it is probable that youths will exhibit future offending.

Actuarial Prediction. **Actuarial prediction** is an aggregate predictive tool. Those youthful offenders who are being considered for diversion, probation, or parole are compared with former offenders who have similar characteristics (Goldson 2001). Performances and records of previous conduct in view of diversion, probation, or parole decisions, serve as the basis for profiling the high-risk recidivist. Certain youths may exhibit characteristics similar to previous juveniles who became recidivists. The expectation is that current youths will likely recidivate as well (D. Jones 2001).

Clinical Prediction. **Clinical prediction** involves professional assessments of diagnostic examinations and test results. The professional training of probation officers, prosecutors, and judges, as they experience working with youthful offenders directly, enables them to forecast probable behaviors of their present clients. Clinical prediction involves administration of psychological tools and personality assessment devices. Certain background and behavioral characteristics are assessed as well. Some persons consider clinical prediction to be superior to actuarial and anamnestic prediction, although there is little support for this claim. In fact, actuarial prediction, the simplest prediction form, is either equal to or better than clinical prediction under a variety of circumstances (Gardner et al. 1996; Quinsey, Rice, and Harris 1995).

Common Elements of Risk Assessment Instruments

Most risk assessment measures for juvenile offenders contain several common elements (Dillingham et al. 1999). Adapting these common elements to youthful offender scenarios, the following elements seem prevalent:

1. Age at first adjudication
2. Prior delinquent behavior (a combined measure of the number and severity of priors)
3. Number of prior commitments to juvenile facilities
4. Drug/chemical abuse
5. Alcohol abuse
6. Family relationships (parental control)
7. School problems
8. Peer relationships

For each of the elements above, some evidence has been found to establish a definite association between these and a youth's recidivism potential. These associations are not always strong, but in an actuarial prediction sense, they provide a basis for assuming that each of these elements has some causal value. The earlier the age of first adjudication and/or contact with the juvenile justice system, the greater the risk of recidivism (Sawicki, Schaeffer, and Thies, 1999). Poor school performance, family problems and a lack of parental control, drug and/or alcohol dependencies, prior commitments to juvenile facilities, and a prior history of juvenile offending are individually and collectively linked with recidivism (Funk, 1999).

For example, the California Youth Authority includes the following variables and response weights as a means of assessing one's risk level:

1. Age at first police contact:
     9 = score 6 points
    10 = score 5 points
    11 = score 4 points
    12 = score 3 points
    13 = score 2 points
    14 = score 1 point
    15 = score 0 points
2. Number of prior police contacts (number):
    (score actual number)
3. Aggression and/or purse snatching:
    score "yes" = 1, "no" = 0
4. Petty theft:
    score "yes" = 1, "no" = 0
5. Use of alcohol or glue:
    score "yes" = 1, "no" = 0
6. Usually three or more others involved in delinquent act:
    score "yes" = 1, "no" = 0

7. Family on welfare:
   score "yes" = 1, "no" = 0

8. Father main support in family:
   score "no" = 1, "yes" = 0

9. Intact family:
   score "no" = 1, "yes" = 0

10. Number of siblings:
    3 = score 1 point
    4 = score 2 points
    5+ = score 3 points

11. Father has criminal record:
    score "yes" = 1, "no" = 0

12. Mother has criminal record:
    score "yes" = 1, "no" = 0

13. Low family supervision:
    score "yes" = 1, "no" = 0

14. Mother rejects:
    score "yes" = 1, "no" = 0

15. Father rejects:
    score "yes" = 1, "no" = 0

16. Parents wanted youth committed:
    score "no" = 1, "yes" = 0

17. Verbal IQ:
    equal to or less than 69 = 4
    70–79 = 3
    80–89 = 2
    90–99 = 1
    100+ = 0

18. Grade level:
    at grade level = 1
    1 year retarded = 2
    2 years retarded = 3
    3 years retarded = 4
    4+ years retarded = 5

19. Negative school attitude:
    score 0–3

20. School disciplinary problems:
    score "yes" = 1, "no" = 0

On the basis of the score obtained, youths might be assigned the following risk levels:

Risk Level Score	Degree of Risk
0–22	Low
21–31	Medium
32+	High

Source: Adapted from the California Youth Authority 2001.

Youths who receive scores of 0–22 are considered low risks, while those with scores of 32 or higher are considered high risks. California Youth Authority officials believe that while these scores do not necessarily indicate that all youths with higher scores will be recidivists and all those with lower scores will be nonrecidivists, there does appear to be some indication that these categorizations are generally valid ones. Thus, these classifications might be used to segregate more serious offenders from less serious ones in secure confinement facilities. Or such scores might be useful in forecasts of future performance in diversion or probationary programs.

When measures or indices such as these are examined critically, it is interesting to note how such important life-influencing decisions are reduced to six or seven predictive criteria. In the case of the instrumentation devised by the California Youth Authority, decisions about youths made by this organization are supplemented with several other important **classification** criteria, such as personality assessment tools, youth interviews, and professional impressions.

The Functions of Classification

1. Classification systems enable authorities to make decisions about appropriate offender program placements.
2. Classification systems help to identify needs and the provision of effective services in specialized treatment programs.
3. Classification assists in determining custody level if confined in either prisons or jails.
4. Classification helps to adjust custody level during confinement, considering behavioral improvement and evidence of rehabilitation.
5. While confined, inmates may be targeted for particular services and/or programs to meet their needs.
6. Classification may be used for offender management and deterrence relative to program or prison rules and requirements.
7. Classification schemes are useful for policy decision making and administrative planning relevant for jail and prison construction, the nature and number of facilities required, and the types of services to be made available within such facilities.
8. Classification systems enable parole boards to make better early-release decisions about eligible offenders.
9. Community corrections agencies can utilize classification schemes to determine those parolees who qualify for participation and those who don't qualify.
10. Classification systems enable assessments of risk and dangerousness to be made generally in anticipation of the type of supervision best suited for particular offenders.
11. Classification schemes assist in decision making relevant for community crime control, the nature of penalties to be imposed, and the determination of punishment.
12. Classification may enable authorities to determine whether selective incapacitation is desirable for particular offenders or offender groupings.

For most states, the following general applications are made of risk assessment instruments at different client-processing stages:

1. To promote better program planning through optimum budgeting and deployment of resources.
2. To target high-risk and high-need offenders for particular custody levels, programs, and services without endangering the safety of others.
3. To apply the fair and appropriate sanctions to particular classes of offenders and raise their level of accountability.
4. To provide mechanisms for evaluating services and programs as well as service and program improvements over time.
5. To maximize public safety as well as public understanding of the diverse functions of corrections by making decision making more open and comprehensible to both citizens and offender-clients.

Several important and desirable characteristics of such predictive models are:

1. The model should be predictively valid.
2. The model should reflect reality.
3. The model should be designed for a dynamic system and not remain fixed over time.
4. The model should serve practical purposes.
5. The model should not be a substitute for good thinking and responsible judgment.
6. The model should be both qualitative and quantitative (Rans 1984, 50).

The state of Washington has a Juvenile Rehabilitation Administration (JRA), an agency charged with the custody and treatment of committed youths. During the mid-1990s, the JRA created a juvenile rehabilitation model that utilizes assessment tools designed to specify appropriate treatment programming for juvenile offenders. The mission of the JRA is to teach offenders accountability, provide preventive and rehabilitative programming and public protection, and reduce repetitive criminal behavior using the least restrictive setting necessary. Under this model, the JRA evaluates committed offenders' risks to the community, articulates competency-based treatment outcomes, and assesses youths' sustained treatment progress while incarcerated. The goal of this model is to effectively move youths through a continuum of care, from structured residential settings through community parole (Schmidt et al. 1998, 104–105). Thus, Washington authorities have devised initial security classification assessment tools and an assessment of community risk. Further, community placement eligibility criteria have been established, together with a variety of rehabilitative treatment programs. Core treatment programming includes substance abuse education, work, vocational and life skills, problem solving, constructive response to frustration, and victim empathy/restoration. Specialized treatment programming is provided for sex offenders, mentally ill offenders, and substance abusers.

Risk Prediction from Arizona and Florida

Below are two different risk prediction instruments devised by Arizona and Florida. As a simple exercise, read the following scenarios involving several hypothetical delinquents. Next, read through the particular risk prediction instruments, paying attention to their instructions for score determinations. Then, complete each instrument and determine the total score for each juvenile. It will be apparent that this task is easier for some instruments than for others. You will need to do several things when you compute scores for each of these juvenile offenders. You will need to keep track of their ages, how many formal and informal delinquency or status offender adjudications they have acquired, and whether they have escaped or attempted escape from a secure juvenile facility. In some of the instruments, you will need to determine whether they are drug- or alcohol-dependent. A brief solution will be provided at the end of these two scenarios.

Scenario 1: Arizona and Jerry J.   Jerry J. lives in Phoenix, Arizona. He is 14 years old. Jerry J. is a member of the Scorpions, a Phoenix juvenile gang. He has been a gang member for three years and has participated in several drive-by shootings, none of which has resulted in fatalities to intended victims. Jerry J. is known to the police. When Jerry J. was 11, he was taken into custody for assaulting another student in his school. This was the result of a referral by the school principal. An intake officer adjusted the case and returned Jerry J. to the custody of his parents. Two months later, Jerry J. was taken into custody again, this time for beating another student with a lead pipe and causing serious bodily injuries. Again, the school principal referred Jerry J. to juvenile authorities for processing, and a delinquency petition was filed. This time, the juvenile court judge heard Jerry J.'s case and adjudicated Jerry J. delinquent on the assault charge. Jerry J. was disposed to probation for one year.

While on probation, Jerry J. joined the Scorpions and was involved in at least three convenience store thefts and five crack cocaine sales. During the last crack cocaine sale, an undercover police officer posing as a crack cocaine customer arrested Jerry J. and two of his gang companions and took them to the police station for processing. Jerry J. appeared again before the same juvenile court judge after a police referral. This time, the judge adjudicated Jerry J. delinquent on the drug charge and disposed him to an 18-month probationary term. In the meantime, a routine drug screen at the local jail where Jerry J. was being detained in preventive detention revealed that he tested positive for cocaine and alcohol use. Under questioning, Jerry J. admitted to using drugs occasionally, as well as consuming alcohol at gang meetings. When Jerry J. was 12 and still on probation, he was taken into custody by police following a burglary report at a local drug store. When officers apprehended Jerry J., he was crawling out of a back window of the drug store with several bottles of Percodan, a prescription pain-reliever. Officers confiscated a loaded .22-caliber pistol that Jerry J. was carrying in his jacket pocket. Officers filed a delinquency petition with the juvenile court, alleging several law violations, including burglary, theft, and carrying a concealed firearm. Jerry J.'s probation officer also referred Jerry J. to the juvenile court and recommended that Jerry J.'s probation program be revoked, since he was in clear violation of his probation program requirements. The juvenile court judge adjudicated Jerry J. delinquent on the firearms charge as well as on the burglary and theft charges. He also revoked Jerry J.'s probation after a two-stage hearing where substantial evidence was presented of Jerry J.'s guilt. Jerry J. was disposed to six months' intensive supervised probation with electronic monitoring.

Subsequently, Jerry J. has been adjudicated delinquent three more times. Police officers filed petitions with the juvenile court on all three occasions. Two of these delinquency adjudications were for felonies (aggravated assault and selling one kilo of cocaine). For the aggravated assault offense, the juvenile court judge disposed Jerry J. to the Arizona State Industrial School, a secure-custody facility, for a term of six months. The judge also revoked Jerry J.'s probation program. A predispositional report filed by the juvenile probation officer disclosed that Jerry J. has frequently been truant from school and has had serious behavioral problems when in school. He has had difficulty relating with other youths. Two weeks ago, Jerry J. was taken into custody and charged with arson, a felony. He and two Scorpion gang members were observed by three eyewitnesses setting fire to the occupied home of a rival gang member. Fortunately, no one was injured in the resulting fire. The juvenile court judge has just adjudicated Jerry J. delinquent on the arson charge and has committed him to the Arizona State Industrial School for two years.

Using the Arizona Department of Juvenile Corrections (ADJC) Risk Assessment form illustrated in Figure 10.1, determine Jerry J.'s total risk score. What is Jerry J.'s risk category? What is Jerry J.'s most serious commitment offense? What is Jerry J.'s most serious prior adjudicated offense?

Scenario 2: Florida and Mary M.   Mary M. is 15 years old. She lives in Tampa, Florida, and is a sophomore in high school. Recently, a juvenile court judge adjudicated Mary M. delinquent for stealing a neighbor's car and joyriding. She drove the car into another state, where she wrecked it. She was accompanied by two other girls, who were subsequently identified as members of a female gang from Tampa. Mary M. has admitted that she, too, is a member of that same gang. The auto theft charge is a third-degree felony. The judge has disposed her to 2 years' probation, together with mandatory psychological and substance-abuse counseling, since she had been using marijuana at the time of her arrest. She is currently receiving both psychological counseling and treatment for her substance abuse. The marijuana possession was a second-degree misdemeanor, although this charge was subsequently dropped pursuant to a plea bargain with the juvenile court prosecutor. A predispositional report prepared by a juvenile probation officer for the juvenile court disclosed the following background factors for Mary M. She began her career of delinquency when she was 12 years of age. At that time, she shoplifted some cosmetics from a local department store. When she was confronted by a store security officer, Mary M. assaulted the officer by pushing her into a display counter. The glass broke and the officer sustained severe lacerations. Mary M. was charged with theft and aggravated assault. The theft was related to a gang initiation. The juvenile court judge adjudicated her delinquent on both charges and ordered her committed to the Florida Industrial School, a secure facility, for a term of 6 months. Mary M. and another inmate escaped from this facility one evening, although they were apprehended three days later and returned to custody. Over the next few months, Mary M. tried to escape from the facility on at least four

ADJC RISK ASSESSMENT

YOUTH NAME _____ K# _____   DATE OF ASSESSMENT _____

COMMITTING COUNTY _____   DATE OF ADMISSION _____ DOB _____

		SCORE

R1   **Number of Referrals**   (__)
1 to 4 0
5 or More ....+1

_____

R2   **Number of Adjudications**   (__)
1 or 2 ....-1
3 or 4 0
5 or More ....+1

_____

R3   **Age at First Juvenile Referral** (__)
12 yrs 5 mos. or Younger.....................................+1
12 yrs 6 mos. or Older.. 0

_____

R4   **Petition Offense History (check applicable below and add for score)**
A.(__) 2 or More Assaultive Offenses.................+1
B.(__) 2 or More Drug Offenses..........................+2
C.(__) 3 or More Property Offenses....................+1
D.(__) Weapons Offense or use in above..............+1

R 4 Sub Total   _____

_____

R5   **Petitions for Felony Offenses**   (__)
0 to 2...0
3 or More..+1

_____

R6   **Affiliation with a Delinquent Gang**
No...0
Yes..+1

_____

R7   **Enrolled in School with no Serious Truancy or Behavioral Problems**
No... 0
Yes..-1

_____

R8   **Known Use of Alcohol or Drugs**
No...-1
Yes.. 0

_____

TOTAL RISK SCORE   _____

RISK CATEGORY (CHECK ONE)		
[ ] LOW(1 or Less)	[ ] MEDIUM (2-4)	[ ] HIGH (5+)

_____
Signature of Staff Completing Assessment Instrument

CURRENT COMMITMENT TYPE (CHECK ONE):   [ ] NEW COMMIT   [ ]ADJC REVOCATION

MOST SERIOUS COMMITMENT OFFENSE:

OFFENSE DESCRIPTION	ARS CODE	F/M CLASS	SUBCLASS	DATE

MOST SERIOUS PRIOR ADJUDICATED OFFENSE:

OFFENSE DESCRIPTION	ARS CODE	F/M CLASS	SUBCLASS	DATE

CLASS: 1,2,3,4,5,6 OR 9 = NOT APPLICABLE
F=FELONY   M=MISDEMEANOR   V=VIOLATION PROB. OR PAROLE   O=OTHER

FIGURE 10.1   The Arizona ADJC Risk Assessment Instrument

different occasions. The juvenile court judge adjudicated her delinquent on an escape charge, and the term of her confinement in the Florida Industrial School was extended to one year. Mary M. was subsequently released from secure confinement at age 13, and she returned to school. Over the next two years, Mary M. was involved in several minor incidents involving low-level misdemeanors. In one instance, she was placed on diversion by the prosecutor, with judicial approval. A part of her diversion was performing 200 hours of community service as well as observance of a curfew. Her juvenile probation officer caught her violating curfew on at least three occasions and filed an affidavit with the juvenile court. The juvenile court judge verbally reprimanded Mary M. on this occasion, but he did not impose other sanctions.

An interview with Mary M.'s parents revealed that Mary M. is incorrigible. The parents say that they have no control over Mary M.'s actions. However, Mary M.'s siblings, a younger brother and a sister, report that their parents, who have physical altercations frequently in front of them and use drugs themselves, are seldom home to monitor them and their sister, Mary M. A counselor has concluded independently that the family has a history of domestic violence and that the home is quite unstable. Mary M.'s mother has been committed to a psychiatric institution in previous years for depression as well as schizophrenia. The mother is currently on medication for the purpose of managing her depression. Mary M.'s father has a previous conviction for receiving stolen property, a second-degree misdemeanor. He has also been previously convicted of sexual battery and served six months in the county jail for this crime. In fact, at the present time, the Florida Department of Human Services is conducting an investigation of Mary M.'s family on charges of alleged child neglect.

Mary M. herself has no obvious developmental disabilities or prior mental illnesses and appears to be in good physical health. However, because of the history of her family, it has been recommended that she should have a psychological assessment to determine her present mental state. Mary M. is currently unemployed and has no marketable skills. Thus, she would be unable to obtain and/or sustain employment if she were expected to work. It has been recommended that she take several vocational/technical courses to improve her skill level. Her peer relations are poor, and she is socially immature and withdrawn. She is easily led by others, as evidenced by the ease with which she was recruited into her gang. Most of Mary M.'s close peers are other gang members. Although she is currently enrolled in school, she has poor attendance. During periods when she has attended school, she has been compliant and not disruptive. According to her teachers, Mary M. reads well and has no obvious learning disabilities. But it has been determined that Mary M. has used marijuana frequently with her gang friends. Mary's home situation has been cited by the juvenile probation officer as a substantial mitigating circumstance, and she recommends a 5-point reduction in Mary M.'s risk score. The probation supervisor, who oversees risk assessment instrument preparation and administration, concurs with this recommendation and has chosen not to override it.

Figure 10.2 shows the Florida Department of Juvenile Justice Supervision Risk Classification Instrument. Notice that it consists of two parts. The first part is a risk assessment scale. The second part is a needs assessment scale.

Figure 10.2 illustrates the Florida Department of Juvenile Justice Classification Matrix. This matrix is used to determine the level of a youth's placement in the Florida Department of Juvenile Justice based on a combination of one's needs assessment score and risk assessment score. Using the information for Mary M. in the scenario above, determine Mary M.'s risk assessment and needs assessment scores. Next, place Mary M. in the Classification Matrix according to the scores you have calculated.

FLORIDA DEPARTMENT OF JUVENILE JUSTICE
SUPERVISION RISK CLASSIFICATION INSTRUMENT

Youth's Name: Sharon H Test _____   Court Docket #: _____
Juvenile Probation Officer: _____   Unit: _____
Date Completed: _____ DJJID: 532950   Referral ID: 1507938 _____

RISK ASSESSMENT

A.   INSTANT OFFENSE (most serious) ....   _____

- Capital or life felony   32 points
- 1st degree felony (violent)   20 points
- 1st degree felony/2nd degree felony (violent)   18 points
- 2nd degree felony/3rd degree felony (violent)   15 points
- 3rd degree felony   7 points
- 1st degree misdemeanor (violent)   5 points
- 1st degree misdemeanor   3 points
- 2nd degree misdemeanor   1 point

B.   PRIOR HISTORY (highest applicable score)

- Meets the criteria for Level 10 placement   7 points
- Has met the definition of a SHO/IRT with this offense   6 points
- Two or more prior non-related felonies resulting in adjudication or withheld adjudication   3 points
- One felony or two or more non-related misdemeanors resulting in adjudication or withheld adjudication   2 points
- One prior misdemeanor resulting in adj. or withheld adj.   1 point

C.   OTHER SCORING FACTORS (combined score) ....   _____

- Current legal status CC/F (2 pts) - committed (4 pts)
- Previous completed CC/F (2 pts) committed (4pts)
- Previous technical violation (1 point. per affidavit)
- Youth 12 years old/under at time of 1st charge (1pt)
- Substance use/abuse involved (1 pt.)
- History of escape or absconding (1pt.)
- Current or previous JASP/community arb. (2 pts each)
- Other previous or current diversion (1 pt. each)
- Domestic violence involved (youth as perpetrator) (2 pts each)
- Gang related offense (2 pt.)

D.   A+B+C = SUBTOTAL   0

Mitigating (maximum 5 pts.).............................(-)   _____
Justification _____

Aggravating-consider pending offenses (max 5) ......(+)   _____
Justification _____

TOTAL: A+B+C – mitigation + aggravating =   0

TOTAL RISK SCORE ____ 0   **TOTAL NEEDS SCORE** ____ 0

CLASSIFICATION DECISION (see matrix on page 3):
☐ Diversion ☐ Minimum ☐ General ☐ Intensive
☐ Level 2 ☐ Level 4 ☐ Level 6 ☐ Level 8/10

OVERRIDE CLASSIFICATION DECISION (if applicable):
☐ Diversion ☐ Minimum ☐ General ☐ Intensive
☐ Level 2 ☐ Level 4 ☐ Level 6 ☐ Level 8/10
OVERRIDE JUSTIFICATION: _____

JPO Initials _____   Date: _____
Supervisor Initials _____   Date: _____

NEEDS ASSESSMENT

A.   FAMILY RELATIONSHIPS (score total points)   _____ 0

- Parents unable/unwilling to control youth   3 pts. ____
- Parent cooperative, some control   1 pt. ____
- Youth in unstable independent living situation   2 pts. ____
- Family history of domestic violence   2 pts. ____
- Family history of abuse/neglect   2 pts. ____
- Parent or sibling with criminal history   1 pt. ____
- Parent with mental illness   2 pts. ____
- Parent with substance abuse   2 pts. ____
- Out of home dependency placement   2 pts. ____
- Current abuse/neglect investigation   3 pts. ____
- Youth is a parent   3 pts. ____

B.   PEER RELATIONSHIPS (score total pts)   _____ 0

- Socially immature   1 pt. ____
- Socially withdrawn   1 pt. ____
- Easily led by others   1 pt. ____
- Exploits or aggressive to others   2 pts. ____
- Peers have delinquent history or gang involvement   3 pts. ____

C.   SIGNIFICANT ADULT RELATIONS (score highest)   _____ 0

- Authority figure relationships are inconsistent   1 pt. ____
- Youth unavailable/unwilling to positively relate to adult authority figures   2 pts ____

D.   EDUCATIONAL (score total pts.) ....   _____ 0

- Poor attendance/not enrolled (under 16)   3 pts. ____
- Disruptive school behavior   2 pts. ____
- Literacy problems   2 pts. ____
- Learning disability   2 pts. ____
- Withdrawn/expelled/suspended   3 pts. ____
- Enrolled and failing   2 pts. ____

E.   YOUTH'S EMPLOYMENT (score total pts)   _____ 0
(youth over 16, not in school or youth with monetary needs)

- Currently developing marketable skills/no school   1 pt. ____
- Needs to develop marketable skills   2 pts. ____
- Currently unemployed   2 pts. ____

F.   DEVELOPMENTAL DISABILITY (score highest)   _____ 0

- Known dev. disability/no current services   3 pts. ____
- Known dev. disability/with current services   2 pts. ____
- Disability suspected/no diagnosis   2 pts. ____

G.   PHYSICAL HEALTH & HYGIENE (score total pts.) ......   _____ 0

- Medical or dental referral needed   1 pt. ____
- Health or hygiene education needed   1 pt. ____
- Handicap or illness limits functioning   3 pts. ____

H.   MENTAL HEALTH (score total pts.) ....   _____ 0

- Assessment needed   2 pts. ____
- Prior history of mental health problems   2 pts. ____
- Currently in treatment   2 pts. ____
- Assessment indicates treatment needs/no current services   3 pts. ____

I.   SUBSTANCE ABUSE (score total pts.)   _____ 0

- Assessment needed   2 pts. ____
- Occasional user   1 pt. ____
- Frequent user   3 pts. ____
- Assessment indicates treatment needs/no services   3 pts. ____
- Receiving treatment services   2 pts. ____

TOTAL NEEDS SCORE   _____ 0

April, 1998   Case Management: Intake   DJJ/IS Form 4
Page 1 of 3

FIGURE 10.2 Florida Department of Juvenile Justice Supervision Risk Classification Instrument

Calculating the ADJC Risk Score for Jerry J. Before determining Jerry J.'s score on the Arizona Risk Assessment instrument, familiarize yourself with the instrument's contents. There are eight categories: (1) number of referrals, (2) number of adjudications, (3) age at first juvenile referral, (4) petition offense history, (5) petitions for felony offenses, (6) affiliation with a delinquent gang, (7) enrolled in school with no serious truancy or behavioral problems, and (8) known use of alcohol or drugs.

First, let's count the number of times Jerry J. has been referred to juvenile court on various charges. We can count *both* referrals *and* delinquency petitions filed against Jerry J., because both actions are intended to bring juveniles

FLORIDA DEPARTMENT OF JUVENILE JUSTICE
SUPERVISION RISK CLASSIFICATION INSTRUMENT

DJJID #: __532950__   Referral ID: __1507938__

JUSTIFICATION: ____

April, 1998   Case Management: Intake   DJJ/IS Form 4
                              Page 2 of 3

FIGURE 10.2 Continued

before the juvenile court. Delinquency petitions are only filed in about half of all juvenile cases that reach the juvenile courts annually throughout the United States. The other types of cases are nonpetitioned cases. In Jerry J.'s case, he was referred by the school principal on two occasions, with a delinquency petition filed on the second occasion. Jerry J. was referred again to juvenile court by police officers for selling crack cocaine. Later, Jerry J. was referred to the juvenile court for burglary, theft, and carrying a concealed weapon. Jerry J.'s probation officer also referred him to the juvenile court because of a probation violation. Subsequently, Jerry J. was referred to juvenile court three more times, all resulting in delinquency adjudications. Two of these offenses were felonies: aggravated assault and selling cocaine. Finally, Jerry J. was most recently re-

**FLORIDA DEPARTMENT OF JUVENILE JUSTICE
CLASSIFICATION MATRIX**

NEEDS	RISK			
	LOW 0 10	**MODERATE** 11 17	**HIGH** 18 24	**VERY HIGH** 25 32
LOW 0 : : : : 15	Diversion	Minimum Supervision General Supervision	Minimum Supervision General Intensive Supervision	Level 4 Level 6 Level 8/10
MODERATE 16 : : : 30	Diversion	Minimum Supervision General Supervision	Intensive Level 2	Level 4 Level 6 Level 8/10
HIGH 31 : : : : 45	Diversion Minimum Supervision	General Supervision	Intensive Level 2 Level 4	Level 6 Level 8/10
VERY HIGH 46+ : : : :	Diversion Minimum Supervision	General Supervision Intensive Supervision	Level 2 Level 4 Level 6	Level 8/10

April, 1998   Case Management: Intake   DJJ/IS Form 4
Page 3 of 3

FIGURE 10.2 Continued

ferred to the juvenile court for arson and adjudicated delinquent on that charge. Therefore, there are at least nine referrals of Jerry J. to juvenile court. Since this is "5 or more," we will give Jerry J. a +1 for R1 as shown in Figure 10.1.

Next, we determine the number of Jerry J.'s adjudications. He was adjudicated delinquent on the school assault charge; the drug charge; the firearms, burglary, and theft charges; three additional adjudications for offenses, including aggravated assault and selling cocaine; and for arson. This adds up to seven delinquency adjudications. For R2, this is "5 or more," and therefore, we score R2 with a +1.

Jerry J.'s age at his first juvenile court referral was 11. For R3, this is "12 years, 5 months or younger," and therefore, we score Jerry J. a +1.

Jerry J.'s petition offense history includes "2 or more assaultive offenses." We score this portion of the risk instrument with a +1. Jerry J. also has "2 or more drug offenses," and therefore, we assign him a +2. Although Jerry J. has participated in several thefts, as mentioned in the scenario, we should count only what police and other authorities actually know about Jerry J. and which types of offenses resulted in petitions filed with the juvenile court. He has a burglary and a theft charge for which petitions have been filed. Since this is not "3 or more property offenses," we do not assign Jerry J. a score. However, we can give Jerry J. a +1 for "weapons offense or use in above." Thus, for the R4 Petition Offense History score, Jerry J. should receive a 4.

R5 is "Petitions for Felony Offenses," and Jerry J. has at least three or more of these. Therefore, we assign him a +1 for R5.

R6 is easy to score. Is Jerry J. a gang member? Yes. Therefore, he receives a +1 for R6.

R7 is also easy to score. Jerry J. has been enrolled in school in the past, but he has serious truancy problems. We must assign him a 0 for R7.

Finally, for R8, Jerry J. is known for his use of alcohol and drugs. We must assign him a 0 for R8.

Summing R1 through R8, we have 1 + 1 + 1 + 4 + 1 + 1+ 0 + 0 = 9. Jerry J.'s total risk assessment score is 9. According to the ADJC Risk Assessment instrument, the Risk Category where we would place Jerry J. is "High" (5+ points).

Notice that there are other items to fill in on this form. One space is for "Most Serious Commitment Offense." We are not in a position to know how Arizona rates the seriousness of aggravated assault in relation to arson. But these are the two offenses resulting in Jerry J.'s commitment to the Arizona State Industrial School. If "arson" were the more serious offense, then we would list this in the first space for "Most Serious Commitment Offense," with an appropriate code and date. It would be a felony. For the "Most Serious Prior Adjudicated Offense," we would have to list "aggravated assault" as the offense, which is also a felony. We would also enter a code for this offense, as well as the date of the adjudication.

Without the accompanying Arizona Department of Juvenile Corrections instruction manual for this instrument, we don't know how Jerry J.'s score of "9" will be used. In all likelihood, it will relate to his placement in the secure facility and the intensity of supervision he will receive while confined. He is definitely a risk to others and must be monitored carefully. However, this score is only one of many criteria that are used in placement and level-of-custody decision making.

It should be noted that if Jerry J. is alternatively considered for admission into a community-based program by the juvenile court judge instead of placement in a secure facility, another form is used by the Arizona Department of Juvenile Corrections. This form is very similar to the form shown in Figure 10.1 and is illustrated in Figure 10.3.

Figure 10.3 is a reassessment form, and it serves to give us an impression of how much Jerry J. has improved his behavior since being admitted into the community-based program. In this form, attention is focused on one's peer relationships within a 30- to 90-day period, whether there have been problems with

ADJC RISK REASSESSMENT

FOR YOUTH IN COMMUNITY PROGRAMS

YOUTH NAME _____ K# _____ DOB _____ DATE OF REASSESSMENT _____

For items 1 - 4 use initial Risk Assessment information

                                                SCORE

RE 1.   **Age At First Referral**   (____)
        12 Years or Less ....+1
        13 Years or Older 0   _____

RE 2.   **Number of Prior Referrals**   (____)
        4 or Less 0
        5 or More ....+1   _____

RE 3.   **Prior Petition Offense History**
        A (____)   3 or More Property ....+1
        B (____)   2 or More Assaultive Offenses ....+1
        C (____)   2 or More Drug Offenses ....+2
        D (____)   Weapons Offense...+1   _____

                              RE 3 SUBTOTAL   _____

RE 4.   **Prior Petitions For Felony Offenses**   (____)
        2 or Less 0
        3 or More ....+1   _____

Score All Following Items for Last 30/90 Days.

RE 5.   **Referrals To Court or For Revocation Hearing (Last 30/90 days)**
        None ....–1
        One ....+1
        Two or More...+2

RE 6.   **Use of Alcohol or Other Drugs (Last 30/90 Days)**
        No...0
        Yes...+1   _____
        Check type (if any)   _____Alcohol   _____ Marijuana   _____ Other Drug

RE 7.   **Peer Relationships (Last 30/90 Days)**
        No Problems 0
        Associates with Delinquent Peers ....+1   _____
        Associates with Gang Members ....+2

RE 8.   **School or Work Adjustment (Last 30/90 Days)** _____ **Where**
        No Problems or Minor Problems..0
        Some Attendance /Behavior Problems.....................................+1   _____
        Serious Work or School Attendance/Behavior Problems.........+2

RE 9.   **Adjustment to Supervision/Compliance with Plan (Last 30/90 Days)**
        No Problems ....–1
        Minor Problems..0
        Serious Compliance Problems with Plan ....+1   _____

                              TOTAL SCORE   _____

RISK CATEGORY (CIRCLE ONE)

LOW (5 or Less) = LEVEL III	MEDIUM (6 - 10) = LEVEL II	HIGH (11 or HIGHER) = LEVEL I

Assigned Supervision Level_____   Override Y/N   Reason _____
                                                           _____

Parole Officer's Signature _____   Date _____

Supervisor's Signature _____   Date _____

FIGURE 10.3   ADJC Risk Reassessment for Youth in Community Programs

school or work adjustment within a similar time interval, and whether the client has had problems adjusting to supervision or compliance with program requirements within the most recent 30- to 90-day period.

    In Jerry J.'s case, if he were placed in a community program instead of being incarcerated, he would be evaluated within a 30- to 90-day period following his community program placement. If he had improved his behavior, there is a good possibility that his risk level (or risk category) could be reduced. This possible risk category reduction may have implications for how closely or loosely Jerry J. is supervised in his community-based program. It is also indicative of whether he is becoming rehabilitated and reintegrated.

Calculating the Florida Risk Assessment Score for Mary M.   The Florida Department of Juvenile Justice Risk Classification Instrument, Figure 10.2, is divided into two parts. One part is "Risk Assessment," while the other is "Needs Assessment." Again, when determining the score for any juvenile, we must first familiarize ourselves with the instrument's contents before computing a risk score. There are three categories (A, B, and C), which refer to (1) the instant offense, (2) prior history, and (3) other scoring factors.

For category A, "Instant Offense," Mary M. has recently been adjudicated delinquent on an auto theft charge, which is a third-degree felony. According to this risk assessment scale, a third-degree felony rates a score of 7 points.

For category B, we are to assign Mary M. the highest applicable score. This means that we are not supposed to add or sum the scores for all categories that fit Mary M. Given her delinquency history since age 12, including her escape from a secure facility, an assault on a store security officer, and gang membership, she probably meets the criteria for "Level 10 placement." According to Florida officials, the risk score derived from this instrument at the time of a youth's arrest is used to make an appropriate recommendation to the state attorney's office (Friedenauer 2002, 1). Let's assume that Mary M. qualifies for Level 10 placement, and therefore we will assign her a 7.

Category C is additive in that we are to consider a number of factors, each associated with specific points. These factors include current legal status (presently committed to a secure facility), previous completed commitment (to a secure facility), previous technical violation (in connection with a probation or parole program or diversion), age at time of first charge, substance use/abuse involvement, history of escape or absconding, current or previous community arbitration (alternative dispute resolution), other previous or current diversion, and a gang-related offense. For each category that applies to Mary M., we should assign a score. Subsequently we will sum the individual scores to determine the combined score for C.

Currently, Mary M. is on probation. However, she has had a previous commitment to the Florida Industrial School. We assign her 4 points for this category. She has a technical violation, violating curfew while on probation, and an affidavit has been filed in connection with this violation. Therefore, Mary M. receives 1 point for this category.

Mary M. began her career of delinquency at age 12. Therefore, she receives 1 point for this category. She is a substance abuser, and therefore she receives 1 point for this category. She has a history of escape from the secure facility where she was placed, and this entitles her to 1 point. She has never participated in alternative dispute resolution, and therefore she receives no points for this category. However, she has been placed on diversion once in the past, and she receives 1 point for this category. Although there is domestic violence in Mary M.'s home, Mary M. has never been the perpetrator. Therefore, she receives no points for this category. Finally, she has had at least one gang-related offense, shoplifting. We assign her 2 points for this category. There are ten categories as subparts of C, and we sum the various subparts as follows: $0 + 4 + 1 + 1 + 1 + 1 + 0 + 1 + 0 + 2 = 11$ points. Mary M.'s score for C is 11.

Summing her scores for categories A, B, and C, we have $7 + 7 + 11 = 25$ points. Notice that for D, adjustments may be made for the presence of aggravating or mitigating circumstances. Anyone completing this risk assessment might choose to focus upon Mary M.'s violent acts, such as pushing the store security officer. They might also focus upon Mary M.'s escape from the Florida Industrial School and subsequent attempts to escape. These factors might be considered as aggravating. However, substantial evidence exists that might constitute mitigating circumstances. Mary M.'s home life is a disaster. She has a dysfunctional family where frequent physical altercations and drug use are evident. Background information about Mary M. from school officials suggest that but for her gang affiliation, Mary M. is a compliant and reasonably intelligent student. In the present scenario, the juvenile probation officer has recommended a 5-point reduction for Mary M., given her home circumstances. The probation supervisor has concurred with this recommendation. Therefore, there will probably be a 5-point reduction in Mary M.'s final score. This would be 25 − 5 = 20 points. Thus, Mary M.'s final risk assessment score would be 20.

One final word about the Florida risk reassessment device is in order. At the very bottom of the risk assessment instrument shown in Figure 10.5, a classification decision is illustrated. But immediately below this classification decision is an override classification decision. **Overrides** are decisions by someone in authority and with pertinent expertise to change whatever classification is yielded from the original risk score that has been computed. For instance, Mary M.'s score of 20 can be overridden for one or more reasons. The nature of the override is either to increase or decrease the resulting score or classification decision.

No risk assessment instrument captures every single facet of one's existence or circumstances. If there are circumstances or facts that are relevant to cases such as Mary M.'s, then the original classification decision may be overridden. For instance, Mary M. may have been coerced into committing burglaries and thefts by her other gang members. Duress might be a mitigating circumstance that is otherwise undetected through conventional measurement methods. Or Mary M. may be emotionally immature for her age. Factors such as these may be detected through interviews with juvenile clients. Perhaps information is yielded through other means, such as reports from school or church officials. In any case, any particular score assigned to a juvenile client may be overridden. It may be raised or lowered, provided that a reasonable justification is articulated to account for the change.

Needs Assessments

Besides measuring a juvenile's potential risk or dangerousness, it is important for juvenile justice practitioners to know what types of problems afflict particular youths. Many youths enter the juvenile justice system who are drug- or alcohol-dependent, have psychological problems, suffer from maladjustments in their homes or schools, or are impaired physically in some respect. Therefore, practitioners must assess juveniles who are processed to determine their respective needs. Sometimes scales are combined to obtain information about *both* risk and needs. These risk/needs assessment instruments enable those conducting such assessments to obtain both types of information from youths in one test administration. Not all juveniles need the same community services. There are diverse community resources available to meet a wide variety of needs exhibited by the youth who enter the juvenile justice system. Some juveniles require minimal intervention, while other youths need extensive treatments and services. Whether youths are confined in secure facilities or allowed to attend their schools and remain with their families in their communities, different provisions often must be made to individualize their needs. Needs assessment instruments are used to determine which specific services and treatments ought to be provided each youth.

For example, in the example of the Florida Risk Classification Instrument described above and our hypothetical case of Mary M., Figure 10.2 contained a needs assessment component as well as a risk assessment component. We calculated the risk assessment component. In the next section, we will compute Mary M.'s needs assessment score based on the scenario information provided previously.

Computing Mary M.'s Florida Needs Assessment Score. Again, we should familiarize ourselves with the needs assessment instrument, the second part of the Risk Classification Instrument as shown in Figure 10.2. There are nine areas covered, including family relationships, peer relationships, significant adult relations, educational factors, youth's employment, developmental disability (if any), physical health and hygiene, mental health, and substance abuse. Some of these areas contain additive components, meaning that we must assign points to juveniles such as Mary M. if certain subparts of these areas pertain to her or her circumstances.

For Part A, Family Relationships, we know from the above scenario about Mary M. that her parents cannot control her. We also know that she lives in an unstable family environment with a family history of domestic violence, abuse, and/or neglect, and that one parent has a criminal history. We also know that the parents use drugs or abuse various substances. Further, there is an ongoing investigation of this allegedly abusive environment being conducted by the Florida Department of Human Services. Mary M. herself is not a parent. There are eleven subparts for Part A. We would score these subparts sequentially as follows: 3 + 0 + 2 + 2 + 2 + 1 + 2 + 2 + 0 + 3 + 0 = 17 points. The Part A calculation is determined as follows:

Parents unable/unwilling to control youth? Yes.	3 points
Parent cooperative, some control? No.	0 points
Youth in unstable independent living situation? Yes.	2 points
Family history of domestic violence? Yes.	2 points
Family history of abuse/neglect? Yes.	2 points
Parent or sibling with criminal history? Yes.	1 point
Parent with mental illness? Yes.	2 points
Parent with substance abuse? Yes.	2 points
Out-of-home dependency placement? No.	0 points
Current abuse/neglect investigation? Yes.	3 points
Youth is a parent? No.	0 points

Part B has five subparts: socially immature, socially withdrawn, easily led by others, exploits or aggressive to others, and peers have delinquent history or gang involvement. We would score these subparts as follows: 1 + 1 + 1 + 0 + 3 = 6 points. The Part B calculation is determined as follows:

Socially immature? Yes.	1 point
Socially withdrawn? Yes.	1 point
Easily led by others? Yes.	1 point
Exploits or aggressive to others? No.	0 points
Peers have delinquent history or gang involvement? Yes.	3 points

Part C deals with significant adult relations. We can assign Mary M. 1 point for "authority figure relationships are inconsistent," although we have no data to suggest that Mary M. is unavailable/unwilling to positively relate to adult authority figures. Thus, for Part C, Mary M.'s score would be 1 point.

For Part D (educational), there are six components: poor attendance/not enrolled, disruptive school behavior, literacy problems, learning disability, withdrawn/expelled/suspended, enrolled and failing. Mary M. has poor attendance at school, although she is not disruptive and has no literacy or learning disability problems. She has not withdrawn from school, nor has she been expelled or suspended. She is not failing her classes, despite her truancy. We would give her 3 points for poor attendance, but "0" points for the other subparts. Her score for Part D, therefore, would be 3 points.

For Part E (youth's employment), since Mary M. is not over 16, these subparts are not relevant for her. She receives a 0 for Part E.

For Part F (developmental disability), Mary M. has no known developmental disabilities. Therefore, she will receive a 0 for this part.

For Part G (physical health and hygiene), Mary M. is in good physical health. She needs no health or hygiene education, and no obvious handicaps or illnesses limit her functioning. Therefore, she receives a 0 for Part G.

For Part H (mental health), there are three subparts: assessment needed, prior history of mental health problems, currently in treatment, and assessment indicates treatment needs/no current services. Mary M. will receive 3 points because of the recommended mental health assessment. Furthermore, she is currently receiving psychological counseling for her substance abuse problems. She receives 2 points for this subpart. Otherwise, no other points apply to Mary M. Part H, therefore, is scored as 3 + 2 = 5 points.

Last, for Part I (substance abuse), an assessment of her substance abuse problem is needed, and she is a frequent user of marijuana. Although a substance abuse assessment is recommended and will likely be conducted, Mary M. is currently receiving mandatory substance-abuse counseling/treatment. We would score Part I as follows: 2 + 0 + 3 + 0 + 2 = 7 points. This score accrues as follows:

Assessment needed? Yes.	2 points
Occasional user? No.	0 points
Frequent user? Yes.	3 points
Assessment indicates treatment needs/no services? No (not yet, anyway).	0 points
Receiving treatment services? Yes.	2 points

If we sum the various parts, we would have the following cumulative score:

Part	Points	Part	Points
A	17	F	0
B	6	G	0
C	1	H	5
D	3	I	7
E	0		

Total = 39 points

Mary M.'s total needs score is 39 points.

Together with this needs assessment score of 39, we can use Mary M.'s risk score of 20 and determine where Mary M. should be placed in the Florida Department of Juvenile Justice Classification Matrix illustrated in Figure 10.2. This matrix cross-tabulates risk and needs scores, with risk score across the top and needs score down the left-hand side. Where these scores intersect in the body of the table define the suggested nature of supervision Mary M. should receive by Florida juvenile corrections officials. Where a needs score of 39 (High) intersects with a risk score of 20 (High), a square is indicated with "Intensive," "Level 2," and "Level 4." Since we have no interpretive booklet from the Florida Department of Juvenile Justice, we don't know what these different levels mean, although we can glean that the levels range from 2 to 10, with 2 being the lowest level and 10 being the highest level. "Intensive" would suggest to us that Mary M. should receive intensive supervision, regardless of the program, community or institutional, where she is ultimately placed. We know from Mary M.'s scenario that the juvenile court judge disposed Mary M. to 2 years' probation, with mandatory psychological and substance-abuse counseling. No doubt there were other conditions, such as community service and/or restitution. This is because she stole a neighbor's car and wrecked it. Some compensation to the neighbor for the loss of the car will be provided. Mary M. will be expected to make some restitution for the car loss.

It should be emphasized that juvenile justice officials do not depend entirely on risk/needs instruments for their information about youth needs. Interviews with youths and their families are often conducted (Virginia Department of Criminal Justice Services 2000). Intake officers acquire extensive information about a youth's background. If certain youths are recidivists and have extensive juvenile records, some indication of their needs will already be on file. Thus, we will know what interventions have been applied in the past and whether these interventions have helped in any way. If not, then we might try alternative interventions and programs (Funk 1999; Wieckowski et al. 1998). Furthermore, the needs of male juvenile offenders often differ from the needs of female juvenile offenders. These gender differences are important and should be taken into consideration whenever assessment instruments are devised (Acoca and Dedel 1998). Another source of information about youths and their needs comes from juvenile probation officers. These court officials compile information about a youth's background and furnish this material to juvenile court judges. Subsequently, dispositions are individualized according to the probation officer's report. This is known as a predisposition report.

PREDISPOSITION REPORTS

Assisting juvenile court judges in their decision making relating to sentencing juvenile offenders during adjudicatory proceedings are predisposition reports that are often filed by juvenile probation officers, especially in serious cases. Predisposition reports contain background information about juveniles, the facts relating to their delinquent acts, and possibly probation officer recommendations for particular dispositions. They serve the function of assisting judges to make more informed sentencing decisions. They also serve as needs assessment devices, where probation officers and other juvenile authorities can determine high-need areas for certain youths and channel them to specific community-based organizations and agencies for particular treatments and services.

The Predisposition Report and Its Preparation

Juvenile court judges in many jurisdictions order the preparation of **predisposition reports,** which are the functional equivalent of presentence investigation reports for adults. Predisposition reports are intended to furnish judges with background information about juveniles to make a more informed sentencing decision (Myers 2001). They also function to assist probation officers and others to target high-need areas for youths and specific services or agencies for individualized referrals. Trester (1981, 89–90) has summarized four important reasons for why predisposition reports should be prepared:

1. These reports provide juvenile court judges with a more complete picture of juvenile offenders and their offenses, including the existence of any aggravating or mitigating circumstances.
2. These reports can assist the court in tailoring the disposition of the case to an offender's needs.
3. These reports may lead to the identification of positive factors that would indicate the likelihood of rehabilitation.
4. These reports provide judges with the offender's treatment history, which might indicate the effectiveness or ineffectiveness of previous dispositions and suggest the need for alternative dispositions.

It is important to recognize that predisposition reports are not required by judges in all jurisdictions. By the same token, legislative mandates obligate officials in other jurisdictions to prepare them for all juveniles to be adjudicated. Also, there are no specific formats universally acceptable in these report preparations. An example of a predispositional report from New Mexico is shown in Box 10.5.

Rogers (1990, 44) indicates that predisposition reports contain insightful information about youths that can be helpful to juvenile court judges prior to sentencing. Six social aspects of a person's life are crucial for investigations, analysis, and treatment. These include: (1) personal health, physical and emotional; (2) family and home situation; (3) recreational activities and use of leisure time; (4) peer group relationships (types of companions); (5) education; and (6) work experience. According to the National Advisory Commission on Criminal Justice Standards and Goals (1976), predisposition reports have been recommended in all cases where the offenders are minors. In actual practice, however, predisposition reports are only prepared at the request of juvenile court judges. No systematic pattern typifies such report preparation in most U.S. jurisdictions.

Rogers (1990, 46) lists the following characteristics that were included in 100 percent of all of the cases he has examined: (1) gender; (2) ethnic status; (3) age at first juvenile court appearance; (4) source of first referral to juvenile court; (5) reason(s) for referral; (6) formal court disposition; (7) youth's initial placement by court; (8) miscellaneous court orders and conditions; (9) type of counsel retained; (10) initial plea; (11) number of prior offenses; (12) age and time of initial offense; (13) number of offenses after first hearing; (14) youth's total offense number; (15) number of companions, first offense; (16) number of detentions; and (17) number of out-of-home placements.

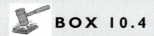 **BOX 10.4**

Dina Pennington Hales
Director, Shawnee County Community Corrections, Topeka, Kansas

Statistics:

B.S. (social work), Southern Colorado State College

Work History and Experiences:

Social work and corrections can be a good mix! I obtained a bachelor's degree in social work from Southern Colorado State College (now Southern Colorado University) in Pueblo, Colorado, in 1972. I joined VISTA, Volunteers in Service to America, the domestic side of the Peace Society of Topeka, Kansas. We worked as community organizers with low-income families by informing them of their rights and responsibilities as tenants in public and private housing. What an incredible opportunity! It really helped me develop organizational skills and learn about the community. It was also my first introduction into the world of laws, regulations, and standards. I served a year and a half in the program and decided to stay in Topeka.

In 1974, I began working at the Shawnee County Youth Center (juvenile detention) and at the Girls Group Home operated by the Youth Center. I worked nights at the Group Home and days at the Youth Center. Because I could sleep at the Group Home, I was only paid half time. What a deal! However, being the only staff on duty at night, I certainly could not sleep! I quickly advanced at the Youth Center under the mentorship of Elmer Whitmore, the Director. He seemed to see what I was capable of, long before I did, and he promoted me to Assistant Director.

My fourteen years at the Youth Center saw many changes in the world of juvenile detention. Initially, we held mostly status offenders: runaways, truants, and young people displaying ungovernable behavior. In 1978 we built a new and smaller facility designed for security and to hold more seri-

ous offenders. Fortunately, during the 1980s, the Office of Juvenile Justice and Delinquency Prevention became more diligent at enforcing the deinstitutionalization of status offenders and removing juveniles from adult jails. The Youth Center population switched to being mostly juveniles alleged or convicted of misdemeanor or felony offenses and waiting for placement. Major changes occurred in 1981 when the Jail, Community Corrections, and Youth Center combined to make the Shawnee County Department of Corrections.

In 1989 I was transferred to the Adult Detention Facility. I was Captain over Classification and Operations the majority of the time. Being the first female to hold that level of management was a challenge. It was assumed by some that I could not know how to run a jail, but I knew how to keep a building secure! Anyone who has worked with both juvenile and adult offenders knows that juveniles present more difficulties. They can dismantle nearly any item claimed to be "secure." One juvenile at the Youth Center completely removed a cinder block using only a toothbrush. Some of my efforts were not appreciated. My management style promoted teamwork, rather than an authoritarian manner. I felt that inmates should be treated respectfully. Staff training in interpersonal communication skills was just as important as training with weapons, self-defense, conducting searches, and report writing. The facility was a new generation, direct supervision jail, and the relationship between the officers and inmates was important to maintaining security. In addition,

(continued)

BOX 10.4 *(Continued)*

I believed that male and female officers should meet the same requirements and likewise offered the same opportunities.

Within four years, I was promoted to Major and operated the Community Corrections Division of the Department of Corrections. This was my first opportunity at operating a field services agency rather than an institution. I was finally out of lockup! Community corrections provided intensive supervised probation for both juvenile and adult offenders.

A short three years later I was transferred to the Youth Center to assist in the development of a new 75-bed juvenile detention center, to be co-located with the jail. It was to open in 1998. In preparation, I had been told that things were different in juvenile detention since I left. There was a new breed of violent, juvenile predators who would just as soon kill you as look at you, I was warned. These kids are cold and unfeeling, I was told. I was skeptical.

One of my first days on the job, I heard a ruckus on the boys' wing and decided to see what was going on. I was never the type to stay in my office. I circulate. Talk to officers. Talk to inmates. Special Housing at the jail was my most frequently visited module. Jeremy (not his real name), a large, handsome 17-year-old African American male, was kicking the 200-pound door to the point that it appeared it could actually pop off the hinges. I approached the door and talked to the young man through the glass window. He spit and cussed and told me in detail what I could do to certain body parts of his, but I kept talking in a low voice so he would have to quiet down to listen to me. He did quiet down and eventually told me why he was upset. Well, this started one of my favorite relationships. Jeremy grew up on the streets of Chicago. His language was alarming. Every female was a 'ho, every buddy was a "nigga," and m-f occurred in every sentence. We talked a lot about other words he could use that would be more acceptable! It was so automatic for him that when staff disciplined him, he often had no idea what he had said wrong. One time, a young girl was giving me a hard time. Jeremy stepped in and said to the girl, "Now don't be talkin' to the head 'ho like that!" He was defending me; we had come a long way in our relationship! Let's just say that it gave me the opportunity to tell him I was not a whore and did not want to be called one. He wanted to know what he should call me. We had several of these types of conversations.

Another three years passed, the new facility was open and running, and I was able to return to Community Corrections. A year later, Community Corrections separated from the Department of Corrections. I was fortunate to be selected as the Director of the newly formed Shawnee County Department of Community Corrections. We still provide intensive supervised probation for adult felony offenders. The juvenile area has really expanded. We provide three juvenile programs. Intensive supervised probation is for misdemeanor and felony offenders referred by the court. Juveniles referred to us were often not successful at standard probation, or their offenses are serious in nature and requiring more stringent monitoring and services. Juvenile offender case management is for juveniles needing out-of-home placement in order to be successful in their efforts to be crime-free. We also provide conditional release supervision for juveniles who have been released from one of the four state juvenile correctional facilities.

Advice to Students:

Thank you for this opportunity to walk down memory (career) lane. Criminal justice is such an exciting field. If you believe you can inspire people to change and that there are really very few bad apples, then I hope you will consider this field of work. First, get a degree. Second, find every opportunity to learn and develop your skills. Third, always remember that when you are dealing with offenders, you are a role model. Be a good one. Use language that is not offensive, always work in a professional manner, and treat everyone with fairness and consistency. Most people make positive changes because they had someone who cared and showed them other ways to behave.

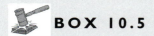 **BOX 10.5**

SAMPLE PREDISPOSITIONAL REPORT FROM NEW MEXICO

CHILDREN, YOUTH AND FAMILIES DEPARTMENT
JUVENILE JUSTICE DIVISION

IDENTIFYING INFORMATION*
*Fictitious names because of
New Mexico confidentiality provisions

NAME: Mary Allen
DOB: October 15, 1988
SSN: n/a
ADDRESS: 301 1st St.
Las Cruces, NM
PHONE NUMBER: (444)(555-1212)
P/G/C: Parents
RELIGIOUS PREF: unknown
PRIMARY LANGUAGE SPOKEN: English

AKA: n/a

COURT INFORMATION

COMPLETED BY: Ann Ames
DATE COMPLETED: October 10, 2002
CASE NUMBER: 123456
CAUSE NUMBER: 7890
JUDGE: Hon. Mark Jones
COUNTY: McNabb
DEFENSE ATTY: Charles Barkin
CCA: unknown

FINAL DISPOSITION: No contest plea
FINAL DISPOSITION DATE: Pending

I. REFERRAL INFORMATION

Current Offense: On 1-02-2002 at 3:40 AM, Mary Allen was taken (by her parents) to the hospital because she was bleeding profusely. Doctors there notified Mary Allen's parents that it was apparent that she had just given birth to a baby. The location of the baby was unknown at the time and doctors suspected that Mary Allen had possibly killed the baby. Police were notified and searched her room where they found a full term baby (deceased) in a trash can in Mary Allen's bedroom. Mary Allen allegedly told police that she did not know she was pregnant, but gave birth to the baby, by herself, on 12-30-01. An autopsy report indicates that the baby girl who was found with the umbilical cord still attached, and wrapped around her neck, was alive at birth and died of asphyxiation. Mary Allen was arrested on 1-11-02 and booked into McNabb County Jail, Juvenile Unit, at approximately 6:00 PM.

On 1-13-02, a petition was filed charging Mary Allen with Count 1: Child Abuse (intentionally caused) (death), or in the alternative; Child Abuse (negligently caused)(death), or in the alternative; Child Abuse (negligently permitted)(death) and Count 2: Tampering with Evidence. Mary Allen's parents were able to post the 10 percent cash deposit of $10,000 bond and Mary Allen was released home on January 14, 2002. A forensic evaluation was ordered at this time.

On September 22, 2002, Mary Allen entered into a plea agreement with the Children's Court Attorney. Mary Allen pleaded No Contest to Alternative Count 1: Child Abuse (negligently permitted)(death). In exchange for the plea, the remaining counts in the petition were dismissed and the state agreed to handle the case in a juvenile setting. There was no agreement as to the disposition in the matter and a Predispositional Report was ordered.

Number of Co-Offenders: 0
Victim Impact Mailed: ❐ Yes   ❐ No   ❐ N/A   Response: ❐ Yes   ❐ No
Victim Requests Restoration:

(continued)

BOX 10.5 (*Continued*)

Victim Impact Summary: A victim impact statement is not applicable in this case. It should be noted, however, that Mary Allen has given two names for the father of her child. Initially, Mary Allen told investigators that she had sexual intercourse with Walter Brooks and that the condom broke. She said she had taken a pregnancy test at Planned Parenthood with negative results. During this officer's conversation with Mary Allen, however, she indicated that the father is John Johnson. She said that Johnson denied that he is the father and that they do not have any contact with each other.

Chronological report attached: ❏ Yes ❏ No

Currently on Probation/Parole: ❏ Yes ❏ No Location:

Prior Supervision:

Cause No.	Begin Date	Type	Length	Expiration	Release Date	Release Type
N/A	10-13-00	Informal supervision	3 months	1-12-01	1-12-01	Now Supervising under conditional release.

Comments: Mary Allen was placed on Informal Supervision after her first referral to the probation department in October 2000. Mary Allen was referred to Juvenile Probation for a citation she had received for Criminal Trespass. Mary Allen and her two sisters were cited as a group of teens were caught loitering at Grady's, a restaurant and popular hangout for youth. Mary Allen came to see this officer at least one time every week, without fail. Mary Allen turned in weekly grade checks from school and attendance was verified.

Prior Commitment to Correctional Facility:

Cause No.	Commit Date	Type	Length	Expiration	Dis.Date	Dis.Type
N/A	N/A	N/A	N/A	N/A	N/A	N/A

Comments: Mary Allen has had no prior commitments to correctional facilities.

Prior Youthful Offender: ❏ Yes ❏ No

Outstanding Restitution: ❏ Yes ❏ No Amount: $0.00

Outstanding Community Service: ❏ Yes ❏ No Hours: 0

II. SOCIAL, EDUCATIONAL, AND SUBSTANCE ABUSE HISTORY

(Please include information on siblings, dependents, employment, parents marital status, primary language spoken in home, current school status, special expectations, truancy, behavior problems, gang activity, weapons, extracurricular activities, alcohol, marijuana, and other drug use.)

A. Social

Mary Allen is the youngest of three daughters born to Martin and Jane Allen. Jean Allen is 19 years old, married, and living with her husband, William Smith, 21, and their infant son, Frederick. Olivia Allen (18), lives in the family home along with Mary Allen. The family lives in a rented house in the northeast heights of Las Cruces and have for the past four years. The home is a three-bedroom home that appears cluttered but clean. The front and back yards seem moderately maintained and the inside is well-furnished. The ashes of Mary Allen's (deceased baby) sit on the fireplace mantel in an urn the shape of an angel. Baby Allen was cremated on 1-28-02, after the Office of Medical Investigators released the body. For weeks after the incident, the mailbox outside the house and the cars belonging to the family and friends were decorated with tiny pink ribbons in remembrance of the baby. Mary Allen has moved out of the bedroom that she resided in at the time of the incident. Mary Allen's parents have moved into that room and report that Mary Allen is unable (emotionally) to go in there. Mary Allen is currently working at Best Industries, as of May 1, 2002. Mary Allen previously worked at McDonald's but lost her job shortly after the events of this case came to light. Mary Allen had to take four months off of work after the incident. She was an emotional wreck, making her "dysfunctional" and therefore unable to complete her job as expected. Taking this time off has taken its toll on the family as well, and Martin Allen was forced to work even more at his job of eleven years. Martin Allen said that he had to "keep the family going" in a time when it seemed everything was falling apart. Mary Allen is currently working with her father at Best Industries where she is working in the mail room. Mary Allen is currently considered a part-time employee although she works 7.5 hours/day. Mary Allen has been there for three months and currently makes $6.50/hour. The remainder of her day is spent on her home schooling. Mary Allen spends much of her weekends babysitting her 5-month-old nephew, Frederick.

Mary Allen attended Las Cruces Elementary School where her mother was the President of the P.T.A. Both Mrs. Allen and her father report that Mary Allen was a good student and did fine in elementary school. Once in middle school, Mary Allen attended Craig Middle School. She and her family lived in the south valley and Mary Allen said she was one of the very few blonde-haired, blue-eyed girls there. Mary Allen reported that she did fine in school, but had problems with peers because of her race. The family eventually moved and Mary Allen began attending Burgess Middle School. Mary Allen reported no problems at Burgess. Once in high school, Mary Allen began attending informal student parties

and that she was very much into marijuana her ninth grade year. Mary Allen became involved with a boyfriend who proved to be a bad influence on her. After her ditching classes became a habit, Mary Allen was referred to a truancy officer and ordered to complete community service. Mary Allen reportedly got back on track after her parents placed her on more structure and restriction. By the time this incident took place, Mary Allen was seemingly doing much better. Mary Allen was in the midterm of her sophomore year when this incident occurred and did not return following her arrest in January 2002. Mary Allen plans to continue with her home schooling until graduation. Incidentally, Mary Allen has done very well in this program and is now classified as a junior, ahead of her schedule in mainstream educational setting. Mary Allen's sister, Olivia, left her school after the incident as well when the publicity brought adverse reactions from her peers. Olivia, however, has since returned to the school and is reportedly not having any problems there. Jean Allen graduated from school before any of these circumstances arose.

As mentioned earlier, Mary Allen was referred to the probation department on one other occasion. In July 2000, police officers working a tac-plan in the Northeast Heights cited Mary Allen and her sisters for trespassing at a local restaurant. Officers were working in an effort to reduce the number of young people loitering in the various parking lots. Mary Allen and her sisters were at Grady's when the three of them were cited. Mary Allen came in to see this officer for her Preliminary Inquiry on 10-13-00 and was placed on informal supervision. Mary Allen made weekly visits with this officer, called in regularly, and turned in school reports as requested. There does not appear to be any other legal history with the family; however, it has been reported that things have been tense at home.

There does not appear to be any physical evidence in the home; however; it has been reported that there is tension and that marital conflict is present. According to the Forensic Evaluation, dated 1-20-01, there were frequent fights about issues relating to

(continued)

BOX 10.5 (*Continued*)

the three daughters, money, and dad's drinking. Martin Allen has been said to have a "long-standing alcohol abuse hell." Counseling was offered initially to help cope with the surrounding offense and any issues exacerbated by it, however, Martin Allen advised that he does not need any more counseling. Martin Allen reports that he will support Mary Allen throughout her counseling, but that he has no intention of continuing himself. Martin Allen reported that he does not believe the incident should be "dwelled on" and that "you have to go on, or it will tear you up." It was unclear if Martin Allen would participate in further counseling or not.

Initially, Martin Allen sought counseling services for his family through the Employee Assistance Program that his employer provides. This program only allowed for five visits and the family quickly exhausted that service. Dr. Martha Ames, a private psychologist, was recommended and Mary Allen has been seeing her for some time now. Mary Allen sees Dr. Ames every two weeks, but no other family member attends. Mary Allen's sessions are on average one hour at a time. Mary Allen reports that she likes Dr. Ames and feels comfortable in working with her.

Mary Allen has admitted to using substances in the past such as marijuana and acid. It is this officer's understanding that Mary Allen used acid on an experimental basis only and that marijuana was her drug of choice while in the ninth grade. It is also this officer's understanding that Mary Allen has not used any marijuana since June 2001. It is a concern, however, that Mary Allen admits to using alcohol on New Year's Eve 2000. This apparently took place at the house with her parents present along with other friends drinking as well. It is disconcerting that Mary Allen's parents would allow minors to drink in their home. This was not typical, however, according to Mary Allen, but rather something of a celebration of the upcoming new year. Mary Allen advised her parents allow drinking on special occasions only.

B. Education/Employment

Diploma:

❐ HS Diploma   ❐ GED Certificate

Graduation date: Pending   GED Date: N/A

Special Education:

❐ Eligible for Sp.Ed.   ❐ Ineligible for Sp.Ed.   ❐ May require Sp.Ed.

Qualifications for Sp.Ed: N/A

Level: N/A   Effective Date: N/A

C. School History

School Name	Type	Program	Prog. Type	Grade/Sp.Ed.	Start Date Stat.
Hardcourt Learning Direct	Home School	Mail/correspondence school	Regular Education	10	03/01/02

Comments: As mentioned earlier, Mary Allen is doing well in school and is now classified as a junior in high school. Mary Allen mails in her school work and completes the assignments that she is provided through the Hardcourt Learning Direct Program. Mary Allen has goals of completing her high school education and eventually obtaining a degree in Auto Mechanics.

D. Mental Health/Substance Use History

Treatment:
    ❏ Prior Treatment Outpatient   ❏ Prior Treatment Outpatient
    Date of Last Psych.   Eval: 4-17-01
Substance Use:
    ❏ Alcohol   Frequency: Special Occasions
    ❏ Marijuana   Frequency: Daily in the past
    ❏ Drugs   Frequency: Experimental
    ❏ Solvents   Frequency:
Date Updated: 11-7-01

Comments: Please refer to Section II above for details.

III. JPPO OVERVIEW RECOMMENDATION

(Include core services, P/G/C, and client's view of needs, issues, and strengths, treatment/residential placement, JPPO areas of concern, and community-based service required if removal of client from home is recommended).

Mary Allen appeared to be very nervous about the outcome of this case. Mary Allen acknowledged that she would like to continue working and complete her education. Mary Allen described herself as a very caring person who is "good minded" and prides herself in her good grades and employment history. Mary Allen's father was equally complimentary in his description of Mary Allen. Martin Allen described Mary Allen as a hard worker, energetic, focused, and good with chores at home, never having to be reminded to do them. The only negative issue that Mary Allen and her father could pinpoint was her need to stay on track with school. Nothing was mentioned in regards to counseling or the deep issues associated with the death of her child.

It is difficult to ascertain what Mary Allen's thoughts are about the incident itself. It is unfortunate that she was able to plead No Contest in that she now can keep her side of the story to herself. It has been very difficult to assess the situation given that much of the very important information will never have to be given by Mary Allen. It impedes treatment as well by not having to talk about the incident or specific actions in the matter as long as that is the case. Mary Allen's own state of mind is at risk. As Dr. Ames described it, Mary Allen has been greatly limited in her ability to work with other students, as she has not been permitted to talk about the offense. Dr. Ames has been hampered in her ability to investigate with Mary Allen and her family the causes of the offense and to directly address them. When weighing the distinction between retribution, safety of the public, and the best interest of the child, it is difficult to suggest that incarceration is the most appropriate outcome. Mary Allen has been afforded the opportunity to show that she can comply with the structure and rules that the probation department can provide and she has done that. Incarcerating her at this point would serve no purpose other than punishment, and this could impede the treatment process even further. Dr. Ames feels that Mary Allen does not lack the capacity for empathy and the concern for others. Further, it is this officer's understanding that Mary Allen does not pose a threat to anyone. The amount of denial in this case is insurmountable and the plea agreement encourages it. It is imperative that Mary Allen be allowed to engage in therapy to the point that she can talk about the incident and work, with her parents, to move past this and begin the lengthy process of intensive therapy. It is equally important that Mary Allen's family engage in therapy. According to the Forensic Evaluation, a likely factor in Mary Allen's situation is the stress in the family characterized by parental alcohol abuse, depression, and chronic marital conflict. The results of these family problems affected the whole family. Mary Allen,

(continued)

BOX 10.5 (*Continued*)

it has been reported, is deficient in coping skills, judgment, problem solving, and decision making. Mary Allen, according to the Forensic, appears to be "overwhelmed by especially stressful circumstances, and to ill-judged behavior at such times." Mary Allen, it reports, "does not seem to be a girl with antisocial or prominent aggressive tendencies, or characteristic tendencies toward remorseless use of others." Given these findings, it would seem appropriate to think that with support and supervision, and with intense therapy to recognize these contributing factors, Mary Allen would seem to be a low risk for repeat offenses and danger to others.

It is this officer's recommendation that Mary Allen be given a term of probation, for an extended period of time, to be determined by the court, but that addresses these crucial elements. It is highly recommended that Mary Allen be monitored closely to determine her progress and participation. It is also recommended that Mary Allen's par-

ents be made party to the petition and monitored for their compliance in therapy as well. A referral to the JIPS program could also be made to address what could be a rocky transition from intense publicity of this case back to more routine circumstances. It is also recommended that Mary Allen continue with intense psychotherapy and address specifics of the incident. The probation department would ideally work with the therapist in maintaining compliance and progress. Incarceration at this point would serve no other purpose than to address punishment and retribution. These issues could be served in the context of probation supervision just as well, while allowing Mary Allen to obtain the therapy that she desperately needs. Periodic Judicial Reviews could be used to further monitor compliance and progress. Community service is advised and possible options with meaningful results could be explored through the context of therapy.

IV. CLINICAL SOCIAL WORKER COMMENTS

(*Must be completed for mandatory referrals and court order*)

Please refer to Forensic Evaluation dated 1-20-02.

Clinical Social Worker

Respectfully Submitted,

Approved:

Jane Clark, JPPO

Chief JPPO/Supervisor

Not all juvenile courts require the preparation of predisposition reports. They take much time to prepare, and their diagnostic information is often limited, since juvenile justice system budgets in many jurisdictions are restricted. In many respects, these reports are comparable to **presentence investigation reports (PSIs)** filed by probation officers in criminal courts for various convicted adult offenders. Unfortunately, there is no consistent pattern regarding the use of such predisposition reports and their preparation among jurisdictions (Rogers and Williams 1995).

In recent years, various juvenile justice reforms have been implemented in many juvenile courts. Some of these reforms have been mandated by U.S. Supreme Court decisions regarding more extensive rights of juvenile offenders. Greater uniformity in handling and less disparity in sentencing are desirable outcomes in the aftermath of extensive informal juvenile processing that characterized the juvenile courts of previous decades. Nevertheless, there continues to exist a great deal of individualism exhibited among juvenile court judges in different jurisdictions and how the various laws and decisions pertaining to juveniles should be interpreted (Minor, Hartmann, and Terry 1997).

Victim-Impact Statements in Predisposition Reports

Predisposition reports may or may not contain a **victim-impact statement.** Presentence investigation reports or PSIs that are prepared for adults who are convicted of crimes in criminal courts are the adult equivalents to predisposition reports. It is more common to see such victim-impact statements in PSI reports, although some predisposition reports contain them in certain jurisdictions (Herman and Wasserman 2001). These statements are often prepared by victims themselves and appended to the report before the judge sees it. They are intended to provide judges with a sense of the physical harm and monetary damage victims have sustained, and thus they are often aggravating factors that weigh heavily against the juvenile to be sentenced (Edwards 2001).

Since 1992, however, there has been a trend among state legislatures to increase the rights of victims of juvenile crime (Herman and Wasserman 2001). By 1996, twenty-two state legislatures had enacted legislation addressing the victims of juvenile crime (Erez and Laster 1999). This state legislation addresses the role of victims in various ways, including:

1. Including victims of juvenile crime in the victim's bill of rights.
2. Notifying the victim upon release of the offender from custody.
3. Increasing opportunities for victims to be heard in juvenile court proceedings.
4. Expanding victim services to victims of juvenile crime.
5. Establishing the authority for victims to be notified of significant hearings (e.g., bail disposition).
6. Providing for release of the name and address of the offender and the offender's parents to the victim upon request.
7. Enhancing sentences if the victim is elderly or handicapped (Torbet et al. 1996, 48). States enacting such legislation include Alabama, Alaska, Arizona, California, Connecticut, Florida, Georgia, Idaho, Iowa, Louisiana, Minnesota, Montana, New Mexico, North Dakota, Pennsylvania, South Dakota, Texas, Utah, Virginia, and Wyoming.

A strong consideration when enacting this legislation is the matter of restitution to victims. Restitution is increasingly regarded as an essential component of fairness in meting out dispositions for juvenile offenders. Offender accountability is heightened as restitution is incorporated into the disposition, especially if there was some type of property loss, damage, physical injury, or death. In reality, however, many states continue to haggle over how reparations will be imposed on either the youths or families or both. Some states have incorporated into their juvenile statutes high dollar limits relating to parental liability whenever their children destroy the property of others or cause serious physical injuries. The theory is that if parents are held accountable, they will hold their own children accountable. Thus, reparations assessed against parents for the wrongdoing of their children is an indirect way of preventing delinquency, or so some state legislatures have contemplated.

SUMMARY

Screening juvenile offenders occurs at various stages of juvenile justice processing. Intake officers perform initial screening functions, apart from those functions performed by law enforcement officers having to do with deciding which juveniles should be arrested. Prosecutors later screen cases further, by purportedly targeting only the most serious juvenile offenders for prosecution. Finally, juvenile court judges make final decisions about offender dispositions in adjudication proceedings. Consideration is given to whether offenders are first-timers, or whether they have prior records of delinquent activity. Chronic violent offenders are among the most serious juveniles processed by the system, although such offenders actually account for a small proportion of all juvenile arrests. However, long-term detainees in juvenile detention facilities are predominantly less serious property offenders with extensive histories of recidivism.

Judges consider aggravating and mitigating circumstances when sentencing offenders (Mears 2002). Aggravating circumstances enhance punishments imposed, and they include whether death or serious bodily injury occurred to victims, whether offenders committed their offenses while on probation or parole, whether they have prior records, whether they played leadership roles in the delinquent activity, whether weapons were used to commit their acts, and whether extreme cruelty was demonstrated toward victims. Mitigating circumstances, or those factors that lessen punishments imposed, include cooperating with authorities to apprehend other delinquents, no prior record of delinquent activity, mental incapacitation or retardation, drug/alcohol dependencies, and whether they committed their acts while under duress. It is up to each judge to establish the weights these factors should receive in deciding a youth's sentence.

Attempts to forecast delinquent conduct have been made by using various risk assessment devices and dangerousness measures. While most of these measures have not been extensively validated, some researchers believe they are of value in forecasting delinquent behavior and ought to be used. The use of such instruments has led some researchers to believe that high-risk youths may be targeted for selective incapacitation, where their behaviors are controlled through lengthy incarceration. However, other investigators believe such selective incapacitation is fundamentally unfair, and that it is inconsistent with constitutional guarantees and safeguards to punish persons for acts they have not as yet committed. Other problems of such measures include false positives and false negatives, or the identification of those who are predicted to be dangerous but turn out not to be dangerous, and those who are predicted not to be dangerous, but turn out to be dangerous anyway. Common elements of such instrumentation include age at first adjudication, number of prior offenses, alcohol and drug abuse, unstable family environments, and poor school performance.

In some jurisdictions, juvenile probation officers prepare predispositional reports for the most serious offenders. These materials contain useful information so that judges may make informed sentencing decisions. No schemes are foolproof, however. Judges experience role conflict as they attempt to balance community interests, which favor due process and just-deserts, against other traditional sentiments that favor rehabilitation and reintegration. The range of sanctions available to juvenile judges include nominal, conditional, and custodial punishments. Depending upon the particular treatment orientation of judges, different punishments imposed can have far-reaching effects on affected juveniles.

For more serious juvenile cases, juvenile probation officers may complete predispositional reports, which are similar to presentence investigation reports for adults. Predispositional reports contain a great deal of information about the juvenile, the events surrounding the offense and its commission, and background details about the juvenile's family, home background, school performance, possible gang affiliation, and peer associates. These predispositional reports are used by juvenile court judges and influence their dispositions of juveniles accordingly. Sometimes, victim-impact statements are appended to these reports, where victims describe how their lives have been disrupted and changed as the result of the juvenile's offending.

QUESTIONS FOR REVIEW

1. What are some qualitative differences between first offenders and repeat offenders? How does being a first offender or a repeat offender make a difference in how one's dangerousness or risk is assessed?

2. What are four different kinds of aggravating circumstances? How does each function to intensify one's punishment?

3. What are four mitigating circumstances? How do judges use these mitigating circumstances to lessen one's punishment?

4. What are some major differences between risk instruments and needs assessments?

5. What is meant by selective incapacitation? How is it used? What are false positives and false negatives? How do such designations occur?

6. What are three types of prediction? Which ones are most effective and why?

7. What is a predisposition report? Who prepares this report? How are such reports used for determining a juvenile's disposition?

8. What is a victim-impact statement? How is it used to modify the severity of one's disposition?

9. What are Violent Juvenile Offender Programs? What are their functions?

10. What are some moral and ethical questions which have been raised about selective incapacitation? Is selective incapacitation successful? Why or why not?

SUGGESTED READINGS

Benda, Brent B., Robert Flynn Corwyn, and Nancy J. Toombs. 2001. From adolescent "first offender" to adult felon: A predictive study of offense progression. *Journal of Offender Rehabilitation* 32:79–108.

Everle, Jane A. and Roland D. Maiuro. 2001. Introduction and commentary: Developmental perspectives on violence and victimization. *Violence and Victims* 16:351–354.

Goldson, Barry. 2001. A rational youth justice? Some critical reflections on the research, policy, and practice relation. *Probation Journal* 48:76–85.

Risler, Edwin A., Richard Sutphen, and John Shields. 2000. Preliminary evaluation of the Juvenile First Offender Risk Assessment Index. *Research on Social Work Practice* 10:111–126.

INTERNET CONNECTIONS

Families and Corrections Network
http://www.fcnetwork.org/

HandsNet
http://www.handsnet.org/

National Center on Education, Disability, and Juvenile Justice
http://www.edjj.org/

Resources for Youth
http://www.preventviolence.org/

CHAPTER 11 | *Nominal Sanctions: Warnings, Diversion, and Alternative Dispute Resolution*

Chapter Outline

Key Terms

Alternative dispute resolution
    (ADR)
Citizen action model
Community Board Program
Community organization model
Community Services Program,
    Inc. (CSP, Inc.)
Cooperating agencies model

Day reporting centers
Diversion
Diversion Plus Program
Mediation
Mediator
Orange County Peer Court
PINS Diversion Program
See Our Side (SOS) Program

Street outreach model
Systems modification model
Teen courts
Youth Service Bureaus (YSBs)
Youth Services/Diversion (YS/D)
    Program

Chapter Objectives

As a result of reading this chapter, you will accomplish the following objectives:

1. Understand what is meant by nominal dispositions.
2. Learn about several important juvenile dispositions, including diversion and alternative dispute resolution, as well as their functions and dysfunctions.
3. Understand what is meant by teen courts and why teen courts are important in delinquent offender processing.
4. Learn about day treatment centers and how they operate in communities as important services for juveniles.

INTRODUCTION

- *A 16-year-old boy sat in front of six teenagers in the high school auditorium in northern California. A retired judge and several school authorities sat nearby to oversee the proceedings. The boy was charged with stealing a book from another student's locker. Several witnesses were called to testify. After hearing the evidence, the youths deliberated and came back with a "guilty" verdict. Their recommended punishment: suspension from school for 30 days and payment of a $250 fine. The youth found guilty of the book theft was asked if he accepted the verdict, and he agreed. Subsequently, he signed some papers agreeing to the school suspension and the payment of the $250 fine. The boy was suspended from school for 30 days and subsequently paid the $250 fine, which was used to further the program known as a teen court.* [Adapted from the Associated Press, "Teen Courts Instead of Juvenile Courts?" April 19, 2002.]

- *Angry over being ordered off his neighbor's property, a 17-year-old Seattle youth got drunk one night with some of his friends. On his way home, he deliberately drove his family's car across the neighbor's yard, ruining the lawn and flower garden. When the neighbor discovered the damage the next morning, he noticed dirt on the wheels of the neighboring vehicle. He called the police, who investigated the incident. After interviewing the neighbors, the police arrested the 17-year-old and charged him with driving while intoxicated and willful destruction of property. Subsequently, a prosecutor scanned the 17-year-old's file and determined that this was his first offense. The youth had been doing well in school and had no prior juvenile record. The prosecutor conferred with the boy's attorney and, after some discussion, they agreed upon diversion, whereby the youth's case would be temporarily suspended from the juvenile justice system. Under the diversion conditions, the youth would be obligated to repay the neighbor for the property damage caused by the automobile. Furthermore, the youth was to remain law-abiding for one year and pay a $25 per month maintenance fee to the county. At the end of that period, if the youth paid the monthly fee, reimbursed the neighbor for his loss, and remained law-abiding, all charges against the youth would be dismissed.* [Adapted from the Associated Press, "Youth Gets Diversion for Mashing Neighbor's Geraniums." May 4, 2002.]

- *Kyle R. is a juvenile who was adjudicated delinquent by a New Jersey juvenile court for aggravated assault. A clinical psychologist and the probation department recommended that Kyle R. should be committed to a secure juvenile facility for at least six months. The juvenile court judge disagreed. Instead, Kyle R. was placed on probation*

*for one year, subject to supervision and other requirements by the local juvenile proba-
tion department. The judge justified her actions by citing no prior delinquency record
on the part of Kyle R. and that there were mitigating factors to be considered, such as
Kyle R.'s mild retardation. Besides his disposition of probation, Kyle R. was ordered to
participate in anger management sessions at a local social services clinic for the duration of his probationary period. Is probation a suitable punishment for aggravated assault? Should one's mental capacity be considered in determining the proper
disposition?* [Adapted from the Associated Press, "Juvenile Draws Probation for Aggravated Assault." July 10, 2002.]

This chapter examines the least punitive and restrictive options imposed
as punishments by juvenile court judges or recommended by intake officers
and/or prosecutors. These options include nominal reprimands, such as verbal
warnings and diversion, as well as the least punitive conditional option, standard probation. Both diversion and standard probation are programs that may
require offenders to perform various acts, such as victim restitution or compensation, community services and other good works, and pay fines or other monetary penalties. Several diversionary programs currently used in various U.S.
jurisdictions will be described. Their effectiveness will also be assessed.

An additional nonadjudicatory option increasingly used in many jurisdictions is the teen court or youth court. Such a court consists of one's peers who
sit in judgment of offenders, usually those who have been charged with petty
offenses. Being judged by and receiving sentences from one's peers seems to
promote greater accountability among youthful offenders. These teen courts
will be described. Another option to full juvenile court adjudication is alternative dispute resolution. The sanctioning mechanism involves a third-party arbi-
trator who mediates between the youthful offender and his or her victim.
Again, the dispute is usually pertaining to something minor, such as destruction of one's property or minor injuries received in an altercation. Agreements
are reached between parties in most instances, and such mechanisms have
proved useful as alternatives to formal court action.

NOMINAL DISPOSITIONS DEFINED

Nominal dispositions are verbal and/or written warnings issued to low-risk juvenile offenders, often first offenders, for the purpose of alerting them to the seriousness of their acts and their potential for receiving severe conditional
punishments if they ever should reoffend. These sanctions are the least punitive alternatives. Nominal dispositions may be imposed by police officers in
their encounters with juveniles. These verbal warnings or reprimands are often
in the form of stationhouse adjustments, where youths are taken into custody
and released to their parents later, without a record being made of the incident.

Juvenile court judges are encouraged in most states to utilize the least restrictive sanctions after adjudicating juveniles as delinquents, status offenders,
or CHINS. The use of incarceration as a sanction is within the judicial powers
of juvenile courts, although these courts are obliged and encouraged to seek
other options as sanctions. Some persons believe that secure confinement as a
disposition is overused and that public safety is better served to the extent that
most juveniles can remain at home within their communities, where a more
therapeutic milieu exists for them to become rehabilitated (Weatherburn and

Baker 2001). One community-based option in Delaware is the Delaware Bay Marine Institute (DBMI), a program that emphasizes sea-related activities and underwater skills. While the results of this research were inconclusive, the fact remains that there are viable alternatives to incarcerating juveniles that may work as well as or better than simply incarcerating them (Brandau 1992). For some persons, even better alternatives include doing little or nothing other than issuing certain juveniles verbal warnings or reprimands.

For example, intake officers may also use nominal dispositions against certain juveniles, if it is perceived that they merit only verbal warnings instead of more punitive sanctions. If petitions against certain juveniles are filed, depending upon the circumstances, judges may find them to be delinquent as alleged in these petitions. However, these adjudications do not automatically bind judges to implement conditional or custodial sanctions. Thus, judges may simply issue warnings to adjudicated juveniles. These warnings are serious, especially after a finding that the juvenile is delinquent. Juveniles with prior records face tougher sentencing options later if they reoffend in the same juvenile court jurisdiction and reappear before the same judges. Actually, various juvenile court actors engage in the process of attempting to forecast a youth's behavior if certain actions are taken or not taken. Some persons have created decision trees to operationalize this process. Ashford and LeCroy (1988) suggest the following decision tree as shown in Figure 11.1.

This juvenile aftercare decision tree begins with the question of whether the youth is violent. Depending upon the answer to this question, the tree branches two different ways, where other questions are posed. Notice that if the answers to successive questions are "yes," the degree of restrictiveness recommended to the juvenile court increases. More "no" answers suggest less restrictiveness. This tree merely conceptualizes court thinking, particularly following an adjudication. However, actors may utilize similar decision trees much earlier in the system. For instance, intake officers and prosecutors may contemplate seriously the use of **diversion** for some youths.

DIVERSION

The Juvenile Justice and Delinquency Prevention Act of 1974 and its subsequent amendments was intended, in part, to deinstitutionalize status offenders and remove them from the jurisdiction of juvenile courts. Another provision of this Act was to ensure that all other adjudicated delinquent offenders would receive the least punitive sentencing options from juvenile court judges in relation to their adjudication offenses. In fact, the National Advisory Committee for Juvenile Justice and Delinquency Prevention declared in 1980 that juvenile court judges should select the least restrictive sentencing alternatives, given the nature of the offense, the age, interests, and needs of the juvenile offender, and the circumstances of the conduct. Thus, judicial actions that appear too lenient are the result of either federal mandates or national recommendations (American Bar Association 2001).

Diversion is not new. It is regarded as a form of deferred prosecution where offenders, especially low-risk ones, can have a chance to prove themselves as law-abiding persons. An early instance of diversion was created by Conrad Printzlien, New York's first chief probation officer. Printzlien was concerned that many youths were stigmatized by rapid prosecution and convic-

INSTRUCTIONS: Starting at the left, circle yes or no for each question.
Refer to decision criteria for clarification of each question. When the
degree of restrictiveness is reached, place an X in the box.

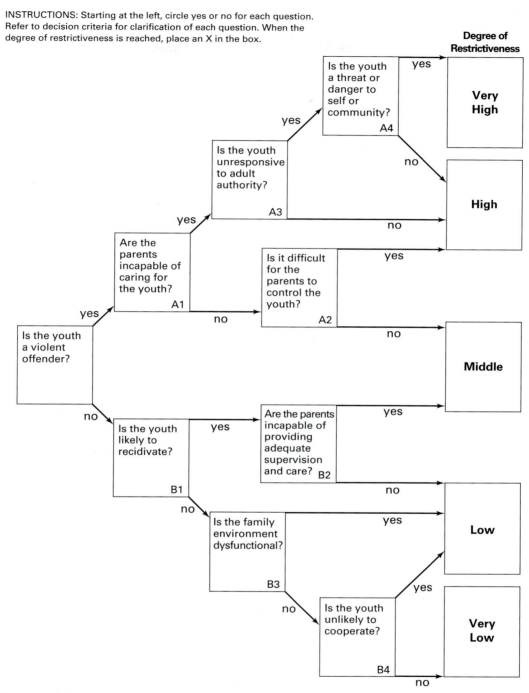

FIGURE 11.1 Juvenile Aftercare Decision Tree (from Ashford and LeCroy, 1988)

tion, and thus he set out to find an alternative to unnecessary and unwarranted
incarceration of juveniles (Rackmill 1996). The result was the Brooklyn Plan, a
deferred prosecution program that provided a way to distinguish situational offenders from more serious chronic and persistent juvenile delinquents. Between 1936 and 1946, 250 youths were handled as divertees. The program
proved successful at decreasing recidivism among divertees and eventually was
operated in other cities besides New York.

According to some persons, a primary, intended consequence of diversion is to remove large numbers of relatively minor offenders from juvenile court processing as quickly as possible (Myers et al. 2000). However, other professionals caution that one unintended consequence of diversion is the development of wider, stronger, and different nets (Feld 2000). This means in the simplest terms that those youngsters diverted from the formal juvenile justice system are captured in nets formed by the community-based agencies. Thus, if we view social control in its broadest terms, this means that more, not fewer, children will fall under some form of social control through diversionary programs.

Some authorities say that diversion of offenders should be aimed at the client population that would otherwise have received formal dispositions if diversion had not occurred (Gavazzi et al. 2000). This client population consists of youths who have committed delinquent acts and not simply status offenses. However, some critics say that status offenders may escalate to more serious offenses if left untreated by the system. Therefore, intervention of some sort is necessary to prevent this escalation of offense seriousness. Status offenders do not necessarily progress to more serious offenses. Sometimes, their apparent involvement in more serious offenses is a function of relabeling of the same acts differently by police (Coumarelos and Weatherburn 1995). On other occasions, status offenders may be upgraded to misdemeanants by juvenile court judges if they fail to obey valid court orders. If a status offender is ordered to attend school and doesn't, this provides the judicial grounds for issuing a contempt of court citation, a misdemeanor. Not everyone favors this particular use of juvenile court contempt power, especially against status offenders. Regardless of whether they are status offenders or have committed serious delinquent acts, divertees often exhibit some recidivism. Therefore, it is true that at least some of these divertees do progress to more serious offenses as some critics allege.

Functions and Dysfunctions of Diversion

Diversion has certain logistical benefits and functions. First, it decreases the caseload of juvenile court prosecutors by shuffling less serious cases to probation departments. Of course, this increases the supervisory responsibilities of probation departments who must manage larger numbers of divertees in addition to juvenile probationers. Another function of diversion is that it seems to reduce recidivism in those jurisdictions where it has been used (Delaware Statistical Analysis Center 1999). Another intended consequence of diversion is to reduce the degree of juvenile institutionalization or placement in either secure or nonsecure incarcerative facilities. A fourth function is that diversion is potentially useful as a long-range crime prevention measure. Finally, diversion reduces certain youth risks, such as suicide attempts as the result of being confined in adult jails or lockups for short periods. The stress and anxiety generated as the result of even short-term confinement for certain juveniles, including their propensity to commit suicide, has been described. At least for some youths, diversion assists in avoiding the stresses of confinement or prosecution (Smith 1991).

One of the dysfunctions of diversion is that it may widen the net by including some youths who otherwise would have received stationhouse adjustments by police or warnings from juvenile court judges (Shelden 1999). Much of this net-widening occurs through changes in police discretion and relabeling of juvenile behaviors as more serious, however. Another dysfunction is that some affected youths may acquire beliefs about the juvenile justice system that it is lenient and will tolerate relatively minor law breaking. The fact that many juvenile offenders are not disposed to secure confinement until their fourth or fifth delinquency adjudications would provide support for these beliefs.

A key problem with applying diversion on a large-scale basis is that not all status offenders or low-level delinquent offenders are suitable as divertees. We cannot say that all status offenders are alike, or that all minor delinquent offenders share the same characteristics. In order for diversion programs to maximize their effectiveness, they should target offenders most amenable to having minimal contact with the juvenile justice system. Ideally, we ought to be able to identify certain youths who are at risk of becoming more serious delinquent offenders or dangerous adult criminals. This means that it is necessary to identify particular factors that qualify certain youths as being at-risk. Thus, diversion could be selectively applied, depending upon whether certain youths possess more risk characteristics than others. Net-widening would be minimized and the sheer operating costs would be reduced substantially (Cohen 1998).

DIVERSION PROGRAMS FOR JUVENILES

Youth Service Bureaus

Diversion programs have operated in the United States for many years. In the early 1960s, **Youth Service Bureaus (YSBs)** were established in numerous jurisdictions in order to accomplish diversions' several objectives. While we still cannot identify precisely those youths considered delinquency-prone or at risk, YSBs were created, in part, as places within communities where delinquent-prone youths could be referred by parents, schools, and law enforcement agencies (Norman 1970). Actually, YSBs were forerunners of our contemporary community-based correctional programs, since they were intended to solicit volunteers from among community residents and to mobilize a variety of resources that could assist in a youth's treatment. The nature of treatments for youths, within the YSB concept, originally included referrals to a variety of community services, educational experiences, and individual or group counseling. YSB organizers attempted to compile lists of existing community services, agencies, organizations, and sponsors who could cooperatively coordinate these resources in the most productive ways to benefit affected juveniles (Romig 1978).

Five model YSB programs have been described. These are (1) the cooperating agencies model, (2) the community organization model, (3) the citizen action model, (4) the street outreach model, and (5) the systems modification model.

The Cooperating Agencies Model.   The **cooperating agencies model** consists of several different community-based agencies and organizations. Each organization or agency furnishes at least one paid full-time worker to the YSB program. As a team, these workers attempt to involve citizens and youth by bringing in interested professionals and others to work with juveniles who might have poor self-concepts or social adjustment problems.

The Community Organization Model.   The **community organization model** utilizes community citizens who work on a strictly voluntary basis. They are encouraged to form a board of directors who will assist them in coordinating diverse community services in ways that can benefit those juveniles serviced. Such organizations provide temporary shelter for runaways or those youths who are experiencing family difficulties or school problems. Thus, these agencies function to accommodate those who need emergency treatment or assistance.

The Citizen Action Model.   As the name implies, citizen involvement in the **citizen action model** is intensified. Community volunteers are attracted from various types of youth services. Each youth referred to these organizations is regarded as a case, and case conferences are held to determine the best treatment approaches to assist youths in solving their problems.

The Street Outreach Model.   The **street outreach model** provides for the establishment of neighborhood centers in business areas, where group and individual therapy may be administered to troubled youths. The accessibility of such centers in business districts is an attractive feature, since it caters to assisting juvenile transients who are roaming those same streets constantly.

The Systems Modification Model.   The **systems modification model** has led to the establishment of community-based facilities that function in relation with other agencies, schools, churches, and institutions to help these other organizations become more effective in supplying the needed youth services (Norman 1970, 15-19).

Youth service bureaus may contribute to the net-widening problem, because they include many youths who might otherwise have avoided prolonged contact with the juvenile justice system. Nevertheless, they have established common patterns that many community-based organizations have found useful as program guides over the years. In retrospect, youth service bureaus failed to live up to their goals relative to effective treatment and services for low-risk offenders. This is particularly true regarding offense-specific crimes such as drug offenses (Inciardi, McBride, and Rivers 1996).

Generally, diversion programs operate in pretty much the same ways for juveniles as they operate for adult offenders. Diversion in the juvenile justice system has the primary objective of avoiding labeling and the stigma associated with involvement in juvenile court (Polan 1994). Diversion may be either unconditional or conditional. Unconditional diversion simply means that the divertee will attend school, behave, and not reappear before the juvenile court for a specified period. Conditional diversion may require juveniles to attend lectures, individual or group psychotherapy, drug or alcohol treatment centers, police department-conducted DUI classes, and/or vocational or educational classes or programs. Successful completion of the diversion program means dismissal of the case. These programs are of variable lengths, but most run for periods of six months to a year (Kassebaum, Marker, and Glancey 1997).

Youth Services/Diversion and Community Service Programs, Inc.

In Orange County, California, the **Youth Services/Diversion (YS/D) Program** and **Community Services Program, Inc. (CSP, Inc.)** were established in the early 1990s to fulfill two goals. These goals are to teach client responsibility and reduce family dysfunction (Polan 1994). Samples of youths from Orange County were selected and subjected to several experimental interventions. Family counseling sessions were established on a regular basis for diverted youths from juvenile court. Youths themselves participated in several self-help programs designed to enhance their self-esteem and confidence. Not all youths and their families completed the project. Those who dropped out were compared with those who finished the program requirements. Evidence suggests that most of those who successfully completed their programs fared better over time by exhibiting reduced recidivism compared with those who dropped out. Some persons suggest that the program is cost-effective and can conceivably be implemented on a large scale in other jurisdictions. One of the most positive benefits of this program accrued to juveniles whose self-concepts and general psychological well-being were improved.

The Diversion Plus Program

An alternative to formal court processing for status and less serious delinquent offenders is the **Diversion Plus Program.** This program was established in Lexington, Kentucky, in July 1991 and operated until November 1992 (Kammer, Minor, and Wells 1997, 52). Besides reducing recidivism among its clients, the goal of the program was to promote conformity to the law without causing stigmatization. Eligibility requirements were that youths had to be (1) between the ages of 11 and 18, (2) charged with a status or less serious delinquent offense, and (3) free of any prior record of delinquency.

The entire program consisted of eight separate sessions during a two-month period, Monday through Friday, from 6:00 P.M. to 9:00 P.M. Group size was limited to twelve persons. The first sessions were designed to orient clients and teach them to work as a group. A variety of exercises were used to promote interpersonal trust and cooperation. Needs of program participants were assessed initially and one-on-one counseling and small group interaction emphasizing active learning occurred through hands-on projects. Each session emphasized a core curriculum emphasizing building self-esteem and self-control, improvement in decision-making processes, independent living skills, career exploration, substance abuse prevention, recreation, and team challenges (p. 52). After learning about a particular topic (e.g., independent living), participants used the knowledge acquired to complete specific tasks (e.g., budgeting money). A point system was used to encourage compliance with program requirements. Points could be earned for participating and completing requirements, and points could be lost for noncompliance. Persons could use their points at the end of the program to purchase items in an auction during the final evening. Also, a $100 gift certificate was given to the person earning the most points.

During the Diversion Plus Program, there were 94 participants. Half were female, and the average age was 14.5 years. Subsequently, 81 clients graduated from the program. Most of the 13 nongraduates terminated the program because of noncompliance. A follow-up showed that 63 percent of the graduates were subsequently rearrested for various charges. Interestingly, the rearrests of status offenders most often involved delinquent offenses. This finding shows for this sample at least that some offense escalation occurred. However, the escalation was from status offending to minor delinquent offending. No strong pattern of escalation to felonious offenses was detected. Thus, it cannot be said in the present instance that high levels of program involvement and completion are sufficient to ensure low recidivism. However, the investigators conjectured that had this program not been available, more youths would have penetrated the juvenile justice system further with perhaps more serious types of offending (Kammer, Minor, and Wells 1997, 54).

The PINS Diversion Program

In New York City, the **PINS Diversion Program** for persons alleged to be in need of supervision (PINS) was instituted in February 1987. Three groups of status offense cases were included: (1) persons in need of supervision, (2) adjournment contemplating dismissal, and (3) dismissal (Steinberg, Levine, and Singer 1992). Data collected from juvenile records during 1989–1990 yielded questionnaire information for a 1986 prediversion group of 693 youths as well as a 1988 postdiversion group of 728 youths. Using out-of-home placements and increased access to community-based services, New York youth counselors worked with numerous PINS cases diverted from New York juvenile courts. Ultimately, the program proved successful at diverting numerous PINS cases from otherwise proceeding to the family court, the numbers of youths subsequently placed in either secure or nonsecure confinement, and the use of court-mandated services. The percentage of cases at intake where formal sanctions were received was reduced from 10 percent to only 4 percent, while the placement rate decreased from 6.8 percent to 4.1 percent (Rabinowitz 1992).

See Our Side (SOS) Program

In Prince George's County, Maryland, a program was established in 1983 called **See Our Side (SOS) Program** (Mitchell and Williams 1986, 70). SOS is referred to by its directors as a juvenile aversion program and dissociates itself from shock programs such as Scared Straight. Basically, SOS seeks to educate juveniles about the realities of life in prison through discussions and hands-on experience and attempts to show them the types of behaviors that can lead to incarceration. Clients coming to SOS are referrals from various sources, including juvenile court, public and private schools, churches, professional counseling agencies, and police and fire departments. Youths served by SOS range in age from 12 to 18, and they do not have be adjudicated as delinquent in order to be eligible for participation. SOS helps any youth who might benefit from such participation.

SOS consists of four, three-hour phases. These are described below.

Phase I: Staff orientation and group counseling session where staff attempt to facilitate discussion and ease tension among the youthful clients; characteristics of jails are discussed, including age and gender breakdowns, race, and types of juvenile behavior that might result in jailing for short periods.

Phase II: A tour of a prison facility.

Phase III: Three inmates discuss with youths what life is like behind bars; inmates who assist in the program are selected on the basis of their emotional maturity, communications skills, and warden recommendations.

Phase IV: Two evaluations are made—the first is an evaluation of SOS sessions by the juveniles; a recidivism evaluation is also conducted for each youth after a one-year lapse from the time they participated in SOS; relative program successfulness can therefore be gauged.

An evaluation of the program by SOS officials in 1985 found that SOS served 327 youths during the first year of operation and that a total of 38 sessions were held. Recidivism of program participants was about 22 percent. Again, this low recidivism rate is favorable. Subsequent evaluations of the SOS program showed that the average rate of client recidivism dropped to only 16 percent. The cost of the program was negligible. During the first year, the program cost was only $280, or about 86 cents per youth served.

Programs similar to SOS are operated in other states. In Tennessee, for instance, the Davidson County (Nashville) Sheriff's Department operates D.E.P.U.T.Y., which stands for Developing, Educating and Promoting Unity among Tennessee Youth (*American Jails* 1998, 98). The program is designed to give young people a look inside a jail without actually being arrested. The program will teach children that jail is not a place they want to be. The program is available to any interested organization, such as Boys and Girls Clubs and scouting groups. Sheriff Gayle Ray shows videos of inmates sharing their personal stories, where they explain when they started to go wrong in their own lives and how alcohol, drugs, and crime lead to a lifetime of problems. Sheriff Ray says, "We are expecting a great deal out of the D.E.P.U.T.Y. program. Children need to know that there's nothing exciting about jail. We want them to unite together and decide to make the right choices—the choices that will keep them out of the jail system."

The Community Board Program

One innovation introduced by the San Francisco juvenile courts is the **Community Board Program,** which is a civil **mediation** mechanism. This program involves first- and second-time juvenile offenders who have been charged with minor offenses, often property offenses, where damage to or loss of property was sustained by one or more victims. The Community Board Program uses volunteers to meet with both offenders and their victims as an alternative to a full juvenile court adjudicatory hearing. Mediation is conducted wherein a mutually satisfactory solution is arranged by the **mediator.**

One of the positive aspects of this program is that victims can meet and confront their attackers. Victims may become involved and empowered. Their face-to-face encounters with youths who victimized them enable victims to tell them of the harm they caused. In a selective way, the mediation program was successful. That is, some types of juveniles directly benefited from their confrontation experience. In a comparative investigation of program evaluation, 113 juveniles who completed mediation were compared with 157 controls. Particularly younger juveniles were the least responsive to mediation, however. Interestingly, in younger-offender cases, recidivism rates were much higher for them compared with youths of similar ages in the control group. Simply put, this mediation program didn't seem to work with particularly youthful offenders. However, older juveniles seemed favorably affected by the confrontation and mediation. Their recidivism rates were much lower compared with comparable controls (URSA Institute 1993).

IMPLICATIONS OF DIVERSION PROGRAMS FOR JUVENILES

One result of the Juvenile Justice and Delinquency Prevention Act of 1974 was to deinstitutionalize status offenders and remove them from the jurisdiction of juvenile courts. This has been done in some jurisdictions, but not in all of them. One result is that there is much variation among jurisdictions about how juvenile offenders are processed and treated (Potter and Kakar 2002). In recent years, however, an increasing number of juvenile courts have imposed dispositions according to offender needs as well as according to what is just and deserved. Better classifications of offenders need to be devised. Additional information is needed about offender characteristics, their backgrounds, and specific circumstances in order that proper punishments and treatments can imposed by juvenile court judges. For diversion programs to be successful, they must be targeted at the most successful juvenile candidates. Most frequently, these are low risk, first offenders or juveniles who are quite young.

Some diversion programs include some rather stringent conditions and may even involve participation in intervention projects designed to remedy certain manifested problems. For example, a sample of 39 juvenile sex offenders was assigned to the Behavioral Studies Program of the Pines Treatment Center in Portsmouth, Virginia (Hunter and Goodwin 1992). All participants received a minimum of six months of verbal satiation, in addition to individual, group and family counseling and other therapies. Youths were also exposed to psychophysiological assessments of changes in their penile circumference by various testing procedures. The result was that deviant sexual arousal was decreased significantly and that the youths had favorably responded to therapy designed to treat their deviant conduct. However, not all divertees are subjected to these or similar experiences. Other studies of diversion interventions for juvenile sex offenders have been similarly successful (Wright 1997).

Juvenile courts have come under attack in recent years as the result of what the public considers excessive judicial leniency in dealing with youthful offenders. Often, juvenile cases are dismissed. This occurs not only during formal adjudicatory proceedings by juvenile court judges, but also by intake officers in earlier screenings of offenders. Thus, it is unreasonable to identify any specific part of the juvenile justice process as unusually lenient in juvenile case processing. All phases of the system seem to be influenced by the rehabilitative philosophy. And for many people, rehabilitation is equated with leniency (Campbell and Retzlaff 2000).

The degree of case attrition through diversions or dismissals has been investigated by several researchers (Bilchik 1996). In the mid-1970s, for example, a study by the National Assessment of Juvenile Corrections reported that about two-thirds of all juvenile referrals were dismissed at either intake or at the judicial hearing (Sarri and Hansenfeld 1976). Studies of juvenile case dismissal rates in later years disclosed similar results, although attrition figures were somewhat lower, ranging from 30 to 54 percent (Ito 1984).

In addition to charges of being too lenient with offenders and dismissing or diverting their cases, the juvenile court has been targeted for other criticisms. Critics say that the juvenile court has failed to distinguish adequately between less serious and more serious offenders; it has often ignored the victims of juvenile violence; it has often failed to correct or rehabilitate juveniles in a manner consistent with its manifest purposes; it has been unconcerned or complacent about juvenile offenders and how they should be punished; it has confined children at times in adult jails; it has failed often to protect juveniles' rights; its services have been too thinly spread; and it has been too resistant to self-examination and suggestions for improvement. But one criticism of these criticisms is that collectively, they do not especially apply to any single juvenile court at a particular point in time. Rather, they are loosely distributed and shared by many juvenile courts. By the same token, there are many juvenile courts operating with few serious flaws (Dembo et al. 2000b).

The goals of diversion can be achieved more effectively, according to some authorities, if divertees are obligated to accept responsibility for their actions through restitution or community service. When youths must do something constructive and repay victims for damages to property, they learn valuable lessons concerning their actions and how they affect others. Sometimes diversion coupled with other program elements has been termed creative diversion and is used throughout the United States in diverse jurisdictions (Bazemore and Senjo 1997).

TEEN COURTS

Increasing numbers of jurisdictions are using **teen courts** as an alternative to juvenile court for determining one's guilt and punishment (LeGalbo and Callahan 2001). Teen courts are informal jury proceedings, where jurors consist of teenagers who hear and decide minor cases. First-offender cases, where status offenses or misdemeanors have been committed, are given priority in a different type of court setting involving one's peers as judges. Judges may divert minor cases to these teen courts (Harrison, Maupin, and Mays 2001). Adults function only as presiding judges, and these persons are often retired judges or lawyers who perform such services voluntarily and in their spare time. The focus of teen courts is upon therapeutic jurisprudence, with a strong emphasis upon rehabilitation. One objective of such courts is to teach empathy to offenders. Victims are encouraged to take an active role in these courts. Youths become actively involved as advisory juries (Minor et al. 1999).

Teen courts are also known as youth courts, peer courts, and student courts. In 1997 there were 78 active teen courts. By 2002 there were 880 youth court programs operating in juvenile justice systems, schools, and community-based organizations throughout the United States (National Youth Court Center 2002, 15). The American Probation and Parole Association has recognized the significance and contributions of teen courts by establishing September 2002 as National Youth Court Month to highlight the activities of youth courts and their contributions to the youth justice system (*APPA Perspectives* 2002, 15).

The Use of Teen Courts

Among the first cities to establish teen courts were Seattle, Washington, and Denver, Colorado (Rothstein 1985, 18). Subsequently, teen courts have been established in many other jurisdictions, including Odessa, Texas. In Odessa, for

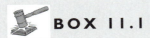 **BOX 11.1**

Kevin I. Minor
Professor and Chair, Department of Correctional and Juvenile Justice Studies, Eastern Kentucky University

Statistics:

Ph.D. (sociology/criminology), Western Michigan University; M.S. (correctional psychology), Emporia State University; B.S. (psychology and criminology), Indiana State University

Background and Experiences:

Presently, I hold the position of professor and chair in the Department of Correctional and Juvenile Justice Studies at Eastern Kentucky University (EKU). Prior to coming to EKU, I taught four years at Southwest Missouri State University. My areas of professional interest include institutional and community corrections, juvenile delinquency and justice, evaluation and applied research, and theory. I have published numerous articles and book chapters on these topics and co-edited two books: *Law-Related Education and Juvenile Justice* (Charles C. Thomas, 1997); and *Prisons Around the World: Studies in International Penology* (William C. Brown, 1992).

I am from Southern Indiana and attended Indiana State University from 1978–1982. It was at Indiana State that I became interested in juvenile justice. I was a first-semester junior majoring in psychology when I took a course in criminology to explore it as a possible minor. During the spring of my junior year, I took a course in juvenile delinquency and then that summer, took a job in an institution for juvenile offenders. From that point on, I was pretty much hooked on the juvenile justice field.

Upon completing the bachelor's degree, I enrolled in the correctional psychology program at Emporia State University in Emporia, Kansas. The program seemed like a nice synthesis of my undergraduate interests, and plus, I was offered a graduate teaching assistantship. About three months

after finishing the bachelor's degree, I began teaching introductory psychology and almost immediately got hooked on teaching as well. I didn't discover how much I enjoyed writing and conducting research until completing a thesis on juvenile delinquency in 1983. The program at Emporia required a one-semester, full-time internship, and I opted to do mine in the Mental Health Unit at the Kansas State Penitentiary in Lansing (not too far from Kansas City). Although penitentiary work was a great learning experience, it was during the internship that I settled upon a career of university teaching and research over being a practitioner.

After applying to and being accepted at several different criminology/criminal justice doctoral programs, I chose Western Michigan University. I liked the opportunity the program there afforded to work toward integrating the academic and applied realms of the field. We studied a lot of abstract material about theory and research methods, but we were encouraged to apply what we learned to concrete issues in the field. It was at Western that I first became interested in conducting evaluation research on criminal and juvenile justice programs. To complete the Ph.D., I wrote a dissertation on the effects of intervention for juvenile probationers.

My interest in program evaluation continued to develop during my first academic job at Southwest Missouri State University; my first few articles on the topic were published while there. Shortly after moving to EKU, I was fortunate enough to develop a relationship with officials at the Kentucky Administrative Office of the Courts (AOC) who were interested in evaluating their law-related education diversion programs. It was collaboration with that office that eventually led me to research teen courts. In 1995, Dr. James Wells and I received a small grant to collect and analyze data on the teen court program in Kentucky, and in one capacity or another, we have been working to evaluate the program ever since.

Some Observations on Teen Court:

What I know about teen court is based on the research I have done with the Kentucky program and on what I have read about the operation of these courts in other jurisdictions. Kentucky's program, which began in 1992, is somewhat different from other teen courts. For one thing, it's a statewide program that is centrally administered by AOC. There are numerous sites across the state, and these vary greatly in size and operation. Also, in Kentucky, teen court is a posttrial diversion program, meaning that juvenile court judges refer youth to teen court only after the youth have pleaded or been found guilty of an offense. And so teen court is an alternative to traditional sentencing rather than traditional adjudication. Each site has a coordinator, who is usually a college student intern. The coordinator works with a local district court judge who presides over teen court sessions. The coordinator and judge are typically the only adults who participate, although at some sites, local attorneys or law students will be present to help educate youth participants about legal principles. Local high school students volunteer to fill all of the other roles—defense attorney, prosecutor, clerk, bailiff, and jurors. Coordinators and high school participants have to complete five weeks of training before taking part in the program.

In Kentucky, juveniles are referred to teen court for less serious felonies, misdemeanors, status offenses, traffic offenses, and other offenses that fall into the low to moderate seriousness range. Although most of these youth do not have extensive prior records, a good number have gone through pretrial diversion programs for past offenses. During a court session, the teen prosecutor presents evidence to jurors about the circumstances surrounding the offense for which the defendant was convicted as well as evidence about the defendant's character. The prosecutor generally argues in support of a stiff penalty. By contrast, the teen defense attorney presents evidence as to why the defendant should receive a more lenient sentence. Both sides are permitted to call and question witnesses. Following presentations from the prosecution and the defense, the judge informs the jurors of the sentences permitted under the law. While jurors deliberate in private, some judges use the time to educate the youth attorneys by giving them feedback on their presentations. Although judges have the authority to override or modify jury sentences, this is seldom done. Following issuance of the sentence, site coordinators work out contracts with offenders concerning the terms and timeframe of the sentence. Coordinators monitor compliance with sentence requirements, and youth who fail to complete these requirements are returned to regular juvenile court. Some typical sentences include community service, letters of apology, essays, curfews, restitution, and counseling.

One of the most important goals of teen court is supposed to be education. Offenders should learn about responsibility and accountability for their behaviors. Offenders and youth participants alike should develop respect and appreciation for the law, legal processes, and civic responsibilities. My impression is that some teen courts accomplish much more than others in this respect, and a crucial factor is the effort made by the presiding judge to promote education. Some judges our research team has observed take great efforts to make teen court a valuable learning experience. Others seem less concerned over what youths learn and more concerned about getting the case processed and a sentence imposed on the guilty party. Most judges do remarkably well at balancing these two concerns. Other goals of teen court are to (1) increase the likelihood of the defendant completing his

(continued)

BOX 11.1 (Continued)

or her sentence and (2) decrease the chances that he or she will get reinvolved in illegal activities. Combined with the educative effects mentioned above is another potentially powerful tool that should promote these two goals—peer influence. By their very nature, teen courts are designed to promote peer (juror) disapproval for illegal behavior and peer reinforcement for positive actions. In short, the idea is that the sentence will somehow mean more and have more positive outcomes when it comes from one's peers.

Research is important because that is the only way we can estimate whether teen courts are accomplishing these goals. Also, research can help us know what needs to be modified to improve a program. Our research into teen court in Kentucky found that over 70 percent of the juveniles referred to teen court between 1994 and 1997 successfully completed their sentences. We also found that, in the year following sentencing, just less than 32 percent were sent back to juvenile court for new offenses; usually these were less serious offenses, such as theft and selling marijuana. Other data we have collected show that high school volunteers who participate in the program gain knowledge of the law and legal processes, have relatively positive attitudes toward teen court, and have relatively positive attitudes toward legal system officials (e.g., police officers, judges, lawyers).

Although defendants certainly have less positive attitudes toward teen court than volunteer participants, the attitude of most defendants is not negative. In fact, over 87 percent of the defendants who were sentenced in teen court during the 1998–1999 term (the most recent term for which we collected attitudinal data) rated their sentences as fair. I think this is an important finding. It has been my experience that when offenders perceive themselves as being treated unfairly by the system, they tend to shift attention away from their own blameworthiness and responsibility toward the faults of legal authorities. In their classic article on techniques of neutralization, Gresham Sykes and David Matza called this "condemnation of condemners," and criminologist Lawrence Sherman has described how perceptions of unfairness and injustice on the part of those being sanctioned can increase future criminal behavior by undermining a sense of shame and promoting attitudes of defiance.

Although peer disapproval for illegal acts and peer approval for prosocial activities can be powerful tools for effecting behavioral change, it is very important that coordinators, judges, and other adult officials carefully monitor interactions between defendants and their peers in teen court. If defendants sense that they are being condemned and rejected by these peers, they can end up being driven further into delinquent subcultures. The object of peer disapproval needs to be the defendant's illegal act and never the defendant's self. In the words of John Braithwaite, an authority on restorative justice, the process needs to be reintegrative instead of disintegrative. At teen court sessions I have observed, both teen participants and adult officials generally do well in this regard. A sense of having been treated with respect by peers during the court session is probably a major factor in so many defendants perceiving their sentences as fair.

Teen court is a noteworthy juvenile justice program in that young people are given active and meaningful roles; they have some control over both the process and outcome. Historically, the juvenile justice system has operated from the assumption that, due to their young age, juveniles are in certain ways less culpable for their illegal acts than adults; they are in greater need of tutelage than punishment from the government. This traditional *parens patriae* orientation has seldom resulted in juveniles having anything other than passive roles. Our experience has been that volunteers and defendants alike tend to comment favorably upon the voice and civic involvement afforded them by teen court. At the same time, there is a tension of sorts between the active, creative role that teen court gives youths and the rules and procedures it imposes on them (e.g., procedures governing how evidence must be presented or rules severely limiting the possible sentences from which jurors may choose). Formal rules and procedures certainly have their place in keeping the process organized and moving toward an end state (i.e., determination of a sentence) and consistent across cases. But if not carefully crafted, rules and procedures can take away both needed flexibility and control on the part of youth. I have observed some teen court sessions where the youths had become so preoccupied with the rules and procedures in which they had been trained that the entire session amounted to the style of rushed, routinized, assembly-line justice that I have seen all too frequently in the adult system.

Many people seem to support the teen court movement for many different reasons, and the movement has certainly expanded on a national scale. But I would caution against supporting it for the wrong reasons. Teen court programs should not be naively embraced as the latest fad or panacea for delinquency. Doing so will only create unrealistic expectations that, in turn, are likely to be frustrated when anticipated results are not quickly forthcoming. Building sound juvenile justice programs requires at least two things: (1) close adherence to principles of effective correctional intervention that are becoming well-established in the professional literature and (2) program development and refinement efforts over time that are guided by careful research.

Advice to Students:

The best advice I can give students who are interested in teen court is to experience it. Find out if there is a program in your area, and if so, try to arrange an internship, co-op, or practicum working in the program. Keep in mind that these programs are not termed "teen court" in all locations; they may be called "youth courts" or "peer courts." Keep in mind also that not all such programs operate out of court agencies; some are operated by schools and other community agencies. Find out if any of your professors are conducting research on teen court programs, and if so, volunteer to assist with data collection or data management. There are also numerous interesting websites to check out. Two of these include http://www.youthcourt.net and http://www.ojjdp.ncjrs.org.

instance, juveniles are referred to teen courts for Class C misdemeanors and minor traffic violations. Defendants range in age from 10 to 16. Traffic citation cases result in teen court referrals by municipal judges, who give youths the option of paying their fines or having their cases heard by the teen court. If youths select the teen court for adjudication, then they do not acquire a juvenile record. The teen court listens to all evidence and decides the matter.

Teen court dispositions are always related closely to community service as well as jury service. Thus, juveniles who are found guilty by teen courts may, in fact, serve on such juries in the future as one of their conditional punishments. Or they may be required to perform up to 22 hours of community service, such as working at the animal shelter, library, or nursing home; picking up trash in parks or ballfields, or working with various community agencies (Rothstein 1985, 22). The teen court program in Odessa has been very successful. Prior to using teen courts, the recidivism rate for all juvenile offenders in the city was between 50 and 60 percent. However, teen court adjudications all but eliminated this recidivism figure. Interestingly, juveniles who are tried by the teen court often develop an interest in the legal system. Rothstein says that teen courts place a high priority on educating young people about their responsibilities of being individuals, family members, and citizens. As a part of one's diversion, conditional options such as restitution, fines, or community service may be imposed in those cases where property damage was incurred as the result of the juvenile's behavior. Juvenile court judges must exercise considerable discretion and impose dispositions that best meet the juvenile's needs and circumstances.

Constructive dispositions are the objective of teen courts in northern Kentucky. In September, October, and November 1992, teen jurors in a Kentucky teen court heard case details in nine different cases (Williamson, Chalk, and Knepper 1993). Referrals to teen court were made from the regular juvenile court, a division of the state's district court. If juveniles are found guilty by the teen court, then the court imposes constructive dispositions involving community service hours. It should be noted that these teen courts do not determine

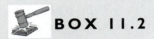 **BOX 11.2**

ON TEEN DRUG COURTS

Teen Drug Courts in North Dakota

How do you keep juvenile offenders away from drugs and out of jail? One preventive measure is to hold them more accountable for their actions and monitor them more closely than traditional supervisory methods. In Fargo and Grand Forks, North Dakota, juvenile court programs are being established to accomplish this objective. Groups of judges, attorneys, juvenile court officers, and addiction counselors have been organized in these two cities for the purpose of establishing teen drug courts. These courts are designed for juveniles between the ages of 14 and 17 who have committed nonviolent crimes and show signs of substance abuse. North Dakota Supreme Court Justice Mary Maring has commented that "Our goal is to get these kids clean. It's a tough program. It involves a high level of accountability." The teens who appear in court will appear weekly before a judge, undergo intensive drug screening, and work with mentors to complete a certain number of community service hours. Money for the program was obtained from the U.S. Department of Justice and the U.S. Attorney General's Office. Under the current program operating in North Dakota, teens with drug and alcohol problems are usually placed on probation and sometimes don't see a juvenile court judge for several months. Some more serious juveniles are locked up in juvenile detention centers at a cost of $30,000 per year per youth, with little or no rehabilitation occurring. The idea of a teen drug court was introduced in 1997 when it was determined by various state officials that North Dakota youth were increasingly involved in drug- and alcohol-related offending. In fact, between 1997 and 1998 the number of drug and alcohol juvenile cases doubled in the state. At least 60 percent of all adjudicated juveniles in North Dakota those years had consumed alcohol or used drugs within 30 days preceding their offending. This is 10 percent higher than national figures. With the juvenile teen drug courts, however, it is expected that closer monitoring and greater accountability of juveniles will cause these numbers of drug and alcohol offenders to decline appreciably.

What do you think of the teen drug court idea? If it works in Grand Forks and Fargo, North Dakota, do you think it would have a chance of working in more urban environments such as New York, Chicago, or Los Angeles?

Source: Adapted from the Associated Press, "Teen Drug Court Nearly Finished: Fargo, Grand Forks Court Close to Completion." December 28, 1999.

one's guilt or innocence—rather, they convene and recommend appropriate dispositions. Teenagers act as prosecutors, defense attorneys, clerks, bailiffs, jury forepersons, and jurors as they carry out roles similar to their counterparts in criminal courts. The Kentucky teen court variety is interesting because accused and judged teens are themselves recruited subsequently to serve as teen jurors. Thus, all defendants are assigned to jury duty following their teen court appearances. When this study was conducted, no youth had been returned to the teen court for noncompliance. Perhaps seeing how the process works from the other side, as jurors, made these teenagers understand the seriousness of what they had done themselves as victimizers in the past.

The Orange County Peer Court

By 1995, there were over 250 teen courts established and active in thirty states (Godwin 1996, 11–12). These courts are not always known as teen courts. In Orange County, California, for example, the **Orange County Peer Court** has been established (Beck 1997, 40). This court is actually a hybrid of both diversion and conventional juvenile justice programs. It is a diversion in that offenses heard do not appear on an offender's record and the informal adjustments are given over to a peer jury. These peer court sessions are held after school in a large high school multipurpose room or auditorium. A volunteer attorney–advisor explains the purpose of the peer court to an audience of high school students and encourages them to maintain proper demeanor. Members of the audience volunteer as jurors. Charges against certain youths are read by a probation officer and jurors are sworn in by a judge. Guilty or not guilty verdicts are rendered by the teen jurors. Sentences cannot include fines or jail time. Typical sentences include combinations of the following: performing community service, making restitution, participating in future peer courts, interviewing victims and writing an essay, obeying curfews, attending drug and alcohol programs, attending school regularly, seeking or maintaining employment, not associating in negative peer relationships, and participating in specialized programs exposing teens to the realities of the criminal justice system (e.g., visiting the county jail). The general purpose of the peer court is rehabilitative. The Orange County Peer Court has been modestly successful in this regard.

DAY REPORTING CENTERS

Goals and Functions of Day Reporting Centers

Some jurisdictions have day treatment program centers, following a day treatment model (National Governor's Association 1991). **Day reporting centers** were established first in England in 1974 to provide intensive supervision for offenders who would otherwise be incarcerated (Larivee 1990). Offenders in English day treatment centers typically lived at home while remaining under the supervision of a correctional administrator. Inmates would either work or attend school, regularly participate in treatment programming, devote at least four hours a week to community service, and observe a strict curfew.

A variation on day treatment programs in England has been attempted in the United States for juvenile offenders. The first U.S. day reporting centers

Day treatment centers offer counseling and other forms of assistance.

were established in Connecticut and Massachusetts in the mid-1980s (Corbett and Harris 1996, 51). During that period, there were thirteen day treatment centers operating. By 1994, there were 114 day treatment centers in twenty-two states.

Day treatment programs are presently operated in most state jurisdictions throughout the United States (Illinois Department of Corrections 2000). Both male and female clients benefit from day treatment services. Since the mid-1970s these programs have helped to expand the continuum of services available to at-risk and delinquent youths (Martin, Olson, and Lurigio 2000). These programs have been developed through the collaborative efforts of educators, judiciary, and social service professionals and provide an effective alternative to out-of-home placements. Many day treatment programs are operated on a year-round basis, offering community-based nonresidential services to at-risk and delinquent youths (Marciniak 2000).

These centers offer offenders a variety of treatments and services. Offenders report to these centers frequently, usually once or twice a day, and treatment and services are provided on site in most instances. For more serious types of problems or illnesses, personnel at these centers will refer clients to the appropriate community services, where they can receive necessary specialized treatments (Corbett and Harris 1996, 51). The types of services provided by 60 percent or more of these day reporting centers include the acquisition of job-seeking skills, drug abuse education, group counseling, job placement services, education, drug treatment, life skills training, individual counseling, transitional housing, and recreation and leisure activities.

The goals of day treatment centers are to provide access to treatment and services, to reduce prison and jail overcrowding, protect the public, and build political support. Eligibility requirements are that offenders should be low-risk delinquents or criminals with a good chance of succeeding while free in the community. Those with serious and violent prior records are usually excluded. Surveillance of day reporting center clients consists of on-site contacts and off-site contacts. On-site contacts average 18 hours per week, where clients must be at these day reporting centers for treatment and special programming during the most intensive phases. Off-site surveillance includes site visits to one's home or dwelling, telephone contact, and visits to one's place of work or school. Although day reporting centers have failure rates among their clientele of about 50 percent, these failure rates are still better than traditional probation programs, where recidivism is as high as 65 to 70 percent (Parent 1996, 52).

Not all day treatment programs are operated for low-risk offenders. In some jurisdictions, such as Wisconsin, day reporting centers are operated as intermediate sanctions for more serious offenders (Craddock and Graham 1996). Furthermore, some of these day treatment programs are offense-specific, such as day treatment for drug offenders. In Boston, Massachusetts, for example, the Metropolitan Day Treatment Center has been operating since 1987 as a residential, transitional facility for inmates released early from local jails. Most of these inmates have had former drug problems and need special assistance in remaining drug free (McDevitt, Domino, and Baum 1997). Also, some day reporting centers are operated almost exclusively for DWI offenders. In Arizona, for instance, a day reporting center functions to reduce recidivism among those convicted of driving while intoxicated (Jones and Lacey 1999). Additionally, some day reporting centers operate almost exclusively for technical probation and parole violators.

Some Examples of Day Reporting Centers

The Moore County Day Reporting Center. The Moore County (North Carolina) Day Reporting Center is a state-funded program that involves youths ages 7 to 16 who have been adjudicated delinquent or undisciplined. The juveniles come to the center every day after school hours to receive various services. Particularly targeted are youths who are nonviolent, who have a substance abuse history, and who need to develop living skills.

Participation in the day reporting center is approved, provided that clients meet the following eligibility requirements:

1. Be a Moore County resident
2. Have not been charged with a serious or violent crime
3. Have an approved residence
4. Have access to a telephone
5. Agree to abide by the conditions of the contract with the day reporting center
6. Meet the requirements for intermediate punishment under the Structured Sentencing Act of 1994.

Youths who come to the center acquire valuable employment skills; participate in general education development (GED) classes; undergo life skills training; participate in random drug testing; have access to a variety of mental health services, including group or individual counseling; participate in vocational rehabilitation programs; participate in health education courses; and undergo cognitive behavioral interventions. The cognitive behavioral interventions program is a 36-session program designed to change a person's thought processes to more law-abiding orientations. Numerous youths have been assisted by this day reporting program. The recidivism rate is quite low, less than 30 percent (Moore County Government 2002).

The Englewood Evening Reporting Center. Some day reporting centers are operated during evening hours. This is true of the Englewood Evening Reporting Center, operated between the hours of 4:00 P.M. and 8:00 P.M. weekdays in Englewood, Illinois, a Chicago suburb. The Englewood center is an alternative detention site to serve local juvenile offenders who would otherwise be ordered held in the Juvenile Temporary Detention Center. The center was opened in 1995. Subsequently, the center has received numerous state awards for the services it provides participating Illinois youth.

A part of the court's Juvenile Alternative Detention initiative, evening reporting centers such as the Englewood center are community-based facilities that operate through partnerships between sponsoring social service organizations and the court. Under the program, the juvenile court judge can order nonviolent juvenile offenders awaiting disposition on a warrant or probation violation to report to the evening reporting center as an alternative to being held in detention. Youths are required to report to the center between the hours of 4:00 P.M. and 8:00 P.M. daily. At these centers, they meet with professional staff who consist of educational specialists, recreational specialists, and three group workers who provide programs, activities, and workshops for a maximum of 25 youths. Transportation to and from the Englewood center and an evening meal are provided.

Chief Judge Donald P. O'Connell of the Cook County Court has said that "The purpose of the Circuit Court's support for establishing evening reporting centers is twofold. First, we are helping at-risk kids avoid the possibility of being rearrested and sent to detention centers by getting them off the street and offering them positive, structured programming. We are able to do this through a low staff to client ratio of five to one which ensures the personal attention simply not possible at the detention center." The expectation is that stronger, safer neighborhoods are fostered by reducing the likelihood of criminal activity and by providing various jobs to community residents.

The average daily cost per client at the Englewood center is $33 per day, which is significantly less than the $100 per day it would cost to hold the juvenile in detention facilities. Funding is provided by the Cook County Court. The Englewood center is operated by the Reach Out and Touch Someone, Inc. and Treatment Alternatives for Safer Communities (TASC), Aunt Martha's Youth Service Center, and the Circuit Court of Cook County Juvenile Department's Probation and Court Service Division. This particular evening reporting center is in a community that has one of the highest rates of juvenile arrests and referrals to detention (Cook County Court 2002).

The Day Reporting Center for Juvenile Firearms Offenses. In McLean County, Illinois, a day reporting center is operated for juveniles who have possessed firearms during the commission of delinquent acts. It is called the Day Reporting Center for Juvenile Firearms Offenses. The purpose of this program is to provide the juvenile court with meaningful sanctions for juveniles possessing firearms. Three components of the program include mandatory public service, public health education addressing the risks of firearms and their possession, and psychological evaluation and appropriate referrals.

Community service is a mandatory component of the program. The purpose of the community service is to assist juveniles in learning how to assume responsibility for themselves and for the community in which they live. Service to the local public will enable the youth to form attachments and commitments that promote civility and safety within the community. Mandatory public health education is designed to instill in the juvenile participants more complete understanding of the personal and public health risks associated with the unlawful use of firearms. And an exhaustive psychological evaluation is required prior to a juvenile's acceptance into the program. All files are meticulously maintained during the juvenile's participation. Referrals to psychological and/or counseling services are made where appropriate.

Each juvenile spends between 1 and 60 days in the program. Juveniles receive tutoring, especially those in need of assistance with schoolwork. Tutoring time can also be used for the completion of homework. The main goal of this portion of the program is to teach the juvenile how to use his or her study time effectively. Group therapy is also included. Group therapy includes presentations by informed authorities on positive peer relationships, drug education, handgun education, esteem building, and understanding of the juvenile court system. Individual therapy is sometimes conducted on a one-to-one basis, depending upon the youth's needs. Basic life skills are imparted in an instructional component of the program, which includes personal hygiene and meal planning, preparation, and cleanup. The goal of this part of the program is to heighten the juvenile's awareness of himself or herself and family members. The program runs Mondays through Fridays, after normal school hours. Juveniles are expected to attend school and keep up with their studies.

There is strong parental input in this day reporting center. The parents' role in rehabilitating the juvenile is large, as they can reinforce the program's message. Parents are responsible for transporting their children to the program, and they have an opportunity to become integrated into the actual program. Program officials maintain daily case notes on each juvenile in the program. Attainment of and progress toward the juvenile's goals is also noted. When the juvenile successfully completes the program, a full report of the juvenile's progress is made to the court. The cost of maintaining each child in the day reporting program is $50 per day compared with $92 per day if the juvenile were placed in secure detention in the McLean County Juvenile Detention Center. The recidivism rate of youths who have successfully completed the program is about 25 percent (McLean County Court Services 2002).

The Pre-Dispositional Supervision Program.   The Pre-Dispositional Supervision (PDS) Program is operated in Geary County, Kansas, through the local community corrections office. The original purpose of the program was to reduce juvenile crime and recidivism. Local law enforcement officials in Geary County believed that the juvenile crime rate was directly related to the high incidence of substance abuse among its youth. Therefore, early assessments and treatments of juveniles arrested for drug-related offenses were believed to be an effective means of decreasing the crime rate.

The predispositional nature of the program is such that juvenile court judges in Geary County are provided with additional information about a youth's suitability for probation prior to disposition. Prior to the program, juvenile court judges were often unaware of a particular juvenile offender's needs and other problems, including behavioral/emotional problems. The predispositional day reporting program operating in Geary County commenced operations in September 1996.

Eligible offenders are restricted to adjudicated youths who have not as yet been disposed (sentenced) by juvenile court judges. Prior to the dispositional hearing, the court can order the juvenile detained or released on bond. As a condition of the bond, the court can order the juvenile to predispositional supervision. The local community corrections department offers predispositional supervision. Juvenile offenders must report to the community corrections day reporting center for an assessment. The day reporting staff conducts a needs assessment as well as a substance abuse assessment, including a urinalysis. Services are provided as needed. A local provider supplies substance abuse assessment and treatment.

The juvenile offender must report to the day reporting center from 8:30 A.M. to 5:00 P.M. daily. During this time, the juvenile participates in academic sessions, job skills training, social skills training, anger management, conflict resolution, and community service for a maximum of 20 hours. All predispositional-ordered youth meet in one classroom and are supervised by two staff members. The staff may utilize electronic monitoring for non-compliant youths. Curfews are generally ordered from 6:00 P.M. to 6:00 A.M., and clients are randomly monitored by the community corrections surveillance officers.

The maximum capacity is 30 clients at any given time, based upon staff and space limitations. The average length of supervision varies between 30 and 60 days. The staff consists of the director and a life skills instructor. The typical length of time clients remain in the predispositional program is four weeks, and the average cost of this experience is $155 per offender. The expenditures include staffing, alcohol and drug evaluations, urinalyses, electronic monitoring, books, and software. The successfulness of this program is reflected by the low 6 percent rate of recidivism among all clientele (Geary County Community Corrections 2002).

ALTERNATIVE DISPUTE RESOLUTION

In New Mexico, many youths are subject to **alternative dispute resolution (ADR)** or mediation to resolve school problems. Melinda Smith (1990, 112) says that the mediation process allows people to resolve conflicts in a nonthreatening and nonpunitive atmosphere. Mediators are third-party neutrals who help people in a dispute to express their points of view, identify their needs, clarify issues, explore solutions, and negotiate satisfactory agreements.

The New Mexico Center for Dispute Resolution operates a school mediation program that trains students in grades 5 through 12 as mediators to intervene in school-based disputes among students (Smith 1990, 112). Smith describes the program as consisting of three components: (1) a conflict resolution curriculum that can be taught either in academic or residential settings, (2) a mediation program that trains residents and staff to help resolve conflicts among themselves, and (3) a reintegration component involving parents and residents developing terms of daily living for when the residents return home.

She further indicates that the program's rationale is that by giving students a model for positive expression and conflict resolution, it can teach them alternatives to violent and self-destructive behavior. By using these skills within the institutional setting, students can be assisted to interact successfully with their peers and adults. A voluntary program, this mediation effort has seemingly reduced juvenile deviance in the jurisdiction. Thus, it may be viewed as an early intervention for preventing juvenile delinquency.

Victim-offender mediation is now established as an important and growing part of alternative dispute resolution (Simms 1997). For juveniles who have committed property offenses, it is often beneficial for them to face their victims and learn how these victims have been affected by their losses. It is believed that their accountability is heightened and that they are more inclined to accept responsibility for whatever they have done (Ostermeyer and Keilitz 1997).

Some victim-offender mediation sessions may involve all parties, including family members, the child's attorney, social service agencies, and others involved in the case. The goal is to work toward an agreement and a restitution plan that everyone approves (Evje and Cushman 2000). This agreement is submitted to the juvenile court judge for approval (Lowry 1997). It is believed that the family-centered nature of the mediation process provides the social support youths need for long-term behavioral change associated with the mediation. No single victim-offender mediation model is workable in all situations, however. Individual factors and circumstances must be considered in order to configure the best mediation plan.

South Carolina has been operating juvenile arbitration programs since 1983. One such program is the Lexington County Juvenile Arbitration Program. Some of the conditions of this program include waiving rights to legal representation and permitting impartial arbitrators to make a determination of guilt at the beginning of the hearing. The juvenile admits guilt and the hearing proceeds to a mutually satisfactory conclusion between the offender and victim. If the juvenile does not admit guilt, then the arbitration proceedings are terminated and the juvenile is sent to the juvenile court. Arbitrators are chosen from the community on the basis of their skill and expertise, and they are given over 20 hours of arbitration training prior to conducting arbitration sessions. During 1995–1996, for instance, 370 juveniles were referred to the Lexington County Juvenile Arbitration Program, with a success rate of 94 percent. Total hours of community service generated by these sessions were 4,666, while the restitution amount collected was $5038. The future of juvenile arbitration in South Carolina is bright and is designed to promote successful prevention/intervention strategies for at-risk juvenile offenders (Alford 1998, 28, 34).

The prevailing correctional philosophy applied to juvenile corrections today as well as to programs for adults is punishment/control rather than treatment/rehabilitation (Wilkinson 1998). But like adults, not all juvenile offenders are the same according to their emotional needs, offense seriousness, educational levels, vocational skills, and honesty. Therefore, it is difficult for judges to prescribe meaningful, categorical punishments for aggregates of youthful offenders facing similar charges (Boutellier et al. 1996). Even if specific predictor variables could be identified, they are not always foolproof for effective program placement decision-making.

SUMMARY

Nominal options available to juvenile court judges include verbal warnings and diversion. Verbal warnings may be committed to writing, so that judges may refer to them if the same juveniles reappear for new offenses at a later date. Diversion is often suggested by either intake probation officers or prosecutors. Diversion is a temporary suspension of a juvenile's case from the juvenile justice system, where various conditions or behavioral requirements are imposed. The result of successfully completing a diversion program may be expungement of one's juvenile record, or at the very least, a reduction in the seriousness of charges against the juvenile.

Various diversion programs exist throughout most jurisdictions. Early versions of diversion programs involved Youth Service Bureaus. Subsequently, various community services were established that were devoted to meeting the diverse needs of juvenile offenders. Several programs have been established, including the Youth Services/Diversion and Community Service Programs, Inc., the Diversion Plus Program, the PINS Diversion Program, the See Our Side (SOS) Program, and the Community Board Program.

One alternative diversionary program is the teen court, sometimes known as a youth court, where one's peers decide the punishment imposed in minor offense cases. Offenders tried by a teen court may be asked to serve on such a court in the future, as one type of conditional punishment imposed upon them. Day treatment programs are used in some jurisdictions. These programs permit youths to attend their schools as well as participate in day treatment activities in late afternoon hours. Such programs provide vocational as well as educational assistance. Another option is to divert youths to alternative dispute resolution programs where mediators resolve disputes between victims and juvenile offenders.

QUESTIONS FOR REVIEW

1. What are nominal dispositions? Do you think they are effective punishments for low-risk juvenile offenders? Why or why not?

2. What is meant by diversion? Who are the primary types of juveniles who are eligible for diversion?

3. What are some of the functions and dysfunctions of diversion?

4. What is a youth services bureau? What are four types of youth service bureaus? Have they been successful at accomplishing their goals? Why or why not?

5. How does the Diversion Plus Program compare with the See Our Side Program? What are the basic components of each?

6. What is meant by the PINS Diversion Program? Is it effective? Why or why not?

7. What are teen courts? What types of juvenile offenders are the best types of clients for teen courts? Why?

8. What are day reporting centers? What are some of their goals and functions?

9. What are two examples of day reporting centers? What are some of their characteristics and which types of juveniles are served by them?

10. What is meant by alternative dispute resolution? Do you think it is an effective way of settling disputes between victims and youthful offenders? Why or why not?

SUGGESTED READINGS

American Bar Association. 2001. *Justice by gender: The lack of appropriate prevention, diversion, and treatment alternatives for girls in the justice system.* Washington, DC: American Bar Association/National Bar Association.

Chernoff, Nina W. and Bernadine H. Watson. 2000. *An investigation of Philadelphia's Youth Aid Panel: A community-based diversion program for first-time youthful offenders.* Philadelphia: Philadelphia District Attorney's Office.

LoGalbo, Anthony P. and Charlene M. Callahan. 2001. An evaluation of the teen court as a juvenile crime diversion program. *Juvenile and Family Court Journal* 52:1–11.

Marciniak, Liz Marie. 2000. The addition of day reporting to intensive supervision probation: A comparison of recidivism rates. *Federal Probation* 64:34–39.

INTERNET CONNECTIONS

CompassPoint Nonprofit Services
http://www.compasspoint.org/

DrugSense
http://www.drugsense.org/

Empowerment Resources
http://www.empowermentresources.com/

Georgia Alliance for Children
http://www.gac.org/

Idaho Youth Ranch
http://www.youthranch.org/

Institute for Global Communications
http://igc.org/iga/gateway/index.html

Nonprofit Consultants ONTAP
http://www.ontap.org/

Nonprofit GENIE
http://www.genie.org/

Resources for Youth
http://www.preventviolence.org/

Vera Institute of Justice
http://www.broadway.vera.org/

CHAPTER 12 | *Juvenile Probation and Community-Based Corrections*

Chapter Outline

Key Terms

American Correctional
   Association (ACA)
Balanced approach
Boston Offender Project (BOP)
Caseloads
Case supervision planning
Community corrections acts
Community service
Conditional probation

Conventional model
Conventional model with
   geographic considerations
Creative sentencing
Electronic monitoring
Electronic monitoring signalling
   devices
Fines
Home confinement

Home incarceration
House arrest
Intensive Aftercare Program
   (IAP)
Intensive supervised probation
   (ISP)
Juvenile intensive supervised
   probation (JISP)
Juvenile Probation Camps (JPCs)

Numbers-game model
Ohio experience
Project New Pride
Recidivism rate
Recidivists
Restitution
San Francisco Project
Second Chance Program

Sexual Offender Treatment
    (SOT) Program
Smart sentencing
SpeakerID Program
Special conditions of probation
Specialized caseloads model
Standard probation
Tagging

Unconditional probation, uncon-
    ditional standard probation
Victim compensation
Victim–offender mediation
Youth-to-Victim Restitution
    Project

Chapter Objectives

As a result of reading this chapter, you will realize the following objectives:

1. Understand what is meant by juvenile probation and parole, as well as the extent to which these sanctions are used in juvenile cases.
2. Become familiar with several important types of probation programs for juveniles.
3. Learn about different dispositional options as conditions of probation, including restitution, fines, community service, and victim compensation.
4. Understand what is meant by home confinement and electronic monitoring for juveniles and how often such options are used in their conditional supervision.
5. Understand what is meant by intermediate punishments for juveniles.
6. Learn about several important intensive supervised probation programs for juveniles, including their weaknesses and strengths.

INTRODUCTION

• *In June 1999, 18-year-old Relvy Ramon Martinez was gunned down behind the Laredo, Texas Country Club. Following the murder, two suspects were apprehended, based in part on the eyewitness testimony of a teenager, Jose Manuel "Joey" Martinez. Both suspects were eventually charged with Martinez's murder, and Pioquinto Mendiza Jr. was convicted in early 2000. A second suspect charged in the murder, Jorge Margarito Aguillon, was acquitted. In September 2000, there was a strange turn of events. Information and evidence developed from the trials of Mendiza and Aguillon revealed that Jose Martinez was more than informant and eyewitness. He became a suspect and actual participant in the murder of Martinez. He was arrested by police and held in a Laredo juvenile detention center for three weeks. On September 22, 2000, he was temporarily released to the custody of his mother and placed on home confinement and electronic monitoring. Martinez's attorney said only that "We are not going to comment on the release other than to say that he will be pleading not guilty to all charges." Court records revealed that Martinez had several other charges pending against him, including an assault charge resulting from a call to police from his mother because the youth became disruptive and would not stop smoking in the house. [Adapted from Robert Garcia, "Juvenile Suspect at Home with Electronic Monitoring." September 23, 2000.]*

• *It happened in Darmstadt, Germany. Several U.S. teens, ages 14, 17, and 18, positioned themselves over a major highway on an overpass. As motorists passed, the youths dropped 20-pound rocks on the cars. Some of the rocks broke through windshields and at least two German drivers were killed in these incidents. Eyewitnesses led to the subsequent arrests of the three teens, who were all children of military personnel at a U.S. military base south of Frankfurt, Germany. The youths faced murder charges and causing accident with intent. Authorities questioned the teens separately in different interrogation rooms. A German prosecutor, Neuber, said that the next stage would be the teens' arraignment, "which we think will come soon." He said that the youths would all be tried as juveniles and that they would face up to 10 years in prison for a juvenile murder conviction. Darmstadt police said that the U.S. teens confessed to hurling volleyball-sized stones, some weighing as much as 20 pounds, from a pedestrian bridge onto a four-lane highway below. A 20-year-old woman and a 41-year-old mother of two were killed, and several other car passengers were seriously injured. Subsequently, the three teenagers were convicted of murder on December 22, 2000 and were sentenced for up to 8 1/2 years in prison for this crime. Prosecutors had demanded 10-year sentences for the trio. Judge Bertram Schmitt said that the teens acted out of boredom and that they sought progressively larger stones after failing at first to hit any vehicles, using the approaching headlights as targets in the darkness. The judge added, "They didn't set out to kill people, but there was a qualified intent. The defendants recognized the possibility that people could die." Ultimately, the stones were as big as breadboxes. Schmitt added that "they kept raising the level of risk until the people in the cars had no chance. It's like a game of Russian roulette except they were not putting their own lives at risk, only those people unknown to them."* [Adapted from the Associated Press, "U.S. Teens Questioned about Stoning Deaths." March 2, 2000; adapted from Katharine Schmidt and the Associated Press, "Three American Teens Convicted of Stoning Deaths." December 23, 2000.]

• *It happened in 1992. At the time, Amy Fisher was 17 and seeing a married man, Joey Buttafuoco. One afternoon, Amy went to Joey Buttafuoco's home and attempted to kill Joey's wife. Although shot in the head and seriously impaired following the shooting, Joey's wife recovered and identified Amy Fisher as her attacker. Subsequently, it was determined that Amy Fisher had begun her affair with Joey Buttafuoco when she was 16. Joey owned a car repair shop. Amy would see Joey frequently for sex. Amy became known as the "Long Island Lolita." Joey was charged with and convicted of statutory rape of a teenager, following his admission that he had had sex with Amy when she was 16. However, Amy was sentenced from 5 to 15 years for the attempted murder of Joey's wife. In June 1997, Amy Fisher applied to the New York Parole Board to consider her for early release. The parole board rejected her application. A parole board member told Amy, "There is a reasonable probability that you would not live and remain at liberty without violating the law. Your release at this time is incompatible with the welfare and safety of the community." A few years later, the parole board finally granted Amy's request for early release and she walked out of prison on May 10, 1999.* [Adapted from the Associated Press, "Fisher Denied in First Parole Bid." June 14, 1997; adapted from the Associated Press, "Long Island Lolita Paroled." May 12, 1999.]

The traditional view of juvenile offenders is that they should receive the least restrictive confinement or punishment if they are adjudicated delinquent. Further, every attempt should be made to rehabilitate them. The cases above illustrate that (1) not all youths are considered by juvenile courts to be capable of becoming rehabilitated; and (2) the least restrictive alternative is not always the best choice for a juvenile, especially for a juvenile with a long record of serious violent offending.

At the other end of the spectrum are the vast majority of youths who are capable of becoming rehabilitated and who should be granted the least restrictive conditions upon their adjudication for various offenses. There is no particular class of delinquent youths who should be diverted from the juvenile justice system. Neither should their cases be thrown out or downgraded by prosecutors. Rather, these youths should be subjected to minimal supervisory conditions and community controls for various periods of time. This chapter describes several nonsecure punishments that juvenile court judges may impose, including an array of intermediate punishment programs for juveniles. Intermediate punishment programs are sanctions that exist somewhere between incarceration and standard probation on the continuum of criminal penalties. Intermediate punishments described here include intensive supervised probation (ISP), juvenile intensive supervised probation (JISP), community-based juvenile corrections, electronic monitoring, home confinement, and shock probation.

The significance of intermediate punishment programs is that they are characterized by a higher degree of supervisory control over juvenile offenders. They are generally considered to be delinquency deterrents and repressive, in the sense that they are intended to promote a strong degree of crime or delinquency control through offender monitoring. Therefore, they deter by controlling offender behaviors and by making it increasingly difficult for individual offenders to deviate from program conditions. Offenders who are closely supervised or monitored have fewer opportunities to reoffend compared with offenders on traditional probationary or diversionary programs. Collectively, intermediate punishment programs are generally intended for more serious habitual or chronic juvenile offenders, although it is not unusual to place certain first offenders in an intermediate punishment program if the first offense is a particularly serious one.

It is not uncommon for juvenile court judges to impose fines and restitution orders in addition to other program requirements, if intermediate punishments are imposed. A brief discussion of the use of fines and victim reparations for juvenile offenders will be presented. Each of the intermediate punishment programs presented will also be assessed in terms of its effectiveness at reducing recidivism.

STANDARD PROBATION FOR JUVENILES

Standard Probation Defined

Standard juvenile probation is fairly simple to understand and considered a routine disposition for most juvenile court judges. Of all dispositional options available to juvenile court judges, standard probation is the one most frequently used. The first probation law was enacted in Massachusetts in 1878, although probation was used much earlier. John Augustus invented probation in Boston in 1841. **Standard probation** is either a conditional or unconditional nonincarcerative disposition for a specified period following an adjudication of delinquency.

There are several types of standard probation programs. Like their diversion program counterparts, probation programs for juveniles are either **unconditional probation** or **conditional probation.** Again, there are many similarities between probation programs devised for adults and those structured for juvenile offenders (Campbell and Schmidt 2000). **Unconditional standard probation,** another term for unconditional probation, basically involves complete freedom of movement for juveniles within their communities, perhaps accompanied by periodic reports by telephone or mail with a probation officer (PO) or the probation department. Because a PO's caseload is often large, with several hundred juvenile clients who must be managed, individualized attention cannot be given to most juveniles on standard probation. The period of unsupervised probation varies among jurisdictions depending upon offense seriousness and other circumstances (Shearer 2002).

Conditional probation programs may include optional conditions and program requirements, such as performing a certain number of hours of public or community service; providing restitution to victims; payment of fines; employment; and/or participation in specific vocational, educational, or therapeutic programs. It is crucial to any probation program that an effective classification system is in place so that juvenile court judges can dispose offenders accordingly. It is common practice for conditional probation programs to contain special conditions and provisions that address different youth needs. These special conditions are usually added by the juvenile court judge on the basis of information provided by juvenile POs (Knupfer 2001).

The terms of standard probation are outlined in Figure 12.1. Although these terms may be accompanied by special conditions, known as **special conditions of probation,** more often than not, no special conditions are attached. Thus, youths disposed to standard probation experience little change in their social routines. Whenever special conditions of probation are attached, they usually mean additional work for probation officers. Some of these conditions might include medical treatments for drug or alcohol dependencies, individual or group therapy or counseling, or participation in a driver's safety course. In some instances involving theft, burglary, or vandalism, restitution provisions may be included, where youths must repay victims for their financial losses. Most standard probation programs in the United States require little, if any, direct contact with the probation office. Logistically, this works out well for probation officers, who are frequently overworked and have enormous client caseloads of 300 or more youths. However, greater caseloads mean less individualized attention devoted to youths by POs, and some of these youths require more supervision than others while on standard probation. Item 12 of the juvenile probation form used by Orange County, California, as shown in Figure 12.1, specifies which, if any, special conditions apply for particular juveniles.

Community service orders are increasingly used, although in some states, juvenile probation departments have found it difficult to find personnel to supervise youthful probationers. For instance, a North Dakota delinquent was ordered to perform 200 hours of community service. The community had about 500 residents, and the work ordered involved park maintenance and general cleanup duties. However, the youth never performed any of this community service, since the probation department did not have the money to pay a juvenile probation officer to monitor the youth for the full 200 hours. Despite these occasional limitations, most probation program conditions today are geared toward heightening offender accountability by having him or her do something constructive (Decker 2000).

In view of the fact that little or no monitoring of juvenile conduct exists in many state probation agencies, standard probation has fairly high rates of recidivism, ranging from 40 to 75 percent. Even certain youth camps operated in various California counties, where some degree of supervision over youths exists, have reported recidivism rates as high as 76 percent among their youthful clientele (Palmer 1994). Therefore, it is often difficult to forecast which juveniles will have the greatest likelihood of reoffending, regardless of the program we are examining (Steen 2001).

Ron Corbett (2000, 28) has recommended the following steps toward a reformed type of juvenile probation:

INSTRUCTIONS:
1. Original to Probation Files
2. Pink to Parents
3. Blue to Minor
4. Goldenrod to Division Officer

ORANGE COUNTY PROBATION DEPARTMENT
INFORMAL PROBATION AGREEMENT

The authority for undertaking a plan of informal probation which may include the use of a crisis resolution home or shelter-care facility is contained in Section 654 of the Welfare and Institutions Code, which is printed in full on the reverse side of this form. Before signing this agreement, please read it and resolve any questions about it with the deputy probation officer.

Minor's Initials

GENERAL RULES AND REQUIREMENTS

_____ 1. You are to report in person and submit written reports to your probation officer as directed.

_____ 2. You are to obey all laws, including traffic rules and regulations. You are not to operate a motor vehicle in any street or highway until properly licensed and insured. You are to report to your probation officer any arrests or law violations immediately.

_____ 3. You are to obey the curfew law of the city or county in which you live or any special curfew imposed by the Court or the probation officer, specifically:_____

_____ 4. You are not to leave the State of California or change your residence without first getting permission from your probation officer. Prior to change of residence, you are to nofity your probation officer of the new address. You are not to live with anyone except your parents or approved guardian without specific permission of your probation officer.

_____ 5. You are to attend school every day, every class, as prescribed by law, and obey all school regulations. Suspension from school and/or truancies/tardiness could result in action being taken by the Probation Department. You are to notify your probation officer by 10:00 a.m. on any school day that you are absent from school. If you are home from school because of illness or suspension, you are not to leave your home that day or night except to keep a doctor's appointment.

_____ 6. You are not to use or possess any intoxicants, alcohol, narcotics, other controlled substances, related paraphernalia, poisons, or illegal drugs; including marijuana. You are not to be with anyone who is using or possessing any illegal intoxicants, narcotics or drugs. Do not inhale or attempt to inhale or consume any substance of any type or nature, such as paint, glue, plant material or any aerosol product. You are not to inject anything into your body uness directed so by a medical doctor.

_____ 7. You are not to frequent any places of business disapproved by your probation officer, parents or guardians, specifically: _____

_____ 8. You are not to associate with individuals disapproved by your probation officer, parents or guardians, specifically: _____ _____

_____ 9. You may be required to participate in any program outlined in Section 654 W&I Code.

_____ 10. You are to seek and maintain counseling if and as directed by the probation officer.

_____ 11. You are not to have any weapons of any description, including firearms, numchucks or martial arts weaponry, and knives of any kind, in your possession while you are on probation, or involve self in activities in which weapons are used, i.e., hunting, target shooting.

_____ 12. You are ordered to obey the following additional terms of probation:
_____
_____

Probation supervision will expire on _____ unless you fail to abide by the above terms and conditions of your probation resulting in court action.

I have personally initialed, read and understand the above rules and requirements of informal probation that apply in my particular case as explained to me by the probation officer. I understand that my failure to comply with the initialed items could result in the petition, that is pending in my case, being filed with the District Attorney.

SIGNED: _____   DATE: _____
                         (minor)

SIGNED: _____   DATE: _____
                         (parent)

SIGNED: _____   DATE: _____
                         (parent)

MICHAEL SHUMACHER
Chief Probation Officer

BY: _____   DATE: _____
                 (Deputy Probation Officer)

FIGURE 12.1 Orange County Probation Department Informal Probation Agreement

1. Let research drive policy. All too often, the field becomes enthralled in the latest fad and rushes to adopt it. Any and all new initiatives should include an evaluation component. Smart programs should be developed, especially programs that emphasize restitution.

2. Emphasize early intervention. Interventions occurring in a youth's early years are far more effective than those attempted when the youth is in his or her midteen years.

3. Emphasize the paying of just debts. Just-deserts and justice should be emphasized in part to change the coddling image persons presently have of juvenile courts. Restitution and community service do much to heighten offender accountability, and they can easily be integrated into a probation or parole program.

4. Make probation character building. Many delinquents lack character, or good habits of thought and action, as well as self-control. Programs that include psychoeducational strategies are better at character-building than those that are strictly punishment-centered.

5. Prioritize violence prevention. Juvenile probation must focus on efforts to suppress violent behavior. Programs that are educational in nature are more profitable in the long run compared with punishment-centered programs. These educational programs are geared to enable youths to learn how to cope more effectively with their environment. Such programs would include anger management training, acquiring skills (social and emotional), improving moral reasoning, and instilling heightened self-esteem (Corbett 2000, 28–29).

Mission-Driven Probation Versus Outcome-Focused Probation. More effective juvenile probation appears to be both mission-driven and outcome-focused. Good juvenile probation is outcome-focused. Both for individual offenders and for entire juvenile probation officer caseloads, outcome-focused probation systematically measures the tangible results of its interventions, compares those results to its goals, and makes itself publicly accountable for any differences. Organizations tend to become whatever they measure. Departments must measure more than their failures (recidivism) and the sanctions they have imposed (Torbet and Griffin 2002, 24). Outcome measures assess whether goals have been achieved. They provide evidence of the degree to which probation supervision goals have or have not been achieved, in essence measuring the department's performance in meeting system goals. Long-term outcomes measure the degree to which probation supervision has impacted youthful offenders after their release, in terms of changing their thinking, behaviors, and attitudes (Torbet and Griffin 2002, 24–25).

Mission-driven juvenile probation is that the work of probation must be directed at achieving clearly articulated and widely shared goals. Getting there requires a commitment to a strategic planning or focus group process that gives a representative cross-section of staff a chance to define their values about the juvenile justice system and juvenile probation in particular and to translate them into action and results. Such an effort will increase staff buy-in and provide a basis for continuous feedback, evaluation, and improvement at the policy program and individual employee levels. Mission statements provide an organizational compass that points in the direction of an agreed-upon destination, and they are central to the operations and activities of any organization. What does juvenile probation stand for in the community? What is it attempting to accomplish? Ultimately, mission statements should be broken down into individual goals that are directed at protecting the public, holding the juvenile accountable for repairing harm caused to victims and the community, and engaging offenders in rehabilitative activities designed to address their most pressing problems and needs (Torbet and Griffin 2002, 22–23).

The Youth-to-Victim Restitution Project

One factor associated with significant reductions in recidivism is restitution (Lemmon and Calhoon 1998). Programs that use restitution and enforce it seem to have lower recidivism rates associated with their youthful clientele (Knupfer 2001). This is because offenders are required to repay victims for damages they inflict and take some responsibility for their actions. In Lincoln, Nebraska, for example, a study evaluated the effectiveness of the **Youth-to-Victim Restitution Project,** a program operated through the Lincoln Juvenile Court. Juveniles are ordered to pay restitution as a condition of probation. In order to assure their compliance, the juvenile court arranges for and supplies their employment at various jobs. Between 1984 and 1993, 183 youths had participated in the restitution project. Jacobs and Moore (1994) found that successful compliance with the court restitution orders was the most significant predictor of recidivism. Specifically, these researchers determined that among the youths ordered to pay restitution, certain variables existed, such as the restitution goal, time given to pay, amount ordered to be paid, and subsequent offenses charged. Youths could be arranged according to a continuum in terms of which youths paid the greatest proportion of restitution. The least amount of recidivism was observed among those who paid the greatest proportion of restitution. Those paying the least amount of restitution or not paying it at all had high rates of delinquency recidivism. Restitution is a powerful deterrent to further offending. At least a financial connection is made between what the youthful offenders did and how much it cost to compensate victims for their losses (Roy 1997). Therefore, these tangible punishments were considered most effective as delinquency deterrents.

The Second Chance Program

A program established in an Iowa county during the early 1990s is the **Second Chance Program** (Leiber and Mawhorr 1995). The Juvenile Court in Iowa placed several samples of adjudicated youths into a program, Second Chance, which included social skills training, pre-employment training, and job placement opportunities as means of reducing recidivism and delinquency. A one-year follow-up showed that while Second Chance youth had similar recidivism rates compared with a control group not participating in the Second Chance program, the Second Chance participants tended to engage in far less serious offenses compared with their experimental controls. Four characteristics tended to be associated with program success and long-term recidivism-free behavior: family involvement, treatment integrity, cultural sensitivity, and follow-up care and monitoring.

Juvenile Probation Camps

In the early 1980s, California experimented with several types of **Juvenile Probation Camps (JPCs)** (Palmer and Wedge 1994). These camps were county-operated and included physical activities, community contacts, and academic

Probation camps offer youths structure, educational opportunities, and self development.

training. These nonincarcerative camps were designed as dispositional alternatives to secure custody for youthful offenders. Eligibility requirements included first-offender status and nonviolent behaviors. Counselors worked with youth who were carefully screened before entering the program. Groups of youths were deliberately small in order to maximize individualized attention for each youth. Older juveniles who participated in these probation camps had lower rates of recidivism compared with younger youths. Overall, the camps were viewed as successful in minimizing recidivism and maximizing rehabilitation of participants. One reason for the lower rates of recidivism among youthful clients was greater direct supervision by camp personnel. This circumstance is not unlike that found in communities where various methods of formal social control, including police and probation officer surveillance, are employed to supervise juvenile probationers and parolees (Bond-Maupin and Maupin 1998).

The Intensive Aftercare Program (IAP)

Between 1988 and 1990, the **Intensive Aftercare Program (IAP)** was designed in Philadelphia and targeted serious youthful offenders (Altschuler and Armstrong 2001). A sample of 46 youths committed to the Bensalem Youth Development Center was compared with a control group of 46 youths who received traditional aftercare probation services. While the IAP participants exhibited lower rates of recidivism compared with those subject to conventional aftercare probation, the differences were not significant. It was reported, however, that IAP officers believed that their interventions with IAP youth were both rapid and positive. Thus, some officials believed that they were able to assist some of these IAP participants from incurring subsequent rearrests (Sontheimer and Goodstein 1993).

The Sexual Offender Treatment (SOT) Program

Not all specialized programs for juvenile probationers are successful. For example, an assessment was made of the **Sexual Offender Treatment (SOT) Program** established by a juvenile probation department of a large Midwestern U.S. metropolitan county in January 1988 (Lab, Shields, and Schondel 1993). The program consisted of 20 peer-group meetings with psycho-socio-educational intervention focus, supplemented by individual family counseling sessions with youths who had been adjudicated delinquent for assorted sex offenses. Subsequently, an experimental program was conducted for 46 youths referred to the SOT program and compared with a control group of 109 youths assigned to nonsexually specific interventions during the same period. Data sources included juvenile court and program records. Essentially, youths handled by the SOT program fared no better than youths processed through normal, nonoffense-specific programming. Thus, these researchers concluded that simply knowing one's symptoms and problems and designing specific interventions for those problems are not always workable. Additional study is needed to identify appropriate treatment factors that might make a difference in reducing their recidivism rates for sexual offending (Seng 2000).

THE SUCCESSFULNESS OF STANDARD JUVENILE PROBATION

The successfulness of standard juvenile probation as well as other probation and parole programs is measured according to the **recidivism rate** accompanying these program alternatives. Recidivism is measured various ways, including rearrests, reconvictions, new adjudications, return to secure confinement, movement from standard probation to intensive supervised probation, and simple probation program condition violations, such as drug use or alcohol and curfew violation. One of the best discussions of **recidivists** and its numerous definitions is *Recidivism* by Michael Maltz (1984).

The most popular meaning of recidivism is a new adjudication as delinquent for reoffending. It is generally the case that, with exceptions, intensive supervision programs have less recidivism associated with them than standard probation. Over the years, a recidivism standard of 30 percent has been established among researchers as the cutting point between a successful probation program and an unsuccessful one. Programs with recidivism rates of 30 percent or less are considered successful, while those programs with more than 30 percent recidivism are not particularly successful. This figure is arbitrary, although it is most often used as a success standard. No program presently has zero percent recidivism.

Probation and Recidivism

Standard probation, which means little or no direct and regular supervision of offenders by probation officers, has a fairly high rate of recidivism among the various state jurisdictions. Recidivism rates for juveniles on standard probation range from 30 percent to 70 percent, depending upon the nature of their offenses and prior records (Tolman 1996).

The following elements appear to be predictive of future criminal activity and reoffending by juveniles: (1) age at first adjudication, (2) a prior criminal record (a combined measure of the number and severity of priors), (3) the number of prior commitments to juvenile facilities, (4) drug/chemical abuse, (5) alcohol abuse, (6) family relationships (parental control), (7) school problems, and (8) peer relationships (Baird 1985, 36).

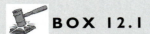 **BOX 12.1**

 **PERSONALITY HIGHLIGHT**

Melissa L. Mojica
Chief Juvenile Probation Officer
Webb County, Texas

Statistics:

Bachelor of Science (government, sociology), Texas Woman's University; Master of Arts (sociology), Texas A & M International University

Work History and Experience:

Presently, I am the Chief Juvenile Probation Officer of Webb County, Texas. I've held this position for the past seven years. I began my career in juvenile justice. I had the privilege of working with the Denton County Juvenile Detention Center as a detention officer under an internship while still a student at Texas Woman's University. It was there that I became interested in this very rewarding field.

Two weeks after graduation, I was hired in Laredo, Texas, as a detention officer with the Webb County Juvenile Department. Two years later, I was promoted to the position of juvenile probation officer. It was at this time that I found out for myself what problems plagued our community.

During my seven and a half years of service as a juvenile probation officer, I learned that treating my clients with respect and setting attainable and measurable goals gave parents and children hope, the hope of success. Since I was dealing with law enforcement agencies on a daily basis, this contact made me appreciate the tremendous responsibility law enforcement officers have to the community and to their fellow officers and colleagues.

Soon thereafter, I was promoted to Case Management Supervisor. In this area, I was responsible for all of the programs and services that were delivered to our clientele. This was challenging because it made me become proactive in setting up programs and/or services. This job also required that I supervise others; I was now in the position of leadership. I held this position for an-

other seven years, and in 1994 I assumed the position of Chief Probation Officer (CPO).

Now, as a CPO, the challenges and opportunities of heading this department are many. When I took over, we were a department of 38 employees. Since that time, we have reached a total of 68 employees. I have had to look at other issues besides the problems that confront our youth, but also in who actually delivers those services. I would say that hiring the "right person" with the "right stuff" has been the most difficult task. It is not enough to have just the minimum qualifications of education and experience; it is what that applicant brings to the table in their own personal skills. I ask myself, "Does this person care? Can he or she be compassionate? Does he or she have the life experience to guide young children and their parents to a place in time when they are no longer in conflict with each other?" Without a solid educational foundation on human behavior and its relationship to society, this becomes just another job and not a career.

Advice to Students:

I encourage all interested students to look into this career field because the youth are our future and, yes, even those involved in the juvenile justice system have an impact on our everyday life; they cannot be written off. People in this profession must do more than just their best; we have got to do better because those kids will be making decisions for us in later years. I'd like to believe that I've handled every case and person with all they were due, but I know in my heart that if I didn't, it wasn't for a lack of trying. Through the trials and tribulations and the stress that the job brings, I cannot imagine having done anything else. Mere words cannot express the feeling one gets in the reward of having imprinted your touch on the lives of many youths. In the hearts and souls of the many that have gone through these doors, they carry my contribution in deed for my community, for their families, and most importantly, for them, our youth.

Christopher Baird (1985) recommends that needs assessments should be individualized, based upon the juvenile's past record and other pertinent characteristics, including the present adjudication offense. The level of supervision should vary according to the degree of risk posed to the public by the juvenile. While Baird furnishes no weighting procedure, so each of the risk factors listed above can be weighted and judges can use these criteria effectively at the sentencing stage, he does describe a supervisory scheme that acts as a guide for juvenile probation and aftercare. This scheme would be applied based on the perceived risk of each juvenile offender. His scheme would include the following:

Regular Supervision
1. Four face-to-face contacts per month with youth.
2. Two face-to-face contacts per month with parents.
3. One face-to-face contact per month with placement staff.
4. One contact with school officials.

Intensive Supervision
1. Six face-to-face contacts per month with youth.
2. Three face-to-face contacts per month with parents.
3. One face-to-face contact per month with placement staff.
4. Two contacts with school officials.

Alternative Care Cases
1. One face-to-face contact per month with youth.
2. Four contacts with agency staff (one must be face-to-face).
3. One contact every two months with parents.

An assignment to any one of these supervision levels should be based on both risk and needs assessments. Baird says that, often, agencies make categorical assignments of juveniles to one level of supervision or another, primarily by referring to the highest level of supervision suggested by two or more scales used (Baird 1985, 38). Each juvenile probation agency prefers specific predictive devices, and some agencies use a combination of them. Again, no scale is foolproof, and the matter of false positives and false negatives arises, as some juveniles receive more supervision than they really require, while others receive less than they need.

At the beginning of the twentieth century, when probation began to be used for juvenile supervision, a report was issued entitled *Juvenile Courts and Probation* (Flexner and Baldwin 1914). Writing seven years following the establishment of the National Probation Association in 1907, Flexner and Baldwin described three important aspects of probation as it applied to juvenile offenders:

1. The period of probation should always be indeterminate because judges cannot possibly fix the period of treatment in advance.
2. To be effective, probation work must be performed by full-time, professionally trained probation officers.
3. Probation is not a judicial function (Hurst 1990, 17).

It is interesting to see how Flexner and Baldwin discounted the value of the judiciary in fixing one's term of probation and performing supervisory functions. They were adamant in the belief that only professional probation officers should engage in such supervisory tasks and that the judicial function should be minimal. The strong treatment orientation of probation is apparent as well, suggesting their belief that probationer treatment programs should be tailored to fit the probationer's needs. Further, they underscored the power originally assigned to probation officers and the leverage that probation officers could exert upon their clients, including possible probation revocation action if program infractions occurred.

An effective probation program is one where probation officers (POs) have an awareness of the juvenile offender's needs and weaknesses. One problem in many existing probation programs is that POs find it hard to establish rapport between themselves and their juvenile clients. A high degree of mistrust exists, in large part because of the age differential between the PO and offender.

Some POs have suggested an approach normally practiced by psychological counselors in developing rapport between themselves and their clients. It has been suggested, for instance, that each PO should (1) thoroughly review the youth's case, including family and juvenile interviews and other background information; (2) engage in introspection and attempt to discover his or her own reactions to adolescents and responses to verbal exchanges; (3) attempt to cultivate a relationship of acceptance rather than rejection and punitiveness; (4) react favorably to a "critical incident," where the juvenile may "screw up" and expect reprimand or punishment but where acceptance and understanding are reflected instead; and (5) follow through with continued support that bolsters juvenile confidence in the PO (Sweet 1985, 90).

Some juveniles are unreachable through any kind of effective exchange. Chronic offenders, hard-core offenders, or psychologically disturbed juveniles frequently reject any attempts by authorities to understand them or assist them in any task (Matson and Barnoski 1997). If some youths are chemically dependent, the fact of substance abuse may interfere with effective interventions of any kind (Lurigio 1996). Where standard probation is not feasible, an intensive supervision program (ISP) is required for certain types of offenders.

INTERMEDIATE PUNISHMENTS FOR JUVENILE OFFENDERS

Intermediate Punishments Defined

Intermediate punishments are community-based sanctions that range from **intensive supervision probation (ISP)** to nonsecure custodial programs. These programs include more intensive monitoring or management of juvenile behaviors through more intensive supervision. They may include home confinement, electronic monitoring, or both. Other community-based services are included, where the goal is to maintain fairly close supervision over youthful offenders. The most successful ISP programs seem to be those that emphasize the social structural causes of delinquency and use greater community participation and agency networking rather than focus upon individual youths' problems. Cognitive-behavioral interventions and participatory problem-solving activities are used as a part of probation department programs designed to reduce offender recidivism and promote long-term law-abiding behaviors (Robertson, Grimes, and Rogers 2001).

Intermediate punishment programs are presently operated in all states for both juvenile and adult offenders. They are sometimes referred to as **creative sentencing,** since they are somewhere between standard probationary dispositions and traditional incarcerative terms that might be imposed by judges. These alternatives to incarceration are regarded as positive interventions for a majority of today's youth who are brought to the attention of the juvenile justice system (English, Pullen, and Chadwick 1996).

The Goals of Intermediate Punishment Programs

There is considerable variation among intermediate punishment programs, although they tend to exhibit similar goals or objectives. These include, but are not limited to:

1. Provision of less expensive sanctions compared with secure confinement.
2. Achievement of lower rates of recidivism compared with standard probation.
3. Greater emphasis on reintegration into communities as the primary correctional goal.
4. Provision of greater range of community services and organizations in a cooperative effort to assist youthful offenders.
5. Minimization of adverse influence of labeling that might stem from secure confinement.
6. Improvement in personal educational and vocational skills of individual offenders, together with acquisition of better self-concepts and greater acceptance of responsibility for one's actions.

In Colorado, for example, an ISP program was established to divert prison-bound youthful offenders (English, Chadwick, and Pullen 1994). Colorado juvenile agency records were obtained for 2,782 offenders who were sentenced to prison; 933 to community corrections; and 3,214 to probation, including 200 sentences to ISP. A twelve-month follow-up of 247 ISP cases matched with comparable samples of offenders sentenced to probation and community corrections was conducted. ISP was successful in diverting offenders from prison, while adequately protecting the public, and at a lower cost than community corrections or prison. The program diverted offenders with rather lengthy juvenile records and adult arrests for violent crimes. ISP offenders were six times as likely to be terminated from the program because of technical violations than for a new crime, which suggests that increased surveillance of these offenders directly detects more technical program infractions. Most of the time, these infractions are not particularly serious (e.g., violating curfew, minor use of alcohol). The cost savings of the Colorado ISP program was substantial. It was estimated by English and her associates that the average daily cost of supervising ISP clients was about $6, while community corrections average daily costs were $33 and prison was $53. These researchers have recommended that their ISP program should be replicated elsewhere to see if similar results are obtained with ISP clients in other jurisdictions. Related research by Woodward and English (1993) has yielded similar findings about ISP programs.

Earlier in 1989, several ISP programs were assessed by Krisberg et al. (1989). These included:

1. The Key Program, Inc. (Massachusetts)
2. The Associated Marine Institutes, Inc. Program (Florida)
3. The Youth Advocate Programs, Inc. (Pennsylvania)
4. The Kentfields Rehabilitation Program (Michigan)
5. The Firestone Community Day Center (California)
6. The Pennsylvania Intensive Probation Supervision Program (Pennsylvania)
7. The Specialized Gang Supervision Program (California)
8. The Hennepin County Surveillance Program (Minnesota)
9. The Ramsey County Juvenile Intensive Supervision Project (Minnesota)
10. The Lucas County Intensive Supervision Unit (Ohio)
11. The Wayne County Intensive Probation Program (Michigan)

Subsequent follow-ups of these programs indicated that while recidivism of participating youths was not entirely eliminated, most of these programs exhibited reasonably low rates of recidivism among participating juveniles. Subsequently, more than a few jurisdictions have reported low rates of recidivism among ISP clients. Some persons refer to these and similar programs under the general category of creative sentencing or **smart sentencing,** inasmuch as they do not require secure confinement and offer meaningful and rehabilitative alternatives to youths who would otherwise be incarcerated (Petersen 1995).

Classification Criteria for Placement in ISP Programs

One problem for juvenile court judges is deciding which juveniles should be assigned to which programs. This is a classification problem, and the level of accuracy associated with juvenile risk prediction instruments is about as poor as adult risk prediction devices. This problem is considered one of correction's greatest challenges (English, Pullen, and Chadwick 1996; McNulty 1996). Nevertheless, judges attempt to make secure or nonsecure confinement decisions on the basis of the following elements:

1. Classification based on risk of continued criminal activity and the offender's need for services.
2. A case management classification system designed to help probation and parole officers develop effective case plans and select appropriate casework strategies.
3. A management information system designed to enhance planning, monitoring, evaluation, and accountability.
4. A work load deployment system that allows agencies to effectively and efficiently allocate their limited resources (Baird 1985, 34).

Chronic recidivists and serious offenders are most often designated for secure confinement. However, an increasing number of community-based programs are being designed to supervise such offenders closely and offer them needed services and treatments. It is helpful to review briefly some of the issues relating to the effectiveness of such instrumentation (Petersen 1995). Depending upon the scores received by various juvenile clients when classified, they may or may not be entitled to assignment to intensive supervised probation or to a community-based program. Theoretically, those youthful offenders who are considered dangerous and violent are poor candidates for inclusion, because it is predicted that they might harm themselves or others, including agency staff or probation officers. Also, those considered not dangerous would be predicted to be good candidates as program clients. However, the flaws of our instrumentation do not always discriminate effectively. Interestingly, some jurisdictions, such as Virginia, report that secure confinement has been used unsuccessfully with violent juveniles, and they appear most responsive when assigned to nonsecure programs, including ISP and community-based projects (Virginia Joint Legislative Audit and Review Commission 1996).

JUVENILE INTENSIVE SUPERVISED PROBATION (JISP)

Juvenile intensive supervised probation (JISP) programs have become increasingly popular for managing nonincarcerated offender populations. JISP will be used to describe the programs developed in different jurisdictions, regardless whether the JISP or JIPS designation is used by individual programs. Since the mid-1960s, these programs have been aimed primarily at supervising adult offenders closely, and in recent years, JISP programs have been designed for juvenile offenders as well. Intensive supervised probation is a highly structured and conditional supervision program for either adult or juvenile offenders that serves as an alternative to incarceration and provides for an acceptable level of public safety. For administrators of secure facilities for juveniles, community-based options such as ISP are desirable, since overcrowding is reduced (Pullen 1996).

Characteristics of JISP Programs

JISP programs for juveniles have been developed and are currently operating in about half of all U.S. jurisdictions. It is important to note that many of these JISP programs are operated on a countywide or citywide basis, rather than on a

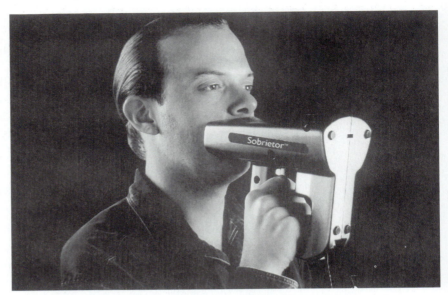

Random alcohol and drug tests are conducted for those under intensive supervised probation.

statewide basis. Thus, it is difficult to find a state jurisdiction with a uniform policy and program information about JISPs that apply to all local agencies within the state. One example of a JISP program operated by a county is the Johnson County (Kansas) Department of Corrections.

The Johnson County, Kansas, Juvenile Intensive Supervision Program. The court grants probation for a set period of time with the specific conditions of each supervision spelled out in the Probation Plan or Conditional Release Contract. Each client must abide by the written rules and regulations of the program, which will be reviewed by the Intensive Supervision Officer (ISO) assigned.

There are levels in the Intensive Supervision Program. Some of the minimum requirements of each level are:

Level I
1. 30 days in length
2. 3 face-to-face contacts with ISO per week
3. 4 random urinalyses/breath analyses per month as directed by the ISO
4. 20 hours of community service
5. Curfew as directed

Level II
1. 60 days in length
2. 2 face-to-face contacts with ISO per week
3. 3 random urinalyses/breath analyses per month as directed by ISO
4. Curfew as directed

Level III
1. 60 days in length
2. 1 face-to-face contact with ISO per week
3. 2 random urinalyses/breath analyses per month as directed by ISO
4. Curfew as directed

Level IV
1. No specified minimum length
2. 1 face-to-face contact with ISO per week for the first 30 days
3. 1 face-to-face contact every other week after a minimum of 30 days
4. 1 random urinalysis/breath analysis per month as directed by ISO

ISOs are also required to have frequent contact with those individuals who play a significant role in the juvenile's life, such as family, friends, treatment providers, sponsors, and so on.

A face-to-face contact may include:

1. Visits to the probation office

2. Visits at employment sites

3. Home visits

4. Meetings at other designated places

The curfew is monitored on a random basis.

Compliance with the previously stated requirements, and any other requirements, will allow the individual to progress through the Intensive Supervision Program (Johnson County Department of Corrections 2002).

Similar to their adult ISP program counterparts, JISP programs are ideally designed for secure incarceration-bound youths and are considered as acceptable alternatives to incarceration. According to Armstrong (1988, 342), this is what JISP programs were always meant to be. Armstrong differentiates JISP programs from other forms of standard probation by citing obvious differences in the amount of officer/client contact during the course of the probationary period. For example, standard probation is considered no more than two face-to-face officer/client contacts per month. He says that JISP programs might differ from standard probation according to the following face-to-face criteria: (1) two or three times per week versus once per month, (2) once per week versus twice per month, or (3) four times per week versus once per week (the latter figure being unusually high for standard probation contact).

The brokerage nature of probation officer dispositions toward their work is evident in the different types of services provided by the different JISP programs investigated by Armstrong (1988). For example, of the fifty-five programs he examined (92 percent of his total program sample), he found that the following range of services, skills, and resources were mentioned as being brokered by POs in different jurisdictions: (1) mental health counseling; (2) drug and alcohol counseling; (3) academic achievement and aptitude testing; (4) vocational and employment training; (5) individual, group, and family counseling; (6) job search and placement programs; (7) alternative education programs; (8) foster grandparents programs; and (9) Big Brother/Big Sister programs.

Wiebush (1990, 26) cautions that not all ISP programs are alike. Nevertheless, many juvenile ISP programs share similarities, including: (1) recognition of the shortcomings of traditional responses to serious and/or chronic offenders (e.g., incarceration or out-of-home placement); (2) severe resource constraints within jurisdictions that compel many probation departments to adopt agency-wide classification and workload deployment systems for targeting a disproportionate share of resources for the most problematic juvenile offenders; (3)

program goals include hopes of reducing the incidence of incarceration in juvenile secure confinement facilities and reduce overcrowding; (4) programs tending to include aggressive supervision and control elements as a part of the get tough movement; and (5) all programs having a vested interest in rehabilitation of youthful offenders (Armstrong 1991).

From these analyses of ISP program content generally, we can glean the following as basic characteristics of ISP programs:

1. Low officer/client caseloads (i.e., 30 or fewer probationers).
2. High levels of offender accountability (e.g., victim restitution, community service, payment of fines, partial defrayment of program expenses).
3. High levels of offender responsibility.
4. High levels of offender control (home confinement, electronic monitoring, frequent face-to-face visits by POs).
5. Frequent checks for arrests, drug and/or alcohol use, and employment/school attendance (drug/alcohol screening, coordination with police departments and juvenile halls, teachers, family) (Fagan and Reinarman 1991).

The Ohio Experience

A comprehensive description of a juvenile intensive supervised probation program is the **Ohio experience** (Wiebush 1990). A comparison was made of three different Ohio counties that used different ISP programs for their juvenile offenders, as well as the Ohio Department of Youth Services (ODYS). The different counties include Delaware County (predominantly rural), Lucas County (Toledo), and Cuyahoga County (Cleveland). The ODYS is state-operated and manages the most serious offenders, since these are exclusively felony offenders on parole from secure confinement. In each of the county jurisdictions, most of the offenders are incarceration-bound, with the exception of the Lucas County juveniles who are disposed to ISP after having their original dispositions of secure confinement reversed by juvenile court judges. Tables 12.1 and 12.2 show the basic parameters of the different Ohio programs as well as the program sizes and staffing patterns.

Table 12.1 shows the different types of agencies involved, the particular program models used by each, and the types of juvenile offender/clients served. Each of the programs uses risk scores for client inclusion, with the exception of the Lucas County program. Table 12.2 shows that all four programs follow a four-phase plan, where the intensity of supervision and surveillance over offenders is gradually reduced after particular time intervals. The ODYS program elects to reevaluate juveniles at three-, five-, and seven-month intervals through the use of a risk assessment device, rather than to graduate them to new phases automatically.

The Delaware JISP program targets those juveniles with a high propensity to recidivate as well as more serious felony offenders who are incarceration-bound. Youths begin the program with a five-day incarceration, followed by two weeks of house arrest. Later, they must observe curfews, attend school and complete school work satisfactorily, report daily to the probation office, and submit to periodic urinalysis. Each youth's progress is monitored by intensive counselors and surveillance staff 16 hours a day, seven days a week. Wiebush says that although the Delaware program has a rather strict approach, it embod-

TABLE 12.1

Basic Parameters of the Ohio Programs: Models, Goals, and Client Selection

Characteristic	Jurisdiction			
	Delaware	*Lucas*	*Cuyahoga*	*ODYS*
Agency type	County probation	County probation	County probation	State parole
Program model	Probation enhancement and alternative incarceration	Alternative to incarceration	Probation enhancement	Probation enhancement
Program goals	Reduced recidivism Reduced commitments Reduced overhead placement	Reduced recidivism Reduced commitments	Reduced recidivism Reduced overhead placement	Reduced recidivism Reduced re-commitment
Primary client selection criterion	High-risk score	Post-commitment status	High-risk score	High-risk score
Additional criteria	Chronic felony offenders; high	Excluded offenses = use of weapon, victim injury, drug trafficking	Status offenders excluded	Metro area resident; 2 + violent offenders included automatically
Philosophy, supervision emphasis	All stress "balanced" approach—relatively equal emphasis on public safety and rehabilitation			

Source: Richard G. Wiebush, "Programmatic Variations in Intensive Supervision for Juveniles: The Ohio Experience," *Perspectives* 14:28 (1990). Reprinted by permission, American Probation and Parole Association and Richard G. Wiebush.

ies rehabilitation as a primary program objective. The Delaware program has about a 40 percent recidivism rate, which is high, although it is better than the 75 percent rate of recidivism among the general juvenile court population of high-risk offenders elsewhere in Ohio jurisdictions.

In Lucas County, program officials select clients from those already serving incarcerative terms and are considered high-risk offenders. Lucas County officials wished to use this particular selection method, since they wanted to avoid any appearance of net-widening that their JISP program might reflect. Drawing from those already incarcerated seemed the best strategy in this case. The Lucas program is similar to the Delaware program in its treatment and control approaches. However, the Lucas program obligates offenders to perform up to 100 hours of community service as a program condition. House arrest,

TABLE 12.2

ISP Program Size and Staffing Patterns

Characteristic	Jurisdiction			
	Delaware	Lucas	Cuyahoga	ODYS
Total agency caseload[a]	225	500	1500	1500
ISP caseload	17	60	360[b]	525
ISP staff/youth ratio (probation/ parole officers)	1:17	1:15	1:30	1:13
Surveillance staff/youth ratio	2:17	2.5:60	3:60	2:39
Team configuration	Court administrator 1 ISP PO 2 surveillance staff (part-time) Student interns Family advocates	1 unit supervisor 4 ISP Pos 2 surveillance staff (full-time) 2 surveillance staff (part-time) 3 comm. service staff (part-time)	1 team leader 2 ISP Pos 3 surveillance staff (full-time)	3 ISP Pos 2 surveillance staff (part-time)
Number of teams	1	1	6	1-3 per region, 14 total
Coverage	7 days; 14 hours/day	7 days; 14 hours/day	7 days; 24 hours/day	7 days; 14 hours/day

[a]Caseload = cases under supervision at any one time.
[b]Projected figure for summer 1989.
Source: Richard G. Wiebush, "Programmatic Variations in Intensive Supervision for Juveniles: The Ohio Experience," *Perspectives* 14:29 (1990). Reprinted by permission, American Probation and Parole Association and Richard G. Wiebush.

curfew, and other Delaware program requirements are also found in the Lucas program. The successfulness of the Lucas program has not been evaluated fully, although it reduced institutional commitments by about 110 percent between 1986 and 1987.

The Cuyahoga County program (Cleveland) was one of the first of several ISP programs in Ohio's metropolitan jurisdictions. It is perhaps the largest county program, with 1500 clients at any given time, as well as six juvenile court judges and 72 supervisory personnel. One innovation of the Cuyahoga program was the development of a team approach to client surveillance and management. This program, like the other county programs, performs certain broker functions by referring its clients to an assortment of community-based services and treatments during the program duration. Currently, there are six teams of surveillance officers who each serve about 60 youths. These teams are comprised of a team leader, two counselors, and three surveillance staff. The nature of contact standards for this and the other three programs are shown in Table 12.3.

The ODYS program operates the state's nine training schools, in addition to supervising the 3,000 youths each year who are released on parole. The ODYS has 93 youth counselors to staff seven regional offices. The ODYS commenced JISP in February 1988 and supervised those high-risk offenders with a predicted future recidivism rate of 75 percent or higher. Since these clients were all prior felony offenders with lengthy adjudication records, they were considered the most serious group to be supervised compared with the other programs. Accordingly, the ODYS supervision and surveillance structure exhibited the greatest degree of offender monitoring. The team approach has been

TABLE 12.3

Contact Standards by Type and Phase

Type of Contact[a]	Jurisdiction[b]			
	Delaware	Lucas	Cuyahoga	ODYS[c]
Phase I				
PO, direct with youth	5/week	2/week	1/week	6.5/month
Family, direct	n.s.	4/month	n.s.	2/month
Surveillance	11/week	14/week	17/week	4/week
Duration (minimum)	21 days	30 days	30 days	90 days
Phase II				
PO, direct with youth	5/week	2/week	1/week	4–6/month
Family, direct	n.s.	2/month	n.s.	2/month
Surveillance	11/week	10/week	8/week	4/week
Duration	28 days	50 days	75 days	60 days
Phase III				
PO, direct with youth	3/week	1/week	1/week	2–6/month
Family, direct	n.s.	2/month	n.s.	1/month
Surveillance	0–11/week	7/week	5/week	2–4/week
Duration	70 days	50 days	75 days	60 days
Phase IV				
PO, direct with youth	1–3/week	2/month	As needed	2–6/month
Family, direct	n.s.	1/month	n.s.	1/month
Surveillance	None	5/week	3/week	2–4/week
Duration	By contract	26 days	75 days	60 days

[a]Surveillance includes direct and telephone contacts.
[b]n.s., not specified.
[c]Ohio Department of Youth Services does not use phase system to govern youth movement through the program. Youths are classified at three, five, and seven months, based on reassessment of risk.
Source: Richard G. Wiebush, "Programmatic Variations in Intensive Supervision for Juveniles: The Ohio Experience," *Perspectives* 14:30 (1990). Reprinted with permission. American Probation and Parole Association and Richard G. Wiebush.

used by the ODYS, with teams consisting of three youth counselors and two surveillance staff.

Because of geographical considerations, some variations have been observed among teams regarding the numbers of offenders supervised as well as the intensity of their supervision or surveillance. Basically, the ODYS program incorporated many of the program conditions that were included in the various county programs. These conditions or components have been divided into control components and treatment components and are shown respectively in Tables 12.4 and 12.5.

Since its creation, the JISP program operated by the ODYS has exhibited a drop in its recidivism rate. On the basis of a comparison of the first year of its operation with recidivism figures for its clients from the previous year, the ODYS program had a 34 percent reduction in its rate of recidivism. Further, a 39 percent reduction in parole revocations occurred. This is significant, considering the high-risk nature of the offender population being managed.

Wiebush notes that all of these programs have required enormous investments of time and energy by high-quality staff. Further, each program has illustrated how best to utilize existing community resources to further its objectives and best serve juvenile clients in need. However, Wiebush says that what is good for Ohio probationers and parolees may not necessarily be suitable for those offenders of other jurisdictions. Nevertheless, these programs function as potential models after which programs in other jurisdictions may be patterned.

Other programs designed for both male and female juvenile offenders have been described (Mardon 1991). The Youth Center in Beloit, Kansas, is the state's only institutional facility for female juvenile offenders. The emphasis of treatment programs at the Youth Center is assisting these female youths to deal with problems of sexual abuse, which many of these offenders have experienced. Besides treatment, the females are exposed to vocational and educa-

TABLE 12.4

Program Components: Control Elements[a]

	Jurisdiction			
Component	Delaware	Lucas	Cuyahoga	ODYS
Surveillance	x	x	x	x
Curfew	x	x	x	x
Front-end detention	x	—[b]	—	—
House arrest	x	x	x	o
Prior permission	x	—	—	—
Electronic surveillance	—	—	o	—
Urinalysis	o	x	o	o
Daily sanctioning (phase system)	x	x	x	—
Hourly school reports	x	x	x	—
Formal graduated sanction schedule	—	x	—	x

[a]x = Mandatory component; — = component not available; o = component optional, varies by youth.
[b]Most Lucas ISP youth do have front-end detention, but it is not mandated.
Source: Richard G. Wiebush, "Programmatic Variations in Intensive Supervision for Juveniles," *Perspectives* 14:31 (1990). Reprinted with permission, American Probation and Parole Association and Richard G. Wiebush.

TABLE 12.5

Program Components: Treatment Elements[a]

| | Jurisdiction | | | |
Component	Delaware	Lucas	Cuyahoga	ODYS
Individualized contracts	x	x	x	x
Individual counseling (non-PO)	o	o	o	o
Family counseling or family conferences	o	x	o	o
Group counseling	x	x	o	o
In-home family services	x	—	x	—
Community sponsors, advocates	—	—	—	—
Alternative education	o	o	o	o
Job training	o	o	o	o
Substance abuse counseling	o	o	o	o
School attendance (or work)	x	x	x	x
Community service	o	x	o	o
Restitution	o	o	o	o

[a]x = Mandatory component; — = component not available; o = component optional, varies by youth.
Source: Richard G. Wiebush, "Programmatic Variations in Intensive Supervision for Juveniles," *Perspectives* 14:32 (1990). Reprinted with permission, American Probation and Parole Association and Richard G. Wiebush.

tional experiences designed to prepare them for useful lives once they are released. Another program described by Mardon is the Fort Smallwood Marine Institute near Baltimore, Maryland. This program was established in 1988. Between 1988 and 1991, approximately 225 delinquent youths have been treated successfully.

Similar programs described by Mardon include the Eckerd Youth Challenge Program, which is a community-based alternative to placing adjudicated youths in training schools. Youths are housed in residences at this site, and they participate in programs designed to improve their interpersonal and living skills. Experiential and action-oriented phases of this program include activities such as hikes, canoe trips, and community service projects.

Strengths and Weaknesses of JISP Programs

A strength of ISP programs is that they are substantially less expensive compared with the costs of incarcerating juvenile offenders. For instance, the Texas Youth Commission reports that juvenile incarceration represents the most expensive criminal justice option, averaging $114 as the daily expenditure per juvenile (Reed 1997). Alternatively, juvenile probation programs manage youths at the rate of $8.25 per day. Various ISP programs in Texas average $28 per day per juvenile.

Another strength is that JISP programs generally report lower rates of recidivism compared with standardized probation and other more conventional nonincarcerative options (Hurley and Hatfield 1996). One reason is that JISP clients are more closely monitored and thus are given less opportunity to reoffend. Another reason is that prospective clients for ISP programs are more

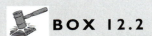

BOX 12.2

PERSONALITY
HIGHLIGHT

Sherry Anderson
Juvenile Probation Officer II
Department of Children, Youth, and Families
Albuquerque, New Mexico

Statistics:

B.S. (corrections), University of Albuquerque; Reality Therapist II, Glasser Institute

Background:

I grew up in Albuquerque, New Mexico, and still live there. In 1973 I graduated from Eldorado High School, and as a senior competed in and won the city and state title as New Mexico's Junior Miss, a scholarship program. I also competed in the national competition for Junior Miss. All three competitions allowed me valuable scholarship monies for college. As a junior in high school, I traveled with Up with People, a performing and scholarship program. It was at this time that I knew I wanted to be involved in a career that would help people. My one-year experience entailed traveling to many cities in the United States as well as Europe. I stayed in homes wherever I traveled. I discovered many families with personal struggles and hurts. They seemed to be encouraged by my words, even though I was quite young. It was an experience that would shape who I am today. After Up with People, college was on the horizon. I used my scholarship to attend the University of Arizona. After one year and while on summer leave, I discovered a criminal justice program at the University of Albuquerque. The duties and job functions of this degree really interested me to the point that I enrolled in this program. I was fortunate to have been nominated for a Rhodes Scholarship (first year that women were chosen). The nomination was based on scholarship performance in college (I graduated summa cum laude) and athletic abilities. After college, my work experiences in the criminal justice field followed, and now, twenty-five years later, I still very much love what I do.

Presently, I am a Juvenile Probation Officer at the Juvenile Justice Center in Albuquerque, New Mexico. Prior to beginning this job in 1978, I had completed a college internship with Pre-Prosecution Probation, a division of the District Attorney's Office. I had also worked for a year in the District Attorney's Office in Roswell, New Mexico, as a Youth Coordinator and Juvenile Parole Officer. I have remained as a Juvenile Probation Officer for most of my career. I did leave for a five-year period in the early 1990s to work for New Mexico Boy's and Girl's Ranches as senior case manager in their foster care program. For many years, I was a field officer supervising youth placed on probation, but as of 2000, I work with youth who have been charged with a criminal offense, but who are being diverted away from the legal system.

Our office in Albuquerque has numerous informal programs where services may be provided. I, too, have created two such informal programs: the Animal Outreach Program and the Food For Kids Program. Regarding the first program, my clients participate in community service with two animal rescue organizations. As for the second program, clients conduct their own food drives, and collected food is given to those children identified in the community as going hungry within their family system. Our office also presents diversion classes for youth who have been cited for first-time misdemeanors. We have classes for those charged with shoplifting, alcohol or drug offenses, assaults or batteries, and criminal trespass. I enjoy teaching in two of these classes because our research indicates that youth are not recidivating. I have also developed a tennis program for youth who have been released from our detention facility and are placed in a program called the Youth Reporting Center. Clients spend their entire day in this program and have access to numerous services and programs. The tennis program is meant to provide a new athletic experience for youth, to promote self-esteem, teach social skills, and deter criminal behavior. And these kids keep me running!

Interesting Experiences:

Throughout my career, I have had many memorable experiences as a juvenile probation officer. When I was a rookie many years ago and somewhat naive regarding youthful criminal behavior, I arrested a young man who pleaded with me not to handcuff him. Well, I handcuffed him, but from the front. I thought this would be a less painful process for this young man. Well, while traveling in the transport vehicle, this youthful offender managed to get the back door open and while the vehicle was moving, jumped out of the car. He did a roll on the street, jumped up and began running away. No, I didn't chase him. I was more concerned what I would tell my chief, and I knew those handcuffs would cost me at least $50 to replace. The lesson I learned: I never handcuffed another youth from the front.

I also recall numerous cases that were quite serious in nature and some quite tragic. I remember a young man who was addicted to drugs and alcohol and who very much wanted my help. He loved music, and so I connected him to numerous sources that would encourage his love for music. Tragically, as a young adult, I next saw this client on the local news. He had kidnapped a woman in the parking lot of a grocery store and was holding her hostage. The SWAT Team was called, and he lost his life as a result. I remember him all the time in that he had made two woodworking items for me. I still have them in my home today.

Another client tragically murdered an infant, and I spent my day recalling the police officer's call to me from the morgue regarding the brutal facts of this case. Or the probationer who educated me about the satanic cult he belonged to and the gruesome details of his life in this cult. Cases that consisted of brutality and tragedy forever remain in my mind, but many of my cases have been positive and even humorous moments. I recall a young man desperately in love with a girl across the street. This young man was painfully shy, and so rather than visiting with her, he chose to send love notes. He was an excellent marksman with a bow. He would get on top of his roof and shoot arrows into the front door where this girl lived. Of course, the love notes were attached to the arrows. Well, her parents were not pleased. In fact, they were quite concerned someone would get hurt. I nicknamed this client "Robin Hood." Actually, I could relate several more stories, but I think you get the idea that life as a juvenile probation officer has never been boring, and sometimes it has been very exciting!

Advice and Insights:

As the department's training officer for all new employees, I try to promote the following insights in hopes that they will discover complete job satisfaction and meaning in their career. I tell them the following:

1. You will make a difference in the lives of many children and families that come to your attention; however, many of these cases will make a difference in you. They will test your ultimate patience and beliefs in human nature, and they will grow you up professionally. In other words, each case has a purpose.

2. Working as a probation or parole officer in the juvenile justice system requires someone who I consider to have a big heart—someone who has an enduring capacity to care about difficult youth. I see professionals who continue on in this field long after their commitment has waned.

(continued)

BOX 12.2 (Continued)

3. You must find some means of relieving the stress this kind of work will create in your professional and personal life. It is helpful to participate in some kind of hobby, interest, exercise, or sport. For me, cycling or playing tennis is a must. Staying healthy is important for sustaining the kind of energy needed for this work.

4. Stay focused and remember why you

are doing this kind of work. It isn't about you, but rather, it is about the children and families you serve. This job requires an enormous amount of commitment, but the rewards are many. It isn't a job for the faint-hearted, but for the bold and courageous.

I wish all of you, future graduates in the juvenile justice field, all the best!

closely screened. More serious offenders are usually excluded, which increases the success rates of included clients (Hoge, Andrews, and Leschied 1995).

A weakness of most JISP programs is that local demands and needs vary to such an extent among jurisdictions that after twenty-five years, we have yet to devise a standard definition of what is meant by intensive supervised probation (Corbett 2000). Thus, the dominant descriptions of current ISP programs appear to be (1) those that are designed as front-end alternatives to secure confinement, (2) those that combine incarceration with some degree of community supervision (shock probation), and (3) those that follow secure confinement.

CASE SUPERVISION PLANNING

Caseload Assignments

Ellsworth's (1988) description of the progress of developing ISP programs in the United States since the early 1960s highlights certain problems that JISP programs are currently facing. One of the first strategies employed by probation departments was the numbers-game reshuffling of **caseloads,** where reduced caseloads for POs were ordered to supposedly improve officer/client interpersonal contact. It was argued that reduced caseloads would necessarily intensify the supervision as well as the supervisory quality of client/offenders. Several recent studies have experimented with varying degrees of officer/client contact and recidivism rates (Center for Legal Studies 2000). PO caseload reductions were mandated by one of the recommendations of the Task Force on Corrections appointed by the President's Commission on Law Enforcement and the Administration of Justice in 1967.

The San Francisco Project

However, a project investigating the differential recidivism rates of probationers supervised more or less intensively and conducted subsequently in San Francisco, known as the **San Francisco Project,** did much to undermine the nation's confidence in manipulating sheer caseload numbers (Banks, Siler, and Rardin 1977). The San Francisco Project compared recidivism rates of probationers supervised by POs with caseloads of 20 and 40, respectively, with the former caseloads defined by probation departments as intensive and the latter caseloads defined as ideal. No significant differences in recidivism rates of probationers were reported between intensive and ideal caseload scenarios. In fact, those POs with caseloads of 20 probationers reported more technical program violations (e.g., curfew violations, traveling violations, drug/alcohol violations) compared with those POs with caseloads of 40 probationers. Greater offender monitoring simply made it possible for POs to spot more program violators.

Despite the methodological and theoretical flaws cited by various critics of the San Francisco Project, the study suggested that something other than sheer numbers of cases assigned POs should be an integral part of the officer/client relation. Ellsworth (1988, 28–29) says that the next step to be taken by probation departments was the construction of risk/needs assessment instruments and classification systems that would enable probation departments to more effectively plan their case assignments. One of these instruments was the Wisconsin Case Classification System, which introduced the idea of case supervision planning through the Client Management Classification interview. This interview purportedly enabled POs to proactively supervise their clients more effectively, since they could identify in advance certain problems that otherwise would interfere with productive officer/client relationships. Therefore, instead of reacting to client problems whenever they surfaced, POs could anticipate certain client problems and take steps to deal with them in advance of their occurrence (Ellsworth 1988, 28).

Subsequently, various probation departments implemented case assignment policies according to a finer degree of specialization than case allocation procedures formerly used. Those offenders with drug abuse problems would be grouped according to this problem and assigned to POs who acquired a drug abuse specialty. Ideally, probation departments would benefit because officers would be assigned cases they enjoyed working with and where their particular skills could be maximized. They would be in a better position to understand client problems and to be better enablers and brokers for their clients, arranging contacts between them and existing community services.

Unfortunately, there have been unanticipated consequences arising from such case supervision planning. Intradepartmental jealousies and a lack of POs with specific competencies have made it either impossible or impractical for certain probation departments to implement case supervision planning fully. Further, specialized case allocations have at times undermined the officer/client relation, since the enforcement nature of PO work has sometimes collapsed through changing interpersonal relationships. In short, some officers have become too close (emotionally) with their offender clients to the extent that they are no longer effective enforcers of other program requirements. Ellsworth (1988, 29) indicates that currently, a basic incompatibility exists between POs who favor a law-and-order approach to PO work (consistent with the get-tough philosophy) and those who favor a rehabilitation or treatment approach that is closely associated with the case planning process. Case supervision planning, therefore, is considered irrelevant by some POs, since, in their view, the primary function of POs is to conduct surveillance activities, control the behaviors of their clients, ensure offender accountability, and ensure offender compliance with program conditions (Crosland 1995).

Models of Case Supervision Planning

Case supervision planning makes more sense if we consider several alternative case assignment strategies that are presently used by different probation departments. The most popular model is the **conventional model,** which is the random assignment of probationers to POs on the basis of one's present caseload in relation to others. This is much like the **numbers-game model,** where total probationers are divided by the total POs in a given department, and each PO is allocated an equal share of the supervisory task. Thus, POs may supervise both very dangerous and nondangerous probationers. Another model is the **conventional model with geographic considerations.** Simply, this is assigning probationers to POs who live in a common geographic area. The intent is to shorten PO travel between clients. Again, little or no consideration is given to an offender's needs or dangerousness in relation to PO skills. The **specialized caseloads model** is the model used for case supervision planning, where offender assignments are made on the basis of client risks and needs and PO skills and interests in dealing with those offender risks and needs. Some POs may have special training and education in psychology or social work or chemical dependency. Thus, if certain clients have psychological problems or chemical dependencies, it is believed that these POs with special skills and education might be more effective in relating to them (Carlson and Parks 1979).

The Balanced Approach

Some of the problems of JISP have been attributable to different caseload assignment models or to other organizational peculiarities and conflicting organizational goals that interfere with the performance of juvenile PO roles. One solution is referred to as the **balanced approach** (Seyko 2001). The balanced approach to juvenile probation is neither a wholly punitive nor rehabilitative formulation, but rather is a more broad-based, constructive approach. It operates on the assumption that decision making must take into consideration the converging interests of all involved parties in the juvenile justice process, including offenders, victims, the community-at-large, and the system itself. No party to the decision making should benefit at the expense of another party; rather, a balancing of interests should be sought. The balanced approach, therefore, simultaneously emphasizes community protection, offender accountability, individualization of treatments, and competency assessment and development.

The balanced approach obligates community leaders and juvenile justice system actors to consider their individual juvenile codes and determine whether a balance exists between offender needs and community interests. Punitive provisions of these codes should address victim needs as well as the needs of juvenile offenders, to the extent that restitution and victim compensation are a part of improving an offender's accountability and acceptance of responsibility. The fairness of the juvenile justice system should be assessed by key community leaders, and a mission statement should be drafted that has the broad support of diverse community organizations. Training programs can be created through the close coordination of chief probation officers in different jurisdictions, where offender needs may be targeted and addressed. All facets of the community and the juvenile justice process should be involved, including juvenile court judges. The high level of community involvement will help to ensure a positive juvenile probation program that will maximize a youth's rehabilitative benefits (Hemmons, Fritsch, and Caeti 1997).

Some ISP programs fail because they often neglect to address many of the problems that include those suggested by the balanced approach. Some of the reasons for why case supervision planning is often unsuccessful are:

1. Purpose: The purposes of case supervision planning have not been thought out carefully.

2. Perceptual differences: Offenders often change only when they find it necessary to change, not because we want them to change.

3. Resistance: We don't always recognize that resistance to change is normal; sometimes we prematurely shift emphasis to an enforcement orientation and rules of probation. Case planning starts to look more like the probation order whenever this occurs.

4. Expectation: Desired change is sought too quickly; we sometimes expect too much from offenders or expect unrealistic changes to be made.

5. Focus: There is a tendency to focus on lesser problems in order to gain "success."

6. Involvement: We often fail to involve offenders in the case planning process.

7. Stereotyping: Case supervision planning is equated with treatment and rehabilitation, and thus, it is often rejected without an adequate consideration of its strengths.

8. Getting too close: Sometimes POs are perceived as getting too close to offenders.

9. Perceptions of accountability: Nonspecific case plans cannot be criticized by supervisors.

10. Use of resources: There is tendency to "burn out" community resources by referring involuntary offenders, those who are not ready to work on their problems.

11. Measurement: Probation successes or failures are not measured according to some case plan, but rather, according to arrests, convictions, or numbers of technical violations; how should success be evaluated or measured?

12. Management: There is a general lack of understanding or support for case supervision planning by management; POs are considered exclusively officers of the court, and judges don't particularly expect offenders to change because of officer "treatments," only that someone shares the blame or accountability whenever offenders commit new crimes or violate one or more of their probationary conditions.

13. Training: Staff members have not been adequately trained in the development, implementation, and evaluation of case plans (Ellsworth 1988, 29–30).

The principles of JISP programs are sound. Basically, implementation problems of one type or another have hindered their successfulness in various jurisdictions (Jones 1990). It is apparent that juvenile probation services will need to coordinate their activities and align their departmental and individual PO performance objectives with those of community-based agencies that are a part of the referral network of services and treatments, in order to maximize goal attainment. Consistent with the balanced approach to managing offenders, Guarino-Ghezzi (1998) recommends that in order for ISP programs to maximize their effectiveness, they should be individualized to a high degree, so that a proper balance of punishment/deterrence and rehabilitation/community protection may be attained. Public safety remains a key goal of any community-based program responsible for serious and violent juvenile offenders (Hemmens, Fritsch, and Caeti 1997). An offender's constitutional rights should be recognized, but at the same time, accountability to victims and the community must be ensured. In the next section, we will examine several specific ISP programs that are considered community-based alternatives in contrast with state- or locally operated public programs.

COMMUNITY-BASED ALTERNATIVES

Community Corrections Acts

Community-based corrections agencies and organizations are not new. An early community-based corrections program for adult offenders was created in California in 1965, known as the Probation Subsidy Program (Lawrence 1985). Originally, these programs were intended to alleviate prison and jail overcrowding by establishing community-based organizations that could accommodate some of the overflow of prison-bound offenders. However, corrections officials soon realized that the potential of such programs was great for offender rehabilitation and reintegration and that juveniles as well as adult offenders could profit from involvement in them.

Many states subsequently passed **community corrections acts** that were aimed at funding local government units to create community facilities that could provide services and other resources to juveniles. Minnesota passed the Community Corrections Act (CCA) in the early 1970s, for example. In 1979 the state undertook a comprehensive examination of the CCA in order to evaluate its effectiveness (Minnesota Crime Control Planning Board 1981).

The evaluation results indicated that the objectives of Minnesota's CCA were all met. In planning and administration, CCA participation led to the emergence of new organizational structures and activities. The improvement was most apparent in the functions of training and budgeting. There were eleven CCA areas established for juvenile offenders. Considerable attention was devoted to programming for juvenile clients. A primary objective of Minnesota's CCA was to retain more juvenile offenders in their communities. In nine out of eleven CCA areas, this goal was achieved. One potentially disturbing finding reported in this evaluation was that juvenile arrest rates were somewhat higher in the CCA areas compared with non-CCA areas. Officials associated with the evaluation were quick to point out that this did not mean that the CCA had a negative effect on public protection from juvenile offenders. Rather, the fact of larger concentrations of juvenile delinquents in given CCA areas explained the higher arrest rates compared with other areas. Statistically accounting for these disproportionate differences, it was concluded that public protection was maintained in ways similar to non-CCA areas, and that individual safety was not compromised despite the higher juvenile arrest rates.

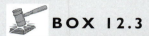

BOX 12.3

Eric Petross, 17, Hacker

It happened in Rawlins, Wyoming. A high school senior was taken into custody by police officers after hacking into his school's computer system and deleting a teacher's class quiz. Eric Petross, 17, was charged with a crime against intellectual property and prosecuted as an adult. The punishment for the crime is a maximum of three years in prison and a $3,000 fine. Police conducted an investigation following a report from a teacher in Petross's electronics class on December 6, 1999, when a teacher found a quiz file missing. Administration files are password-protected and not accessible by students. However, Petross had told some of his classmates that he had gotten a command from the Internet that would enable him to override all commands and passwords.

With the advent of computers, are we seeing a new kind of juvenile delinquency emerging? Will increasing numbers of juveniles be engaging in computer crimes? How should such crimes be punished compared with drug, property, and violent offenses? What do you think?

Source: Adapted from the Associated Press, "Senior Accused of Hacking," January 4, 2000.

The overall objective of community corrections agencies is to develop and deliver front-end solutions and alternative sanctions in lieu of state incarceration (Shawnee County Department of Community Corrections 2002, 1). In 1984, the **American Correctional Association (ACA)** Task Force on Community Corrections Legislation recommended that community corrections acts should not target violent offenders. Rather, the states should be selective about who meets their program requirements. It was recommended that (1) states should continue to house violent juvenile offenders in secure facilities; (2) judges and prosecutors should continue to explore various punishment options in lieu of incarceration; and (3) local communities should develop programs with additional funding from state appropriations (Huskey 1984, 45). The ACA Task Force identified the following elements as essential to the success of any community corrections act:

1. There should be restrictions on funding high-cost capital projects as well as conventional probation services.

2. Local communities should participate on a voluntary basis and may withdraw at any time.

3. Advisory boards should submit annual criminal justice plans to local governments.

4. There should be a logical formula in place for allocating community corrections funds.

5. Incarceration-bound juveniles should be targeted, rather than adding additional punishments for those who otherwise would remain in their communities (in short, avoid net-widening).

6. Financial subsidies should be provided to local government and community-based corrections agencies.

7. Local advisory boards in each community should function to assess program needs and effectiveness, and to propose improvements in the local juvenile justice system and educate the general public about the benefits of intermediate punishments.

8. A performance factor should be implemented to insure that funds are used to achieve specific goals of the act.

Shawnee County (KS) Community Corrections.   A good example of a contemporary view of community corrections acts in action within specific cities and counties is the Shawnee County, Kansas, community corrections program (Shawnee County Department of Community Corrections 2002, 1). Originally, a Community Corrections Act (CCA) was passed in 1978 in Kansas, and Shawnee County was one of the first counties to join in the CCA and begin programming. At first there were only nine counties involved. In 1989 Kansas mandated that all counties should have community corrections services. In 1994 juvenile services were included. And in 1996–1997, juvenile offender services were transferred from the Kansas Department of Corrections to the Juvenile Justice Authority (JJA).

One original purpose of the Kansas CCA was the diversion of prison-bound offenders from institutions to community-based intermediate sanction programs. With the changes brought about by the implementation of sentencing guidelines, offenders are formally sentenced to probation pursuant to the guidelines' computation of sentence. In 2002 the Department of Community Corrections supervised chronic or violent offenders within the community. Effective community-based programming involves intensive supervision of these clients, together with solution-focused case management services that assist offenders in becoming productive members of society.

When Shawnee County Community Corrections (SCCC) was established, it was one of three units within the Shawnee County Department of Corrections. The Department of Corrections included the jail, a juvenile detention center, and community corrections. In 2000, community corrections became a separate department. Presently, the mission of the SCCC is to (1) provide highly structured community supervision to felony offenders, (2) hold offenders accountable to their victims and to the community, and (3) improve the offenders' ability to live productively and lawfully.

The juvenile community corrections program is a state and local partnership. It is designed to (1) promote public safety, (2) hold juvenile offenders accountable for their behavior, and (3) improve the ability of youth to live productively and responsibly in their communities. In this respect, the juvenile program reflects the basic elements of the balanced approach.

Program goals are attained in the following manner. For the goal of public safety, manageable caseloads are maintained, allowing staff to closely supervise offenders in the community. For the goal of enforcing court-ordered sanctions, supervision plans are devised that meet the requirements of the court and provide structure, which will improve the offender's ability to successfully complete the terms of his/her probation program. For the aim of restoring losses to crime victims, payment of restitution by offenders is overseen, including the collection of court costs and supervision of community service work. Finally, for the aim of assisting offenders to change their behaviors, offender participation in services provided by community corrections or community resources is enforced through close offender monitoring to ensure their compliance. Services include drug treatment, job search and maintenance skills, literacy enhancement, and life skills.

Several supervisory options are available, depending upon the juvenile offender's needs. For example, a juvenile intensive supervised probation program includes intensive monitoring and provides an intermediate sanction between standard probation and placement in a juvenile correctional facility for adjudicated juvenile offenders. The juvenile offender community case management program consists of services provided for juvenile offenders who have been placed by the court in the care and custody of the JJA. The court may order out-of-home placement for certain juvenile offenders after all other reasonable efforts have been made to address the problems that caused their illegal behavior. Case management services are provided to assist juveniles and their caregivers to find resources that will meet their needs. Finally, the juvenile conditional release supervision program provides monitoring of juveniles who have been released from one of four JJA-operated juvenile correctional facilities and returned to the community. Community corrections officers monitor these juveniles so that they comply with the conditions of their release. These officers also assist juveniles in accomplishing their aftercare plans.

The juvenile justice process followed in Shawnee County is as follows:

Arrest

Juvenile Detention Center (if danger to self or others during court process)

Adjudication (court determines juvenile committed offense; juvenile is adjudicated a delinquent offender)

Sentencing alternatives:

1. Place juvenile offender in parent's custody (to follow terms and conditions of the court, including making restitution).

2. Place juvenile offender on probation through court services for a fixed period (to follow terms and conditions of the court, including making restitution).

3. Place juvenile offender on intensive supervised probation for a fixed period through community corrections (to follow terms and conditions of the court, including making restitution; reporting to ISO as required; submit to drug screens; use no alcohol or illegal drugs; follow mental health or drug treatment plan; perform community service work—20 hours; attend school; employment, if not enrolled in school; no firearms; other conditions as ordered by the court).

4. Place juvenile offender in custody of JJA (case management through community corrections) once reasonable efforts have been met for juveniles requiring more services (supervision plan may include similar items as intensive supervised probation and may require placement out of the home).

5. Commit juvenile offender to a juvenile correctional facility (incarceration).

6. Conditional release supervision (follow conditional release requirements; similar requirements as outlined under intensive supervised probation).

Education programs are important features of most community corrections programs.

On any given day in Topeka and the Shawnee area, there are about 465 juvenile misdemeanor or felony offenders on probation supervised by court services. Approximately 35 juvenile misdemeanor or felony offenders are on intensive supervised probation, while 90 juvenile misdemeanor or felony offenders are on community case management supervision. About 15 juvenile offenders are on conditional release and are supervised by community corrections, while 40 juvenile offenders are in a state juvenile correctional facility supervised by community corrections for reintegration planning. Overall, 645 juveniles from Shawnee County are on some type of supervision for a criminal offense. Shawnee County has approximately 165,000 people.

Approximately 2,915 adults and juveniles are in the county criminal or juvenile justice system each day. This figure does not include ex-offenders or alleged offenders. The cost of having an offender on intensive supervised probation is about $2,650 a year compared with $18,775 per year in a Kansas correctional facility. All offenders are screened and evaluated according to their risk to reoffend. A risk assessment form is the instrument used for this evaluation. The higher one's score, the more intense their supervision. Offenders are reassessed at different time intervals in order to allow for progress in their individual programs. This reassessment may reduce the intensity of their future supervision if they are doing well. Besides frequent meetings with each offender, the intensive supervision officer will have contact with the offenders' employers, counselors, teachers, families, and law enforcement agencies. Random drug/alcohol screens are also conducted (Shawnee County Department of Community Corrections 2002, 1–4). The successfulness of this community corrections program has been assessed in recent years. Between 1999 and 2002, the amount of recidivism among juvenile clients has been approximately 12 percent. This low recidivism rate suggests that at least in Shawnee County, Kansas, the community corrections program is fulfilling its diverse objectives.

The Boston Offender Project

Sometimes, it is prudent to seek a compromise relating to the custody imposed in various juvenile probation programs, where a degree of secure custody over juveniles is necessary for a short time, but where nonsecure supervision would also be permitted and desirable. One of the most frustrating aggregates of juvenile offenders is that small minority who commits violent offenses. These are sometimes known as the chronic 6 percent or violent few, since a small number of offenders accounts for a large proportion of violent offenses annually (King 1996). Judges and probation officers are often at a loss for strategies to identify and deal effectively with such offenders. Often, the options are secure custody in a reform school or a waiver to criminal courts, presumably for more stringent punishments and longer dispositions of confinement. Some professionals in juvenile corrections continued to believe, however, that other options were available, provided that the time and resources could be allocated properly.

In 1981, an experimental program was commenced in Boston to give some of these professionals their chance to put into practice what they believed could be done in theory. The Massachusetts Department of Youth Services was awarded a grant to implement what eventually became known as the **Boston Offender Project (BOP).** BOP was one of five demonstration sites selected. Its target was violent juveniles, and the program goals included reducing recidivism among them, enhancing public protection by increasing accountability for major violators, and improving the likelihood of successful reintegration of juveniles into society by focusing upon these offenders' academic and vocational skills (Murphy 1985, 26). BOP sought to improve the typical handling of a violent juvenile case in the following ways:

1. By developing three coordinated phases of treatment that include initial placement in a small, locked, secure-treatment program, followed by planned transition into a halfway house, and finally, a gradual return to the juvenile's home community.

2. By assuring the delivery of comprehensive services by assigning particularly experienced caseworkers responsible for working intensively with a caseload of not more than eight violent offenders and their families.

3. By providing services focused on increasing the educational level of offenders and tying educational programs to the marketplace, significantly increasing the prospects of meaningful employment (Murphy 1985, 26).

BOP was similar to shock probation, in that violent juvenile offenders would experience some confinement in a secure facility, but after a short time, they would be released to less secure surroundings. Thus, a shock element was included, at least implicitly, in the BOP structure.

The BOP has several important features compared with the treatment received by those juveniles in the control group. First, diagnostic assessments of juveniles in BOP went well beyond standard psychological assessments, and these measures were administered on an ongoing basis to chart developments in psychological, vocational, and medical areas. Second, caseworkers in the BOP program were three times more experienced (in numbers of years) compared with standard program caseworkers. A third important difference was that BOP caseworker loads were limited to seven, while caseloads for workers in the standard program were as high as twenty-five.

A fourth feature was that BOP caseworkers were actively involved in the treatment phase, while the standard program caseworker involvement was passive. A fifth feature of BOP was that caseworker visits to juveniles were eight times as frequent per month compared with standard program visits. A sixth BOP feature was an automatic assignment to nonsecure residential facilities once the first secure phase of the program was completed. For standard program participants, this was not necessarily an option. Furthermore, in the BOP program, continued violence would subject a participant to regression, so that the offender could be placed back in secure confinement. In the standard program, there was only limited flexibility to make this program shift. Finally, the standard program was terminated for youths when they reached 18 years of age, while the BOP could be discontinued or continued before or after age 18, depending upon caseworker judgment.

Some important differences between the two groups emerged over the next several years. For instance, 79 percent of BOP clients found unsubsidized employment compared with only 29 percent of the control group. Also, only about a third of the BOP clients had been rearrested. This was about half the rearrest rate exhibited by the control group. Thus, while the BOP may not be the most perfect solution to the problem of violent juvenile offenders, it does offer a viable, middle-ground alternative that has demonstrable success, at least with some offenders. For the chronic, hard-core, and most dangerous offenders, secure confinement is one of the last resorts as a judicial option.

Project New Pride

One of the most popular probation programs is **Project New Pride,** which was established in Denver, Colorado, in 1973. It has been widely used as a model for probation programs in other jurisdictions in subsequent years (Laurence and West 1985). New Pride is a blend of education, counseling, employment, and cultural education directed at those more serious offenders between the ages of 14 and 17. Juveniles eligible for the New Pride program must have at least two prior convictions for serious misdemeanors and/or felonies, and they must be formally charged or adjudicated for another offense when referred to New Pride. There are very few females in New Pride, only about 10 or 15 percent. This is not deliberate exclusion, but rather, females tend to have lower rates of recidivism and commit less serious offenses compared with their male delinquent counterparts. Those who are deliberately excluded are offenders previously diagnosed as severely psychotic or who have committed forcible rape.

Project New Pride's goals include (1) reintegrating participants into their communities through school participation or employment, and (2) reducing recidivism rates among offenders. The project emphasizes schooling, employment, and closeness with families. It is a community-based project and utilizes professional probation officers as well as volunteers. The project staff offer employment counseling services and job placement, tutoring for school assignments and projects, and vocational training. Project New Pride personnel will help juveniles fill out job application forms and answer other questions relevant for effective job-hunting and success in school. The goals of Project New Pride seem obtainable. Over the years, recidivism rates have been low, less than 20 percent. Furthermore, nearly half the juveniles who have participated in various New Pride projects through the United States have returned to finish their high school education or have completed the GED.

Delinquent youths are given useful vocational opportunities as a part of their rehabilitation.

Community-based programs are particularly advantageous for youths because they provide opportunities for them to remain integrated into their communities. At the same time, youths receive assistance from agency referrals to available services and treatments. Altschuler and Armstrong (1990, 170) suggest that community-based correctional programs and other intensive probation supervision programs can maximize their effectiveness and assistance to youthful clients if they attempt to realize five important principles. These include:

1. Preparing youths for gradually increased responsibility and freedom in the community.
2. Helping youths become involved in the community and getting the community to interact with them.
3. Working with youths and their families, peers, schools and employers to identify the qualities necessary for success.
4. Developing new resources and supports where needed.
5. Monitoring and testing youths and the community on their abilities to interact.

In the next section, we will examine three increasingly important intermediate punishments that seem to be working well with adult and juvenile offenders alike. These include (1) electronic monitoring, (2) home confinement, and (3) shock probation.

ELECTRONIC MONITORING

Electronic Monitoring Defined

Electronic monitoring or **tagging** is the use of telemetry devices to verify that an offender is at a specified location during specified times (Johnston 2000). Electronic monitoring is also a system of home confinement aimed at monitoring,

Electronic monitoring is useful for identifying an offender's whereabouts.

controlling, and modifying the behavior of defendants or offenders (Vollum and Hale 2002, 1). The offender wears an electronic bracelet/anklet or other electronic device in accordance with conditions set by the courts. The tagged person is monitored by computer for 24 hours a day and is supervised by a private company or a combination of a company and the criminal justice authority, usually a probation department. The person must remain in the home under surveillance, unless authorized to leave for employment, school, participation in community treatment programs, or similar activities. Electronic monitoring tends to be used for less serious, nonviolent offenders who are identified by a risk formula (Alpha Enterprises 1996).

Electronic monitoring devices were first used in 1964 as an alternative to incarcerating certain mental patients and parolees (Gable 1986). Subsequently, electronic monitoring was extended to include monitoring office work, employee testing for security clearances, and many other applications (Roy 1997). Other countries are currently experimenting with electronic monitoring. In British Columbia, Canada, for instance, the Corrections Branch's Electronic Monitoring System was pilot-tested in 1988 and used widely in 1992 (Mainprize 1992). England and the Netherlands are also using electronic monitoring for managing certain adult and youthful offenders (Spaans and Verwers 1997; Whitfield 1997).

The Second Judicial District Judge Jack Love of New Mexico is credited with implementing a pilot electronic monitoring project in 1983 for persons convicted of drunk driving and certain white collar offenses, such as embezzlement (Houk 1984). Subsequent to its use for probationers, the New Mexico State Supreme Court approved the program, since it required the voluntariness and consent of probationers as a condition of their probation programs. Judge Love directed that certain probationers should wear either anklets or bracelets that emitted electronic signals that could be intercepted by their probation officers who conducted surveillance operations. After a short period of such judicial experimentation, other jurisdictions decided to conduct their own experiments for offender monitoring with electronic devices. Eventually, experiments were underway, not only for probationers, but for parolees and inmates of jails and prisons.

How Much Electronic Monitoring Is There in the United States?

Accurate statistical information about the extent and use of electronic monitoring in the United States for either juveniles or adults is difficult to obtain. Most of this information is based on estimated usage rather than actual usage. Some of this information is derived from sales figures reported by firms that manufacture electronic monitoring equipment, such as BI, Inc. Sales figures are often misleading, since jurisdictions that order electronic monitoring equipment may replace older equipment, or they may only use some of this equipment rather than all of it at any given time. The numbers of electronically monitored clients fluctuate daily, and there are great variations in the amount of time clients spend being monitored. However, the amount of time spent on electronic monitoring averages about twelve to fifteen weeks. Other information is obtained from those jurisdictions interested enough in reporting such information (Schmidt 1998).

Contemporary surveys that seek accurate information about electronic monitoring usage throughout the United States only obtain such information from about 25 percent of the jurisdictions canvassed. For instance, in August 1991, the International Association of Residential and Community Alternatives undertook a survey of its members from which it received a 25 percent response rate (Schmidt 1998).

Considering all of these limitations, virtually every report about electronic monitoring shows that its frequency is increasing annually. For instance, in 1987, 826 persons were being electronically monitored. By 1988 that figure had grown to 2,277. In 1989, the figure had climbed to 6,490. In 1990, an estimated 12,000 persons were being electronically monitored. In 1997, a report was issued showing that 31,236 probationers and parolees were being electronically monitored (Schmidt 1998, 11). A 1998 report disclosed that 95,000 electronic monitoring units were being used in approximately 1,500 programs in the United States (National Law Enforcement and Corrections Technology Center 1999, 1).

It has been estimated that in 2000 there were at least 100,000 adult and juvenile offenders on electronic monitoring programs in all states (Maguire and Pastore 2002). Over 10,000 youths were involved in electronic monitoring programs by 2000 (American Correctional Association 2002). The average cost of using this equipment in different probation and parole departments ranges from $5 to $25 per day, depending upon the intensity of the surveillance by POs. This is at least half of the cost of maintaining a juvenile or adult under some type of detention per day. The Administrative Office of the U.S. Courts reports that under the U.S. Probation and Pretrial Services System, there were 5,720 convicted offenders and 3,165 pretrial defendants on some form of electronic monitoring in 2000 (Administrative Office of the U.S. Courts 2001, 2).

Types of Signalling Devices

There are at least four types of **electronic monitoring signalling devices.** First, a continuous-signal device consists of a miniature transmitter that is strapped to the probationer's wrist. The transmitter broadcasts an encoded signal that is received by a receiver-dialer in the offender's home. The signal is relayed to a central receiver over the telephone lines. A second type of monitor is the programmed contact device, which is similar to the continuous-signal device. However, in this case, a central computer from the probation office is programmed to call the offender's home at random hours to verify the probationer's whereabouts. Offenders must answer their telephones, insert the wristlet-transmitter into the telephone device, and their voices and signal emissions are verified by computer (Cadigan 2001).

A third monitor is a cellular device. This is a transmitter worn by offenders and emits a radio signal that may be received by a local area monitoring system. Up to 25 probationers may be monitored at once with such a system. The fourth type of monitor is the continuous signalling transmitter that is also worn by the offender. This type of transmitter also sends out continuous signals that may be intercepted by portable receiving units in the possession of probation officers. These are quite popular, since POs may conduct drive-bys and verify whether offenders are at home during curfew hours when they are supposed to be.

These wristlet anklet transmitters are certainly not tamperproof. They are similar in plastic construction to the wristlet ID tags given patients at the time of hospital admissions. However, these electronic devices are somewhat more sturdy. Nevertheless, the plastic is such that it is easy to remove. It is easily seen whether the device has been tampered with (e.g., stretched, burned, mutilated), since it is impossible to reattach without special equipment in the possession of the probation department. If tampering has occurred and probationers have attempted to defeat the intent of the device, they may be subject to probation revocation. This offense may be punished by incarceration.

Types of Offenders on Electronic Monitoring

The types of offenders placed on electronic monitoring are selected because of their low likelihood of reoffending and the fact that their crimes are less serious, usually property offenses (Jones and Ross 1997). Thus, there is a certain amount of creaming that occurs, where those most likely to succeed are selected. This is one reason why electronic monitoring exhibits low recidivism rates among its clientele in numerous jurisdictions (Virginia Department of Criminal Justice Services 1998). However, in recent years, electronic monitoring has been extended to include more violent types of juvenile offenders, such

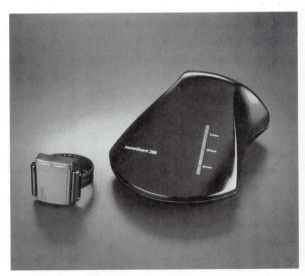

A plastic electronic monitoring device worn by certain youthful offenders.

as violent juvenile parolees (Finn and Muirhead-Steves 2002). One reason is that juvenile correctional facilities are increasingly overcrowded to the point where more dangerous juveniles must be released short of serving their full terms. The public is increasingly concerned about community safety. One result is the greater use of electronic monitoring equipment for such offenders to verify their whereabouts and exert a minimum amount of behavioral control.

Gradually, the use of electronic monitoring devices was extended to include both low- and high-risk juvenile offenders. In Knoxville, Tennessee, for example, electronic monitoring is used to a limited degree with juvenile probationers, but only as a last resort. Thus, juvenile offenders who have failed in other types of probation programs or community-based agencies are placed in an electronic monitoring program prior to being placed in secure confinement. If they do not comply with their electronic monitoring program conditions, they will be sent to secure confinement at one of the state's several public and private secure confinement facilities (Knox County Juvenile Services 2002).

Electronic monitoring is used in most jurisdictions for both adult and juvenile offenders (Cohn 2000). Electronic monitoring should not be viewed as a panacea for every low-risk offender, however. Some selectivity is necessary to ensure that persons who do not require electronic monitoring are not monitored, thus increasing the cost-effectiveness of the program (Connelly, Cohn, and Johnston 1998).

When the alternative to electronic monitoring is jail, most offenders, juveniles or otherwise, prefer electronic monitoring to confinement in a jail cell (Payne and Gainey 1998). There are significant punitive dimensions of electronic monitoring, including both physical and psychological. One's presence is required in a particular place at a particular time, and computer checks of one's whereabouts are frequent enough to cause some clients stress. Being confined to one's house as a punishment is more serious than it sounds. Many electronically monitored clients point out that the electronic monitoring program is in many ways equivalent to a jail sentence and is very much a punishment (American Correctional Association 1996).

The SpeakerID Program

Some jurisdictions, such as the Dane County, Wisconsin Sheriff's Office, have implemented a **SpeakerID Program** (Listug 1996, 85). SpeakerID is a voice verification monitoring system allowing law enforcement and criminal justice agencies to monitor low-risk offenders under probation or house arrest. Implemented in October 1994, the SpeakerID program is a completely automated system that calls clients at their authorized locations at random times. Prior to using SpeakerID, the Dade County Sheriff's Office used traditional ankle bracelets and wristlets as described earlier. The SpeakerID system started out with only 8 to 12 offenders. In 1996 there were between 30 and 35 offenders participating in this system. When offenders answer their telephones, they are asked specific questions. Voice matches are verified perfectly, and thus there is little likelihood that any particular offender can fool the system with a previously recorded tape or some other device. Because of the automated nature of the system, SpeakerID is cost-effective. Apart from initial start-up costs, the SpeakerID system costs about $3 per day per monitored offender. This compares very favorably with jail and prison costs of $40 and $49 per prisoner per day in Wisconsin jails and prisons.

Some Criticisms of Electronic Monitoring

Some limitations of electronic monitoring programs are that they are quite expensive to implement initially (Boone 1996). The direct costs associated with their purchase or lease are seemingly prohibitive to local jurisdictions that are used to incarcerating juveniles and defraying their maintenance costs over an extended period. However, once a given jurisdiction has installed such equipment, it eventually pays for itself and functions to reduce overall incarcerative expenses that otherwise would have been incurred had these same youths been placed in secure confinement.

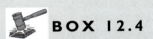 **BOX 12.4**

 **PERSONALITY HIGHLIGHT**

James L. Anderson
Vice President, Re-Entry Services, BI Incorporated, Colorado

Statistics:

B.S. (business accounting), Colorado State University; J. D., University of Northern Colorado; Graduate of National Institute of Trial Lawyers; board member of the Colorado Legal Aid Society; certified Moral Recognition Therapy cognitive skills trainer

Background:

Currently, I lead a division of BI Incorporated called Re-Entry Services. I work with community corrections officials nationwide to help develop programs that transition prisoners from incarceration to community life successfully. I look at success in terms of what's good for both the offender and the community. BI formed this division as a natural extension to the company's technology division, which uses community offender supervision tools such as electronic monitoring, voice verification, and remote alcohol testing.

After graduating from law school in the 1970s, I went to work as an attorney for the Colorado State Public Defender's Office for several years. During that time, I developed an interest that is still strong today—dealing with high-risk offenders who will eventually return to the community. Both the community and the offenders were not getting what they needed, and as a result, recidivism was rampant. To a large extent, this is true today, although we are beginning to see changes for the better. For a few years, I worked as a general counsel for Washing-

ton DC-based ACTION, which oversaw the Peace Corps and VISTA.

Based on my experience in the criminal justice system, I formed a company in the early 1990s called Peregrine Corrections. We started the company with the belief that neither punishment nor treatment alone can have a lasting impact on criminal behavior. Instead, we believed a balanced combination of accountability and treatment does yield positive results. Convincing the first local agency that we knew what we were talking about was challenging, but after we overcame that hurdle, we quickly moved into many jurisdictions in the Rocky Mountain region and then beyond. In 1997 we joined BI, the clear leader in developing reliable supervision technology for community corrections.

Experiences and Insights:

I have been fortunate over the years to meet and work closely with experts in many segments of our industry. These include public policymakers such as state and national legislators, county commissioners, and city leaders; individuals who drive correctional operations for both juveniles and adults, such as sheriffs and heads of departments of corrections; and people focused on human behavior and what makes people tick. This is a diverse mix of very smart people focused on protecting the public and changing people's lives for the better.

One recent experience in my current position stands out. We had gone to the Illinois Department of Corrections in 1998 and presented to officials about the virtues of our re-entry day reporting centers. They said okay, give it a try in the toughest neighborhood in Chicago. As we were getting the program off the ground, we sought the support of a very active and strong Catholic Church in the neighborhood, St. Sabina. Not only did members of the congregation become employees of the center, but also the church as a whole became a powerful ally politically. In fact, we hold graduation ceremonies for offenders who exit the program successfully at the church. St. Sabina is one of the reasons our program in South Side Chicago has been able to drop recidivism rates more than 40 percent among a very tough population.

At the core, there is a common thread among criminal offenders—bad decision making and poor values, especially in their early years as juveniles. If we focus upon getting to the people who have given up on society and pose one of the biggest threats to our way of life in this country, we can make a difference. For the most part, people involved in correction agencies are conservative by nature. That's good and understandable when you consider the stakes involved, although this can sometimes be a detriment to incorporating new practices that may save money or improve results. The initial challenge in corrections is to balance what is tried and true with new ideas that may improve outcomes. Sometimes there is a tendency to focus on only one element of an offender's time in the corrections system. Instead, I think we could improve results by stepping back and looking at the big picture. Most juvenile offenders have substance abuse problems; many have difficulty managing anger; most have no job skills; and many have inadequate living conditions. By assessing the juvenile's situa-

tion and developing a plan of attack for his or her return to society, we will improve the likelihood that that person will contribute to his or her community and avoid reincarceration.

Community corrections is an exciting segment of criminal justice. It is fast-moving and young. As local, state, and federal agencies look to alleviate prison and jail overcrowding, manage tight budgets, and improve overall results, they are going to look to community corrections for innovative ideas. One of the exciting new developments in the last decade is the proliferation of specialty courts such as drug, family, and re-entry courts. In particular, the number of drug courts nationally has grown from 12 to more than 1,000 since 1994. Their success is rooted in the approach: Offenders are required to undergo drug treatment, frequent drug testing, close monitoring, and regular court visits. This approach was designed to insure short-term accountability in the criminal adjudication process and a long-term reduction in recidivism. Our Re-Entry program borrows some of the key components of these specialty courts.

Advice to Students:

Don't be afraid to take on the hard challenges in corrections, and don't give up along the way. This is an honorable profession that is going to need some of the best thinkers we have to change people who have abandoned our values and culture and pose a real threat to our country. People who will succeed in community corrections will be able to look at the big picture and blend the best practices from a number of disciplines, such as psychiatry, psychology, operations, business, and communications. The exciting news is that people who choose this profession are going to help solve one of the large unmet needs of our time. Keep abreast of new approaches to behavior change and look for areas in corrections where they can be incorporated into the process. Demand excellence from the field, the programs, and the processes we develop and implement in community corrections.

Also, electronic monitoring programs require some training on the part of the users (Nieto 1998). While those using such systems do not need to be computer geniuses, some computer training is helpful. Electronic monitoring is a delinquency deterrent for many offenders (Johnston 2000). However, it is not foolproof. In spite of the fact that they may be easily tampered with, electronic wristlets and anklets only help to verify an offender's whereabouts. They do not provide television images of these persons and whatever they may be doing. One federal probation officer has reported that one of his federal probationers on electronic monitoring was running a successful stolen property business out of his own home. Thus, he was able to continue his criminal activity unabated, despite the home confinement constraints imposed by electronics.

Electronic monitoring has also been criticized as possibly violative of the Fourth Amendment search-and-seizure provision, where, it is alleged by some critics, electronic eavesdropping might be conducted within one's home or bedroom. This argument is without serious constitutional merit, since the primary function of such monitoring is to verify an offender's whereabouts. Some sophisticated types of monitoring systems are equipped with closed-circuit television transmissions, such as those advertised by the Bell Telephone Company as viewer-phones of the future. But even if such monitoring were so equipped, this additional feature would only intrude where offenders wished it to intrude, such as their living rooms or kitchens.

The fact is that many offenders may be inexpensively tracked through these monitoring systems and their whereabouts can be verified without time-consuming face-to-face checks (Cohn 2000). For instance, a single juvenile probation officer may conduct drive-bys of client residences during evening hours and receive their transmitted signals with a portable unit. This silent means of detection is intended only to enforce one program element; namely, observance of curfews. Other checks, such as those conducted for illegal drug or alcohol use, must be verified directly, through proper testing and expert confirmation. As we will see, electronic monitoring is increasingly used in tandem with another sentencing option—home confinement (Boone 1996).

Summarizing the arguments for and against electronic monitoring, proponents of electronic monitoring say that it (1) assists offenders in avoiding the criminogenic atmosphere of prisons or jails and helps reintegrate them into their communities; (2) permits offenders to retain jobs and support families; (3) assists probation officers in their monitoring activities and has potential for easing their caseload responsibilities; (4) gives judges and other officials considerable flexibility in sentencing offenders; (5) has the potential of reducing recidivism rate more than existing probationary alternatives; (6) is potentially useful for decreasing jail and prison populations; (7) is more cost-effective in relation to incarceration; and (8) allows for pretrial release monitoring as well as for special treatment cases such as substance abusers, the mentally retarded, women who are pregnant, and juveniles.

Those against electronic monitoring say that (1) some potential exists for race, ethnic, or socioeconomic bias by requiring offenders to have telephones or to pay for expensive monitoring equipment and/or fees (ironically, some jurisdictions report that many offenders enjoy better living conditions in jail or prison custody compared with their residences outside of prison); (2) public safety may be compromised through the failure of these programs to guarantee that offenders will go straight and not endanger citizens by committing new offenses while free in the community; (3) it may be too coercive, and it may be unrealistic for officials to expect full offender compliance with such a stringent system; (4) little consistent information exists about the impact of electronic monitoring on recidivism rates compared with other probationary alternatives; (5) persons frequently selected for participation are persons who probably don't need to be monitored anyway; (6) technological problems exist making electronic monitoring somewhat unreliable; (7) it may result in widening the net by being prescribed for offenders who otherwise would receive less costly standard probation; (8) it raises right to privacy, civil liberties, and other constitutional issues such as Fourth Amendment search-and-seizure concerns; (9) much of the public interprets this option as going easy on offenders and perceives electronic monitoring as a nonpunitive alternative; and (10) the costs of electronic monitoring may be more than published estimates.

HOME CONFINEMENT OR HOUSE ARREST

The use of one's home as the principal place of confinement is not new. In biblical times, St. Paul was sentenced in Rome to house arrest for two years, where he performed tentmaker services for others. **Home confinement** is a program of intermediate punishment involving the use of the offender's residence for mandatory incarceration during evening hours after a curfew and on weekends (Cadigan 2001).

Florida introduced the contemporary use of home confinement in 1983 (Boone 1996). At that time, corrections officials considered the use of homes as incarcerative facilities as acceptable alternatives to prisons or jails for certain low-risk offenders. Home confinement was a very inexpensive way of maintaining supervisory control over those offenders who were deemed not in need of costly incarceration. When Florida began its home confinement program, it was established under the Correctional Reform Act of 1983. This Act provided that the home could be used as a form of intensive supervised custody in the community. This highly individualized program is intended primarily to restrict

Home confinement with curfew is increasingly used as an alternative to incarceration.

offender movement within the community, home, or nonresidential placement, together with specific sanctions such as curfew, payment of fines, community service, and other requirements. When Florida started to use home confinement as a punishment, prison costs averaged $30 per inmate per day, while home confinement required an expenditure of about $3 per offender per day. In the late 1990s prison maintenance costs per prisoner were in excess of $75 per day in most jurisdictions, while home confinement costs stabilized at about $5 per day (Tonry 1997). Although Florida officials consider **home incarceration** or **house arrest** punitive, some persons disagree. They believe that incarceration should be in a jail or prison, if it is meaningful incarceration (Landreville 1999).

Functions and Goals of Home Confinement Programs

The functions and goals of home confinement programs include the following:

1. To continue the offender's punishment while permitting the offender to live in his/her dwelling under general or close supervision.
2. To enable offenders to perform jobs in their communities to support themselves and their families.
3. To reduce jail and prison overcrowding.
4. To maximize public safety by ensuring that only the most qualified clients enter home confinement programs and are properly supervised.
5. To reduce the costs of offender supervision.
6. To promote rehabilitation and reintegration by permitting offenders to live under appropriate supervision within their communities.

In many jurisdictions, including U.S. federal probation, home confinement is used together with electronic monitoring (Administrative Office of the U.S. Courts 2001). The National Juvenile Detention Association has significantly encouraged different jurisdictions to adopt home confinement and other nonincarcerative alternatives as ways of dealing with low-risk juvenile offenders. Executive Director Earl Dunlop says that "the vast majority of kids do not need to be locked up. Our emphasis is upon detention services, the process—home prevention, electronic monitoring, staff supervision—not detention services, the place" (*Corrections Today* 1999a, 20).

Relatively little is known about the extent to which home confinement is used as a sentencing alternative for juvenile offenders. Since probation is so widely used as the sanction of choice except for the most chronic recidivists, home confinement is most often applied as an accompanying condition of electronic monitoring (Bowers 2000). However, this type of sentencing may be redundant, since curfew for juvenile offenders means home confinement anyway, especially during evening hours. As a day disposition, home confinement for juveniles would probably be counterproductive, since juveniles are often obligated to finish their schooling as a probation program condition. Again, since school hours are during the daytime, it would not make sense to deprive juveniles of school opportunities through some type of home confinement.

A survey of several home detention and electronic monitoring programs was conducted and reported by Baumer, Maxfield, and Mendelsohn (1993).

Three separate programs were established in Marion County, Indiana, in 1986 to electronically supervise both adults and juveniles in (1) postconviction, (2) pretrial, and (3) juvenile burglary. The postconviction program was designed for adult offenders convicted of nonviolent offenses that can be suspended as an alternative to incarceration. Actually, Indiana law provides that convicted offenders must be sentenced to a term of incarceration. After this sentence is imposed, it is suspended and offenders are placed on electronic monitoring and house arrest. The pretrial program involves defendants charged with nonviolent crimes and who are screened according to their criminal history, living arrangements, and length of stay at the jail before their trials. Persons who qualify are placed into a programmed contact system identical to that furnished for convicted offenders.

The juvenile burglary program was commenced in June 1989 by the Juvenile Division of the Marion County Superior Court. All juveniles initially charged with burglary and convicted of either burglary or theft are targeted. Participating juveniles must be eligible for either probation or a suspended sentence; thus, more violent and serious juvenile offenders are automatically excluded. Juveniles assigned to home confinement can also receive a blend of treatments, including electronically programmed contact, manual monitoring, and random home visits by police officers (Baumer, Maxfield, and Mendelsohn 1993, 125–126). These researchers report favorable results with all three programs, especially with the juvenile burglary program. The participating youths had low rates of absconding and recidivism compared with adult offenders. Thus, public safety as a program goal was reasonably achieved. Although these investigators suggest further study concerning the feasibility of applying home confinement and programmed electronic monitoring systems with juveniles, Marion County's efforts thus far have been very favorable.

Home confinement is also useful for certain types of offenders who are drug- or alcohol-dependent. Probation officers can visit the homes of certain drug-dependent clients and perform instant checks to determine whether they have used alcohol or drugs in the recent past. While access to drugs or alcohol is relatively easy when a client is confined to his or her home, the threat of a random drug/alcohol test by a PO is often a sufficient deterrent (Latessa and Allen 1999). Needs assessments for certain offenders can determine which services they require, and they are relatively mobile to seek these services with probation department approval (Tonry 1997).

Advantages and Disadvantages of Home Confinement

Among the advantages of home confinement are that (1) it is cost effective, (2) it has social benefits, (3) it is responsive to local citizen and offender needs, and (4) it is easily implemented and is timely in view of jail and prison overcrowding. Some of the disadvantages of home confinement are: (1) House arrest may actually widen the net of social control, (2) it may narrow the net of social control by not being a sufficiently severe sentence, (3) it focuses primarily upon offender surveillance, (4) it is intrusive and possibly illegal, (5) race and class bias may enter into participant selection, and (6) it may compromise public safety.

Wilderness experiences promote self-esteem and build confidence.

OTHER JISP PROGRAM CONDITIONS

Briefly reviewing judicial dispositional options, at one end of the sentencing spectrum, they may adjudicate youths as delinquent, impose nominal sanctions, and take no further action other than to record the event. Therefore, if the same juveniles reappear before the same judge in the future, sterner measures may be taken in imposing new dispositions. Or the judge may divert juveniles to particular community agencies for special treatment. Juveniles with psychological problems or who are emotionally disturbed, sex offenders, or those with drug and/or alcohol dependencies may be targeted for special community treatments. At the other end of the spectrum of punishments are the most drastic alternatives of custodial sanctions, ranging from the placement of juveniles in nonsecure foster homes and camp ranches, or secure facilities, such as reform schools and industrial schools. These nonsecure and secure forms of placement and/or incarceration are usually reserved for the most serious offenders (Latessa and Allen 1999).

Probation is the most commonly used sentencing option. Probation is either unconditional or conditional. This chapter has examined several conditional intermediate punishments, including intensive probation supervision and community-based programs. A youth's assignment to any of these programs may or may not include conditions. Apart from the more intensive monitoring and supervision by POs, juveniles may be expected to comply with one or more conditions, including restitution, if financial loss was suffered by one or more victims in cases of vandalism, property damage, or physical injury. Also, fines may be imposed. Or the judge may specify some form of community service. All of these conditions may be an integral part of a juvenile's probation program. Violation of or failure to comply with one or more of these conditions may result in a probation revocation action. Probation officers function as the link between juvenile offenders and the courts regarding a youth's compliance with these program conditions.

Restitution, Fines, Victim Compensation, and Victim–Offender Mediation

Restitution.   An increasingly important feature of probation programs is **restitution** (Brumbaugh and Birkbeck 1999). Several models of restitution have been described. These include:

1. The financial/community service model, which stresses the offender's financial accountability and community service to pay for damages.
2. The victim/offender mediation model, which focuses upon victim–offender reconciliation.
3. The victim/reparations model, where juveniles compensate their victims directly for their offenses (Schneider and Schneider 1985).

The potential significance of restitution, coupled with probation, is that it suggests a reduction in recidivism among juvenile offenders. In a restitution program in Atlanta, Georgia, for example, 258 juvenile offenders participated in several experimental treatment programs, where one of the programs included restitution. The restitution offender group had a 26 percent reduction in recidivism compared with other juveniles where restitution was not included as a condition (Schneider and Schneider 1985). But other observers caution that if restitution is not properly implemented by the court or carefully supervised, it serves little deterrent purpose (Roy 1995).

Fines and Victim Compensation.   Beyond reductions in recidivism, restitution, payment of **fines,** and **victim compensation** also increase offender accountability. Given the present philosophical direction of juvenile courts, this condition is consistent with enhancing a youth's acceptance of responsibility for wrongful actions committed against others and the financial harm it has caused (Arthur 2000). Many of these programs include restitution as a part of their program requirements. Restitution orders may be imposed by juvenile court judges with or without accompanying dispositions of secure confinement (O'Mahony 2000).

Victim–Offender Mediation.   There is growing interest in programs for juvenile offenders that heighten their accountability, especially toward their victims. Since 1980, there has been growing awareness of and interest in **victim–offender mediation** as a means of resolving disputes between the juvenile perpetrator and his or her victim. Victim–offender mediation is bringing together victims, offenders, and other members of the community to hold offenders accountable not only for their crimes but for the harm they caused to victims (Bazemore and Umbreit 2001). These programs provide an opportunity for crime victims and offenders to meet face-to-face to talk about the impact of the crime on their lives and to develop a plan for repairing the harm. Most of these programs work with juvenile offenders, although a growing number are involving adult offenders (Umbreit, Coates, and Vos 2001, 29). Sometimes referred to as restorative justice, victim–offender mediation was quite prevalent throughout the world in 2000, with over 1,300 programs in 18 countries (Umbreit, Coates, and Vos 2001). In 2000, there were 300 victim–offender mediation programs in the United States. One unique feature of such programs is that they are dialogue-driven rather than settlement-driven. While not all victims are to-tally satisfied with the outcomes of such programs, most report being satisfied with having the opportunity of sharing their stories and their pain resulting from the crime event. Many juveniles report being surprised at learning about the impact their actions had on various victims they confront.

Community Service

Associated with restitution orders is **community service.** Community service may be performed in different ways, ranging from cutting courthouse lawns and cleaning up public parks to painting homes for the elderly or repairing fences on private farms. Youths typically earn wages for this service, and these wages are usually donated to a victim compensation fund. The different types of com-munity service activities are limited only by the imagination of the juvenile court and community leaders. Similar to restitution, community service orders are intended to increase offender accountability and individual responsibility (Myers et al. 2000).

SUMMARY

Standard probation is a commonly used dispositional option. This type of pro-bation may be either conditional or unconditional, where supervision by juve-nile probation officers is optional and at the judge's discretion. Conditions ordinarily include victim compensation or restitution, community service, or payment of fines. Standard probation programs include the Youth-to-Victim Restitution Project, the Second Chance Program, juvenile probation camps, the Intensive Aftercare Program, and the Sexual Offender Treatment Program.

Intermediate punishments are sanctions that juvenile court judges may im-pose that lie somewhere between standard probation and incarceration. Popu-lar intermediate punishments include intensive supervised probation, community-based programs, electronic monitoring, home confinement, and shock probation. The significance of such programs is that the more intensified supervision and monitoring of juvenile offenders will deter them from commit-ting new offenses. Generally, recidivism figures seem to show that these pro-grams are successful in reducing delinquency fairly effectively.

Intensive supervised probation (ISP) increases the number of PO/client contacts as well as accompanying conditions, such as payment of fines, curfew, drug and alcohol checks, restitution orders, and individual or group therapy. Ohio and other states have operated juvenile intensive supervised probation (JISP) programs for juvenile offenders for many years. Ohio JISP programs sug-gest that JISP may be implemented differently, depending upon the jurisdic-tion. Yet, similar results are obtained regarding offender desistance from further offending. Ordinarily, juveniles are screened for participation through the use of risk/needs assessment instruments. Some experts suggest a balanced ap-proach to juvenile ISP, including both punitive and rehabilitative dimensions. Overall objectives are to increase offender accountability and personal respon-sibility.

Community-based programs include the Boston Offender Project, which is aimed at reintegrating youths into their communities, and Project New Pride, which focuses upon building self-esteem and independence, as well as offering employment assistance to youthful clients. Other intermediate punishments include electronic monitoring and home confinement, where offenders wear electronic bracelets or anklets that emit electronic signals which can be received by POs to verify an offender's whereabouts. Homes are used as incarcerative facilities, and PO checks verify one's presence. Both of these programs are geared to help cut the costs of incarcerating juvenile offenders. Also imposed as punishments are fines, restitution, and community service. It is presumed that such conditional penalties enhance one's accountability and improve an offender's responsibility to victims and society. Various victim–offender mediation programs and restorative justice are used to resolve disputes between youthful perpetrators and their victims.

QUESTIONS FOR REVIEW

1. What is meant by standard probation? What are some characteristics of it?

2. What was the Youth-to-Victim Restitution Project? What types of clients did it serve?

3. What is a juvenile probation camp? What is meant by intensive aftercare?

4. What is meant by intermediate punishments? How do intermediate punishments differ from standard probation?

5. What are some goals of intermediate punishments? What are some of the criteria for placement in intensive supervised probation programs?

6. What is the Ohio experience? What are some of its prominent characteristics?

7. What is meant by case supervision planning? What was the San Francisco Project and what did it find?

8. What is meant by the balanced approach? Is it successful in dealing with delinquent offenders? Why or why not?

9. What are home confinement and electronic monitoring? Who are the juvenile clients who are disposed to electronic monitoring and/or home confinement? What are the goals and functions of these respective programs?

10. What is victim–offender mediation? Under what conditions is it used? How successful is victim–offender mediation in resolving disputes between juvenile perpetrators and their victims?

SUGGESTED READINGS

Altschuler, David M. and Troy L. Armstrong. 2001. Reintegrating high-risk juvenile offenders into communities: Experiences and prospects. *Corrections Management Quarterly* 5:72–88.

Evie, Audrey and Robert C. Cushman. 2000. *A summary of the evaluations of six California victim–offender reconciliation programs.* Sacramento: Judicial Council of California, Center for Families, Children and the Courts.

Gowen, Darren. 2001. Analysis of competing risks in the federal home confinement program. *The Journal of Offender Monitoring* 14:5–9.

Jonson-Reid, Melissa and Richard P. Barth. 2000. From placement to prison: The path to adolescent incarceration from child welfare supervised foster or group care. *Children and Youth Services Review* 22:493–516.

Meisel, Joshua S. 2001. Relationships and juvenile offenders: The effects of intensive aftercare supervision. *Prison Journal* 81:206–245.

INTERNET CONNECTIONS

American Jail Association
http://www.corrections.com/aja/

Correctional Educational Connections
http://www.io.com/~ellie/

The Fortune Society
http://www.fortunesociety.org/

Helping.org
http://www.helping.org/

Intensive Aftercare for High Risk Juveniles
http://www.csus.edu/ssis/cdcps/IAPPAGE.htm

Sentencing Project
http://www.sentencingproject.org/

ServiceLeader
http://www.serviceleader.org/

<table>
<tr><td>**CHAPTER 13**</td><td>*Juvenile Corrections:*
Custodial Sanctions and Parole</td></tr>
</table>

Chapter Outline

Key Terms
Chapter Objectives
Introduction
Goals of Juvenile Corrections
Current Juvenile Custodial
   Alternatives
Nonsecure Confinement

Secure Confinement: Variations
Persistent Problems of Nonsecure
   and Secure Confinement
Juvenile Parole
Recidivism and Parole Revocation
Examples of Probation and Parole
   Revocation for Juveniles

Selected Issues in Juvenile
   Corrections
Summary
Questions for Review
Suggested Readings
Internet Connections

Key Terms

About face
Army model
Boot camps
Combination sentences
Detention centers
Detention hearing
Foster homes
Group homes
Halfway houses
Homeward Bound
IMPACT (Intensive Motivational
   Program of Alternative Cor-
   rectional Treatment)

Intermittent sentences
Jail as a condition of probation
Juvenile offender laws
Long-term detention
Minimum due process rights
Mixed sentences
Parole revocation
Parole revocation hearing
Parolees
Privatization
Probation revocation hearing

Project Outward Bound
Regimented Inmate Discipline
   (RID) Program
Scared Straight
Shock incarceration
Shock parole
Shock probation
Short-term confinement
Split sentences
VisionQuest
Wilderness experiments

> ## Chapter Objectives
>
> *As a result of reading this chapter, you will realize the following objectives:*
>
> 1. Understand the different components and goals of juvenile corrections.
> 2. Differentiate between nonsecure and secure confinement, as well as examine some of the programs associated with nonsecure treatment of juvenile offenders.
> 3. Learn about various types of custodial facilities for juveniles and their relative successfulness in fostering juvenile rehabilitation and reintegration.
> 4. Learn about several important correctional issues as they apply to juvenile offenders.
> 5. Learn about juvenile parole and the characteristics of parole programs.
> 6. Understand the process of juvenile probation and parole revocation.
> 7. Learn about some of the leading U.S. Supreme Court cases that apply to juvenile probation and parole as well as the revocation process.

INTRODUCTION

• *It happened in McMinnville, Oregon. Shelly Leann Hammitt, 28, was a secretary with the Amity High School. Everything seemed normal at the time. But something was wrong on the Amity campus. Hammitt was having sex with several of the high schoolers. The discovery of Hammitt's indiscretions came about when some of the male students bragged to others about having sex with her. "If anything, they thought it was a sign of manhood, of status among their peers," said defense attorney Mark Bierly. "They were bragging to the other kids in school," he added. When it was learned that Hammitt was having sex with some of the male students, an investigation revealed that at least four male students were involved. They were having sex with Hammitt in homes and vehicles off school grounds. The boys were 17 years old at the time. Since the incidents, three of the boys have turned 18. Hammitt was arrested on January 21, 1997, and charged with child sexual abuse and contributing to the sexual delinquency of a minor. When interviewed, Hammitt said as she sobbed, "I wish I could understand how it happened, but the truth is, I don't know. I only know it was wrong." Hammitt was sentenced to 30 days in jail and five years' probation. How accountable are the juveniles for having sexual relations with a school staff member? What punishments should be imposed for their behavior, if any? What do you think?* [Adapted from the Associated Press, "High School Secretary Jailed for Having Sex with Students." April 11, 1997.]

• *Want a jail in your neighborhood? Probably not. The citizens of New England, North Dakota don't want one there either. As overcrowding in jails, prisons, and juvenile correctional facilities continues to grow unchecked, federal, state, and local governments are turning toward the community for short- and long-term solutions to accommodating inmate overflow. Community corrections is a growing enterprise. In southwestern North Dakota, near Dickinson, federal authorities have been plagued with the problem of growing juvenile delinquency. The federal system has no juvenile court, although the Native American reservations controlled by the federal government mean that whenever juveniles are adjudicated delinquent for serious offenses, they must be placed in secure juvenile facilities <u>somewhere</u>. The growing delinquency problem has caused federal agencies to consider converting unused building space into juvenile detention housing.*

In 1998 federal authorities moved to renovate several buildings that were once a school in New England. New England St. Mary's School was closed in 1997, leaving approximately 57,000 square feet of space available. The federal government acquired the buildings and grounds and implemented a renovation program designed to convert the facility into a short-term detention center for juveniles. The new facility would be called the Southwest Multi-County Correction Center. Some New England citizens were outraged. The Citizens for a Progressive New England moved to prevent the renovation by having a federal court issue an injunction against the authorities who were initiating the conversion. Consisting of 92 members, the Citizens for a Progressive New England contend that the juvenile facility would endanger property values and the security of neighbors in the community, which is located about 25 miles south of Dickinson. An attorney for the group, Loren McCray, said that "on its face, there's a potential for property values to drop for those homes" near the former school. Proponents of the center say that the new juvenile facility will provide needed jobs and boost the local community economy. Further, they say that fears about community safety are unfounded. "These are wild assumptions that something bad will happen," said Dickinson attorney Tom Priebe, calling the injunction a pretty drastic remedy. More than a few communities oppose construction of juvenile or adult facilities in their neighborhoods. While research has generally shown that property values near these sites are unaffected, the prospect of having dangerous juveniles housed nearby may cause some community concern. What do you think about having any kind of correctional facility constructed near or within a community? [Adapted from the Associated Press, "New England Juvenile Jail Prevails in First Round of Court Battle." November 14, 1998.]

• It happened in Tyler, Texas. A 17-year-old girl was accused of shooting her parents to death while they slept on Christmas morning. Stephanie Catherine Barron, 17, was taken into custody and held for investigation following the murders of her parents, Stephen Wayne Barron, 44, and Carla Barron, 43. Deputies received a call about the shooting around 4:00 A.M. They arrived at the Barron home near Tyler, Texas, and found Stephen Barron and his wife, Carla, shot in the head in their bedroom. A handgun was recovered from the bedroom. Stephanie Barron told deputies that she thought there was an intruder in the house and she heard gunshots coming from her parents' bedroom. She said she hid in her closet, and then she ran to her grandparents' house next door. After several hours of investigation, police placed Stephanie Barron under arrest for the double murder. No motive was immediately apparent. What should be Stephanie's punishment if convicted of the double murder? What do you think? [Adapted from the Associated Press, "Girl Suspected in Holiday Killings." December 27, 1999.]

Youthful offenders under age 18 are attracting the attention of the nation as they enter incarcerative facilities (Owens 1999, 102). In 2000, there were 352,000 juveniles under some form of correctional supervision in 51 jurisdictions in the United States (Maguire and Pastore 2002). About 74,300 of these juveniles were being held in secure and nonsecure facilities (with limited community privileges). There were approximately 2 million admissions and discharges of juveniles from secure confinement facilities during 2000. Minority youths made up 65 percent of those confined. Sheer admission rates of juveniles to confinement of any kind, even for a few hours, are staggering. In 1990 there were 690,000 admissions of juveniles to detention centers and other facilities. By 2000, over 1 million youths were admitted to detention centers for a few hours or longer (Maguire and Pastore 2002).

One of the most important components of the juvenile justice system is juvenile corrections. Juvenile corrections encompasses all personnel, agencies, and institutions that supervise youthful offenders. We have previously examined various nominal and conditional options that related to supervising juveniles who are placed on diversion or disposed to probation or intermediate punishment programs. This chapter describes several custodial sentencing options, the most severe sanctions that juvenile court judges may impose. These sanctions are usually administered to youthful offenders who have been adjudicated as delinquent and considered sufficiently serious or dangerous to merit close supervision or secure confinement.

First, some of the more important goals of juvenile corrections will be described. Next, an overview of several custodial sentencing options will be provided. This overview will be followed by a description of some of the more popular nonsecure and secure custodial alternatives. Because some juvenile offenders require greater discipline and harsher treatment than others, secure confinement facilities vary in their degree of supervision and control exerted over juvenile inmates. These facilities and programs will be described and assessed.

Juveniles released from nonsecure or secure confinement are often placed on parole for limited periods. Those juveniles placed on parole are ordinarily expected to abide by various parole conditions in order to fulfill their parole programs successfully. Some of these conditions and parole programs will be described. If juveniles violate one or more parole conditions, their parole may be revoked. Parole revocation may mean that juveniles will be returned to their original custodial institutions. This revocation process will be described. Finally, several key issues in juvenile corrections will be presented. These issues include the privatization of juvenile corrections, housing juveniles in adult lockups or jail facilities, classifying offenders for their subsequent placement, and offender recidivism.

GOALS OF JUVENILE CORRECTIONS

Various goals of juvenile corrections include (1) deterrence, (2) rehabilitation and reintegration, (3) prevention, (4) punishment and retribution, and (5) isolation and control. These goals may at times appear to be in conflict. For instance, some jurisdictions stress delinquency prevention through keeping juveniles away from the juvenile justice system through diversion and warnings. However, other jurisdictions get tough with juveniles by providing more certain and stringent penalties for their offenses. A middle ground stresses both discipline and reform.

Deterrence

Significant deterrent elements of juvenile correctional programs include clearly stated rules and formal sanctions, anticriminal modeling and reinforcement, and a high degree of empathy and trust between the juvenile client and staff (Armstrong 2001). Traditional counseling, institutionalization, and diversion, according to some investigators, are considered largely ineffective (Goldsmith 2001; Jurich, Casper, and Hull 2001). A natural intervention may occur apart from any particular program designed to deter. As youths grow older, their offending tends to reach a plateau and then decline. Thus, many youths simply outgrow delinquency as they become older.

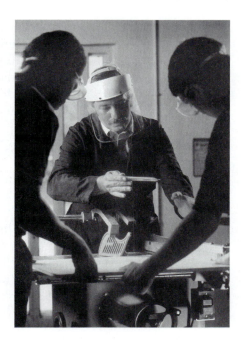

Vocational and educational training are useful features of rehabilitative correctional programs.

Rehabilitation and Reintegration

Various juvenile correctional programs stress internalizing responsibilities for one's actions, while other programs attempt to inculcate youths with social and motor skills. Other programs attempt to diagnose and treat youths who are emotionally disturbed (Moore, Sprengelmeyer, and Chamberlain 2001). Alternative medical and social therapies are often used. Group homes are becoming increasingly popular as alternatives to incarceration, since a broader array of services can be extended to juveniles with special needs.

Prevention

Delinquency prevention seems to be a function of many factors (Altschuler and Armstrong 2001). One factor is early preschool intervention. Early preschool intervention programs seem to have modest successfulness. In 1962 the Perry Preschool Project was implemented in Ypsilanti, Michigan (Berrueta-Clement et al. 1984). Nearly 70 percent of the children who participated in the program had no future reported offenses as juveniles and only 16 percent were ever arrested for delinquent acts. However, about half of the nonparticipants in the same school had future reported offenses as juveniles and 25 percent were subsequently arrested for delinquency.

Punishment and Retribution

Some persons want to see youths, especially violent ones, punished rather than rehabilitated (Mears 2001). One major impact of the get-tough-on-crime policy adopted by many jurisdictions is that the juvenile justice system seems to be diverting a larger portion of its serious offenders to criminal courts where they may conceivably receive harsher punishments (Wilson and Petersilia 2002).

This may be one reaction to widespread allegations that the juvenile courts are too lenient in their sentencing of violent offenders or that the punishment options available to juvenile court judges are not sufficiently severe. For those juveniles who remain within the juvenile justice system for processing, secure confinement for longer periods seems to be the court's primary response to citizen allegations of excessive leniency.

Isolation and Control

Apprehension and incarceration of juvenile offenders, especially chronic recidivists, are believed important to isolating them and limiting their opportunities to reoffend (Steen 2001; Tombs, Chang, and Lu 1999). In principle, this philosophy is similar to selective incapacitation. However, the average length of juvenile incarcerative terms in public facilities in the United States is less than 10 months (Maguire and Pastore 2002). Thus, incarceration by itself may be of limited value in controlling the amount of juvenile delinquency (Lobley, Smith, and Stern 2001).

CURRENT JUVENILE CUSTODIAL ALTERNATIVES

The custodial options available to juvenile court judges are of two general types: nonsecure and secure. Nonsecure custodial facilities are those that permit youths freedom of movement within the community. Youths are generally free to leave the premises of their facilities, although they are compelled to observe various rules, such as curfew, avoidance of alcoholic beverages and drugs, and participation in specific programs that are tailored to their particular needs.

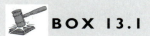 **BOX 13.1**

EIGHTH-GRADER TAKES FOUR LOADED GUNS TO SCHOOL

Santa Fe, Texas

A 13-year-old boy was arrested following a tip given to a teacher that he had brought some guns and knives to school in his gym bag. The boy was taken to the principal's office and his bag was searched. The search revealed four guns: a .380-caliber handgun, a .22-caliber handgun, a 9mm pistol, and a .38-caliber handgun. The pistols were loaded. Sources said that the boy had moved to the school district less than three weeks ago. It wasn't known at the time whether there was any intent on the boy's part to harm other students or teachers.

However, a second boy was also arrested for possessing a switchblade knife that had been given to him by the 13-year-old. Neither boy was identified to the press because of their status as juvenile offenders.

Should the identity of juveniles, especially those with guns, be withheld from the public? Potentially serious consequences could have resulted from this incident. How do you think the boy should be processed? Should the boy be treated as a delinquent offender and face juvenile court? What do you think?

Source: Adapted from the Associated Press, "Boy Takes Four Pistols to School," April 8, 2000.

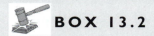

BOX 13.2

MAKE A THREAT, GET ARRESTED

Columbine High School Revisited

It certainly isn't funny. An off-hand remark was made by one student to another at Columbine High School in Golden, Colorado, about six months following one of the bloodiest shootings in recent history involving high school students. A 17-year-old student allegedly told another student one afternoon that he planned to "finish the job" started by two student killers who had murdered 12 Columbine High School students, a teacher, and themselves in an armed attack in April 1999. Shortly after making that statement, the student was arrested by police after the other student reported the incident to authorities and police. The boy was being held on $500,000 bond and remained in police custody since his arrest on October 19, 1999. His name was withheld from the news because of his age. Chief Deputy District Attorney Mark Pautler said his office cannot discuss the charges or details, but he said that they are based on writings and other communications that prompted many Columbine students to stay home on October 20, the six-month anniversary of the shooting rampage. The student was being held on charges of inciting destruction of life or property and one count of misdemeanor theft.

What would an appropriate punishment be for someone who makes threats following a student shooting? Should these remarks be considered "freedom of speech," or should they be taken seriously? Are police and school authorities overreacting to such incidents when they occur? When do you draw the line about who should or should not be taken seriously when they threaten to kill others? Should a zero tolerance policy be just that? What do you think?

Source: Adapted from the Associated Press, "Columbine Student Arraigned." November 23, 1999.

These types of nonsecure facilities include foster homes; group homes and halfway houses; and camps, ranches, experience programs, and wilderness projects (Peterson, Ruck, and Koegl 2001; Platt 2001).

Secure custodial facilities are the juvenile counterpart to adult prisons or penitentiaries. Such institutions are known by different names among the states. For example, secure, long-term secure confinement facilities might be called youth centers or youth facilities (Alaska, California, Colorado, District of Columbia, Illinois, Kansas, Maine, Missouri), juvenile institutions (Arkansas), schools (California, Connecticut, New Mexico), schools for boys (Delaware), training schools or centers (Florida, Indiana, Iowa, Oregon), youth development centers (Georgia, Nebraska), youth services centers (Idaho), secure centers (New York), industry schools (New York), and youth development centers (Tennessee). This listing is not intended to be comprehensive, but it illustrates the variety of designations states use to refer to their long-term, secure confinement facilities. Table 13.1 shows a distribution of juveniles confined in all states and the District of Columbia for 2000. The number of facilities includes both secure and nonsecure institutions, excluding day reporting centers and treatment centers. Also included in Table 13.1 is the rated capacity of the combined facilities for each state, together with the actual daily capacity.

TABLE 13.1

Juvenile Secure and Nonsecure Population for 2000, by State, Number of Facilities, Rated Capacity, and Actual Daily Capacity.*

State	No. of Facilities	Rated Capacity	Average Daily Capacity
Alabama	12	815	793
Alaska	6	265	271
Arizona	4	474	502
Arkansas	6	256	196
California	16	11,419	11,801
Colorado	11	699	772
Connecticut	4	264	273
Delaware	6	3,266	3,203
District of Columbia	19	6,211	6,433
Florida	49	4,085	4,690
Georgia	31	3,260	3,533
Hawaii	1	50	71
Idaho	5	300	291
Illinois	12	1,895	1,892
Indiana	11	1,434	1,363
Iowa	2	311	302
Kansas	4	535	535
Kentucky	12	954	954
Louisiana	4	1,670	1,458
Maine	2	167	167
Maryland	17	2,486	2,321
Massachusetts	29	3,268	3,268
Michigan	19	812	812
Minnesota	4	163	163
Missouri	17	763	763
Montana	6	123	123
Nebraska	4	333	333
Nevada	3	396	392
New Hampshire	2	135	135
New Jersey	24	3,175	3,175
New Mexico	4	665	665
New York	44	3,191	3,191
North Carolina	21	1,658	1,658
North Dakota	2	175	175
Ohio	23	2,147	2,147
Oklahoma	4	319	319
Oregon	14	1,140	1,140
Pennsylvania	23	754	754
Rhode Island	2	336	336
South Carolina	9	1,110	1,110
South Dakota	5	429	429
Tennessee	4	564	564
Texas	15	5,968	5,968
Utah	18	1,796	1,796
Vermont	1	30	30
Virginia	11	1,535	1,535
Washington	13	1,180	1,180
West Virginia	8	286	286
Wisconsin	12	939	939
Wyoming	2	166	166
Totals	577	74,372	75,368

* Nonsecure confinement facilities include youth centers, halfway houses, ranches, and other facilities designed to hold juveniles 24 hours a day, with limited community privileges. Because of the nature of reporting from individual jurisdictions, precise male–female breakdowns are frequently not provided. However, independent information from the American Correctional Association (2002) discloses that females made up approximately 10 percent of the secure and nonsecure juvenile population.

NONSECURE CONFINEMENT

Nonsecure confinement involves placing certain youths in (1) foster homes; (2) group homes and halfway houses; and (3) camps, ranches, experience programs, and wilderness projects.

Foster Homes

If the juvenile's natural parents are considered unfit, or if the juvenile is abandoned or orphaned, **foster homes** are often used for temporary placement. Those youths placed in foster homes are not necessarily law violators. They may be children in need of supervision (CHINS). Foster home placement provides youths with a substitute family. A stable family environment is believed by the courts to be beneficial in many cases where youths have no consistent adult supervision or are unmanageable or unruly in their own households. In 1996, approximately 3,300 youths were under the supervision of foster homes in state-operated public placement programs (American Correctional Association 2002).

A survey of 266 specialist foster family care programs was conducted in the early 1990s to determine how well these programs were assisting placed juveniles (Galaway et al. 1995). While foster care programs are not directly designed to cater to hardcore delinquents, about half of all foster home placements involved adjudicated delinquent youths. Delinquent youths tended to be slightly older on the average compared with nondelinquent youths who participated in these foster care programs. Furthermore, delinquent youths spent less time in foster care before being released. Recidivism rates among delinquent youths tended to be much lower compared with other delinquent youths placed either on probation or in secure confinement.

Foster home placements are useful in many cases where youths have been apprehended for status offenses. Most families who accept youths into their homes have been investigated by state or local authorities in advance to determine their fitness as foster parents. Socioeconomic factors and home stability are considered important for child placements. Foster parents often typify middle-aged, middle-class citizens with above-average educational backgrounds. Despite these positive features, it is unlikely that foster homes are able to provide the high intensity of adult supervision required by more hardcore juvenile offenders. Further, it is unlikely that these parents can furnish the quality of special treatments that might prove effective in the youth's possible rehabilitation or societal reintegration. Most foster parents simply are not trained as counselors, social workers, or psychologists. For many nonserious youths, however, a home environment, particularly a stable one, has certain therapeutic benefits (Acoca and Austin 1996).

Group Homes and Halfway Houses

Another nonsecure option for juvenile court judges is the assignment of juveniles to **group homes** and **halfway houses.** Placing youths in group homes is considered an intermediate option available to juvenile court judges. Group homes or halfway houses are community-based operations that may be either publicly or privately administered. The notion of a halfway house is frequently used to refer to community homes used by adult parolees recently released from prison. These halfway houses provide a temporary base of operations for parolees as they seek employment and readjustment within their communities. Therefore, they are perceived as transitional residences halfway between incarceration and full freedom of life "on the outside." To many ex-inmates, exposure to unregulated community life is a traumatic transition from the rigidity of prison culture. Many ex-inmates need time to readjust. The rules of halfway houses provide limited structure as well as freedom of access to the outside during the transitory stage (Towberman 1994).

Usually, group homes will have counselors or residents to act as parental figures for youths in groups of ten to twenty. Certain group homes, referred to as family group homes, are actually family-operated, and thus, they are in a sense an extension of foster homes for larger numbers of youths. In group homes, nonsecure supervision of juvenile clients is practiced. About 3,000 youths were in group homes during 2000 (American Correctional Association 2002).

No model or ideal group home exists in the nation to be emulated by all jurisdictions, and what works well for youths in some communities may not be effective in other jurisdictions. However, most successful group homes have strong structural components, where all residents are obligated to participate in relevant program components, where predictable consequences for rule violations are rigorously enforced, and where constant monitoring by staff workers occurs (Kadish et al. 2001). Thus, juveniles have the best of both worlds—they can live in a home-like environment and visit with family and friends in a home setting. Yet they must comply with strict rules governing curfew, program participation, and other court-imposed conditions. In an examination of nine facilities located in five counties in southwestern Pennsylvania, for example, all of the facilities operated under the principles of community-based treatment and relied on behavior modification as the major program. Little victimization occurred, especially where supervision was fairly intensive.

Community centers offer various training programs to assist youths in being more self-sufficient.

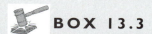

BOX 13.3

Deborah R. Dick
Superintendent, Edna Tamayo Halfway House
Texas Youth Commission

Statistics:

B.S. (psychology), Corpus Christi State University

Background and Interests:

I am currently the Superintendent of the Edna Tamayo Halfway House, which is one of the nine halfway houses operated by the Texas Youth Commission. The youth served at Edna Tamayo House are all male, ranging in ages from 12 to 21 years old, and may have been committed for offenses ranging from burglary to murder. My career with the Texas Youth Commission began in 1982 when I did an internship at the Neuces Halfway House through the Criminal Justice Department at Corpus Christi State University. Once I had completed my internship and received my bachelor's degree in psychology in July 1983, I began my career at that time at Neuces House as a Juvenile Corrections Officer. Since then, I have increased my level of job responsibility by moving up through the agency as a parole officer, case analyst, assistant superintendent of a halfway house, and eventually to my present position as superintendent.

Experiences:

My experiences with the Texas Youth Commission have afforded me the opportunity to sample many different aspects of the criminal justice system. I have had the unique privilege of actually completing each job task associated with all positions in the halfway house. This has enabled me to have a clear understanding of the demands, frustrations, and rewards employees may feel. The halfway house system is designed to assist youth reintegrate into the community via a medium restriction program prior to being released home on parole or alternate placement.

Youths at the Tamayo House are required to attend school if they have not as yet obtained their GED or high school diploma, complete community service hours, and obtain employment. A superintendent of a halfway house is faced with several challenges. First, there is the community challenge—making sure that the youths released will be positive members of the community and follow the law. Second, there are the youth—ensuring their protection and then cultivating their trust in society. Youth who are placed in the halfway house have been in a high-restriction facility and have earned the privilege of transition to a less-restrictive halfway house, prior to the expiration of their minimum length of stay.

Insights I would like to share with anyone wanting a career in corrections are as follows:

1. It is not your typical 9:00 A.M. to 5:00 P.M. job. Be prepared to work on holidays, birthdays, weekends, and not necessarily an eight-hour shift, whenever the need arises. However, the key is to hire trustworthy and competent employees and train them properly. This will limit the need to remain on campus extensively.

2. Never get too comfortable with the youth or clients you serve. Remember why you met them.

3. Just when you think you have experienced everything, that one new experience is right around the corner.

4. This is a tough career. Always remember to take care of yourself physically, mentally, and emotionally.

(continued)

BOX 13.3 (*Continued*)

5. You will have many youths who you work with who will disappoint you. However, just before you begin to wonder why you work in this field, one youth will come along and renew your faith in your career.

6. Last, dealing with the youth or clients is a lot easier than dealing with employees!

Advice to Students:

My advice to you is to complete an internship or volunteer in the field if possible. This will enable you to experience your career choice and give you a picture of what to expect. This is a tough career, but a very rewarding one. You must realize that you cannot help everyone, only those who wish to be helped. Never forget where you have been and where you are when dealing with your career. As an administrator, I try never to forget my days as a juvenile corrections officer. And last, appreciate all of the hard work your employees do for you.

Privately or publicly operated, group homes require juvenile clients to observe the rights of others, participate in various vocational or educational training programs, attend school, participate in therapy or receive prescribed medical treatment, and observe curfew. Urinalyses or other tests may be conducted randomly as checks to see whether juveniles are taking drugs or consuming alcohol contrary to group home policy. If one or more program violations occur, group home officials may report these infractions to juvenile court judges who retain dispositional control over the youths. Assignment to a group home or any other type of confinement is usually for a determinate period.

Positively, group homes provide youths with the companionship of other juveniles. Problem sharing often occurs through planned group discussions, where the subjects might include peer relations in school to suicide prevention. Staff are available to assist youths to secure employment, work certain difficult school problems, and absorb emotional burdens arising from difficult interpersonal relationships. However, these homes are sometimes staffed by community volunteers with little training or experience with youth problems. Certain risks and legal liabilities may be incurred as the result of well-intentioned but bad advice or inadequate assistance (Pratt and Winston 1999). Currently, limited regulations exist among states for how group homes are established and operated (Leon, Dziegielewski, and Tubiak 1999). Training programs for group home staff are scarce in most jurisdictions, and few standards exist relating to staff preparation and qualifications. Therefore, considerable variation exists among group homes relating to the quality of services they can extend to the juveniles they serve (Arthur 2000).

One way that group homes can improve their effectiveness is for staff workers and home administrators to develop associations with various community interests. Kearon (1990) has made several recommendations including the following:

1. Develop a network in every community of voluntary service delivery systems, such as day treatment, nonsecure shelter and group homes, and small, nonsecure institutional care centers.

2. Increase staffing levels in these systems.

3. For the most disturbed and abused youth, who will inevitably escape from a nonsecure setting, establish perimeter-secure facilities.

4. Ensure that authorities intervene with youths at crucial entry points such as bus and railway terminals.

5. Educate youths in facilities about AIDS and at-risk behavior and make voluntary testing available and provide these services as outreach centers to youths still on the streets.

Depending on how youths are screened, some youths are more suited than others for placement under conditions where supervision may be minimal (Schafer 1998). For instance, the Texas Youth Commission operated Independent Living, where selected youths were placed away from home, such as in an apartment, and possibly received some temporary financial support from the Commission (Texas Youth Commission 1990). Some Independent Living youths engaged in new delinquent offenses, but their recidivism rate was low (9 percent). Rearrests where no charges were subsequently placed against youths also yielded a successful result for Independent Living participants. Compared with standard juvenile parolees, who had a 52 percent rearrest rate, Independent Living participants had a rearrest rate of only 33 percent. One factor cited by Texas authorities was the additional trust and confidence in these youths by the Texas Youth Commission, as well as the living and financial support while these youths attended school or looked for work.

Sometimes the simple fact that youths are the subject of an experiment can have a halo effect for them. That is, they may behave well because they know they are being studied. An Intensive Aftercare Probation Program of the Philadelphia Family Court was investigated by Sontheimer, Goodstein, and Kovacevic in 1990. Between December 1988 and January 1990, 90 juveniles were released into this aftercare program and assigned to probation officers with maximum caseloads of 12 youths each. These youths were compared with a control group of juveniles whose probation officers had average caseloads of 90 clients each. While the overall results were not impressive, the more intensively supervised Aftercare Probation Program youths had a rearrest rate of 50 percent compared with a 64 percent rearrest rate of conventionally supervised youthful probationers. The risk-management component was cited as the major factor leading to lower rates of rearrest. Similar successful experiences with intensive supervision of juvenile parolees have been reported elsewhere (Springer 1991).

Missouri Division of Youth Services Aftercare Program. Professionals in the field agree that the ultimate measure of success for residential or institutional treatment programs is the assurance that youths exiting such facilities maintain positive gains and refrain from reoffending or engaging in otherwise problematic behaviors upon return to the community (Glover and Bumby 2001, 68). The Missouri Division of Youth Services has taken some aggressive steps to ensure that youths who go through their juvenile justice system are not simply released and forgotten once they have been punished. The Missouri Division of Youth Services is a subpart of the Department of Social Services. Missouri's approach to juvenile justice includes a balanced focus on rehabilitation and community safety. Thus, Missouri has established various regionally based treatment programs that are designed to serve youths and their families close to home.

Each of these facilities is small, ranging in size from ten to thirty beds. Youths are placed in these facilities in groups of ten in order to provide greater individualized attention to them and their respective needs. A consistent, safe, caring, and structured environment is provided (Glover and Bumby 2001, 69). The services and approaches the Department of Youth Services (DYS) provides include:

1. A continuum of security and programming, ranging from community-based and nonresidential programs, such as alternative living and day treatment, to residential programs, including group homes, and moderate and secure care placements.

2. Comprehensive, standardized needs and risk assessments that enhance classification and placement decisions and facilitate development of individualized treatment plans.

3. An emphasis on individualized psychosocial, educational, and vocational needs.

4. Community-based partnerships for job placement and alternative education.

5. Incorporation of treatment outcome exploration, quality assurance and program reviews to evaluate efficacy and improve service delivery.

6. Demonstrated investment and commitment toward collaboration with local juvenile courts in early intervention and prevention efforts through the provision of more than $6 million for diversionary programs.

7. A singular case management system in which a service coordinator follows each youth throughout his/her tenure with the DYS (Glover and Bumby 2001, 69).

The ultimate goal of the Missouri program is to successfully reintegrate delinquent youths into their communities. The system does this by ensuring that comprehensive and appropriate transitional and aftercare services are delivered. The Missouri aftercare program consists of an indefinite period of time where youths remain on PO caseloads but have already transitioned into the community. The range of services offered to youths includes family therapy, drug and alcohol counseling, general equivalency diploma (GED) preparation, community service, sex offender groups, mentoring services, and college and vocational programming (Glover and Bumby 2001, 71). POs work with individual youths to make sure that they work on meeting program expectations, maintain curfew if imposed, attend school, and perform other responsibilities, such as restitution to victims or community service. The Missouri program includes extensive day treatment programming and a jobs program to assist those youths in need of work and finding it. Considerable emphasis is placed upon family therapy, where entire families are involved in rehabilitation and reintegration. While not all youths who go through the Missouri program complete it successfully, the results thus far are quite favorable. Recidivism rates are lower compared with traditional probation programming, and many youths report successful transition experiences and moral improvement (Glover and Bumby 2001, 75).

Camps, Ranches, Experience Programs, Wilderness Projects

Camps, ranches, or camp ranches are nonsecure facilities that are sometimes referred to as **wilderness experiments** or experience programs (MacKenzie and Wilson 2001). A less expensive alternative to the incarceration of juvenile offenders, even those considered chronic, is participation in experience programs (Gover and MacKenzie 2000; Maryland Governor's Independent Assessment Team 1999). Experience programs include a wide array of outdoor programs designed to improve a juvenile's self-worth, self-concept, pride, and trust in others (Fendrich and Archer 1998).

Three Springs Wilderness School.   In Trenton, Alabama, a wilderness-based residential treatment program was established in the late 1980s (McCord 1995). Screening juveniles was accomplished through interviews with residential counselors and an administration of the Minnesota Multiphasic Personality Inventory (MMPI), a widely used personality assessment device. The MMPI results helped to profile and select 46 juvenile participants. These juveniles were clustered into three groups, according to their MMPI scores. One group was labeled nonconformist. Those in this group exhibited the following characteristics: anger, resentment, passivity-aggressivity, immaturity, and narcissism. A second group, labeled as party animal, tended to exhibit hedonism, extroversion, rule-avoidance, and defiance toward authority. The third group, emotionally disturbed, were primarily distressed. According to the different characteristics exhibited by these three groups, specialized treatments were configured to fit those with particular needs. The results of the treatment experiences were considered positive by staff researchers, indicating that the MMPI might be a useful tool as a means of differentiating between juveniles and their individual needs in subsequent wilderness experiments. These data have received independent support from other research under different treatment conditions (Swenson and Kennedy 1995). In this latter research, scales were used for youth selection including the Child Behavior Checklist, the Multidimensional Measure of Children's Perceptions of Control, the Perceived Contingency Behavioral Domain Scale, and the Piers-Harris Self-Concept Scale.

Appel Program.   In Williamson County, Texas, a wilderness challenge program was created in 1988 (Harris et al. 1993). This program involved weekly two-hour meetings, two one-day sessions, and two half-day sessions held over a twelve-week period. Unlike many of the programs designed for juveniles, the APPEL program was designed to complement other correctional services, particularly those offered by various community supervision agencies. The challenge curriculum has an articulated mission that addresses the documented, underlying problems of a large proportion of youthful community corrections clients. These wilderness treatments are relative low in cost and can be easily adopted by community corrections agencies.

Project Outward Bound.   Another wilderness project, **Project Outward Bound** is one of more than 200 programs of its type in the United States today.

Outward Bound was first introduced in Colorado in 1962 with objectives emphasizing personal survival in the wilderness. Youths participated in various outdoor activities including rock climbing, solo survival, camping, and long-range hiking during a three-week period (Castellano and Soderstrom 1990). Program officials were not concerned with equipping these juveniles with survival skills per se, but rather, they wanted to instill within the participants a feeling of self-confidence and self-assurance to cope with other types of problems in their communities.

Homeward Bound.   A program known as **Homeward Bound** was established in Massachusetts in 1970. Homeward Bound was designed to provide juveniles with mature responsibilities through the acquisition of survival skills and wilderness experiences. A six-week training program subjected 32 youths to endurance training, physical fitness, and performing community service (Claggett et al. 1992). Additionally, officials of the program worked with the boys to develop a release program when they completed the project requirements successfully. During the evenings, the juveniles were given instruction in ecology, search and rescue, and overnight treks.

Toward the end of the program, the boys were subjected to a test—surviving a three-day, three-night trip in the wilderness to prove that each boy had acquired the necessary survival skills. Recidivism rates among these boys were lower than for boys who had been institutionalized in industrial or reform schools. Although these programs serve limited numbers of juveniles and some authorities question their value in deterring further delinquency, some evidence suggests that these wilderness experiences generate less recidivism among participants compared with those youths who are institutionalized in industrial schools under conditions of close custody and monitoring (Claggett et al. 1992).

VisionQuest.   A well-established wilderness program is **VisionQuest,** a private, for-profit enterprise operated from Tucson, Arizona. Currently, VisionQuest operates in about fifteen states, serves about 500 juveniles annually, and is about half of the cost of secure institutionalization (Kohl 1996). Among the various jurisdictions that have used VisionQuest for its juvenile probationers is San Diego County, California (Armstrong et al. 1990).

Juvenile offenders selected for participation in the VisionQuest program in San Diego were secure incarceration-bound offenders with several prior arrests and placements with the California Youth Authority. VisionQuest staff members conducted interviews with certain juveniles who were tentatively selected for inclusion in the program. On the basis of VisionQuest staff recommendations, juvenile court judges would assign these juveniles to VisionQuest, where they would be under an indeterminate disposition of from six months to a year or more (Greenwood 1990).

Peter Greenwood describes the VisionQuest experiences of youths as follows. They immediately find themselves in a rustic type of boot camp environment, where they live in an Indian tepee with six to ten other youths and two junior staff. They sleep on the ground and engage in a strenuous physical fitness program. They complete regular school work. Failure to perform their daily chores adequately results in an immediate confrontation between them and senior staff. They participate in an orientation and outdoor training program, which takes several months to complete. Eventually, they take a wagon train on the back roads of the Western states to Canada, averaging about 24 miles a day, for four to six months. All the while, they are given increased responsibilities, including breaking horses that VisionQuest acquires annually. Eventually, they attend the VisionQuest group home in Arizona where it is determined whether they can be reintegrated into their communities (Greenwood 1990, 20–21).

SECURE CONFINEMENT: VARIATIONS

Shock Probation

Shock probation is an intermediate punishment where offenders are initially disposed to incarcerative terms; after a period of time, between 90 and 180 days, youths are removed from secure confinement and obligated to serve the remainder of their disposition on probation. The actual term, shock probation, was coined by Ohio authorities in 1964. Shock probation is also known as **shock parole,** because it technically involves a release from jail or prison after serving some amount of time in incarceration (MacKenzie and Wilson 2001).

Sometimes shock probation is used synonymously with **combination sentences** or **split sentences.** Other terms, such as **intermittent sentences, mixed sentences,** or **jail as a condition of probation,** are also used interchangeably with shock probation, although they have somewhat different meanings. Combination sentences or split sentences occur whenever judges sentence offenders to a term, a portion of which includes incarceration and a term of which includes probation. Mixed sentences occur whenever offenders have been convicted of two or more offenses and judges sentence them to separate sentences for each conviction offense. Intermittent sentences occur whenever judges sentence offenders to terms such as weekend confinement only. Jail as a condition of probation is a sentence that prescribes a specified amount of jail incarceration prior to serving the remainder of the sentence on probation (Gover and MacKenzie 2000).

Technically, shock probation is none of these. Youths disposed to shock probation don't know they have received such dispositions. The judge disposes them to incarceration. The youths have no way of knowing that within three or four months, they will be yanked out of incarceration, brought before the same judge, and disposed to probation. This new probationary disposition is contingent upon their good behavior while they are incarcerated. Thus, they are shocked or traumatized by their incarceration. When they are redisposed to probation later, they should be sufficiently shocked to avoid further offending. But recidivism figures suggest it doesn't always work that way.

Shock probation is a misnomer in a sense. If we recall that probation is a disposition in lieu of incarceration, then it seems peculiar to incarcerate these offenders first, and then release them later and call them probationers. This practice is more accurately shock parole, since these are previously incarcerated offenders who are resentenced to a supervised release program. But also since a parole board does not grant them parole, we are uncertain about what they should be called other than shock probationers. In any case, the intended effect of incarceration is to scare offenders sufficiently so that they refrain from reoffending. Simply, their incarcerative experiences are so shocking that they don't want to face further incarceration (Maryland Governor's Independent Assessment Team 1999).

Shock probation is sometimes erroneously compared with **Scared Straight,** a New Jersey program implemented in the late 1970s. Scared Straight sought to frighten samples of hardcore delinquent youths by having them confront inmates in a Rahway, New Jersey, prison. Inmates would yell at and belittle them, calling them names, cursing, and yelling. Inmates would tell them about sexual assaults and other prison unpleasantries in an attempt to get them to refrain from reoffending. However, the program was unsuccessful (Finckenauer and Gavin 1999). Despite early favorable reports of recidivism rates of less than 20 percent, the actual rate of recidivism among these participating youths was considerably higher. Furthermore, another control group not exposed to Scared Straight had a lower recidivism rate.

Boot Camps

The juvenile version of shock probation or **shock incarceration** is perhaps best exemplified by juvenile **boot camps** (MacKenzie and Wilson 2001). Also known as the **Army model,** boot camp programs are patterned after basic training for new military recruits. Juvenile offenders are given a taste of hard military life, and such regimented activities and structure for up to 180 days are often sufficient to shock them into giving up their lives of delinquency or crime and staying out of jail (Gover and MacKenzie 2000). Boot camp programs in various states have been established, including the Regimented Inmate Discipline program in Mississippi, the **About Face** program in Louisiana, and the shock incarceration program in Georgia. These are paramilitary-type programs that emphasize strict military discipline and physical training

What Are Boot Camps?   Boot camps are highly regimented, military-style, short-term correctional programs (90 to 180 days) where offenders are provided with strict discipline, physical training, and hard labor resembling some as-

Boot camps stress physical exercise as part of a rigorous rehabilitative regimen.

pects of military basic training. When successfully completed, boot camps provide for transfers of participants to community-based facilities for nonsecure supervision. By 1993, boot camps had been formally established in over half of the states (Florida Office of Program Policy Analysis 1995). In 1995, there were thirty-five federal and state boot camps being operated, with a total of 9,304 inmate-clients. Of these, there were 626 females. Of the 9,304 inmate-clients, 455 were juvenile offenders distributed throughout nine locally operated programs (Bourque, Han, and Hill 1996:3). By 1996 there were forty-eight residential boot camps for adjudicated juveniles operating in twenty-seven states (MacKenzie et al. 2001:1).

Some persons regard boot camps as the latest correctional reform (Styve et al. 2000). Other professionals are skeptical about their success potential (Zachariah 2002). Much depends upon how particular boot camps are operated and for how long. Boot camp programs are operated for as short a time as 30 days or as long as 180 days. While boot camps were officially established in 1983 by the Georgia Department of Corrections Special Alternative Incarceration (SAI), the general idea for boot camps originated some time earlier in late 1970s, also in Georgia (MacKenzie et al. 2001).

The Rationale for Boot Camps. Boot camps have been established as an alternative to long-term traditional incarceration. Austin, Jones, and Bolyard outline a brief rationale for boot camps:

1. A substantial number of youthful first-time offenders now incarcerated will respond to a short but intensive period of confinement followed by a longer period of intensive community supervision.

2. These youthful offenders will benefit from a military-type atmosphere that instills a sense of self-discipline and physical conditioning that was lacking in their lives.

3. These same youths need exposure to relevant educational, vocational training, drug treatment, and general counseling services to develop more positive and law-abiding values and become better prepared to secure legitimate future employment.

4. The costs involved will be less than a traditional criminal justice sanction that imprisons the offender for a substantially longer period of time (Austin, Jones, and Bolyard, 1993:1).

Boot Camp Goals. Boot camps have several general goals, including:

1. To provide rehabilitation and reintegration. In 1986, the Orleans (Louisiana) Parish Prison System established a boot camp program called About Face (Caldas 1990). This program sought to improve offenders' sense of purpose, self-discipline, self-control, and self-confidence through physical conditioning, educational programs, and social skills training, all within the framework of strict military discipline. One early criticism of this Louisiana program was the amount of inexperience among boot camp staff. Over time, however, this criticism was minimized (MacKenzie and Shaw 1993, 463–466).

2. To provide discipline. Boot camps are designed to improve discipline. Certain boot camps, especially those aimed at younger offenders, must

Boot camps are based on the military model to instill discipline and respect for authority.

deal with adjudicated juvenile offenders who usually resist authority and refuse to listen or learn in traditional classroom or treatment environments (MacKenzie and Wilson 2001). Physical conditioning and structure are most frequently stressed in these programs. But most boot camp programs also include educational elements pertaining to literacy, academic and vocational education, intensive value clarification, and resocialization (Styve et al. 2000).

3. To promote deterrence. The sudden immersion of convicted offenders into a military-style atmosphere is a frightening experience for many participants. The rigorous approach to formal rules and authority was a challenging dimension of boot camp programs for most participants (Shaw and MacKenzie 1992). Mack (1992:63–65) reports that of the many clients who have participated in the Rikers Boot Camp High Impact Incarceration Program (HIIP), only 23 percent have recidivated compared with 28 percent of those released from traditional incarceration. While these recidivism rate differences are not substantial, the direction of the difference says something about the potential deterrent value of boot camp programs.

4. To ease prison and jail overcrowding. Boot camps are believed to have a long-term impact on jail and prison overcrowding. Theoretically, this is possible because of the low recidivism rates among boot camp participants. The short-term nature of confinement in boot camp programs with the participant's subsequent return to the community helps to ease the overcrowding problem in correctional settings. It is believed that boot camp experiences are significant in creating more positive attitudes among participants (Gover and MacKenzie 2000).

5. To provide vocational and rehabilitative services. An integral feature of most boot camp programs is the inclusion of some form of educational and/or vocational training. A New York Shock Incarceration program makes it possible for participants to work on GED diplomas and provides elementary educational instruction (New York State Department of Correctional Services 1992). Educational training is also a key feature of

IMPACT, or **Intensive Motivational Program of Alternative Correctional Treatment** in Louisiana jurisdictions. As an alternative to traditional incarceration, boot camps do much to promote greater social and educational adjustment for clients reentering their communities.

Profiling Boot Camp Participants.   Who can participate in boot camps or shock incarceration programs? Participants may or may not be able to enter or withdraw from boot camps voluntarily. It depends on the particular program. Most boot camp participants are prison-bound youthful offenders convicted of less serious, nonviolent crimes, and who have never been previously incarcerated (Zachariah 2002).

Participants may either be referred to these programs by judges or corrections departments or they may volunteer. They may or may not be accepted, and if they complete their programs successfully, they may or may not be released under supervision into their communities. Screening of boot camp participants is extremely important. For instance, a boot camp program in California, LEAD, sponsored by the California Youth Authority, conducted screenings for 365 eligible juveniles during 1992–1993. Only 180 were admitted into the LEAD program, while only 107 graduated successfully and were granted parole after four months (Bottcher and Isorena 1994).

Representative Boot Camps.   Several boot camps described below are indicative of the general nature of boot camps in the various states that have them.

The Camp Monterey Shock Incarceration Facility.   New York State has a major boot camp project with the following features:

Boot camps offer useful vocational training as well as educational opportunities.

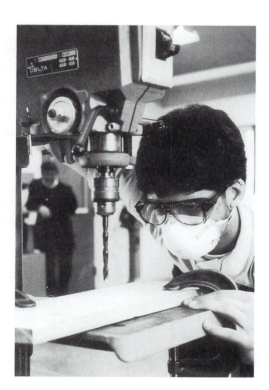

1. It accommodates 250 participants in minimum-security institution.
2. It has 131 staff (83 custody positions).
3. Participants are screened and must meet statutory criteria; three-fourths volunteer; one-third of applicants are rejected.
4. Inmates form platoons and live in open dormitories.
5. Successful program completion leads to parole board releases to an intensive probation supervision program called "aftershock."
6. Programs include physical training, drill, and eight hours daily of hard labor.
7. Inmates must participate in therapeutic community meetings, compulsory adult basic education courses, mandatory individual counseling, and mandatory recreation.
8. All must attend alcohol and substance abuse treatment.
9. All must participate in job seeking skills training and re-entry planning.

The Oklahoma Regimented Inmate Discipline Program (RID). Oklahoma has a **Regimented Inmate Discipline Program (RID)** with the following features:

1. 145-bed facility at the Lexington Assessment and Reception Center; also houses 600 long-term general population inmates as medium security.
2. Offenders screened according to statutory criteria and may volunteer.
3. Inmates living in single or double-bunk cells.
4. Strict discipline, drill, physical training; housekeeping and institutional maintenance.
5. Six hours daily of in educational/vocational programs.
6. Drug abuse programs, individual and group counseling.
7. Subsequently, participant resentencing by judges to intensive supervised probation or "community custody," perhaps commencing at a halfway house.

The Georgia Special Alternative Program (SAI). This program includes the following characteristics:

1. This is a program for male offenders.
2. Judges control selection process, and SAI is a "condition of probation"; if successful, boot camp graduates are released, since judges do not ordinarily resentence them to probation.
3. The program includes physical training, drill, hard work; two exercise and drill periods daily, with eight-hour hard labor periods in between.
4. Participants perform limited community services.
5. There is little emphasis on counseling or treatment.
6. Inmates do receive drug abuse education and information about sexually transmitted diseases.
7. Inmates are double-bunked in two 25-cell units at Dodge, and at Burris, 100 inmates are single-bunked in four 25-cell units (MacKenzie, Shaw, and Gowdy 1993).

Because many of these boot camp programs have been established since about the late 1980s and early 1990s, extensive evaluation research about general boot camp program effectiveness has not been abundant (Zachariah 2002). However, indications from available research are that boot camps generally are effective at reducing recidivism among participants. Currently, some states, such as Georgia, report relatively high rates of recidivism among boot camp clientele, whereas New York and Oklahoma have much lower recidivism rates. Besides reducing recidivism, boot camps might also be effective at saving taxpayers money over time. For various states, operating boot camps is considerably cheaper than using traditional incarceration for particular offenders. In some instances, the cost savings is considerable.

PERSISTENT PROBLEMS OF NONSECURE AND SECURE CONFINEMENT

Secure juvenile incarcerative facilities in the United States are known by various names. Further, not all of these secure confinement facilities are alike. While many institutions provide only custodial services for chronic or more serious juvenile offenders, other incarcerative facilities offer an array of services and treatments, depending upon the diverse needs of the juveniles confined. Clarifying the mission and goals of corrections agencies helps staff to do a better job supervising youthful clientele. Institutional rules tend to be couched in a more meaningful context, and incarcerated youth are able to cope more effectively with their confinement (Butts and Adams 2001).

Architecture and Officer Training

In recent years, however, numerous improvements have been made generally in the overall quality of juvenile secure confinement facilities throughout the United States. Evidence of improvement in juvenile corrections is the massive efforts made by authorities in numerous jurisdictions to design and build more adequately equipped juvenile facilities that minimize youthful inmate problems of idle time and overcrowding. Private interests, including the Corrections Corporation of America, have assisted as well in providing more modern designs and plant operations for secure juvenile facilities in various states such as California and Tennessee (Mendel 2001).

Besides constructing more attractive physical plants in which to house hardcore offenders, juvenile corrections planners have also made efforts to improve the quality of all levels of the staff who administer and supervise juvenile inmates. Entering juveniles exhibit a myriad of personal and social problems. Some youths are psychologically disturbed and suicidal. Others are distinctly antisocial and violent. Correctional officers at these facilities must be prepared for virtually any behavior that might arise (Altschuler and Armstrong 2001). In an effort to prepare correctional officers to cope with various types of inmate problems, several local and national organizations have established training courses to heighten an officer's awareness of problems and skills to deal with them. Santa Clara County (San Jose), California, has one of the largest direct supervision jails in the nation. It has over 4,500 bookings per month, as well as at least 600 psychiatric referrals. A portion of these bookings and referrals are juveniles. Recognizing that staff training should be a major priority, administrators from the Custody and Mental Health Services established a training experience for officers, including classes in suicide identification and intervention, psychiatric illnesses, management of assaultive behavior, and communication skills (Quinlan and Motte 1990, 22–23).

In Tacoma, Washington, Pierce County Sheriff Raymond A. Fjetland has developed a program, the Master Correctional Officer Program, which is designed to increase the performance of staff correctional officers for future roles within the corrections division (Tess and Bogue 1988, 66). The program includes three stages, the entry level, the senior level, and the master level. Officers must accumulate points in various educational and on-the-job training areas, including weapons qualification, comprehensive written examinations, and frequent performance evaluations. Thus, Sheriff Fjetland has helped to establish a program that provides officer incentives to advance as well as to acquire more effective skills to deal with offenders of all types and ages. Greater professionalism, expertise, and productivity are the outcomes of this innovative continuous motivator program.

Both male and female correctional officers are targeted for additional training to cope with inmate problems. Formerly, it has been alleged by some critics that female correctional officers tend to lack the same degree of authority of their male officer counterparts when dealing with inmates. However, programs such as on-the-job training and self-improvement courses sponsored and conducted by the American Correctional Association have done much to improve correctional officer credibility and performance. According to ACA standards, correctional officers should have at least 160 hours of orientation and training during their first year of employment. Certification is awarded after satisfactorily completing the ACA training course (American Correctional Association 2002; Jurich, Casper, and Hull 2001).

Juvenile Detention Resource Centers

The U.S. Department of Justice's Office of Juvenile Justice and Delinquency Prevention (OJJDP) promulgated specific guidelines for all juvenile detention facilities in the early 1980s. These guidelines were published as *Guidelines for the Development of Policies and Procedures for Juvenile Detention Facilities.* The goal of the OJJDP was to establish national juvenile detention resource centers around the United States in various jurisdictions that would provide information, technical assistance, and training to juvenile detention professionals who wished to participate (Criswell 1987, 22). The ultimate aim of these juvenile detention centers was to provide juveniles with better and more adequate services and assistance (Matson, Bretl, and Wolf 2000). Such **detention centers** have done much to improve juvenile incarceration standards throughout the nation. The ACA has been actively involved in assisting different jurisdictions in their efforts to establish juvenile detention resource centers and operate them successfully (Russell 2001). The educational dimension of such centers can assist in transmitting knowledge about communicable diseases, such as AIDS, and inform adolescents about the risks of sexual misconduct. Other positive contributions of these centers might be to assist youths in managing their anger and providing them with opportunities to improve their general mental health (Butts and Adams 2001).

Short- and Long-Term Facilities

Secure juvenile confinement facilities in the United States are either short-term or long-term. Short-term confinement facilities are designed to accommodate juveniles on a temporary basis. These juveniles are either awaiting a later juvenile court adjudication, subsequent foster home or group home placement, or a transfer to criminal court. Whether a juvenile is held for a period of time in detention depends upon the outcome of a **detention hearing,** where the appropriateness of the detention is determined.

Sometimes youths will be placed in short-term confinement because their identity is unknown and it is desirable that they should not be confined in adult lockups or jails. Other youths are violent and must be detained temporarily until more appropriate placements may be made. The designations short-term and long-term may range from a few days to several years, although the average duration of **long-term detention** across all offender categories nationally is about six to seven months. The average short-term incarceration in public facilities for juveniles is about 30 days (Maguire and Pastore 2002).

Some **short-term confinement** is preventive detention or pretrial detention, where juveniles are awaiting formal adjudicatory proceedings. While some authorities question the legality of jailing juveniles or holding them in detention centers prior to their cases being heard by juvenile court judges, the U.S. Supreme Court has upheld the constitutionality of pretrial or preventive detention of juveniles, especially dangerous ones, in the case of *Schall v. Martin* (1984). One objective of pretrial detention is to prevent certain dangerous juveniles from committing new pretrial crimes. Juvenile court judges must make a determination of whether certain juveniles should be held in pretrial detention or released into the custody of parents or guardians. While their discretion is not perfect, many juvenile court judges exercise good judgment in determining which juveniles should be temporarily detained.

Fagan and Guggenheim (1996) studied juvenile court judge discretion with two groups of juveniles—one group consisting of a cohort of 69 juveniles predicted to be dangerous, requiring custody but were released, and a control group of 64 other juveniles. A sample of juvenile court judges predicted which juveniles from the two groups would have the greatest likelihood of being rearrested prior to their trials. Judges predicted with 40 percent accuracy which juveniles would be rearrested and who were actually rearrested. However, they made a high rate of false positive predictions. Sixty percent of those determined to be dangerous by these judges and who were predicted to reoffend did not commit new offenses prior to their trials. Eighty-five percent of the control group did not reoffend either. Thus, the study showed that some ambiguity existed about the criteria that should be used for dangerousness forecasts made by juvenile court judges.

Some Criticisms of Incarcerating Juveniles

There are numerous proponents and opponents of juvenile secure confinement of any kind. Those favoring incarceration cite the disruption of lifestyle and separation from other delinquent youths as a positive dimension. For example, youths who have been involved with delinquent gangs or friends who engage in frequent law-breaking would probably benefit from incarceration, since these unfavorable associations would be interrupted or terminate (Fried and Reppucci 2001). Of course, juveniles can always return to their old ways when released from incarceration. There is nothing the juvenile justice system can do to prevent these reunions. But at least the pattern of interaction that contributed to the delinquent behavior initially is temporarily interrupted.

Another argument favoring incarceration of juveniles is that long-term secure confinement is a deserved punishment for their actions. This is consistent with the just-deserts philosophy that seems to typify contemporary thinking about juvenile punishment. There is a noticeable trend away from thinking about the best interests of youths and toward thinking about ways to make them more accountable for their actions. This shift has prompted debate among juvenile justice scholars about the true functions of juvenile courts and the ultimate aims of the sanctions they impose (Feld 2001).

For some critics, the question of whether juvenile incarceration is rehabilitative is irrelevant. The fact is, juvenile incarceration restricts a juvenile's mobility and is seen as a deterrent to delinquent conduct. We don't know for sure how much of a deterrent effect is achieved through incarcerating juveniles. But incarceration does suffice as a punishment. If juveniles break the law, they should be punished. Thus, incarceration may be viewed as a form of retribution. Some types of screening mechanisms seem fruitful for targeting particular youths for special treatments. The Juvenile Justice Assessment Instrument (JJAI) has been used successfully in selected jurisdictions in order to determine the best treatment and interventions while youths are confined (Stein, Lewis and Yeager 1993). Areas measured by the JJAI include the offense; aggressive acts; use of weapons; chronology of living situations; school history; family medical, psychiatric, and behavioral history; social history; sexual abuse; physical abuse and witnessing family violence; psychiatric history; psychomotor/dissociative symptoms; medical/neurological history; and scars.

Opponents to long-term secure confinement of juveniles believe, among other things, that there are possibly adverse labeling effects from confinement with other offenders. Thus, juveniles might acquire labels of themselves as ju-

Secure confinement is most often reserved for the most serious youthful offenders.

venile delinquents and persist in reoffending when released from incarceration later. However, it might be maintained that if they are incarcerated, they know they are delinquents anyway. Will they necessarily acquire stronger self-definitions of delinquents beyond those they already possess? In some respects, it is status-enhancing for youthful offenders to have been confined in some joint or juvenile secure confinement facility, so that they may brag to others about their experiences later. No doubt, confinement of any kind will add at least one dimension to a person's reputation as a delinquent offender among other offenders in the community.

Most of the successful incarcerative programs for juveniles have built-in educational and vocational components, many of which are voluntary (Houchins 2001). It seems to make a difference whether confined juveniles are forced to take vocational or educational courses or whether they can enroll in such programs on a voluntary basis (Kadish et al. 2001). For example, a literacy program in the South Carolina Department of Youth Services was investigated in 1990–1991. The sample consisted of 415 participants enrolled in the General Educational Development (GED) program. While few differences were exhibited between those forced to enroll in this program and those who voluntarily entered it, the volunteers seemed to make a better adjustment in a subsequent follow-up program evaluation (U.S. General Accounting Office 1996a). Providing needed psychological and medical services also seems to make a difference in those institutions managing hardcore offenders. Some evidence also supports efforts to intervene in offense-specific matters such as sex crimes for qualified juveniles (Tsytsarev, Manger, and Lodrini 2000).

In the state of Washington, for example, juveniles as young as 14 may be sent to the Department of Corrections (Fleming and Winkler 1999, 132). However, separate housing units are provided for more youthful offenders before they are placed in the general inmate population. Washington officials have established a number of successful multidisciplinary, psychological, and case management programs to treat incarcerated youths. Juveniles are exposed to an offense cycle group, where they are taught to think critically about their crimes and what led up to their behaviors. They also receive anger management training, victim awareness experience, social skills, assertiveness skills, problem-solving activities, and cognitive-behavioral awareness. They are compelled to follow a mandatory dress code and maintain a healthy regimen of exercise. Whether these youths want this training and exposure or not, they must have it. These services are believed beneficial to their law-abiding behavior in future years.

Other arguments suggest that the effects of imprisonment on a juvenile's self-image and propensity to commit new offenses are negligible (Fried and Reppucci 2001). Thus, incarceration as a punishment may be the primary result, without any tangible, long-range benefits such as self-improvement or reduction in recidivism. At least there does not appear to be any consistent or reliable evidence that detaining juveniles automatically causes them to escalate to more serious offenses or to become adult criminals. According to some analysts, the peak ages of juvenile criminality fall between the sixteenth and twentieth birthdays, with participation rates falling off rapidly. Thus, incarceration for a fixed period may naturally ease the delinquency rate, at least for some of the more chronic offenders. Some opponents note that racial, ethnic, and gender factors are more operative in secure confinement decisions than legal factors (Wooldredge et al. 1994).

Despite how many youths are incarcerated, however, there is little disagreement that more juveniles are incarcerated than need to be incarcerated (Levinson and Greene 1999). Observers estimate that at least half of all currently incarcerated youths could be released with little fear for community safety or further recidivism (U.S. General Accounting Office 1996a).

One program that appears to have promise as a deterrent to further delinquency has been pioneered in Missouri. It is called the Missouri Intensive Case Monitoring System (Onek 1994). In 1994 there were five programs in various Department of Youth Services regions throughout Missouri. In 1991, 215 youths were tracked by researchers at Southeastern Missouri State University. Each delinquent youth was paired with a college student to act as an intensive case monitor. Participating youths benefited in various ways from the closeness of the monitoring, together with the valuable assistance, frequent contact, and mentoring of older college students. At the same time, criminal justice students who participated as mentors benefited as well from the real-world experience of assisting juvenile delinquents. Thus, a very cost-effective alternative was created and proved successful as an alternative to out-of-home placements.

Example of Residential Failure

Not all residential programs for juveniles are successful. One such program was operated for a brief period in Kane County, Illinois, under the direction of the Court Services Department. The Kane County Youth Home was established and designed to house up to nine male delinquents, aged 13 through 17, who had been previously adjudicated delinquent and deemed in need of intensive services that could not be provided otherwise on an outpatient basis (Kearney 1994). The program failed because the essential balance between safety and trust could not be achieved. Staff workers could not be hired, trained, or evaluated primarily as residential treatment workers. The program director, court service hierarchy, and child care workers' theory and philosophy of change contrasted dramatically with the therapists' philosophy. Thus, the program philosophy itself was self-contradictory. Through no fault of their own, the youths served by the program were destined to "fail," simply because the administrators and practitioners could not agree on which philosophy should govern the youths' treatment. Kearney has observed that in order to be successful, such programs should have the following three essential components: (1) they must have a consistent philosophy of management shared by all participants; (2) persons should be hired and trained according to that philosophy; and (3) administration of the program should be consonant with the program philosophy, including any changes introduced into program operations. Thus, the program itself was probably workable. However, staff disagreements about how best to implement the program led to its demise.

Example of Program Success

Kent State University's Department of Criminal Justice established a Juvenile Justice Assistants Program in December 1990 (Babb and Kratcoski 1994). The goals of the program were to maximize the community-based treatment potential for unruly, delinquent, or victimized youths. To ensure the effectiveness of this program, program coordinators screened prospective employees in recruitment, training, and placement over a one-year period. About 45 juvenile justice assistants were hired and devoted a minimum of 200 hours to juvenile courts and justice agencies in a five-county area.

During the first eighteen months of the program, 69 assistants were assigned to placement agencies for further training, together with service to the agency and its clients. Ultimately, more than 11,400 hours of training and service had been completed in approximately 25 agencies. Students involved in the program were able to assist numerous clientele during this same period. Thus, a successful internship/field experience was converted into a meaningful assistance program with juvenile justice assistants. A director oversaw the project and ensured that all program goals were consistent and implemented evenly. Any staff–client problems were dealt with immediately. Equitable solutions were found. The study yielded little recidivism among participating clientele during a follow-up period.

JUVENILE PAROLE

Juvenile Parole Defined

Parole for juveniles is similar to parole for adult offenders. Those juveniles who have been detained in various institutions for long periods may be released prior to serving their full sentences. Generally, parole is a conditional supervised release from incarceration granted to youths who have served a portion of their original sentences (Archwamety and Katsiyannis 2000). They are known as **parolees.**

Purposes of Parole for Juveniles

The general purposes of parole are:

1. To reward good behavior while youths have been detained.
2. To alleviate overcrowding.
3. To permit youths to become reintegrated back into their communities and enhance their rehabilitation potential.
4. To deter youths from future offending by ensuring their continued supervision under juvenile parole officers.

Some authorities also believe that the prospect of earning parole might induce greater compliance to institutional rules among incarcerated youths. Also, parole is seen by some persons as a continuation of the juvenile's punishment, since parole programs are most often conditional in nature (e.g., observance of curfew, school attendance, staying out of trouble, periodic drug and alcohol urinalyses, participation in counseling programs, and vocational and educational training). Many juvenile justice professionals agree that early-release decision making should not necessarily be automatic. Rather, releases should be based upon a well-defined mission, strategy, and a matching continuum of care, which might also include assorted aftercare enhancements (Lewis and Howard 2000).

Minnesota Department of Corrections

JUVENILE PAROLE AGREEMENT

WHEREAS, it appears to the Commissioner of Corrections that

_____
(NAME)

☐ presently in custody at _____, and

☐ presently on parole, and

WHEREAS, the said Commissioner, after careful consideration, believes that parole at

this time is in the best interests of this said individual and the public.

Now, THEREFORE, be it known that the Commissioner of Corrections, under authority

vested by law,   ☐ grants parole to,

☐ continues parole for,   _____
(NAME)

and does authorize his/her release from the institution with the parole plan which has been

approved. Upon being paroled and released he/she shall be and remain in legal custody and

under the control of the Commissioner of Corrections subject to the rules, regulations, and

conditions of this parole as set forth on the reverse side of this agreement.

Signed this_____day of_____19_____.

**COMMISSIONER OF CORRECTIONS
BY:**

_____
(HEARING OFFICER)

DISTRIBUTION:
Original—Central Office
2nd Copy—Parolee
3rd Copy—Agent
4th Copy—Inst. File
CR-00100-03

☐ New Parole Agreement

☐ Restructured Parole Agreement

FIGURE 13.1 Juvenile parole agreement

A standard parole agreement from the Minnesota Department of Corrections for juveniles is shown in Figure 13.1. Notice that this agreement specifies that the particular juvenile must remain in the legal custody and control of the Commissioner of Corrections "subject to the rules, regulations, and conditions of this parole as set forth on the reverse side of this agreement." While the reverse side of this agreement is not shown here, this reverse side provides sufficient space for the juvenile parole board to specify one or more program conditions, such as mandatory attendance at vocational/educational training schools, therapy or counseling, community service, restitution orders, or fine payments and maintenance fees. The parole plan is actually a continuation of the youth's punishment.

Often, the public thinks that if the youth is free from custody, he or she is completely unrestricted. This is not true. Both probation and parole are considered punishments. The behavioral conditions specified under either parole or probation may be very restrictive. Also, it is ordinarily the case that juvenile probation/parole officers have unlimited access to the premises where the youth is located. This intrusion by parole officers is unrestricted so that if youths are using drugs or in possession of illegal contraband, it can be detected by surprise, through an unannounced visit from an officer at any time of the day or night.

How Many Juveniles Are on Parole?

The American Correctional Association (2002) estimates that over 24,000 juveniles were in nonsecure, state-operated halfway houses and other community-based facilities in 2000. Also, there were over 90,000 youths in secure institutions and training schools. It has been estimated that approximately 6,000 youths were under other forms of state-controlled supervision as parolees, although no precise figures are available.

Characteristics of Juvenile Parolees

Selected studies of juvenile parolees indicate that a majority are male, black and between 17 and 19 years of age (Maguire and Pastore 2002). Some jurisdictions, such as New York, have **juvenile offender laws.** These laws define 13-, 14-, 15-, and 16-year-olds as adults under certain conditions, whenever they are charged with committing specified felonies. They may be tried as adults and convicted. When they are subsequently released from institutionalization, they are placed under adult parole supervision. Many other jurisdictions do not have such juvenile offender laws but have waiver or transfer provisions for particularly serious juvenile offenders.

Juvenile parolees share many of the same programs used to supervise youthful probationers. Intensive supervised probation programs are used for both probationers and parolees in many jurisdictions. Further, juvenile parole officers often perform dual roles as juvenile parole officers as they supervise both types of offenders.

Juvenile Parole Policy

Between November 1987 and November 1988, Ashford and LeCroy (1993, 186) undertook an investigation of the various state juvenile parole programs and provisions. They sent letters and questionnaires to all state juvenile jurisdictions, soliciting any available information on their juvenile paroling policies. Their response rate was 94 percent, with forty-seven of the fifty states responding. One interesting result of their survey was the development of a typology of juvenile parole. Ashford and LeCroy discovered eight different kinds of juvenile parole used more or less frequently among the states. These were listed as follows:

1. Determinate parole (length of parole is linked closely with the period of commitment specified by the court; paroling authorities cannot extend confinement period of juvenile beyond original commitment length prescribed by judge; juvenile can be released short of serving the full sentence).

2. Determinate parole set by administrative agency (parole release date is set immediately following youth's arrival at secure facility).

3. Presumptive minimum with limits on the extension of the supervision period for a fixed or determinate length of time (minimum confinement period is specified, and youth must be paroled after that date unless there is a showing of bad conduct).

4. Presumptive minimum with limits on the extension of supervision for an indeterminate period (parole should terminate after fixed period of time; parole period is indeterminate, where PO has discretion to extend parole period with justification; parole length can extend until youth reaches age of majority and leaves juvenile court jurisdiction).

5. Presumptive minimum with discretionary extension of supervision for an indeterminate period (same as 4 except PO has discretion to extend parole length of juvenile with no explicit upper age limit; lacks explicit standards limiting the extension of parole).

6. Indeterminate parole with a specified maximum and a discretionary minimum length of supervision (follows Model Juvenile Court Act of 1968, providing limits for confinement but allows parole board authority to specify length of confinement and period of supervised release within these limits).

7. Indeterminate parole with legal minimum and maximum periods of supervision (parole board is vested with vast power to parole youths at any time with minimum and maximum confinement periods; more liberal than 1 and 2 above).

8. Indeterminate or purely discretionary parole (length of parole unspecified; may maintain youths on parole until youths reach the age of majority; at this time, parole is discontinued; may release youths from parole at any time during this period) (Ashford and LeCroy 1993, 187–191). The most popular parole type is 8; the least popular is 1.

Deciding Who Should Be Paroled

The decision to parole particular juveniles is left to different agencies and bodies, depending upon the jurisdiction. In most state jurisdictions, the dispositions imposed are indeterminate (Josi and Sechrest 1999). In thirty-two states, early-release decisions are left up to the particular juvenile correction agency, whereas six states use parole boards exclusively, and five other states depend upon the original sentencing judge's decision. Only a few states had determinate sentencing schemes for youthful offenders, and therefore, their early release would be established by statute in much the same way as it is for adult offenders.

In New Jersey, for instance, a seven-member parole board appointed by the governor grants early release to both adult and juvenile inmates. In Utah, a Youth Parole Authority exists, which is a part-time board consisting of three citizens and four staff members from the Utah Division of Youth Corrections. Ideally, paroling authorities utilize objective decision-making criteria in determining which youths should be released short of serving their full incarcerative terms. Often discrepancies exist between what the paroling authority actually does and what it is supposed to do. Thus, some criticisms have been to the effect that the primary early-release criteria are related to one's former institutional behavior rather than to other factors, such as one's prospects for successful adaptation to community life, employment, and participation in educational or vocational programs (Cavender and Knepper 1992).

Many parole boards for both adults and juveniles are comprised of persons who make subjective judgments about inmates on the basis of many factors beyond so-called objective criteria. Predispositional reports prepared by juvenile probation officers, records of institutional behavior, a youth's appearance and demeanor during the parole hearing, and the presence of witnesses or victims may exert unknown impacts upon individual parole board members. Parole decision making is not an exact science. Where elements of subjectivity intrude into the decision making process, a juvenile's rights are seemingly undermined. Thus, parole board decision making profiles in various jurisdictions may exhibit evidence of early-release disparities attributable to racial, ethnic, gender, or socioeconomic factors.

RECIDIVISM AND PAROLE REVOCATION

Parole revocation is the termination of a parole program, usually for one or more program violations. When a parole is terminated, regardless of who does the terminating, there are several possible outcomes. One is that the offender will be returned to secure confinement. This is the most severe result. A less harsh alternative is that offenders will be shifted to a different kind of parole program. For instance, if a juvenile is assigned to a halfway house as a part of the parole program, the rules of the halfway house must be observed. If one or more rules are violated, such as failing to observe curfew, failing drug or alcohol urinalyses, or committing new offenses, a report is filed with the court or the juvenile corrections authority for possible revocation action. If it is decided later that parole should be terminated, the result may be to place the offender under house arrest or home confinement, coupled with electronic monitoring. Thus, the juvenile would be required to wear an electronic wristlet or anklet and remain on the premises for specified periods. Other program conditions would be applied as well. The fact is that one is not automatically returned to incarceration following a **parole revocation hearing.**

Usually, if a return to incarceration is not indicated, the options available to judges, parole boards, or others are limited only by the array of supervisory resources in the given jurisdiction. These options ordinarily involve more intensive supervision or monitoring of offender behaviors. Severe overcrowding in many juvenile incarcerative facilities discourages revocation action that would return large numbers of offenders to industrial schools or youth centers. Intermediate punishments, therefore, function well to accommodate larger numbers of serious offenders, including those who have their parole revoked (Visher, Lattimore, and Linster 1991).

The process of parole revocation for juveniles is not as clear-cut as it is for adult offenders. The U.S. Supreme Court has not ruled thus far concerning how juvenile parole revocation actions should be completed. Furthermore, very little is known about the actual numbers of juveniles who are paroled annually. Reliable statistical information about the extent of juvenile parole revocation throughout the United States simply does not exist.

Prior to several significant U.S. Supreme Court decisions, either parole or probation revocation could be accomplished for adult offenders on the basis of reports filed by probation or parole officers that offenders were in violation of one or more conditions of their programs. Criminal court judges, those ordinarily in charge of determining whether to terminate one's probationary status, could decide this issue on the basis of available evidence against offenders. For adult parolees, former decision making relative to terminating their parole could be made by parole boards without much fanfare from offenders. In short, parole officers and others might simply present evidence that one or more infractions or violations of probation or parole conditions had been committed. These infractions, then, could form the basis for revoking probation or parole as well as a justification for these decisions.

A probationer's or parolee's right to due process in any probation or parole revocation action was largely ignored prior to 1967. Thus, technical violations, such as failing to submit monthly reports, violating curfew, filing a falsified report, or drinking alcoholic beverages "to excess," might result in an unfavorable recommendation from a person's PO that the probation or parole program should be terminated. Popular television shows sometimes portray parole officers as threatening their clients with parole revocation: "Do this or else I'll have you back in the joint!", meaning a return to prison for adult offenders. Currently, it is not so easy to accomplish either type of revocation.

For adult parolees as well as for adult probationers, revocations for either probation or parole are currently two-stage proceedings. The landmark cases that have directly affected parolees and probationers and their rights are: *Mempa v. Rhay* (1967), *Morrissey v. Brewer* (1972), *Gagnon v. Scarpelli* (1973). While these landmark cases pertain to adult probationers and parolees, they have significance for juvenile probationers and parolees. The significance is that juvenile justice policies are often formulated or influenced on the basis of U.S. Supreme Court decisions about the rights of inmates, parolees, or probationers, and the procedures involved in their processing throughout the criminal justice system. Thus, these cases are not binding on juvenile court judges or juvenile paroling authorities. But they provide a legal basis for specific actions in pertinent juvenile cases, if the juvenile justice system chooses to recognize them as precedent-setting.

Mempa v. Rhay (1967)

Jerry Mempa was convicted in criminal court of joyriding in a stolen vehicle on June 17, 1959, in Spokane, Washington. The judge placed him on probation for two years. A few months later, Mempa was involved in a burglary on September 15, 1959. The county prosecutor in Spokane requested that Mempa's probation be revoked. Mempa admitted that he committed the burglary to police. At a **probation revocation hearing** conducted later, the sole testimony about his involvement in the burglary came from his probation officer, who obtained his factual information largely from police reports. Mempa, an indigent, was not permitted to offer statements in his own behalf, nor was he provided counsel, nor was he asked if he wanted counsel, nor was he permitted to cross-examine the probation officer about the officer's incriminating statements. The judge revoked Mempa's probation and sentenced him to 10 years in the Washington State Penitentiary.

A short time later, Mempa filed a writ of *habeas corpus,* which essentially challenges the fact of his confinement and the nature of it. He alleged that he had been denied the right to counsel in his probation revocation hearing, and thus, he claimed his due process rights had been violated in part. The Washington Supreme Court denied his petition, but the U.S. Supreme Court elected to hear it on appeal. The U.S. Supreme Court overturned the Washington Supreme Court and ruled in Mempa's favor. Specifically, the U.S. Supreme Court said that Mempa was entitled to an attorney but was denied one. Furthermore, and perhaps most important, the Court declared that a probation revocation hearing is a "critical stage" that falls within the due process provisions of the Fourteenth Amendment. Critical stages refer to any stages of the criminal justice process where a defendant is in jeopardy. If defendants are accused of crimes, or arraigned, or prosecuted, their due process rights "attach" or become relevant. Thus, they are entitled to attorneys at any of these critical stages, since they are in jeopardy of losing their freedom. This ruling did not mean that Mempa would be entirely free from further court action. However, it did provide for a rehearing, and his 10-year sentence in the Washington State Penitentiary was set aside.

Morrissey v. Brewer (1972)

In 1967, John Morrissey was convicted in an Iowa court for falsely drawing checks. He was sentenced to "not more than 7 years" in the Iowa State Prison. Subsequently, he was paroled in June 1968. Seven months later, his parole officer learned that Morrissey had bought an automobile under an assumed name and operated it without permission, had obtained credit cards giving false information, and had given false information to an insurance company when he became involved in an automobile accident. Further, Morrissey had given his PO a false address for his residence. After interviewing Morrissey, Morrissey's PO filed a report recommending that Morrissey's parole be revoked. The parole violations involved all of the infractions and false information noted above. In his own defense, Morrissey claimed to be "sick" and had been prevented from maintaining continuous contact with his PO during the car-buying, credit-card accumulating, and automobile accident period. The PO countered by alleging that Morrissey was "continually violating the rules." The Iowa Parole Board revoked Morrissey's parole and he was returned to the Iowa State Prison to serve the remainder of his sentence.

During his parole revocation hearing, he was not represented by counsel, nor was he permitted to testify in his own behalf, nor was he permitted to cross-examine witnesses against him, nor was he advised in writing of the charges against him, nor was there any disclosure of the evidence against him. Further, the Iowa Parole Board gave no reasons to Morrissey for their revocation action. Morrissey appealed to the Iowa Supreme Court, which rejected his appeal. The U.S. Supreme Court decided to hear his appeal, however, and overturned the

Iowa Supreme Court and Iowa Parole Board actions. The Court did not specifically address the issue of whether Morrissey should have been represented by counsel, but it did establish the foundation for a two-stage parole revocation proceeding. The first or preliminary stage or hearing would be conducted at the time of arrest or confinement, and its purpose would be to determine whether probable cause exists that the parolee actually committed the alleged parole violations. The second stage or hearing would be more involved and designed to establish the parolee's punishment the alleged violations. Currently, all parolees in all states must be extended the following rights relating to **minimum due process rights:**

1. The right to have written notice of the alleged violations of parole conditions.
2. The right to have disclosed to the parolee any evidence of the alleged violation.
3. The right of the parolee to be heard in person and to present exculpatory evidence as well as witnesses in his or her behalf.
4. The right to confront and cross-examine adverse witnesses, unless cause exists why they should not be cross-examined.
5. The right to a judgment by a neutral and detached body, such as the parole board itself.
6. The right to a written statement of the reasons for the parole revocation.

Thus, the primary significance of the *Morrissey* case was that it established minimum due process rights for all parolees and created a two-stage proceeding where alleged infractions of parole conditions could be examined objectively and where a full hearing could be conducted to determine the most appropriate offender disposition.

Gagnon v. Scarpelli (1973)

Because the matter of representation by counsel was not specifically addressed in the *Morrissey* case, the U.S. Supreme Court heard yet another parolee's case concerning a parole revocation action and where court-appointed counsel had not been provided. Gerald Scarpelli was convicted of robbery in July 1965 in a Wisconsin court. At his sentencing on August 5, 1965, Scarpelli was sentenced to 15 years in prison, but the judge suspended the sentence and placed him on probation for 7 years. Believe it or not, the following day, August 6, 1965, Gerald Scarpelli was arrested and charged with burglary. The judge immediately revoked his probation and ordered Scarpelli placed in the Wisconsin State Reformatory for a 15-year term.

At this point, Scarpelli's case becomes a little complicated. During his early stay in prison, Scarpelli filed a *habeas corpus* petition with the court, alleging that his due process rights were violated when his probation was revoked. He was not represented by counsel and he was not permitted a hearing. However, Scarpelli was paroled from prison in 1968. Nevertheless, the U.S. Supreme Court acted on his original *habeas corpus* petition filed earlier and ruled in his favor. The U.S. Supreme Court held that Scarpelli was indeed denied the right to counsel and had not been given a hearing in the probation revocation action. While this might seem to be a hollow victory, since Scarpelli was already free on parole, the case had profound significance on both subsequent parole and probation revocation actions. The U.S. Supreme Court, referring to the *Morrissey* case that it had heard the previous year (1972), said that "a probation revocation, like parole revocation, is not a stage of a criminal prosecution, but does result in loss of liberty . . . We hold that a probationer, like a parolee, is entitled to a preliminary hearing and a final revocation hearing in the conditions specified in *Morrissey v. Brewer.*"

The significance of *Scarpelli* case is that it equated probation with parole regarding revocation hearings. While the Court did not say that all probationers and parolees have a right to be represented by counsel in all probation and parole revocation hearings, it did say that counsel should be provided in cases where the parolee or probationer makes a timely claim contesting the allegations. This U.S. Supreme Court decision has been liberally interpreted by the courts and parole boards in all jurisdictions. Thus, while no constitutional basis currently exists for providing counsel in *all* probation or parole revocation proceedings, most of these proceedings usually involve defense counsel if legitimate requests are made in advance by probationers or parolees.

Some persons are understandably perplexed by the seemingly excessive time interval that lapses between when questioned events occur, such as probation revocation actions which may be unconstitutionally conducted, and when the U.S. Supreme Court gets around to hearing such petitions or claims and deciding cases. It is not unusual for these time intervals to be five or six years, or even longer. The wheels of justice move slowly, especially the wheels of U.S. Supreme Court actions. Interestingly, of the more than 3,500 cases that are presented to the U.S. Supreme Court annually for hearing, only about 150 to 175 cases are heard where decisions are written. Four or more Justices must agree to hear any specific case, and even then, their convening time may expire before certain cases are heard. It is beyond the scope of this text to discuss the process by which U.S. Supreme Court cases are initiated and processed, but this short discussion serves to explain the apparent slowness in rendering significant opinions in landmark cases.

For juveniles, these three cases are important because they provide juvenile courts and juvenile paroling authorities within juvenile corrections with certain guidelines to follow. These guidelines are not mandatory or binding, since these U.S. Supreme Court rulings pertain to adults rather than to juveniles. However, the law is not always abundantly clear regarding its application in a wide variety of different cases. While it may be anticipated that the U.S. Supreme Court will eventually address probation and parole revocation issues that pertain to juvenile offenders, we can only use adult guidelines for the present.

Currently, probation and parole revocation proceedings for juveniles differ widely among jurisdictions. Knepper and Cavender (1990), for instance, indicate that in a Western state they examined, informal hearings were conducted by a juvenile parole board outside of the presence of juveniles. In such informal settings, decisions about parole revocations were made. Subsequently, juveniles were brought before the board and advised in a more formal hearing of the rightness of the board's decision about the revocation action taken. This is strongly indicative of the continuation of *parens patriae* in juvenile matters. In other jurisdictions, explicit criteria exist for determining court or parole board actions relating to juvenile parolees who violate program rules or commit new offenses. Statutory constraints may or may not be in place to regulate judicial or parole board decision making in these situations. Again, the cases of *Morrissey, Scarpelli,* and *Mempa* are not binding on juvenile probation or parole revocation actions in any state jurisdiction.

EXAMPLES OF PROBATION AND PAROLE REVOCATION FOR JUVENILES

Since there is no federal law governing juvenile probation or parole revocation, we must examine state statutes and decisions to determine the types of situations and circumstances where the probation or parole programs of juveniles have been revoked. This will give us some indication of what practices are prevalent among the states, as well as the grounds used in such revocation actions.

Juvenile Probation and Parole Revocation Cases

Several cases have been reported involving revocations of juvenile probation and parole. These are reported below. There are considerably more juvenile probation revocation cases reported than parole revocation cases, the former outnumbering the latter by as much as 20 to 1. Thus, most of the cases below are probation revocation cases. It is important to note, however, that the same grounds used to revoke one's probation program are also used to revoke one's parole program. Thus, for all practical purposes, each jurisdiction can use these grounds almost interchangeably, whether it is for probation or parole revocation actions.

Can a probation program be revoked on the basis of hearsay evidence from the juvenile's probation officer? No.

Matter of Todd D., 732 N.Y.S.2d 488 (N.Y.Sup.App.Div.Nov.) (2001). Todd D., a juvenile, was suspected by his probation officer of violating certain rules associated with his probation program. The PO filed a petition with the court seeking to have Todd D.'s probation program revoked. The petition contained mostly unsupported allegations about what the PO believed true about Todd D., included his suspicions about Todd D.'s behavior in violating various components of his probation program. However, no tangible evidence was presented (e.g., the results of urinalyses, drug tests, informant testimony) to back up the PO's suspicions. Under the New York Family Court Act, any petition seeking to revoke the probation of a juvenile must be verified and subscribed by the probation service or the appropriate presentment agency. Such petition must stipulate the condition or conditions of the order violated and a reasonable description of the time, place, and manner in which the violation occurred. Nonhearsay allegations of the factual part of the petition or of any supporting depositions must establish, if true, every violation charged. Since the petition contained no such nonhearsay evidence, other than the unsupported suspicions of the PO that reflected his personal opinions and knowledge, the petition to revoke the Todd D.'s probation program was dismissed.

Can a juvenile's probation be revoked because of the juvenile's failure to follow a judge's verbal (rather than written) order to attend vocational school training? No.

Matter of Appeal in Maricopa County, 915 P.2d 1250 (Ariz.App. April) (1996). A juvenile was verbally ordered by a judge to attend Valley Vocational School in Arizona as a condition of his probation. No written order requiring such attendance was provided, however. Later, evidence was presented to the juvenile court that the juvenile had failed to attend the Valley Vocational School. The judge brought the youth before him and revoked his probation. The youth appealed, contending that there had been no written order requiring his attendance at the vocational school. In this case, the appellate court in Arizona reversed the juvenile court judge's revocation order. They concluded that probation revocation for juveniles is an area where the adult criminal requirement regarding written notice of the terms of probation upon which revocation is based must appropriately be applied in juvenile cases as a matter of due process and general fairness. The appeals court noted that although there had been a verbal order from the judge to require the youth's attendance at the vocational school, it was not sufficiently important, since a written order was issued to revoke one's probation. The court said, "If an order is important enough to warrant a revocation petition, the order first must be reduced to writing and given to [the] probationer."

Can a juvenile have his or her probation revoked and be prosecuted for an offense that is the same type of offense for which probation was initially granted, without a violation of one's double jeopardy rights? Yes.

Ignacio R. v. Superior Court, 114 Cal.Rptr.2d 375 (Cal.App.Dec.) (2001). Ignacio R., a juvenile, was placed on probation following his adjudication for a delinquent offense. Subsequently, Ignacio R. was apprehended by police committing the same type of offense for which he was originally adjudicated. A juvenile court prosecutor sought to prosecute Ignacio R. in juvenile court for the new offense. In the meantime, the juvenile court judge revoked Ignacio R.'s probation and ordered him detained subsequent to a new adjudicatory hearing. Ignacio appealed, contending that having his probation program revoked and being prosecuted for the same type of offense involved in the original probation order was the equivalent of double jeopardy, and thus his constitutional right against double jeopardy was being violated. The appellate court upheld the new prosecution and probation revocation, holding that the revocation of probation in the present case merely changed the level of restriction on the juvenile's liberty; it did not result in an additional punishment in relation to the offense for which probation was originally granted.

Can a juvenile's probation program be revoked following the juvenile's admission to certain alleged probation program violations if such admissions were not made knowingly and intelligently? No.

D.R. v. Commonwealth, 64 S.W.3d 292, (Ky.App.Dec.) (2001). D.R., a juvenile, was charged with violating one or more conditions of his probation program following a delinquency adjudication. D.R. was not advised of his right against self-incrimination prior to giving testimony in his own behalf at the probation revocation hearing before the juvenile court judge. Following the hearing, D.R.'s probation was revoked and D.R. appealed, arguing that his admissions were not made knowingly and intelligently. The appellate court reversed the juvenile court and reinstated D.R.'s probation, holding that unless a juvenile knowingly and intelligently makes admissions concerning probation program violations, and if that juvenile is not informed of the consequences of an admission of guilty, then he is presumed not informed of his constitutional rights and the rights he was waiving by admitting his guilt.

Can a juvenile's probation program be revoked if the juvenile court judge fails to state in writing the specific reasons for revoking the probation program and the specific nature of the program infractions? No.

A.D. v. State, 778 So.2d 244 (Ala.Crim.App.) (2001). A.D., a juvenile was adjudicated delinquent for fighting at school. He was placed on probation and ordered to obey the law, conduct himself properly, cooperate with probation services, comply with electronic monitoring, and not leave the county of his residence. Subsequently, a juvenile PO filed a complaint seeking to revoke A.D.'s aftercare status claiming that A.D. had violated the terms of his aftercare by assaulting a school employee, by being absent from class with authorization, and by using profane language. A juvenile court judge ordered A.D.'s probation revoked, stating that A.D. had caused chaos at the high school and was completely unamenable to treatment. An Alabama appellate court set aside the juvenile court judge's revocation order, holding that in Alabama, a court must provide a written order stating the evidence relied upon and the reasons for revoking probation. Because the juvenile court failed to state the specific reason for revoking A.D.'s aftercare status, and because it did not set out the evidence it relied upon, the matter had to be remanded.

Can juvenile court judges place juveniles on probation and order them committed to a specific detention facility if they fail to obey their probation orders? No.

Dept. of Juvenile Justice v. K.B., 784 So.2d 556 (Fla.Dist.App.May) (2001). K.B., a juvenile, was adjudicated delinquent and disposed to probation for a period of time. The juvenile court judge declared that if K.B. violated one or more probationary conditions, he would therefore be committed to a specific residential commitment facility, which he referred to by name. The probation orders were reviewed by an appellate court and the juvenile court judge's mixed probation order was vacated. The appellate court held that it is beyond the jurisdiction of a juvenile court judge to order a youth committed to a specific detention facility if one or more probation program conditions are violated. This is the responsibility of the Department of Juvenile Justice, which has the sole authority to dictate where a juvenile will be placed if found in violation of probation. Juvenile court judges have the authority to place youths on probation and to specify probation program conditions; however, they cannot include in those probation orders an assignment to a specific facility if the juvenile violates one or more probationary terms.

Can a juvenile court judge impose an indefinite period of community control on a juvenile adjudicated delinquent? No.

J.A.L. v. State, 778 So.2d 408 (Fla.Dist.App.Jan.) (2001). J.A.L., a juvenile, was adjudicated delinquent and disposed by the juvenile court judge to an indefinite period of time in Florida's community control program, which is a community-based probation program. J.A.L. appealed the indefinite probationary term, and the Florida court of appeals remanded the case back to the juvenile court judge for a new disposition. The court held that juvenile court judges cannot impose indefinite probationary periods for adjudicated juveniles. Terms of probation must be for specific time intervals and not indefinite ones.

Can a juvenile's probation be revoked on the basis of uncross-examined testimony from a police officer at a probation revocation hearing? No.

Commonwealth v. Emmanuel E., 754 N.E.2d 1067 (2001).   Emmanuel E., a juvenile, was adjudicated delinquent and placed on probation. Subsequently, a police officer testified at a probation revocation hearing concerning one or more probation program condition violations allegedly committed by Emmanuel E. Emmanuel E. was prohibited from confronting and cross-examining the police officer. Emmanuel E. appealed, alleging that his right to confront and cross-examine his accuser was violated, and therefore, the probation revocation order should be set aside. An appellate court agreed with Emmanuel E. and reversed the juvenile court judge. Juveniles are entitled to confront and cross-examine their accuser. The police officer in this case testified on the basis of hearsay evidence, and there was no exception to the hearsay rule in this case. Furthermore, there was no showing of good cause for why the police officer's cross-examination was not permitted.

Is it permissible to hold juveniles in detention prior to their hearing on the matter of revoking their probation? Yes.

D.H. v. Esteves, 790 So.2d 1275 (Fla.Dist.App.Aug.) (2001).   D.H., a juvenile, was placed on probation following an adjudication of delinquency. Subsequently, D.H. was taken into custody by police officers for alleged violations of certain probation program conditions. A hearing was set for 21 days following D.H.'s being taken into custody. During that period, D.H. was held in detention. D.H. filed a writ of *habeas corpus* demanding to be freed from detention. The appellate court denied his writ and held that the detention order was perfectly proper under the circumstances. The court had the authority to hold D.H. in detention prior to the hearing on the probation revocation.

Can a juvenile court judge impose a lawful order committing a youth to a youth authority after that youth has become an adult? No.

Matter of D.C., 49 S.W.3d 26 (Tex.App.April) (2001).   D.C., an 18-year-old adult, was ordered committed to the Texas Youth Commission by a juvenile court judge after a finding that he had violated a probation program condition. D.C. appealed, contending that the juvenile court judge no longer had jurisdiction over D.C., since the probation program violation occurred after D.C. turned 18 years of age, the age of adulthood in Texas. The appellate court reversed the judge's commitment order, holding that once a juvenile reaches the age of his majority or adulthood, the probationary term under the original disposition ceases to apply. Therefore, if an adult violates a probation condition that was imposed as a part of a probation program when the person was a juvenile, the probation condition no longer applies, since probation ceases once the person becomes an adult.

Can juvenile parole boards terminate a juvenile's commitment to an institution and grant parole despite a judge's order to continue the juvenile's commitment for a period of time until the juvenile is 21? No.

In re Ruben D., 18 P.3d 1063 (N.M.App.Feb.) (2001).   Ruben D., a juvenile, was committed to an industrial school for a period of years. From time to time, the juvenile court judge would review Ruben D.'s institutional behavior and progress. On the basis of these reports, the judge would decide to extend

Ruben D.'s commitment to the institution for additional one-year periods. Following one such order by the juvenile court judge that extended Ruben D.'s commitment to the institution for one more year, the juvenile parole board convened and acknowledged that Ruben D.'s original commitment order had expired. The parole board did not acknowledge the extension of the commitment order by the juvenile court judge. Ruben D. appealed, contending that he should be paroled because of the juvenile parole board's acknowledgment that his commitment term had expired. The appellate court upheld the juvenile court judge's authority to extend Ruben D.'s commitment by one-year periods until Ruben D. reached 21 years of age. The order that extended the commitment of Ruben D. was affirmed.

Can a juvenile have his or her parole program revoked for violating an implied rather than written order requiring him to participate in a particular aftercare program following release from commitment? No.

K.G. v. State, 759 So.2d 752 (Fla.Dist.App.June) (2000). K.G., a female juvenile, was adjudicated delinquent and committed to a juvenile secure facility. Subsequently, K.G. was paroled. The parole board implied that it would be a good idea for K.G. to participate in a particular aftercare program involving treatment for substance abuse, which was a problem K.G. had prior to being committed initially. K.G. did not participate in the particular aftercare program and the parole board sought to revoke her parole program. K.G. appealed, contending that there were no specific orders requiring her to participate in the aftercare program following the completion of the term of commitment. The appellate court reversed the parole board, holding that there was no showing that K.G. had been properly transferred to the aftercare program following the term of commitment. In order for a violation of one's parole program to be upheld, a valid written order by the parole board must have been violated. Since no written orders had been violated, K.G. was reinstated into her parole program.

SELECTED ISSUES IN JUVENILE CORRECTIONS

Investigations of the rate of secure confinement of juveniles during the past two centuries have disclosed that the rate of juvenile institutionalization has increased, especially during the most recent decades (Goodstein and Sontheimer 1997). Many of those youths detained for fairly long periods of 30 days or longer are less serious misdemeanants and status offenders. For this and other reasons, juvenile corrections has been under attack from various sectors for years. This attack comes from many quarters, and it coincides with a general attack on the criminal justice system for its apparent failure to stem the increasing wave of crime in the United States. Sentencing reforms, correctional reforms, experiments with probation and parole alternatives, and a host of other options have been attempted in an apparent effort to cure or control delinquents and criminals (Bottcher, Isorena, and Belnas 1996).

In 1985, the United Nations and National Council of Juvenile and Family Court Judges adopted policy statements about the juvenile justice system that bear directly on juvenile corrections. The issues to be discussed in this final section may be better understood in the context of these statements. Several recommendations have been made by Dwyer and McNally (1987, 50–51). These are that:

1. Primary dispositions of juvenile courts should be to have a flexible range for restricting freedom with the primary goal focused on the restoration to full liberty rather than let the punishment fit the crime; that no case dispositions should be of a mandatory nature, but rather, they should be left to the discretion of the judge based on predetermined dispositional guidelines; that in no case should a juvenile under 18 years of age be subject to capital punishment.

2. Individualized treatment of juveniles should be continued, including the development of medical, psychiatric, and educational programs that range from least to most restrictive, according to individual need.

3. While being held accountable, chronic, serious juvenile offenders should be retained within the jurisdiction of the juvenile court. As a resource, specialized programs and facilities need to be developed that focus on restorations rather than punishment.

4. Policymakers, reformers, and researchers should continue to strive for a greater understanding as to the causes and most desired response to juvenile crime; that research should be broad-based rather than limited to management, control, and punishment strategies.

5. Where the juvenile court judge believes that the juvenile under consideration is nonamenable to the services of the court and based on the youth's present charges, past record in court, and his or her age and mental status, the judge may waive jurisdiction; that in all juvenile cases the court of original jurisdiction be that of the juvenile court; that the discretion to waive be left to the juvenile court judge; that the proportionality of punishment would be appropriate with these cases, but the most high-risk offenders should be treated in small, but secure, facilities.

Each of the issues discussed below is affected directly by these recommendations and policy statements. While these statements are not obligatory for any jurisdiction, they do suggest opinions and positions of a relevant segment of concerned citizens—juvenile court judges and juvenile corrections personnel. These issues include (1) the privatization of juvenile corrections, (2) the classification of juvenile offenders, and (3) juveniles held in adult jails and lockups.

The Privatization of Juvenile Corrections

Juvenile corrections has many of the same problems as adult corrections. Chronic overcrowding in secure confinement facilities is extensive among jurisdictions. Existing facilities in many states are deteriorating rapidly. Furthermore, there are disproportionate representations of black, Hispanic, and Native American youths (American Correctional Association 2002). With the current emphasis on more punitive juvenile sentencing policies, it is unlikely that significant improvements in the quality of juvenile incarcerative facilities will be implemented in the near future. **Privatization** is believed by some authorities to be one solution to overcrowded publicly operated facilities. Privatization is the establishment and operation of correctional services and institutions by nongovernmental interests, including private corporations and businesspersons (Armstrong 2001).

Nonsecure and secure facilities are both publicly and privately operated. Florida is one of several states experimenting with various forms of private ju-

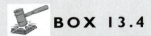 **BOX 13.4**

John Robinson
Managing Director, Quality Assurance
Corrections Corporation of America

Statistics:

B.A. (sociology), Lenior-Rhyne College; member, North American Association of Wardens and Superintendents; American Correctional Association; National Juvenile Court Services Association; Tennessee Juvenile Court Services Association; National Juvenile Detention Association; National Association of Juvenile Correctional Agencies.

Background and Experience:

Presently, I serve as Managing Director, Quality Assurance for Corrections Corporation of America (CCA). I joined the company in 1984 as Assistant Facility Administrator of the Houston Processing Center. In 1985 I became the Facility Administrator for CCA's first juvenile facilities, Tall Trees and Shelby Training Center, in Memphis, Tennessee. In 1988, I was appointed Director of Juvenile Services Development at CCA's corporate office, and in 1990, I was transferred to the company's operations division as a director. In 2001, CCA created a new quality assurance department and I was appointed to head that department. My corrections career began in 1972 with the Virginia Department of Corrections, where I worked in various capacities until I joined CCA in 1984.

I came to corrections, as many did in earlier days, looking for a job, and found a career. I graduated from college in 1972 with a degree in sociology and a lifelong interest in athletics. I was hoping to find a job in the recreational field and was getting married the following summer. Through relatives, I found out about a juvenile correctional facility in Virginia that needed teachers, and so I applied, was hired, and reported to Richmond right after my wedding. It was quite an experience with which to begin my corrections career. I was hired as a math teacher—my worst academic subject—with the hopes of transferring into the facility's programs or recreation department.

Nowadays, corrections professionals receive extensive training prior to beginning their positions. Then, I arrived at work my first day, was given a key to the classroom and told, "They're all yours." And there I was, with thirty youth in the classroom. I think the theory for new staff in those days was the "learn by the seat of one's pants" philosophy. I eventually transferred as an instructor in the physical education department, and later I became assistant principal, then assistant superintendent of the entire facility. I worked there from 1972 until I joined CCA in 1984. I'd planned to be at the Virginia facility for two years, and I didn't think I had an interest in corrections, although it became my career. I got involved, and found that working in corrections, especially with youth, was tremendously rewarding.

CCA co-founder Don Hutto was the director of the Virginia Department of Corrections for part of my tenure at the Virginia facility. I knew him, respected him, and followed his public sector career and move to CCA. And so, when the call came from CCA, I was interested. At the time I was contacted about joining CCA, privatization of major institutions was still just a concept. I made the decision and never looked back. It was definitely a risk, but I had confidence in the people who were building the company. I was hired as an assistant warden at the Houston Processing Center, CCA's first design/build facility contract, helped to start and prepare that facility for ACA accreditation, and a few months later, I became the warden. Next, I moved to CCA's Tall Trees and Shelby Training Center, both juvenile facilities, in November 1985. Tall Trees, a nonsecure residential facility for the juvenile court of Memphis and Shelby County, was already in operation with CCA assuming management of the facility in January 1984. Shelby Training Center was being built at the time, and so I was able to provide input in areas ranging from construction to programs. Shelby Training Center was the first secure training school in the country to be designed, built, and managed by the private sector. Both Tall Trees and Shelby Training Center were accredited by the ACA while I was administrator.

In 1988 I was promoted to Director of Business Development with an emphasis on CCA's juvenile market. We experienced many successes, contracting with Delaware, Nevada, and Tennessee. I also worked on other projects, including CCA's Leavenworth Detention Center in Kansas, the first private maximum-security facility under direct contract with a federal agency, and Winn Correctional Center in Louisiana, the first privately operated medium-security prison in the United States. CCA's Operations Division was growing so rapidly at the time that I was eventually asked to return to that department as Director of Operational Support. CCA was in a major growth phase during the mid-1990s, and during my time in the operations department, implemented its divisional concept: Our approximately 70 facilities in the field were divided into three divisions, each managed by a senior divisional director, to provide direct oversight and guidance. I was one of CCA's first senior divisional directors, and as the company's residential juvenile expert, supervised CCA's juvenile facilities in my division, as well as some adult facilities and jails. As CCA grew, we eventually expanded this concept from three to five operating divisions. I served as a divisional director until the creation of a new Quality Assurance department in 2001, and was appointed managing director of that department. In this role, I oversee our company's quality assurance efforts, from facility compliance with

corporate and facility policy and procedures, agency management contracts and industry standards, to setting benchmarks for facility performance. We are responsible for maintaining, and continually improving, the level of service our customers expect. In addition to helping facilities maintain compliance, we collect and analyze audit data, providing information to key management staff for the purpose of ongoing evaluation of all programs, services, and policies.

Interesting Experiences:

Juveniles are an interesting challenge to manage—they are both rewarding and entertaining to work with. Sometimes, they do things that are downright funny. The Virginia facility where I began my career was located way out in the country. Part of our security team consisted of bloodhounds: If kids took off, we'd use bloodhounds to help track them, and 95 percent of the time, we found them. As assistant superintendent, I received a call one night during a snowstorm informing me that two juveniles had escaped. We began to track them with the dogs and quickly realized that they had left a trail of footprints in the snow. We didn't need the tracking dogs—it was an easy matter to follow the footprints to the hayloft of a nearby barn, and there sat the two boys. It was almost comical. The boys hadn't stopped to consider the fact that they'd left their footprints in the snow.

One of my proudest achievements during my tenure at Beaumont was the founding of the facility's first football team, which competed on the junior varsity level against other institutions as well as public schools. For many of these kids formerly on the street, it was their first experience with athletics. We provided them structure, and they flourished. The team had a 6–2 record its first year, and many of these kids had never participated in organized sports. They proved to be very talented and showed that they could make good decisions, with some leadership and guidance. It was very rewarding to watch these kids benefit from

(continued)

BOX 13.4 (*Continued*)

contributing to a team and reaching for common goals and then celebrating once they reached them. Some went on to play in school, which was especially rewarding to hear. I like to think that the rewards of teamwork may have played a part in attracting them back to school and keeping them there.

No particular event at CCA stands out as more significant than others; however, my tenure at CCA's Shelby Training Center was especially meaningful. CCA was in its earliest days, and due to the dire need for housing space for juveniles in that area, we were asked to convert and operate a small temporary facility for 30 juveniles, prior to Shelby Training Center's opening. Our staff was brand new to corrections and to CCA, and the experience we had in these temporary quarters was invaluable. Our population increased from 30 to 60. It required that staff learn quickly, be resourceful and attentive, and implement solutions. When we moved into the new Shelby Training Center facility, operations went like clockwork, because our folks had cut their teeth in a very difficult environment to supervise. I'm very proud of the Tall Trees and Shelby Training Center programs. Despite the newness of the CCA concept, we provided two important aspects to the care continuum in the Memphis/Shelby County area. Thanks to the support of the juvenile court, we were never treated as a contractor, but as a widely accepted arm of the local system. Our work there provided an early model for privatization—a model that would and continues to work today.

On the other end of the security spectrum, our Okeechobee Juvenile Offender Corrections Center (OJOCC) in Florida is another success story. We had a hard time selling the facility concept to the local community. The facility houses Level 10 offenders—the toughest juveniles in the system—as well as runs a Level 8 sex offender program for the Florida Department of Juvenile Justice. I think OJOCC is actually one of our best juvenile facilities. We utilize a JROTC program and other aspects of military science there, from making beds daily to drill instruction, to provide structure and build a regime into youth's daily activity. I think we actually do better with harder-to-manage inmate populations. We won over the county with our performance in operations and security and pleased our contracting agency as well. On a recent review, the facility scored a "commendable" level—a very high rating on the audit scale—from the state's quality assurance agency.

Insights:

The juvenile population in the United States continues to grow and become more violent. Fifteen or twenty years ago, you'd see juveniles in facilities for very minor offenses. Now they're in for murder, armed robbery, and assault with a deadly weapon. In Memphis, 84 percent of the youth at the Shelby Training Center were from a single household, which was the number one problem in my opinion—there was no dominant male figure in the home, often five or six other siblings, and a mother who couldn't provide what they needed. These kids are out on the street with no curfews, robbing and stealing—some to help support their families, others for reasons ranging from gangs to drugs. Likewise, the corrections field has changed since that time as well. During the 1970s, when I began my career, there was a fraction of the number of academic degree programs in criminal justice. The criminal justice field has become more popular and grown in depth and breadth. I believe our training and orientation is better, and facility design has certainly improved.

One thing has remained constant: Managing a youthful population is definitely a challenge. One of CCA's former officers, who began his career with the company as an administrator, said he'd take the toughest adult prison block before having to deal with juveniles. The management approach is different for juveniles. It takes staff with different areas of expertise than an adult facility. In a youth facility, for example, you need more than a case manager: You must have skilled counselors with an understanding of child development and juvenile justice. Different approaches and programs are required because youthful offenders are in a certain cognitive stage of social development, whereas adult inmates have already completed those formative years. It's a challenge, but also an opportunity, because dealing with youth gives us a greater opportunity to impact their emotional development and, hopefully, make changes for the better.

Juveniles are more compulsive and less rational than adults. Adult inmates understand what's expected of them and take advantage of the programs and services available. There are exceptions, but for the most part, adult inmates understand the rules and regulations and will do what they have to do in order to "do their time" and make it profitable, if possible. Juveniles are at a point in their lives where their thought processes are not mature, and they retaliate against people or issues they don't agree with in the same way they would on the street. They have underdeveloped communications skills, are less aware of the consequences, and will try anything. Adults understand the consequences of their actions, while youth will act first and ask questions later. They are very manipulative—for example, if they don't like a roommate, they will act out in the hopes of getting a single cell. As corrections professionals, we must understand their motivation for certain actions and confront them with it, in order to effectively manage their behavior.

Training is different for corrections employees in juvenile facilities, too. A juvenile population necessitates training in self-defense, because for the most part, facilities use no weapons or chemical agents in dealing with youthful offenders. Therefore, staff have potentially dangerous clients on their hands: aggressive teenagers who often have the size and strength of their adult counterparts, with whom staff are expected to deal without the additional support of weapons. It takes teamwork, extensive training, and good communication. CCA supervises all inmates—youth and adult—through direct supervision. We don't just watch inmates from a control room. Communication is incredibly important.

CCA doesn't have a "model" for juvenile facilities, because we respond to agency needs individually. Our juvenile facilities have different programs, approaches, and locales. What makes us successful is by utilizing different approaches, we find out what works. We cull our best practices and apply them to the other facilities we manage. State and local correctional systems do not have that advantage—they can read or network with other professionals at conferences, but they only have the experiences within their own continuum. We have practical experience to build upon in determining the most effective approaches with different populations. While we don't have a "footprint" for juvenile programs, we do utilize a very structured approach.

What made CCA successful in our early days was the commitment to quality from day one. Our co-founder, Don Hutto, was committed to American Correctional Association standards and brought the ACA into the process early in our history, when ACA accreditation was just starting in the industry. It made CCA different and provided an instant track record, as well as great credibility, and it encouraged our colleagues in the industry to look into privatization as a viable option. Being a private company is one of the biggest motivations we have to do a good job. No one is scrutinized as much as we are. In addition to our contractual partners and industry standards, we are also responsible to our company shareholders and the financial community. Moreover, we keep employees motivated to do a good job because they own a piece of the company. They have a vested interest in our success, and therefore, they look at things differently, from efficiency to innovation. Finally, CCA's recruitment of quality staff from a variety of areas—not just corrections practitioners—has worked well for the company. We have tenured corrections professionals from the public and private sector, as well as people with expertise in basic business, finance,

(continued)

BOX 13.4 (Continued)

marketing, and other related fields. It's a good mix. They learn from us about corrections, and we learn from them about how to run a good business operation. That's what has made CCA successful.

Advice to Students:

Two decades ago, there were very few undergraduate or graduate programs in the criminal justice field. Many corrections professionals entered the field from a programs–or social services–related background, such as sociology. Individuals who are truly interested in making corrections a long-term career—and I highly recommend doing so—should experience all aspects of corrections, in order to develop a sound basis of knowledge to build upon and to be an effective manager. While the academic tools to prepare students for a corrections career are more developed than ever before, practical experience is a "must." Students should spend some time working in entry-level po-

sitions, whether as a full-time job or an internship, to get a better perspective and a broader background. It's necessary in order to learn the field. To be a better supervisor, one should have spent some time in the positions he or she manages. Only then can you truly understand what it takes to be a good correctional officer, counselor, or security supervisor. When hiring staff, I have always looked for hands-on, hard experience on the front lines. It's also important to secure experience on both sides of the corrections continuum: programs and security. Often, I see individuals pursue one track or another exclusively, as they advance their careers. The best corrections administrators have experience across the board. It helps make them more well-rounded, in addition to being excellent management: correctional staff regard supervisors who have served in the trenches as they've advanced their career with a great deal of respect.

venile secure confinement. Historically, Florida sought to rehabilitate youths through incarceration including placement of serious offenders in reform or training schools (Rivers, Dembo, and Anwyl 1998). The first school for male juveniles opened in Florida in 1900, and by 1972, four schools were operating in various jurisdictions throughout the state. But because of serious institutional overcrowding and the ineffectiveness of program treatments, Florida officials decided to shift their incarcerative priorities to the development of less secure, community-based facilities (Pingree 1984, 60). Florida's objectives are to (1) reduce the number of juveniles actually placed in secure confinement facilities, and (2) to provide juveniles with a broader base of community options that will be instrumental in helping them to acquire vocational training and education. Much emphasis is placed on assisting youths with psychological problems as well. Thus, trained counselors work closely with Florida juvenile offenders to meet their psychological and social needs more effectively. The Florida model has served as an example for other jurisdictions in later years (Rivers, Dembo, Anwyl 1998).

Several important issues relating to the privatization of corrections, for both adult and juvenile offenders, have been outlined (Robbins 1986, 29). These are:

1. What standards will govern the operation of the institution?
2. Who will monitor the implementation of the standards?

3. Will the public still have access to the facility?

4. What recourse will members of the public have if they do not approve of how the institution is operated?

5. Who will be responsible for maintaining security and using force at the institution?

6. Who will be responsible for maintaining security if the private personnel go on strike?

7. Where will the responsibility for [incarcerative] disciplinary procedures lie?

8. Will the company be able to refuse to accept certain inmates, such as those with AIDS?

9. What options will be available to the government if the corporation substantially raises its fees?

10. What safeguards will prevent a private contractor from making a low initial bid to obtain a contract and then raising the price after the government is no longer immediately able to reassume the task of operating the facility?

11. What will happen if the company declares bankruptcy?

12. What safeguards will prevent private vendors, after gaining a foothold in the corrections field, from lobbying for philosophical changes for their greater profit?

13. What options will the public have if they do not approve of how the institution is operated?

Currently, juvenile corrections has a large share of the privatization business. The Corrections Corporation of America (CCA), headquartered in Nashville, Tennessee, currently operates numerous facilities for both adults and juveniles throughout the United States. The CCA began operating several juvenile facilities in Tennessee in 1985, although there have been continuing debates and controversies over the years about the effectiveness of private corrections for the state (Kyle 1998, 88, 158). Other private interests are increasingly entering these correctional areas to provide services and supervisory tasks, often at less cost to taxpayers than government-operated facilities (Geis, Mobley, and Shichor 1999).

Favorably for privatization, private interests can often cut the red tape associated with secure confinement operations (Armstrong 2001). The private sector can work cooperatively with the public sector in providing the best of both worlds for offenders. Private sector operations can reward employees more quickly for excellent service performed, and new operational ideas may be implemented more quickly in private operations compared with government organizations. Further, many of those involved in private corrections operations have formerly been employed in administrative and staff capacities in public corrections agencies and institutions. Thus, they possess experience to do the job and do it well (Haas and Alpert 1999).

The profit issue is often raised by opponents of privatization of corrections (U.S. National Institute of Justice 2000; Witke 1999). In turn, this profit motive may inspire private interests to keep inmates confined for longer periods to maximize profits. However, it is apparent that the current state of chronic overcrowding in both adult and juvenile incarcerative facilities will continue, regardless of whether these institutions are privately or publicly operated (Seiter 1999). Also, if private interests can make a profit while providing quality services to inmates at less cost to government, this seems to be a compelling argument in favor of greater privatization (Wright 1998).

The Classification of Juvenile Offenders

Classification of any offender is made difficult by the fact that the state-of-the-art is such in predictions of risk and dangerousness that little future behavior can be accurately forecasted (Jones and Harris 1999). This holds for juveniles as well as adults. We know that status offenders may or may not escalate to more serious offenses, with the prevailing sentiment favoring or implying nonescalation (Crowe 2000). Fully effective classification schemes have not yet been devised, although we know that on the basis of descriptions of existing aggregates of offenders, factors such as gender, age, nature of offense, seriousness of offense, race or ethnicity, and socioeconomic status are more or less correlated.

The flaws of various classification schemes are made more apparent when program failures are detected in large numbers. Juvenile court judges make the wrong judgments and decisions about juvenile placements (Young 1999). Intake officers make similar errors of classification when conducting initial screenings of juveniles. The issue of false positives and false negatives is raised here, because some youths may be unfairly penalized for what authorities believe are valid predictive criteria of future dangerousness. By the same token, some youths are underpenalized, because it is believed, wrongly, that they will not pose risks or commit serious offenses in the future. But these same offenders do pose risks (Dillingham et al. 1999).

Guarino-Ghezzi (1989, 112–114) has suggested that a systematic classification model can be devised by incorporating objective predictors of an offender's risk of recidivism into the intake assessment. She believes that an objective risk classification procedure can accomplish the following objectives:

1. Increase control over juvenile offenders who are placed in community settings.
2. Increase agency accountability for placement decisions.
3. Increase consistency in decision making.
4. Direct allocation of scarce resources.
5. Increase support for budget requests.

Guarino-Ghezzi (1989, 116) says that with few exceptions, administrative control factors are often given low priority whenever classification models are designed. But she encourages their adoption, since they are crucial in influencing how private vendors will react toward youths (in a privatization context, for instance), how youths will adjust to their programs, determining which youths are most likely to cause behavioral problems and assault staff, and whether gang involvement is indicated (possibly requiring a youth's separation from other gang members upon arrival at a new facility). Some results of more effective classification schemes include greater staff accountability, greater staff and inmate safety, and more effective programming relative to individual offenders and their needs.

Juveniles Held in Adult Jails or Lockups

The most apparent problems with celling juveniles in adult lockups or jails are that (1) youths are subject to potential sexual assault from older inmates and (2) youths are often traumatized by the jailing experience (Kerle 1998). This latter problem leads to another problem that is even more serious—jail suicides. Juveniles are especially suicide-prone during the first 24 hours of their incarceration in jails. Thus, it is little consolation that states such as Illinois pass laws prohibiting a juvenile's confinement in adult jails for periods longer than six hours (Huskey 1990). And Dale (1988, 46) says that a juvenile's potential sexual exploitation does not always involve other, older inmates. In Ironton, Ohio, for example, Dale reports a case of sexual assault against a detained juvenile status offender by a corrections officer. Although a $40,000 judgment was subsequently awarded the youth, no amount of money can remove completely the trauma to a juvenile resulting from such a violent sexual incident (*Doe v. Burwell* 1981).

Currently, there are organized movements in many jurisdictions to mandate the permanent removal of juveniles from adult jails, even on temporary bases (Reed 1997). Civil rights suits as well as class action claims are being filed by and on behalf of many juveniles currently detained in adult facilities (Howell and Krisberg 1998). In the Iowa case of *Hendrickson v. Griggs* (1987), a federal district judge, Donald E. O'Brien, ruled that the Juvenile Justice and Delinquency Prevention Act could be used as the basis for a lawsuit seeking the permanent removal of juveniles from adult jails. Much remains to be done to rectify a situation that seems more within the purview of the juvenile justice system rather than within the criminal justice system (Reddington and Anderson 1996).

SUMMARY

Juvenile corrections encompasses all personnel, agencies, and institutions that supervise youthful offenders. Besides nominal and conditional sanctions that juvenile courts may impose, nonsecure and secure custodial sanctions may also be administered. Nonsecure detention includes programs that permit limited access to communities, but where various conditions are imposed, including the observance of curfews, regular urinalyses for the detection of illegal drugs or alcohol, participation in individual or group therapy, and vocational or educational coursework. Secure detention includes youth centers, industrial schools, and other prisonlike institutions where a youth's movements are confined to the premises.

The goals of juvenile corrections are rehabilitation and community reintegration, delinquency prevention, punishment and retribution, and isolation and control. Currently, the "get-tough" movement is pervasive throughout the juvenile justice system, and the emphasis is upon juvenile offender accountability and punishment. However, rehabilitative aims of detention have not been neglected. Foster home placements, group homes, halfway houses, camps and ranches, and wilderness experiences or experience programs are considered nonsecure types of sanctions that juvenile courts can impose. Their successfulness varies according to the type of program, although most authorities believe that youths tend to benefit from these experiences. VisionQuest is one of the better-known experience programs designed to provide participants with a greater degree of self-reliance and an improved self-concept. Outdoor skills are stressed, together with group discussions and activities that enable youths to function independently in a socially healthy environment.

Juvenile detention has undergone substantial reforms in recent years. The establishment of juvenile detention resource centers has improved the quality of detention staff and has helped to expand the service options available to detained youths. Major detention issues concern whether youths should be detained in adult jails or lockups and whether privatization should be used to accommodate growing numbers of youthful offenders. Better classification schemes are being designed to make more favorable placements of juveniles in either nonsecure or secure detention institutions.

Youths may be paroled from secure facilities through informal processes in most jurisdictions. Although U.S. Supreme Court caselaw relating to juvenile probation and parole revocation is rare, several adult probation and parole revocation cases have been instrumental in guiding juvenile courts and juvenile corrections in establishing more objective guidelines for both early-release and parole/probation revocation decision making. These adult decisions are not binding on individual juvenile parole boards or juvenile court judges, however. Most decision making relating to juvenile probation or parole revocation is made at the state appellate or supreme court levels.

Selected issues in juvenile corrections include the privatization of juvenile corrections, classifying juvenile offenders, and whether juveniles should be held in adult jails or lockups. The privatization issue is presently a pervasive one, and there are both proponents and opponents of privatization of juvenile corrections. However, private operation of juvenile correctional facilities has been occurring for several decades, and there are no successful court challenges to the privatization of juvenile corrections thus far. In all cases where private enterprise operates facilities to house and/or supervise juvenile offenders, these operations are thoroughly inspected and approved by the states utilizing private services. And private contractors are licensed and operate at the direction and under the control of state juvenile justice officials.

Classification of juvenile offenders for correctional purposes is less well-established compared with classification for adult offenders. Most states currently are developing or revising classification mechanisms for juveniles, although instrumental flaws are pervasive similar to those that affect the validity and reliability of adult classification instrumentation. Each year, classification devices are being revised and/or developed to more adequately assess offender needs as well as risks posed by particular juveniles. Noticeable improvements in such instrumentation have assisted various agencies and communities in establishing better services for juvenile offenders as well as more effective placements in secure and nonsecure facilities.

It is likely the case that some juveniles will continue to be housed for brief periods in adult jails or lockups. Short-term detention of juveniles in adult facilities is both reasonable and constitutional, particularly where it is difficult to determine a youth's identity or age. Initiatives have been implemented in virtually every jurisdiction in the United States to remove juveniles from adult jails. However, these initiatives have been hampered by many factors, including limited accommodations for juvenile offenders whenever they are arrested or taken into custody by police in various jurisdictions.

QUESTIONS FOR REVIEW

1. What are the goals of juvenile corrections? How do these goals differ from one another?

2. What are foster homes? How do they differ from group homes?

3. What are halfway houses? What are their functions and goals?

4. What are wilderness experiences and what are their functions?

5. What is meant by shock probation? What are several different types of shock probation? What are some major differences between each?

6. What is a boot camp? What are some specific goals and features of boot camps? Are they effective? Why or why not?

7. What are some major differences between short- and long-term secure juvenile facilities?

8. What is meant by juvenile parole? How much juvenile parole is there? Is juvenile parole successful? Why or why not?

9. What are three key adult probation and parole revocation cases that have guided state juvenile probation and parole revocation decision making?

10. What are three examples of probation and parole revocation cases for juveniles?

SUGGESTED READINGS

Armstrong, Gaylene Styve. 2001. *Private vs. public operation of juvenile correctional facilities.* New York: LFB Scholarly Publishing.

Butts, Jeffrey and William Adams. 2001. *Anticipating space needs in juvenile detention and correctional facilities.* Washington, DC: U.S. Department of Justice.

Crowe, Ann H. 2000. *Jurisdictional technical assistance package for juvenile corrections.* Washington, DC: Office of Juvenile Justice and Delinquency Prevention.

MacKenzie, Doris Layton et al. 2001. The impact of boot camps and traditional institutions on juvenile residents: Perceptions, adjustments, and change. *Journal of Research in Crime and Delinquency* 38:279–313.

Mears, Daniel P. 2001. Getting tough with juvenile offenders: Explaining support for sanctioning youths as adults. *Criminal Justice and Behavior* 18:206–226.

INTERNET CONNECTIONS

American Correctional Association
http://www.aca.org/

Boot Camps
http://www.boot-camps-info.com

Boot Camp Information
http://www.ncjrs.org/txtfiles/evalboot.txt

Close Cheltenham Now!
http://www.closecheltenham.org/

Corrections Connection
http://www.corrections.com

Debt to Society
http://www.motherjones.com/prisons/

Engaged Zen Foundation
http://www.engaged-zen.org/

Families Against Mandatory Minimums
http://www.famm.org/index2.htm

Federal Bureau of Prisons
http://www.bop.gov/bopmain.html

Fortune Society
http://www.fortunesociety.org/

Howard League
http://www.howardleague.org/

John Howard Association
http://www.johnhowardassociation.org/

Juvenile Boot Camps
http://www.juvenile-boot-camps.com/?source=overture

National Coalition to Abolish the Death Penalty
http://www.ncadp.org/

National Institute of Corrections
http://www.bop.gov/nicpg/nicmain.html

Other Side of the Wall
http://www.prisonwall.org/

Penal Reform
http://www.penalreform.org/

Prison Industry
http://www.corpwatch.org/

Prison Issues Desk
http://www.prisonactivist.org/

Stop Prison Rape
http://www.spr.org/index.html

Teen Boot Camps
http://www.teenbootcamps.com/resources/BootCamps.html

Glossary

About Face Georgia boot camp program. (See also **Boot camps**)

Acceptance of responsibility Genuine admission or acknowledgment of wrong-doing; in federal presentence investigation reports, for example, convicted offenders may write an explanation and apology for the crime(s) they committed; a provision that may be considered in deciding whether leniency should be extended to offenders during the sentencing phase of their processing.

Act to Regulate the Treatment and Control of Dependent, Neglected, and Delinquent Children Delinquency Act passed by Illinois legislature in 1899; established first juvenile court among states.

Actuarial justice When the traditional orientation of juvenile justice, rehabilitation and individualized treatment, has been supplanted by the goal of efficient offender processing.

Actuarial prediction Projection of future inmate behavior based on a class of offenders similar to those considered for parole.

Addams, Jane Established Hull House in Chicago during 1880s; assisted wayward and homeless youths.

Adjudication Judgment or action on a petition filed with the juvenile court by others.

Adjudication hearing Formal proceeding involving a prosecuting attorney and a defense attorney where evidence is presented and the juvenile's guilt or innocence is determined by the juvenile judge; about one-fifth of all jurisdictions permit jury trials for juveniles under certain circumstances, with or without judicial approval.

Adversarial proceedings Opponent-driven court litigation, where one side opposes the other; prosecution seeks to convict or find defendants guilty, while defense counsel seeks to defend their clients and seek their acquittal.

Aftercare A wide variety of programs and services available to both adult and juvenile probationers and parolees; includes halfway houses, psychological counseling services, community-based correctional agencies, employment assistance, and medical treatment for offenders or ex-offenders.

Age of majority Chronological date when one reaches adulthood, usually either 18 or 21, when juveniles are no longer under the jurisdiction of the juvenile courts but, rather, the criminal courts; also age of consent.

Aggravating circumstances Factors that may enhance the severity of one's sentence; these include brutality of act, whether serious bodily injury or death occurred to a victim during crime commission, and whether offender was on probation or parole when crime was committed.

Alternative dispute resolution (ADR) Procedure whereby a criminal case is redefined as a civil one and the case is decided by an impartial arbiter, where both parties agree to amicable settlement; criminal court is not used for resolving such matters; usually reserved for minor offenses; court-approved mediation programs where civilians are selected from community to help resolve minor delinquency, status offense, and abuse/neglect cases without formal judicial hearings.

American Correctional Association (ACA) Established in 1870 to disseminate information about correctional programs and correctional training; designed to foster professionalism throughout correctional community.

Anamnestic prediction Projection of inmate behavior according to past circumstances.

Anomie Condition of feelings of helplessness and normlessness.

Anomie theory Robert Merton's theory, influenced by Emile Durkheim, alleging that persons acquire desires for culturally approved goals to strive to achieve, but they adopt innovative, sometimes deviant, means to achieve these goals (e.g., someone may desire a nice home but lack or reject the institutionalized means to achieve this goal, instead using bank robbery, an innovative mean, to obtain money to realize the culturally approved goal). Implies normlessness.

Army model (See Boot camps)

Arraignment Following booking, a critical stage of the criminal justice process where defendants are asked to enter a plea to criminal charges, a trial date is established, and a formal list of charges is provided.

Arrest Taking persons into custody and restraining them until they can be brought before court to answer the charges against them.

Assessment centers Organizations selecting entry-level officers for correctional work; assessment centers hire correctional officers and probation or parole officers.

Assumptions Statements of fact about the real world or events; examples of assumptions might be, "All societies have laws," or "The greater the deviant conduct, the greater the group pressure on the deviant to conform to group norms."

Atavism Positivist school of thought arguing that a biological condition renders a person incapable of living within the social constraints of a society; according to Cesare Lombroso, the physical characteristics that distinguish born criminals from the general population and are evolutionary throwbacks to animals or primitive people.

At-risk youths Any juveniles who are considered more susceptible to the influence of gangs and delinquent peers; tend to be characterized as having less developed reading skills, greater immaturity, lower socioeconomic status, parental dysfunction, and who are otherwise disadvantaged by their socioeconomic and environmental circumstances.

Automatic transfer laws Jurisdictional laws that provide for automatic waivers of juveniles to criminal court for processing; legislatively prescribed directive to transfer juveniles of specified ages who have committed especially serious offenses to jurisdiction of criminal courts.

Bail Surety provided by defendants or others to guarantee their subsequent appearance in court to face criminal charges; bail is available to anyone entitled to bail; bail is denied when suspects are considered dangerous or likely to flee.

Bail bond Written guarantee, often accompanied by money or other securities, that the person charged with an offense will remain within the court's jurisdiction to face trial at a time in the future.

Balanced approach Probation orientation that simultaneously emphasizes community protection, offender accountability, individualization of treatments, and competency assessment and development.

Banishment Sanction used to punish offenders by barring them from a specified number of miles from settlements or towns; often a capital punishment, since those banished could not obtain food or water to survive the isolation.

Barker balancing test Speedy trial standard, where delays are considered in terms of the reason, length, existence of prejudice against the defendant by the prosecutor, and the assertion of the defendant's speedy trial rights [from the case of *Barker v. Wingo,* 407 U.S. 514 (1972)].

Beats Patrol areas assigned to police officers in neighborhoods.

Beccaria, Cesare (1738–1794) Developed classical school of criminology; considered "father of classical criminology"; wrote *Essays on Crimes and Punishments;* believed corporal punishment unjust and ineffective; believed that crime could be prevented by plain legal codes specifying prohibited behaviors and punishments; promoted just-deserts philosophy; also endorsed a *utilitarianism* approach to criminal conduct and its punishment by suggesting that useful, purposeful, and reasonable punishments ought to be formulated and applied; also viewed criminal conduct as pleasurable to criminals and felt that they sought pleasure and avoided pain; thus, pain might function as a deterrent to criminal behavior.

Bench trials Proceedings where guilt or innocence of defendant is determined by the judge rather than a jury.

Beyond a reasonable doubt Evidentiary standard used in criminal courts to establish guilt or innocence of criminal defendant.

Big Brothers/Big Sisters Program Federation of over 500 agencies to serve children and adolescents; adults relate on a one-to-one basis with youths to promote their self-esteem and self-sufficiency; utilizes volunteers who attempt to instill responsibility, excellence, and leadership among assisted youths.

Biological determinism View in criminology holding that criminal behavior has physiological basis; genes, foods and food additives, hormones, and inheritance are all believed to play a role in determining individual behavior; one's genetic makeup causes certain behaviors to become manifest, such as criminality.

Blended sentencing Any type of sentencing procedure where either a criminal or juvenile court judge can impose *both* juvenile and/or adult incarcerative penalties.

Bonding theory A key concept in a number of theoretical formulations. Emile Durkheim's notion that deviant behavior is controlled to the degree that group members feel morally bound to one another, are committed to common goals and share a collective con-science; in social control theory, the elements of attachment, commitment, involvement, and belief; explanation of criminal behavior implying that criminality is the result of a loosening of bonds or attachments with society; builds on differential association theory. Primarily designed to account for juvenile delinquency.

Booking Process of making written report of arrest, including name and address of arrested persons, the alleged crimes, arresting officers, place and time of arrest, physical description of suspect, photographs (sometimes called "mug shots"), and fingerprints.

Boot camps Also known as the Army model, programs patterned after basic training for new military recruits. Juvenile offenders are given a taste of hard military life, and such regimented activities and structure for up to 180 days are often sufficient to "shock" them into giving up their lives of delinquency or crime and staying out of jail.

Boston Offender Project (BOP) Experimental program in Boston targeted for violent juveniles; program goals include reducing recidivism among them, enhancing public protection by increasing accountability for major violators, and improving the likelihood of successful reintegration of juveniles into society by focusing upon these offenders' academic and vocational skills.

Bridewell Workhouse Sixteenth-century London jail (sometimes gaol) established in 1557; known for providing cheap labor to business and mercantile interests; jailers and sheriffs profited from prisoner exploitation.

Bullying Prevention Program Targets bullies in elementary, middle, and high schools; vests school authorities with intervention powers to establish class rules for disciplining bullies and bullying behavior through student committees.

Capital punishment Imposition of the death penalty for the most serious crimes; may be administered by electrocution, lethal injection, gas, hanging, or shooting.

Career escalation Moving as a juvenile offender to progressively more serious offenses as new offenses are committed; committing new violent offenses after adjudications for property offenses would be career escalation; committing progressively more serious offenses.

CASASTART Program Targets high-risk youths who are exposed to drugs and delinquent activity; decreases risk factors by greater community involvement.

Caseloads Number of cases a probation or parole officer is assigned according to some standard such as a week, month, or year; caseloads vary among jurisdictions.

Case supervision planning A means whereby a probation or parole department makes assignments of probationers or parolees to probation officers or parole officers.

Certification Similar to waivers or transfers; in some jurisdictions, juveniles are certified or designated as adults for the purpose of pursuing a criminal prosecution against them.

Chancellors Civil servants who acted on behalf of King of England during Middle Ages; chancellors held court and settled property disputes, trespass cases, and minor property offenses; thievery, vagrancy, and public drunkenness.

Chancery courts Court of equity rooted in early English common law where civil disputes are resolved; also responsible for juvenile matters and adjudicating family matters such as divorce; has jurisdiction over contract disputes, property boundary claims, and exchanges of goods disputes.

Children at risk (See **At-risk youths**)

Children in need of supervision (CHINS) Any children determined by the juvenile court and other agencies to be in need of community care or supervision.

Children's tribunals Informal court mechanisms originating in Massachusetts to deal with children charged with crimes apart from system of criminal courts for adults.

Childsavers, Child-saving movement Organized effort during early 1800s in United States, comprised primarily of upper and middle class interests who sought to provide assistance to wayward youths; assistance was often food and shelter, although social, educational, and religious values were introduced to children later in compulsory schooling.

Chronic offenders Habitual offenders; repeat offenders; persistent offenders; youths who commit frequent delinquent acts.

Citizen action model Youth Service Bureau model using community volunteers to actively intervene and assist in the lives of delinquency-prone youths.

Civil tribunals (See **Children's tribunals**)

Classical school Line of thought that assumes that people are rational beings who choose between good and evil.

Classical theory A criminological perspective indicating that people have free will to choose either criminal or conventional behavior; people choose to commit crime for reasons of greed or personal need; crime can be controlled by criminal sanctions, which should be proportionate to the guilt of the perpetrator.

Classification Means used by prisons and probation/parole agencies to separate offenders according to offense seriousness, type of offense, and other criteria; no classification system has been demonstrably successful at effective prisoner or client placements.

Cleared by arrest Term used by FBI in the *Uniform Crime Reports* to indicate that someone has been arrested for a reported crime; does not necessarily mean that the crime has been solved or that the actual criminals who committed the crime have been apprehended or convicted.

Clinical prediction Forecast of inmate behavior based upon professional's expert training and working directly with offenders.

Combination sentences Occur whenever judges sentence offenders to a term, a portion of which includes incarceration and a term of which includes probation.

Common law Authority based on court decrees and judgments that recognize, affirm, and enforce certain usages and customs of the people; laws determined by judges in accordance with their rulings.

Community Board Program Civil mediation mechanism utilizing volunteers to mediate between victims and offenders.

Community corrections acts Enabling legislation by individual states to fund local government units to provide community facilities, services, and resources to juveniles who are considered at risk of becoming delinquent or who are already delinquent and need treatment/services.

Community organization model Youth Services Bureau model that uses citizens on a voluntary basis to assist delinquency-prone youth.

Community policing Major police reform that broadens the police mission from a narrow focus on crime to a mandate that encourages the police to explore creative solutions for a host of community concerns, including crime, fear of crime, disorder, and neighborhood decay; rests on belief that only by working together will citizens and police be able to improve the quality of life in their communities, with the police not only as enforcers, but also as advisors, facilitators, and supporters of new community-based police-supervised initiatives.

Community reintegration model Operating theory whereby offender who has been incarcerated is able to live in community under some supervision and gradually adjust to life outside of prison or jail.

Community service Any activity imposed on a probationer or parolee involving work in one's neighborhood or city, performed in part to repay victims and the city for injuries or damages caused by one's unlawful actions.

Community Service Program, Inc. (CSP, Inc.) Established in Orange County, California; designed to instill self-confidence in youths, reduce parental and familial dysfunction, and establish self-reliance and esteem through family counseling therapy and sessions.

Compulsory School Act Passed in 1899 by Colorado; targeted those youths who were habitually absent from school; encompassed youths who wandered the streets during school hours; originally designed to enforce truancy laws; erroneously regarded as first juvenile court act, which was actually passed in Illinois in 1899.

Concentric zone hypothesis Series of rings originating from a city center, such as Chicago, and emanating outward, forming various zones characterized by different socioeconomic conditions; believed to contain areas of high delinquency and crime.

Concurrent jurisdiction Power to file charges against juveniles in either criminal courts or juvenile courts.

Conditional dispositions Results of a delinquency adjudication that obligate youths to comply with one or more conditions of a probation program, such as restitution, community service, work study, therapy, educational participation, or victim compensation.

Conditional probation Program where divertee is involved in some degree of local monitoring by probation officers or personnel affiliated with local probation departments.

Confidentiality privilege Right between defendant and his or her attorney where certain information cannot be disclosed to prosecutors or others because of the attorney-client relation; for juveniles, records have been maintained under secure circumstances with limited access, and only then accessed by those in authority with a clear law enforcement purpose.

Conformity Robert K. Merton's mode of adaptation characterized by persons who accept institutionalized means to achieve culturally approved goals.

Consent decrees Formal agreements that involve children, their parents, and the juvenile court, where youths are placed under the court's supervision without an official finding of delinquency, with judicial approval.

Containment theory Explanation elaborated by Walter Reckless and others that positive self-image enables persons otherwise disposed toward criminal behavior to avoid criminal conduct and conform to societal values. Every person is a part of an external structure and has a protective internal structure providing defense, protection, and/or insulation against one's peers, such as delinquents.

Contempt of court Any citation by a judge against anyone in court who disrupts the proceedings or does anything to interfere with judicial decrees or pronouncements.

Conventional model Caseload assignment model where probation or parole officers are assigned clients randomly.

Conventional model with geographic considerations Similar to conventional model; caseload assignment model is based upon the travel time required for POs to meet with offender-clients regularly.

Convictions Judgments of a court, based on a jury or judicial verdict, or on the guilty pleas of defendants, that the defendants are guilty of the offenses alleged.

Cooperating agencies model Youth Service Bureau model where several agencies act as a team to provide delinquency-prone youths with needed services.

C.O.P.Y. Kids (Community Opportunities Program for Youth) Spokane, Washington, program for disadvantaged youth commenced in 1992; youth participated in arts and crafts and learned valuable work skills.

Corporate gangs Juvenile gangs emulate organized crime; profit-motivated gangs that rely on illicit activities, such as drug trafficking, to further their profit interests.

Corrections Aggregate of programs, services, facilities, and organizations responsible for the management of people who have been accused or convicted of criminal offenses.

Court of record Any court where a written record is kept of court proceedings.

Court reporters Court officials who keep a written word-for-word and/or tape-recorded record of court proceedings.

Court unification Proposal that seeks to centralize and integrate the diverse functions of all courts of general, concurrent, and exclusive jurisdiction into a more simplified and uncomplicated scheme.

Courts of equity (See **Chancery courts**)

Creative sentencing Broad class of punishments as alternatives to incarceration that are designed to fit the particular crimes; may involve community service, restitution, fines, becoming involved in educational or vocational training programs, or becoming affiliated with other "good works" activity.

Crime control model Criminal justice program that emphasizes containment of dangerous offenders and societal protection; a way of controlling delinquency by incapacitating juvenile offenders through some secure detention or through intensive supervision programs operated by community-based agencies.

Criminal-exclusive blend Form of sentencing by a criminal court judge where either juvenile or adult sentences of incarceration can be imposed, but not both.

Criminal-inclusive blend Form of sentencing by a criminal court judge where both juvenile and adult sentences can be imposed simultaneously.

Criminal informations Charges filed by prosecutors directly against defendants; usually involve minor crimes.

Criminal justice Interdisciplinary field studying nature and operations of organizations providing justice services to society; consists of lawmaking bodies including state legislatures and Congress, local, state, and federal agencies that try to enforce the law.

Criminal justice professional Anyone interested in studying the criminal justice system; may have a Ph.D. or master's degree in criminal justice or a related field; may be a practitioner, such as a police officer, corrections officer, probation or parole officer, prosecutor, or judge.

Criminal justice system, criminal justice process Interrelated set of agencies and organizations designed to control criminal behavior, to detect crime, and to apprehend, process, prosecute, punish, and/or rehabilitate criminal offenders.

Criminogenic environment Setting where juveniles may feel like criminals or may acquire the characteristics or labels of criminals; settings include courtrooms and prisons.

Criminologist Professional or scholar who studies crime, criminal law, criminals and criminal behavior, examining the etiology of crime and criminal behavior and crime trends.

Criminology Study of crime, the science of crime and criminal behavior, the forms of criminal behavior, the causes of crime, the definition of criminality, and the societal reaction to crime.

Cultural transmission theory Explanation emphasizing transmission of criminal behavior through socialization. Views delinquency as socially learned behavior transmitted from one generation to the next in disorganized urban areas.

Curfew violators Youths who violate laws and ordinances of communities prohibiting youths on the streets after certain evening hours, such as 10:00 P.M.; curfew itself is a delinquency prevention strategy.

Custodial dispositions Either nonsecure or secure options resulting from a delinquency adjudication; juveniles may be placed in foster homes, group homes, community-based correctional facilities, or secure detention facilities that are either publicly or privately operated.

Dangerousness Defined differently in several jurisdictions; prior record of violent offenses; potential to commit future violent crimes if released; propensity to inflict injury; predicted risk of convicted offender or prison or jail inmate; likelihood of inflicting harm upon others.

D.A.R.E. (Drug Abuse Resistance Education) Intervention program sponsored and implemented by the Los Angeles Police Department; utilizes officers familiar with drugs and drug laws who visit schools in their precincts and speak to youths about how to say "no" to drugs; children are taught how to recognize illegal drugs, different types of drugs, as well as their adverse effects.

Day reporting centers Established in England in 1974 to provide intensive supervision for low-risk offenders who lived in neighborhoods; continued in various U.S. jurisdictions today to manage treatment programs, supervise fee collection, and other responsibilities, such as drug-testing and counseling.

Death penalty Sentence that terminates the life of an offender, either through lethal gas, electrocution, lethal injection, hanging, or by firing squad.

Decarceration Type of deinstitutionalization where juveniles charged with status offenses are still under court jurisdiction and subject to filing of petitions; detention of youths is prohibited; youths may be removed from their homes and placed in nonsecure facilities, put on probation, required to attend treatment or service programs, and subjected to other behavioral restraints.

Defendant Anyone charged with one or more crimes.

Defense attorneys Advocates for juvenile defendants; represent the interests and defend the rights of juveniles in either juvenile or criminal courts.

Deinstitutionalization of status offenses (DSO) Eliminating status offenses from broad category of delinquent acts and removing juveniles from or precluding their confinement in juvenile correctional facilities; the process of removing status offenses from jurisdiction of juvenile court so that status offenders cannot be subject to secure confinement.

Delinquency Act committed by an infant of not more than a specified age who has violated criminal laws or engages in disobedient, indecent, or immoral conduct, and is in need of treatment, rehabilitation, or supervision; status acquired through an adjudicatory proceeding by juvenile court.

Delinquent child Infant of not more than a specified age who has violated criminal laws or engages in disobedient, indecent, or immoral conduct and is in need of treatment, rehabilitation, or supervision.

Demand waiver Requests by juveniles to have their cases transferred from juvenile courts to criminal courts.

Dependent and neglected children Youths considered by social services or the juvenile court to be in need of some type of adult supervision.

Detention centers Juvenile secure facilities used for serious and violent juveniles who are awaiting an adjudication hearing.

Detention hearing Judicial or quasi-judicial proceeding held to determine whether it is appropriate to continue to hold or detain a juvenile in a shelter facility.

Determinism Concept holding that persons do not have a free will but rather are subject to the influence of various forces over which they have little or no control.

Differential association theory Edwin Sutherland's theory of deviance and criminality through associations with others who are deviant or criminal; theory includes dimensions of frequency, duration, priority, and intensity; persons become criminal or delinquent because of a preponderance of learned definitions that are favorable to violating the law over learned definitions unfavorable to it.

Differential reinforcement theory Explanation that combines elements of labeling theory and a psychological phenomenon known as conditioning; persons are rewarded for engaging in desirable behavior and punished for deviant conduct.

Direct file Prosecutorial waiver of jurisdiction to a criminal court; an action taken against a juvenile who has committed an especially serious offense, where that juvenile's case is transferred to criminal court for the purpose of a criminal prosecution.

Discretionary powers Relating to the police role, police discretion is the distribution of nonnegotiable coercive force employed in accordance with the dictates of an intuitive grasp of situational exigencies; police have authority to use force to enforce the law, if in the officer's opinion, the situation demands it.

Discretionary waivers Transfers of juveniles to criminal courts by judges, at their discretion or in their judgment; also known as **judicial waivers.**

Dispose To decide the punishment to be imposed on a juvenile following an adjudication hearing.

Dispositions Punishments resulting from a delinquency adjudication; may be nominal, conditional, or custodial.

Diversion Official halting or suspension of legal proceedings against criminal defendants after a recorded justice system entry, and possible referral of those persons to treatment or care programs administered by a nonjustice or private agency. See also **Pretrial release.**

Diversion Plus Program Established in Lexington, Kentucky, in 1991, designed to reduce recidivism and promote conformity to the law without stigmatization; youths targeted included first offenders, low-risk delinquent offenders, and any youth without a prior juvenile record; consists of a series of weekly meetings and self-help sessions, stressing self-esteem and self-control, substance abuse prevention, and independent living, one-on-one counseling, and small group interaction.

Divestiture Strategy for deinstitutionalizing status offenders, where juvenile courts cannot detain, petition, adjudicate, or place youths on probation for any status offense; according to legislatively created statutes, juvenile court does not accept most, if not all, status offense cases.

Double jeopardy Subjecting persons to prosecution more than once in the same jurisdiction for the same offense, usually without new or vital evidence; prohibited by the Fifth Amendment.

Drift theory David Matza's term denoting a state of limbo in which youths move in and out of delinquency and in which their lifestyles embrace both conventional and deviant values.

Due process Basic constitutional right to a fair trial, presumption of innocence until guilt is proven beyond a reasonable doubt, the opportunity to be heard, to be aware of a matter that is pending, to make an informed choice whether to acquiesce or contest, and to provide the reasons for such a choice before a judicial official.

Due process model Treatment model based upon one's constitutional right to a fair trial, to have an opportunity to be heard, to be aware of matters that are pending, to a presumption of innocence until guilt has been established beyond a reasonable doubt, to make an informed choice whether to acquiesce or contest, and to provide the reasons for such a choice before a judicial officer.

Ectomorphs Body type described by Sheldon; persons are thin, sensitive, delicate.

Ego The part of one's personality that represents the identity of the individual and actual behavior.

Electronic monitoring Use of electronic devices that emit electronic signals; these devices, anklets or wristlets, are worn by offenders, probationers, and parolees; the purpose of such monitoring is to monitor an offender's presence in a given environment where the offender is required to remain or to verify the offender's whereabouts.

Electronic monitoring signalling devices Apparatuses worn about the wrist or leg that are designed to monitor an offender's presence in a given environment where the offender is required to remain.

Endomorphs Body type described by Sheldon; persons are fat, soft, plump, jolly.

Exculpatory evidence Information considered beneficial to defendants, tending to show their innocence.

Expungement orders Deletion of one's arrest record from official sources; in most jurisdictions, juvenile delinquency records are expunged when the youth reaches the age of majority or adulthood.

Extralegal factors Characteristics influencing intake decisions, such as juvenile offender attitudes, school grades and standing, gender, race, ethnicity, socioeconomic status, and age.

Faith in Families Multi-Systematic Therapy Program (MST) Operated by the Henry and Rilla White Foundation in Bronson, Florida; attempts to modify youth behaviors by working with their interpersonal environment, including family, therapists, and peer groups; subjects taught include self-control, anger management, self-reflectiveness, and problem-solving skills.

False negatives Offenders predicted not to be dangerous who turn out to be dangerous.

False positives Offenders predicted to be dangerous who turn out not to be dangerous.

Family model Established under the Juvenile Law of 1948, exist in all Japanese jurisdictions and hear any matters pertaining to juvenile delinquency, child abuse and neglect, and child custody matters; both status offenders and delinquents appear before Family Court judges; similar to juvenile court judges in U.S. jurisdictions, Family Court judges have considerable discretionary authority; decide cases within the *parens patriae* context.

FAST Track Program Rural and urban intervention program targeting girls and boys of many ethnicities; designed to provide severe and chronic misconduct problems for high-risk children.

Felonies Crimes punishable by imprisonment in prison for a term of one or more years; major crimes; any index offense.

Fines Financial penalties imposed at time of sentencing convicted offenders; most criminal statutes contain provisions for the imposition of monetary penalties as sentencing options.

First offender Criminal who has no previous criminal records; this person may have committed crimes, but he or she has only been caught for the instant offense.

Flat time Frequent known as hard time, meaning the actual amount of time one must serve while incarcerated.

Foster homes Temporary placement of youths in need of supervision or control; usually families volunteer to act as foster parents and maintain placed youths for short-term care.

Friends for the Love of Reading Project Self-help program and offshoot of District of Columbia Book Buddies Program designed to assist youths with poor reading abilities to improve their reading skills; involves parents and volunteers on a one-to-one basis with youths.

Gangs Groups who form an allegiance for a common purpose and engage in unlawful or criminal activity; any group gathered together on a continuing basis to engage in or commit antisocial behavior.

Gemeinschaft Term created by Ferdinand Tönnies, a social theorist, to describe small, traditional communities where informal punishments were used to punish those who violated community laws.

Gesellschaft Term created by Ferdinand Tönnies, a social theorist, to describe more formalized, larger communities and cities that relied on written documents and laws to regulate social conduct.

Get-tough movement General orientation toward criminals and juvenile delinquents that favors the maximum penalties and punishments for crime and delinquency; any action toward toughening of strengthening sentencing provisions or dispositions involving adults or juveniles.

Grand juries Investigative bodies whose numbers vary among states; duties include determining probable cause regarding commission of a crime and returning formal charges against suspects. See **True bill** and **No bill**.

G.R.E.A.T. (Gang Resistance Education and Training) Established in Phoenix, Arizona; police officers visit schools and help youths understand how to cope with peer pressure to commit delinquent acts; topics of educational programs include victim rights, drugs and neighborhoods, conflict resolution, and need fulfillment.

Group homes Also known as group centers or foster homes, these are facilities for juveniles that provide limited supervision and support; juveniles live in home-like environment with other juveniles and participate in therapeutic programs and counseling; considered nonsecure custodial.

Guardians ad litem Special authorities appointed by the court in which particular litigation is pending to represent a youth, ward, or unborn person in that particular litigation.

Habeas corpus Writ meaning "produce the body"; used by prisoners to challenge the nature and length of their confinement.

Halfway houses Nonconfining residential facilities intended to provide alternative to incarceration as a period of readjustment of offenders to the community after confinement.

Hands-off doctrine Policy practiced by the federal courts, where official court policy was not to intervene in matters relating to adult corrections; belief that correctional superintendents and wardens and departments of corrections are in best position to make decisions about welfare of inmates; applied to juvenile corrections and juvenile courts similarly.

Hard time Also known as flat time, actual amount of secure confinement juveniles must serve as the result of a custodial disposition from a juvenile court judge.

Hedonism Jeremy Bentham's term indicating that people avoid pain and pursue pleasure.

Hidden delinquency Infractions reported by surveys of high school youths; considered "hidden" because it most often is undetected by police officers; disclosed delinquency through self-report surveys.

Home confinement Program intended to house offenders in their own homes with or without electronic devices; reduces prison overcrowding and prisoner costs; intermediate punishment involving the use of offender residences for mandatory incarceration during evening hours after a curfew and on weekends.

Home incarceration (See Home confinement)

Homeward Bound Established in Massachusetts in 1970; designed to provide juveniles with mature responsibilities through the acquisition of survival skills and wilderness experiences. A six-week training program subjected 32 youths to endurance training, physical fitness, and performing community service.

Hospital of Saint Michael Custodial institution established at request of Pope in Rome in 1704; provided for unruly youths and others who violated the law; youths were assigned tasks, including semi-skilled and skilled labor, which enabled them to get jobs when released.

House arrest (See **Home confinement**)

Houses of refuge Workhouses, the first of which was established in 1824 as a means of separating juveniles from the adult correctional process.

Id Sigmund Freud's term to depict that part of personality concerned with individual gratification; the "I want" part of a person, formed in one's early years.

Illinois Juvenile Court Act Legislation passed by Illinois legislature in 1899 providing for the first juvenile court and treatment programs for various types of juvenile offenders.

IMPACT (Intensive Motivational Program of Alternative Correctional Treatment Boot camp program operated in New York; incorporates educational training with strict physical and behavioral requirements.

Incident Specific criminal act involving one crime and one or more victims.

Inculpatory evidence Information considered adverse to defendants or tending to show their guilt.

Indentured servants, indentured servant system Voluntary slave pattern where persons without money for passage from England entered into a contract with merchants or businessmen, usually for seven years, wherein merchants would pay for their voyage fare to the American colonies from England in exchange for their labor.

Index crimes Any violations of the law listed by the *Uniform Crime Reports* under **Index offenses** (e.g., homicide, rape, aggravated assault, robbery, burglary, larceny, arson).

Index offenses Specific felonies used by the Federal Bureau of Investigation in the *Uniform Crime Reports* to chart crime trends; there are eight index offenses listed prior to 1988 (aggravated assault, larceny, burglary, vehicular theft, arson, robbery, forcible rape, murder).

Indictments Charges or written accusations found and presented by a grand jury that a particular defendant probably committed a crime.

Infants Legal term applicable to juveniles who have not attained the age of majority; in most states, age of majority is 18.

Informations Sometimes called criminal informations; written accusations made by a public prosecutor against a person for some criminal offense, without an indictment; usually restricted to minor crimes or misdemeanors.

Initial appearance Formal proceeding during which the judge advises a defendant of the charges against him or her.

Innovation Robert K. Merton's mode of adaptation where persons reject institutionalized means to achieve culturally approved goals; instead, they engage in illegal acts, considered innovative, to achieve their goals.

Intake Critical phase where a determination is made by a juvenile probation officer or other official whether to release juveniles to their parent's custody, detain juveniles in formal detention facilities for a later court appearance, or release them to parents pending a later court appearance.

Intake hearings, intake screenings Proceedings where juvenile official, such as juvenile probation officer, conducts an interview with a youth charged with a delinquent or status offense.

Intake officer Juvenile probation officer who conducts screenings and preliminary interviews with alleged juvenile delinquents or status offenders and their families.

Intensive Aftercare Program (IAP) Philadelphia-based intervention for serious youthful offenders involving intensive counseling and training for acquiring self-help skills; recidivism of participants greatly reduced during study period of 1980–1990.

Intensive supervised probation (ISP) Controlled probation overseen by probation officer; involves close monitoring of offender activities by various means (also known as *Intensive probation supervision* or IPS).

Intensive supervision program Offender supervision program with following characteristics: (1) low officer/client caseloads (i.e., 30 or fewer probationers); (2) high levels of offender accountability (e.g., victim restitution, community service, payment of fines, partial defrayment of program expenses); (3) high levels of offender responsibility; (4) high levels of offender control (home confinement, electronic monitoring, frequent face-to-face visits by POs); (5) frequent checks for arrests, drug and/or alcohol use, and employment/school attendance (drug/alcohol screening, coordination with police departments and juvenile halls, teachers, family).

Interagency Agreement Plan Early intervention plan instituted in San Diego County, California, in 1982 for the purpose of reducing delinquency; graduated sanctions used for repeat offenders; youths held accountable for their actions; gradual increase of services and punishments for repeat offenders.

Intermediate punishments Sanctions involving sanctions existing somewhere between incarceration and probation on a continuum of criminal penalties; may include home incarceration and electronic monitoring.

Intermittent sentences Occur whenever judges sentence offenders to terms such as weekend confinement only.

Interstitial area In concentric zone hypothesis, area nearest the center of a city undergoing change, such as urban renewal; characterized by high rates of crime.

Jail as a condition of probation Sentence where judge imposes some jail time to be served before probation commences; also known as **shock probation.**

Jail removal initiative Action sponsored by the Office of Juvenile Justice and Delinquency Prevention and the Juvenile Justice and Delinquency Prevention Act of 1974 to deinstitutionalize juveniles from secure facilities, such as jails.

Jails City or county operated and financed facilities to contain those offenders who are serving short sentences; jails also house more serious prisoners from state or federal prisons through contracts to alleviate overcrowding; jails also house pretrial detainees, witnesses, juveniles, vagrants, and others.

Judicial waivers Decision by juvenile judge to waive juvenile to jurisdiction of criminal court.

Judicious nonintervention Similar to a "do nothing" policy of delinquency nonintervention.

Jurisdiction Power of a court to hear and determine a particular type of case; also refers to territory within which court may exercise authority such as a city, county, or state.

Jury (See **Petit jury**)

Jury trials Proceedings where guilt or innocence of defendant is determined by jury instead of by the judge.

Just-deserts/justice model Stresses offender accountability as a means to punish youthful offenders; uses victim compensation plans, restitution, and community services as ways of making offenders pay for their offenses; philosophy that emphasizes punishment as a primary objective of sentencing, fixed sentences, abolition of parole, and an abandonment of the rehabilitative ideal; rehabilitation is functional to the extent that offenders join rehabilitative programs voluntarily.

Juvenile-contiguous blend Form of sentencing by a juvenile court judge where the judge can impose a disposition beyond the normal jurisdictional range for juvenile offenders; e.g., a judge may impose a 30-year term on a 14-year-old offender, but the juvenile is entitled to a hearing when he or she reaches the age of majority to determine whether the remainder of the sentence shall be served.

Juvenile court records Formal or informal statement concerning an adjudication hearing involving sustained allegations against a juvenile; a written document of one's prior delinquency or status offending.

Juvenile courts Formal proceeding with jurisdiction over juveniles, juvenile delinquents, status offenders, dependent or neglected children, children in need of supervision, or infants.

Juvenile delinquency Violation of the law by a person prior to his or her eighteenth birthday; any illegal behavior committed by someone within a given age range punishable by juvenile court jurisdiction; whatever the juvenile court believes should be brought within its jurisdiction; violation of any state or local law or ordinance by anyone who has not as yet achieved the age of their majority.

Juvenile delinquents Infant of not more than a specified age who has violated criminal laws or engages in disobedient, indecent, or immoral conduct and is in need of treatment, rehabilitation, or supervision.

Juvenile-exclusive blend Sentencing form where a juvenile court judge can impose either adult or juvenile incarceration as a disposition and sentence but not both.

Juvenile-inclusive blend Form of sentencing where a juvenile court judge can impose *both* adult and juvenile incarceration simultaneously.

Juvenile intensive supervised probation (JISP) Ohio-operated program for youthful offenders, including home confinement, electronic monitoring, and other intensive probation supervision methods.

Juvenile Justice and Delinquency Prevention Act of 1974 (JJDPA) Legislation recommending various alternatives to incarcerating youths, including deinstitutionalization of status offending, removal of youths from secure confinement, and other rehabilitative treatments.

Juvenile justice system Stages through which juveniles are processed, sentenced, and corrected after arrests for juvenile delinquency.

Juvenile Mentoring Program (JUMP) Federally funded program administered by the Office of Juvenile Justice and Delinquency Prevention; promotes bonding between an adult and a juvenile relating on a one-to-one basis over time; designed to improve school performance and decrease gang participation and delinquency.

Juvenile offender Any infant or child who has violated juvenile laws.

Juvenile offender laws Regulations providing for automatic transfer of juveniles of certain ages to criminal courts for processing, provided they have committed especially serious crimes.

Juvenile Probation Camps (JPCs) California county-operated camps for delinquent youth placed on probation in early 1980s; including physical activities, community contacts, and academic training.

Juveniles Persons who have not reached the age of majority or adulthood.

Labeling Process whereby persons acquire self-definitions that are deviant or criminal; process occurs through labels applied to them by others

Labeling theory Explanation of deviant conduct attributed to Edwin Lemert whereby persons acquire self-definitions that are deviant or criminal; persons perceive themselves as deviant or criminal through labels applied to them by others; the more people are involved in the criminal justice system, the more they acquire self-definitions consistent with the criminal label.

Law enforcement officers Any persons sworn to uphold and enforce local, state, or federal laws.

Legal factors Variables influencing the intake decision relating to the factual information about delinquent acts; crime seriousness, type of crime committed, prior record of delinquency adjudications, and evidence of inculpatory or exculpatory nature.

Legislative waiver Provision that compels juvenile court to remand certain youths to criminal courts because of specific offenses that have been committed or alleged.

Libido Sigmund Freud's term describing the sex drive he believed innate in everyone.

Life-without-parole Penalty imposed as maximum punishment in states that do not have death penalty; provides for permanent incarceration of offenders in prisons, without parole eligibility; early release may be attained through accumulation of good time credits.

Litigation explosion Rapid escalation of case filings before appellate courts, often based upon a landmark case extending rights to particular segments of the population, such as jail or prison inmates or juveniles.

Lockups Short-term confinement facility; usually a small jail where drunks and disorderly persons are held for brief periods.

Lombroso, Cesare (1835–1909) Founder of the school of thought linking criminal behavior with abnormal, unusual physical characteristics.

Long-term detention Period of incarceration of juvenile offenders in secure facilities that averages 180 days in the United States.

Looking-glass self Concept originated by Charles Horton Cooley where persons learn appropriate ways of behaving by paying attention to how others view and react to them.

Mandatory waiver Automatic transfer of certain juveniles to criminal court on the basis of (1) their age and (2) the seriousness of their offense; e.g., a 17-year-old in Illinois who allegedly committed homicide would be subject to mandatory transfer to criminal court for the purpose of a criminal prosecution.

Mediation A process whereby a third party intervenes between a perpetrator and a victim to work out a noncriminal or civil resolution to a problem that might otherwise result in a delinquency adjudication or criminal conviction.

Mediator Third-party arbiter in alternative dispute resolution.

Medical model Known as the treatment model, this model considers criminal behavior as an illness to be treated; delinquency is also a disease subject to treatment.

Mesomorphs Body type described by Sheldon; persons are strong, muscular, aggressive, tough.

Midwestern Prevention Project Multifaceted program for adolescent drug abuse prevention; targets middle and late adolescents; assists youths to recognize pressures to use drugs and to avoid such pressures.

Minimum due process rights (See **Due process**)

Miranda warning Sanction given to suspects by police officers advising them of their legal rights to counsel, to refuse to answer questions, to avoid self-incrimination, and other privileges.

Misdemeanor Crime punishable by confinement in city or county jail for a period of less than one year; a lesser offense.

Mistrial Trial ending before defendant's guilt or innocence can be established; usually results from hung jury where jurors unable to reach agreement on one's guilt or innocence; also occurs because of substantial irregularities in trial conduct.

Mitigating circumstances Factors that lessen the severity of the crime and/or sentence; such factors include old age, cooperation with police in apprehending other offenders, and lack of intent to inflict injury.

Mixed sentences Punishments imposed whenever offenders have been convicted of two or more offenses and judges sentence them to separate sentences for each conviction offense.

Modes of adaptation Ways that persons who occupy a particular social position adjust to cultural goals and the institutionalized means to reach those goals.

Monitoring the Future Survey Study of 3,000 high school students annually by Institute for Social Research at University of Michigan; attempts to discover hidden delinquency not ordinarily disclosed by published public reports.

National Crime Victimization Survey (NCVS) Published in cooperation with the U.S. Bureau of the Census, a random survey of 60,000 households, including 127,000 persons 12 years of age or older; includes 50,000 businesses; measures crime committed against specific victims interviewed and not necessarily reported to law enforcement officers.

National Juvenile Court Data Archive Compendium of national statistical information and data bases about juvenile delinquency available through the National Center for Juvenile Justice, under the sponsorship of the Office of Juvenile Justice and Delinquency Prevention (OJJDP); involves acquisition of court dispositional records and publishing periodic reports of juvenile offenses and adjudicatory outcomes from different jurisdictions.

National Youth Gang Survey (NYGS) Conducted annually since 1995, purpose of survey is to identify and describe critical gang components and characteristics.

National Youth Survey Study of large numbers of youths annually or at other intervals to assess hidden delinquency among high school students.

Needs assessment (See **Risk/needs assessment instruments**)

Net-widening Pulling juveniles into juvenile justice system who would not otherwise be involved in delinquent activity; applies to many status offenders (also known as *widening the net*).

Neutralization theory Explanation holds that delinquents experience guilt when involved in delinquent activities and that they respect leaders of the legitimate social order; their delinquency is episodic rather than chronic, and they adhere to conventional values while "drifting" into periods of illegal behavior. In order to drift, the delinquent must first neutralize legal and moral values.

New York House of Refuge Established in New York City in 1825 by the Society for the Prevention of Pauperism; school managed largely status offenders; compulsory education provided; strict prison-like regimen was considered detrimental to youthful clientele.

No bill, no true bill Decision issued by grand jury indicating no basis exists for charges against defendant; charges are usually dropped or dismissed later by judge.

Nolle prosequi Decision by prosecution to decline to pursue criminal case against defendant.

Nominal dispositions Adjudicatory disposition resulting in lenient penalties such as warnings and/or probation.

Noninterventionist model Philosophy of juvenile delinquent treatment meaning the absence of any direct intervention with certain juveniles who have been taken into custody.

Nonsecure custody, nonsecure confinement Custodial disposition where a juvenile is placed in a group home, foster care, or other arrangement where he or she is permitted to leave with permission of parents, guardians, or supervisors.

Numbers-game model Caseload assignment model for probation or parole officers where total number of offender/clients is divided by number of officers.

Office of Juvenile Justice and Delinquency Prevention (OJJDP) Agency established by Congress under the Juvenile Justice and Delinquency Prevention Act of 1974; designed to remove status offenders from jurisdiction of juvenile courts and dispose of their cases less formally.

Ohio experience Program for juvenile delinquents in various Ohio counties where home confinement, electronic monitoring, and other forms of intensive supervised probation are used; emphasis is upon public safety, offender accountability, and offender rehabilitation.

Once an adult/always an adult provision Ruling that once a juvenile has been transferred to criminal court to be prosecuted as an adult, regardless of the criminal court outcome, the juvenile can never be subject to the jurisdiction of juvenile courts in the future; in short, the juvenile, once transferred, will always be treated as an adult if future crimes are committed, even though the youth is still not of adult age.

Orange County Peer Court Established in Orange County, California; teen court consists of high school students who volunteer for different court positions, including prosecutors, defense counsel, and jurors; intent is to vest youths with responsibility and accountability in deciding whether other youths charged with delinquency or status offenses are guilty or innocent through jury process; judge presides, together with community volunteers.

Overrides Actions by an authority in an institution or agency that overrules a score or assessment made of a client or inmate; raw scores or assessments or recommendations can be overruled; function of override is to upgrade seriousness of offense status or downgrade seriousness of offense status, thus changing the level of custody at which one is maintained in secure confinement; may also affect the type and nature of community programming for particular offenders.

Parens patriae Literally "parent of the country" and refers to doctrine where state oversees the welfare of youth; originally established by King of England and administered through chancellors.

Parole Status of offenders conditionally released from a confinement facility prior to expiration of their sentences, placed under supervision of a parole agency.

Parole board Committee of persons who determine whether prisoners should be released prior to serving their full terms prescribed by original sentences in court.

Parolee Offender who has served some time in jail or prison, but has been released prior to serving entire sentence imposed upon conviction.

Parole revocation Two-stage proceeding that may result of a parolee's reincarceration in jail or prison; first stage is a preliminary hearing to determine whether parolee violated any specific parole condition; second stage is to determine whether parole should be cancelled and the offender reincarcerated.

Parole revocation hearing Formal proceeding where a parole board decides whether a parolee's parole program should be terminated or changed because of one or more program infractions.

PATHS Program Promoting Alternative THinking Strategies program aimed to promote emotional and social competencies and to reduce aggression and related emotional and behavioral problems among elementary school children.

Pathways Developmental sequences over the course of one's adolescence that are associated with serious, chronic, and violent offenders.

Perry Preschool Program Program that provides high-level early childhood education to disadvantaged children in order to improve their later school life and performance.

Petitions Official documents filed in juvenile courts on juvenile's behalf, specifying reasons for the youth's court appearance; document asserts that juveniles fall within the categories of dependent or neglected, status offender, or delinquent, and the reasons for such assertions are usually provided.

Petit jury Traditional jury that hears evidence of crime in jury trial and decides a defendant's guilt or innocence.

Philadelphia Society for Alleviating the Miseries of Public Prisons Philanthropic society established by the Quakers in Pennsylvania in 1787; attempted to establish prison reforms to improve living conditions of inmates; brought food, clothing, and religious instruction to inmates.

PINS Diversion Program New York program established in 1987 to divert youths in need of supervision to out-of-home placements, such as foster care.

Pittsburgh Youth Study (PYS) Longitudinal investigation of 1,517 inner-city boys between 1986–1996; studied factors involved in what caused delinquency among some youths and why others did not become delinquent.

Placed Judicial disposition where juvenile is disposed to a group or foster home or other type of out-of-home care; also includes secure confinement in an industrial school or comparable facility.

Placement One of several optional dispositions available to juvenile court judges following formal or informal proceedings against juveniles where either delinquent or status offenses have been alleged; adjudication proceedings yield a court decision about whether facts alleged in petition are true; if so, a disposition is imposed that may be placement in a foster or group home, wilderness experience, camp, ranch, or secure institution.

Plea bargains, plea bargaining Preconviction agreement between the defendant and the state whereby the defendant pleads guilty with the expectation of either a reduction in the charges, a promise of sentencing leniency, or some other government concession short of the maximum penalties that could be imposed under the law.

Police discretion Range of behavioral choices available to police officers within the limits of their power.

Poor Laws Regulations in English Middle Ages designed to punish debtors by imprisoning them until they could pay their debts; imprisonment was for life, or until someone could pay the debtor's debts for them.

Positive school of criminology School of criminological thought emphasizing analysis of criminal behaviors through empirical indicators such as physical features compared with biochemical explanations. Postulates that human behavior is a product of social, biological, psychological, or economic forces. Also known as Italian School.

Positivism Branch of social science that uses the scientific method of the natural sciences and that suggests that human behavior is a product of social, biological, psychological, or economic factors.

Prediction Assessment of some expected future behavior of a person including criminal acts, arrests, or convictions.

Predictors of dangerousness and risk Assessment devices that attempt to forecast one's potential for violence or risk to others; any factors that are used in such instruments.

Predisposition reports Documents prepared by juvenile intake officer for juvenile judge; purpose of report is to furnish the judge with background about juveniles to make a more informed sentencing decision; similar to PSI report.

Preliminary hearing, preliminary examination Proceeding where both prosecutor and defense counsel present some evidence against and on behalf of defendants; proceeding to determine whether probable cause exists to believe that a crime was committed and that the particular defendant committed the crime.

Preponderance of the evidence Standard used in civil courts to determine defendant or plaintiff liability.

Presentence investigation reports (PSI) Inquiry conducted about a convicted defendant at the request of the judge; purpose of inquiry is to determine worthiness of defendant for parole or sentencing leniency.

Presentments Charge brought against a defendant by grand jury acting on its own authority.

Presumptive waiver Requirement that shifts the burden to the juvenile for defending against their transfer to criminal court by showing that they are capable of being rehabilitated; following automatic or legislative waiver, juveniles can challenge the waiver in a hearing where they must demonstrate to the court's satisfaction their capability of becoming reformed.

Pretrial detention Holding delinquent or criminal suspects in incarcerative facilities pending their forthcoming adjudicatory hearing or trial.

Preventive detention Constitutional right of police to detain suspects prior to trial without bail when suspects are likely to flee from the jurisdiction or pose serious risks to others.

Primary deviation Part of labeling process whenever youths engage in occasional pranks and not especially serious violations of the law.

Prisons Incarcerative facilities designed to house long-term serious offenders; operated by state or federal government; houses inmates for terms longer than one year.

Privatization Trend in prison and jail management and correctional operations generally where private interests are becoming increasingly involved in the management and operations of correctional institutions.

Proactive units Police officer youth squads assigned special duties of aggressively patrolling high-delinquency areas in an effort to deter gangs from operating.

Probable cause Reasonable belief that a crime has been committed and that the person accused of crime committed it.

Probation Sentence not involving confinement that imposes conditions and retains authority in sentencing court to modify conditions of sentence or resentence offender for probation violations.

Probation revocation hearing Proceeding wherein it is determined whether to revoke a probationer's probation program because of one or more violations.

Project New Pride One of the most popular probation programs established in Denver, Colorado, in 1973; a blend of education, counseling, employment, and cultural education directed at those more serious offenders between the ages of 14 and 17; juveniles eligible for the New Pride program must have at least two prior convictions for serious misdemeanors and/or felonies; goals include (1) reintegrating participants into their communities through school participation or employment, and (2) reducing recidivism rates among offenders.

Project Outward Bound (See **Wilderness experiments**)

Propositions Statements about the real world that lack the high degree of certainty associated with assumptions; examples of propositions are, "Burnout among probation officers may be mitigated or lessened through job enlargement and giving officers greater input in organizational decision making," or "Two-officer patrol units are less susceptible to misconduct and corruption than one-officer patrol units."

Prosecution and the courts Organizations that pursue cases against criminal suspects and determine whether they are guilty of innocent of crimes alleged.

Prosecutors Court officials who commence civil and criminal proceedings against defendants. Represent state or government interest, prosecuting defendants on behalf of state or government.

Psychoanalytic theory Sigmund Freud's theory of personality formation through the id, ego, and superego at various stages of childhood; maintains that early life experiences influence adult behavior.

Psychological theories Explanations linking criminal behavior with mental states or conditions, antisocial personality traits, and early psychological moral development.

Radical nonintervention Similar to a "do-nothing" policy of delinquency nonintervention.

Reactive units Police youth squad units that respond to calls for service whenever gangs are terrorizing neighborhoods.

Reality therapy model Equivalent of shock probation, where short incarcerative sentences are believed to provide "shock" value for juvenile offenders and scare them from reoffending behaviors.

Rebellion Mode of adaptation suggested by Robert K. Merton where persons reject institutional means to achieve culturally approved goals and created their own goals and means to use and seek.

Recidivism New crime committed by an offender who has served time or was placed on probation for previous offense; tendency to repeat crimes.

Recidivism rate Proportion of offenders who, when released from probation or parole, commit further crimes.

Recidivists Offenders who have committed previous offenses.

Reeve Chief law enforcement officer of English counties, known as **shires.**

Referrals Any citation of a juvenile to juvenile court by a law enforcement officer, interested citizen, family member, or school official; usually based upon law violations, delinquency, or unruly conduct.

Reform schools Different types of vocational institutions designed to both punish and rehabilitate youthful offenders; operated much like prisons as total institutions.

Regimented Inmate Discipline Program (RID) Oklahoma Department of Corrections program operated in Lexington, Oklahoma, for juveniles; program stresses military-type discipline and accountability; facilities are secure and privately operated.

Rehabilitation model Concept of youth management similar to medical model, where juvenile delinquents are believed to be suffering from social and psychological handicaps; provides experiences to build self-concept; experiences stress educational and social remedies.

Relabeling Redefinition of juvenile behaviors as more or less serious than previously defined; example would be police officers who relabel or redefine certain juvenile behaviors, for example, defining curfew violation as loitering for purposes of committing a felony, such as burglary or robbery; relabeling is associated with political jurisdictions that have deinstitutionalized status offenders or have divested juvenile courts of their authority over specific types of juvenile offenders; as one result, police officers lose power, or their discretionary authority, to warn such juveniles or take them into custody; new law may mandate removing such juveniles to community social services rather than to jails; in retaliation, some officers may relabel status behaviors as criminal ones in order to preserve their discretionary authority over juveniles.

Release on own recognizance (ROR) Arrangement where a defendant is able to be set free temporarily to await a later trial without having to post a bail bond; persons released on ROR are usually well known or have strong ties to the community and have not been charged with serious crimes.

Repeat offender Any juvenile or adult with a prior record of delinquency or criminality.

Restitution Stipulation by court that offenders must compensate victims for their financial losses resulting from crime; compensation for psychological, physical, or financial loss by victim; may be imposed as a part of an incarcerative sentence.

Restorative justice Mediation between victims and offenders whereby offenders accept responsibility for their actions and agree to reimburse victims for their losses; may involve community service and other penalties agreeable to both parties in a form of arbitration with a neutral third party acting as arbiter.

Restorative policing Police-based family group conferencing uses police, victims, youths, and their families to discuss the harm caused by the youth and creates an agreement to repair the harm; similar to restorative justice.

Retreatism Mode of adaptation suggested by Robert K. Merton where persons reject culturally approved goals and institutionalized means and do little or nothing to achieve; homeless persons, vagrants, and others sometimes fit the retreatist profile.

Reverse waiver Motion to transfer juvenile's case from criminal court to juvenile court following a legislative or automatic waiver action.

Reverse waiver hearings, reverse waiver actions Formal proceedings to contest automatic transfer of juveniles to jurisdiction of criminal courts; used in jurisdictions with automatic transfer laws.

Risk Potential likelihood for someone to engage in further delinquency or criminality.

Risk/needs assessment instruments Predictive devices intended to forecast offender propensity to commit new offenses or recidivate.

Ritualism Mode of adaptation suggested by Robert K. Merton where persons reject culturally approved goals but work toward lesser goals through institutionalized means.

Runaway Juvenile who leaves home for longterm periods without parental consent or supervision; unruly youth who cannot be controlled or managed by parents or guardians.

San Francisco Project Project that compared recidivism rates of probationers supervised by POs with caseloads of 20 and 40 respectively and found no significant differences in recidivism rates of probationers were reported between "intensive" and "ideal" caseload scenarios.

Scared Straight Juvenile delinquency prevention program that sought to frighten samples of hardcore delinquent youths by having them confront inmates in a Rahway, New Jersey, prison; inmates would yell at and belittle them, calling them names, cursing, and yelling; inmates would tell them about sexual assaults and other prison unpleasantries in an attempt to get them to refrain from reoffending.

Scavenger gangs Groups formed primarily as a means of socializing and for mutual protection.

Screening Procedure used by prosecutor to define which cases have prosecutive merit and which ones do not; some screening bureaus are made up of police and lawyers with trial experience.

Sealing records of juveniles (See **Expungement orders**)

Second Chance Program Probation program operated in Iowa in early 1990s to provide delinquent youths with opportunities to acquire skills, vocational and educational training, pre-employment training, and job placement services.

Secondary deviation Part of labeling theory that suggests that violations of the law become a part of one's normal behavior rather than just occasional pranks.

Secure custody, secure confinement Incarceration of juvenile offender in facility that restricts movement in community; similar to adult penal facility involving total incarceration.

See Our Side (SOS) Program Juvenile aversion program in Prince George's County, Maryland, designed to prevent delinquency.

Selective incapacitation Incarcerating individuals who show a high likelihood of repeating their previous offenses; based on forecasts of potential for recidivism; includes but not limited to dangerousness.

Self-reports, self-report information Surveys of youths (or adults) based upon disclosures these persons might make about the types of offenses they have committed and how frequently they have committed them; considered more accurate than official estimates.

Sentencing hearing Formal proceeding where convicted offender receives a punishment by the court.

Sexual Offender Treatment (SOT) Program Treatment program for juvenile offenders adjudicated delinquent on sex charges; includes psycho-social-educational interventions, therapies, and counseling.

Shire Early English county.

Shock incarceration (See **Shock probation**)

Shock parole (See **Shock probation**)

Shock probation Intermediate punishment where offenders are initially sentenced to terms of secure detention; after a period of time, between 90 and 180 days, youths are removed from detention and sentenced to serve the remainder of their sentences on probation; term, shock probation, was coined by Ohio authorities in 1964.

Short-term confinement Placement in any incarcerative institution for either adults or juveniles where the period of confinement is less than one year; jails are considered short-term facilities.

Situationally based discretion Confronting crime in the streets on the basis of immediate situational factors, time of night, presence of weapons, numbers of offenders; requires extensive personal judgments by police officers.

Smart sentencing (See **Creative sentencing**)

Social control theory Explanation of criminal behavior that focuses upon control mechanisms, techniques, and strategies for regulating human behavior, leading to conformity or obedience to society's rules, and which posits that deviance results when social controls are weakened or break down, so that individuals are not motivated to conform to them.

Social learning theory Applied to criminal behavior, theory stressing importance of learning through modeling others who are criminal; criminal behavior is a function of copying or learning criminal conduct from others.

Society for the Prevention of Pauperism Philanthropic society that established first public reformatory in New York in 1825, the New York House of Refuge.

Sociobiology Scientific study of causal relation between genetic structure and social behavior.

Socioeconomic status (SES) Station or level of economic attainment one enjoys through work; acquisition of wealth; the divisions between various levels of society according to material goods acquired.

Sociological theories Explanations of criminal conduct that emphasize social conditions that bear upon the individual as the causes of criminal behavior.

Solitary confinement Segregation of prisoners into individual cells; originally used at Walnut Street Jail in Philadelphia, Pennsylvania, in 1790.

Sourcebook of Criminal Justice Statistics

Compendium of statistical information about juvenile and adult offenders, court facts, statistics, and trends, probation and parole figures, and considerable additional information; published annually by the Hindelang Criminal Justice Research Center at the University of Albany, SUNY; funded by grant from the U. S. Department of Justice, Bureau of Justice Statistics.

SpeakerID Program Electronic voice verification system used as a part of electronic monitoring to verify the identity of the person called by the probation or parole agency.

Special conditions of probation Extra requirements written into a standard probation agreement, including possible vocational or educational training, counseling, drug or alcohol treatment, attendance at meetings, restitution, community service.

Specialized caseloads model Case assignment method based on POs' unique skills and knowledge relative to offender drug or alcohol problems; some POs are assigned particular clients with unique problems that require more than average PO expertise.

Split sentences (See **Combination sentences**)

Standard of proof Norms used by courts to determine validity of claims or allegations of wrongdoing against offenders; civil standards of proof are "clear and convincing evidence" and "preponderance of evidence," while criminal standard is "beyond a reasonable doubt."

Standard probation Probationers conform to all terms of their probation program, but their contact with probation officers is minimal; often, their contact is by telephone or letter once or twice a month.

Stationhouse adjustments Decisions made by police officers about certain juveniles taken into custody and brought to police stations for processing and investigation; adjustments often result in verbal reprimands and release to custody of parents.

Status offender Anyone committing a status offense, including runaway behavior, truancy, curfew violation, loitering.

Status offenses Violation of statute or ordinance by minor, which, if committed by adult, would not be considered either a felony or a misdemeanor; also any acts committed by juveniles that would (1) bring them to the attention of juvenile courts and (2) not be crimes if committed by adults.

Statute of limitations Maximum time period within which a prosecution can be brought against a defendant for a particular offense; many criminal statutes have 3- or 6-year statute of limitations periods; there is no statute of limitations on homicide charges.

Statutory exclusion Provisions that automatically exclude certain juveniles and offenses from the jurisdiction of the juvenile courts; e.g., murder, aggravated rape, armed robbery.

Stigmas, stigmatize, stigmatization Social process whereby offenders acquire undesirable characteristics as the result of imprisonment or court appearances; undesirable criminal or delinquent labels are assigned those who are processed through the criminal and juvenile justice systems.

Stop Assaultive Children (SAC) Program Activity started in Phoenix, Arizona, in late 1980s and designed for those youths who have committed serious family violence; children are detained in a juvenile facility for a short time, and their release is contingent upon being law-abiding, observing curfew, and other conditions; their prosecution is deferred; must participate in counseling; may include volunteer work.

Strain theory A criminological theory positing that a gap between culturally approved goals and legitimate means of achieving them causes frustration that leads to criminal behavior.

Strategic leniency Less harsh dispositions meted out to certain offenders believed to be nonviolent and least likely to reoffend.

Street outreach model Youth Service Bureau model establishing neighborhood centers for youths who are delinquency-prone, where youths can have things to do other than hang out on the streets.

Subculture of delinquency A culture within a culture where the use of violence in certain social situations is commonplace and normative; Marvin Wolfgang and Franco Ferracuti devised this concept to depict a set of norms apart from mainstream conventional society in which the theme of vio-

lence is pervasive and dominant; learned through socialization with others as an alternative lifestyle.

Superego Sigmund Freud's label for that part of personality concerned with moral values.

Sustained petitions Adjudication resulting in a finding that the facts alleged in a petition are true; a finding that the juvenile committed the offenses alleged that resulted in an adjudication and disposition.

Sweat shops Exploitative businesses and industries that employed child labor and demanded long work hours for low pay.

Systems modification model Youth Service Bureau model involving the establishment of community-based facilities for delinquency-prone youths; associations of churches, schools, and neighborhood businesses organizing to assist youths.

Tagging Being equipped with an electronic wristlet or anklet for the purpose of monitoring one's whereabouts.

Taken into custody For juveniles, not technically an arrest; law enforcement officers may pick up juvenile hitchhikers or runaways and take them into custody, meaning that the juveniles are taken to a care facility where their parents or legal guardians can be located.

Teen courts Tribunals consisting of teenagers who judge other teenagers charged with minor offenses; much like regular juries in criminal courts, where juvenile prosecutors and defense counsel argue cases against specific juvenile offenders; juries decide punishment with judicial approval.

Territorial gangs Groups of youths organized to defend a fixed amount of territory, such as several city blocks.

Theory A set of propositions from which a large number of new observations can be deduced; an integrated body of definitions, assumptions, and propositions related in such a way to explain and predict relations between two or more variables.

Totality of circumstances Sometimes used as the standard whereby offender guilt is determined or where search and seizure warrants may be obtained; officers consider entire set of circumstances surrounding apparently illegal event and act accordingly.

Traditional model Juvenile court proceedings characterized by less formal adjudications, greater use of detention.

Transfer hearings Proceeding to determine whether juveniles should be certified as adults for purposes of being subjected to jurisdiction of adult criminal courts where more severe penalties may be imposed.

Transfers Proceedings where juveniles are remanded to the jurisdiction of criminal courts; also known as **certifications** and **waivers.**

Transportation Early British practice of sending undesirables, misfits, and convicted offenders to remote territories and islands controlled by England.

Treatment model (See **Medical model**)

Truants Juveniles who are habitually absent from school without excuse.

True bill Indictment or charge against defendant brought by grand jury after considering inculpatory evidence presented by prosecutor.

Unconditional probation, unconditional standard probation Form of conditional release without special restrictions or requirements placed on offender's behavior other than standard probation agreement terms; no formal controls operate to control or monitor divertee's behavior.

Uniform Crime Reports (UCR) Official source of crime information published by Federal Bureau of Investigation annually; accepts information from reporting law enforcement agencies about criminal arrests; classifies crimes according to various index criteria; tabulates information about offender age, gender, race, and other attributes.

Victim compensation Financial restitution payable to victims by either the state or convicted offenders.

Victim-impact statement Appendage to a predisposition report or presentence investigation report that addresses the effect of the defendant's actions against victims or anyone harmed by the crime or delinquent act; usually compiled by the victim.

Victimization Basic measure of the occurrence of a crime; a specific criminal act affecting a specific victim.

Victim–offender mediation Third-party intervention mechanism whereby perpetrator and victim work out civil solution to otherwise criminal or delinquent action.

Violent Juvenile Offender Programs (VJOP) Procedures designed to provide positive interventions and treatments; reintegrative programs, including transitional residential programs for those youths who have been subject to long-term detention; provides for social networking, provision of educational opportunities for youths, social learning, and goal-oriented behavioral skills.

VisionQuest Carefully regulated, intensive supervision program designed to improve the social and psychological experiences of juveniles; reintegrative program to improve one's educational and social skills; wilderness program.

Waiver (See **Transfer**)

Waiver hearing Request by prosecutor to transfer juvenile charged with various offenses to a criminal or adult court for prosecution; waiver motions make it possible to sustain adult criminal penalties.

Waiver motion Formal request by prosecutor to send juvenile's case from juvenile court to criminal court.

Walnut Street Jail Reconstructed from earlier Philadelphia Jail in 1790; first real attempt by jail officials to classify and segregate prisoners according to age, gender, and crime seriousness; introduced idea of solitary confinement.

Wilderness experiments Experience programs that include a wide array of outdoor programs designed to improve a juvenile's self-worth, self-concept, pride, and trust in others.

Without prejudice To dismiss charges, but those same charges can be brought again later against the same defendant.

With prejudice To dismiss charges, but those same charges cannot be brought again later against the same defendant.

Workhouses Early penal facilities designed to use prison labor for profit by private interests; operated in shires in mid-sixteenth century and later.

XYY theory Explanation of criminal behavior suggesting that some criminals are born with extra Y chromosome, characterized as the "aggressive" chromosome compared with the passive X chromosome; extra Y chromosome produces greater agitation, greater aggressiveness, and criminal propensities.

Youth Service Bureaus (YSBs) Various types of diversion programs operated in the United States for delinquency-prone youth.

Youth Services/Diversion (YS/D) Program Established in Orange County, California, with the goals of reducing family dysfunction and teaching youth responsibility; instilling self-esteem and self-confidence through family counseling sessions.

Youth squads Teams of police officers in police departments whose responsibility is to focus upon particular delinquency problems and resolve them.

Youth-to-Victim Restitution Project Program operated by the juvenile court in Lincoln, Nebraska, based on the principle that youths must repay whatever damages they inflicted on victims; enforcement of restitution orders decreased recidivism among delinquent offenders.

Zone of transition An area nearest center of city center undergoing rapid social change; believed to contain high rates of crime and delinquency.

References

ACOCA, LESLIE AND JAMES AUSTIN. 1996. *The crisis: The Women Offender Sentencing Study and Alternative Sentencing Recommendations Project: Women in prison.* Washington, DC: National Council on Crime and Delinquency.

ACOCA, LESLIE AND KELLY DEDEL. 1998. *No place to hide: Understanding and meeting the needs of girls in the California juvenile justice system.* San Francisco: National Council on Crime and Delinquency.

ADAMS, MIKE S. 1996. Labeling and differential association: Toward a general social learning theory of crime and deviance. *American Journal of Criminal Justice* 20: 147–164.

ADAMS, MIKE S., JAMES D. JOHNSON, AND T. DAVID EVANS. 1998. Racial differences in informal labeling effects. *Deviant Behavior* 19:157–171.

ADMINISTRATIVE OFFICE OF THE U.S. COURTS. 2001. *The U.S. probation and pretrial services system.* Washington, DC: Administrative Office of the U.S. Courts.

ALEXANDER, RUDOLPH JR. 2000. *Counseling, treatment, and intervention methods with juvenile and adult offenders.* Belmont, CA: Thomson Learning.

ALFORD, SUSAN. 1998. The effectiveness of juvenile arbitration in South Carolina: Professionals need not apply. *APPA Perspectives* 22:28–34.

ALOISI, MICHAEL AND JENNIFER LeBAROON. 2001. *The Juvenile Justice Commission's stabilization and reintegration program: An updated recidivism analysis.* Trenton, NJ: Juvenile Justice Commission Research and Evaluation Unit, New Jersey Department of Law and Public Safety.

ALPHA ENTERPRISES. 1996. *Electronic monitoring of offenders.* New York: Author.

ALTSCHULER, DAVID M. AND TROY L. ARMSTRONG.1990. Designing an intensive aftercare program for high-risk juveniles. *Corrections Today* 52:170–171.

ALTSCHULER, DAVID M. AND TROY L. ARMSTRONG. 2001. Reintegrating high-risk juvenile offenders into communities: Experiences and prospects. *Corrections Management Quarterly* 5:72–88.

AMERICAN BAR ASSOCIATION. 1997. *The state of criminal justice.* Washington, DC: Criminal Justice Section, American Bar Association.

———. 2001. *Justice by gender: The lack of appropriate prevention, diversion, and treatment alternatives for girls in the justice system.* Washington, DC: American Bar Association/National Bar Association.

AMERICAN CORRECTIONAL ASSOCIATION. 1996. *Community corrections.* Lanham, MD: Author.

———. 2001. *Probation and parole directory, 2001–2003.* Lanham, MD: Author.

———. 2002. *2001 directory.* College Park, MD: Author.

AMERICAN JAILS. 1998. Tennessee: A new sheriff's office program gives children a look inside jail. *American Jails* 12:98.

ANDERSON, DENNIS R. AND DONALD F. SCHOEN. 1985. Diversion programs: Effect of stigmatization on juvenile status offenders. *Juvenile and Family Court Journal* 36:13–25.

ANDERSSON, TOMMY ET AL. 1999. The co-occurrence of alcohol problems and criminality in the transition from adolescence to young adulthood: A prospective longitudinal study of young men. *Studies on Crime and Crime Prevention* 8:169–188.

ANNON, JACK S. 1996. Treatment programs for sex offenders. *American Journal of Forensic Psychology* 14:49–54.

APPA PERSPECTIVES. 2002. APPA news: APPA adopts resolution supporting youth courts. *APPA Perspectives* 26:15.

APPIER, JANIS. 1990. Juvenile crime control: Los Angeles law enforcement and the zoot-suit riots. *Criminal Justice History: An International Annual, Vol. 11,* Louis A. Knafla (ed.). Westport, CT: Meckler.

ARCHWAMETY, TEARA AND ANTONIS KATSIYANNIS. 2000. Academic remediation, parole violations, and recidivism rates among delinquent youths. *Remedial and Special Education* 21:161–170.

ARDOVINI, JOANNE AND LEWIS WALKER. 2000. Juvenile boot camps and the reclamation of our youth: Some food for thought. *Juvenile and Family Court Journal* 51:21–29.

ARMOR, JERRY C. AND VINCENT KEITH JACKSON. 1995. Juvenile gang activity in Alabama. *Journal of Gang Research* 2:29–35.

ARMSTRONG, GAYLENE STYVE. 2001. *Private vs. public operation of juvenile correctional facilities.* New York: LFB Scholarly Publishing.

ARMSTRONG, TROY L. 1988. National survey of juvenile intensive probation supervision, Part I. *Criminal Justice Abstracts* 20:342–348.

ARMSTRONG, TROY L., ED. 1991. *Intensive interventions with high-risk youths: Promising approaches in juvenile probation and parole.* Monsey, NY: Criminal Justice Press.

ARMSTRONG, TROY L. ET AL. 1990. Juveniles and crime: Using the balanced approach with unbalanced youth. *APPA Perspectives* 14:8–38.

ARRIGONA, NANCY, SHARON BIRCH, AND MICHAEL DAILEY. 1996. *Top priority: Preparing the juvenile justice system for the twenty-first century.* Austin, TX: Criminal Justice Policy Council.

ARRIGONA, NANCY, GARRETT HODGSON, AND TOM REED. 1999. *An overview of juvenile certification in Texas.* Austin, TX: Texas Criminal Justice Policy Council.

ARTHUR, LINDSAY G. 2000. Punishment doesn't work! *Juvenile and Family Court Journal* 51:37–42.

ASHFORD, JOSE B. AND CRAIG WINSTON LECROY. 1988. Decision-making for juvenile offenders in aftercare. *Juvenile and Family Court Journal* 39:45–58.

ASHFORD, JOSE B. AND CRAIG WINSTON LECROY. 1993. Juvenile parole policy in the United States: Determinate versus indeterminate models. *Justice Quarterly* 10:179–195.

ASHFORD, JOSE, BRUCE D. SALES, AND WILLIAM H. REID. 2000. *Treating adult and juvenile offenders with special needs.* Washington, DC: American Psychological Association.

ASSOCIATED PRESS. 1997. Girl found guilty in toddler's death. February 18, 1997.

———. 2001. Arkansas gets tough on violent youths. March 5, 2001.

AUSTIN, JAMES, MICHAEL JONES, AND MELISSA BOLYARD. 1993. *The growing use of jail boot camps: The current state of the art.* Washington, DC: U.S. Department of Justice, Office of Justice Programs.

AWAD, GEORGE A. AND ELISABETH B. SAUNDERS. 1991. Male adolescent sexual assaulters: Clinical observations. *Journal of Interpersonal Violence* 6:446–460.

AYERS, WILLIAM. 1997. *A kind and just parent: The children of juvenile court.* Boston: Beacon Press.

BABB, SUSAN AND PETER C. KRATCOSKI. 1994. The juvenile justice assistants program. *Juvenile and Family Court Journal* 45:43–499.

BAILEY, ANN LESLIE. 1983. Waiver of Miranda rights by juveniles: Is parental presence a necessary safeguard? *Journal of Family Law* 21:725–743.

BAIRD, S. CHRISTOPHER. 1985. Classifying juveniles: Making the most of an important management tool. *Corrections Today* 47:32–38.

BAKER, MYRIAM L., JANE NADY SIGMON, AND M. ELAINE NUGENT. 2001. *Truancy reduction: Keeping students in school.* Washington, DC: Office of Juvenile Justice and Delinquency Prevention.

BANDURA, ALBERT AND RICHARD WALTERS. 1959. *Adolescent aggression.* New York: Ronald Press.

BANKS, J., T. R. SILER, AND R. L. RARDIN. 1977. Past and present findings in intensive adult probation. *Federal Probation* 41:20–25.

BANKSTON, CARL L. III. 1998. Youth gangs and the new second generation: A review essay. *Aggression and Violent Behavior* 3:35–45.

BANKSTON, CARL L. III AND STEPHEN J. CALDAS. 1996. Adolescents and deviance in a Vietnamese American community: A theoretical synthesis. *Deviant Behavior* 17:159–181.

BARNUM, RICHARD. 1987. Biomedical problems in juvenile delinquency: Issues in diagnosis and treatment. In *From children to citizens,* James Q. Wilson and Glenn C. Loury, eds. New York: Springer-Verlag.

BAUMER, TERRY L., MICHAEL G. MAXFIELD, AND ROBERT MENDELSOHN. 1993. A comparative analysis of three electronically monitored home detention programs. *Justice Quarterly* 10:121–142.

BAYENS, GERALD. 1999. Characteristics of juveniles confined in Kansas adult jails and prisons, 1995–1997. *American Jails* 12:59–64.

BAZEMORE, S. GORDON. 1997. What's "new" about the balanced approach? *Juvenile and Family Court Journal* 48:1–22.

BAZEMORE, S. GORDON AND SCOTT SENJO. 1997. Policing encounters with juveniles revisited: An exploratory study of themes and styles of community policing. *Policing: An International Journal of Police Strategy and Management* 20:60–82.

BAZEMORE, GORDON AND MARK S. UMBREIT. 2001. *A comparison of four restorative conferencing models.* Washington, DC: Office of Juvenile Justice and Delinquency Prevention.

BECCARIA, CESARE BONESANA. 1764. *On crimes and punishments.* Indianapolis, IN: Bobbs-Merrill, 1963, reprinted edition.

BECK, ALLEN J., JENNIFER C. KARBERG, AND PAIGE M. HARRISON. 2002. *Prison and jail inmates at midyear 2001.* Washington, DC: Bureau of Justice Statistics.

BECK, ROBERT J. 1997. Communications in a teen court: Implications for probation. *Federal Probation* 61:40–48.

BECKER, HOWARD S. 1963. *Outsiders: Studies in the sociology of deviance.* New York: Free Press.

BEDAU, HUGO ADAM. 1992. *The case against the death penalty.* Washington, DC: American Civil Liberties Union, Capital Punishment Project.

BEGER, RANDALL R. 1994. Illinois juvenile justice: An emerging dual system. *Crime and Delinquency* 40:54–68.

BEIER, A. L. 1985. *Masterless men: The vagrancy problem in England: 1560–1640.* London, UK: Methuen.

BELL, CARL C. 2002. Violence prevention 101: Implications for policy development. In *Perspectives on crime and justice: 2000–2001 lecture series,* Alfred Blumstein, Laurence Steinberg, Carl C. Bell, and Margaret A. Berger, eds. Washington, DC: National Institute of Justice.

BENDA, BRENT B. 1999. A study of recidivism of serious and persistent offenders among adolescents. *Journal of Criminal Justice* 27:111–126.

BENDA, BRENT B. AND ROBERT FLYNN CORWYN. 2000. A test of the validity of delinquency syndrome construct in a homogeneous sample. *Journal of Adolescence* 23:497–511.

BENDA, BRENT B., ROBERT FLYNN CORWYN, AND NANCY J. TOOMBS. 2001. From adolescent "serious offender" to adult felon: A predictive study of offense progression. *Journal of Offender Rehabilitation* 32:79–108.

BENTHAM, JEREMY. 1790. *An introduction to the principles of morals and legislation.* (reprinted edition). New York: Hafner, 1948.

BERENSON, DAVID AND LEE UNDERWOOD. 2001. *Juvenile sex offender programming: A resource guide.* Washington, DC: U.S. Office of Juvenile Justice and Delinquency Prevention.

BERRUETA-CLEMENT, JOHN R. ET AL. 1984. Preschool's effects on social responsibility. In *Changed lives: The effects of the Perry Preschool Program on youths through age 19,* John R. Berruta-Clement et al., eds. Ypsilanti, MI: High/Scope Press.

BERSET, VALERIE. 2001. The delinquency of siblings. *Kriminologisches Bulletin de Criminologie* 27:33–49.

BEYER, MARTY, THOMAS GRISSO, AND MALCOLM YOUNG. 1997. *More than meets the eye: Rethinking assessment, competency, and sentencing for a harsher era of juvenile justice.* Washington, DC: American Bar Association Juvenile Justice Center.

BILCHIK, SHAY. 1996. *State responses to serious and violent juvenile crime.* Pittsburgh, PA: National Center for Juvenile Justice.

————. 1998. *Mental health disorders and substance abuse problems among juveniles.* Washington, DC: U.S. Department of Justice.

BINDER, ARNOLD AND GILBERT GEIS. 1984. Ad populum argumentation in criminology: Juvenile diversion as rhetoric. *Crime and Delinquency* 30:309–333.

BIRKBECK, CHRISTOPHER. 1998. *Controlling New Mexico juveniles' possession of firearms.* Albuquerque: New Mexico Criminal and Juvenile Justice Coordinating Council.

BISHOP, DONNA M. 2000. Juvenile offenders in the adult criminal justice system. In *Crime and justice: A review of research, Vol. 27,* Michael Tonry, ed. Chicago: University of Chicago Press.

BISHOP, DONNA M. AND CHARLES E. FRAZIER. 1992. Gender bias in juvenile justice processing: Implications of the JJDP Act. *Journal of Criminal Law and Criminology* 82:1162–1186.

BISHOP, DONNA M. AND CHARLES E. FRAZIER. 1996. Race effects in juvenile justice decision making: Findings of a statewide analysis. *Journal of Criminal Law and Criminology* 86:392–414.

BISHOP, DONNA M. ET AL. 1996. The transfer of juveniles to criminal court: Does it make a difference? *Crime and Delinquency* 42:171–191.

BISHOP, DONNA M. ET AL. 2001. *Juvenile transfers to criminal court in Florida: The 1994 reforms.* Washington, DC: U.S. Department of Justice.

BLACK, HENRY CAMPBELL. 1990. *Black's law dictionary.* St. Paul, MN: West Publishing Company.

BLACK, MEGHAN C. 2001. *Juvenile delinquency probation caseload, 1989–1998.* Washington, DC: U.S. Department of Justice.

BLAKEMORE, JEROME L. AND GLENDA M. BLAKEMORE. 1998. African-American street gangs: A quest for identity. *Journal of Human Behavior in the Social Environment* 1:203–223.

BLOOM, BARBARA ET AL. 2002. Moving toward justice for female juvenile offenders in the new millennium: Modeling gender-specific policies and programs. *Journal of Contemporary Criminal Justice* 37:37–56.

BOHM, ROBERT M. AND RONALD E. VOGEL. 1994. A comparison of factors associated with uninformed and informed death penalty opinions. *Journal of Criminal Justice* 22:125–143.

BOND-MAUPIN, LISA J. AND JAMES R. MAUPIN. 1998. Juvenile justice decision making in a rural Hispanic community. *Journal of Criminal Justice* 26:373–384.

BOONE, HARRY N. JR. 1996. Electronic home confinement: Judicial and legislative perspectives. *APPA Perspectives* 20:18–25.

BOTTCHER, JEAN. 2001. Social practices and gender: How gender relates to delinquency in the everyday lives of high-risk youths. *Criminology: An Interdisciplinary Journal* 39:893–932.

BOTTCHER, JEAN AND TERESA ISORENA. 1994. *LEAD: A boot camp and intensive parole program: An implementation and process evaluation of the first year.* Sacramento, CA: Research Division, California Youth Authority.

BOTTCHER, JEAN, TERESA ISORENA, AND MARIETTA BELNAS. 1996. *LEAD: A boot camp and intensive parole program: An impact evaluation.* Sacramento, CA: California Department of the Youth Authority.

BOURQUE, BLAIR B., MEL HAN AND SARAH M. HILL. 1996. *A national survey of aftercare provisions for boot camp graduates.* Washington, DC: U.S. Department of Justice.

BOUTELLIER, HANS ET AL. 1996. Restorative justice and mediation. *European Journal on Criminal Policy and Research* 4:7–130.

BOWERS, DAN M. 2000. Home detention systems. *Corrections Today* 62:102–106.

BRAITHWAITE, JOHN ET AL. 1993. Symposium on the future of research in crime and delinquency. *Journal of Research in Crime and Delinquency* 30:381–533.

BRANDAU, TIMOTHY J. 1992. *An alternative to incarceration for juvenile delinquents: The Delaware Bay Marine Institute.* Ann Arbor, MI: University Microfilms International.

BRANTLEY, ALAN C. AND ANDREW W. DIROSA. 1994. Gangs: A national perspective. *FBI LAW Enforcement Bulletin* 63:1–7.

BRIDGES, GEORGE S. AND SARA STEEN. 1998. Racial disparities in official assessments of juvenile offenders: Attributional stereotypes as mediating mechanisms. *American Sociological Review* 63:554–570.

BROIDY, LISA M. 2001. A test of general strain theory. *Criminology* 39:9–36.

BROOKS, R. R. W. AND S. H. JEON. 2001. Race, income, and perceptions of the U.S. court system. *Behavioral Sciences and the Law* 19:249–264.

BROWNING, KATHARINE AND ROLF LOEBER. 1999. *Highlights of findings from the Pittsburgh Youth Study.* Washington, DC: Office of Juvenile Justice and Delinquency Prevention Programs.

BRUCE, MARINO A. 2000. Inequality and delinquency: Sorting outcome, class, and race effects. *Race and Society* 2:133–148.

BRUMBAUGH, SUSAN AND CHRIS BIRKBECK. 1999. *Sentencing in New Mexico: 1997 follow-up.* Albuquerque: New Mexico Criminal and Juvenile Justice Coordinating Council.

BUMBY, KURT M. 1994. Psychological considerations in abuse-motivated patricides: Children who kill their abusive parents. *Journal of Psychiatry and Law* 22:51–90.

BURGESS, ROBERT AND RONALD AKERS. 1966. Differential association-reinforcement theory of criminal behavior. *Social Problems* 14:128–147.

BURRUSS, GEORGE W. JR. AND KIMBERLY KEMPF-LEONARD. 2002. The questionable advantage of defense counsel in juvenile court. *Justice Quarterly* 19:37–68.

BUTTS, JEFFREY A. 1996a. *Offenders in juvenile court, 1994.* Washington, DC: Office of Juvenile Justice and Delinquency Prevention.

————. 1996b. Speedy trial in juvenile court. *American Journal of Criminal Law* 23:515–561.

BUTTS, JEFFREY A. AND WILLIAM ADAMS. 2001. *Anticipating space needs in juvenile detention and correctional facilities.* Washington, DC: U.S. Department of Justice.

BUTTS, JEFFREY A. AND JEFFREY GABLE. 1992. *Juvenile detention in Cook County and the feasibility of alternatives.* Pittsburgh, PA: National Center for Juvenile Justice.

BUTTS, JEFFREY A. AND GREGORY J. HALEMBA. 1996. *Waiting for justice: Moving young offenders through the juvenile court process.* Pittsburgh: National Center for Juvenile Justice.

BUTTS, JEFFREY A. AND JOSEPH B. SANBORN JR. 1999. Is juvenile justice just too slow? *Judicature* 83:16–24.

BUTTS, JEFFREY A. AND HOWARD N. SNYDER. 1997. *The youngest delinquents: Offenders under age 15.* Washington, DC: Office of Juvenile Justice and Delinquency Prevention.

BUTTS, JEFFREY A. ET AL. 1996. *Juvenile court statistics 1993: Statistics report.* Washington, DC: Office of Juvenile Justice and Delinquency Prevention.

CADIGAN, TIMOTHY P. 2001. PACTS. *Federal Probation* 65:25–30.

CAETI, TORY J., CRAIG HEMMENS, AND VELMER S. BURTON JR. 1996. Juvenile right to counsel: A national comparison of state legal codes. *American Journal of Criminal Law* 23:611–632.

CAHALAN, MARGARET W. 1986. *Historical corrections statistics in the United States, 1850–1984.* Washington, DC: U.S. Department of Justice.

CAIN, TRAVIS ANN. 2002. *JUMP.* Washington, DC: Office of Juvenile Justice and Delinquency Prevention.

CALDAS, STEPHEN J. 1990. Intensive incarceration programs offer hope of rehabilitation to a fortunate few: Orleans parish prison does an "about face." *International Journal of Offender Therapy and Comparative Criminology* 34:67–76.

CALIFORNIA OFFICE OF CRIMINAL JUSTICE PLANNING. 1984. *Governor's youth crime prevention program.* Sacramento, CA: California Office of Criminal Justice Planning.

CALIFORNIA SCHOOL VIOLENCE PREVENTION AND RESPONSE TASK FORCE. 2000. *School violence prevention and response.* Sacramento, CA: California School Violence Prevention and Response Task Force.

CALIFORNIA YOUTH AUTHORITY. 2001. *Risk and needs assessment of youthful offenders.* Sacramento: California Youth Authority.

CAMERON, MARGARET AND COLIN MacDOUGAL. 2000. Crime prevention through sport and physical activity. *Trends and Issues in Crime and Criminal Justice* 165:1–6.

CAMPBELL, JUSTIN S. AND PAUL RETZLAFF. 2000. Juvenile diversion interventions: Participant description and outcomes. *Journal of Offender Rehabilitation* 32:57–73.

CAMPBELL, MARY ANN AND FRED SCHMIDT. 2000. Comparison of mental health and legal factors in the disposition outcome of young offenders. *Criminal Justice and Behavior* 27:688–715.

CARLSON, BONNIE. 1986. Children's beliefs about punishment. *American Journal of Orthopsychiatry* 56:308–312.

CARLSON, ERIC AND EVALYN PARKS. 1979. *Critical issues in adult probation: Issues in probation management.* Washington, DC: U.S. Department of Justice.

CARPENTER, PATRICIA AND SALEK SANDBERG. 1985. Further psychodrama and delinquent adolescents. *Adolescence* 20:599–604.

CARPENTER, PATRICIA AND DENNIS P. SUGRUE. 1984. Psychoeducation in an outpatient setting—designing a heterogeneous population of juvenile delinquents. *Adolescence* 19:113–122.

CARRINGTON, PETER J. AND SHARON MOYER. 1990. The effect of defence counsel on plea and outcome in juvenile court. *Canadian Journal of Criminology* 32:621–637.

CARSTARPHEN, NIKE AND ILANA SHAPIRO. 1997. Facilitating between gang members and the police. *Negotiation Journal* 13:185–207.

CASELLA, RONNIE. 2001. *At zero tolerance: Punishment, prevention, and school violence.* New York: Peter Lang Publishing.

CASTELLANO, THOMAS C. 1986. The justice model in the juvenile justice system: Washington state's experience. *Law and Policy* 8:479–506.

CASTELLANO, THOMAS C. AND MICHAEL FERGUSON. 1998. *A time study of juvenile probation services in Illinois.* Carbondale: Southern Illinois University, Center for the Study of Crime, Delinquency, and Corrections.

CASTELLANO, THOMAS C. AND IRINA R. SODERSTROM. 1990. *Wilderness challenges and recidivism: A program evaluation.* Carbondale: University of Southern Illinois, Center for the Study of Crime, Delinquency and Corrections.

CAVENDER, GRAY AND PAUL KNEPPER. 1992. Strange interlude: An analysis of juvenile parole revocation decision making. *Social Problems* 339:387–399.

CENTER FOR LEGAL STUDIES. 2000. *An implementation evaluation of the specialized sex offender probation projects in Coles, Madison, and Vermillion counties.* Springfield, IL: Center for Legal Studies, Institute of Public Affairs, University of Illinois.

CENTER FOR THE STUDY AND PREVENTION OF VIOLENCE. 2002. *Perry Preschool Program.* Boulder, CO: University of Colorado, Boulder.

CHAFFIN, MARK, BARBARA L. BONNER, AND ROBERT F. HILL. 2001. Family preservation and family support programs: Child maltreatment outcomes across client risk levels and program types. *Child Abuse and Neglect* 25:1269–1289.

CHAMBLISS, LAUREN, BERARDINE DOHRN, AND STEVEN DRIZIN. 2000. *Second chances: 100 years of the children's court: Giving kids a chance to make a better choice.* Washington, DC: Justice Policy Institute.

CHAMPION, DEAN J. 1992. *The use of attorneys in juvenile courts in five states: A trend analysis, 1980–1989.* Pittsburgh, PA: National Center for Juvenile Justice.

———. 1994. *Measuring offender risk: A criminal justice sourcebook.* Westport, CT: Greenwood Press.

———. 1999, November. The use of attorneys in juvenile courts in five states: A trend analysis, 1980–1995. Unpublished paper presented at American Society of Criminology meetings, Toronto, CAN.

———. 2002. *Probation, parole, and community corrections. 4th ed.* Upper Saddle River, NJ: Prentice Hall.

CHAMPION, DEAN J. AND G. LARRY MAYS. 1991. *Juvenile transfer hearings: Some trends and implications for juvenile justice.* New York: Praeger.

CHEN, XIAOMING. 2000. Educating and correcting juvenile delinquents: The Chinese approaches. *The Journal of Correctional Education* 51:334–346.

CHESNEY-LIND, MEDA AND WAYNE MATSUO. 1995. *Juvenile crime and juvenile justice in Hawaii.* Philadelphia: Center for the Study of Youth Policy, University of Pennsylvania.

CHESNEY-LIND, MEDA AND VICKIE V. PARAMORE. 2001. Are girls getting more violent? Exploring juvenile robbery trends. *Journal of Contemporary Criminal Justice* 17:142–166.

CHESNEY-LIND, MEDA ET AL. 1998. *Trends in delinquency and gang membership.* Honolulu, HI: Center for Youth Research, University of Hawaii at Manoa.

CHRISTIANSON, SCOTT. 1998. *With liberty for some: 500 years of imprisonment in America.* Boston: Northeastern University Press.

CLAGGETT, ARTHUR F. ET AL. 1992. Corrections—innovative practices, inmate behavior dynamics, policy analysis, personnel. *Journal of Offender Rehabilitation* 17:1–211.

CLARKE, ELIZABETH E. 1994. *Treatment of juveniles as adults: A report on trends in automatic transfer to criminal court in Cook County, Illinois.* Chicago: Children and Families Justice Center.

CLAYTON, SUSAN. 1999. Children's initiatives: Louisiana corrections makes prevention a policy. *Corrections Today* 61:116–118.

COALITION FOR JUVENILE JUSTICE. 1994. *No easy answers: Juvenile justice in a climate of fear.* Washington, DC: Coalition for Juvenile Justice.

———. 1997. *False images? The news media and juvenile crime.* Washington, DC: Coalition for Juvenile Justice.

———. 1998. *A celebration or a wake? The juvenile court after 100 years.* Washington, DC: Coalition for Juvenile Justice.

COCOZZA, JOSEPH J. AND KATHLEEN SKOWYRA. 2000. Youth with mental health disorders: Issues and emerging responses. *Juvenile Justice* 7:3–13.

COFFEY, ANDREW. 1995. *The history of Florida's juvenile detention: A statutory focus.* Ft. Lauderdale, FL: Center for the Study of Youth Policy, Nova Southeastern University.

COHEN, ALBERT K. 1955. *Delinquent boys.* New York: Free Press.

COHEN, MARK A. 1998. The monetary value of saving high-risk youth. *Journal of Quantitative Criminology* 14:5–33.

COHN, ALVIN W. 1994. The future of juvenile justice administration: Evolution v. revolution. *Juvenile and Family Court Journal* 45:51–63.

————. 2000. Electronic monitoring and graduated sanctions. *Journal of Offender Monitoring* 13:19–20, 24.

COLEMAN, JAMES E. JR. 1998. The ABA's proposed moratorium on the death penalty. *Law and Contemporary Problems* 61:1–231.

COLEMAN ADVOCATES FOR CHILDREN AND YOUTH. 1996. *Reality vs. myth: Is San Francisco soft on juvenile crime?* San Francisco: Center on Juvenile and Criminal Justice.

COLLINS, DAMIAN AND ROBIN A. KEARNS. 2001. Under curfew and under siege? Legal geographies of young people. *Geoforum* 32:389–403.

CONLEY, DARLENE J. 1994. Adding color to a black and white picture: Using qualitative data to explain racial disproportionality in the juvenile justice system. *Journal of Research in Crime and Delinquency* 31:135–148.

CONNELLY, LINDA, ALVIN W. COHN, AND WENDY JOHNSTON. 1998. EM: What's wrong, what can be done? Four experts speak. *Journal of Offender Monitoring* 11:5–12.

COOK, KIMBERLY J. 1998. A passion to punish: Abortion opponents who favor the death penalty. *Justice Quarterly* 15:329–346.

COOK COUNTY COURT. 2002. *The Englewood evening reporting center.* Chicago: Cook County Court.

COOKE, GERALD. 2001. Patricide. *Journal of Threat Assessment* 1:35–45.

COOPER, CAROLINE S. ET AL. 1994. Differentiated case management: What is it? How Effective has it been? *Judges' Journal* 33:2–15.

CORBETT, RONALD P. 2000. Juvenile probation on the eve of the next millennium. *APPA Perspectives* 24:22–30.

CORBETT, RONALD P. AND M. KAY HARRIS. 1996. Day reporting centers: An evolving intermediate sanction. *Federal Probation* 60:51–54.

CORDER, BILLIE F. ET AL. 1986. Characteristics of two types of juvenile rapists: Implications for treatment and prediction. *Journal of Offender Counseling* 7:10–17.

CORRECTIONS TODAY. 1999a. National Juvenile Detention Association: Leading the juvenile detention field. *Corrections Today* 61:20.

————. 1999b. Rise in number of girls in Colorado jails. *Corrections Today* 61:12.

COSTANZO, MARK AND LAWRENCE T. WHITE EDS. 1994. The death penalty in the United States. *Journal of Social Issues* 50:1–197.

COSTANZO, SAMUEL A. 1990. Juvenile academy serves as facility without walls. *Corrections Today* 52:112–126.

COSTELLO, BARBARA J. 2000. Techniques of neutralization and self-esteem: A critical test of social control and neutralization theory. *Deviant Behavior* 21:307–329.

COTHERN, LYNN. 2000. *Juveniles and the death penalty.* Washington, DC: U.S. Department of Justice.

COUMARELOS, CHRISTINE AND DON WEATHERBURN. 1995. Targeting intervention strategies to reduce juvenile recidivism. *Australian and New Zealand Journal of Criminology* 28:35–72.

CRADDOCK, AMY AND LAURA A. GRAHAM. 1996. *Day reporting centers as an intermediate sanction: Evaluation of programs operated by the ATTIC Correctional Services.* Chapel Hill, NC: Pacific Institute for Research and Evaluation.

CREWS, GORDON A. AND REID H. MONTGOMERY. 2001. *Chasing shadows: Confronting juvenile violence in America.* Upper Saddle River, NJ: Prentice Hall.

CRISWELL, JOHN E. 1987. Juvenile detention resource centers: Florida's experience provides a model for the nation in juvenile detention. *Corrections Today* 49:22–26.

CROSLAND, PAUL. 1995. Searching for proof of probation officer effectiveness. *Probation Journal* 42:126–134.

CROWE, ANN H. 2000. *Jurisdictional technical assistance package for juvenile corrections.* Washington, DC: U.S. Office of Juvenile Justice and Delinquency Prevention.

CUNNINGHAM, PHILLIPPE B. AND SCOTT W. HENGGELER. 2001. Implementation of an empirically based drug and violence prevention and intervention program in public school settings. *Journal of Clinical Child Psychology* 30:221–232.

CURRAN, DANIEL J. 1984. The myth of a "new" female delinquent. *Crime and Delinquency* 30:386–399.

CURRY, G. DAVID. 1998. Female gang involvement. *Journal of Research on Crime and Delinquency* 35:100–118.

CURRY, G. DAVID AND SCOTT H. DECKER. 1998. *Confronting gangs: Crime and community.* Los Angeles, CA: Roxbury Publishing Company.

CURRY, G. DAVID, SCOTT H. DECKER, AND ARLEN EGLEY JR. 2002. Gang involvement and delinquency in a middle school population. *Justice Quarterly* 19:275–292.

CURTIN, JOHN C. 1997. *Equity and the underclass in criminal justice: Pieces for a left-hand stride.* Dubuque, IA: Kendall/Hunt.

DAHLBERG, LINDA L. AND LLOYD B. POTTER. 2001. Youth violence: Developmental pathways and prevention challenges. *American Journal of Preventive Medicine* 20:3–14.

DAHLEN, DONALD C. 1986. *Models of court management.* Millwood, NY: Associated Faculty Press.

DALE, MICHAEL J. 1988. Detaining juveniles in adult jails and lockups: An analysis of rights and liabilities. *American Jails* 1:46–50.

DALLEY, LANETTE PATRICE. 1997. *Montana's imprisoned mothers and their children: A case study on separation, reunification and legal issues.* Ann Arbor, MI: University Microfilms International.

DANIELS, STEPHEN. 1984. The problem of caseloads and studying court activities over time. *American Bar Association Research Journal* 4:751–795.

DANILA, BIRGIT, JEFFREY ANNON, AND M. DOUGLAS ANGLIN. 1997. *State demand and treatment needs assessment study: Dependence and abuse of alcohol and other drugs among California arrestees.* Los Angeles: Drug Abuse Research Center, University of California at Los Angeles.

DANNER, MONA J.E. AND DIANNE CYR CARMODY. 2001. Missing gender in cases of infamous school violence: Investigating research and media explanations. *Justice Quarterly* 18:87–114.

DARBY, PATRIC J. ET AL. 1998. Analysis of 112 juveniles who committed homicide: Characteristics and a closer look at family abuse. *Journal of Family Violence* 13:365–375.

DAVIDSON, GERALD E. 1987. Treatment and behavior change in juvenile delinquents. In *Handbook on Crime and Delinquency Prevention,* Elmer H. Johnson, ed. Westport, CT: Greenwood Press.

DAVIDSON, WILLIAM S. ET AL. 1987. Diversion of juvenile offenders: An experimental comparison. *Journal of Consulting and Clinical Psychology* 55:68–75.

DAVIES, ANDREW AND GEOFFREY PEARSON, EDS. 1999. History of crime and modernity. *British Journal of Criminology* 39:1–174.

DAVIS, ROBERT C. AND BARBARA E. SMITH. 1994. The effects of victim impact statements on sentencing decisions: A test in an urban setting. *Justice Quarterly* 11:453–512.

DAWSON, ROBERT O. 1995. *State bar section report on juvenile law: Special legislative issue.* Washington, DC: U.S. Government Printing Office.

DEAN, CHARLES W., J. DAVID HIRSCHEL, AND ROBERT BRAME. 1996. Minorities and juvenile case dispositions. *Justice System Journal* 18:267–285.

DEANGELO, ANDREW J. 1988. Diversion programs in the juvenile justice system: An alternative method of treatment for juvenile offenders. *Juvenile and Family Court Journal* 39:21–28.

DECKER, SCOTT H. 2000. *Increasing school safety through juvenile accountability programs.* Washington, DC: U.S. Office of Juvenile Justice and Delinquency Prevention.

DECKER, SCOTT H. AND C.W. KOHFELD. 1990. The deterrent effect of capital punishment in the five most active execution states: A time series analysis. *Criminal Justice Review* 15:173–191.

DEFRANCES, CAROL J. AND GREG W. STEADMAN. 1998. *Prosecutors in state courts 1996.* Washington, DC: U.S. Bureau of Justice Statistics.

DEFRANCES, CAROL J. AND KEVIN J. STROM. 1997. *Juveniles prosecuted in state criminal courts.* Washington, DC: U.S. Bureau of Justice Statistics.

DEJONG, CHRISTINA AND KENNETH C. JACKSON. 1998. Putting race into context: Race, juvenile justice processing, and urbanization. *Justice Quarterly* 15:487–504.

DELAWARE STATISTICAL ANALYSIS CENTER. 1999. *Evaluation of the Delaware juvenile drug court intervention.* Dover, DE: Delaware Statistical Analysis Center.

DEL CARMEN, ROLANDO V., MARY PARKER, AND FRANCES P. REDDINGTON. 1998. *Briefs of leading cases in juvenile justice.* Cincinnati, OH: Anderson Publishing Company.

DELORTO, THERESA E. AND FRANCIS T. CULLEN. 1985. The impact of moral development on delinquent involvement. *International Journal of Comparative and Applied Criminal Justice* 9:129–143.

DEMBO, RICHARD, ED. 2001. Family empowerment as an intervention strategy in juvenile delinquency. *Journal of Offender Rehabilitation* 33:1–109.

DEMBO, RICHARD, KIMBERLY PACHECO, AND JAMES SCHMEIDLER. 1997. Drug use and delinquent behavior among high risk youths. *Journal of Child and Adolescent Substance Abuse* 6:1–25.

DEMBO, RICHARD ET AL. 1995. Predictors of recidivism to a juvenile assessment center. *International Journal of the Addictions* 30:1425–1452.

DEMBO, RICHARD ET AL. 2000a. A longitudinal study of the impact of a family empowerment intervention on juvenile offender psychosocial functioning: An expanded assessment. *Journal of Child and Adolescent Substance Abuse* 10:1–7.

DEMBO, RICHARD ET AL. 2000b. Youth recidivism twelve months after a family empowerment intervention. *Journal of Offender Rehabilitation* 31:29–65.

DEZOLT, ERNEST M., LINDA M. SCHMIDT, AND DONNA C. GILCHER. 1996. The "tabula rasa" intervention project for delinquent gang-involved females. *Journal of Gang Research* 3:37–43.

DICATALDO, FRANK AND THOMAS GRISSO. 1995. A typology of juvenile offenders based on the judgments of juvenile court professionals. *Criminal Justice and Behavior* 22:246–262.

DIETRICH, KIM N. ET AL. 2001. Early exposure to lead and juvenile delinquency. *Neurotoxicology and Teratology* 23:511–518.

DILLINGHAM, DAVID D. ET AL. 1999. *Annual issue 1999: Classification and risk assessment.* Longmont, CO: U.S. National Institute of Corrections.

DODGE, KENNETH A. 2001. The science of youth violence prevention: Progressing from developmental epidemiology to efficacy to effectiveness to public policy. *American Journal of Preventive Medicine* 20:63–70.

DOUGHERTY, JOYCE. 1988. Negotiating justice in the juvenile justice system: A comparison of adult plea bargaining and juvenile intake. *Federal Probation* 52:72–80.

DUFFIELD, IAN AND JAMES BRADLEY. 1997. *Representing convicts: New perspectives on convict forced labour migration.* London, UK: Leicester University Press.

DUKES, RICHARD L., RUBEN O. MARTINEZ, AND JUDITH A. STEIN. 1997. Precursors and consequences of membership in youth gangs. *Youth and Society* 29:139–165.

DWYER, DIANE C. AND ROGER B. MCNALLY. 1987. Juvenile justice: Reform, retain, and reaffirm. *Federal Probation* 51:47–51.

EDWARDS, IAN. 2001. Victim participation in sentencing: The problems of incoherence. *Howard Journal of Criminal Justice* 40:39–54.

EGLEY, ARLEN JR. 2000. *Highlights of the 1999 National Youth Gang Survey.* Washington, DC: U.S. Department of Justice.

ELLIOTT, DELBERT S. 1994a. 1993 presidential address: Serious violent offenders: Onset, developmental course, and termination. *Criminology* 32:1–21.

———. 1994b. *Youth violence: An overview.* Boulder, CO: Center for the Study and Prevention of Violence.

ELLIS, LEE. 1985. Evolution and the nonlegal equivalent of aggressive criminal behavior. *Aggressive Behavior* 12:57–71.

ELLIS, LEE AND JAMES N. MCDONALD. 2001. Crime, delinquency, and social status: A reconsideration. *Journal of Offender Rehabilitation* 32:3–22.

ELLSWORTH, THOMAS. 1988. Case supervision planning: The forgotten component of intensive probation supervision. *Federal Probation* 52:28–33.

ELLSWORTH, THOMAS, MICHELLE T. KINSELLA, AND KIMBERLEE MASSIN. 1992. Prosecuting juveniles: *Parens patriae* and due process in the 1990s. *Justice Professional* 7:53–67.

ELTRINGHAM, SIMON AND JAN ALDRIDGE. 2000. The extent of children's knowledge of court as estimated by guardians ad litem. *Child Abuse Review* 9:275–286.

EMERSON, ROBERT M. 1969. *Judging delinquents.* Chicago: Aldine.

EMPEY, LAMAR T. AND JEROME RABOW. 1961. The Provo experiment in delinquency rehabilitation. *American Sociological Review* 26:679–695.

ENGLISH, KIM, SUSAN M. CHADWICK, AND SUZANNE K. PULLEN. 1994. *Colorado's intensive supervision probation: Report of findings.* Denver, CO: Division of Criminal Justice.

ENGLISH, KIM, SUZANNE PULLEN, AND SUSAN M. CHADWICK. 1996. *Comparison of intensive supervision probation and community corrections clientele.* Denver, CO: Colorado Division of Criminal Justice.

EREZ, EDNA AND KATHY LASTER. 1999. Neutralizing victim reform: Legal professionals' perspectives on victims and impact statements. *Crime and Delinquency* 45:530–553.

ERICKSON, KRISTAN GLASGOW AND ROBERT CROSNOE. 2000. A social process model of adolescent deviance: Combining social control and differential association perspectives. *Journal of Youth and Adolescence* 29:395–425.

ESBENSEN, FINN-AAGE AND L. THOMAS WINFREE. 1998. Race and gender differences between gang and nongang youths: Results from a multisite survey. *Justice Quarterly* 15:505–526.

ESBENSEN, FINN-AAGE ET AL. 2001. How great is G.R.E.A.T.? Results from a longitudinal quasi-experimental design. *Criminology and Public Policy* 1:87–115.

ESKRIDGE, CHRIS W., ED. 1996. *Criminal justice: Concepts and issues. 2d ed.* Los Angeles: Roxbury Publishing Company.

ESTRADA, FELIPE. 2001. Juvenile violence as a social problem: Trends, media attention, and societal response. *The British Journal of Criminology* 41:639–655.

EVANS, DONALD. 1996. Electronic monitoring: Testimony to Ontario's Standing Committee on Administration of Justice. *APPA Perspectives* 20:8–10.

EVANS, ROBERT C. ET AL. 1996. A cross-cultural comparison of the self-concepts of imprisoned young offenders by country, race, and parental status. *International Journal of Comparative and Applied Criminal-Justice* 20:157–176.

EVERLE, JANE A. AND ROLAND D. MAIURO. 2001. Introduction and commentary: Developmental perspectives on violence and victimization. *Violence and Victims* 16:351–354.

EVJE, AUDREY AND ROBERT C. CUSHMAN. 2000. *A summary of the evaluations of six California victim offender reconciliation programs.* Sacramento, CA: Judicial Council of California, Center for Families, Children, and the Courts.

FADER, JAMIE J. ET AL. 2001. Factors involved in decisions on commitment to delinquency programs for first-time juvenile offenders. *Justice Quarterly* 18:323–341.

FAGAN, JEFFREY A. 1990. Treatment and reintegration of violent juvenile offenders: Experimental results. *Justice Quarterly* 7:233–263.

FAGAN, JEFFREY A. AND MARTIN GUGGENHEIM. 1996. Preventive detention and the judicial prediction of dangerousness for juveniles: A natural experiment. *Journal of Criminal Law and Criminology* 86:415–448.

FAGAN, JEFFREY AND CRAIG REINARMAN. 1991. The social context of intensive supervision: Organizational and ecological influences on community treatment. In *Intensive interventions with high-risk youths: Promising approaches in juvenile probation and parole,* Troy L. Armstrong, ed. Monsey, NY: Criminal Justice Press.

FAGAN, JEFFREY AND FRANKLIN E. ZIMRING, EDS. 2000. *The changing borders of juvenile justice: Transfer of adolescents to the criminal court.* Chicago: The University of Chicago Press, John D. and Catherine T. MacArthur Foundation Series on Mental Health and Development.

FEDER, LYNETTE AND ROBERT F. BORUCH, EDS. 2000. The need for experimental research in criminal justice settings. *Crime and Delinquency* 46:291–434.

FEDERAL BUREAU OF INVESTIGATION. 2002. *Crime trends 2001: Preliminary figures.* Washington, DC: U.S. Department of Justice (June 24, 2002).

FELD, BARRY C. 1988a. The juvenile court meets the principle of offense: Punishment, treatment, and the difference it makes. *Boston University Law Review* 68:821–915.

———. 1988b. *In re Gault* revisited: A cross-state comparison of the right to counsel in juvenile court. *Crime and Delinquency* 34:393–424.

———. 1993a. Criminalizing the American juvenile court. In *Crime and Justice: A Review of Research, Vol.*

17, Michael Tonry, ed. Chicago: University of Chicago Press.

———. 1993b. Juvenile (in)justice and the criminal court alternative. *Crime and Delinquency* 39:403–424.

———. 1995. Violent youth and public policy: A case study of juvenile justice law reform. *Minnesota Law Review* 79:965–1128.

———. 2000. *Cases and materials on juvenile justice administration.* St. Paul, MN: West Group.

———. 2001. Race, youth violence, and the changing jurisprudence of waiver. *Behavioral Sciences and the Law* 19:3–22.

FELSON, RICHARD B., ERIC P. BAUMER, AND STEVEN F. MESSNER. 2000. Acquaintance robbery. *Journal of Research in Crime and Delinquency* 37:284–305.

FENDRICH, MICHAEL AND MELANIE ARCHER. 1998. Long-term rearrest rates in a sample of adjudicated delinquents: Evaluating the impact of alternative programs. *Prison Journal* 78:360–389.

FENDRICH, MICHAEL AND YANCHUN XU. 1994. The validity of drug reports from juvenile arrestees. *International Journal of the Addictions* 29:971–985.

FERRI, ENRICO. 1901. *Criminal sociology.* Boston: Little, Brown.

FINCKENAUER, JAMES O. AND PATRICIA W. GAVIN. 1999. *Scared Straight: The panacea phenomenon revisited.* Prospect Heights, IL: Waveland Press.

FINKELHOR, DAVID AND RICHARD K. ORMROD. 2001a. *Child abuse reported to the police.* Washington, DC: Office of Juvenile Justice and Delinquency Prevention.

———. 2001b. Factors in the underreporting of crimes against juveniles. *Child Maltreatment* 6:219–229.

FINN, MARY A. AND SUZANNE MUIRHEAD-STEVES. 2002. The effectiveness of electronic monitoring with violent male parolees. *Justice Quarterly* 19:293–312.

FISHBEIN, DIANA AND ROBERT THATCHER. 1986. New diagnostic methods in criminology: Assessing organic sources of behavioral disorder. *Journal of Research in Crime and Delinquency* 23:240–267.

FISHER, BONNIE S., FRANCIS T. CULLEN, AND MICHAEL G. TURNER. 2000. *The sexual victimization of college women.* Washington, DC: U.S. Bureau of Justice Statistics.

FLANGO, VICTOR E. 1994. Court unification and quality of state courts. *Justice System Journal* 16:33–55.

FLANNERY, DANIEL J. AND C. RONALD HUFF, EDS. 1999. *Youth violence: Prevention, intervention, and social policy.* Washington, DC: American Psychiatric Press.

FLEMING, GARY AND GERALD WINKLER. 1999. Sending them to prison: Washington state learns to accommodate female youthful offenders in prison. *Corrections Today* 61:132–136.

FLEXNER, BERNARD AND ROGER N. BALDWIN. 1914. *Juvenile courts and probation.* New York: Harcourt.

FLORIDA ADVISORY COUNCIL ON INTERGOVERNMENTAL RELATIONS. 1994. *Intergovernmental impacts of the 1994 Juvenile Justice Reform Bill.* Tallahassee: Florida Advisory Council on Intergovernmental Relations.

FLORIDA DEPARTMENT OF JUVENILE JUSTICE. 1999. *CINS physically-secure pilot program.* Tallahassee: Florida Department of Juvenile Justice Accountability Board.

———. 2000. *Determining best practices in Florida's juvenile boot camps.* Tallahassee: Florida Department of Juvenile Justice, Bureau of Data and Research.

FLORIDA DEPARTMENT OF JUVENILE JUSTICE BUREAU OF DATA AND RESEARCH. 2000. *The fiscal impact of reducing juvenile crime.* Tallahassee: Florida Department of Juvenile Justice, Bureau of Data and Research.

FLORIDA OFFICE OF PROGRAM POLICY ANALYSIS. 1995. *Status report on boot camps in Florida administered by the Department of Corrections and Department of Juvenile*

Justice. Tallahassee: Florida Office of Program Policy Analysis and Government Accountability.

FORST, MARTIN L. ED. 1995. *The new juvenile justice.* Chicago: Nelson-Hall.

FOX, JAMES ALAN AND MARIANNE W. ZAWITZ. 1999. *Homicide trends in the United States.* Washington, DC: U.S. Department of Justice.

FRIED, CARRIE S. 2001. Juvenile curfews: Are they an effective and constitutional means of combating juvenile violence? *Behavioral Sciences and the Law* 19:127–141.

FRIED, CARRIE S. AND N. DICKON REPPUCCI. 2001. Criminal decision making: The development of adolescent judgment, criminal responsibility, and culpability. *Law and Human Behavior* 25:45–61.

FRIEDENAUER, KURT C. 2002. *Florida department of juvenile justice pre-disposition report.* Tallahassee: State of Florida Department of Juvenile Justice.

FRITSCH, ERIC AND CRAIG HEMMENS. 1995. Juvenile waiver in the United States 1979–1995: A comparison and analysis of state waiver statutes. *Juvenile and Family Court Journal* 46:17–35.

FUNK, T. MARKUS. 1996. A mere youthful indiscretion? Reexamining the policy of expunging juvenile delinquency records. *University of Michigan Journal of Law Reform* 29:885–938.

FUNK, STEPHANIE J. 1999. Risk assessment for juveniles on probation: A focus on gender. *Criminal Justice and Behavior* 26:44–68.

GABLE, RALPH KIRKLAND. 1986. Application of personal telemonitoring to current problems in corrections. *Journal of Criminal Justice* 14:167–176.

GAFFNEY, EDWARD MCGLYNN JR. ET AL. 1997. Juvenile crime: Policy proposals on guns and violence, gangs and drugs: Symposium issue. *Valparaiso University Law Review* 31:1–332.

GALAWAY, BURT ET AL. 1995. Specialist foster family care for delinquent youth. *Federal Probation* 59:19–27.

GARDNER, SANDRA. 1983. *Street gangs.* New York: Franklin Watts.

GARDNER, WILLIAM ET AL. 1996. Clinical versus actuarial predictions of violence in patients with mental illnesses. *Journal of Consulting and Clinical Psychology* 64:602–609.

GAVAZZI, STEPHEN M. ET AL. 2000. The Growing Up FAST Diversion Program: An example of juvenile justice system program development for outcome evaluation. *Aggression and Violent Behavior* 5:159–175.

GEARY COUNTY COMMUNITY CORRECTIONS. 2002. *Pre-dispositional supervision program.* Geary County, KS: Geary County Community Corrections.

GEIS, GILBERT, ALAN MOBLEY, AND DAVID SHICHOR. 1999. Private prisons, criminological research, and conflict of interest: A case study. *Crime and Delinquency* 45:372–388.

GELBER, SEYMOUR. 1990. The juvenile justice system: Vision for the future. *Juvenile and Family Court Journal* 41:15–18.

GELSTHORPE, LORAINE R. 1987. The differential treatment of males and females in the criminal justice system. In *Sex, gender and care work,* Gordon Horobin, ed. Aberdeen, UK: Department of Social Work, University of Aberdeen.

GERAGHTY, THOMAS F. ET AL. 1997. Symposium on the future of the juvenile court. *Journal of Criminal Law and Criminology* 88:1–241.

GILLIARD, DARRELL K. AND ALLEN J. BECK. 1998. *Prisoners in 1997.* Washington, DC: U.S. Department of Justice.

GITTENS, JOAN. (1994). *Poor relations: The children of the state of Illinois, 1818–1990.* Urbana: University of Illinois Press.

GLASER, BRIAN A. ET AL. 2001. Multi-observer assessment of problem behavior in adjudicated youths: Patterns of discrepancies. *Child and Family Behavior Therapy* 23:33–45.

GLICK, BARRY. 1998. Kids in adult correctional systems: An understanding of adolescent development can aid staff in managing youthful offender populations. *Corrections Today* 60:96–102.

GLICK, BARRY AND ARNOLD P. GOLDSTEIN, EDS. 1995. *Managing delinquency: Programs that work.* Laurel, MD: American Correctional Association.

GLICK, BARRY AND WILLIAM STURGEON. 1999. Rising to the challenge: Identifying and meeting the needs of juvenile offenders with special needs. *Corrections Today* 61:105–166.

GLOVER, KIT AND KURT BUMBY. 2001. Reentry at the point of entry. *Corrections Today* 63:68–75.

GLUECK, SHELDON AND ELEANOR GLUECK. 1950. *Unraveling juvenile delinquency.* New York: Commonwealth Fund.

GODFREY, MICHAEL J. AND VINCENT SCHIRALDI. 1995. *How have homicide rates been affected by California's death penalty?* San Francisco: Center on Juvenile and Criminal Justice.

GODWIN, T.M. 1996. *Peer justice and youth empowerment: An implementation guide for teen court programs.* Washington, DC: National Highway Safety Administration, Department of Transportation.

GOFFMAN, ERVING. 1961. *Asylums.* Garden City, NY: Anchor Press.

GOLD, MARTIN. 1987. Social ecology. In *Handbook of juvenile delinquency,* Herbert C. Quay (ed.). New York: John Wiley and Sons.

GOLDKAMP, JOHN S. ET AL. 1999. *Implementing local criminal justice strategies: Developing measures of performance in 36 Bureau of Justice assistance open solicitation sites.* Philadelphia, PA: Crime and Justice Research Institute.

GOLDSMITH, HERBERT R. 2001. The interaction of management and treatment in a residential youth corrections treatment setting. *Residential Treatment for Children and Youth* 18:23–32.

GOLDSON, BARRY. 2001. A rational youth justice? Some critical reflections on the research, policy, and practice relation. *Probation Journal* 48:76–85.

GOODSTEIN, LYNNE AND HENRY SONTHEIMER. 1997. The implementation of an intensive aftercare program for serious juvenile offenders: A case study. *Criminal Justice and Behavior* 24:332–359.

GORDON, ROBERT A. 1986, August. IQ—commensurability of black-white differences in crime and delinquency. Unpublished paper presented at the annual meeting of the American Psychological Association. Washington, DC.

GORING, CHARLES. 1913. *The English convict.* London, UK: His Majesty's Stationery Office.

GOTTFREDSON, DENISE C. AND WILLIAM H. BARTON. 1997. *Closing institutions for juvenile offenders: The Maryland experience.* Lewiston, NY: Edwin Mellin Press.

GOTTFREDSON, DENISE C., GARY D. GOTTFREDSON, AND STEPHANIE A. WEISMAN. 2001. The timing of delinquent behavior and its implications for after-school programs. *Criminology and Public Policy* 1:61–86.

GOTTFREDSON, MICHAEL D. AND CAROLYN UIHLEIN. 1992. *Rationality in juvenile justice decision making.* Sacramento, CA: Justice Policy Research Corporation.

GOTTFREDSON, STEPHEN D. AND DON M. GOTTFREDSON. 1990. *Classification, prediction, and criminal justice policy: Final report to the National Institute of Justice.* Washington, DC: U.S. National Institute of Justice.

GOVER, ANGELA R. AND DORIS LAYTON MACKENZIE. 2000. Importation and deprivation explanations of juveniles' adjustment to correctional facilities. *International Journal of Offender Therapy and Comparative Criminology* 44:450–467.

GRAY, PATRICIA. 1999. Community corrections and the experiences of young male offenders in the Hong Kong youth justice system. *Journal of Social Policy* 28:577–594.

GREENBERG, M.T., C. KUSCHE, AND S.F. MIHALIC. 1998. *Blueprints for violence prevention, book ten: Promoting Alternative Thinking Strategies (PATHS)*. Boulder, CO: Center for the Study and Prevention of Violence.

GREENWOOD, PETER W. 1986a. "Differences in Criminal Behavior and Court Responses Among Juvenile and Young Adult Defendants." In Michael Tonry and Norval Morris (eds.) *Crime and Justice: An Annual Review of Research*. Chicago: University of Chicago Press.

———, ed. 1986b. *Intervention strategies for chronic juvenile offenders: Some new perspectives*. Westport, CT: Greenwood Press.

———. 1990. Reflections on three promising programs. *Perspectives* 14:20–24.

———. 1999. *Costs and benefits of early childhood intervention*. Washington, DC: U.S. Department of Justice.

GRIFFIN, BRENDA S. AND CHARLES T. GRIFFIN. 1978. *Juvenile delinquency in perspective*. New York: Harper and Row.

GRIFFIN, PATRICK. 2000. *Frequently asked questions: State juvenile justice state profiles*. Pittsburgh, PA: National Center for Juvenile Justice.

GRIFFIN, PATRICK, PATRICIA TORBET, AND LINDA SZYMANSKI. 1998. *Trying juveniles as adults in criminal courts: An analysis of state transfer provisions*. Washington, DC: U.S. Office of Juvenile Justice and Delinquency Prevention.

GRISSO, THOMAS. 1980. Juveniles' capacities to waive Miranda rights: An empirical analysis. *California Law Review* 68:1134–1166.

———. 1998. *Forensic evaluation of juveniles*. Sarasota, FL: Professional Resource Press.

GUARINO-GHEZZI, SUSAN. 1989. Classifying juveniles: A formula for case-by-case assessment. *Corrections Today* 51:112–116.

———. 1994. Reintegrative police surveillance of juvenile offenders: Forging an urban model. *Crime and Delinquency* 40:131–153.

———. 1998. Balancing juvenile justice. *Corrections Management Quarterly* 2:31–92.

GUARINO-GHEZZI, SUSAN AND BRYAN CARR. 1996. Juvenile offenders vs. the police: A community dilemma. *Caribbean Journal of Criminology and Social Psychology* 1:24–43.

GULLOTTA, THOMAS P., GERALD R. ADAMS, AND RAYMOND MONTEMAYOR, EDS. 1998. *Delinquent violent youth: Theory and interventions*. Thousand Oaks, CA: Sage.

HAAS, KENNETH C. AND GEOFFREY P. ALPERT, EDS. 1999. *The dilemmas of corrections: Contemporary readings*. Prospect Heights, IL: Waveland Press.

HAAS, MICHAEL. 1988. Violent schools—unsafe schools. *Journal of Conflict Resolution* 32:727–758.

HAGAN, JOHN AND BILL MCCARTHY. 1997. *Mean streets: Youth crime and homelessness*. Cambridge, UK: Cambridge University Press.

HAGEDORN, JOHN M. 1998. Gang violence in the postindustrial era. In Michael Tonry and Mark H. Moore, eds., *Youth violence*. Chicago: University of Chicago Press.

HAHN, PAUL H. 1984. *The juvenile offender and the law*. Cincinnati, OH: Anderson.

HALE, ROBERT L. 1997. *A review of juvenile executions in America*. Lewiston, NY: Edwin Mellen Press.

HANKE, PENELOPE J. 1996. Putting school crime into perspective: Self-reported school victimizations of high school seniors. *Journal of Criminal Justice* 24:207–226.

HARRELL, ADELE ET AL. 2002. Breaking the cycle of drugs and crime: Findings from the Birmingham BTC demonstration. *Criminology and Public Policy* 1:189–216.

HARRIS, PATRICIA M. 1988. Juvenile sentence reform and its evaluation: A demonstration of the need for more precise measures of offense seriousness in juvenile justice research. *Evaluation Review* 12:655–666.

HARRIS, PATRICIA M. ET AL. 1993. A wilderness challenge program as correctional treatment. *Journal of Offender Rehabilitation* 19:149–164.

HARRIS, RICHARD J. 2000. *Operation Safe Streets Governor's Task Force*. Dover, DE: Delaware Statistical Analysis Center.

HARRISON, PAIGE, JAMES R. MAUPIN, AND G. LARRY MAYS. 2001. Teen court: An examination of processes and outcomes. *Crime and Delinquency* 47:243–264.

HAYES, HENNESSEY D. AND MICHAEL R. GEERKEN. 1997. The idea of selective release. *Justice Quarterly* 14:353–370.

HAZLEHURST, KAYLEEN AND CAMERON HAZLEHURST, EDS. 1998. *Gangs and youth subcultures: International explorations*. New Brunswick, NJ: Transaction Publishers.

HEATH, G. ADAIR ET AL. 1988. Childhood firesetting. In *Modern perspectives in psychosocial pathology,* John G. Howells, ed. New York: Brunner/Mazel.

HEIDE, KATHLEEN M. 1999. *Young killers: The challenge of juvenile homicide*. Thousand Oaks, CA: Sage.

HEITGERD, JANET L., AND ROBERT J. BURSIK. 1987. Extracommunity dynamics and the ecology of delinquency. *American Journal of Sociology* 92:775–787.

HEMMENS, CRAIG AND KATHERINE BENNETT. 1999. Juvenile curfews and the courts: Judicial response to a not-so-new crime control strategy. *Crime and Delinquency* 45:99–121.

HEMMENS, CRAIG, ERIC FRITSCH, AND TORY J. CAETI. 1997. Juvenile justice code purpose clauses: The power of words. *Criminal Justice Policy Review* 8:221–246.

HENDERSON, THOMAS A. ET AL. 1984. *The significance of judicial structure: The effect of unification on trial court operations*. Washington, DC: U.S. Government Printing Office.

HERMAN, SUSAN AND CRESSIDA WASSERMAN. 2001. A role for victims in offender reentry. *Crime and Delinquency* 47:428–445.

HESS, ALBERT G. AND PRISCILLA F. CLEMENT, EDS. 1993. *History of juvenile delinquency: A collection of essays on crime committed by young offenders*. GER: Scientia Verlag.

HIL, RICHARD AND ANTHONY MCMAHON. 2001. *Families, crime, and juvenile justice*. New York: Peter Lang.

HILLBRAND, MARC ET AL. 1999. Patricides: Characteristics of offenders and victims, legal factors, and treatment issues. *Aggression and Violent Behavior* 4:179–190.

HINDMAN, JAN AND JAMES M. PETERS. 2001. Polygraph testing leads to better understanding adult and juvenile sex offenders. *Federal Probation* 65:8–15.

HIRSCHI, TRAVIS. 1969. *Causes of delinquency*. Berkeley, CA: University of California Press.

HOATH, DAVID R., FRANK W. SCHNEIDER, AND MEYER W. STARR. 1998. Police job satisfaction as a function of career orientation and position tenure: Implications for selection and community policing. *Journal of Criminal Justice* 26:337–347.

HODGES, KAY AND CHEONG SEOK KIM. 2000. Psychometric study of the child and adolescent functional assessment scale: Prediction of contact with the law and poor school attendance. *Journal of Abnormal Child Psychology* 28:287–297.

HODGKINSON, PETER ET AL. 1996. *Capital punishment in the United States of America: A review of the issues.* London, UK: Parliamentary Human Rights Group.

HOGE, ROBERT D. 2001. *The juvenile offender: Theory, research, and applications.* Boston: Kluwer Academic Publishers.

HOGE, ROBERT D., D.A. ANDREWS, AND ALAN W. LESCHIED. 1995. Investigation of variables associated with probation and custody dispositions in a sample of juveniles. *Journal of Clinical Child Psychology* 24:279–286.

HOLDEN, GWEN A. AND ROBERT A. KAPLER. 1995. Deinstitutionalizing status offenders: A record of progress. *Juvenile Justice* 2:3–10.

HOLMES, SHIRLEY R. 2000. Homicide in school: A preliminary discussion. *Journal of Gang Research* 7:29–36.

HOLSINGER, ALEX M. AND EDWARD J. LATESSA. 1999. An empirical evaluation of a sanction continuum: Pathways through the juvenile justice system. *Journal of Criminal Justice* 27:155–172.

HOOTON, EARNEST A. 1939. *Crime and the man.* Cambridge, MA: Harvard University Press.

HORNICK, JOSEPH ET AL. 1996. *A police reference manual on crime prevention and diversion with youth.* Ottawa, CAN: Solicitor General Canada.

HORNICK, JOSEPH P. AND SHULI RODAL. 1995. *The use of diversion and alternatives to traditional youth court: An international comparison.* Calgary, CAN: Canadian Research Institute for Law and the Family.

HOUCHINS, DAVID E. 2001. Developing the self-determination of incarcerated students. *The Journal of Correctional Education* 52:141–147.

HOUK, JULIE M. 1984. Electronic monitoring of probationers: A step toward big brother? *Golden Gate University Law Review* 14:431–446.

HOUSTON, JAMES G. 2001. *Crime, policy, and criminal behavior in America.* Lewiston, NY: Edwin Mellen Press.

HOWELL, JAMES C. 1998. *Youth gangs: An overview.* Washington, DC: U.S. Department of Justice.

HOWELL, JAMES C. AND SCOTT H. DECKER. 1999. *The youth gangs, drugs, and violence connection.* Washington, DC: Office of Juvenile Justice and Delinquency Prevention Programs.

HOWELL, JAMES C. AND BARRY KRISBERG, EDS. 1998. Juveniles in custody. *Crime and Delinquency* 44:483–601.

HOWELL, JAMES C. AND JAMES P. LYNCH. 2000. *Youth gangs in schools.* Washington, DC: U.S. Department of Justice.

HOWELL, WALTER. 1999. Philadelphia's "Adopt-a-School" partnership to prevent delinquency. *Corrections Today* 61:26–28.

HOWITT, PAMELA S. AND EUGENE A. MOORE. 1991. The efficacy of intensive early intervention: An evaluation of the Oakland County Probate Court early offender program. *Juvenile and Family Court Journal* 42:25–36.

HSIEH, CHING CHI. 1993. *Extralegal bias in juvenile justice processing: An application of status characteristic theory.* Ann Arbor, MI: University Microfilms International.

HUGHES, STELLA P. AND ANNE L. SCHNEIDER. 1989. Victim-offender mediation: A survey of program characteristics and perceptions of effectiveness. *Crime and Delinquency* 35:217–233.

HUNTER, JOHN A. JR. AND DENNIS W. GOODWIN. 1992. The clinical utility of satiation therapy with juvenile sexual offenders: Variations and efficacy. *Annals of Sex Research* 5:71–80.

HURLEY, DANIEL J. AND JERRY M. HATFIELD 1996. *Illinois probation intake study.* Chicago: Illinois Criminal Justice Information Authority.

HURST, HUNTER. 1990. Juvenile probation in retrospect. *Perspectives* 14:16–24.

HUSKEY, BOBBIE L. 1984. Community corrections acts. *Corrections Today* 46:45.

———. 1990. In Illinois: Law forces change in juvenile lockups. *Corrections Today* 52:122–123.

ILLINOIS DEPARTMENT OF CORRECTIONS. 2000. *Two year report on Illinois Department of Corrections' Chicago Southside Day Reporting Center.* Springfield, IL: Illinois Department of Corrections.

INCIARDI, JAMES A., DUANE C. MCBRIDE, AND JAMES E. RIVERS. 1996. *Drug control and the courts.* Thousand Oaks, CA: Sage Publications.

IRELAND, TIMOTHY O., CAROLYN A. SMITH, AND TERENCE P. THORNBERRY. 2002. Developmental issues in the impact of child maltreatment on later delinquency and drug use. *Criminology* 40:359–400.

ITO, JEANNE A. 1984. *Measuring the performance of different types of juvenile courts.* Williamsburg, VA: National Center for State Courts.

JACKSON, LONNIE. 1998. *Gangbusters: Strategies for prevention and intervention.* Lanham, MD: American Correctional Association.

JACOBS, SUSAN AND DAVID C. MOORE. 1994. Successful restitution as a predictor of juvenile recidivism. *Juvenile and Family Court Journal* 45:3–14.

JACOBSON, WENDY B. 2000. *Safe from the start: Taking action on children exposed to violence.* Washington, DC: Office of Juvenile Justice and Delinquency Prevention.

JANG, SUNG JOON. 2002. The effects of family, school, peers, and attitudes on adolescents' drug use: Do they vary with age? *Justice Quarterly* 19:97–126.

JARJOURA, G. ROGER AND DAVID C. MAY. 2000. Integrated criminological theories to explain violent forms of delinquency. *Caribbean Journal of Criminology and Social Psychology* 5:81–102.

JENNINGS, MARY ANN AND JOHN GUNTHER. 2000. Juvenile delinquency in search of a practice model: Family health, differential association, and social control. *Journal of Family Social Work* 5:75–89.

JENSEN, ERIC L. AND LINDA K. METSGER. 1994. A test of the deterrent effect of legislative waiver on violent juvenile crime. *Crime and Delinquency* 40:96–104.

JENSON, JEFFREY M. ET AL. 1995. *Racial disproportionality in the Utah juvenile justice system: Final report.* Salt Lake City, UT: Social Research Institute, University of Utah.

JOE, KAREN A.1995. The dynamics of running away, deinstitutionalization policies and the police. *Juvenile and Family Court Journal* 46:43–55.

JOHNSON COUNTY DEPARTMENT OF CORRECTIONS. 2002. *Juvenile ISP conditions and guidelines.* Johnson County, KS: Johnson County Department of Corrections.

JOHNSTON, JAMES B. AND PHILIP E. SECRET. 1995. The effects of court structure on juvenile court decisionmaking. *Journal of Criminal Justice* 23:63–82.

JOHNSTON, WENDY. 2000. An innovative solution to the problem of juvenile offenders in Missouri. *The Journal of Offender Monitoring* 13:18–38.

JONES, BERNADETTE. 1990, November. Intensive probation services in Philadelphia County. Unpublished paper presented at the American Society of Criminology meetings, Baltimore, MD.

JONES, DENIS. 2001. "Misjudged youth": A critique of the Audit Commission's reports on youth justice. *British Journal of Criminology* 41:362–380.

JONES, MARK AND DARRELL L. ROSS. 1997. Electronic house arrest and boot camp in North Carolina: Comparing recidivism. *Criminal Justice Policy Review* 8:383–403.

JONES, MICHAEL A. AND BARRY KRISBERG. 1994. *Images and reality: Juvenile crime, youth violence and public policy.* San Francisco: National Council on Crime and Delinquency.

JONES, PETER R. AND PHILIP W. HARRIS. 1999. Developing an empirically based typology of delinquent youths. *Journal of Quantitative Criminology* 15:251–276.

JONES, PETER R. ET AL. 2001. Identifying chronic juvenile offenders. *Justice Quarterly* 18:479–507.

JONES, RALPH K. AND JOHN H. LACEY. 1999. *Evaluation of a day reporting center for repeat DWI offenders.* Winchester, MA: Mid-America Research Institute.

JOSI, DON A. AND DALE K. SECHREST. 1999. A pragmatic approach to parole aftercare: Evaluation of a community reintegration program for high-risk youthful offenders. *Justice Quarterly* 16:51–80.

JURICH, SONIA, MARTA CASPER, AND KIM A. HULL. 2001. Training correctional educators: A needs assessment study. *The Journal of Correctional Education* 52:23–27.

KADISH, TARA E. ET AL. 2001. Identifying the developmental strengths of juvenile offenders: Assessing four life-skills dimensions. *Journal of Addictions and Offender Counseling* 31:85–95.

KAKAR, SUMAN. 1998. Delinquency prevention through family and neighborhood empowerment. *Studies on Crime and Prevention* 7:107–125.

KAKAR, SUMAN, MARIE-LUISE FRIEDEMANN, AND LINDA PECK. 2002. Girls in detention: The results of focus group discussion interviews and official records review. *Journal of Contemporary Criminal Justice* 18:57–73.

KAMERMAN, SHEILA B. AND ALFRED J. KAHN, EDS. 1990. Social services for children, youth, and families in the United States. *Children and Youth Services Review* 12:170–184.

KAMMER, JAMES J., KEVIN I. MINOR, AND JAMES B. WELLS. 1997. An outcome study of the Diversion Plus Program for juvenile offenders. *Federal Probation* 61:51–56.

KAPP, STEPHEN A., IRA SCHWARTZ, AND IRWIN EPSTEIN. 1994. Adult imprisonment of males released from residential childcare: A longitudinal study. *Residential Treatment for Children and Youth* 12:19–36.

KASINSKY, RENEE GOLDSMITH. 1994. Child neglect and "unfit" mothers: Child savers in the progressive era and today. *Women and Criminal Justice* 6:97–129.

KASSEBAUM, GENE, NANCY L. MARKER, AND PATRICIA GLANCEY. 1997. *A plan for the prevention, resolution, and controls for the problem of youth on the run.* Honolulu, HI: Center for Youth Research, Social Science Research Institute, University of Hawaii at Manoa.

KATZ, CHARLES M., VINCENT J. WEBB, AND DAVID R. SCHAEFER. 2000. The validity of police gang intelligence lists: Examining differences in delinquency between documented gang members and nondocumented delinquents. *Police Quarterly* 3:413–437.

KAUFMAN, PHILLIP ET AL. 1998. *Indicators of school crime and safety 1998.* Washington, DC: U.S. Department of Justice.

KEARNEY, EDMUND M. 1994. A clinical corrections approach: The failure of a residential juvenile delinquency treatment center. *Juvenile and Family Court Journal* 45:33–41.

KEARON, WILLIAM G. 1990. Deinstitutionalization, street children, and the coming AIDS epidemic in the adolescent population. *Juvenile and Family Court Journal* 41:9–18.

KEILITZ, SUSAN L. ET AL. 1997. *Domestic violence and child custody disputes: A resource handbook for judges and court managers.* Williamsburg, VA: National Center for State Courts.

KELLEHER, MICHAEL D. 1998. *When good kids kill.* Westport, CT: Praeger.

KEMPF-LEONARD, KIMBERLY AND ERICKA S.L. PETERSON. 2000. Expanding realms of the new penology: The advent of actuarial justice for juveniles. *Punishment and Society* 2:66–97.

KEMPF-LEONARD, KIMBERLY AND LISA L. SAMPLE. 2000. Disparity based on sex: Is gender-specific treatment warranted? *Justice Quarterly* 17:89–128.

KEMPF-LEONARD, KIMBERLY, PAUL E. TRACY, AND JAMES C. HOWELL. 2001. Serious, violent, and chronic juvenile offenders: The relationship of delinquency career types to adult criminality. *Justice Quarterly* 18:449–478.

KENDRICK, DOUGLAS T. AND VIRGIL SHEETS. 1993. Homicidal fantasies. *Ethnology and Sociobiology* 14:231–246.

KERLE, KENNETH E. 1998. *American jails: Looking to the future.* Boston: Butterworth-Heinemann.

KING, TAMMY CALLIHAN. 1996. *Fifteen years later: A partial retest of the "violent few" study of 1978.* Ann Arbor, MI: University Microfilms International.

KINGREE, J.B., RONALD BRAITHWAITE, AND TAMMY WOODRING. 2001. Psychosocial and behavioral problems in relation to recent experience as a runaway among adolescent detainees. *Criminal Justice and Behavior* 28:190–205.

KITSUSE, JOHN I. 1962. Societal reaction to deviant behavior: Problems of theory and method. *Social Problems* 9:247–256.

KLEIN, MALCOLM W., L. ROSENZWEIG, AND M. BATES. 1975. The ambiguous juvenile arrest. *Criminology* 24:185–194.

KLUG, ELIZABETH A. 2001. Geographical disparities among trying and sentencing juveniles. *Corrections Today* 63:100–107.

KNEPPER, PAUL AND SHANNON M. BARTON. 1996. Informal sources of delay in child management proceedings: Evidence from the Kentucky Court Improvement Project. *Juvenile and Family Court Journal* 47:23–37.

KNEPPER, PAUL AND GRAY CAVENDER. 1990, April. Decision-making and the typification of juveniles on parole. Unpublished paper presented at the Academy of Criminal Justice Science meetings, Denver, CO.

KNIGHT, KAREN WITCHCOFF AND TONY TRIPODI. 1996. Societal bonding and delinquency: An empirical test of Hirschi's theory of control. *Journal of Offender Rehabilitation* 23:117–129.

KNOX, GEORGE W., BRAD MARTIN, AND EDWARD D. TROMANHAUSER. 1995. Preliminary results of the 1995 National Prosecutor's Survey. *Journal of Gang Research* 2:59–71.

KNOX COUNTY JUVENILE SERVICES. 2002. *Electronic monitoring and house arrest for juveniles: A status report.* Knoxville, TN: Knox County Juvenile Services.

KNUPFER, ANNE MEIS. 2001. *Reform and resistance: Gender, delinquency, and America's first juvenile court.* New York: Routledge.

KOHL, SENATOR HERB. 1996. *Promises made, promises broken: The failure to fund crime prevention programs that work.* Washington, DC: Committee on the Judiciary, United States Senate.

KOHLBERG, L. 1981. *The philosophy of moral development.* New York: Harper and Row.

KOWALSKI, MELANIE AND TULLIO CAPUTO. 1999. Recidivism in youth court: An examination of the impact of age, gender, and prior record. *Canadian Journal of Criminology* 41:57–84.

KRAUSE, WESLEY AND MARILYN D. McSHANE. 1994. A deinstitutionalization retrospective: Relabeling the status offender. *Journal of Crime and Justice* 17:45–67.

KRETSCHMER, ERNEST. 1936. *Physique and character.* London, UK: Kegan Paul, Trench, and Trubner.

KRISBERG, BARRY ET AL. 1989. *Demonstration of post-adjudication non-residential intensive supervision programs: Selected program summaries.* San Francisco: National Council on Crime and Delinquency.

KURTZ, P. DAVID, MARTHA M. GIDDINGS, AND RICHARD SUTPHEN. 1993. A prospective investigation of racial disparity in the juvenile justice system. *Juvenile and Family Court Journal* 44:43–59.

KYLE, JIM. 1998. The privatization debate continues: Tennessee's experience highlights scope of controversy over private prisons. *Corrections Today* 60:88–158.

LAB, STEVEN P. 1984. Patterns in juvenile misbehavior. *Crime and Delinquency* 30:293–308.

LAB, STEVEN P., GLENN SHIELDS, AND CONNIE SCHONDEL. 1993. Research note: An evaluation of juvenile sexual offender treatment. *Crime and Delinquency* 39:543–553.

LAHEY, MARY ANNE, BRUCE A. CHRISTENSON, AND ROBERT J. ROSSI. 2000. *Analysis of trial court unification in California.* Sacramento, CA: Judicial Council of California.

LAGRANGE, TERESA C. 1999. The impact of neighborhoods, schools, and malls on the spatial distribution of property damage. *Journal of Research in Crime and Delinquency* 36:393–422.

LANDREVILLE, P. 1999. Electronic surveillance of delinquents: A growing trend. *Deviance et Societe* 23:105–121.

LANGAN, PATRICK A. AND DAVID J. LEVIN. 2002. *Recidivism of prisoners released in 1994.* Washington, DC: U.S. Department of Justice, Office of Justice Programs (June, 2002).

LANSING, SHARON. 1999. *Parental responsibility and juvenile delinquency: A comparative analysis of laws in New York and other states.* Albany, NY: Office of Justice Systems Analysis Public Policy Report, Division of Criminal Justice Services.

LARIVEE, JOHN. 1990. On the outside: Corrections in the community. *Corrections Today* 52:84–106.

LATESSA, EDWARD J. AND HARRY E. ALLEN. 1999. *Corrections in the community,* 2d ed. Cincinnati, OH: Anderson Publishing Company.

LAUB, JOHN H. 1987, November. Reanalyzing the Glueck data: A new look at unraveling juvenile delinquency. Unpublished paper presented at the American Society of Criminology meetings. Montreal, CAN.

LAURENCE, S. E. AND B. R. WEST. 1985. *National evaluation of the New Pride Replication Program: Final report, Vol. I.* Lafayette, CA: Pacific Institute for Research and Evaluation.

LAURITSEN, JANET L. 2001. The social ecology of violent victimization: Individual and contextual effects in the NCVS. *Journal of Quantitative Criminology* 17:3–32.

LAVIN, G. K., S. TRABKA, AND E. M. KAHN. 1984. Group therapy with aggressive and delinquent adolescents. In *The aggressive adolescent: Clinical perspectives,* C. R. Keith, ed. New York: Free Press.

LAWRENCE, RICHARD A. 1984. The role of legal counsel in juveniles' understanding of their rights. *Juvenile and Family Court Journal* 34:49–58.

———. 1985. School performance, containment theory, and delinquent behavior. *Youth and Society* 7:69–95.

LEE, LEONA. 1995. Factors influencing intake disposition in a juvenile court. *Juvenile and Family Court Journal* 46:43–61.

———. 1996. Predictors of juvenile court dispositions. *Journal of Crime and Justice* 19:149–166.

LEFLORE, LARRY. 1988. Delinquent youths and family. *Adolescence* 23:629–642.

LEIBER, MICHAEL J. 1995. Toward clarification of the concept of "minority" status and decision making in juvenile court proceedings. *Journal of Crime and Justice* 18:79–108.

LEIBER, MICHAEL J. AND TINA L. MAWHORR. 1995. Evaluating the use of social skills training and employment with delinquent youth. *Journal of Criminal Justice* 23:127–141.

LEIBER, MICHAEL J., MAHESH K. NALLA, AND MARGARET FARNWORTH. 1998. Explaining juveniles' attitudes toward the police. *Justice Quarterly* 15:151–174.

LEIBER, MICHAEL J. AND JAYNE M. STAIRS. 1999. Race, contexts, and the use of intake diversion. *Journal of Research in Crime and Delinquency* 36:56–86.

LEMERT, EDWIN M. 1951. *Social pathology.* New York: McGraw-Hill.

———. 1967a. *Human deviance, social problems, and social control.* Englewood Cliffs, NJ: Prentice-Hall.

———. 1967b. The juvenile court—quests and realities. In *Task force report: Juvenile delinquency and youth crime.* Washington, DC: President's Commission on Law Enforcement and the Administration of Justice.

LEMMON, ROBIN A. AND SHARON K. CALHOON 1998. Predicting juvenile recidivism using the Indiana department of correction's risk assessment instrument. *Juvenile and Family Court Journal* 49:55–62.

LEON, ANA M., SOPHIA F. DZIEGIELEWSKI, AND CHRISTINE TUBIAK. 1999. A program evaluation of a juvenile halfway house: Considerations for strengthening program components. *Evaluation and Program Planning* 22:141–153.

LEONARD, KIMBERLY KEMPF, CARL E. POPE, AND WILLIAM H. FEYERHERM. 1995. *Minorities in juvenile justice.* Thousand Oaks, CA: Sage.

LEVINE, IRENE, ED. 1996. Preventing violence among youth: Introduction. *American Journal of Orthopsychiatry* 66:320–389.

LEVINSON, ROBERT H. AND JOHN J. GREENE JR. 1999. New "boys" on the block: A study of prison inmates under the age of 18. *Corrections Today* 61:60–68.

LEVITT, STEVEN D. 1998. The relationship between crime reporting and police: Implications for the use of *Uniform Crime Reports. Journal of Quantitative Criminology* 14:61–81.

LEVY, KENNETH C. 2001. The relationship between adolescent attitudes towards authority, self-concept, and delinquency. *Adolescence* 36:333–346.

LEWIS, ALAN DANA AND TIMOTHY J. HOWARD. 2000. Parole officers' perceptions of juvenile offenders within a balanced and restorative model of justice. *Federal Probation* 64:40–45.

LIBERMAN, AKIVA, LAURA WINTERFIELD, AND JEROME MCELROY. 1996. *Minority overrepresentation among juveniles in New York City's adult and juvenile court systems.* New York: New York City Criminal Justice Agency.

LIEB, ROXANNE, LEE FISH, AND TODD CROSBY. 1994. *A summary of state trends in juvenile justice.* Olympia, WA: Washington State Institute for Public Policy.

LINDSTROM, PETER. 1996. Family interaction, neighborhood context and deviant behavior: A research note. *Studies on Crime and Crime Prevention* 5:113–119.

LISTUG, DAVID. 1996. Wisconsin sheriff's office saves money and resources. *American Jails* 10:85–86.

LITTLE HOOVER COMMISSION. 1990. *Runaway/homeless youths: California's efforts to recycle society's throwaways.* Sacramento, CA: Little Hoover Commission.

LOBLEY, DAVID, DAVID SMITH, AND CHRISTINA STERN. 2001. *Freagarrach: An evaluation of a project for persistent juvenile offenders.* Edinburgh, Scotland: The Scottish Executive Central Research Unit.

LOCKE, THOMAS P. ET AL. 1986. An evaluation of a juvenile education program in a state penitentiary. *Evaluation Review* 10:281–298.

LoGALBO, ANTHONY P. AND CHARLENE M. CALLAHAN 2001. An evaluation of the teen court as a juvenile crime diversion program. *Juvenile and Family Court* 52:1–11.

LOGAN, CHARLES H. AND SHARLA P. RAUSCH. 1985. Why de-institutionalizing status offenders is pointless. *Crime and Delinquency* 31:501–517.

LOMBARDO, RITA AND JANET DiGiorgio-MILLER. 1988. Concepts and techniques in working with juvenile sex offenders. *Journal of Offender Counseling Services and Rehabilitation* 13:39–53.

LOUCKS, ALEXANDER AND EDWARD ZAMBLE. 1999. Predictors of recidivism in serious female offenders: Canada searches for predictors common to both men and women. *Corrections Today* 61:26–32.

LOWRY, JOLENE M. 1997. Family group conferences as a form of court-approved alternative dispute resolution in child abuse and neglect cases. *University of Michigan Journal of Law Reform* 31:57–92.

LURIGIO, ARTHUR J., ED. 1996. *Community corrections in America: New directions and sounder investments for persons with mental illness and codisorders.* Seattle, WA: National Coalition for Mental and Substance Abuse Health Care in the Justice System.

LUTZE, FAITH E. 2001. The influence of a shock incarceration program on inmate adjustment and attitudinal change. *Journal of Criminal Justice* 29:255–267.

LYNAM, DONALD R. 1996. Early identification of chronic offenders: Who is the fledgling psychopath? *Psychological Bulletin* 120:209–234.

MACALLAIR, DAN AND RALPH COURTNEY. 1995. *Rebutting juvenile waiver laws: Strategies for defense attorneys in California fitness hearings.* San Francisco: National Council for Crime and Delinquency.

MacDONALD, JOHN M. AND MEDA CHESNEY-LIND. 2001. Gender bias and juvenile justice revisited: A multiyear analysis. *Crime and Delinquency* 47:173–195.

MACK, DENNIS E.1992. High impact incarceration program: Rikers boot camp. *American Jails* 6:63–65.

MacKENZIE, DORIS LAYTON AND EUGENE E. HEBERT, EDS. 1996. *Correctional boot camps: A Tough intermediate sanction.* Washington, DC: U.S. National Institute of Justice.

MacKENZIE, DORIS LAYTON AND JAMES W. SHAW. 1993. The impact of shock incarceration on technical violations and new criminal activities. *Justice Quarterly* 10:463–487.

MacKENZIE, DORIS LAYTON, JAMES W. SHAW, AND VONCILE B. GOWDY. 1993. *An evaluation of shock incarceration in Louisiana.* Washington, DC: U.S. Department of Justice, Office of Justice Programs.

MacKENZIE, DORIS LAYTON AND DAVID B. WILSON. 2001. The impact of boot camps and traditional institutions on juvenile residents: Perceptions, adjustments, and change. *Journal of Research in Crime and Delinquency* 38:279–313.

MacKENZIE, DORIS LAYTON ET AL. 2001. *A national study comparing the environments of boot camps with traditional facilities for juvenile offenders.* Washington, DC: U.S. Department of Justice.

MAGUIRE, KATHLEEN AND ANN L. PASTORE. 2002. *Bureau of Justice statistics sourcebook of criminal justice statistics—2000.* Albany, NY: The Hindelang Criminal Justice Research Center, State University of New York at Albany.

MAINE LEGISLATIVE OFFICE OF POLICY AND LEGAL ANALYSIS. 2000. *Task force to study the implementation of alternative programs and interventions for violent and chronically disruptive students.* Augusta: Maine Legislative Office of Policy and Legal Analysis.

MAINPRIZE, STEPHEN. 1992. Electronic monitoring in corrections: Assessing cost effectiveness and the potential for widening the net of social control. *Canadian Journal of Criminology* 34:161–180.

MALES, MIKE A. 2000. Vernon, Connecticut's juvenile curfew: The circumstances of youths cited and effects on crime. *Criminal Justice Policy Review* 11:254–267.

MALONEY, DENNIS M., DENNIS ROMIG AND TROY ARMSTRONG. 1988. Juvenile probation: The balanced approach. *Juvenile and Family Court Journal* 39:1–63.

MALTZ, MICHAEL D. 1984. *Recidivism.* Orlando, FL: Academic Press.

MANFREDI, CHRISTOPHER P. 1998. *The U.S. Supreme Court and juvenile justice.* Lawrence: University Press of Kansas.

MARCINIAK, LIZ MARIE. 2000. The addition of day reporting to intensive supervision probation: A comparison of recidivism rates. *Federal Probation* 20:34–39.

MARDON, STEVEN 1991. Training America's youth. *Corrections Today* 53:32–65.

MARSH, FRANK H. AND JANET KATZ, EDS. 1985. *Biology, crime, and ethics: A study of biological explanations for criminal behavior.* Cincinnati, OH: Anderson Publishing Company.

MARTIN, CHRISTINE, DAVID E. OLSON, AND ARTHUR J. LURIGIO. 2000. *An evaluation of the Cook County sheriff's day reporting center program: Rearrest and reincarceration after discharge.* Chicago: Illinois Criminal Justice Information Authority.

MARYLAND GOVERNOR'S INDEPENDENT ASSESSMENT TEAM. 1999. *Report of the Governor's Independent Assessment Team on juvenile boot camps.* Baltimore: Maryland Governor's Independent Assessment Team.

MASSACHUSETTS STATISTICAL ANALYSIS CENTER. 2001. *Implementation of the Juvenile Justice Reform Act: Youthful offenders in Massachusetts.* Boston: Massachusetts Statistical Analysis Center.

MATESE, MARK A. AND JOHN A. TUELL. 1998. *Update on the comprehensive strategy for serious, violent, and chronic juvenile offenders.* Washington, DC: U.S. Department of Justice.

MATSON, SCOTT AND ROBERT BARNOSKI. 1997. *Assessing risk: Washington state juvenile court early intervention program.* Olympia, WA: Washington State Institute for Public Policy.

MATSON, STEVEN C., DEBORAH BRETL, AND KRISTINE WOLF. 2000. Health care needs of detained youth. *Journal of Correctional Health Care* 7:245–261.

MATSUEDA, ROSS L. AND KATHLEEN ANDERSON. 1998. The dynamics of delinquent peers and delinquent behavior. *Criminology* 36:269–308.

MATZA, DAVID. 1964. *Delinquency and drift.* New York: Wiley.

MAZEROLLE, PAUL. 1998. Gender, general strain, and delinquency: An empirical examination. *Justice Quarterly* 15:65–91.

MAZEROLLE, PAUL AND JEFF MAAHS. 2000. General strain and delinquency: An alternative examination of conditioning influences. *Justice Quarterly* 17:753–778.

MAZEROLLE, PAUL ET AL. 2000. Onset age, persistence, and offending versatility: Comparisons across gender. *Criminology* 38:1143–1172.

McANANY, PATRICK D., DOUG THOMSON, AND DAVID FOGEL, EDS.1984. *Probation and justice: A reconsideration of a mission.* Cambridge, MA: Oelgeschlager, Gunn, and Hain.

McCARTER, SUSAN AINSLEY. 1997. *Understanding the overrepresentation of minorities in Virginia's juvenile justice system.* Ann Arbor, MI: University Microfilms International.

McCold, Paul and Benjamin Wachtel. 1998. *Restorative policing experiment: The Bethlehem Police Family Group Conferencing Project.* Bethlehem, PA: Real Justice.

McCord, David M. 1995. Toward a typology of wilderness-based residential treatment program participants. *Residential Treatment for Children and Youth* 12:51–60.

McCord, Joan, ed. 1995. *Coercion and punishment in long-term perspectives.* New York: Cambridge University Press.

McCord, Joan, Cathy Spatz Widom, and Nancy A. Crowell, eds. 2001. *Juvenile crime, juvenile justice.* Washington, DC: National Academy Press.

McDevitt, Jack, Marla Domino, and Katrina Baum. 1997. *Metropolitan day reporting center: An evaluation.* Boston: Center for Criminal Justice Policy Research, Northeastern University.

McDowall, David, Colin Loftin, and Brian Wiersema. 2000. The impact of youth curfew laws on juvenile crime rates. *Crime and Delinquency* 46:76–91.

McGee, Zina T. and Spencer R. Baker. 2002. Impact of violence on problem behavior among adolescents. *Journal of Contemporary Criminal Justice* 18:74–93.

McGill, D.E., S.F. Mihalic, and J.K. Grotpeter. 1998. *Blueprints for violence prevention, book two: Big Brothers/Big Sisters of America.* Boulder, CO: Center for the Study and Prevention of Violence.

McLaren, Kaye L. 2000. *Tough is not enough—Getting smart about youth crime: A review of research on what works to reduce offending by young people.* Wellington, NZ: Ministry of Youth Affairs.

McLean County Court Services. 2002. *Day reporting center for juveniles possessing firearms.* McLean County, IL: McLean County Court Services.

McNulty, Elizabeth. 1996. *Arizona Juvenile Transfer Study: Juveniles transferred to adult court 1994.* Phoenix, AZ: Administrative Office of the Courts, Arizona Supreme Court.

Mears, Daniel P. 2000. Assessing the effectiveness of juvenile justice reforms: A closer look at the criteria and the impacts on diverse stakeholders. *Law and Society* 22:175–202.

———. 2001. Getting tough with juvenile offenders: Explaining support for sanctioning youths as adults. *Criminal Justice and Behavior* 28:206–226.

———. 2002. Sentencing guidelines and the transformation of juvenile justice in the 21st century. *Journal of Contemporary Criminal Justice* 18:6–19.

Mears, Daniel P. and William R. Kelly. 1999. Assessments and intake processes in juvenile justice processing: Emerging policy considerations. *Crime and Delinquency* 45:508–529.

Meisel, Joshua S. 2001. Relationships and juvenile offenders: The effects of intensive aftercare supervision. *Prison Journal* 81:206–245.

Menard, Scott 1995. A developmental test of Mertonian anomie theory. *Journal of Research in Crime and Delinquency* 32:136–174.

Mendel, Richard A. 1995. *Prevention or pork? A hard-headed look at youth-oriented anti-crime programs.* Washington, DC: American Youth Policy Forum.

———. 2001. *Less cost, more safety: Guiding lights for reform in juvenile justice.* Washington, DC: American Youth Policy Forum.

Menon, Ramdas and Jeffrey A. Jordan. 1997. *Juvenile justice in Texas: Factors correlated with processing decisions.* College Station, TX: Public Policy Research Institute, Texas A & M University.

Mentaberry, Mary. 1999. *Model courts serve abused and neglected children.* Washington, DC: U.S. Department of Justice.

Merlo, Alida V., Peter J. Benekos, and William J. Cook. 1997. "Getting tough" with youth: Legislative waiver as crime control. *Juvenile and Family Court Journal* 48:1–15.

Merton, Robert K. 1957. *Social theory and social structure.* New York: Free Press.

MetaMetrics, Inc. 1984. *Evaluation of the Breakthrough Foundation Youth At Risk Program: The 10-day course and followup program.* Washington, DC: Author.

Miller, Edward. 1990. Executing minors and the mentally retarded: The retribution and deterrence rationales. *Rutgers Law Review* 43:15–52.

Miller, Jody and Scott H. Decker. 2001. Young women and gang violence: Gender, street offending, and violent victimization in gangs. *Justice Quarterly* 18:115–140.

Miller, J. Mitchell, William J. Ruefle, and Richard A. Wright. 1997. Ideology and gang policy: Beyond the false dichotomy. *Journal of Gang Research* 5:9–20.

Miller, Neal. 1995. *State laws on prosecutors' and judges' use of juvenile records.* Washington, DC: U.S. National Institute of Justice.

Miller, Walter B. 2001. *The growth of youth gang problems in the United States: 1970–1998.* Washington, DC: U.S. Office of Juvenile Justice and Delinquency Prevention.

Mills, Martin. 2001. *Challenging violence in schools: An issue of masculinities.* Buckingham, UK: Open University Press.

Minnesota Crime Control Planning Board. 1981. *Minnesota Community Corrections Act evaluation.* St. Paul, MN: Minnesota Crime Control Planning Board.

Minnesota Office of the Legislative Auditor. 1995. *Guardians ad litem.* St. Paul: Minnesota Office of the Legislative Auditor Program Evaluation Division.

Minor, Kevin I., David J. Hartmann, and Sue Terry. 1997. Predictors of juvenile court actions and recidivism. *Crime and Delinquency* 43:328–344.

Minor, Kevin I. et al. 1999. Sentence completion and recidivism among juveniles referred to teen courts. *Crime and Delinquency* 45:467–480.

Mitchell, John J. and Sharon A. Williams. 1986. SOS: Reducing juvenile recidivism. *Corrections Today* 48:70–71.

Moak, Stacy C. and Lisa H. Wallace. 2000. Attitudes of Louisiana practitioners toward rehabilitation of juvenile offenders. *American Journal of Criminal Justice* 24:271–285.

Molidor, Christian E. 1996. Female gang members: A profile of aggression and victimization. *Social Work* 41:251–257.

Mones, Paul. 1984. Too many rights or not enough? A study of the juvenile related decisions of the West Virginia Supreme Court of Appeals. *Journal of Juvenile Law* 8:32–57.

Moon, Melissa M. et al. 2000. Putting kids to death: Specifying public support for juvenile capital punishment. *Justice Quarterly* 17:663–684.

Moore, Joan. 1993. Gangs, drugs, and violence. In S. Cummings and D.J. Monti, eds., *Gangs: The origins and impact of contemporary youth gangs in the United States.* Albany, NY: SUNY Press.

Moore, Joan and John Hagedorn. 2001. *Female gangs: A focus on research.* Washington, DC: Office of Juvenile Justice and Delinquency Prevention.

Moore, Kevin J., Peter G. Sprengelmeyer, and Patricia Chamberlain. 2001. Community-based treatment for adjudicated delinquents: The Oregon Social Learning Center's "Monitor" multidimensional treatment foster care program. *Residential Treatment for Children and Youth* 18:87–97.

MOORE, MARK H. AND STEWART WAKELING. 1997. Juvenile justice: Shoring up the foundations. In *Crime and justice: A review of research, vol. 22,* Michael Tonry, ed. Chicago: University of Chicago Press.

MOORE, RICHARD G. AND DAVE KUKER. 1993. *A description and discussion of minority overrepresentation in Iowa's juvenile justice system.* Des Moines: Iowa Division of Criminal and Juvenile Justice Planning.

MOORE COUNTY GOVERNMENT. 2002. *Moore County day reporting center.* Moore County, NC: Author.

MUNCIE, JOHN. 1999. *Youth and crime: A critical introduction.* London, UK: Sage.

MURPHY, EDWARD M. 1985. Handling violent juveniles. *Corrections Today* 47:26–30.

MUSSER, DENISE CASAMENTO. 2001. Public access to juvenile records. *Corrections Today* 63:112–113.

MYERS, DAVID L. 1999. *Excluding violent youths from juvenile court: The effectiveness of legislative waiver.* Ann Arbor, MI: University Microfilms International.

———. 2001. *Excluding violent youths from juvenile court: The effectiveness of legislative waiver.* New York: LFB Scholarly Publishing LLC.

MYERS, MATTHEW L. 1973. Legal rights in a juvenile correctional institution. *Journal of Law Reform* 7:242–266.

MYERS, WADE C. AND KERRILYN SCOTT. 1998. Psychotic and conduct disorder symptoms in juvenile murderers. *Homicide Studies* 2:160–175.

MYERS, WADE C. ET AL. 2000. Project Back-on-Track at one year: A delinquency treatment program for early-career juvenile offenders. *Journal of the American Academy of Child and Adolescent Psychiatry* 39:1127–1134.

NAFFINE, NGAIRE AND JOY WUNDERSITZ. 1991. Lawyers in the Children's Court: An Australian's perspective. *Crime and Delinquency* 37:374–392.

NAGOSHI, JACK T. 1986. *Juvenile recidivism: Third Circuit Court.* Honolulu: Youth Development and Research Center, University of Hawaii-Manoa.

NATIONAL ADVISORY COMMISSION ON CRIMINAL JUSTICE STANDARDS AND GOALS. 1976. *Task force report on juvenile justice and delinquency prevention.* Washington, DC: Law Enforcement Assistance Administration.

NATIONAL COUNCIL OF JUVENILE AND FAMILY COURT JUDGES. 1998. *The Janiculum Project: Recommendations.* Reno, NV: National Council of Juvenile and Family Court Judges.

NATIONAL CENTER FOR JUVENILE JUSTICE. 2001. *Petitioned cases to juvenile courts 1997.* Pittsburgh, PA: National Center for Juvenile Justice.

NATIONAL GANG CRIME RESEARCH CENTER. 1997. The facts about female gang members. *Journal of Gang Research* 4:41–59.

———. 2000. Preliminary results of Project GANGMILL: A special report of the National Gang Crime Research Center. *Journal of Gang Research* 7:38–76.

NATIONAL GANG INVESTIGATOR'S ASSOCIATION. 2002. *Female gangs in the United States.* Washington, DC: National Gang Investigator's Association.

NATIONAL GOVERNOR'S ASSOCIATION. 1991. *Kids in trouble: Coordinating social and correctional service systems for youth.* Washington, DC: National Governor's Association.

NATIONAL LAW ENFORCEMENT AND CORRECTIONS TECHNOLOGY CENTER. 1999. *Keeping track of electronic monitoring.* Washington, DC: National Law Enforcement and Corrections Technology Center.

NATIONAL YOUTH COURT CENTER. 2002. APPA adopts resolution supporting youth courts. *APPA Perspectives* 26:15.

NATIONAL YOUTH GANG CENTER. 2000. *1998 National Youth Gang Survey.* Washington, DC: U.S. Department of Justice.

NEBRASKA COMMISSION ON LAW ENFORCEMENT AND CRIMINAL JUSTICE. 1995. *Juvenile offenders in Nebraska.* Lincoln, NE: Nebraska Commission on Law Enforcement and Criminal Justice.

NEELY, DAVID E. 1997. The social reality of street gangs. *Journal of Gang Research* 4:37–46.

NEW MEXICO JUVENILE JUSTICE DIVISION. 2002. *Juvenile justice probation and parole manual.* Albuquerque: New Mexico Juvenile Justice Division.

NEW YORK COMMISSION. 1994. *Preliminary report to the governor.* New York: New York Commission for the Study of Youth Crime and Violence and the Reform of the Juvenile Justice System.

NEW YORK STATE DEPARTMENT OF CORRECTIONAL SERVICES. 1992. *Guidelines for volunteer services.* Albany: New York State Department of Correctional Services.

NIARHOS, FRANCES JOHNSON AND DONALD K. ROUTH. 1992. The role of clinical assessments in the juvenile court: Predictors of juvenile dispositions and recidivism. *Journal of Clinical Child Psychology* 21:151–159.

NIETO, MARCUS. 1998. *Probation for adult and juvenile offenders: Options for improved accountability.* Sacramento, CA: California Research Bureau.

NORMAN, SHERWOOD. 1970. *The youth service bureau: A key to delinquency prevention.* Hackensack, NJ: National Council on Crime and Delinquency.

OFFICE OF JUVENILE JUSTICE AND DELINQUENCY PREVENTION. 2002. *Female delinquents.* Washington, DC: U.S. Government Printing Office.

OLWEUS, D., S. LIMBER, AND S.F. MIHALIC. 1999. *Blueprints for violence prevention, book nine: Bullying Prevention Program.* Boulder, CO: Center for the Study and Prevention of Violence.

O'MAHONY, DAVID. 2000. Young people, crime, and criminal justice: Patterns and prospects for the future. *Youth and Society* 33:60–80.

ONEK, DAVID. 1994. *Pairing college students with delinquents: The Missouri Intensive Case Monitoring Program.* San Francisco: National Council on Crime and Delinquency.

ORLANDO, FRANK A., ALLEN F. BREED AND ROBERT L. SMITH. 1987. *Juvenile justice reform: A critique of the A.L.E.C. code.* Minneapolis: Hubert Humphrey Institute of Public Affairs, University of Minnesota.

OSTERMEYER, MELINDA AND SUSAN L. KEILITZ. 1997. *Monitoring and evaluating court-based dispute resolution programs: A guide for judges and court managers.* Williamsburg, VA: National Center for State Courts.

O'SULLIVAN, KATE, NANCY ROSE, AND THOMAS MURPHY. 2001. *PEPNet: Connecting juvenile offenders to education and employment.* Washington, DC: Office of Juvenile Justice and Delinquency Prevention.

OWENS, TALMADGE JR. 1999. Dual track management of the youthful offender. *Corrections Today* 61:102–105.

PAGE, ROBERT W. 1993. Family courts: An effective judicial approach to the resolution of family disputes. *Juvenile and Family Court Journal* 44:3–60.

PALLONE, NATHANIEL J., ED. 1994. Young victims, young offenders: Current issues in policy and treatment. *Journal of Offender Rehabilitation* 21:1–237.

PALMER, TED. 1994. *A profile of correctional effectiveness and new directions for research.* Albany, NY: State University of New York Press.

PALMER, TED AND ROBERT WEDGE. 1994. *California's juvenile probation camps: A validation study.* Sacramento, CA: Research Division, California Department of the Youth Authority.

PARENT, DALE G. 1996. Day reporting centers: An evolving intermediate sanction. *Federal Probation* 60:51–54.

PAYNE, BRIAN K. AND RANDY R. GAINEY. 1998. A qualitative assessment of the pains experienced on electronic monitoring. *International Journal of Offender Therapy and Comparative Criminology* 42:149–163.

PENNELL, SUSAN AND CHRISTINE CURTIS. 1982. *Juvenile violence and gang-related crime.* San Diego, CA: San Diego Association of Governments.

PENNELL, SUSAN, CHRISTINE CURTIS, AND DENNIS C. SCHECK. 1990. Controlling juvenile delinquency: An evaluation of an interagency strategy. *Crime and Delinquency* 36:257–275.

PENTZ, M.A., S.F. MIHALIC, AND J.K. GROTPETER. 1998. *Blueprints for violence prevention, book one: The Midwestern Prevention Project.* Boulder, CO: Center for the Study and Prevention of Violence.

PETERSEN, REBECCA D. 1995. Expert policy in juvenile justice: Patterns of claimsmaking and issues of power in a program construction. *Policy Studies Journal* 23:636–651.

PETERSON, B. MICHELLE, MARTIN D. RUCK, AND CHRISTOPHER J. KOEGL. 2001. Youth court dispositions: Perceptions of Canadian juvenile offenders. *International Journal of Offender Therapy and Comparative Criminology* 45:593–605.

PINGREE, DAVID H. 1984. Florida youth services. *Corrections Today* 46:60–62.

PIPER, ELIZABETH SPEAR. 1983. *Patterns of violent juvenile recidivism.* Ann Arbor, MI: University Microfilms International.

PIQUERO, ALEX R. 2002. Crime in emerging adulthood. *Criminology* 40:137–170.

PITTS, JOHN. 2001. *The new politics of youth crime: Discipline or solidarity?* Houndsmills, Basingstroke, Hampshire, UK: Palgrave.

PLATT, ANTHONY M. 2001. Social insecurity: The transformation of American criminal justice. *Social Justice* 28:138–155.

PLATT, ANTHONY N. 1969. *The child savers: The invention of delinquency.* Chicago: University of Chicago Press.

PLEYDON, ANNE P. AND JOSEPH G. SCHNER. 2001. Female adolescent friendship and delinquent behavior. *Adolescence* 36:189–205.

PODKOPACZ, MARCY RASMUSSEN. 1996. *The juvenile court's final decisions: An empirical examination of transferring juveniles to adult court.* Ann Arbor, MI: University Microfilms International.

PODKOPACZ, MARCY RASMUSSEN, AND BARRY C. FELD. 1996. The end of the line: An empirical study of judicial waiver. *Journal of Criminal Law and Criminology* 86:449–492.

POE-YAMAGATA, EILEEN AND JEFFREY A. BUTTS. 1996. *Female offenders in the juvenile justice system: Statistics summary.* Washington, DC: U.S. Office of Juvenile Justice and Delinquency Prevention.

POLAN, SUSAN LORI. 1994. *CSP revisited: An evaluation of juvenile diversion.* Ann Arbor, MI: University Microfilms International.

POLLACK, IRA AND CARLOS SUNDERMANN. 2001. Creating safe schools: A comprehensive approach. *Juvenile Justice* 8:13–20.

PORTERFIELD, AUSTIN L. 1943. Delinquency and its outcome in court and college. *American Journal of Sociology* 49:199–208.

POTTER, ROBERTO HUGH AND SUMAN KAKAR. 2002. The diversion decision-making process from the juvenile court practitioners' perspective. *Journal of Contemporary Criminal Justice* 18:20–38.

POULOS, TAMMY MEREDITH AND STAN ORCHOWSKY. 1994. Serious juvenile offenders: Predicting the probability of transfer to criminal court. *Crime and Delinquency* 40:3–17.

PRATT, JOHN AND ROGER GRIMSHAW. 1985. A juvenile justice pre-court tribunal at work. *Howard Journal of Criminal Justice* 24:213–228.

PRATT, TRAVIS C. AND MELISSA R. WINSTON. 1999. The search for the frugal grail: An empirical assessment of the cost-effectiveness of public vs. private correctional facilities. *Criminal Justice Policy Review* 10:447–471.

PRENZLER, TIM AND HENNESSEY HAYES. 1999. Victim-offender mediation and the gatekeeping role of police. *International Journal of Police Science and Management* 2:17–32.

PULLEN, SUZANNE. 1996. *Evaluation of the reasoning and rehabilitation cognitive skills development program as implemented in juvenile ISP in Colorado.* Denver, CO: Colorado Division of Criminal Justice.

PURITZ, PATRICIA ET AL. 1995. *A call for justice: An assessment of access to counsel and quality of representation in delinquency proceedings.* Washington, DC: Juvenile Justice Center, American Bar Association.

PUZZANCHERA, CHARLES M. 2000. *Delinquency cases waived to criminal court, 1988–1997.* Washington, DC: U.S. Department of Justice.

———. 2001. *Delinquency cases waived to criminal court, 1989–1998.* Washington, DC: U.S. Department of Justice.

QUINLAN, JUDITH AND ELAINE MOTTE. 1990. Psychiatric training for officers: An effective tool for increased officer and inmate safety. *American Jails* 4:22–25.

QUINSEY, VERNON L., MARNIE E. RICE, AND GRANT T. HARRIS. 1995. Actuarial prediction of sexual recidivism. *Journal of Interpersonal Violence* 10:85–105.

RABINOWITZ, MARTIN. 1992. *PINS diversion in New York City: Research findings, volume 1.* New York: Office of the Deputy Mayor for Public Safety.

RACKMILL, STEPHEN J. 1996. Printzlien's legacy, the "Brooklyn Plan," A.K.A. deferred prosecution. *Federal Probation* 60:8–15.

RADELET, MICHAEL R., HUGO ADAM BEDAU, AND CONSTANCE E. PUTNAM. 1992. *In spite of innocence: The ordeal of 400 Americans wrongly convicted of crimes punishable by death.* Boston: Northeastern University Press.

RANKIN, JOSEPH H. AND L. EDWARD WELLS. 1985. From status to delinquent offenses: Escalation? *Journal of Criminal Justice* 13:171–180.

RANS, LAUREL L. 1984. The validity of models to predict violence in community and prison settings. *Corrections Today* 46:50–63.

REBELLON, CESAR J. 2002. Reconsidering the broken homes/delinquency relationship and exploring its mediating mechanisms. *Criminology* 40:103–136.

RECKLESS, WALTER. 1967. *The crime problem.* New York: Appleton-Century-Crofts.

REDDINGTON, FRANCES P. AND JAMES F. ANDERSON. 1996. Juveniles in jail and the legal responsibilities: The more things change, the more they stay the same. *Journal for Juvenile Justice and Detention Services* 11:47–54.

REED, TOM. 1997. *Apples to apples: Comparing the operational costs of juvenile and adult correctional programs in Texas.* Austin: Texas Criminal Justice Policy Council.

REESE, WILLIAM A. III AND RUSSELL L. CURTIS JR. 1991. Paternalism and the female status offender: Remanding the juvenile justice double standard. *Social Science Journal* 28:63–83.

REGINI, LISA A. 1998. Combating gangs: The need for innovation. *FBI Law Enforcement Bulletin* 67:25–32.

REGOLI, ROBERT, ELIZABETH WILDERMAN, AND MARK POGREBIN. 1985. Using an alternative evaluation measure for assessing juvenile diversion programs. *Children and Youth Services Review* 7:21–38.

REINEMAN, JOHN OTTO. 1969. The influence of social change on the treatment of the juvenile offender. *The Pennsylvania Association on Probation, Parole, and Correction Quarterly* 26:22–27.

REYNOLDS, K. MICHAEL, RUTH SEYDLITZ, AND PAMELA JENKINS. 2000. Do juvenile curfew laws work? A time-series analysis of the New Orleans law. *Justice Quarterly* 17:205–230.

REYNOLDS, K. MICHAEL ET AL. 1999. Contradictions and consensus: Youths speak out about juvenile curfews. *Journal of Crime and Justice* 22:171–192.

RIGHTHAND, SUE AND CARLANN WELCH. 2001. *Juveniles who have sexually offended: A review of the professional literature.* Washington, DC: U.S. Office of Juvenile Justice and Delinquency Prevention.

RISLER, EDWIN A., RICHARD SUTPHEN, AND JOHN SHIELDS. 2000. Preliminary validation of the Juvenile First Offender Risk Assessment Index. *Research on Social Work and Practice* 10:111–126.

RIVERS, JAMES E., RICHARD DEMBO, AND ROBERT S. ANWYL. 1998. The Hillsborough County, Florida Juvenile Assessment Center: A prototype. *Prison Journal* 78:439–450.

ROBBINS, IRA P. 1986. Privatization of corrections: Defining the issues. *Federal Probation* 50:24–30.

ROBERTS, ALBERT R. 1989. *Juvenile justice: Politics, programs and services.* Chicago: Dorsey Press.

ROBERTS, LEONARD H. 1985. The historic roots of American prison reform: A story of progress and failure. *Journal of Correctional Education* 36:106–109.

ROBERTSON, ANGELA A., PAUL W. GRIMES, AND KEVIN E. ROGERS. 2001. A short-run, cost-benefit analysis of community-based interventions for juvenile offenders. *Crime and Delinquency* 47:265–284.

ROBINSON, JOHN H., ED. 1991. Symposium on serious juvenile crime. *Notre Dame Journal of Law, Ethics, and Public Policy* 5:257–264.

ROGERS, JOSEPH W. 1990. The predisposition report: Maintaining the promise of individualized juvenile justice. *Federal Probation* 54:43–57.

ROGERS, JOSEPH W. AND JAMES D. WILLIAMS. 1995. The predispositional report, decision making, and juvenile court policy. *Juvenile and Family Court Journal* 45:47–57.

ROLEFF, TAMARA L., ED. 1996. *The legal system: Opposing viewpoints.* San Diego, CA: Greenhaven Press.

ROMERO, ESTRELLA ET AL. 2001. Values and antisocial behavior among Spanish adolescents. *Journal of Genetic Psychology.*

ROMIG, DENNIS A. 1978. *Justice for our children.* Lexington, MA: Lexington Books.

ROSENBAUM, JILL LESLIE. 1996. A violent few: Gang girls in the California Youth Authority. *Journal of Gang Research* 3:17–33.

ROSENBLATT, JENNIFER A. AND MICHAEL J. FURLONG. 1997. Assessing the reliability and validity of student self-reports of campus violence. *Journal of Youth and Adolescence* 26:187–202.

ROSSUM, RALPH A., BENEDICT J. KOLLER AND CHRISTOPHER MANFREDI. 1987. *Juvenile justice reform: A model for the states.* Claremont, CA: Rose Institute of State and Local Government and the American Legislative Exchange Council.

ROTHSTEIN, NATALIE. 1985. Teen court. *Corrections Today* 47:18–22.

ROTTMAN, DAVID B. AND WILLIAM E. HEWITT. 1996. *Trial court structure and performance: A contemporary reappraisal.* Williamsburg, VA: National Center for State Courts.

ROWE, DAVID C. AND D. WAYNE OSGOOD. 1984. Heredity and sociological theories of delinquency: A reconsideration. *American Sociological Review* 49:526–540.

ROWE, DAVID C., ALEXANDER T. VAZSONYI, AND DANIEL J. FLANNERY. 1995. Sex differences in crime? Do means and within-sex variation have similar causes? *Journal of Research in Crime and Delinquency* 32:84–100.

ROY, SUDIPTO. 1995. Juvenile restitution and recidivism in a midwestern county. *Federal Probation* 59:55–62.

———. 1997. Five years of electronic monitoring of adults and juveniles in Lake County, Indiana: A comparative study on factors related to failure. *Journal of Crime and Justice* 20:141–160.

RUBACK, R. BARRY AND KIM S. MENARD. 2001. Rural-urban differences in sexual victimization and reporting. *Criminal Justice and Behavior* 28:131–155.

RUBACK, R. BARRY AND PAULA J. VARDAMAN. 1997. Decision making in delinquency cases: The role of race and juveniles' admission/denial of the crime. *Law and Human Behavior* 21:47–69.

RUDDELL, RICK, G. LARRY MAYS, AND DENNIS M. GIEVER. 1998. Transferring juveniles to adult courts: Recent trends and issues in Canada and the United States. *Juvenile and Family Court Journal* 49:1–15.

RUSSELL, BETTY G. 2001. The TAMAR Project: Addressing trauma issues of offenders in jails. *American Jails* 15:41–44.

SALERNO, ANTHONY W. 1991. The child saver movement: Altruism or conspiracy? *Juvenile and Family Court Journal* 42:37–49.

SAMPSON, ROBERT J. 2002. Transcending tradition: New directions in community research, Chicago style. *Criminology* 40:213–230.

SANBORN, JOSEPH B. JR. 1993a. Philosophical, legal and systemic aspects of juvenile court plea bargaining. *Crime and Delinquency* 39:509–527.

———. 1993b. The right to a public jury trial: A need for today's juvenile court. *Judicature* 76:230–238.

———. 1994. The juvenile, the court, or the community: Whose best interests are currently being promoted in juvenile court? *Justice System Journal* 17:249–266.

———. 1995. How parents can affect the processing of delinquents in the juvenile court. *Criminal Justice Policy Review* 7:1–266.

SANDYS, MARLA AND EDMUND F. MCGARRELL. 1995. Attitudes toward capital punishment: Preference for the penalty or mere acceptance? *Journal of Research in Crime and Delinquency* 32:191–213.

SANGSTER, JOAN. 2000. Masking and unmasking the sexual abuse of children: Perceptions of violence against children in "The Badlands" of Ontario. *Journal of Family History* 25:504–525.

SARRI, R.C. AND Y. HANSENFELD, EDS. 1976. *Brought to justice? Juveniles, the courts and the law.* Ann Arbor, MI: National Assessment of Juvenile Corrections.

SAWICKI, DONNA RAU, BEATRIX SCHAEFFER, AND JEANIE THIES. 1999. Predicting successful outcomes for serious and chronic juveniles in residential placement. *Juvenile and Family Court Journal* 50:21–31.

SCAHILL, MEGHAN C. 2000. *Female delinquency cases, 1997.* Washington, DC: U.S. Department of Justice.

SCHAFER, N.E. 1998. *A comparison by race of juvenile referrals in Alaska.* Anchorage: Justice Center, University of Alaska.

SCHIRALDI, VINCENT AND JASON ZIEDENBERG. 1997. *The pods of Elmore County: A glimpse into the rhetoric behind the juvenile crime bill.* Washington, DC: Justice Policy Institute.

SCHLOSSMAN, STEVEN AND ALEXANDER PISCIOTTA. 1986. Identifying and treating serious juvenile offenders: The view from California and New York in the 1920s. In *Intervention strategies for chronic juvenile offenders: Some new perspectives,* Peter W. Greenwood (ed). New York: Greenwood Press.

SCHMIDT, ANNESLEY K. 1998. Electronic monitoring: What does the literature tell us? *Federal Probation* 62:10–19.

SCHMIDT, RIK ET AL. 1998. Measuring success: The Washington state juvenile rehabilitation model. *Corrections Today* 60:104–106.

SCHNEIDER, ANNE LARSON AND PETER R. SCHNEIDER.1985. The impact of restitution on recidivism of juvenile offenders: An experiment in Clayton County, Georgia. *Criminal Justice Review* 10:1–10.

SCHNEIDER, ERIC C. 1992. *In the web of class: Delinquents and reformers in Boston, 1810s–1930s.* New York: New York University Press.

———. 1999. *Vampires, dragons, and Egyptian kings: Youth gangs in postwar New York.* Princeton, NJ: Princeton University Press.

SCHOSSLER, WILLIAM AND MIKE POWERS. 1999. We make house calls: A fresh approach to treating juvenile offenders. *Corrections Today* 61:112–115.

SCHUR, EDWIN. 1973. *Radical nonintervention: Rethinking the delinquency problem.* Englewood Cliffs, NJ: Prentice-Hall.

SCHWARTZ, IRA M., ED. 1999. Will the juvenile court system survive? *Annals of the American Academy of Political and Social Sciences* 564:8–184.

SCHWARTZ, IRA M. AND WILLIAM H. BARTON, EDS. 1994. *Reforming juvenile detention: No more hidden closets.* Columbus, OH: Ohio State University Press.

SEALOCK, MIRIAM D. AND SALLY S. SIMPSON. 1998. Unraveling bias in arrest decisions: The role of juvenile offender type-scripts. *Justice Quarterly* 15:427–457.

SECRET, PHILIP E. AND JAMES B. JOHNSTON. 1996. Specialized juvenile courts: Do they make a difference in judicial decision making? *Journal of Crime and Justice* 19:159–180.

———. 1997. The effect of race on juvenile justice decision making in Nebraska: Detention, adjudication, and disposition, 1988–1993. *Justice Quarterly* 14:445–478.

SEITER, RICHARD P., ED. 1999. The new millennium: Challenges for correctional leadership. *Corrections Management Quarterly* 3:1–82.

SENG, MAGNUS. 2000. Sex offenders on probation. *APPA Perspectives* 24:31–39.

SEYKO, RONALD J. 2001. Balanced approach and restorative justice efforts in Allegheny County, Pennsylvania. *Prison Journal* 81:187–205.

SHANNON, LYLE W.1998. *Alcohol, drugs, delinquency, and crime: Looking back to the future.* New York: St. Martin's Press.

SHAW, CLIFFORD R. AND HENRY D. MCKAY. 1972. *Juvenile delinquency and urban areas.* Rev. ed. Chicago: University of Chicago Press.

SHAW, JAMES W. AND DORIS LAYTON MACKENZIE. 1992. The one-year community supervision performance of drug offenders and Louisiana DOC-identified substance abusers graduating from shock incarceration. *Journal of Criminal Justice* 20:501–516.

SHAWNEE COUNTY DEPARTMENT OF COMMUNITY CORRECTIONS. 2002. *Shawnee County Community Corrections.* Topeka, KS: Author.

SHEARER, ROBERT A. 2002. Probation strategies of juvenile and adult pre-service trainees. *Federal Probation* 66:33–42.

SHELDEN, RANDALL G. 1998. Confronting the ghost of Mary Ann Crouse: Gender bias in the juvenile justice system. *Juvenile and Family Court Journal* 49:11–26.

———. 1999. *Detention diversion advocacy: An evaluation.* Washington, DC: U.S. Office of Juvenile Justice and Delinquency Prevention.

SHELDEN, RANDALL G. AND JOHN A. HORVATH. 1987. Intake processing in a juvenile court: A comparison of legal and nonlegal variables. *Juvenile and Family Court Journal* 38:13–19.

SHELDEN, RANDALL G., SHARON K. TRACY, AND WILLIAM B. BROWN. 2001. *Youth gangs in American society.* 2d ed. Belmont, CA: Wadsworth.

SHELDON, WILLIAM H. 1949. *The varieties of delinquent youth.* New York: Harper.

SHEPHERD, ROBERT E. JR. 2002. *A brief history of the juvenile court in America: Centennial celebration, doing justice to juvenile justice.* Reno, NV: National Council of Family Court Judges.

SHEPPARD, DAVID. 1999. *Strategies to reduce gun violence.* Washington, DC: U.S. Department of Justice.

SHINE, JAMES AND DWIGHT PRICE. 1992. Prosecutors and juvenile justice: New roles and perspectives. In *Juvenile justice and public policy: Toward a national agenda,* I.M. Schwartz, ed. New York: Lexington Books.

SHOEMAKER, DONALD J. 2000. *Theories of delinquency.* 4th ed. New York: Oxford University Press.

SHORT, JAMES F. JR. AND F. IVAN NYE. 1958. *Extent of unrecorded juvenile delinquency: Tentative conclusions. Journal of Criminal Law and Police Science* 49:296–302.

SICKMUND, MELISSA. 2000. *Offenders in juvenile court, 1997.* Washington, DC: U.S. Department of Justice.

SILVER, ERIC AND LISA L. MILLER 2002. A cautionary note on the use of actuarial risk assessment tools for social control. *Crime and Delinquency* 48:138–161.

SIMMONS, JOHN A. ET AL. 1995. *Punishment: A philosophy and public affairs reader.* Princeton, NJ: Princeton University Press.

SIMMS, STUART O. 1997. Communities in crisis: Effective juvenile justice programs involve all sectors of the community. *Corrections Today* 59:78–80.

———. 1998. Restorative juvenile justice: Maryland's legislature reaffirms commitment to juvenile justice reform. *Corrections Today* 59:94–113.

SMALL, MARGARET AND KELLIE DRESSLER TETRICK. 2001. School violence: An overview. *Juvenile Justice* 8:3–12.

SMITH, BEVERLY A.1989. Female admissions and paroles of the Western House of Refuge in the 1880s: An historical example of community corrections. *Journal of Research in Crime and Delinquency* 26:36–66.

SMITH, CAROLYN A. AND MARVIN D. KROHN. 1991. *Delinquency and family life: The role of ethnicity.* New York: Hindelang Criminal Justice Research Center.

SMITH, J. STEVEN. 1991. A lesson from Indiana: Detention is an invaluable part of the system, but it's not the solution to all youths' problems. *Corrections Today* 53:56–60.

SMITH, MELINDA. 1990. New Mexico youths use mediation to settle their problems peacefully. *Corrections Today* 52:112–114.

SMITH, ROBERT R. AND VICTOR S. LOMBARDO. 2002. Evaluation report of the juvenile mediation program. *Corrections Compendium* 27:1–3, 19.

SMITH, WILLIAM R. AND MICHAEL F. ALOISI. 1999. Prediction of recidivism among "Second Timers" in the juvenile justice system: Efficiency in screening chronic offenders. *American Journal of Criminal Justice* 23:201–222.

SMITH, WILLIAM R., MICHAEL F. ALOISI, AND HARVEY M. GOLDSTEIN. 1996. *Early court intervention: A research and demonstration project.* Washington, DC: U.S. Office of Juvenile Justice.

SMITH, WILLIAM R. AND RANDALL D. SMITH. 1998. The consequences of error: Recidivism prediction and civil-libertarian ratios. *Journal of Criminal Justice* 26:481–502.

SNELL, TRACY L. 2001. *Capital punishment 2000.* Washington, DC: Bureau of Justice Statistics.

SNYDER, HOWARD N. 1988. *Court careers of juvenile offenders.* Pittsburgh, PA: National Center for Juvenile Justice.

SNYDER, HOWARD N. AND MELISSA SICKMUND. 1995. *Juvenile offenders and victims: A focus on violence.* Washington, DC: U.S. Office of Juvenile Justice and Delinquency Prevention.

———. 1999. *Juvenile offenders and victims: 1999 national report.* Washington, DC: U.S. Department of Justice, Office of Justice Programs, Office of Juvenile Justice and Delinquency Prevention.

SNYDER, HOWARD N., MELISSA SICKMUND AND EILEEN POE-YAMAGATA. 1996. *Juvenile offenders and victims: 1996 update on violence: Statistics summary.* Pittsburgh: National Center for Juvenile Justice.

———. 2000. *Juvenile transfers to criminal court in the 1990s: Lessons learned from four studies.* Washington, DC: U.S. Office of Juvenile Justice and Delinquency Prevention.

SONTHEIMER, HENRY AND LYNNE GOODSTEIN. 1993. An evaluation of juvenile intensive aftercare probation: Aftercare versus system response effects. *Justice Quarterly* 10:197–227.

SONTHEIMER, HENRY, LYNNE GOODSTEIN, AND MICHAEL KOVACEVIC. 1990. *Evaluation of the Omnibus Criminal Justice Improvement Act of 1986.* Columbia, SC: South Carolina State Reorganization Commission.

SORENSEN, JON AND DONALD H. WALLACE. 1999. Prosecutorial discretion in seeking death: An analysis of racial disparity in the pretrial stages of case processing in a midwestern county. *Justice Quarterly* 16:559–578.

SORENSON, ANN AND DAVID BROWNFIELD. 1995. Adolescent drug use and a general theory of crime: An analysis of theoretical integration. *Canadian Journal of Criminology* 37:19–37.

SPAANS, E.C. AND C. VERWERS. 1997. *Electronic monitoring in the Netherlands: Results of the experiment.* The Hague, NETH: Netherlands Ministry of Justice.

SPRINGER, J. FRED. 1991. Selective aftercare for juvenile parolees: Administrative environment and placement decisions. In *Intensive interventions with high-risk youths: Promising approaches in juvenile probation and Parole.* Monsey, NY: Criminal Justice Press.

SPRUIT, J.E. ET AL. 1998. Forensic history. *International Journal of Law and Psychiatry* 21:315–446.

STAHL, ANNE L. 2001. *Drug offense cases in juvenile courts, 1989–1998.* Washington, DC: U.S. Department of Justice.

STALANS, LORETTA J. AND GARY T. HENRY. 1994. Societal views of justice for adolescents accused of murder: Inconsistency between community sentiment and automatic legislative transfers. *Law and Human Behavior* 18:675–696.

STANLEY, CHRIS. 2001. Will youth justice work? *Probation Journal* 48:93–101.

STASTNY, CHARLES AND GABRIELLE TYRNAUER. 1982. *Who rules the joint? The changing political culture of maximum-security prisons in America.* Lexington, MA: Lexington Books.

STEEN, SARA. 2001. Contested portrayals: Medical and legal social control of juvenile sex offenders. *Sociological Quarterly* 42:325–350.

STEIN, ABBY, DOROTHY OTNOW LEWIS, AND CATHERINE A. YEAGER. 1993. The juvenile justice assessment instrument. *Juvenile and Family Court Journal* 44:91–102.

STEINBERG, KAREN LESLIE, MURRAY LEVINE, AND SIMON SINGER. 1992. *All things in moderation: The ACD adjudication among status offense cases.* Buffalo, NY: Baldy Center for Law and Social Policy, SUNY at Buffalo.

STEINBERG, LAURENCE. 2002. The juvenile psychopath: Fads, fictions, and facts. In *Perspectives on crime and justice: 2001–2002 lecture series,* Alfred Blumstein, Laurence Steinberg, Carl C. Bell, and Margaret A. Berger, eds. Washington, DC: National Institute of Justice.

STEINHART, DAVID. 1994. *Holding high ground: Preserving a justice system for children in a time of fear and turbulence.* Bolinas, CA: Common Knowledge Press.

STREIB, VICTOR L. 1987. *The death penalty for juveniles.* Bloomington, IN: Indiana University Press.

STUTT, HOWARD, ED. 1986. *Learning disabilities and the young offender: Arrest to disposition.* Ottawa, CAN: Canadian Association for Children and Adults with Learning Disabilities.

STYVE, GAYLENE J. ET AL. 2000. Perceived conditions of confinement: A national evaluation of juvenile boot camps and traditional facilities. *Law and Human Behavior* 24:297–308.

SUTHERLAND, EDWIN H. 1939. *Principles of criminology.* Philadelphia: Lippincott.

———. 1951. Critique of Sheldon's varieties of delinquent youth. *American Sociological Review* 16:10–13.

SUTPHEN, RICHARD D., BRUCE A. THYER, AND P. DAVID KURTZ. 1995. Multisystemic treatment of high-risk juvenile offenders. *International Journal of Offender Therapy and Comparative Criminology* 39:327–334.

SUTTON, JOHN R. 1985. The juvenile court and social welfare: Dynamics of progressive reform. *Law and Society Review* 19:107–145.

SWANSON, CHERYL G. 1998. Juvenile mentoring in jail: A partnership with higher education. *American Jails* 12:38–43.

SWEET, JOSEPH. 1985. Probation as therapy. *Corrections Today* 47:89–90.

SWENSON, CYNTHIA CUPIT AND WALLACE A. KENNEDY. 1995. Perceived control and treatment outcome with chronic adolescent offenders. *Adolescence* 30:565–578.

TAXMAN, FAYE S. AND LORI ELIS. 1999. Expediting court dispositions: Quick results, uncertain outcomes. *Journal of Research in Crime and Delinquency* 36:30–55.

TEITELBAUM, LEE E. ET AL. 1980. Children's Rights Symposium. *New Mexico Law Review* 10:235–429.

TERRELL, NATHANIEL EUGENE. 1997. Aggravated and sexual assaults among homeless and runaway adolescents. *Youth and Society* 28:267–290.

TERRY, WALLACE. 1997. He shows them a way out of violence. *Parade Magazine* January 26, 1997:4–7.

TESS, GENE AND KATHRYN BOGUE. 1988. Master correctional officer program: An idea with a future. *American Jails* 1:66–67.

TEXAS YOUTH COMMISSION. 1990. *Independent living: An evaluation.* Austin: Texas Youth Commission Department of Research and Planning.

TOLMAN, RICHARD M. 1996. Expanding sanctions for batterers: What can we do besides jailing and counseling them? In *Future interventions with battered women and their families,* Jeffrey L. Edleson and Zvi Eisikovits, eds. Thousand Oaks, CA: Sage.

TOMBS, BARBARA S., KUNLUN CHANG, AND FENGFANG LU. 1999. *Kansas juvenile correctional facilities: Population projections, trends, and profiles.* Topeka: Kansas Sentencing Commission.

TONRY, MICHAEL. 1997. *Intermediate sanctions in sentencing guidelines.* Washington, DC: U.S. National Institute of Justice.

TOOMBS, NANCY J., BRENT B. BENDA, AND ROBERT F. CORWYN. 2000. Violent youths in boot camps for non-violent offenders. *Journal of Offender Rehabilitation* 31:113–133.

TORBET, PATRICIA AND PATRICK GRIFFIN. 2002. Mission-driven, performance-based, and outcome-focused probation. *APPA Perspectives* 26:22–25.

TORBET, PATRICIA AND LINDA SZYMANSKI. 1998. *State legislative responses to violent juvenile crime: 1996–1997 update.* Washington, DC: U.S. Department of Justice.

TORBET, PATRICIA ET AL. 1996. *State responses to serious and violent juvenile crime.* Washington, DC: Office of Juvenile Justice and Delinquency Prevention.

TORBET, PATRICIA ET AL. 2000. *Juveniles facing criminal sanctions: Three states that changed the rules.* Washington, DC: U.S. Office of Juvenile Justice and Delinquency Prevention.

TOROK, WAYNE C. AND KENNETH S. TRUMP. 1994. Gang intervention: Police and school collaboration. *FBI Law Enforcement Bulletin* 63:13–17.

TOWBERMAN, DONNA B. 1992. A national survey of juvenile risk assessment. *Juvenile and Family Court Journal* 43:61–67.

———. 1994. Racial bias in the criminal justice system: Shifting the focus from outcome to underlying causes. *Juvenile and Family Court Journal* 45:15–25.

TRAVIS, LAWRENCE F. AND FRANCIS T. CULLEN. 1984. Radical intervention: The myth of doing no harm. *Federal Probation* 48:29–32.

TREANOR, WILLIAM W. AND ADRIENNE E. VOLENIK. 1987. *The new right's juvenile crime and justice agenda for the states: A legislator's briefing book.* Washington, DC: American Youth Work Center.

TRESTER, HAROLD B. 1981. *Supervision of the offender.* Englewood Cliffs, NJ: Prentice-Hall.

TRIPLETT, RUTH AND LAURA B. MYERS. 1995. Evaluating contextual patterns of delinquency: Gender-based differences. *Justice Quarterly* 12:59–84.

TROJANOWICZ, ROBERT AND BONNIE BUCQUEROUX. 1990. *Community policing: A contemporary perspective.* Cincinnati, OH: Anderson.

TSYTSAREV, SERGEI, JENNIFER MANGER, AND DEBORAH LODRINI. 2000. The use of reinforcement and punishment on incarcerated and probated, substance-abusing juvenile offenders. *International Journal of Offender Therapy and Comparative Criminology* 44:22–32.

TYGART, CLARENCE E.1988. Strain theory and public school vandalism: Academic tracking, school social status, and students' academic achievement. *Youth and Society* 20:106–118.

UDESHI, RAJ C.1998. *The super block project.* Chicago: Chicago Community Policing Evaluation.

UMBREIT, MARK S., ROBERT B. COATES, AND BETTY VOS. 2001. The impact of victim-offender mediation: Two decades of research. *Federal Probation* 65:29–35.

UNIVERSITY OF NEW MEXICO. 1996. *Evaluation of the juvenile community corrections program.* Albuquerque, NM: Juvenile Justice Division, New Mexico Children, Youth, and Families Department.

U.S. DEPARTMENT OF JUSTICE. 1976. *Two hundred years of American criminal justice: An LEAA bicentennial study.* Washington, DC: Law Enforcement Assistance Administration.

———. 2001. *Youth gang homicides in the 1990s.* Washington, DC: U.S. Government Printing Office.

———. 2002. *2001 preliminary report on crime in the United States.* Washington, DC: U.S. Government Printing Office.

U.S. GENERAL ACCOUNTING OFFICE. 1991. *Noncriminal juveniles: Detentions have been reduced but better monitoring is needed.* Washington, DC: U.S. General Accounting Office.

———. 1994a. *Juvenile justice: Admissions of minors with preadult disorders to private psychiatric hospitals.* Washington, DC: U.S. General Accounting Office.

———. 1994b. *Residential care: Some high-risk youth benefit, but more study needed.* Washington, DC: U.S. General Accounting Office.

———. 1995a. *Juvenile justice: Minimal gender bias occurred in processing noncriminal juveniles.* Washington, DC: U.S. General Accounting Office.

———. 1995b. *Juvenile justice: Representation rates varied as did counsel's impact on court outcomes.* Washington, DC: U.S. General Accounting Office.

———. 1996a. *At-risk and delinquent youth: Multiple federal programs raise efficiency questions.* Washington, DC: U.S. General Accounting Office.

———. 1996b. *Juvenile justice: Status of delinquency prevention program and description of local projects.* Washington, DC: U.S. General Accounting Office.

U.S. HOUSE OF REPRESENTATIVES. 1995. *Correcting revolving door justice: New approaches to recidivism.* Washington, DC: U.S. Government Printing Office.

U.S. NATIONAL INSTITUTE OF JUSTICE. 1998. *Arrestee drug abuse monitoring program (ADAM) 1997: Annual report on adult and juvenile arrestees.* Washington, DC: U.S. National Institute of Justice.

———. 2000. *Boundary changes in criminal justice organizations.* Washington, DC: U.S. National Institute of Justice.

URSA INSTITUTE. 1993. *Community involvement in mediation of first and second time juvenile offenders project of the Community Board Program of San Francisco.* San Francisco: URSA Institute.

VAN DALEN, ANNACLARE. 2001. Juvenile violence and addiction: Tangled roots in childhood trauma. *Journal of Social Work Practice in the Addictions* 1:25–40.

VAN DIETEN, MARILYN. 2002. Implementing best practices: A story from the field. *APPA Perspectives* 26:40–45.

VAN HOFER, HANNS. 2000. Criminal violence and youth in Sweden: A long-term perspective. *Journal of Scandinavian Studies in Criminology and Crime Prevention* 1:56–72.

VIGIL, JAMES DIEGO. 1999. Streets and schools: How educators can help Chicano marginalized gang youth. *Harvard Educational Review* 69:270–288.

VIRGINIA COMMISSION ON YOUTH. 1993. *Report of the study of serious juvenile offenders.* Richmond: Commonwealth of Virginia.

———. 1994a. *Report of the Virginia study of confidentiality of juvenile records.* Richmond: Virginia Commission on Youth.

———. 1994b. *Report on the study of serious juvenile offenders*. Richmond: Virginia Commission on Youth.

———. 1998. *Study of truants and runaways*. Richmond: Virginia Commission on Youth.

VIRGINIA DEPARTMENT OF CRIMINAL JUSTICE SERVICES. 1998. *Report on evaluation of the Richmond City Continuum of Juvenile Justice Services Pilot Program*. Richmond: Virginia Department of Criminal Justice Services, Criminal Justice Research Center.

———. 2000. *Evaluation of the Richmond City Continuum of Juvenile Justice Services Pilot Program*. Richmond: Virginia Department of Criminal Justice Services, Criminal Justice Research Center.

VIRGINIA JOINT LEGISLATIVE AUDIT AND REVIEW COMMISSION. 1996. *Juvenile delinquents and status offenders*. Richmond: Virginia Joint Legislative Audit and Review Commission.

VISHER, CHRISTY A. 1987. Incapacitation and crime control: Does a "lock 'em up" strategy reduce crime? *Justice Quarterly* 4:513–543.

VISHER, CHRISTY A., PAMELA K. LATTIMORE, AND RICHARD L. LINSTER. 1991. Predicting the recidivism of serious youthful offenders using survival models. *Criminology* 29:329–366.

VOLLUM, SCOTT AND CHRIS HALE.2002. Electronic monitoring: A research review. *Corrections Compendium* 27: 1–4, 23–27.

VON EYE, ALEXANDER AND CHRISTOF SCHUSTER. 2001. Methodology for research on adolescence: The need for innovation. *The Journal of Adolescent Research* 16:95–102.

WADSWORTH, TIM. 2000. Labor markets, delinquency and social control theory: An empirical assessment of the mediating process. *Social Forces* 78:1041–1066.

WALKER, JEFFERY T. 1992. Ecology and delinquency in 1990: A partial replication and update of Shaw and McKay's study in Little Rock, Arkansas. Huntsville, TX: Sam Houston State University.

WALKER, NANCY E. 2001. The United Nations Convention on the Rights of a Child: A basis for the prohibition of juvenile capital punishment in the United States. *Behavioral Sciences and the Law* 19:143–169.

WALKER, SAMUEL. 2001. *Sense and nonsense about crime*. 5th ed. Pacific Grove, CA: Brooks/Cole.

WALSH, ANTHONY. 1987. Cognitive functioning and delinquency. *International Journal of Offender Therapy and Comparative Criminology* 31:285–289.

———. 2000. Behavior genetics and anomie/strain theory. *Criminology* 38:1075–1108.

WANG, JOHN Z. 2000. A corporation-based gang prevention approach: Possible? Preliminary report of a corporate survey. *Journal of Gang Research* 7:13–28.

WARR, MARK. 1993. Age, peers, and delinquency. *Criminology* 31:17–40.

WEATHERBURN, DON AND JOANNE BAKER. 2001. Transient offenders in the 1996 Secondary School Survey: A cautionary note on juvenile justice diversion. *Current Issues in Criminal Justice* 13:60–73.

WEEDON, JOEY R. 2002. Budgetary concerns within states may not end reforms. *On the Line* 25:1–2.

WERNER, EMMY E. 1987. Vulnerability and resiliency in children at risk for delinquency: A longitudinal study from birth to adulthood. In *Prevention of delinquent behavior,* John D. Burchard and Sara Burchard, eds. Newbury Park, CA: Sage.

WHITBECK, LES B., DANNY R. HOYT, AND KEVIN A. ACKLEY. 1997. Families of homeless and runaway adolescents: A comparison of parent/caretaker and adolescent perspectives on parenting, family violence and adolescent conduct. *Child Abuse and Neglect* 21:517–528.

WHITEHEAD, JOHN T. 1998. "Good-ol' boys" and the chair: Death penalty attitudes of policy makers in Tennessee. *Crime and Delinquency* 44:245–256.

WHITFIELD, DICK. 1997. *Tackling the tag: The electronic monitoring of offenders*. Winchester, UK: Waterside Press.

WICKSTROM, PEER-OLOF H. AND ROLF LOEBER. 2000. Do disadvantaged neighborhoods cause well-adjusted children to become adolescent delinquents? A study of male juvenile serious offending, individual risk and protective factors, and neighborhood context. *Criminology* 38:1109–1142.

WIEBUSH, RICHARD G. 1990. The Ohio experience: Programmatic variations in intensive supervision for juveniles. *Perspectives* 14:26–35.

WIECKOWSKI, EDWARD ET AL. 1998. Deviant sexual behavior in children and young adolescents: Frequency and patterns. *Sexual Abuse: A Journal of Research and Treatment* 10:293–303.

WILKINSON, REGINALD A. 1998. Community justice in Ohio: Department implements variety of programs to "restore" the community. *Corrections Today* 59:100–142.

WILLIAMS, KATHERINE AND MARCIA I. COHEN. 1993. *Determinants of disproportionate representation of minority juveniles in secure settings: Final report, preliminary findings and recommendations*. Fairfax, VA: Fairfax Juvenile and Domestic Relations District Court.

WILLIAMSON, DEBORAH, MICHELLE CHALK, AND PAUL KNEPPER. 1993. Teen court: Juvenile justice for the 21st century? *Federal Probation* 57:54–58.

WILSON, E. O. 1975. *Sociobiology: The new synthesis*. Cambridge, MA: Harvard University Press.

WILSON, JAMES Q. AND RICHARD J. HERRNSTEIN. 1985. *Crime and human nature*. New York: Simon and Schuster.

WILSON, JAMES Q. AND JOAN PETERSILIA. 2002. *Crime: Public policies for crime control*. Oakland, CA: Institute for Contemporary Studies Press.

WILSON, JOHN J. 2001. *1998 National Youth Gang Survey*. Washington, DC: Office of Juvenile Justice and Delinquency Prevention.

WINOKUR, KRISTIN PARSONS. 1999. *Facing the challenge: A profile of Florida's female juvenile commitment programs*. Tallahassee: Florida Department of Juvenile Research.

WITKE, LEONARD R., ED. 1999. *Planning and design guide for secure adult and juvenile facilities*. Lanham, MD: American Correctional Association.

WITKIN, HERMAN. 1976. Criminality in *XYY* and *XXY* men. *Science* 193:547–555.

WITMER, DENISE. 2002. *Parenting of adolescents*. New York: About, Inc.

WOLFGANG, MARVIN AND FRANCO FERRACUTI. 1967. *The subculture of violence*. London: Tavistock.

WOLFGANG, MARVIN, ROBERT M. FIGLIO, AND THORSTEN SELLIN. 1972. *Delinquency in a birth cohort*. Chicago: University of Chicago Press.

WOOD, GINA E. 2001. Increasing collaboration between family courts and juvenile justice. *Corrections Today* 63:116–122.

WOODEN, WAYNE S. AND RANDY BLAZAK. 2001. *Renegade kids, suburban outlaws: From youth culture to delinquency. 2d ed.* Belmont, CA: Wadsworth Publishing Company.

WOODWARD, BILL AND KIM ENGLISH. 1993. *Juvenile Intensive Supervision Probation Pilot Project: Phase one study*. Denver, CO: Colorado Department of Public Safety.

WOOLDREDGE, JOHN ET AL. 1994. Effectiveness of culturally specific community treatment for African American juvenile felons. *Crime and Delinquency* 40:589–598.

WORDES, MADELINE, TIMOTHY S. BYNUM AND CHARLES J. CORLEY. 1994. Locking up youth: The impact of race on detention decisions. *Journal of Research in Crime and Delinquency* 31:149–165.

WORLD ALMANAC BOOKS. 2002. *The world almanac and book of facts, 2001.* Mahwah, NJ: Funk & Wagnalls Corporation.

WORLING, JAMES R.1995. Adolescent sex offenders against females: Differences based on the age of their victims. *International Journal of Offender Therapy and Comparative Criminology* 39:276–293.

WORRALL, JOHN L. AND OTWIN MARENIN.1998. Emerging liability issues in the implementation and adoption of community oriented policing. *Policing* 21: 121–136.

WRIGHT, JOHN PAUL ET AL.2001. "The root of all evil?" An exploratory study of money and delinquent involvement. *Justice Quarterly* 18: 239–268.

WRIGHT, KEVIN N., ED. 1998. Reinventing corrections. *Corrections Management Quarterly* 2: 1–88.

WRIGHT, LINDA E. 1997. Juvenile crime in rural areas. *Justice System Journal* 19: 355–364.

WU, BOSHIU. 1997. The effect of race on juvenile justice processing. *Juvenile and Family Court Journal* 48:43–51.

WU, BOHSIU, STEPHEN CERNKOVICH, AND CHRISTOPHER S. DUNN. 1997. Assessing the effects of race and class on juvenile justice processing in Ohio. *Journal of Criminal Justice* 25:265–277.

YEAGER, CLAY R., JOHN A. HERB AND JOHN H. LEMMON. 1989. *The impact of court unification on juvenile probation systems in Pennsylvania.* Shippensburg, PA: Center for Juvenile Justice Training and Research, Shippensburg University.

YOUNG, DELTON W. 1999. *Wayward kids: Understanding and treating antisocial youth.* Northvale, NJ: Jason Aronson.

ZACHARIAH, JOHN K. 2002. *An overview of boot camp goals, components, and results.* Washington, DC: Koch Crime Institute.

ZASLAW, JAY G. 1989. Stop assaultive children—Project SAC offers hope for violent juveniles. *Corrections Today* 51:48–50.

———. 1999. Young women in the juvenile justice system. *APPA Perspectives* 23:33–38.

ZHANG, LENING. 1997. Informal reactions and delinquency. *Criminal Justice and Behavior* 24:129–150.

ZIEDENBERG, JASON AND VINCENT SCHIRALDI. 1998. The risks juveniles face: Housing juveniles in adult institutions is self-destructive and self-defeating. *Corrections Today* 60:22–28.

ZIEDENBERG, JASON ET AL. 2001. Drugs and disparity: The racial impact of Illinois' practice of transferring young drug offenders to adult court. Washington, DC: Building Blocks for Youth.

ZIGLER, EDWARD AND NANCY W. HALL. 1987. The implications of early intervention efforts for the primary prevention of juvenile delinquency. In *From children to citizens: Volume III, Families, schools, and delinquency,* James Q. Wilson and Glenn C. Loury, eds. New York: Springer-Verlag.

ZIMRING, FRANKLIN E. 1998. *American youth violence.* New York: Oxford University Press.

Juvenile Agency Telephone/Fax/Web Addresses

Alabama	(334) 215-3800	(334) 215-1453	http://archives/state.al.us/officials/rdas/youthser.htm
Alaska	(907) 465-2212	(907) 465-2333	www.hss.state.ak.us/djj
Arizona	(602) 542-4302	(602) 542-5156	www.juvenile.state.az.us
Arkansas	(501) 682-8654	(501) 682-1339	www.state.ar.us/dhs/dys
California	(916) 262-1467	(916) 262-1483	www.cya.ca.gov
Colorado	(303) 866-7345	(303) 866-7344	www.cdhs.state.co.us/dyc.home.htm
Connecticut	(860) 550-6300	(860) 566-7947	www.state.ct.us/dcf
Delaware	(302) 633-2620	(302) 633-2636	www.state.de.us/kids
District of Columbia	(301) 497-8100	(301) 497-8510	http://dhs.washington.dc.us/
Florida	(850) 413-7313	(850) 922-2992	www.myflorida.com
Georgia	(404) 657-2401	(404) 657-2473	www.djj.state.ga.us
Hawaii	(808) 587-5700	(808) 587-5734	www.state.hi.us/dhs
Idaho	(208) 334-5100	(208) 334-5120	www.djc.state.id.us
Illinois	(217) 522-2666	(217) 522-9583	www.idoc.state.il.us
Indiana	(317) 232-1746	(317) 233-4948	www.state.in.us/indcorrection
Iowa	(515) 281-5452	(515) 281-4980	www.dhs.state.ia.us/ACFS/ACFS.asp
Kansas	(785) 296-4213	(785) 296-1412	http://jja.state.ks.us
Kentucky	(502) 573-2738	(502) 573-4308	http://djj.state.ky.us
Louisiana	(225) 342-3106	(225) 342-4441	www.corrections.state.la.us
Maine	(207) 287-4365	(207) 287-4370	http://janus.state.me.us/corrections
Maryland	(410) 230-3100	(410) 333-4199	www.djj.state.md.us
Massachusetts	(617) 727-7575	(617) 951-2409	www.state.ma.us/eohhs/agencies/dys.htm
Michigan	(517) 373-2000	(517) 335-6101	www.mfia.state.mi.us/
Minnesota	(651) 642-0288	(651) 603-6768	www.doc.state.mn.us
Mississippi	(601) 359-4972	(601) 359-4970	www.mdhs.state.ms.us/dys.html
Missouri	(573) 751-3324	(573) 526-4494	www.dss.state.mo.us/
Montana	(406) 444-3930	(406) 444-4920	www.cor.state.mt.us
Nebraska	(402) 471-8410	(402) 471-9034	www.hhs.state.ne.us/jus/jusindex.htm
Nevada	(702) 486-5095	(702) 486-5089	http://dcfs.state.nv.us/page22.html
New Hampshire	(603) 625-5471	(603) 669-1203	www.dyds.state.nh.us
New Jersey	(609) 530-5200	(609) 530-5037	www.state.nj.us/lps/jjctemp.htm
New Mexico	(505) 827-7629	(505) 827-8408	http://www.state.nm.us/cyfd/index.htm
New York State	(518) 473-8437	(518) 473-9131	www.dfa.state.ny.us
New York City	(212) 925-7779	(212) 431-4874	www.ci.nyc.ny.us/html/djj/home.html
North Carolina	(919) 733-3388	(919) 733-6809	www.juvjus.state.nc.us
North Dakota	(701) 328-6390	(701) 328-6651	www.lnotes.state.nd.us/dhs/dhsweb.nsf
Ohio	(614) 466-8783	(614) 752-9078	www.state.oh.us/dys
Oklahoma	(405) 530-2800	(405) 530-2890	www.state.ok.us/-oja
Oregon	(503) 373-7205	(503) 373-7622	www.oya.state.or.us
Pennsylvania	(717) 787-9532	(717) 787-1529	www.dpw.state.pa.us/ocyf/ocyfjj.asp
Rhode Island	(401) 462-7200	(401) 464-2152	www.state.ri.us
South Carolina	(803) 896-9749	(803) 896-9767	www.state.sc.us/djj
South Dakota	(605) 773-3478	(605) 773-3194	www.state.sd.us/corrections/juvenile.htm
Tennessee	(615) 741-9701	(615) 532-8079	www.state.tn.us/youth
Texas	(512) 424-6001	(512) 424-6010	www.tyc.state.tx.us/index.html
Utah	(801) 538-4330	(801) 538-4334	www.hsdyc.state.ut.us
Vermont	(802) 241-2100	(802) 241-2980	www.state.vt.us/srs
Virginia	(804) 371-0700	(804) 371-0773	www.djj.state.va.us
Washington	(360) 902-7804	(360) 902-7848	www.wa.gov/dshs/jra
West Virginia	(304) 558-6029	(304) 558-6032	www.wvdjs.state.wv.us
Wisconsin	(608) 266-9342	(608) 267-3661	www.wi-doc.com/index_juvenile.htm
Wyoming	(307) 777-7564	(307) 777-7747	http://dfsweb.state.wy.us/1main.htm

Case Index

Name Index

Subject Index

Wisconsin Case Classification
System, 445
Without prejudice, 282
Workhouses, 8

X

XYY theory, 89–90

Y

Youth at Risk Program, 110
Youth Gang Response System, 125
Youth gangs, 217–223

corporate, 217
defined, 217
myths, 218–221
numbers, 217
scavenger, 217
territorial, 217
types, 217
Youth Self-Report, 250
Youth Service Bureaus (YSBs),
397–398
citizen action model, 398
community organization model,
398
cooperating agencies model, 397

street outreach model, 398
systems modification model, 398
Youth Services/Diversion (YS/D) Program, 398–399
Youth Services/Diversion and Community Services Programs, Inc.,
398–399
Youth squads, 216
Youth-to-Victim Restitution Project,
425

Z

Zone of transition, 98